Attila Fenyves, Christa Kissling, Stefan Perner, Daniel Rubin (eds)

**Compulsory Liability Insurance from a European Perspective**

# Tort and Insurance Law

Edited by the
European Centre of Tort
and Insurance Law

together with the
Institute for European Tort Law
of the Austrian Academy of Sciences
and the University of Graz

## Volume 35

# Compulsory Liability Insurance from a European Perspective

Attila Fenyves
Christa Kissling
Stefan Perner
Daniel Rubin (eds)

With Contributions by

Hubert Bär • Diana Cerini • Herman Cousy • Petr Dobiáš • Michael Faure • Özlem Gürses • Helmut Heiss • Robert Koch • Anna Teresa Memola • Franz Merli • Jaana Norio-Timonen • Stefan Perner • Daniel Rubin • Andrea Stäubli • Péter Takáts • Bernard Tettamanti • Caroline Van Schoubroeck • Jean-Claude Werz

DE GRUYTER

European Centre of Tort and Insurance Law
Reichsratsstraße 17/2
A-1010 Vienna
Tel: +43 1 4277 29650
Fax: +43 1 4277 29670
E-Mail: ectil@ectil.org

Institute for European Tort Law
Reichsratsstraße 17/2
A-1010 Vienna
Tel: +43 1 4277 29651
Fax: +43 1 4277 29670
E-Mail: etl@oeaw.ac.at

ISBN 978-3-11-048469-4
e-ISBN 978-3-11-048617-9

**Bibliographic information published by the Deutsche Nationalbibliothek**
The Deutsche Nationalbibliothek lists this publication in the Deutsche Nationalbibliografie; detailed bibliographic data are available on the Internet at http://dnb.dnb.de.


Typesetting: jürgen ullrich typosatz, 86720 Nördlingen
Printing and binding: Hubert & Co. GmbH & Co. KG, Göttingen
♾ Printed on acid-free paper
Printed in Germany

www.degruyter.com

# Preface

Statutory obligations to take out liability insurance are, in practice, the most important means to ensure compensability of damage arising from dangerous activities. However, in contrast to the significant practical impact, academic research on the topic has not been extensive so far. Therefore, the editors were glad that the representative of the Swiss Insurance Association in the Supervisory Board of the European Centre of Tort and Insurance Law (ECTIL), Hubert Bär, encouraged us to undertake a study on the law of Compulsory Liability Insurance in Europe. Based on his proposal, the Supervisory Board of ECTIL decided in 2012 to conduct a study on the topic in cooperation with the Institute for European Tort Law of the Austrian Academy of Sciences and the University of Graz (ETL), Vienna. An extensive Questionnaire was sent out to the project participants in June 2013. The book at hand presents the results of this project.

In the study, compulsory liability insurance was examined from nine national perspectives (Austria, Belgium, the Czech Republic, Finland, Germany, Hungary, Italy, Switzerland, and the United Kingdom). However, the book does not only contain reports from European key jurisdictions. As statutory obligations to take out compulsory liability insurance might conflict with basic rights and fundamental freedoms, the editors also decided to take constitutional as well as European law into account. Due to the economic importance of the topic, we also included a chapter on the economic analysis of compulsory liability insurance and aspects of insurability. Moreover, the editors were pleased that the Project Group 'Restatement of European Insurance Contract Law', chaired by Helmut Heiss, agreed to cooperate. Therefore, a chapter on the perspective of the Principles of European Insurance Contract Law (PEICL) is also included. All these aspects allowed the editors – and hopefully the reader – to come to terms with the fact that the French report, which had initially been scheduled, could not be finalised and is therefore not included in the volume.

The country reports (and the Annex containing a compilation of rules on compulsory liability insurance in the nine national legal systems) were completed by the end of 2014. The special reports – which build upon the findings of the country reports – were subsequently drafted and finished by summer 2015. The authors of the country reports were then given the chance to update their reports until the end of 2015.

The editors – also on behalf of ECTIL and ETL – express their gratitude to Vienna University of Economics and Business (WU) for hosting the public conference, with the aim of presenting and discussing the results of the study, in its premises on 13 June 2016. We would also like to thank Donna Stockenhuber for taking over the time-consuming task of proof-reading the entire manuscript, Fiona Salter-Townshend for helping the editors with the translation of their texts, Kathrin Karner-Strobach for formatting and copy-editing, Andrew Bell for reading parts of the publisher's proofs, and Alexander Longin for compiling the Index. Without their invaluable help, it would have been impossible to publish this volume in due course. We also thank Laura Weissel for assistance at the beginning of the project. Additionally, we thank the whole staff of ECTIL and ETL for their help with the conference, in particular Lisa Zeiler for organising the conference and Julian Pehm for supporting the conference with his graphics expertise. Last but not least, we owe a great debt of gratitude to Helmut Koziol, the former managing director and since April 2016 vice-director of ECTIL, for his valuable advice and support.

Vienna/Linz, May 2016

Attila Fenyves
Christa Kissling
Stefan Perner
Daniel Rubin

# Table of Contents

## Introduction and Questionnaire



## Country Reports

## Annex: Rules on Compulsory Liability Insurance

# Introduction and Questionnaire

Daniel Rubin
# Introduction

## I. Choice of Subject Matter

This study focuses on a comparison of European legal systems with regard to the scope and content of their rules on compulsory liability insurance. Emphasis is laid on topics relating to the *system* of compulsory liability as it has been shaped by different legal orders. The subject matter of the study was chosen due to the following observations. 1

Liability insurance shifts the economic loss linked to liability away from the tortfeasor's (ie the insurance holder's) funds to the insurance company which distributes it among its insurance holders that constitute a community at risk through their premium payments. This makes liability insurance, if made compulsory by law, a rather *complex* legal *phenomenon* worth closer examination: On the one hand, there is its strong practical impact on the fulfilment of liability claims since it ensures that they *are met*.[1] It is therefore an important legal tool for the *factual functioning* of national *tort laws* while at the same time lawmakers need to cope with the structural challenges inherent to compulsory liability insurance, one of these being that compulsory liability insurance stands in tension with the preventive function of tort law.[2] Since, as any insurance, it creates the problem of the insurance holder's (meaning in our case: the injurer's) *moral hazard*: The sheer existence of liability insurance cover leads to a decline in the level of care and risk prevention of the insured due to the fact that his assets are relieved from bearing the financial consequences of liability and therefore of his tortious actions.[3] Thus, compulsory liability insurance cover has, as a rule, the side effect of inducing the insured to lose his otherwise existing incentive to behave carefully vis-à-vis the goods of others in order to avoid liability.[4] In other words: compulsory liability insurance itself has the negative effect of *increasing* the *risk of liability*. 2

Nevertheless, lawmakers are not sufficiently concerned with the issue of moral hazard that they would refrain from stipulating compulsory liability in- 3

---

1 Cf *H Koziol*, Basic Questions of Tort Law from a Germanic Perspective (2012) no 2/71.

2 On this cf *Koziol* (fn 1) no 2/70.

3 Cf *M Faure*, Liability Insurance: Economic Perspectives (in this book) no 25; *B Tettamanti/H Bär/J-C Werz*, Compulsory Liability Insurance in a Changing Legal Environment – An Insurance and Reinsurance Perspective (in this book) no 43.

4 Cf *Tettamanti/Bär/Werz* (fn 3) no 43 ('policy holder hazard') and no 96.

surance for all kinds of activities. This is due to the described *strong positive effect* of liability insurance on the *compensatory* function of tort law.[5] Therefore liability insurance is prescribed as mandatory in different legal systems for many professions, hazardous activities and operations of dangerous plants/vehicles.[6]

4 As a consequence, the issue of moral hazard *remains a problem to be solved* by national lawmakers[7] as are *further structural problems* linked to any compulsory liability insurance scheme. One of them is the fact that compulsory liability insurance *cannot* provide *bullet-proof protection*[8] to potential victims as its functioning relies on the conclusion of a contract fulfilling the statutory requirements. For other structural questions arising in the context of compulsory liability insurance, see in the following (no 5).

## II. Research Aims

5 This study aims for a better understanding of how compulsory liability insurance might best work.[9] For this purpose it was deemed helpful to compare the existing shape of compulsory liability insurance schemes in various European legal orders in order to see which solutions they provide both to solve the problems addressed above and, in particular, to address the following questions:

1. Do lawmakers apply any *general criteria* – and if so, which – when deciding to prescribe compulsory liability insurance for certain activities and professions whereas for others not?[10]
2. What *aims* do lawmakers predominantly pursue when stipulating an obligation to take out liability insurance: is it only the protection of the injured party or are there other objectives to be achieved as well?[11]
3. Do legal orders contain a *proper term for compulsory liability insurance* vested with a specific content?[12] In other words: What are the *criteria* that need to be met if a legal order speaks of compulsory liability insurance in a

---

**5** On this cf *Koziol* (fn 1) no 2/71; see also *Faure* (fn 3) no 27.

**6** Cf *Koziol* (fn 1) no 2/71; further cf in detail the Annexes at the end of this book.

**7** As for possible solutions see *D Rubin*, Comparative Report (in this book) no 38 and *D Rubin*, Conclusions (in this book) 8 ff.

**8** See *Rubin*, Conclusions (fn 7) no 17 ff.

**9** In other words: How does it best fulfil its purposes? On these see *Rubin*, Conclusions (fn 7) no 1.

**10** See Questions 1 and 2 of the Questionnaire.

**11** See Questions 5 and 6 of the Questionnaire.

**12** See Questions 3 and 4 of the Questionnaire.

technical sense? On the one hand, the answer to this depends on the aims that are pursued with compulsory liability insurance (see the previous question). On the other hand, the answer has an impact on how the following two questions (4 and 5) are to be solved.

4. What is the *mandatory content* of cover stipulated by rules on compulsory liability insurance?[13] For example, *which legal interests* are protected by those rules?[14] Further, what are the *boundaries* of their protection – ie, which *risk exclusions* from the compulsory cover are either already foreseen by law or are admissible in the insurance contract?[15]
5. Do legal systems provide *coherent legal consequences* once a compulsory liability contract has been concluded?[16] These consequences most notably refer to the *injured party's protection* regarding the following aspects:
   - Are there any *restrictions* to the injurer's general freedom to make *contractual dispositions* over his claim against the insurer?[17]
   - Does the injured party enjoy protection against the *damaging party's insolvency*?[18]
   - Further: Is the insurer, if it is *freed* from its obligation to pay compensation, *banned from relying* on this fact *in relation to the victim*?[19] The same question applies for the case that the *insurance contract has* already *ended* by the time relevant for the duty to provide cover[20] or that it was, from the beginning, *not effectively concluded.*[21]
6. What consequences does a *breach of the duty* to take out a liability insurance contract (with the prescribed content of cover) entail?[22]

---

**13** See Questions 7–11, 13 and 14 of the Questionnaire.
**14** See Questions 7–9 of the Questionnaire.
**15** See Questions 13 and 14 of the Questionnaire.
**16** See Question 2 of the Questionnaire.
**17** See Question 17 of the Questionnaire.
**18** See Question 18 of the Questionnaire.
**19** See Question 21 of the Questionnaire.
**20** See Question 22 of the Questionnaire.
**21** See Question 23 of the Questionnaire.
**22** See Questions 12 and 29 of the Questionnaire.

# III. Methodology

6 This research was conducted on the grounds of a Questionnaire drafted by the editors in discussion with *Hubert Bär* from the Swiss Insurance Association whose helpful contribution is gratefully acknowledged.[23] The Questionnaire is divided into eight main sections:

I. *The Term Compulsory Liability Insurance,*
II. *Aims* (of compulsory liability insurance),
III. *Content of Insurance Cover,*
IV. *Protection Mechanisms,*
V. *Supervision and Sanctions.*

Further, for the sake of completeness of this study:

VI. *Statutory Provisions required by the Constitution or the European Convention on Human Rights (ECHR),*[24]
VII. *Reform Efforts* (for the respective legal order),
VIII. *Compulsory Liability Insurance and Liability Law.*

7 *Nine legal orders* were selected for the reports responding to the Questionnaire: *Austria, Belgium,* the *Czech Republic, Finland, Germany, Hungary, Italy, Switzerland,* and the *United Kingdom.* The choice was made in order to cover the major legal families of Europe: The *Germanic* family is represented by Austria, Germany and Switzerland, the *Romanic* legal family by Belgium and Italy, the *common law* by the United Kingdom, the *Nordic systems* by Finland and the *post-communist countries*[25] by the Czech Republic and Hungary. A national expert either from academia or from practice (with academic experience) submitted a report for each of these countries.[26] The reports are supplemented by Annexes containing overviews of statutory provisions establishing duties to take out liability insurance.[27]

---

**23** On the Questionnaire method in general cf, with further reference, *E Karner/K Oliphant*, Liability for Loss of Housekeeping Capacity in Comparative Perspective, in: E Karner/K Oliphant (eds), Loss of Housekeeping Capacity (2012) no 6 fn 5.

**24** The evaluation of this section was left to a special report; see below fn 30.

**25** Although, as far as private law is concerned, they are not a proper legal family bonded by common legal roots.

**26** The authors of the country reports are (in alphabetical order according to the country's name): *Daniel Rubin* (Austria); *Herman Cousy/Caroline Van Schoubroeck* (Belgium); *Petr Dobiáš* (Czech Republic); *Jaana Norio-Timonen* (Finland); *Robert Koch* (Germany); *Péter Takáts* (Hungary); *Diana Cerini* (Italy); *Andrea Stäubli* (Switzerland); *Özlem Gürses* (United Kingdom).

**27** They are furnished by the authors of the country reports. The Italian Annex was co-written by *Anna Teresa Memola.*

The study combines the Questionnaire with a separate analysis of the compulsory liability insurance rules laid down in the *Principles of European Insurance Contract Law* (PEICL)[28] as they can be (within their scope) considered as equal to a legal system. PEICL are to be seen as a Restatement providing a model law for European insurance contracts that reflects the most feasible solutions found in current insurance law on national levels.[29] 8

Other special reports of this study deal with the framework set by (national) *constitutional law*[30] and by *EU law*[31] relating to compulsory liability insurance. 9

Further, an important aspect of this work consisted in examining compulsory liability insurance from an *Economic Analysis of Law* viewpoint.[32] 10

Last but not least the *insurers'* (and reinsurers') *perspective* was also taken into account to better understand the practical problems that are to be faced by legislators when stipulating duties to take out compulsory liability insurance.[33] 11

---

**28** *H Heiss*, Compulsory Liability Insurance in the Principles of European Insurance Contract Law (PEICL) (in this book).

**29** On this cf *Heiss* (fn 28) no 6.

**30** *F Merli*, Compulsory Liability Insurance and Constitutional Law (in this book).

**31** *S Perner*, Compulsory Liability Insurance and European Union Law (in this book).

**32** See the special report on the subject matter by *Faure* (fn 3).

**33** *Tettamanti/Bär/Werz* (fn 3).

# Questionnaire

## I. The Term Compulsory Liability Insurance

1. Indicate the rules within your legal system that set out a duty to take out liability insurance. In this context, also take into account the implementation of international treaties (eg, the International Convention on Civil Liability for Bunker Oil Pollution Damage, 2001).
2. Is there a coherent 'law of compulsory liability insurance' in your legal system?
3. Is there a specific term for compulsory liability insurance in your legal system? How is it defined?
4. In which of the following cases does compulsory liability insurance apply according to prevailing opinion?
   a) Duties to take out liability insurance which are not directly based on the law but on an order or decision issued by administrative authorities?
   b) Duties to take out liability insurance that are not based directly on the law but on the statutes of a professional or other self-governing body?
   c) Duties to take out liability insurance that are not based on any public law but on a private law provision (eg, governing the relationship between employer and employee)?
   d) Duties to take out liability insurance that are not based on any public law but on a private law rule that is established by case law (and, eg, governs the relationship between employer and employee)?
   e) Cases in which there is no duty to take out liability insurance but liability insurance cover is a prerequisite for the admissibility of carrying out a particular activity?
   f) Cases of alternative financial security, in which the duty to provide for financial security may be fulfilled either by taking out liability insurance or other forms of financial security (eg, bank guarantees)?
   g) Cases in which the duty to have insurance has only been created by a contractual agreement between potential injuring party and victim?

## II. Aims

5. What are the aims of the rules that impose an obligation to take out liability insurance:
   a) the protection of the victim,
   b) the protection of the insurance holder,
   c) the protection of the victim and the insurance holder,
   d) other aims, eg internalising the costs in the interests of society?
6. Do the rules that prescribe a form of alternative financial security (see above Question 4.f) pursue the same aims as those rules that exclusively set out a duty to have liability insurance (ie with no other alternative financial security options)?

## III. Content of Insurance Cover

7. Are the duties to take out liability insurance laid down by law only to cover extra-contractual compensation duties or also those arising out of contractual infringements?
8. a) Are there duties to take out liability insurance aimed not only at the protection of absolutely protected rights (eg, property, bodily integrity) but additionally at compensating pure economic loss?
   b) Are there duties to take out liability insurance that are directed only or at least predominantly at the compensation of pure economic loss?
9. Are there provisions that require the insurance of a third party's liability interest – for instance, that the employer must take out liability insurance for the benefit of an employee?
10. To what extent do the rules requiring the compulsory conclusion of a liability insurance policy also specify the specific contents of the insurance coverage:
    a) Is there always a (sufficiently well-defined) specification of the risk to be insured?
    b) Are there provisions that require unlimited coverage?
    c) If unlimited coverage is not required (see above Question b), is a minimum or maximum insurance sum always specified?
    d) Are there general statutory rules to be applicable if the respective law that requires compulsory insurance only makes incomplete stipulations regarding the content of the insurance coverage? An example of this would be § 114 para 1 of the German Insurance Contract Act (*Versicherungsvertragsgesetz*, VVG) 2008.

11. Is it admissible to restrict the insurance cover by agreeing:
    a) risk exclusion clauses,
    b) deductibles,
    c) aggregate limits,
    d) claims series clauses,
    e) other clauses?
12. What are the consequences if the liability insurance contract concluded in order to fulfil the insurance obligation contravenes what the law stipulates as to contents (see above Questions 10 and 11)?
13. a) Are statutory stipulations as to the contents of the policy (eg, regarding the amount of the insurance sum, the ban on certain risk exclusion clauses, on deductibles, etc, see above Questions 10 and 11) also binding in favour of the insurance holder? Or is it nonetheless possible for the liability insurer and the insurance holder acting within their internal relationship to agree risk exclusion clauses, deductibles, aggregate limits, and claims series clauses, etc (see above Questions 10 and 11), releasing the insurer from its liability to pay?
    b) If it is possible for liability insurer and insurance holder acting within their internal relationship to agree a release from the obligation to pay (see above Question a): What consequences does this entail? Must the insurer first pay out to the victim and can then have recourse to the insurance holder? Or is another construction provided for the relationship between insurer, insurance holder and victim?
14. a) Does your general (voluntary) liability insurance law include a statutory risk exclusion in respect of intentional damage by the insurance holder or the insured person?
    b) If the general liability insurance law contains a statutory risk exclusion in respect of intentional damage inflicted by the insurance holder (see above Question a): Does this also apply in cases of compulsory liability insurance?

## IV. Protection Mechanisms

15. Are insurers obliged to contract when they offer liability insurance policies covering a risk for which the insurance holder is obliged to obtain cover?
16. If there is no obligation to contract: Are there comparable mechanisms provided to ensure that an insurance agreement is concluded?
17. Is the insurance holder prohibited from disposing over his cover entitlement to the disadvantage of the victim (eg, by surrendering his entitlement)?

18. Does the victim enjoy special protection against insolvency on the part of the insurance holder with regard to the sum payable by the liability insurer?
19. a) In what manner can the victim obtain the insurance payment?
    b) Does the victim have a direct right of action against the liability insurer (*action directe*) in the case of voluntary or compulsory liability insurance?
20. When settling the claim, is the liability insurer obliged to observe a certain procedure in the interests of the victim? For instance, must it pay the victim an advance within a certain period?
21. a) In the context of its relationship with the victim, can the liability insurer rely on the fact that vis-à-vis the insurance holder (= damaging party) it is freed from the obligation to pay, eg, due to the insurance holder breaching an obligation of conduct/warranty (*Obliegenheitsverletzung*) or due to him defaulting on premiums?
    b) Does the law distinguish on the basis of the ground for the release from the obligation to pay so that in some cases the insurer may not invoke its release from such obligation vis-à-vis the victim?
    c) If the insurer must still pay the victim despite being released from its obligation to pay vis-à-vis the insurance holder (see above Question b), may it take recourse against the latter?
22. a) Within its relationship to the victim, can the liability insurer invoke the fact that the insurance agreement had already ended by the time relevant in respect of the duty to provide cover?
    b) If the insurer must pay the victim despite the termination of the insurance agreement by the time relevant for the duty to provide cover (see above Question a), can it take recourse against the insurance holder?
23. a) Are there cases in which a damaging party does not effectively conclude the required liability insurance and the victim injured by him nonetheless receives compensation for his loss from a liability insurer or another compensation scheme (eg, a guarantee fund)?
    b) In the event that the policy taken out was not in fact effectively concluded, is it necessary to distinguish on the basis of the ground for this ineffectiveness, eg, whether the reason for the contract not coming into effect was:
       i) a lack of legal capacity on the part of the insurance holder,
       ii) lack of consent,
       iii) *falsa procuratio* (unauthorised agency)?
    c) Can the liability insurer (or the alternative compensation scheme) that must provide cover even though the insurance policy was not effec-

tively concluded (see above Questions a and b) have recourse against the damaging party?

24. a) Are there cases in which a damaging party does not take out any liability insurance, ie not even an ineffective insurance policy (see above Question 23), and the victim whom he injured is still compensated for his damage by a liability insurer or another compensation scheme (guarantee fund, etc)?
    b) Can the liability insurer (or the alternative compensation scheme) that must provide cover despite the total absence of any insurance agreement (see above Question a) have recourse against the damaging party?
25. Is the victim protected against the insolvency of the liability insurer?
26. Are there rules that serve in particular the protection of the victim when the liability insurance was only concluded voluntarily – ie without it being compulsory?

## V. Supervision and Sanctions

27. a) In which cases must the insurance holder prove to an authority before commencing an activity requiring insurance that he has taken out the respective prescribed liability insurance cover (see above Question 4.e)?
    b) Must the insurer inform an authority when liability insurance taken out to meet an insurance obligation ends?
    c) Is the insurer also under a duty to inform when a liability insurance agreement is in existence but it has no duty to provide cover – eg, due to defaults on premium payments?
    d) What are the consequences when the duties to inform of the end of contract or the release from payment obligations (see above Questions b and c) are violated?
28. Is there some official body (authority, professional chamber) where an injured party can find out whether and where the injuring party who inflicted damage upon him in the course of an activity requiring insurance has liability insurance?
29. Are there (public law) sanctions against the party who was required to take out insurance if such does not take out the compulsory liability insurance? Examples of this would be a ban on carrying out the activity that requires the insurance or the imposition of an administrative or judicial penalty.

## VI. Statutory Provisions required by the Constitution or the European Convention on Human Rights (ECHR)

30. What has been said regarding the compatibility of the duties to take out liability insurance with your country's constitution and the ECHR? Please take into account case law and academic literature.
31. Does the constitution or the ECHR make any stipulations regarding the contents of such duties to take out liability insurance? Please take into account case law and academic literature.

## VII. Reform Efforts

32. Are there efforts towards reforming the law regarding compulsory liability insurance?

## VIII. Compulsory Liability Insurance and Liability Law

33. Is, at the legislative level, any connection discernible between the nature of liability (in particular in the case of strict liability) and the imposition of compulsory liability insurance?

# Country Reports

Daniel Rubin

# Compulsory Liability Insurance in Austria

## I. The Term Compulsory Liability Insurance

1. *Indicate the rules within your legal system that set out a duty to take out liability insurance. In this context, also take into account the implementation of international treaties (eg, the International Convention on Civil Liability for Bunker Oil Pollution Damage, 2001).*

In Austria there are *over 50 federal laws* that set out an obligation to take out li- 1
ability insurance. The same can be attested at the level of *provincial laws*. In respect of both, see the lists in Annex: Rules on Compulsory Liability Insurance in Austria (at the end of this book).

2. *Is there a coherent 'law of compulsory liability insurance' in your legal system?*

Austrian legal teaching is in agreement that this is *not* the case.[1] In this respect 2
it is criticised that there is not even the beginning of a coherent legislative system in respect of either the question of when there is a legislative duty to have such cover in the first place or, in such case, what this cover includes.[2] Thus, for example, architects are still not obliged to take out liability insurance. The obligation for doctors[3] and operators of hospitals[4] as well as for builders[5] was also only introduced relatively recently. Furthermore, there is no uniform standard for when the legislator prescribes compulsory financial security, whether pure

---

1 *M Hinteregger*, Die Pflichthaftpflichtversicherung aus zivilrechtlicher Sicht, Versicherungsrundschau (VR) 2005, 44, 55; *A Fenyves*, Versicherungsvertragsrechtliche Grundfragen der Pflichthaftpflichtversicherung, VR 2005, 70, 70; see also *G Ertl*, Versicherungspflicht light, ecolex 2007, 586, 586.

2 *Fenyves*, VR 2005, 70, 70; *Hinteregger*, VR 2005, 44, 55; *M Schauer*, Rechtsprobleme der Haftpflichtversicherungen im KMG, WAG und ÜbG, in: Festschrift (FS) H Krejci II (2001) 1270 (on the second question).

3 § 52d Medical Doctors Act (Ärztegesetz, ÄrzteG), in force since August 2010.

4 § 5c Hospitals and Health Resorts Act (Krankenanstalten- und Kuranstaltengesetz, KAKuG), in force since August 2010.

5 § 99 Trade Act (Gewerbeordnung, GewO), in force since August 2012.

liability insurance is required or liability insurance is just an optional way to fulfil the requirement (on the latter see below under Question 4.f).[6]

3 However, the beginnings of a system can be discerned insofar as the legislator *usually* ties the requirement of liability insurance to *strict liability* when it legislates for such.[7] Nonetheless, there are exceptions in this regard too for which no reason is apparent.[8]

3. *Is there a specific term for compulsory liability insurance in your legal system? How is it defined?*

4 In Austrian law there is the distinct, legally relevant term *Pflichthaftpflichtversicherung*, which translates literally as 'compulsory liability insurance'. It is found in *§ 158b VersVG*, which uses the verbum legale *Pflichtversicherung* (in English: compulsory insurance) as a synonym for *Pflichthaftpflichtversicherung*: § 158b Insurance Contract Act (*Versicherungsvertragsgesetz*, VersVG) defines this as 'a liability insurance which is legally required to be concluded (compulsory insurance)'. Thus, the term compulsory liability insurance is *ambiguous* in the Austrian legal field: On the one hand, as a *technical legal term* with a specific normative meaning, it determines the external elements of § 158b VersVG. Thus, in the context of Question 4 below, the issue of when there is compulsory liability insurance under Austrian law is none other than the issue of the scope of § 158b VersVG (cf below no 5). On the other hand, the term 'compulsory liability insurance' also has a *non-technical meaning*, which includes the cases relevant under § 158b VersVG but goes beyond these too: the non-technical term relates to any and all legislative norms that prescribe the conclusion of liability insurance, whether these satisfy the requirements of § 158b VersVG or not.

5 The normative significance of the *specific term* compulsory liability insurance pursuant to § 158b VersVG consists in its link to special, private insurance law rules, namely those of *§§ 158c–158i VersVG*. The subsumption of a particular insurance contract under the term compulsory insurance is hence equivalent to

---

6 *B Raschauer*, Die Pflichthaftpflichtversicherung aus verfassungsrechtlicher Sicht, VR 2005, 35, 35; *D Rubin*, Der Begriff der Pflichthaftpflichtversicherung – Zum Anwendungsbereich der §§ 158c ff VersVG, VR 9 (2007) 21, 28 f.

7 See the list in Annex: Rules on Compulsory Liability Insurance in Austria (at the end of this book) I.1.

8 Strict liability regimes that have been established without compulsory liability regimes are: § 160 ff Mineralrohstoffgesetz for mining damage, the Liability Act of the German Empire (Reichshaftpflichtgesetz) for systems to transport and supply electricity and gas (except for natural gas), finally § 53 Forestry Act (Forstgesetz) in respect of certain facilities that cause air pollution damaging to forests.

deciding that the above-mentioned provisions are applicable to this contract.[9] In other words, the technical legal term 'compulsory insurance' under § 158b VersVG serves to define the external elements for such legal consequences, as are prescribed by the subsequent provisions in *§ 158c ff VersVG*.[10]

These predominantly govern the legal *relationship between the injured party and the liability insurer*. The central provision is *§ 158c VersVG*,[11] which aims to ensure that the injured third party receives the benefits from the liability insurer even if the insurance contract is not in order, ie when the damaging party has no *contractual entitlement* to insurance cover from his liability insurer: § 158c VersVG therefore simulates the existence of an entitlement to cover 'in view of the third party' both in the event of *the insurer being free of the duty to pay out* (para 1 leg cit) and also when no *valid insurance contract* exists (any longer) at the time of the (not) insured event (para 2 leg cit); see for more detail on this below no 61 ff (§ 158c *para 1* VersVG) and no 65 ff (§ 158c *para 2* VersVG). 6

Consequently, a statutory obligation in the sense of § 158b VersVG to take out liability insurance requires that it is established (at least also) to *protect the injured party*.[12] For further criteria under § 158b, see below Question 4. 7

4. *In which of the following cases does compulsory liability insurance apply according to prevailing opinion?*

a) *Duties to take out liability insurance which are not directly based on the law but on an order or decision issued by administrative authorities?*

There is consensus that a 'statutory duty' in the sense of § 158b is established by so-called laws in the substantive sense,[13] hence by any *general-abstract legal norm*.[14] This also includes *decrees* (*Verordnungen*) issued by the adminis- 8

9 *Rubin*, VR 9 (2007) 21, 22; cf also *Fenyves*, VR 2005, 70, 72; *Raschauer*, VR 2005, 35, 35 f.
10 *Rubin*, VR 9 (2007) 21, 22.
11 *Schauer* (fn 2) 1279; *Fenyves*, VR 2005, 70, 72; *D Rubin*, Wertpapierdienstleistungsunternehmer und ihre Deckungsvorsorge im WAG 2007, ecolex 2008, 17, 17.
12 *Rubin*, VR 9 (2007) 21, 24 f; cf also *Hinteregger*, VR 2005, 44, 45.
13 *M Baumann* in: H Honsell (ed), Berliner Kommentar (hereinafter: BK) zum VVG (1998) Vorbem zu §§ 149–158k no 14; *M Schauer*, Einige Rechtsfragen der obligatorischen Haftpflichtversicherung für Notare, Österreichische Notariatszeitung (NZ) 1999, 305, 307.
14 *Fenyves*, VR 2005, 70, 72; *Rubin*, VR 9 (2007) 21, 22; *W Kath*, Regress des Versicherers (2011) 305.

trative authorities,[15] insofar as they are sufficiently well-defined by a statutory law.[16]

9 If, on the other hand, liability insurance cover is prescribed by a *decision* (*Bescheid*) issued by an administrative authority, then prevailing opinion draws a *distinction* as to whether the law makes this *mandatory* or the law allows the authority issuing the decision *discretion* in this respect: in the former case the existence of compulsory liability insurance is affirmed, in the latter it is negated.[17]

*b) Duties to take out liability insurance that are not based directly on the law but on the statutes of a professional or other self-governing body?*

10 Compulsory liability insurance in the sense of § 158b VersVG may also be required by the relevant *statutes* (= regulations) of *self-governing professional bodies* (professional associations).[18]

*c) Duties to take out liability insurance that are not based on any public law but on a private law provision (eg, governing the relationship between employer and employee)?*

11 There are a few laws governing solely private law (contractual) relationships that provide a basis for an obligation to take out liability insurance. Examples include § 30 para 1 no 4 Condominium Act (*Wohnungseigentumsgesetz*, WEG) 2002 and § 24 para 7 Associations Act (*Vereinsgesetz*, VerG). According to prevailing opinion, however, compulsory liability insurance laws in the sense of § 158b VersVG are always of a *public law nature.*[19] This is presumably because private law duties to take out liability insurance are in fact not aimed at the protection of the injured party (see on this above no 7).

---

15 *Fenyves*, VR 2005, 70, 72; *A Vonkilch*, Die Haftung der Zertifizierungsdiensteanbieter nach dem SigG und ihre Pflichtversicherung, VR 2001, 122, 126; *U Knappmann* in: J Prölss/A Martin (hereinafter: PM), Kommentar zum VVG (27th edn 2004) § 158b no 1.

16 *Raschauer*, VR 2005, 35, 35.

17 *Fenyves*, VR 2005, 70, 72; *Kath* (fn 14) 306; *M Hübsch* in: Berliner Kommentar (BK) zum VVG (1998) § 158b no 3.

18 Cf *D Rubin* in: A Fenyves/M Schauer (eds), Kommentar zum VersVG (2014) § 158b no 9; *Schauer*, NZ 1999, 305, 307.

19 Oberster Gerichtshof (Supreme Court, OGH) 7 Ob 27/62 Juristische Blätter (JBl) 1962, 563; *Raschauer*, VR 2005, 35, 36 f; *Schauer*, NZ 1999, 305, 306 f.

*d) Duties to take out liability insurance that are not based on any public law but on a private law rule that is established by case law (and, eg, governs the relationship between employer and employee)?*

Case law infers from the *employer's duty of care* towards employees (§ 1157 Civil Code [ABGB]) that such is obliged to safeguard the employee from compensation claims of third parties, in the case of accident-prone activities, by taking out adequate liability insurance. The cases decided so far relate to the drivers of hazardous goods transports.[20] This does *not involve* compulsory liability insurance in the technical sense *pursuant to § 158b VersVG* either, see above no 11. 12

*e) Cases in which there is no duty to take out liability insurance but liability insurance cover is a prerequisite for the admissibility of carrying out a particular activity?*

Such constellations are frequent in the Austrian administrative law landscape. *Examples* include § 52d para 1 Medical Doctors Act (*Ärztegesetz*, ÄrzteG); § 26c para 1 Dentists Act (*Zahnärztegesetz*, ZÄG); § 44 para 1 no 2 Natural Gas Act (*Gaswirtschaftsgesetz*, GWG 2011) (operators of natural gas networks); § 137c para 1 Trade Act (*Gewerbeordnung*, GewO) (insurance brokers), § 12 para 1 no 3, § 18 para 1 no 2 and para 2 no 2, § 20 para 2, § 72 para 1 lit c, § 106 para 1 lit c, § 120b para 4, § 132 para 2, § 140b para 5 no 3 Aviation Act (*Luftfahrtgesetz*, LFG) (keepers of aerial vehicles); § 28 Postal Market Act (*Postmarktgesetz*) (postal services); § 4 para 2 no 2 Securities Supervision Act (*Wertpapieraufsichtsgesetz*, WAG 2007) (investment services providers); on all of these see Annex: Rules on Compulsory Liability Insurance in Austria. 13

The term compulsory liability insurance under § 158b VersVG also includes these cases and is not limited to constellations in which the law prescribes liability insurance cover as an obligation of conduct.[21] 14

**20** See Supreme Court (OGH) 9 ObA 129/90; cf further references in *H Krejci* in: P Rummel (ed), ABGB – Kommentar zum Allgemeinen bürgerlichen Gesetzbuch (3rd edn 2000) § 1157 no 43.

**21** *Rubin*, ecolex 2008, 17, 18; *idem*, VR 9 (2007) 21, 26 f; cf also *Schauer* (fn 2) 1280, 1283; cf on the other hand *Ertl*, ecolex 2007, 586, 586.

*f) Cases of alternative financial security, in which the duty to provide for financial security may be fulfilled either by taking out liability insurance or other forms of financial security (eg, bank guarantees)?*

15 *Examples* for such so-called alternative liability insurance can be found in § 137c Trade Act (GewO), § 7 para 1 no 6 Signature Act (*Signaturgesetz*, SigG), § 10 para 1 Nuclear Liability Act (*Atomhaftungsgesetz*, AtomHG), § 79j para 1 sent 1 Act on Genetic Engineering (*Gentechnikgesetz*, GTG) and in § 16 Product Liability Act (*Produkthaftungsgesetz*, PHG); on all of these see also Annex: Rules on Compulsory Liability Insurance in Austria. In legal teaching it is sometimes pointed out that the legislator usually requires this form of financial security instead of exclusive compulsory insurance without alternative when it considers the risk of damage to be insured less serious but still worth to be covered by mandatory financial security to be taken out by the potential tortfeasor.[22]

16 If the party required to provide financial security decides to take out such *alternative liability insurance*, then, according to prevailing, albeit disputed, opinion, this is not to be categorised as compulsory liability insurance under § 158b ff.[23]

*g) Cases in which the duty to have insurance has only been created by a contractual agreement between potential injuring party and victim?*

17 Any duty to take out insurance that is based on a contract – even with the *exchequer*[24] – does *not* fall under § 158b.[25] According to prevailing opinion, this even applies to *collective bargaining agreements*.[26]

---

**22** *Hinteregger*, VR 2005, 44, 51; *Kath* (fn 14) 309.

**23** See the Justice Committee Report (*Justizausschussbericht*) on PHG 438 BlgNR 17. GP 1f; *M Schauer*, Das österreichische Versicherungsvertragsrecht (3rd edn 1995) 392; BK/*Hübsch* (fn 17) § 158b no 2; *Vonkilch*, VR 2001, 122, 126; *Hinteregger*, VR 2005, 44, 45, 51f; *Raschauer*, VR 2005, 35, 35; *Fenyves*, VR 2005, 70, 72f; *Kath* (fn 14) 307ff. With another view, on the other hand, *KM Goretzky*, Die Leistungspflicht des Versicherers nach § 158c VVG (1998) 88; *Rubin*, VR 9 (2007) 21, 25ff.

**24** *T Langheid* in: W Römer/T Langheid (hereinafter: RL), Versicherungsvertragsgesetz (VVG) (2nd edn 2002) § 158b no 2.

**25** *Fenyves*, VR 2005, 70, 72; PM/*Knappmann* (fn 15) § 158b no 1; BK/*Baumann* (fn 13) Vorbem zu §§ 149–158k no 15.

**26** BK/*Hübsch* (fn 17) § 158b no 3.

# II. Aims

5. *What are the aims of the rules that impose an obligation to take out liability insurance:*

*a) the protection of the victim,*

There is consensus that the *main aim* of rules imposing compulsory liability insurance is usually to *protect the injured party* against the insolvency of the injuring party.[27] It is assumed that legislative duties to take out liability insurance are linked to the observation that certain activities are particularly likely to endanger third party interests.[28] In order to counterbalance this, the legislator ensures that victims' compensation claims resulting from this endangerment are then actually satisfied.[29] 18

*b) the protection of the insurance holder,*

No rules are provided that solely serve the protection of the insurance holder. 19
Some laws, however, impose an obligation to insure third party liability interests, ie to take out liability insurance for the account of a third party. Such duties usually *solely* serve the *protection of the insured party.*[30] Therefore, this situation does *not qualify* as compulsory liability insurance in the sense of § 158b ff either;[31] see above no 7.

This constellation arises above all when the (co-)insured party *may not be* 20
*exposed to any duties to compensate* potential victims, but may only be exposed to rights of recourse from the principal, who at the same time is the addressee of the duty to obtain insurance for the relevant activity (on behalf of a third party). An example of this is, in particular, § 9a para 7 Judges Service Act (*Richterdienstgesetz*, RDG).[32] In other cases, in particular a *systematic-teleological interpretation* of the respective duty to obtain insurance can show that the duty to

27 *Raschauer*, VR 2005, 35, 36; *Hinteregger*, VR 2005, 44, 45f; *M Hinteregger*, Haftung und Versicherung, in: FS für Rudolf Reischauer (2010) 511; *Rubin*, VR 9 (2007) 21, 21f, 30; *Kath* (fn 14) 311; RL/*Langheid* (fn 24) § 158b no 1. See likewise Erläuterungen zur Regierungsvorlage (Explanatory remarks on the government bill, ErläutRV) zu § 21a RAO 1638 BlgNR 20. GP, 17; ErläutRV zu § 30 NO 1633 BlgNR 20. GP, 12.

28 Cf *Raschauer*, VR 2005, 35, 36; *Hinteregger*, VR 2005, 44, 52.

29 Cf RL/*Langheid* (fn 24) § 158b no 1.

30 *Rubin*, VR 9 (2007) 21, 25.

31 *Hinteregger*, VR 2005, 44, 45; *Rubin*, VR 9 (2007) 21, 24f; *Kath* (fn 14) 306.

32 *Rubin*, VR 9 (2007) 21, 25 fn 43.

take out liability insurance exists only in the interest of the insured, which is the case for instance with § 48 Medical Devices Act (*Medizinproduktegesetz*, MPG),[33] § 7 Development Aid Workers Act (*Entwicklungshelfergesetz*)[34] and § 6 para 2 Railway Ordinance (*Eisenbahnverordnung*, EisbVO 2003).

*c) the protection of the victim and the insurance holder,*

21 Legal teaching often points out that the statutory establishment of a duty to obtain liability insurance not only serves the protection of the victim but frequently *also* that of *the insurance holder*.[35] Nevertheless, in my view this can only be said with certainty in respect of cases in which the relevant sectoral legislation provides for legal consequences that favour the insurance holder. This is true above all in the context of motor vehicle liability insurance: here, on the one hand, the range of the obligations of conduct (*Obliegenheiten*) that may be imposed on the insurance holder are limited (see § 5 Motor Vehicle Liability Insurance Act [*Kraftfahrzeug-Haftpflichtversicherungsgesetz* 1994, KHVG]). And, on the other hand, there is a limit on the amount (§ 7 KHVG) that the insurer can claim in recourse against the insurance holder when it is released from the duty to pay out benefits to such because such breached an obligation of conduct (*Obliegenheit*) under the insurance agreement (§ 24 para 4 KHVG; on this recourse in general see below no 64).

*d) other aims, eg internalising the costs in the interests of society?*

22 Legal teaching notes that compulsory liability insurance also has the purpose of effecting a continual *internalisation* of the costs of damage among potential injuring parties.[36] Furthermore it is pointed out that the legislator draws on the *redistribution of the damage* by means of compulsory liability insurance – by shifting these costs to the risk community – in order to make activities it considers desirable available to a larger circle of people.[37]

---

**33** *Rubin*, VR 9 (2007) 21, 25 fn 40; *Hinteregger*, VR 2005, 44, 45; see, however, *Raschauer*, VR 2005, 35, 35.

**34** *Rubin*, VR 9 (2007) 21, 25 fn 41; *Hinteregger*, VR 2005, 44, 45.

**35** BK/*Hübsch* (fn 17) § 158b no 5; *W Lemmel*, Länderbericht Österreich, in: J Basedow/T Fock (eds), Europäisches Versicherungsvertragsrecht II (2002) 1009; largely of the same opinion *Raschauer*, VR 2005, 35, 36.

**36** *Hinteregger*, VR 2005, 44, 46 f; *Hinteregger*, FS Reischauer (fn 27) 515 f; *Rubin*, VR 9 (2007) 21, 31 f.

**37** *Raschauer*, VR 2005, 35, 36. See on this also *Hinteregger*, FS Reischauer (fn 27) 517 f.

6. *Do the rules that prescribe a form of alternative financial security (see above Question 4.f) pursue the same aims as those rules that exclusively set out a duty to have liability insurance (ie with no other alternative financial security options)?*

This is partly affirmed in legal teaching, in that it is assumed that these rules primarily serve the protection of the victim.[38] Sometimes, on the other hand, it is assumed that this can only be determined by teleological interpretation of the respective sectoral legislation that lays down the duty to provide financial security.[39] 23

# III. Content of Insurance Cover

7. *Are the duties to take out liability insurance laid down by law only to cover extra-contractual compensation duties or also those arising out of contractual infringements?*

There are examples in this respect for *both cases*: *extra-contractual compensation duties* are covered above all by rules that prescribe insurance duties in respect of strict liability and thus also delictual liability, for instance § 59 Motor Vehicles Act (*Kraftfahrgesetz*, KFG), §§ 6f and 10 para 2 Nuclear Liability Act (AtomHG), § 79j para 1 sents 2 and 3 Act on Genetic Engineering (GTG), § 44 Natural Gas Act (GWG), § 164 para 1 Aviation Act (LFG), § 13 Pipelines Act (*Rohrleitungsgesetz*) and § 103 Cableway Act (*Seilbahngesetz*, SeilbG). Above all the insurance duties of the prospectus auditor under § 8 para 2 Capital Market Act (*Kapitalmarktgesetz*, KMG) and the court-appointed expert witness and interpreter under § 2a Expert Witnesses and Interpreters Act (*Sachverständigen- und Dolmetschergesetz*, SDG) relate to extra-contractual albeit not delictual compensation duties. 24

Compulsory liability insurance for *compensation claims arising from a contract* is prescribed in particular by: § 52d Medical Doctors Act (ÄrzteG), § 5c Hospitals and Health Resorts Act (*Krankenanstalten- und Kuranstaltengesetz*, KAKuG), § 30 Code on Notaries (*Notariatsordnung*, NO), § 21a Patent Attorneys Act (*Patentanwaltsgesetz*), § 21a Attorney Code (*Rechtsanwaltsordnung*, RAO), § 136a para 12 Trade Act (GewO) (commercial financial advisors), § 117 para 7 GewO (real estate trustees) and § 137c GewO (insurance brokers). 25

38 *Rubin*, VR 9 (2007) 21, 30.
39 *Fenyves*, VR 2005, 70, 73; *Kath* (fn 14) 308.

8.a) *Are there duties to take out liability insurance aimed not only at the protection of absolutely protected rights (eg, property, bodily integrity) but additionally at compensating pure economic loss?*

26 It is only rarely provided for *expressly*; examples include in particular § 2 para 1 Motor Vehicle Liability Insurance Act (KHVG) and a respective duty for builders under § 99 para 7 Trade Act (GewO).

27 If the respective sectoral legislation does not expressly restrict the insurance duty to damage sustained by absolutely protected legal goods, this must include liability for all primary pecuniary damage that represents a *typical liability risk of the activity requiring insurance*. This is in general the outcome of the teleological interpretation of the respective sectoral legislation. Thus, for instance, the liability insurance of a gynaecologist must also pay for the increased child support costs incurred by parents of a child with a disability in cases of wrongful birth.[40]

b) *Are there duties to take out liability insurance that are directed only or at least predominantly at the compensation of pure economic loss?*

28 This is true for those cases in which there is a duty to take out professional liability insurance and for which the *liability risk* related to the activity that must be insured is *typically limited to primary pecuniary damage*. In this case, the duty to take out insurance only extends to obtaining liability insurance for pecuniary damage. Sometimes this is already provided for in the wording of the relevant sectoral legislation, for example, in § 7 para 1 no 4 and § 10 Accountancy Act (*Bilanzbuchhaltungsgesetz*, BiBuG) (accountants), § 117 para 7 Trade Act (GewO) (real estate trustees) and § 136a para 12 GewO (commercial financial advisors).

9. *Are there provisions that require the insurance of a third party's liability interest – for instance, that the employer must take out liability insurance for the benefit of an employee?*

29 *Two groups* of rules are relevant here:

30 The *first group* exclusively involves obligations to insure third party liability interests, ie solely to take out *liability insurance for the account of a third party*. This is the case above all when the (co-)insured party may *not be exposed to compensations duties* vis-à-vis the potential victim, but only to the recourse rights of the principal, who is also the addressee of the insurance obligation for

40 For this on § 52d Medical Doctors Act (Ärztegesetz) cf *W Fitsch*, Über Wirkung und unerwünschte Wirkung fragen Sie Ihren Haftpflichtversicherer, VR 10 (2011) 22, 23.

the activity at stake. An example of this is, in particular, § 9a para 7 Judges Services Act (RDG).[41] In other cases, a systematic-teleological interpretation of the respective insurance obligation may show that it exists only in the interest of the insured, for example, in the case of § 48 Medical Devices Act (MPG),[42] § 7 Development Aid Workers Act (*Entwicklungshelfergesetz*)[43] and § 6 para 2 Railway Ordinance 2003 (EisbVO 2003). These obligations exclusively serve the protection of the insured.[44] Therefore, this does *not constitute compulsory liability insurance* in the sense of § 158b ff either;[45] cf above no 7.

The *second group of rules* prescribes *liability insurance on behalf of a third party* in addition to covering the liability interests of the party obliged to take out the insurance. An example of this is § 2 para 2 Motor Vehicle Liability Insurance Act (KHVG) 1994, which accordingly specifies the insurance obligation for keepers of motor vehicles under § 59 Motor Vehicle Act (KFG) (mandatory co-insurance of the driver authorised by the keeper to drive the car subject to the insurance). Another example is provided by § 21a para 3 Attorney Code (RAO) in favour of lawyers in an attorney-at-law partnership. 31

It is noteworthy that entrepreneurs who are obliged by law to obtain insurance for their activity usually *do not have to co-insure their employees*. This applies, for example, also to hospital staff (no duty to co-insure under § 5c Hospitals and Health Resorts Act, KAKuG). Some help is provided by the case law mentioned above in no 12, which infers a corresponding duty of employers to co-insure from the general *employers' duty of care* in the case of employee activity that is particularly likely to pose liability risks. 32

*10. To what extent do the rules requiring the compulsory conclusion of a liability insurance policy also specify the specific contents of the insurance coverage:*

*a) Is there always a (sufficiently well-defined) specification of the risk to be insured?*

No, there are no exact specifications for the primary formulation of the contingency to be insured against.[46] One typical formulation would be that a certain 33

41 *Rubin*, VR 9 (2007) 21, 25 fn 43.
42 *Rubin*, VR 9 (2007) 21, 25 fn 40; *Hinteregger*, VR 2005, 44, 45; see, however, *Raschauer*, VR 2005, 35, 35.
43 *Rubin*, VR 9 (2007) 21, 25 fn 41; *Hinteregger*, VR 2005, 44, 45.
44 *Rubin*, VR 9 (2007) 21, 25.
45 *Hinteregger*, VR 2005, 44, 45; *Rubin*, VR 9 (2007) 21, 24 f; *Kath* (fn 14) 306.
46 Cf also *Fenyves*, VR 2005, 70, 73.

party engaging in a commercial activity 'must *take out* liability insurance for pecuniary losses *for their working activity*'; this is the case, for example, under § 117 para 7 Trade Act (GewO) (real estate trustees) and § 136a para 12 GewO (financial advisors). Or one might think of the obligation certain freelance workers are under to prove before embarking on their activity that they have 'liability insurance ... to cover compensation claims arising out of their professional activity' (§ 21a para 1 Attorney Code [RAO] and § 21a para 1 Patent Attorneys Act [*Patentanwaltsgesetz*]; almost identical is § 30 para 1 Code on Notaries [NO]).

34 Even less concretely defined specifications of the risk to be insured can be found, for example, '*corresponding liability insurance* must be obtained' (§ 103 Cableway Act [*SeilbG*]; with the same meaning, § 28 para 1 no 2 Postal Market Act [*Postmarktgesetz*]). Or: that liability insurance must be taken out 'in a *manner* and with a *scope* that is usual *in proper business relations*' (§ 12 para 7 Accreditation Act [*Akkreditierungsgesetz*, AkkG] 2012 and § 16 Product Liability Act [PHG][47]).

*b) Are there provisions that require unlimited coverage?*

35 No.

*c) If unlimited coverage is not required (see above Question b), is a minimum or maximum insurance sum always specified?*

36 Minimum insurance sums are *usually* prescribed whereas maximum insurance sums are not to be found in Austrian law.

37 In some cases, on the other hand, the law only states that 'sufficient' liability insurance must be obtained, thus, for example, in § 32 para 1 no 12 Pharmaceutical Products Act (*Arzneimittelgesetz*, AMG), § 37 para 8 and § 48 Medical Devices Act (MPG) and § 21 para 7 Environmental Management Act (*Umweltmanagementgesetz*, UMG) (environmental consultants).

38 Sometimes the law only states that there must be '*adequate liability insurance*' or liability insurance with a *scope* that is '*usual in due and proper business relations*'; see the examples above in no 34.

47 Further examples in *Fenyves*, VR 2005, 70, 73 fn 24.

*d) Are there general statutory rules to be applicable if the respective law that requires compulsory insurance only makes incomplete stipulations regarding the content of the insurance coverage? An example of this would be § 114 para 1 of the German Insurance Contract Act (Versicherungsvertragsgesetz, VVG) 2008.*

No. 39

*11. Is it admissible to restrict the insurance cover by agreeing:*

*a) risk exclusion clauses,*

Only a few pieces of sectoral legislation deal with the question of whether and 40
by which risk exclusion clauses the insurance cover they prescribe may be limited. A relatively detailed list is found in § 4 Motor Vehicle Liability Insurance Act (KHVG). Furthermore, there are limitations on the insurance duty itself in some strict liability laws in cases of force majeure, above all, for instance, in § 6 para 1 and § 7 para 1 Nuclear Liability Act (AtomHG). Such rules are rather seldom as in this context (force majeure) the operator of the respective dangerous plant is not liable in the first place. Insofar as they apply, there is, as aforementioned, no insurance duty on the part of the party liable.

Otherwise it is predominantly assumed that risk exclusion clauses may 'be 41
agreed *within the usual framework*'.[48] In other words, prevailing opinion is that risk exclusion clauses are possible but may not '*materially undermine*' the *protection of the victim.*[49] The opinions presented here do not distinguish in this respect between the internal relationship between the insurer and the injuring party and the external relationship of the insurer to the victim.

*b) deductibles,*

The statutory *minimum insurance sum* must be paid *in full* to the victim. There- 42
fore, it is inadmissible to agree a deductible *vis-à-vis the victim.*[50] This is the case unless the respective sectoral legislation separately sets out the admissibility of

**48** ErläutRV zu § 21a RAO 1638 BlgNR 20. GP, 17; ErläutRV zu § 30 NO 1633 BlgNR 20. GP, 12; see also *Fenyves*, VR 2005, 70, 73 f.

**49** OGH 7 Ob 152/06p Versicherungsrechtliche Entscheidungen (VersE) 2173; 7 Ob 33/10v VersE 2348; *Fenyves*, VR 2005, 70, 74.

**50** ErläutRV zu § 21a RAO 1638 BlgNR 20. GP, 17; ErläutRV zu § 30 NO 1633 BlgNR 20. GP, 12.

such,[51] for instance in § 99 para 7 Trade Act (GewO) (*builders*) and § 117 para 7 GewO (*real estate trustees*). This applies, however, only vis-à-vis the victim. Within the internal relationship to the *insurance holder* it is *in principle possible to agree deductibles.*[52] In two cases this is also stipulated in the respective law, namely in § 11 para 3 Certified Public Accountants and Tax Advisors Act (*Wirtschaftstreuhandberufsgesetz*, WTBG) (*tax advisors* and *auditors*) and § 10 para 3 Accountancy Act (BiBuG) (*accountants*). Even where the insurance duty also serves the *protection of the insurance holder*, as is the case especially, for example, in motor vehicle liability insurance (see above no 21), deductibles can be agreed validly vis-à-vis the insurance holder. This follows in particular from § 12 Motor Vehicle Liability Insurance Act (KHVG).

*c) aggregate limits,*

43 The statements made above in no 42 apply accordingly here as well.[53] Aggregate limits are also in principle only admissible within the internal relationship, see here too § 11 para 3 Certified Public Accountants and Tax Advisors Act (WTBG) and § 10 para 3 Accountancy Act (BiBuG). However, there are a number of provisions that also allow aggregate limits vis-à-vis the victim. Examples of this are § 52d para 2 Medical Doctors Act (ÄrzteG), § 5c para 2 Hospitals and Health Resorts Act (KAKuG), § 99 para 7 Trade Act (GewO) (*builders*) and § 117 para 7 GewO (*real estate trustees*), § 136a para 12 GewO (*commercial financial advisors*), § 137c para 1 GewO (*insurance brokers*) and § 26c para 2 Dentists Act (ZÄG).

*d) claims series clauses,*

44 The statements above in no 42 apply once again accordingly.[54]

*e) other clauses?*

45 The statements above in no 42 apply to the *limitation* on the basis of the insurance contract *of the subsequent coverage* (the insurer's duty to pay even after the expiry of the insurance cover).[55] Beyond this, there are provisions that *expressly prohibit* limitations on subsequent coverage to the detriment of the vic-

51 *Fenyves*, VR 2005, 70, 75.
52 Ibid.
53 Cf *Fenyves*, VR 2005, 70, 75f.
54 Cf *Fenyves*, VR 2005, 70, 76.
55 Cf *Fenyves*, VR 2005, 70, 75f.

tim. Examples include § 21a para 5 Attorney Code (RAO), § 30 para 4 Code on Notaries (NO), § 2a para 3 Expert Witnesses and Interpreters Act (SDG) (court appointed expert witnesses and interpreters), § 39 para 2 no 1 Psychologists Act (*Psychologengesetz*) 2013. Sometimes too, the law merely sets out a minimum period for the subsequent coverage, for example, in § 6 para 1 Nuclear Liability Act (AtomHG).[56]

12. *What are the consequences if the liability insurance contract concluded in order to fulfil the insurance obligation contravenes what the law stipulates as to contents (see above Questions 10 and 11)?*

Insofar as such amount to inadmissible limitations of the insurance cover (see above nos 41–45), they are *null and void* under *§ 879 Civil Code* (ABGB). 46

13.a) *Are statutory stipulations as to the contents of the policy (eg, regarding the amount of the insurance sum, the ban on certain risk exclusion clauses, on deductibles, etc, see above Questions 10 and 11) also binding in favour of the insurance holder? Or is it nonetheless possible for the liability insurer and the insurance holder acting within their internal relationship to agree risk exclusion clauses, deductibles, aggregate limits, and claims series clauses, etc (see above Questions 10 and 11), releasing the insurer from its liability to pay?*

In principle the latter case is assumed; see in detail above nos 42–45. 47

b) *If it is possible for liability insurer and insurance holder acting within their internal relationship to agree a release from the obligation to pay (see above Question a): What consequences does this entail? Must the insurer first pay out to the victim and can then have recourse to the insurance holder? Or is another construction provided for the relationship between insurer, insurance holder and victim?*

In those cases in which cover is validly excluded by agreement only vis-à-vis the insurance holder, the insurer has a contractual duty only to provide cover in relation to the victim. Therefore, the insurer has a *right of recourse* against the insurance holder. This is either contractually agreed in the first place[57] or follows in my opinion by analogy from § 158f VersVG (on this, see below no 64). 48

**56** On this *Fenyves*, VR 2005, 70, 77.
**57** On this *Schauer*, NZ 1999, 305, 311 (notaries).

*14.a) Does your general (voluntary) liability insurance law include a statutory risk exclusion in respect of intentional damage by the insurance holder or the insured person?*

49 Such a subjective risk exclusion is prescribed by *§ 152 Insurance Contract Act* (VersVG), though *dolus eventualis* is sufficient.[58] If (solely) the *insurance holder* (and not the co-insured) can be accused of intention, § 152 VersVG (only) applies to him.

*b) If the general liability insurance law contains a statutory risk exclusion in respect of intentional damage inflicted by the insurance holder (see above Question a): Does this also apply in cases of compulsory liability insurance?*

50 Yes. There is consensus that § 152 VersVG also applies vis-à-vis the victim where there is *compulsory liability insurance.*[59]

## IV. Protection Mechanisms

*15. Are insurers obliged to contract when they offer liability insurance policies covering a risk for which the insurance holder is obliged to obtain cover?*

51 There is in principle no obligation to contract upon insurers that offer compulsory liability insurance policies either. Only in the case of *motor vehicle liability insurance* is there any such obligation if three insurers have refused to provide liability insurance cover to a particular motor vehicle keeper (for details see § 25 Motor Vehicle Liability Act [KHVG]). An analogous procedure was considered by the legislator in respect of compulsory liability insurance of doctors too,[60] but never introduced.

*16. If there is no obligation to contract: Are there comparable mechanisms provided to ensure that an insurance agreement is concluded?*

52 No. This is why academic teaching also criticises the fact that consequently it lies within the power of the liability insurer to deny people access to activities

---

**58** *Schauer* (fn 23) 396.

**59** OGH 7 Ob 33/10v VersE 2348; *Schauer* (fn 23) 413; *R Beckmann* in: H Honsell (ed), Berliner Kommentar (BK) zum VVG (1998) § 158c no 34.

**60** See the ErläutRV zu § 52d ÄrzteG 779 BlgNR 24. GP, 22.

requiring insurance simply because they belong to a group with a greater risk of causing damage.[61]

*17. Is the insurance holder prohibited from disposing over his cover entitlement to the disadvantage of the victim (eg, by surrendering his entitlement)?*

§ 156 para 1 VersVG stipulates that '*legal transactions* over the compensation claim arising out of the insurance relationship ... [are] ineffective vis-à-vis the third party'. From this rule, it thus follows that *only paying out to the victim can have the effect of discharging the insurer's debt,*[62] unless the victim was, by way of exception, already satisfied by the insurance holder. Therefore, the insurance holder may normally cede in particular his cover entitlement solely and exclusively to the victim.[63] The above-mentioned rule additionally stipulates that this claim is also *removed* from the *executionary grasp of the creditors* of the insurance holder. In this manner, § 156 para 1 VersVG ensures that the insurance holder's cover entitlement is *reserved to satisfy* the insurance holder's duty to compensate *the victim*. This rule already applies to both compulsory and voluntary liability insurance. 53

*18. Does the victim enjoy special protection against insolvency on the part of the insurance holder with regard to the sum payable by the liability insurer?*

§ 157 VersVG grants the victim in the event of insolvency of the injuring party a right to *separate satisfaction* out of the entitlement to cover from the liability insurer. This rule complements § 156 para 1 VersVG (on this see above no 53) and ensures that, even if the injuring party becomes insolvent, only the victim will have access to the insurance benefit from any (even voluntary) liability insurance. 54

*19.a) In what manner can the victim obtain the insurance payment?*

The victim's access to the injuring party's entitlement to cover from his liability insurer is subject – just as in the case of voluntary liability insurance – as a rule to the *general debt and enforcement rules*. The victim may thus only seize the entitlement and have it transferred to him *by means of executionary enforcement* on the basis of a final, enforceable judgment in a liability proceeding against 55

61 *Hinteregger*, FS Reischauer (fn 27) 518.
62 *Schauer* (fn 23) 410. On the procedure cf in more detail below no 55 ff.
63 *W Voit/U Knappmann* in: Prölss/Martin, VVG (27th edn 2004) § 156 nos 4 and 10.

the insurance holder, in order to assert the cover entitlement against the insurer by means of a subrogatory measure.[64]

*b) Does the victim have a direct right of action against the liability insurer (action directe) in the case of voluntary or compulsory liability insurance?*

56 At present in the case of *ten types of compulsory liability cover*, the respective sectoral legislation grants the victim a separate claim (*action directe*) against the insurer. These are: § 26 Motor Vehicle Liability Act (KHVG) (motor vehicle keepers), § 4a para 3 Pharmacy Act (*Apothekengesetz*), § 52d para 6 Medical Doctors Act (ÄrzteG), § 24 Nuclear Liability Act (AtomHG), § 5c para 3 Hospitals and Health Resorts Act (KAKuG), § 166 Aviation Act (LFG) (keepers of aircraft vehicles), § 34 para 6 Music Therapy Act (*Musiktherapiegesetz*), § 39 para 5 Psychologists Act 2013 (*Psychologengesetz 2013*), § 16b para 3 Psychotherapy Act (*Psychotherapiegesetz*) and § 26c para 6 Dentists Act (ZÄG). The sectoral legislation creates a *joint obligation* between injuring party and insurer in these cases.[65]

57 In addition, the Austrian Supreme Court (*Oberster Gerichtshof*, OGH) proceeds on the basis that § 4 para 3 no 1 Securities Supervision Act (WAG) 2007 (investment service providers) is also to be regarded as a statutory provision prescribing the *action directe*.[66]

*20. When settling the claim, is the liability insurer obliged to observe a certain procedure in the interests of the victim? For instance, must it pay the victim an advance within a certain period?*

58 The liability insurer may as a rule only satisfy its duty to compensate by means of *payment to the victim* (§ 156 para 1 VersVG); see in more detail above no 53.

59 'It must pay the compensation within two weeks from the date on which ... the third party's claim ... was established by *final judgment*' (§ 154 para 1 VersVG). The same applies, according to this rule, when the insurance holder – *in agreement with the insurer*[67] – *satisfies* the injured third party (but in this case the insurer has to pay to the insurance holder, see above no 53) or *acknowledges*

64 OGH 7 Ob 60/79 VersE 962; *Schauer* (fn 23) 410; *idem*, NZ 1999, 305, 311.

65 See, eg, § 26 sent 2 KHVG, § 52d para 6 sent 2 ÄrzteG, § 24 para 1 sent 2 AtomHG, § 5c para 3 sent 2 KAKuG, § 166 sent 2 LuftFG, § 26c para 6 sent 2 ZÄG.

66 Thus, on the previous rule (§ 20 para 5 WAG 1996) OGH 7 Ob 152/06p = VersE 2173; with another opinion *Schauer* (fn 2) 1287; *Rubin*, ecolex 2008, 17, 19 fn 26; leaving it open *Fenyves*, VR 2005, 70, 78.

67 Cf PM/*Voit*/*Knappmann* (fn 63) § 154 no 3.

the debt or agrees a *settlement* with respect to such third party's compensation claim. Prior to these points in time, specified in § 154 para 1 VersVG, the liability insurer's payment is thus not yet due. This applies in the same way to *compulsory* and *voluntary* liability insurance.

Only in the context of *motor vehicle liability insurance* does an *earlier due* 60
*date* come into question: here the insurer 'must offer the compensation payment to the injured third party within three months from the point in time when such notified it of the damaging event, if such is not disputed as to the merits or amount' (§ 29a para 1 Motor Vehicle Liability Act [KHVG]). If, however, inquiries by the insurer are necessary in order to establish the duty to provide cover and if these are 'not yet completed within the period specified in para 1, then the injured third party may demand ... *payments on account* in the minimum amount that the insurer must pay according to the respective case' (§ 29a para 2 KHVG).

*21.a) In the context of its relationship with the victim, can the liability insurer rely on the fact that vis-à-vis the insurance holder (= damaging party) it is freed from the obligation to pay, eg, due to the insurance holder breaching an obligation of conduct/warranty (Obliegenheitsverletzung) or due to him defaulting on premiums?*

This is true in general. However, if liability insurance is concluded on the basis 61
of an *insurance duty serving to protect the victim* (= compulsory liability insurance in the technical sense pursuant to § 158b VersVG; see above nos 7 and 18), then § 158c para 1 VersVG (cf above no 6) applies: 'If the insurer is freed in full or in part from the duty to pay vis-à-vis the insurance holder, nonetheless its obligation in view of the third party remains.' Thus, according to prevailing opinion, the legislator *simulates* in the interest of the victim the existence of an *obligation of the insurer to provide cover* that does not in fact currently exist based on the insurance contract.[68] The victim is thus enabled to obtain the simulated cover entitlement of the injuring party by way of execution measures (cf above no 55).

This fictional cover provided by § 158c para 1 VersVG in this respect in- 62
cludes all cases where the insurer is freed from having to pay while the *insurance policy* is *in effect*, in particular thus when the insurer is freed due to the insurance holder *defaulting on premiums*,[69] *breaching obligations of conduct* (*Obliegenheitsverletzung*)[70] and there is an *increase in risk*.[71]

---

**68** OGH 7 Ob 108/11z VersE 2392 = EvBl 2011/154 (*Rubin*).
**69** OGH 1 Ob 960/52 SZ 26/93; *Schauer*, NZ 1999, 305, 311; RL/*Langheid* (fn 24) § 158c no 2.
**70** OGH 7 Ob 37/81 VersE 1047; *Schauer*, NZ 1999, 305, 311.
**71** OGH 7 Ob 37/81 VersE 1047; RL/*Langheid* (fn 24) § 158c no 2.

*b) Does the law distinguish on the basis of the ground for the release from the obligation to pay so that in some cases the insurer may not invoke its release from such obligation vis-à-vis the victim?*

63 If fictional cover pursuant to § 158c VersVG as described above in no 62 applies, the insurer is only liable to the injured third party 'within the scope of the officially determined minimum insurance sum and the risk to be covered according to the contract' (§ 158c para 3 VersVG). This means that agreed risk exclusion clauses also have effect vis-à-vis the victim.[72] Accordingly, it is important to *distinguish* precisely between freedom from the obligation to pay due to breach of a *duty of conduct* (*Obliegenheitsverletzung*) and such freedom on the basis of a *risk exclusion clause*.[73]

*c) If the insurer must still pay the victim despite being released from its obligation to pay vis-à-vis the insurance holder (see above Question b), may it take recourse against the latter?*

64 Yes. If the insurer has satisfied the victim's compensation claim pursuant to § 158c VersVG (see on this above no 63), this is *transferred ex lege to the insurer* to the extent of the satisfaction (§ 158f VersVG). This claim is the necessary counterbalance to the insurer's duty to take out cover as stipulated by § 158c VersVG, since such cannot be required ultimately to bear the liability burden given the lack of a contractual obligation towards the injuring party.[74]

*22.a) Within its relationship to the victim, can the liability insurer invoke the fact that the insurance agreement had already ended by the time relevant in respect of the duty to provide cover?*

65 This is true in general but not, however, when there is compulsory liability insurance in the sense of § 158b VersVG (see above nos 5–7). In this case, *§ 158c para 2 VersVG simulates* the *continued existence* of the insurance cover (see above also no 6). The insurer may *only end* its further liability thus effected by *informing* the *supervisory authority* responsible for the insurance holder about the termination of the insurance contract. One month after this information is received by the authority, the fictional cover is extinguished. According to some

**72** 7 Ob 33/10v VersE 2348; *Schauer* (fn 23) 413.
**73** BK/*Beckmann* (fn 59) § 158c no 34.
**74** *Rubin*, VR 9 (2007) 21, 24; *Rubin*, ecolex 2008, 17, 18.

special rules, which insofar supersede § 158c VersVG, this period can also be two[75] or three[76] months, and in some cases it is shortened to two weeks.[77]

*b) If the insurer must pay the victim despite the termination of the insurance agreement by the time relevant for the duty to provide cover (see above Question a), can it take recourse against the insurance holder?*

Yes. The same applies as stated above in no 64. **66**

*23.a) Are there cases in which a damaging party does not effectively conclude the required liability insurance and the victim injured by him nonetheless receives compensation for his loss from a liability insurer or another compensation scheme (eg, a guarantee fund)?*

Here too – for example, in the case that a contract is contested on the basis of **67** fraud in the inducement[78] – *§ 158c para 2 VersVG* also applies (on this see above no 65ff).

*b) In the event that the policy taken out was not in fact effectively concluded, is it necessary to distinguish on the basis of the ground for this ineffectiveness, eg, whether the reason for the contract not coming into effect was:*

*i) a lack of legal capacity on the part of the insurance holder,*

According to prevailing opinion, this case also falls under § 158c para 2 **68** VersVG.[79]

*ii) lack of consent,*

It is a minimum requirement for the fictional cover under § 158c para 2 VersVG **69** that there is at least the *external appearance of a liability insurance contract,*

---

**75** For example, according to § 99 para 9 GewO (builders), § 117 para 9 GewO (real estate trustees), § 136a para 12 GewO (commercial financial advisors), § 137c para 4 GewO (insurance brokers).

**76** Cf § 24 para 2 KHVG.

**77** § 30 para 5 NO (notaries), § 21a para 6 RAO (lawyers) and § 21a para 6 Patentanwaltsgesetz.

**78** *M Gruber*, Kfz-Zulassung – Amtshaftung bei Leistungsfreiheit des Haftpflichtversicherers, Zeitschrift für Verkehrsrecht (ZVR) 1991, 33, 36.

**79** *Gruber*, ZVR 1991, 33, 36.

even if such has not effectively been concluded.[80] Thus, the application of § 158c para 2 VersVG is denied in the case of an *obvious lack of consent* between the insurer and the (merely seeming) insurance holder;[81] in the case of *lack of consent which was not apparent* on the other hand, it is affirmed.[82]

*iii) falsa procuratio (unauthorised agency)?*

70 To date legal writing has only dealt with *falsa procuratio* on the side of the *insurer*: in such case the applicability of § 158c para 2 VersVG is affirmed, however, only provided that the insurer is 'in a legal relationship of some form' with the *falsus procurator*.[83]

*c) Can the liability insurer (or the alternative compensation scheme) that must provide cover even though the insurance policy was not effectively concluded (see above Questions a and b) have recourse against the damaging party?*

71 Yes. The same as stated above in no 64 applies.

*24.a) Are there cases in which a damaging party does not take out any liability insurance, ie not even an ineffective insurance policy (see above Question 23), and the victim whom he injured is still compensated for his damage by a liability insurer or another compensation scheme (guarantee fund, etc)?*

72 In this case no *protection* for the victim comes into question even *under § 158c para 2 VersVG* (see above no 65ff). There is only an alternative protection mechanism as far as *motor vehicle liability insurance* is concerned: a victim who has suffered a bodily injury or damage to property has a claim against the Professional Association of Insurers (*Fachverband der Versicherungsunternehmen*)[84] for such benefit as would be due in the case of a valid insurance contract (§ 4 para 1 no 1 Act on Compensation for Road Traffic Victims [*Verkehrsopfer-Entschädigungsgesetz*, VOEG]).

---

**80** PM/*Knappmann* (fn 15) § 158c no 8; BK/*Beckmann* (fn 59) § 158c no 18.
**81** PM/*Knappmann* (fn 15) § 158c no 8; BK/*Beckmann* (fn 59) § 158c no 18.
**82** PM/*Knappmann* (fn 15) § 158c no 7; BK/*Beckmann* (fn 59) § 158c no 17.
**83** PM/*Knappmann* (fn 15) § 158c no 8.
**84** This is a section of the Austrian Federal Economic Chamber with partial legal capacity.

b) *Can the liability insurer (or the alternative compensation scheme) that must provide cover despite the total absence of any insurance agreement (see above Question a) have recourse against the damaging party?*

Here there is *cessio legis* as well: the victim's compensation claim against the injuring party passes over to the Professional Association of Insurers (see above no 72) 'insofar as such has paid the victim a benefit' (§ 13 VOEG). 73

25. *Is the victim protected against the insolvency of the liability insurer?*

This is only the case in respect of *motor vehicle insurance*: in this field the victim who has suffered a bodily injury or property damage obtains a claim to an equivalent to the insurance benefit against the Professional Association of Insurers (§ 4 para 1 no 5 VOEG).[85] 74

In all other cases there is general, limited protection of insurance claims: these *have to be fulfilled before the other insolvency claims* in the event that the insurer is insolvent (§ 94 para 1 Insurance Supervision Act [*Versicherungsaufsichtsgesetz*, VAG]). 75

26. *Are there rules that serve in particular the protection of the victim when the liability insurance was only concluded voluntarily – ie without it being compulsory?*

This protection is provided in the form of *§ 156 para 1 VersVG* (on this see above nos 53 and 58) and *§ 157 VersVG* (on this see above no 54). A further rule on the protection of the victim can be found in *§ 156 para 3 VersVG*: this sets out what must apply when there are *several victims* and the *liability insurance sum is not sufficient* to remedy their damage in full. In this case, all victims will be satisfied pro rata in accordance with the extent of their respective compensation claims. If another victim only appears after the whole insurance sum has been distributed and if the insurer can be blamed for the fact that such was not considered, then the insurer shall compensate the relevant victim despite having already paid out the entire insurance sum; this compensation shall be in the proportion that this victim would have been entitled to had he been considered in good time. According to academic teaching, the insurer in turn then has a claim for 76

85 Take note of the limitation pursuant to § 5 para 2 VOEG. On this professional association cf above no 72 fn 84.

enrichment in respect of this payment against the insurance holder pursuant to § 1042 Civil Code (ABGB).[86]

# V. Supervision and Sanctions

*27.a) In which cases must the insurance holder prove to an authority before commencing an activity requiring insurance that he has taken out the respective prescribed liability insurance cover (see above Question 4.e)?*

77 If the law prescribes the conclusion of liability insurance, this usually means that this is set out as a *prerequisite for exercising* a certain hazardous activity. Thus, the existence of the liability insurance must normally be proven to the competent supervisory authority before the respective activity is begun. There are *two types of rule* here: firstly, the duty to have insurance is limited to the above-described function of being a *prerequisite for exercising a certain activity*. These are the cases addressed in Question 4.e (above no 13). Or, secondly, on the other hand, the conclusion of liability insurance is *additionally* also the object of an *obligation* in the technical sense. Most types of compulsory liability insurance fall within this category, for example, § 3 para 4 lit f in conjunction with § 5c Hospitals and Health Resorts Act (KAKuG) (hospitals), § 3b para 1 no 5 in conjunction with § 5c KAKuG (out-patient clinics), § 30 para 1 Code on Notaries (NO), § 1 para 2 lit g in conjunction with 21a para 1 Attorney Code (RAO), § 10 Accountancy Act (BiBuG), § 199 Trade Act (GewO) (builders), § 117 GewO (real estate trustees), § 136a GewO (commercial financial advisors), § 137c GewO (insurance brokers) and § 23 para 1 no 3 and § 79j para 1 sent 1 Gene Technology Act (GTG) (works with genetically modified organisms).

78 Only rarely is the conclusion of a (compulsory) liability insurance policy *not a prerequisite for the permit* required for the exercise of an activity, but solely the object of an obligation. An example of this is § 16 Product Liability Act (PHG).

*b) Must the insurer inform an authority when liability insurance taken out to meet an insurance obligation ends?*

79 There is no *general rule* that imposes such a duty on compulsory liability insurers. Instead *§ 158c para 2 VersVG* prescribes, however, (in respect of compulsory liability insurance in the sense of § 158b VersVG [see above no 4ff]) *fictional*

86 BK/*Baumann* (fn 13) § 156 no 61 (referring to § 812 BGB, the German equivalent to § 1042 ABGB).

*cover*, as long as the insurer does not inform the supervisory authority (more on this above in no 65ff). This fiction is more advantageous to the victim than an insurer's duty to inform in that it allows the victim to receive a payment from the liability insurer although such may not have been at any fault in respect of the omission to notify the supervisory authority.

*Additionally*, however, more recently enacted sectoral legislation mostly *requires the compulsory liability insurer* to *inform* the *supervisory authority* (in the sense of § 158c para 2 VersVG) as soon as the insurance cover ends. Examples of this are § 52d para 5 Medical Doctors Act, § 26c para 5 Dentists Act (ZÄG), § 5c para 4 Hospitals and Health Resorts Act (KAKuG), § 39 para 3 Psychologists Act 2013, § 30 para 5 Code on Notaries (NO), § 21a para 6 Attorney Code (RAO), § 21a para 6 Patent Attorney Act, § 10 para 5 Accountancy Act (BiBuG), § 13 para 4 Pipelines Act and § 61 para 4 Motor Vehicle Act (KFG). 80

c) *Is the insurer also under a duty to inform when a liability insurance agreement is in existence but it has no duty to provide cover – eg, due to defaults on premium payments?*

Here too there is no *general obligation* to inform, as the liability insurer is once again subject to the *fictional cover pursuant to § 158c VersVG* in any case, this time under *para 1* (see above no 61ff). Regardless of this, there are several rules – albeit a smaller number than in respect of the previous Question – which do set out a statutory duty to inform. Examples are once again § 52d para 5 Medical Doctors Act, § 26c para 5 Dentists Act (ZÄG), § 5c para 4 Hospitals and Health Resorts Act (KAKuG), § 39 para 3 Psychologists Act 2013, § 30 para 5 Code on Notaries (NO), § 21a para 6 Attorney Code (RAO), § 21a para 6 Patent Attorney Act, § 10 para 5 Accountancy Act (BiBuG) as well as § 61 para 3 Motor Vehicle Act (KFG) (as regards the motor vehicle liability insurer being free from the duty to pay out due to the insurance holder's default on premium payments). 81

d) *What are the consequences when the duties to inform of the end of contract or the release from payment obligations (see above Questions b and c) are violated?*

The violation of this duty to notify *is frequently not attached to any consequences*: none of the sectoral legislation that sets out such duties expressly provides for any administrative penalty or other form of sanction for the insurer which fails to fulfil such duty. However, violating the duty to provide such information is penalised in any constellation in which the respective law makes non-compliance with the duties it imposes a *general administrative offence*. This 82 is the case, for example, in respect of *motor vehicle liability insurance* pursuant to § 134 para 1 Motor Vehicle Act (KFG). The Insurance Supervision Act (VAG), on the other hand, contains specially formulated administrative offence definitions in § 107b to cover the breach of insurers' duties to notify; however, this does not affect the cases of interest here. *Neither are any compensation duties* on the part of the insurer conceivable, as in any case the fictional cover pursuant to § 158c VersVG applies. Therefore, no recoverable harm can be sustained by the victim due to the insurer's failure to notify.

*28. Is there some official body (authority, professional chamber) where an injured party can find out whether and where the injuring party who inflicted damage upon him in the course of an activity requiring insurance has liability insurance?*

83 This must generally be answered in the *negative*. Only in very few cases does the law provide for such bodies from which the victim can obtain information about whether an injuring party has compulsory liability insurance: this applies, on the one hand, in respect of *motor vehicle liability insurance* (the Professional Association of Insurers[87] has a duty to provide information pursuant to § 31a para 4 Motor Vehicle Liability Act, KHVG) and, on the other hand, for the liability insurance of *insurance brokers* (information from the insurance broker register pursuant to § 365e para 1 and 5 Trade Act [GewO] in combination with § 365a para 1 no 12 GewO, § 365b para 1 no 9 GewO).

*29. Are there (public law) sanctions against the party who was required to take out insurance if such does not take out the compulsory liability insurance? Examples of this would be a ban on carrying out the activity that requires the insurance or the imposition of an administrative or judicial penalty.*

84 There are *two possible forms* of administrative law sanctions which are also often cumulatively imposed:

85 1. In the majority of cases the competent supervisory authority – mostly only after a certain period has elapsed in which the duty to take out liability insurance should have been fulfilled – must revoke a permit to carry out an activity which requires insurance. Examples include: §§ 44 para 1 lit b and c and 61 para 5 KFG (motor vehicle holders),[88] § 30 para 2 Code on Notaries (NO), § 21a para 2 Attorney Code (RAO), § 99 para 10 Trade Act (GewO) (builders), § 117

**87** On this professional association cf above no 72 fn 84.
**88** Cf in more detail on this *Gruber*, ZVR 1991, 33, 34 f.

para 10 GewO (real estate trustees), § 136a para 12 GewO (commercial financial advisors), § 137c para 5 GewO (insurance brokers).

2. In many cases, carrying out an activity that requires insurance without such liability insurance is punishable by *administrative penalty* (*Verwaltungsstrafe*) – albeit usually only after the permit has been revoked by the supervisory authority (on this see above). Examples of this are: § 134 para 1 KFG (keepers of motor vehicles), § 186 para 1 NO (using a fake permit to carry out the activities of a notary after such has been suspended pursuant to § 30 para 2 NO), § 57 para 1 RAO (using a fake permit to act as an attorney-at-law when such has been revoked under § 21a para 2 RAO), § 92 para 1 in combination with § 367 no 28 Trade Act (GewO) (all activities falling under the GewO [see the previous no]), § 25 Nuclear Liability Act (AtomHG), and § 109 para 2 no 3 Act on Genetic Engineering (GTG). 86

# VI. Statutory Provisions required by the Constitution or the European Convention on Human Rights (ECHR)

30. *What has been said regarding the compatibility of the duties to take out liability insurance with your country's constitution and the ECHR? Please take into account case law and academic literature.*

The position held is that it lies within the margin of appreciation of the legislator to stipulate compulsory liability insurance for the carrying out of certain activities.[89] In academic teaching, it is pointed out in this respect that, from a fundamental rights perspective, the legislator must take the cost-benefit relation into account when setting out such insurance requirements. This means that a duty to take out insurance is only to be selected as the way to accomplish a goal when it proves to be the most suitable way that comes into consideration to accomplish such legislative goal.[90] The requirement to take out insurance would seem, however, to be regarded without further ado by the Constitutional Court (*Verfassungsgerichtshof*, VfGH) as a suitable means to protect clients (cf above no 18) and also to protect a profession against loss of confidence (cf also no 21).[91] 87

**89** *Raschauer*, VR 2005, 35, 40 f.

**90** Cf *Raschauer*, VR 2005, 35, 41.

**91** Cf VfGH B 1721/10 VfSlg 19.588/2011 in connection with the duty on attorneys-at-law related to compulsory liability insurance, under § 10a para 7 RAO. According to this rule, attorneys-at-

31. *Does the constitution or the ECHR make any stipulations regarding the contents of such duties to take out liability insurance? Please take into account case law and academic literature.*

88 It is pointed out, for example, in relation to the insurance duty for attorneys-at-law (§ 21a RAO), that the statutory professional liability may not be so high as to form a 'disproportionate hindrance to carrying out the profession'.[92]

## VII. Reform Efforts

32. *Are there efforts towards reforming the law regarding compulsory liability insurance?*

89 As far as is discernible, no reforms in the sense of an overall reform of the law on compulsory liability insurance are pending. However, the law on compulsory liability insurance is subject to constant change due to the permanent expansion of activities requiring insurance. Thus, for example, only recently the Psychologists Act (*Psychologengesetz*) 2013 introduced compulsory liability insurance for psychologists (under its § 39) as per 25 October 2013.

## VIII. Compulsory Liability Insurance and Liability Law

33. *Is, at the legislative level, any connection discernible between the nature of liability (in particular in the case of strict liability) and the imposition of compulsory liability insurance?*

90 In Austrian law there is a strong *correlation* between the implementation of *strict liability* and safeguarding it with *compulsory liability insurance*, cf on this above no 3.

---

law must pay contributions to finance the insurance premiums for the trustee facilities of the Bar Association.

92 ErläutRV zu § 21a RAO 1638 BlgNR 20. GP, 16; *Raschauer*, VR 2005, 35, 41.

Herman Cousy and Caroline Van Schoubroeck

# Compulsory Liability Insurance in Belgium

## I. The Term Compulsory Liability Insurance

1. *Indicate the rules within your legal system that set out a duty to take out liability insurance. In this context, also take into account the implementation of international treaties (eg, the International Convention on Civil Liability for Bunker Oil Pollution Damage, 2001).*

To answer Question 1, relating to 'rules within the legal system that set out a duty to take out liability insurance', it is useful to follow the guidance of the description of 'compulsory insurance' that is used by the Belgian financial supervisory authority, the Financial Services and Market Authority (FSMA) (www.fsma.be). This description has no binding force but has a high moral authority and is used as a convenient instrument in the majority of the legal doctrine.[1] 1

According to this definition, insurance is considered to be compulsory:

'a) if a (federal or regional) legislative prescription, or any other normative prescription that is taken in pursuance thereof, or a EU regulation, explicitly imposes an insurance obligation;
b) if such a prescription as in a) provides one of the following sanctions:
   - a penal or administrative sanction;
   - a prohibition to exercise an activity or to take an action;
   - the *ex officio* affiliation with an alternative (public or private) organism or fund;
   - the total or partial recourse against the (non-insured) person of the sums paid (advanced) by such institution or fund.

Cases where the taking out of insurance is required by law as a condition for obtaining a subsidy, or where insurance is imposed by a contractual obligation, or where the law im-

---

1 *J Rogge*, De verplichte verzekering: een ongedefinieerde notie, in: X (ed), Liber amicorum H Bocken (2009) 242; *M Fontaine*, Les assurances obligatoires. Technique et opportunité (1983) Revue générale des assurances et des responsabilités (RGAR) no 10.587, 1 (concerning the list drafted by the former Office de Contrôle des Assurances, now replaced by the FSMA); *H De Rode*, Les assurances de responsabilité. Evolution et perspectives, in: B Dubuisson and others (eds), Mélanges offerts à Marcel Fontaine (2003) 703, 705. For an older, more succinct, and thus highly incomplete 'typology' of compulsory insurances in Belgium, see *H Claassens*, Les obligations d'assurance en Belgique présentées en un premier essai de typologie, in: J Rogge/B Dubuisson (eds), L'obligation d'assurance. Analyse économique et juridique, Dossier Bulletin des assurances (Bull Ass) 7 (2001) 29–46; *H Claassens*, Verplichte verzekeringen: een nieuw verschijnsel in België? (1977–78) Rechtskundig Weekblad (RW) col 145–180.

poses the (minimal) extent of cover in (otherwise) non-compulsory insurance, are not considered as instances of compulsory insurance'.[2]

This FSMA definition refers to any compulsory insurance but can be, and indeed is, considered to be applicable to compulsory liability insurance in particular. The delimitation of what liability insurance contracts are does not appear too problematic among Belgian doctrinal writers. For the sake of completeness, let it be remembered that there is a legal definition of liability insurance contracts. According to art 141 Insurance Act of 4 April 2014 (IA 2014) (former art 1 Insurance Contract Act of 25 June 1992 – ICA 1992),[3] these are contracts of insurance against a claim for compensation based on a loss occurrence provided for by the contract and to keep the insured's estate indemnified, within the limits of cover, for any debt arising from a proven liability.

On the basis of these definitions and guidelines, the FSMA publishes a (regularly updated) list of more than 150 acts, decrees or executive regulations (both at the federal and regional level) imposing compulsory insurance (see no 13). The title, date and place of publication in the Moniteur Belge (MB)[4] of all the different laws and regulations are to be found in the Annex: Rules on Compulsory Liability Insurance in Belgium (at the end of this book).

2 The classifications or nomenclatures of international organisations such as WTO, WTO GATS and UNO do not appear to acknowledge or use the concept of compulsory insurance (except in the context of 'compulsory social security services').[5] The OECD glossary contains a definition of 'compulsory insurance', defining it as 'any form of insurance whose purchase is required by law'.[6]

---

2 *K Bernauw*/*J Rogge*, National report Belgium, AIDA World Conference Paris 2010, <http://www.aida.org.uk/pastcong.asp>, 5; *E Denoël*, Assurances des responsabilités civiles extra-contractuelles découlant de la vie privée (1987) Bulletin des assurances (Bull Ass) 34–69.

3 Note: by an Act of 4 April 2014, the Belgian legislator has incorporated the existing Insurance Contract Act of 11 June 1874 and the Insurance Contract Act on Land Insurance of 25 June 1992 (Loi sur le contrat d'assurance terrestre) into a coordinated legislation called Act on Insurance (Loi relative aux assurances), hereinafter translated as Insurance Act and cited as 'IA 2014'. Since the coordination implied renumbering of the articles of the existing Act, any reference to articles of the IA 2014 will be accompanied by a reference to the corresponding articles of the former Insurance Contract Act on Land Insurance of 25 June 1992, cited as 'ICA 1992'.

4 <www.ejustice.just.fgov.be/cgi/welcome.pl>.

5 *Bernauw*/*Rogge* (fn 2) 9.

6 See *OECD*, Insurance Regulation and supervision in economics in transition, OECD proceedings, Paris, OECD publications, 1997.

In EU law: art 8 of the 2nd Non-Life Directive 88/357/EC of 22 June 1988 provides for a specific conflict of law rule as regards 'compulsory insurance'. As is well known, this has essentially been copied by the EU Regulation (EC) No 593/2008 of 17 June 2008 (Rome I Regulation) on the law applicable to contractual obligations. Article 7 para 4 provides for additional rules that apply to insurance contracts covering a risk for which a Member State imposes an obligation to take out insurance. Neither the Directive nor the Regulation gives a definition of what is meant by compulsory insurance. However, recital 99 of the EU Services Directive states 'it is not necessary for an obligation of appropriate insurance to be laid down by law. It should be sufficient if an insurance obligation is part of the ethical rules laid down by professional bodies'.[7] 3

Borderline cases: some doubts are still uttered in doctrinal writings about certain kinds of obligatory insurance. Bernauw/Rogge mention the (third party liability) insurance cover that is part of the standard conditions imposed by public tender legislation; or the compulsory insurance that is only one of the various alternatives to provide the required financial solvency guarantee (said authors propose that the insurance is considered to be 'compulsory' if the insurance alternative is chosen by the parties).[8] 4

*2. Is there a coherent 'law of compulsory liability insurance' in your legal system?*

A 'law of compulsory insurance' does not exist in the sense of a coherent set of rules that apply to compulsory liability insurance in general with the important exception of the rule laid down in art 151 IA 2014 (former art 87 ICA 1992) (see below nos 7f and 63f; as for the text of the provision see below no 63). 5

Article 150 IA 2014 (former art 86 ICA 1992), which confers upon the injured party a right of his own (*ius proprium*) and a 'direct action' against the liability insurer applies, however, to all types of liability insurance, including compulsory liability insurance (see below nos 61f and 72). 6

To be more precise, these arts 150–152 IA 2014 Part 4 (former ICA 1992) apply to all liability insurance, both compulsory and non-compulsory, falling under the scope of 'land insurance contracts'. Insurance contracts not falling under the scope of the IA 2014 Part 4 remain governed by the IA 2014 Part 5 (former

7 EU Directive 2006/123/EC of 12 December 2006 on services in the internal market, Official Journal (OJ) L 376, 27.12.2006, 36–68. See regarding the insurance Directives *H Claassens*, De verplichte verzekeringen in het aanstaande Europa van de verzekeringen, in: L'Europe de l'assurance. Les directives de la troisième génération (1992) 261–267.

8 *Bernauw/Rogge* (fn 2) 9.

Insurance Act 1874), like maritime, transport and aviation insurance. IA 2014 Part 5, like the Insurance Act 1874, did not (and still does not) clearly acknowledge the mere concept of liability insurance.

7 Another issue concerns the question of which defences can be raised by the insurer against a 'direct action' of the injured party. Article 151 IA 2014 (former art 87 ICA 1992) contains an explicit rule on the opposability of defences the insurer can raise against the injured party. The rule makes a distinction according to whether the liability insurance is or is not compulsory. If one deals with compulsory liability insurance, the liability insurer is barred by art 151, § 1 IA 2014 (former art 87, § 1 ICA 1992) from raising against the injured party any civil liability defences, such as nullities, deductibles or forfeitures which derive from law or contract and have their cause in an act either prior or subsequent to the insured event. In addition, art 151, § 1, para 2 IA 2014 (former art 87, § 1, para 2) specifies that the annulment, cancellation,[9] expiry or suspension of the contract that took place before the occurrence of the insured event may be relied upon as against the injured party.

8 Article 151, § 2 IA 2014 (former art 87, § 2 ICA 1992) provides that in all other types of liability insurance (ie in non-compulsory insurance), the insurer may rely, as against the injured party, only upon defences which derive from law or contract if they have their cause in an act prior to the insured event (see below nos 63 and 65). Let it be repeated that, as was mentioned hereabove (see no 5), neither the IA 2014 nor the ICA 1992 nor any other legislative provision provides for a clear definition of what makes (liability) insurance 'compulsory', although it is important to know which insurance is considered to be 'compulsory' in the meaning of the cited art 151 IA 2014 (former art 87 ICA 1992).

9 Already before the ICA 1992, the rule of the non-opposability of certain defences against the injured party had been established, and was thus well known, at least as regards one particular type of compulsory liability insurance, ie the Compulsory Motor Vehicle Liability Insurance, governed by the Belgian Act of 1 July 1956, later replaced by the Act of 21 November 1989 (hereafter cited as Compulsory Motor Vehicle Liability Insurance Act 1989) (both Acts finding their original basis in the Benelux Convention of 24 May 1966, and the common provisions in the annex thereof, which introduce common rules on the subject matter, and still govern the subject matter).

10 As was already the case in these Act(s) on Motor Vehicle Liability Insurance, the IA 2014 (and former ICA 1992) contains a rule that concerns the right of recourse of the liability insurer. According to art 152 IA 2014 (former art 88 ICA

9 Annulment (Nichtigerklärung) has an *ex tunc* effect; cancellation (Kundigung) operates *ex nunc*.

1992), the insurer may reserve a right of recourse against the policyholder and, if appropriate, against the insured other than the policyholder, to the extent that it could have refused or reduced the benefit pursuant to the law or under the insurance contract (see below no 83).

3. *Is there a specific term for compulsory liability insurance in your legal system? How is it defined?*

Apart from the description (see above no 1) as used by the Belgian supervisory authority, FSMA, no other definitions are found in Belgian law. 11

4. *In which of the following cases does compulsory liability insurance apply according to prevailing opinion?*

On the basis of the description used by the Belgian supervisory authority FSMA (see above nos 1 and 3), the concept of compulsory insurance applies in the following cases: 12

a) *Duties to take out liability insurance which are not directly based on the law but on an order or decision issued by administrative authorities?*

The duty to take out liability insurance will be considered as compulsory insurance if the public authority's order or decision is directly based on a general normative legal prescription, which are: EU Regulation, Act of Parliament, Royal Decree (federal level), Decree or Decision of Community or Regional government (level of Communities and Regions).[10] 13

b) *Duties to take out liability insurance that are not based directly on the law but on the statutes of a professional or other self-governing body?*

According to the prevailing opinion, a duty to take out insurance that is based on the bylaws of a professional or other self-governing body would only be considered as compulsory insurance if their decision is thereafter incorporated in a general normative legal prescription as defined in no 13.[11] 14

Even if a normative legal prescription gives a professional or self-governing body the competence, but not the duty, to impose compulsory insurance, such 15

---

**10** *Bernauw/Rogge* (fn 2) 4. See also the answer to Question 1, no 4 (borderline cases).

**11** See Cour de cassation (Cass) 19 October 2001, <www.cass.be> regarding professional liability of architects concerning Royal Decree of 25 April 2007.

insurance would not be considered as legally imposed compulsory insurance but solely as insurance that is made mandatory by a deontological requirement (eg art 17 Act of 30 April 2007, coordinating Act of 22 July 1953 on auditors; the same conclusion applies to the deontological obligation of attorneys to take out professional liability insurance).

The answer would be different in those cases where the ethical rule that imposes an insurance obligation is explicitly approved or confirmed or ratified by a legal or regulatory provision, since in this way the ethical rule acquires legal force (eg Royal Decree of 25 April 2007 on the compulsory insurance for architects).[12]

*c) Duties to take out liability insurance that are not based on any public law but on a private law provision (eg, governing the relationship between employer and employee)?*

16 Insurance that is imposed by a contractual obligation is not compulsory insurance. Even insurance that is compulsory by virtue of collective agreements (such as collective labour agreements) is not considered to be compulsory insurance.[13] The answer would probably be different if the contractual obligation to take out insurance were itself imposed by law. However, we are not aware of any examples. It appears that to achieve such result, the legislator would rather impose the duty to insure directly upon one of the parties, than requiring the parties to insert a contractual clause to this effect.

*d) Duties to take out liability insurance that are not based on any public law but on a private law rule that is established by case law (and, eg, governs the relationship between employer and employee)?*

17 According to the prevailing opinion (see above nos 1 and 13), the duty to take out insurance that is based on a rule that is established by case law would not be

---

**12** *V Callewaert*, Actualités législatives et jurisprudentielles dans les assurances de la responsabilité, in: C Paris/B Dubuisson (eds), Actualités en droit des assurances (2008) 224; *B Dubuisson*, L'action directe et l'action récursoire, in: B Dubuisson/P Jadoul (eds), La loi du 25 juin 1992 sur le contrat d'assurance terrestre. Dix années d'application (2002) 158; *C Van Schoubroeck*, Professionele aansprakelijkheidsverzekering en de Europese Interne Markt (1994) 336 ff.

**13** For contractual agreements in general cf *M Fontaine*, Droit des assurances (2010) 59. For collective (labour) agreements cf *H De Rode/M Collignon*, Les assurances obligatoires en Europe, in: J Rogge/B Dubuisson (eds), L'obligation d'assurance. Analyse économique et juridique, Bull Ass 7 (2001) 52; *Dubuisson* (fn 12) 157.

considered as being compulsory insurance. We are not aware of any examples of such 'case law imposed' insurance under Belgian law.

e) *Cases in which there is no duty to take out liability insurance but liability insurance cover is a prerequisite for the admissibility of carrying out a particular activity?*

In accordance with the description of the FSMA, this duty is considered to be compulsory insurance if it is imposed by a normative legal prescription (see nos 1–4 and 13). However, insurance that is a prerequisite to be entitled to a subsidy is not. The underlying idea in the last case is that the activity can be carried out without obtaining a subsidy, and thus without the need for insurance.[14] **18**

f) *Cases of alternative financial security, in which the duty to provide for financial security may be fulfilled either by taking out liability insurance or other forms of financial security (eg, bank guarantees)?*

The fact that an alternative financial security can be opted for, to replace the compulsory insurance, does not take away the characterisation of compulsory insurance (eg arts 33 and 50 of the Act of 22 April 1999 on accountancy and tax professions). **19**

The financial security or guarantee itself is not considered to be compulsory insurance.[15] **20**

g) *Cases in which the duty to have insurance has only been created by a contractual agreement between potential injuring party and victim?*

These cases are clearly not considered as compulsory insurance. **21**

When insurance cover (including compulsory liability insurance) is imposed by the authorities as part of the standard conditions that are imposed by a public tender legislation (or regulation), this is considered as a borderline case, but one where the compulsory insurance qualification can be justified.[16]

---

**14** *Dubuisson* (fn 12) 159.

**15** *H Bocken*, Rechtstreekse verzekeringen ten behoeve van derden en andere wisseloplossingen voor aansprakelijkheid en aansprakelijkheidsverzekering. Een typologie, in: J Rogge (ed), Liber Amicorum René Van Gompel. Studies in verzekeringen (1998) 30.

**16** *Bernauw/Rogge* (fn 2) 9.

## II. Aims

5. *What are the aims of the rules that impose an obligation to take out liability insurance:*

22 It must be admitted that the legislator has made extensive, not to say excessive, use of compulsory insurance, often without clarifying the motives or aims.[17]

The legislature should be reluctant to impose compulsory insurance. Arguments invoked against a mandatory rule are in particular the need for regular monitoring, insufficient knowledge and experience of the risk and problems of capacity and of price.[18]

The aims of the legislative (or normative) prescriptions imposing an obligation to take out liability insurance can be listed as follows:

a) *the protection of the victim,*

23 The protection of the injured party against the insolvency of the liable person is a very important reason to impose compulsory insurance. Liability insurance does not close the so-called 'liability gap', but is intended to close the 'solvency gap'. The compulsory character of insurance is intended to bridge the 'insurance gap'.[19]

The protection of the injured party is considered to be necessary, inter alia because of the catastrophic nature of the risk (eg fire and explosion in public places), the (widespread nature of the) activity (eg traffic accidents, professional activities), or the possible number of casualties (eg hunting).[20]

---

**17** *Fontaine* (1983) RGAR no 10.587, 2; *B Dubuisson*, L'assurance obligatoire: introduction, in: J Rogge/B Dubuisson (eds), L'obligation d'assurance. Analyse économique et juridique, Bull Ass 7 (2001) 1. For an elaborated list of possible motives and justifications for imposing compulsory insurance, see *Rogge* (fn 1) 243; *Bernauw/Rogge* (fn 2) 10. For an overview of aims and justifications of compulsory insurance at a European level, see *De Rode/Collignon* (fn 13) 68; compare *J Kullmann*, L'accompagnement juridique de l'obigation d'assurance en France, in: J Rogge/B Dubuisson (eds), L'obligation d'assurance. Analyse économique et juridique, Bull Ass 7 (2001) 81–102.

**18** *Dubuisson* (fn 17) 1.

**19** See *H Cousy*, Tort Liability and Liability Insurance: A Difficult Relationship, in: H Koziol/BC Steininger (eds), European Tort Law 2001 (2002) 18.

**20** Cf *Fontaine* (1983) RGAR no 10.587, 2: in some cases insurance is made compulsory when aggravated criteria of insurance are introduced; *De Rode/Collignon* (fn 13) 63: these authors also point out that the legislator's intention 'non seulement d'assurer la protection des victimes et des responsables contre les risques jugés importants, mais aussi l'intention d'assurer par ce

*b) the protection of the insurance holder,*

The protection of the insured against the financial implication of heavy losses or liability claims is an important argument to impose compulsory insurance.[21] It is of course true that liability insurance does not give the insured person total financial protection, especially when the liability cover contains (as is usually the case) deductibles and caps or ceilings. Cases where the law, while imposing compulsory insurance, also limits the maximum amount of liability that can be incurred are rare. One example of such legislation is found in the legislation on public accountants which introduces a maximum amount of liability per control task (€ 3 million, raised to € 12 million when the control concerns a public company) (art 17 para 1 Act of 22 July 1953 on the Institute of Public Accountants as coordinated by Act of 30 April 2007). One other example is the rule that the liability of a company of notaries is limited to € 5 million and their obligation to take out compulsory liability insurance is also limited to € 5 million (art 50, § 4 Act of 25 ventôse Year XI, as modified by the Act of 25 April 2014). Putting maximum amounts on liability is here intended to promote insurability, but equally serves to give effective protection to the insured. 24

*c) the protection of the victim and the insurance holder,*

Establishing the spread of risks (mutualisation, solidarity) by apportioning them over a large number of participants may not be among the explicitly mentioned objectives or goals of the legislator or regulators while imposing compulsory liability insurance, but risk spreading and alleviation of costs belong so much to the essence of insurance that they necessarily enter into the aims and goals of the public authority, while imposing an obligation to insure. As *Dubuisson* explains, by generalising the taking out of insurance to large classes of the population, an optimal degree of risk spreading is achieved, which in turn will have the effect of lowering premium levels and thereby making the insurance accessible to all.[22] 25

moyen un meilleur équilibre entre la situation du consommateur, jugé en état d'infériorité et celle du professionnel, considéré en position de supériorité économique et technique'.

**21** *Fontaine* (1983) RGAR no 10.587, 2.

**22** *Dubuisson* (fn 17) 1.

*d) other aims, eg internalising the costs in the interests of society?*

26 Avoiding losses having to be borne by the public treasury.

Insurance solutions also free public authorities that are faced with protecting the population against catastrophic distress or against other burdens, such as the need to calculate and collect contributions, the need for available and capable personnel who can intervene in the loss assessing procedure. Examples are found in the replacement of public security funds and comparable devices by 'insurance solutions' (eg compensation scheme for motor vehicle accidents, terrorism [Act of 1 April 2007] or natural catastrophes [arts 130–132 IA 2014, former art 68-8/68-10 ICA 1992]).

A striking example of a case where the legislator has organised a scheme of compulsory cover of accidental harm with the explicit aim of alleviating the public budget is the enactment of a regime of compensation of non-motorised victims of traffic accidents involving a motor vehicle (art 29bis Compulsory Motor Vehicle Liability Insurance Act 1989, as introduced in 1995).[23] This compensation regime is not liability insurance, but an autonomous legal obligation weighing on the motor vehicle liability insurer of an involved motor vehicle (or the owner of an involved train or tram) to compensate victims' injuries and damage to clothes.[24] The Belgian system of compensation for damage caused by traffic accidents was indeed justified by a double objective, ie indemnification of the victim in the first place, but at the same time also alleviation of the (public) social security system. This system, and thus the public budget, are freed from the costs of compensating victims of traffic accidents where liability cannot be proven. Indeed, in these cases the losses caused to the (uncompensated) traffic victims would otherwise ultimately be borne by the state's social security mechanism.

Another example where the imposition of compulsory insurance is clearly inspired by (inter alia) the desire to alleviate the public budget is the compulsory coverage of natural disasters.[25] Let it be noted, however, that the present Belgian legal system does not directly impose on its citizens an obligation to cover natural catastrophes, but 'indirectly' achieves a comparable result by

---

**23** *De Rode/Collignon* (fn 13) 64.
**24** See *C Van Schoubroeck*, Traffic Accident Compensation in Belgium: An Example for Europe? (2003) 10 Maastricht Journal of European and Comparative Law 199–213; *C Van Schoubroeck*, The Belgian Traffic Accident Compensation System, in: K Ludwichowska (ed), Kompensacja szkód komunikacyjnych-nowoczesne rozwiązania ubezpieczeniowe. Traffic Accident Compensation – Modern Insurance Solutions (2011) 97–117.
**25** *De Rode/Collignon* (fn 13) 64.

requiring non-compulsory home insurance to ensure cover against natural catastrophes.

It has also been underlined that the requirement of compulsory insurance is sometimes intended to accompany a more general move to 'reinforce' a liability regime (eg a regime of strict liability).[26] 27

6. *Do the rules that prescribe a form of alternative financial security (see above Question 4.f) pursue the same aims as those rules that exclusively set out a duty to have liability insurance (ie with no other alternative financial security options)?*

We have no indications to the contrary. The choice between the vehicle of compulsory insurance and alternative systems achieving a comparable goal must be made in the light of a balancing of the advantages (see hereabove no 22ff) and the disadvantages (penalising the good risks, giving an undesired social function to a commercial insurer in a competitive market, extreme administration costs, inevitable standardisation of insurance conditions impeding innovation, possible moral hazard problems) of the insurance solution. Such balancing must be made on the basis of criteria such as necessity and proportionality. The proportionality test consists in finding out which one of the alternative methods or systems can achieve goals comparable to those of compulsory insurance while creating fewer disadvantages.[27] 28

# III. Content of Insurance Cover

7. *Are the duties to take out liability insurance laid down by law only to cover extra-contractual compensation duties or also those arising out of contractual infringements?*

Generally speaking compulsory insurance can cover extra-contractual as well as contractual liabilities. 29

Several legislative prescriptions impose an obligation to cover civil contractual liability, for example, compulsory liability insurance regarding architects (art 2, § 4 and art 9 Act of 20 February 1939, as modified), insurance intermediaries (art 268, § 1, 3° IA 2014, former art 10 Act of 27 March 1995), travel agents and tour operators (art 36 Act of 16 February 1994), notaries (arts 34ter and 50, § 4

26 See *De Rode/Collignon* (fn 13) 63.
27 *Dubuisson* (fn 17) 3.

Act of 25 ventôse Year XI, as modified by the Act of 25 April 2014), and veterinarians (art 4 Act of 28 August 1991, as modified by art 3 Act of 19 March 2014).

The liability risk covered is the professional liability, ie the liability incurred because one has not carried out professional activities according to the required professional standards.

*8.a) Are there duties to take out liability insurance aimed not only at the protection of absolutely protected rights (eg, property, bodily integrity) but additionally at compensating pure economic loss?*

30 See below the answer to Question 8.b, no 31.

*b) Are there duties to take out liability insurance that are directed only or at least predominantly at the compensation of pure economic loss?*

31 Under Belgian law, economic loss (consequential loss as well as pure economic loss) is compensated in the case of extra-contractual as well as contractual liability.[28] Consequently, in the legislation on compulsory insurance, the distinction between damage caused by the violation of protected rights and pure economic loss is not made and all damage must be covered.

Indeed, the Belgian law of civil liability does not make a distinction between the different kinds of damage in determining which type of damage or loss must be the object of repair or compensation. Under Belgian law, which is in this respect quite similar to French law, the general rule concerning civil (non-contractual) liability under arts 1382–1383 Civil Code is that there are (only) three conditions for liability: faulty behaviour, damage and a causal relation between them.

Damage is described as the difference between the actual situation of the victim and the hypothetical situation in which the person would have been if he had not been victimised. In order to be recoverable, the damage has to be: (i) certain (the likelihood of damage must be such that a judge cannot seriously consider the contrary, even if it remains theoretically possible that the expected damage may never materialise), (ii) personal to the victim (the primary victim and also the persons not directly harmed but suffering any damage of their own because of a relationship with the primary victim[29]) and

---

**28** See *B Weyts*, Economische schade (2013) Revue de Droit Commercial (RDC) 1018, 1022.

**29** Legal systems, like the French and the Belgian, which do not specify especially protected legal interests, do not encounter (the same) difficulties in defining which interferences with bodily integrity and health are actionable in tort. Under Belgian law, any harm done to a le-

(iii) should follow from the violation of a legitimate interest (not necessarily a subjective right).[30]

*Lucrum cessans* (loss of profit) and *damnum emergens* are to be compensated.[31] Under Belgian law, all damage as it appears *in concreto* must be compensated, ie the right to *restitutio ad integrum*, though not for more (*in concreto* and full). As a result pecuniary as well as non-pecuniary loss has to be compensated without distinction and to its full extent.[32] The Belgian law of damages does not allow punitive damages. Caps or thresholds are not frequently used under Belgian law (eg Act of 30 July 1979 on the strict liability of the exploiter and compulsory insurance coverage regarding damage caused by fire and explosions in public buildings provides a maximum liability cover).

9. *Are there provisions that require the insurance of a third party's liability interest – for instance, that the employer must take out liability insurance for the benefit of an employee?*

The most typical example of a situation in which the law obliges a person to take out insurance that covers the liability of a third person is found in the legislation on compulsory motor vehicle liability insurance. 32

In accordance with the above cited Benelux Convention of 1966 and with the European Directive 2009/103/EC of 16 September 2009 on Motor Vehicle Liability Insurance, art 2 of the Belgian Compulsory Motor Vehicle Liability Insurance Act 1989 obliges each owner who brings a motor vehicle into circulation to take out liability insurance that conforms with the provisions of this Act. One of the requirements is that the insurance must cover the liability not only of the owner but also of each driver or keeper of the vehicle, and also the liability of passengers. In addition, the policy must cover the vicarious liability of certain persons, such as the liability of the employer for acts of his employee connected to the use of the vehicle (art 3).

There are numerous other instances where the obligatory cover includes the liability of persons other than the policyholder who possess an insurable interest. 33

gitimate interest may give rise to liability if the harm is certain. Thus any disturbance of living conditions suffered by the primary victims and secondary victims ('victims par ricochet') is regarded as eligible for compensation.

**30** See Cass 16 January 1939, Pasicrisie Belge (Pas) 1939 I 25.

**31** See *H Cousy/A Vanderspikken*, Damages under Belgian Law, in: U Magnus (ed), Unification of Tort Law: Damages (2001) 27–51.

**32** See *H Cousy/D Droshout*, Non-Pecuniary Loss under Belgian Law, in: WVH Rogers (ed), Damages for Non-Pecuniary Loss in a Comparative Perspective (2001) 28–53.

Examples are:

34 Where liberal professionals are obliged to cover their professional liability, it is sometimes specified that the policy must not only cover the personal liability of the (natural or legal) person who exercises the profession, but also their vicarious liability for acts of employees, and collaborators (eg art 4 Act of 11 February 2013 on syndic). Sometimes it is specified that the policy must not only cover the (natural or legal) person who exercises the profession, but also the liability of his employees and collaborators when acting on his behalf (eg art 3 Royal Decree of 25 April 2007 concerning the compulsory insurance of land surveyors).

35 When the profession subject to compulsory liability insurance is exercised by a legal person, some Acts provide that the policy must also cover the liability of the members of the board, the directors and officers whenever they act on account of the legal person in the context of the exercise of the profession (see eg literally art 3 Royal Decree of 25 April 2007 on compulsory insurance for architects provided for by the Act of 20 February 1939).

36 The Act of 7 May 2004 concerning experiments on the human person imposes a duty to take out insurance on the commissioner, covering his own liability as well as the liability of each person who intervenes in the carrying out of the experiment, irrespective of the legal ties that exist between the commissioner, the intervening person and the participant (art 5, no 9 and art 29 Act of 7 May 2004).

37 *Warning*: In studying the Belgian law of compulsory insurance, one should not commit the error of considering the Belgian law of workers' accident compensation as an example of liability insurance. Under Belgian law this compulsory insurance is personal insurance that must be taken out by the employer on behalf of employees who are insured persons.[33]

38 Similarly the insurance that must be taken out by medical banks that take human bodily material in custody covers the damage that the donor suffers caused by the removal of the organs, regardless of the cause of the damage (art 17, § 4 Act of 19 December 2008 on the collection and use of human bodily material).

33 Cass 14 January 2013 (2013) Pas 77, <www.cass.be>.

*10. To what extent do the rules requiring the compulsory conclusion of a liability insurance policy also specify the specific contents of the insurance coverage:*

*a) Is there always a (sufficiently well-defined) specification of the risk to be insured?*

There is no general rule or principle that prescribes to what extent the law **39**
which imposes a duty to take out insurance must describe the essential contents of the insurance coverage.

As a consequence, the specification of the risk that must be covered, and especially the terms and conditions of such cover, vary greatly from one legislative prescription to another.

The matter has been discussed in the legal doctrine and the absence of sufficient specifications in many laws and regulations imposing the liability insurance duty has often been criticised,[34] even by the representative of the public authority.[35]

Many older laws and regulations provide the insurance obligation without **40**
further clarification of the insurance conditions, or they are so vague that it is nearly impossible to verify whether the duty to insure has effectively been fulfilled (eg 'taking into account the size and risks of the construction site', art 65sexies Royal Decree of 25 January 2001 and Act of 4 August 1996 on construction site safety coordinators).

More recent legal prescriptions are in general more detailed and explicit. **41**
Good examples are the two Royal Decrees of 25 April 2007 respectively on the compulsory liability insurance of architects and land surveyors, and the Royal Decree of 19 December 2006 on the extra-contractual liability of organisations engaging volunteers.

Even in the hypothesis that the law or regulation do contain detailed speci- **42**
fications as to the mandatory insurance conditions and content of the policy, the question arises how and by whom the compliance of the policy with the obligations will be verified.[36]

The FSMA (see above no 1) does not appear to systematically exercise such control. By virtue of the EU insurance directives, the supervisory authorities

**34** *Fontaine* (fn 13) no 75; *Callewaert* (fn 12) 255.

**35** *H Conruyt*, L'autorité publique face au problème de l'obligation d'assurance, in: J Rogge/B Dubuisson (eds), L'obligation d'assurance. Analyse économique et juridique, Bull Ass 7 (2001) 135–137; *De Rode/Collignon* (fn 13) 66.

**36** For a short comparative overview, see *De Rode/Collignon* (fn 13) 66; *Fontaine* (1983) RGAR no 10.587, 3.

have the authority to exercise an ex post systematic control of policy conditions and documents concerning compulsory non-life insurance contracts (see art 65 Act of 9 July 1975 on the supervision of insurance companies; art 26 IA 2014).

A better way, in the sense of a more effective way than that exercised by the FSMA, to control the conformity is the one which is found in the law on public accountants, where the task of controlling the adequacy of the insurance cover is imposed upon the Council of the Institute of Public Accountancy (a professional self-governing body) (art 17 para 3 Act of 22 July 1953 on the Institute of Public Accountants as coordinated by Act of 30 April 2007).

*b) Are there provisions that require unlimited coverage?*

43 Under Belgian law there is only one law that explicitly provides unlimited cover in compulsory insurance. Article 3 Compulsory Motor Vehicle Liability Insurance Act 1989 requires, still (!), unlimited coverage for damage caused by bodily injury. Since a legislative change by the Act of 12 January 2007, this art 3, § 2 allows the King to limit the coverage for damage caused by bodily harm to a level that may not be lower than € 100 million (plus indexation) per claim. As of today such Royal Decree has not been enacted. Thus, for damage caused by bodily injury, the duty to take out unlimited cover remains.

The legislative change of art 3, § 2 Act of 21 November 1989 by the Act of 12 January 2007 allows the insurer to limit coverage for damage to goods to a level that may not be lower than € 100 million (plus indexation) per claim. Since the concept of 'unlimited cover' of a liability debt appears to be outdated and indeed contrary to each and every actuarial logic, the law has been adapted.

Whenever the legislation that imposes the obligation to take out insurance does not specify the minimum insured amount, such rule is not understood as requiring cover for an unlimited amount.

*c) If unlimited coverage is not required (see above Question b), is a minimum or maximum insurance sum always specified?*

44 As appears from the answer in nos 39–41, quite often the minimum and maximum amounts of cover are not further specified.

d) *Are there general statutory rules to be applicable if the respective law that requires compulsory insurance only makes incomplete stipulations regarding the content of the insurance coverage? An example of this would be § 114 para 1 of the German Insurance Contract Act (Versicherungsvertragsgesetz, VVG) 2008.*

Such general or legislative clause is indeed lacking. A sort of 'default legisla- 45
tion' would be a good solution.

11. *Is it admissible to restrict the insurance cover by agreeing: a) risk exclusion clauses, b) deductibles, c) aggregate limits, d) claims series clauses, e) other clauses?*

Whenever the normative legal prescription which imposes the obligation to take 46
out insurance prescribes in detail the contents of the cover, these provisions are of course mandatory, and derogatory clauses in the policy would be null and void.

However, when the contents of the cover are not prescribed by law, the insurer must be considered to be allowed to specify the contents and limits of the cover, as long as these limitations do not lead to emptying the cover of its essential content and meaning.

12. *What are the consequences if the liability insurance contract concluded in order to fulfil the insurance obligation contravenes what the law stipulates as to contents (see above Questions 10 and 11)?*

The starting point is that any normative legal prescription (like a Royal Decree) 47
taken in pursuance of a legislative act, must be considered to be mandatory (*un droit impératif*).

Contractual arrangements that violate the mandatory provisions are voidable (art 56 IA 2014, former art 3 ICA 1992). If the prescription is simply 'mandatory', the nullity of the contractual arrangement is called 'relative', which means that the nullity must be claimed by the party whose interest is protected by the mandatory law.[37] If the legal provision is one that protects not only the interest of one of the parties, but also the public order (*ordre public*), derogating contracts or clauses will be considered to be absolutely void (*nullité absolue*)

---

**37** On the difference between absolute and relative nullity, *W Van Gerven*, Verbintenissenrecht (2001) 146 f.

which means that the judge must pronounce the nullity *ex officio*.[38] As a general rule the provisions that make insurance compulsory do so to protect the third party victim and thus are mandatory.

48 The mandatory rules (*normes impératives*) not only have a negative effect (limiting the freedom of the parties to derogate from the rule) but also a positive effect, consisting in obliging the judge to give effect to the mandatory legal rules on the rights and obligations of the parties. By so doing, the legal prescriptions are so to speak incorporated into the contract, even in the absence of any clause to that effect and notwithstanding any derogatory clause.[39]

49 It may be interesting to compare this sanction, consisting in a form of conversion (of a contract or clause that is void into another valid contract or clause that satisfies the mandatory legal rule) with the legally provided conversion that is found in art 19bis Act on Insurance Supervision of 9 July 1975 (see also art 22 IA 2014). This article concerns only the conformity of the insurance clauses with the (mandatory) provisions of the Insurance Supervision Act and the regulations taken in pursuance thereof. This sanction prescribes that contract clauses and contracts that are not in conformity with these provisions are assumed, as from the time of the conclusion of the contract, to have been drafted in conformity with these provisions. The reconversion of contracts and clauses is here operated by force of law.

*13.a) Are statutory stipulations as to the contents of the policy (eg, regarding the amount of the insurance sum, the ban on certain risk exclusion clauses, on deductibles, etc, see above Questions 10 and 11) also binding in favour of the insurance holder? Or is it nonetheless possible for the liability insurer and the insurance holder acting within their internal relationship to agree risk exclusion clauses, deductibles, aggregate limits, and claims series clauses, etc (see above Questions 10 and 11), releasing the insurer from its liability to pay?*

50 Statutory rules that prescribe the contents of a (liability) insurance policy are mandatory. Contractual derogations from such rules are null and void (the nullity will be relative insofar as the legislator's intention, while imposing compulsory insurance will, as a rule, be the protection of private interests [see above

**38** For more details and references to the extensive doctrinal literature on the subject matter, see *B Dubuisson*, La norme impérative dans le droit du contrat d'assurance, in: C Van Schoubroeck/H Cousy (eds), Liber Amicorum Hubert Claassens (1998) 109–135.
**39** See *Dubuisson* (fn 38) 112.

no 47f]). If they contain a limitation of the intended protection,[40] as was explained, the nullity of the derogatory policy clauses leads to a sort of legal conversion, in the sense that the legal rule (on obligatory content of the contract) takes the place of the contractual rule. Thus, if an insurance policy contains, for example, an exclusion clause that is not allowed or that is prohibited by a legal provision, the insurer will not be allowed to claim application of the contract clause. If the policy provides for a lower amount of cover than that which is legally prescribed, the injured party can claim cover up to the minimum cover that is legally required.

As to the question of whether the statutory stipulations concerning the contents of the policy will also be binding in favour of the policy holder, the answer must, in our view, be affirmative. The mandatory nature of the legal provision prohibits the parties from limiting their adherence to such provision to the 'external' relationship between the liability insurer and the injured person, including and by the same token, prevents them from relying on derogating clauses in their 'internal' relationship. The consequence of this is that the insurer will have to pay to the injured party in accordance with the legal stipulations, without having the possibility to exercise a recourse action against the insured.

*b) If it is possible for liability insurer and insurance holder acting within their internal relationship to agree a release from the obligation to pay (see above Question a): What consequence does this entail? Must the insurer first pay out to the victim and can then have recourse to the insurance holder? Or is another construction provided for the relationship between insurer, insurance holder and victim?*

See answer to Question 13.a, no 50. 51

*14.a) Does your general (voluntary) liability insurance law include statutory risk exclusion in respect of intentional damage by the insurance holder or the insured person?*

According to art 62, § 1 IA 2014 (former art 8, § 1 ICA 1992) 'notwithstanding any 52
agreement to the contrary, the insurer shall not be required to provide a benefit to any person who intentionally caused the insured event'. This rule does not make any distinction between the policyholder and the insured. This rule is

---

**40** One agrees that derogatory clauses that extend the protection offered by the mandatory rule are valid, *Dubuisson* (fn 38) 114.

considered to be a rule of public order (*ordre public*).[41] However, it is generally accepted and common practice to cover the liability for intentional fault of minors younger than sixteen/fourteen years old.[42]

According to the case law of the highest court (*Cour de cassation*), intentionally causing damage in the meaning of the cited provision requires an act which is willfully committed and with the intent to cause damage (any damage): there is no requirement that the insured had the intention to cause particular or the occurred damage (no *dolus directus*).[43]

The highest court ruled that the sanction for an intentional fault must be considered to be a forfeiture (loss of right).[44] In accordance with this case law of the highest court, this forfeiture has its cause in an act occurring prior to the insured event (see art 151, § 2 IA 2014 [former art 87, § 2 ICA 1992] as discussed hereafter in no 60ff: in non-compulsory liability insurance, the insurer may rely, as against the injured party, only upon defences, nullity and forfeitures which derive from law or contract and have their cause in an act occurring prior to the insured event).[45]

However, as regards compulsory insurance, the rule is the non-opposability of defences against the third party (art 151, § 1 IA 2014 [former art 87, § 1 ICA 1992, see nos 7f and 63–65]). Thus the insurer cannot raise against the third party the defence that the damage causing event was caused intentionally.

53 The insurer of any liability insurance cannot be obliged to give cover for the person causing damage intentionally ('*who* intentionally caused the insured event'), but must cover the person who is vicariously liable for the tortfeasor (eg the insurer must cover the parents who are vicariously liable for the acts of their minor child, but can refuse to cover the personal liability of this child).[46]

54 In all cases in which the insurer was not allowed to invoke the intentionally caused insured event against the third party, the insurer can provide for a recourse action against his policy holder or insured, upon the conditions of art 152 IA 2014 (former art 88 ICA 1992), and will do so in practice.

**41** *Dubuisson* (fn 38) 114.

**42** *C Van Schoubroeck*, Verzekeringen en jeugdbeschermingsrecht: een moeilijke verhouding? in: J Put (ed), Jeugdbeschermingsrecht, Themis School voor Postacademische Juridische vorming KU Leuven 2013–2014 (2014) 83.

**43** Cass 24 April 2009 (2009) Arresten Cassatie (Arr Cass) 1111; (2010) Tijdschrift Belgisch Handelsrecht (TBH) 56, cmt *H Cousy*; Cass 26 October 2011 (2012) Nieuw Juridisch Weekblad (NjW) 214, cmt *G Jocqué*.

**44** Cass 14 May 2012, <www.cass.be>.

**45** Cass 18 November 2011 (2011) Pas 2554.

**46** Cass 25 March 2003 (2003) RDC, cmt *G Jocqué*; Cass 4 June 2012 (2012) Pas 1271.

b) *If the general liability insurance law contains statutory risk exclusion in respect of intentional damage inflicted by the insurance holder (see above Question a): Does this also apply in cases of compulsory liability insurance?*

The rule equally applies to compulsory insurance (see answer to Question 14, no 52f). 55

# IV. Protection Mechanisms

15. *Are insurers obliged to contract when they offer liability insurance policies covering a risk for which the insurance holder is obliged to obtain cover?*

Under Belgian law a legal rule that obliges an insurer to underwrite a liability insurance contract even in cases where insurance is obligatory for the policyholder does not exist. In other words, also with respect to compulsory liability insurance, the insurer enjoys his contract and underwriting freedom.[47] 56

16. *If there is no obligation to contract: Are there comparable mechanisms provided to ensure that an insurance agreement is concluded?*

Under Belgian law, however, the legislator has taken steps to ensure, or at least enhance, the chances of obtaining certain mandatory insurance to those who are under a duty to obtain this insurance. 57

The best known example is the creation, in 2002 by art 9bis Compulsory Motor Vehicle Liability Insurance Act 1989, of an official body, the *Bureau de Tarification/Tariferingsbureau*. Those who cannot obtain motor vehicle liability insurance cover in the commercial market, or who can only obtain cover at an unreasonably high premium or deductible (the calculation of which is further specified in art 9bis of the Act) can file an application with the Bureau and request it to determine a more reasonable premium level (that takes into account the particular risk of the policyholder as well as its effect on the other insured persons). The insured will actually obtain cover at the given premium tariff from one of the (few larger) insurance companies that manage this system. These participating insurance companies are entitled to spread the negative saldo of the specific portfolio of 'tariffied insured' to the community of motor vehicle liability insurers. 58

47 *Fontaine* (fn 13) fn 166: 'l'obligation d'assurance n'équivaut pas au droit à l'assurance'.

Although some authors have characterised the system as the beginning of a right to obtain insurance cover (*droit à l'assurance*), the system, which is to a large extent inspired by the French *Bureau National de Tarification*, does not really attribute such a right.[48] The system is rather conceived to make it possible to spread the costs created by bad drivers who pay insufficient premiums, over the community of insurers, and thus of the insureds, in the given branch.[49] A similar system of intervention of a *Bureau de tarification* is created in the framework of insurance against natural disasters (floods, earthquakes, rising sewage water and landslides), introduced by art 3 Act of 21 May 2003 and amended afterwards, in art 123 IA 2014 (former art 68–1ff ICA 1992). However, this regulation does not deal with liability insurance and the insured is not obliged to conclude a fire insurance contract. However, if the insured concludes a fire insurance contract covering damage caused by fire to his house, the insurer is under the obligation to include the natural disaster cover in all (non-compulsory) fire insurance policies for the so-called non-industrial risks (*risques simples* as defined in art 121, § 2 IA 2014 (former art 67, § 2 ICA 1992) and art 5 Royal Decree of 24 December 1992).

*17. Is the insurance holder prohibited from disposing over his cover entitlement to the disadvantage of the victim (eg, by surrendering his entitlement)?*

59 As is explained hereafter in the answer to Question 18, the Belgian legislator has, ever since 1992, generalised the system of the 'direct action' of the victim against the third party liability insurer (which formerly existed only within compulsory motor vehicle liability insurance) to all types of liability insurance. One of the functions of the direct action is a protective one, which means that the 'direct action' protects the victim against any misuse (in the sense of a deleterious use) by the policyholder/insured of his own claim for cover against the liability insurer.[50] At the same time the existence of the 'direct action' makes an assignment by the insured to the victim of the insured's claim against the liability insurer superfluous. Indeed, by vesting the victim with a direct action, in-

48 *Dubuisson* (fn 17) 3; *H Claassens*, Du droit de l'assurance au droit à l'assurance, avec ou sans frontières, in: J Rogge (ed), Liber amicorum René Van Gompel (1998) 39–58.

49 Compare with the situation in France where a comparable 'Bureau Central de Tarification' functions, *Kullmann* (fn 17) 94.

50 *E Dirix/E Decorte*, Zekerheidsrechten (2006) 392; cf *H Cousy*, Pikante details over een beruchte driehoeksverhouding: de rechtstreekse vordering in de aansprakelijkheidsverzekering, in: H Bocken (ed), Aansprakelijkheid, aansprakelijkheidsverzekering en andere schadevergoedingssystemen (2007) 429.

cluding a *ius proprium* against the liability insurer, there is no need or use for a transfer of rights by the insured himself.

*18. Does the victim enjoy special protection against insolvency on the part of the insurance holder with regard to the sum payable by the liability insurer?*

This question, as well as a number of the following questions (and more specifi- **60**
cally Questions 19.a and b, 21.a, b and c, 22.a and b, and 25), can be answered as follows.

Under Belgian law, all of these questions are treated with, and to a large extent solved, by the system of the own right of the third party (*ius proprium*) and the direct action which apply to all liability insurance classes (arts 150 and 151 IA 2014, former art 86f ICA 1992). This own right and direct action of the third party was first introduced in certain specific legislation, the most important examples of which are fire insurance (own right of the owner and neighbours against the liability insurer of the tenant in art 38 of the Insurance Contract Act of 11 June 1874), art 11 Act of 1 July 1956 on Compulsory Motor Vehicle Liability Insurance, art 8 of the Act of 30 July 1979 Concerning the Prevention of Fire and Explosions and Concerning the Compulsory Insurance of Civil Liability in the case of Fire and Explosions in Places accessible by the General Public (see below nos 66 and 92), and later generalised by art 86 of the ICA 1992 to all compulsory liability insurance falling under the scope of 'land insurance contracts'.

The general lines of the system, as laid down in arts 150 and 151 IA 2014 (former art 86f ICA 1992) have been exposed hereabove (see nos 7–9). Further details of this system can be summarised as follows.

The law starts by giving the victim not only a direct action, but in the first **61**
place an 'own right' (*ius proprium*) against the liability insurer, ie a right to obtain compensation which is not proceeding *ex contractu* as in the case of a stipulation to the benefit of a third party (*stipulation pour autrui*), but a right *ex lege*. This own right and direct action can be exercised when a valid liability insurance contract exists at the moment of occurrence of the insured event. To vest the victim with a direct action, it is sufficient that an insurance contract was concluded, even if later the nullity of the contract (see above no 47) or a clause is observed. The victim would lose his direct right of action if a judge decided on the nullity of the contract before the accident occurred.

The advantage of having his own right *ex lege* consists first in the fact that the victim does not enter into a *concursus creditorum* situation with the other creditors of the insured on the assets of the insured claim against the insurer. In the absence of a direct action, the claim against the liability insurer would form part of the bankrupt estate of the policyholder or insured and would therefore be distributed among all creditors, the victim being only one of them and receiving only a share of it. The direct action prevents this result, since the direct action is not part of the bankrupt estate of the policyholder or the insured.[51] In addition, the third party does not depend upon the initiative or actions by the insured. Finally, the insurer has to pay the compensation directly to the third party. Consequently, the third party is protected against the insolvency of the policyholder.

62 The (substantive) own right that the third party has against the insurer is accompanied by his (procedural) right to bring an action directly against the insurer (accessory to the substantive right).

The direct action is a measure of 'procedural economy' (*économie de procedure*). The possibility for the third party to bring a direct action directly against the liability insurer does not prevent this victim from lodging (simultaneously) a claim against the insured (without of course ever obtaining compensation for an amount greater than the damage suffered). This own right is governed by a specific prescription rule (art 88, § 2 and art 89, § 4 IA 2014, former art 34, § 2 and art 35, § 4 ICA 1992).

63 That the victim has an own right against the liability insurer explains why the insurer is denied the right to invoke a number of defences against the direct action of the third party.

Contrary to, for example, the situation under English law (as represented in the famous quote of Lord Denning 'that the third party cannot have the plums without the duff'), which means that the victim must take the insured and the rights of the insured against the insurer in the state in which he finds them, the Belgian rule of the 'non-opposability of nullities, defences and forfeitures' (art 151 IA 2014 [former art 87 ICA 1992], see above no 7f) goes very far to protect the victim in particular with regard to compulsory liability insurance.

Article 151 IA 2014 (former art 87 ICA 1992) states:

> '§ 1. In compulsory liability insurance, the insurer cannot raise against the third party civil liability defences, deductibles, nullities and forfeitures which derive from law or contract, and have their cause in an act prior or subsequent to the insured event.
>
> Nonetheless, the annulment, cancellation, expiry or suspension of the contract before the occurrence of the insured event may be relied upon as against the injured party.
>
> § 2. In other types of civil liability insurance the insurer may rely, as against the injured party, only upon defences, nullities and forfeitures which derive from law or contract and have their cause in an act occurring prior to the insured event.

---

51 Cf *J Basedow et al*, Principles of European Insurance Contract Law (PEICL) (2nd edn 2016) Comm C4 to art 15.101.

> The King may, however, extend the scope of subsection 1 to any type of non-compulsory civil liability insurance prescribed by him'.[52]

To better understand the scope of art 151, one can state that in compulsory insurance the independence of the rights of the third party to the contract are guaranteed and the insurer can only raise the following defences against the victim: 64

a) *No liability*. The third person did not suffer damage for which the insured person is liable.

b) *No insurance contract* (*non-assurance*). At the time of the insured event there was no valid insurance contract: because there had never been a contract, or because the expiry, cancellation, annulment or suspension had its effect before the occurrence of the insured event. Borderline cases occur when the insured benefits from an insurance cover but not precisely for the risk that materialised and caused the damage to the injured party. For example, the much debated question whether a motorbike (a moped) with artificially raised power is a *different* risk than the one that was the object of insurance, or rather an *aggravated* risk (non-opposable defence), was solved by the Benelux Court which decided that it must be considered as an aggravated risk (which defence cannot be raised against the third party).[53]

c) *No cover*. The insurer must only pay within the borders of the contractually agreed cover. The contractual clauses that define the extent and contents of the cover (positively or negatively by means of exclusions) can be raised against the third party claimant. However, if the law that makes the insurance compulsory specifies the content or the minimum cover that must be covered by the insurance contract, only those exclusions or limitations of cover that are expressly allowed by law can be raised against the claimant (see above no 50).

An exception to this rule is that in compulsory liability insurance the deductible, etc (see above no 63) cannot be raised against the third party. The insurer has to pay out to the third party but can make use of a recourse right against the policyholder to obtain reimbursement of the amount of the deductible (arts 87 and 88 ICA 1992) (this rule originated in motor vehicle liability insurance and was generalised by the Act of 22 August 2002 through incorporation into art 87, § 1 ICA 1992).

As far as compulsory insurance is concerned, art 87 ICA 1992 (art 151 ICA 2014) enumerates the defences that cannot be raised against the injured person

---

**52** The concept of 'the occurrence of the insured event' means 'the occurrence of the damage', Cass 27 June 2013, <www.cass.be>.

**53** Benelux Court 15 December 1989 (1989) Benelux Jurisprudence 70.

(the third party as the article states), no matter whether these defences find their cause in an act before or after the occurrence of the event.

Examples of such non-opposable defences (finding their cause in an act which occurred before the event) are: netting, forfeiture for an intentional fault or shortcoming of the insured, the nullity of the contract because of intentional non-disclosure of the risk (unless the nullity was already judicially decided before the insured event), the reduction of cover because of non-intentional non-disclosure of the elements of the risk or their aggravation. The non-opposability, however, does not extend to defences that are based on the absence of liability, the non-existence of the contract or the exceeding of the scope of the cover.

65 As far as non-compulsory insurance is concerned, the rule is that defences, nullities and forfeitures which derive from law or contract can be raised against the third party, except those that have their cause in an act occurring after the moment of the insured event.

The logic of this is that the rights of the third party against the insurer are limited by the extent of the cover obligation of the insurer at the moment of the insured event.

66 A remarkable rule about the opposability of the defences of *non-assurance* is encountered in the Act of 30 July 1979 concerning the prevention of fire and explosions and concerning the compulsory insurance of the civil liability for fire and explosion which occur in certain places accessible to the general public, as defined in the Royal Decree of 5 August 1991 (eg schools, churches, airports; see Question 27.a, no 92). Whereas art 8bis, § 6 of the Act of 1979 contains the (classical) rule about the non-opposability against the injured party of defences such as the nullity and loss of right (accompanied by a possibility of recourse actions for the insurer), art 8bis, § 7 of the Act of 1979 adds that the insurer can raise the defences of termination, annulment, resolution, cancellation and suspension of the contract or of the cover, whatever the reason may be, only with respect to claims that are filed more than thirty days after the notification of these facts to the mayor of the town where the institution is located.

*19.a) In what manner can the victim obtain the insurance payment?*

67 See answer to Question 18, nos 60–64.

*b) Does the victim have a direct right of action against the liability insurer (action directe) in the case of voluntary or compulsory liability insurance?*

68 See answer to Question 18, nos 60–65.

*20. When settling the claim, is the liability insurer obliged to observe a certain procedure in the interests of the victim? For instance, must it pay the victim an advance within a certain period?*

The general civil law principle, laid down in art 1134 Civil Code that all contracts must be carried out in good faith, obliges insurers to indemnify the victim within reasonable time. **69**

Whereas such good faith requirement does not by itself seem to oblige insurers to pay the victim in advance, insurers have done so in disaster situations where several insurers are involved and the discussions concern not so much the question whether someone will be held liable, but rather the question which one of the defendants will be held liable. A recent example of such situation is the case of the Ghislengien gas pipe explosion and the Act of 13 November 2011 on the compensation of major technological disasters, which was inspired by the manner in which this major catastrophe was handled by the insurance companies on an *ad hoc* settlement procedure. Victims of disasters falling under the scope of this Act have the right to claim compensation for bodily injury and non-pecuniary loss directly from the Motor Vehicle Fund although the disaster may have no relation with traffic accidents. The Common Guarantee Fund for Motor Vehicles is presently called Common Guarantee Fund because of the described widening of its tasks. The precise conditions for compensation by the Fund, and the procedure to be followed are described in arts 6–15 of the mentioned Act. The Fund, funded by the liability insurers active on the Belgian market (art 16, §§ 2–6), pays out the compensation and is subrogated to the rights of the victim against the tortfeasor (and his insurer) (art 17). In the case of absence of (proven) liability, the Fund can, under certain conditions, claim reimbursement from the National Disaster Fund (art 20). **70**

A detailed procedure to be followed by the insurer in paying the third party exists in motor vehicle liability insurance. Articles 13 and 14 of the Compulsory Motor Vehicle Liability Insurance Act 1989 transpose the provisions of art 22 EU Directive 2009/103/EC on Compulsory Motor Vehicle Liability Insurance. These articles oblige the insurer to propose an advance payment in case the liability is not contested but the damage is not quantifiable yet. In the case of infringement, the insurer has to pay double interest based on the granted compensation. In case the liability is contested, the insurer has an obligation to inform the third party of the reasons why he does not compensate within three months of the third party's claim for compensation, upon the threat of having to pay a fine of € 250 per day. **71**

A special issue occurs in the situation of serial damage where there are several victims and where the total amount of the claims exceeds the insured sum. **72**

This issue was first resolved under Belgian law in the Act on Compulsory Motor Vehicle Liability Insurance of 1989 (art 12, § 2 transposing the rule of the Benelux Convention). By the Act of 22 August 2002 this provision was transferred to the ICA 1992 and is now applicable to all liability insurance classes. Article 150, § 3 IA 2014 (former art 86, § 3 ICA 1992) prescribes that in case there is more than one injured party and the total amount of compensation payable exceeds the sum insured, the rights of the injured parties against the insurer shall be reduced proportionally to the extent of this sum. In a situation of serial damage, where insurers do not know all the victims of a particular damaging event, the cited article allows the insurer to pay out the money according to the above mentioned proportional rule. Insofar as the insurer effectuates such payments in good faith, his obligation towards the other victims will be limited to turning out the remainder of the totality of the insured amount.[54]

*21.a) In the context of its relationship with the victim, can the liability insurer rely on the fact that vis-à-vis the insurance holder (= damaging party) it is freed from the obligation to pay, eg, due to the insurance holder breaching an obligation of conduct/warranty (Obliegenheitsverletzung) or due to him defaulting on premiums?*

73 See answer to Question 18, nos 63–65.

*b) Does the law distinguish on the basis of the ground for the release from the obligation to pay so that in some cases the insurer may not invoke its release from such obligation vis-à-vis the victim?*

74 See answer to Question 18, nos 63–65.

*c) If the insurer must still pay the victim despite being released from its obligation to pay vis-à-vis the insurance holder (see above Question b), may it take recourse against the latter?*

75 See answer to Question 23.c, no 83.

54 On the practical implications of this rule, see *L Schuermans*, Het paard van Troje is niet opgetuigd. Pleidooi voor een efficiënte afwikkeling van massaschade (2005–06) RW 721–727.

*22.a) Within its relationship to the victim, can the liability insurer invoke the fact that the insurance agreement had already ended by the time relevant in respect of the duty to provide cover?*

See answer to Question 18, no 64. 76

*b) If the insurer must pay the victim despite the termination of the insurance agreement by the time relevant for the duty to provide cover (see above Question a), can it take recourse against the insurance holder?*

See answer to Question 18, no 64 and answer to Question 23.c, no 83. 77

*23.a) Are there cases in which a damaging party does not effectively conclude the required liability insurance and the victim injured by him nonetheless receives compensation for his loss from a liability insurer or another compensation scheme (eg, a guarantee fund)?*

In Belgium, like in other EU Member States, a first example of a guarantee fund 78
that covers the losses or part of the losses of an injured party in cases where the liable person has not concluded the legally required liability insurance is found in the field of motor vehicle liability insurance. The Belgian legislation, which in substance has existed since 1956 but has now been brought into line with the (coordinating) EU Directive (2009/103/EC) of 16 September 2009, is found in the Compulsory Motor Vehicle Liability Insurance Act 1989 (art 19bis-2ff and in the Royal Decree of 11 July 2003).

Article 19bis-2 of the Act provides the establishment of a 'Motor Vehicle Guarantee Fund', presently (because of the widening of its tasks beyond motor vehicle insurance) called *Fonds Commun de Garantie*, Common Guarantee Fund, the statutes of which had to be and were approved by Royal Decree. One of the manifold tasks of the Fund (information, indemnification of traffic victims, identification of non-insured vehicles) consists in indemnifying the losses caused by a motor vehicle when no insurance undertaking is held to indemnify because the duty to conclude an insurance contract was not fulfilled (art 19bis-11, § 1, 8°).

A more recent example of a fund that is invested with the task of compen- 79
sating the victim in the case of the absence of an adequate liability insurance (whether it is compulsory to take out this insurance or not) covering the provider of health care who is liable, is the Fund for Medical Loss. This Fund intervenes in cases where patients suffer loss as a consequence of certain medical accidents without liability or in cases where the provider of care is liable but not or insufficiently insured, or where he contests his liability (arts 4 and 5 Act of

31 March 2010 concerning the compensation of loss that is suffered as a consequence of health care treatment).

b) *In the event that the policy taken out was not in fact effectively concluded, is it necessary to distinguish on the basis of the ground for this ineffectiveness, eg, whether the reason for the contract not coming into effect was:*

i) *a lack of legal capacity on the part of the insurance holder,*

**80** No such distinctions are made by art 87, § 1 ICA 1992 (see above no 63f).

ii) *lack of consent,*

**81** No such distinctions are made by art 87, § 1 ICA 1992 (see above no 63f).

iii) *falsa procuratio (unauthorised agency)?*

**82** No such distinctions are made by art 87, § 1 ICA 1992 (see above no 63f).

c) *Can the liability insurer (or the alternative compensation scheme) that must provide cover even though the insurance policy was not effectively concluded (see above Questions a and b) have recourse against the damaging party?*

**83** In those cases where the insurer has paid out totally or partially the direct claim of the injured party, in spite of the legal or contractual defences, nullities and forfeitures that the insurer could have invoked in the absence of the legally organised own right and direct claim according to arts 150 and 151 IA 2014 (former arts 86 and 87 ICA 1992), the law explicitly confirms the right of the insurer to reserve itself a right of recourse against the policyholder in the insurance policy, and, if appropriate, against the insured other than the policyholder, to the extent that he could have refused or reduced (vis-à-vis the policyholder/the insured) the benefit pursuant to law or to the insurance contract (art 152 IA 2014, former art 88 ICA 1992).

According to art 152, § 2 IA 2014, the insurer shall notify the policyholder or, as the case may be, the insured other than the policyholder, of its intention to seek recourse as soon as it is informed of the facts justifying its decision. In addition, the grounds for recourse have to be stipulated in the contract. This recourse right is therefore considered to be a contractual right.

Although art 152, § 3 IA 2014 gives the King the power to limit the cases and the extent of recourse, so far no use has been made of this.

The Compulsory Motor Vehicle Liability Insurance Act 1989 provides for the possibility of the Common Guarantee Fund to exercise a recourse against the (uninsured, or not effectively insured) liable person and, as the case may be, against their insurers[55] (art 19bis-14 of the Act 1989). Here the right of recourse is not based on a contractual stipulation between the Fund and the liable person but on a specifically legally provided right of subrogation of the Fund into the rights of the injured party against the liable person for the amount paid out to the victim. 84

When the Medical Fund, as provided in the Act of 31 March 2010 concerning the compensation of loss that is suffered as a consequence of health care treatment, has compensated the injured party, this Fund has a legal recourse right against the health care provider or its liability insurer. However, neither the health care provider nor its insurer or the judge are bound by the amount of compensation the Fund has paid out (art 4 para 2, arts 28, 30–32 of the Act of 31 March 2010). 85

*24.a) Are there cases in which a damaging party does not take out any liability insurance, ie not even an ineffective insurance policy (see above Question 23), and the victim whom he injured is still compensated for his damage by a liability insurer or another compensation scheme (guarantee fund, etc)?*

The question has been answered under Question 23.a, no 78f. 86

*b) Can the liability insurer (or the alternative compensation scheme) that must provide cover despite the total absence of any insurance agreement (see above Question a) have recourse against the damaging party?*

As appears from the answer to Question 18 (no 64) concerning the direct action of the third party and the defences that can be raised against him by the liability insurer, the defence that no insurance contract was ever concluded covering the risk in question (thus a situation of 'absence of insurance') can be successfully raised against the injured party. In such a situation the insurer is exempted from payment, and there will be no need for a recourse action. 87

The situation is, however, different in the case of a guarantee fund that is legally called to cover victims in cases where the tortfeasor did not take out insurance while being legally obliged to do so. Under Belgian law this is the case in motor vehicle liability insurance. The Common Guarantee Fund is, by virtue 88

55 Eg in case the insurance company had not appointed a claims handler (art 19bis-1, § 1, 6° Act 1989). This is based on the EU Directive 2009.

of the cited art 19bis-14, subrogated to the rights of the victim against the liable person (and, as the case may be, against the liability insurer) to the extent that the Fund has indemnified the victim (see above Question 23.c, no 84).

89 Another example is the recourse of the Fund for Medical Loss according to arts 28, 30–32 Act of 31 March 2010 concerning the compensation of loss that is suffered as a consequence of health care treatment (see above Question 23.c at no 85).

*25. Is the victim protected against the insolvency of the liability insurer?*

90 Yes, but only if a guarantee fund has been set up by the concerned liability insurers. In Belgium this is only the case in motor vehicle liability insurance, where the Common Guarantee Fund exists (see answer to Question 23.a, no 78).

*26. Are there rules that serve in particular the protection of the victim when the liability insurance was only concluded voluntarily – ie without it being compulsory?*

91 The system of the own right of the third party and direct action, together with the system of limited opposability of defences, protects a third party against a number of problems (see art 150f, § 2 IA 2014, former arts 86 and 87, § 2 ICA 1992, see above nos 7–9, 60–65 and 72).

## V. Supervision and Sanctions

*27.a) In which cases must the insurance holder prove to an authority before commencing an activity requiring insurance that he has taken out the respective prescribed liability insurance cover (see above Question 4.e)?*

92 There is no general legal regime that organises the control and implementation of the duty. A few of the specific legal provisions are here described.

a) Article 2 Compulsory Motor Vehicle Liability Insurance Act 1989 provides that vehicles are not allowed to participate in public traffic unless they are covered by liability insurance (to be taken out, as a rule, by the owner of the vehicle or, in absence, by the custodian) that is in accordance with the conditions that are prescribed by this Act.

Article 6 of this Act provides that no motor vehicle may be registered (to obtain a licence plate) if it is not covered by the legally required and prescribed insurance cover. The system is organised in such way that the owner of the vehicle must prove, with a document that is delivered to him by the liability insurer, to the authority that delivers the licence plate that insurance cover was obtained.

Therefore an additional measure of control is provided for by art 7 of this Act that obliges the insurer to deliver to the policyholder proof of the existence of an insurance contract. A Royal Decree of 13 February 1991 (that contains a number of executive measures of the Act of 1989) prescribes that the proof, referred to by art 7 of the Act, will be the international insurance certificate that is delivered by the 'Belgian Bureau of Automobile Insurers' (the green card). In Belgium, the green card thus also fulfils a function in the domestic field: the yearly renewed green card testifies that the vehicle is insured in accordance with the law and that the (last) yearly premium was paid.[56]

b) Act of 30 July 1979 concerning the prevention of fire and explosions and concerning the compulsory insurance of civil liability, and the Royal Decree of 5 August 1991 (both concerning public institutions that are accessible to the public, see nos 60, 66 and 92).

Liability insurance is a prerequisite for the accessibility of a building to the public (art 8 para 3 Act of 31 July 1979). The Royal Decree prescribes that the insurer must deliver to the policyholder a (legally defined) certificate (that proves the existence of the compulsory insurance) and that a duplicate must be sent to the mayor of the town where the institution is located. In addition the insurer shall enter all the contracts (number, name and address of the parties, location of the insured institution, duration of the contract and the insured amount) in a repertory. In this repertory the notifications that the insurer has to make, according to art 8bis, § 7 of the 1979 Act, concerning the termination of the contract shall also be registered.

On the one hand, art 8bis, § 6 Act 1979 contains the (classical) rule about the non-opposability of defences against the injured party such as nullity (exceptions) and loss of right (accompanied by a possibility of recourse actions for the insurer) while, on the other hand, art 8bis, § 7 of this Act also contains a remarkable rule about the opposability of the defences of '*non-assurance*' (see no 66).

c) In all cases where the insurance is imposed as a condition to obtain authorisation to an activity or profession, the authorising authority will control whether the insurance has been taken out, and whether the conditions are in accordance with the legal requirements.

**56** Art 6 of the Royal Decree of 13 February 1991.

*b) Must the insurer inform an authority when liability insurance taken out to meet an insurance obligation ends?*

93 Such a rule is only rarely prescribed. An exception is art 8bis, § 9 of Act of 30 July of 1979, described in the answer to Question 27.a, no 92. Another example is art 268, § 1, 3° IA 2014 (former art 10, 4° Act of 27 March 1995 on [re]insurance mediation) which states that the contract must provide that the insurer must inform the supervisory authority that the contract has been terminated.

*c) Is the insurer also under a duty to inform when a liability insurance agreement is in existence but it has no duty to provide cover – eg, due to defaults on premium payments?*

94 Such a rule is only rarely prescribed. For example, art 8bis, § 7 of Act of 30 July of 1979, described in the course of the answer to Question 27.a, no 92. Another example is the duty of the motor vehicle liability insurer to inform the Common Guarantee Fund every month of any changes in the database that the law requires it to manage (art 19bis-6, § 3 Act of 21 November 1989 and art 17 Royal Decree of 11 July 2003).

*d) What are the consequences when the duties to inform of the end of contract or the release from payment obligations (see above Questions b and c) are violated?*

95 In the example of art 8bis, § 7 Act of 1979, described in the answer to Question 27.a, no 92, this article provides the sanction of the non-opposability of defences such as the termination of the contract, or suspension of the coverage due to non-payment of the premium.

*28. Is there some official body (authority, professional chamber) where an injured party can find out whether and where the injuring party who inflicted damage upon him in the course of an activity requiring insurance has liability insurance?*

96 One would expect the FSMA (see above no 1) to be able to offer such service. The FSMA is in charge of a number of supervisory tasks vis-à-vis insurers, ie control of the respect of conduct of business rules, consumer protection and information (thus not prudential control).

In reality the FSMA is not equipped to systematically offer this service. Consumers will rather turn to the information desk of consumer organisations (in Belgium eg Test Achat/Test Aankoop).

According to the prescriptions of the EU Directive 2009/103/EC, an information centre has been set up with regard to motor vehicle liability insurance (art 19bis-6j ff Compulsory Motor Vehicle Liability Insurance Act 1989) which in Belgium is managed by the Common Guarantee Fund (see above nos 78 and 88).

*29. Are there (public law) sanctions against the party who was required to take out insurance if such does not take out the compulsory liability insurance? Examples of this would be a ban on carrying out the activity that requires the insurance or the imposition of an administrative or judicial penalty.*

The Compulsory Motor Vehicle Liability Insurance Act 1989 imposes penal sanctions on the owner and the holder of the vehicle (art 22). 97

In case insurance is a requirement to obtain an authorisation, the authorisation is not obtained or withdrawn. If no general rule to that effect exists, it follows from the way in which the requirement of liability insurance is circumscribed in the legislation or regulation (be it varying ways as appears from the numerous illustrations in the Annex: Rules on Compulsory Liability Insurance in Belgium at the end of this book).

A professional authority or organisation can impose disciplinary measures.

# VI. Statutory Provisions required by the Constitution or the European Convention on Human Rights (ECHR)

*30. What has been said regarding the compatibility of the duties to take out liability insurance with your country's constitution and the ECHR? Please take into account case law and academic literature.*

The legislative difference in treatment between compulsory and non-compulsory liability insurance in the rule on the opposability of defences the insurer can raise against the third party (art 151 IA 2014 [former art 87 ICA 1992], see nos 7f and 63–65) was (unsuccessfully) challenged before the Belgian Constitutional Court. The Court decided that the constitutional rule of equal treatment and non-discrimination (arts 10 and 11 Constitution) was not violated, because the difference in treatment in this case appeared to be justified by an objective criterion, ie the compulsory or non-compulsory character of the insurance. Whereas the opposability of defences against the injured party in non-com- 98 pulsory liability insurance is based on the maintaining of the freedom to contract, the legislative derogations to this general rule in the case of compulsory insurance appear, in the opinion of the Constitutional Court, to be justified by the considerations that underlie the legislative option to make the insurance compulsory.[57]

*31. Does the constitution or the ECHR make any stipulations regarding the contents of such duties to take out liability insurance? Please take into account case law and academic literature.*

99 The Belgian Constitution does not make any stipulations regarding the contents of such duties to take out liability insurance.

We did not examine the case law of the European Court of Human Rights.

## VII. Reform Efforts

*32. Are there efforts towards reforming the law regarding compulsory liability insurance?*

100 Not to our knowledge.

## VIII. Compulsory Liability Insurance and Liability Law

*33. Is, at the legislative level, any connection discernible between the nature of liability (in particular in the case of strict liability) and the imposition of compulsory liability insurance?*

101 Apart from the aims and goals described in the answers to Question 5 (above nos 22–27), the requirement of compulsory insurance can also be intended to accompany a more general move to 'reinforce' a liability regime (eg a regime of strict liability), see above no 27.[58] Important examples are the strict liability and

57 Constitutional Court, 28 October 2004, case 167/2004, <www.const-court.be>; MB 13 December 2004, <http://staatsblad.be>.
58 See *De Rode/Collignon* (fn 13) 63.

duty to take out insurance of organisations making use of volunteers (art 6 Act of 3 July 2005) and the strict liability and duty to take out insurance of operators of buildings accessible to the general public (art 8, § 3 Act of 31 July 1979).[59] Motor vehicle liability is not a regime of strict liability.

**59** For a general comment on the subject matter of Question 33, see also *Cousy* (fn 19) 18–55.

Petr Dobiáš

# Compulsory Liability Insurance in the Czech Republic

## I. The Term Compulsory Liability Insurance

1. *Indicate the rules within your legal system that set out a duty to take out liability insurance. In this context, also take into account the implementation of international treaties (eg, the International Convention on Civil Liability for Bunker Oil Pollution Damage, 2001).*

General rules are contained in §§ 2779–2781[1] Civil Code (No 89/2012 Coll, *občanský zákoník*),[2] for other rules in special laws compare Annex: Rules on Compulsory Liability Insurance in the Czech Republic (at the end of this book). 1

In a few cases, the duty to take out liability insurance is contained directly in international treaties (International Convention on Civil Liability for Bunker Oil Pollution Damage 2001, Vienna Convention on Civil Liability for Nuclear Damage[3] 1963 and Protocol on the Privileges and Immunities of the International Seabed Authority 1998). 2

---

1 An unofficial translation of §§ 2779–2781 Civil Code is as follows:

§ 2779

(1) If another law obliges the concrete person to conclude the insurance contract, it is possible to deviate from the provisions of this section only if it is allowed by the other law and it will not lead to the reduction of the scope of insurance stipulated by the other law.

(2) The duty of the insurer to conclude the insurance contract stipulated by another law is imposed upon him in such a manner that the duty to provide indemnity will arise also in the case of the wilful act of the policyholder, insured or other person.

§ 2780

In the case of compulsory liability insurance, the insurer may refuse to provide indemnity only in the case that the victim or another person with the victim's knowledge participated in the disclosure of deliberately false or grossly misleading information or provided incomplete answers to questions rendered in written form.

§ 2781

The insurer has the right to withdraw from the contract only if this is stipulated in another law. This does not preclude contractual stipulations imposing rights of recourse in relation to the policyholder or insured in the case of the breach of its duties.

2 Cf below nos 3–5, 7, 30, 35–40, 42, 44, 49, 55, 59 and 85 and fn 12 and 18.

3 But it should be noted that arts V, VI, VII, IX and XV of the Vienna Convention on Civil Liability for Nuclear Damage 1963 were transfomed into §§ 13, 36–38 of the Act No 18/1997 Coll on the Peaceful Use of Nuclear Energy and Ionising Radiation.

*2. Is there a coherent 'law of compulsory liability insurance' in your legal system?*

3 There is no coherent 'law of compulsory liability insurance' in the Czech legal system because the duty and conditions to take out liability insurance are defined in different ways in specific laws (for an overview of these laws see Annex: Rules on Compulsory Liability Insurance in the Czech Republic). This leads to divergences in terminology (eg limitation of insured sum). However, as already mentioned above (cf no 1), general provisions are contained in §§ 2779–2781 Civil Code.

*3. Is there a specific term for compulsory liability insurance in your legal system? How is it defined?*

4 The specific term for compulsory liability insurance is *povinné pojištění odpovědnosti za škodu*. The Civil Code (§§ 2779–2781) only deals with compulsory insurance in general. Whereas compulsory liability insurance is not defined in laws or case law, it is briefly described by M Karfíková and V Přikryl: 'Compulsory contractual insurance originates in the same way as voluntary insurance, but in contrast, there is an obligation to conclude the contract imposed by law. This duty is imposed by law especially for activities which can be the source of an increased risk of damage to others.'[4] In a similar way, compulsory liability insurance is defined by L Bohman and M Wawerková as follows: 'If a special law entails an obligation to conclude the insurance contract for someone who belongs to a group of people exercising a specific type of activity which is a source of danger for others or who is in possession of a specific property, then we speak of compulsory contractual insurance.'[5]

*4. In which of the following cases does compulsory liability insurance apply according to prevailing opinion?*

*a) Duties to take out liability insurance which are not directly based on the law but on an order or decision issued by administrative authorities?*

5 Currently, according to § 2779 Civil Code, it is not allowed to lay down a duty to take out liability insurance which is not directly based on the law but on an or-

---

4 *M Karfíková/V Přikryl*, Pojišťovací právo (2010) 285 ff.

5 *L Bohman/M Wawerková*, Zákon o pojistné smlouvě – komentář (2009) 47. This definition is also accepted in *J Švestka/J Dvořák/J Fiala et al*, Občanský zákoník, komentář, vol VI, §§ 2521–3081 (2014) 488 ff.

der or decision issued by administrative authorities. According to § 4 para 3 of the Decree of the government No 1/1988 Coll (repealed by the Act No 127/1990 Coll) on the Sale of Goods and Rendition of Services by the Citizens Based on the Permission of the People's Committee, in the permit, the state body could order the citizen to conclude a liability insurance contract covering work injury or occupational disease for a prescribed period.

Public authorities can only exceptionally stipulate the amount of the in- 6
sured sum on the basis of the law (eg Ministry for Environment – § 57 para 2 Act No 185/2001 Coll on Waste). This leads to a situation that in some cases (cf eg §§ 6–8 Act No 159/1999 Coll on Certain Conditions for Undertakings in Travel Services), it is the insurance company which has to judge whether the insurance sum is adequate. The above-mentioned insufficient state of legal regulation should be resolved by the amendment of Act No 159/1999 Coll on Certain Conditions for Undertakings in Travel Services. The amendment (Act No 341/2015 Coll, entered into force on 29 December 2015) is a tightening of the information duty of Travel Agencies in relation to the insurer and Ministry of Regional Development and a strengthening of the penalties which could be imposed to the Travel Agencies for the breach of the information duty.

*b) Duties to take out liability insurance that are not based directly on the law but on the statutes of a professional or other self-governing body?*

According to § 2779 Civil Code, it is not allowed to impose duties to take out 7
liability insurance that are not based on the law but on the statutes of a professional or other self-governing body. Under this condition, professional or other self-governing bodies can prescribe the scope of cover and premiums only on the ground that a formal law has prescribed the duty itself (eg Czech Bar Association – cf § 24c Act No 85/1996 Coll on the Legal Profession; further: Czech Medical Chamber, Czech Dental Chamber and Czech Chamber of Pharmacists – cf § 9 para 2 lit e Act No 220/1991 Coll on Czech Medical Chamber, Czech Dental Chamber and Czech Chamber of Pharmacists; or Chamber of Patent Attorneys Czech Republic – cf § 42 Act No 417/2004 Coll on Patent Attorneys and on a Modification of the Act on Measures for Protection of Industrial Property).

The Association of Real Estate Agencies of the Czech Republic indeed pre- 8
scribes an insurance duty in relation to the risks connected with real estate activities of its members, but membership in this association is not compulsory for real estate agents and custodians. The Association of Real Estate Agencies is an association within the meaning of § 214 para 1 Civil Code ('At least three persons driven by a common interest may implement this interest by forming an associa-

tion as a self-governing and voluntary group of members to associate with each other.'). This contractual scheme is therefore not regarded as compulsory liability insurance.

c) *Duties to take out liability insurance that are not based on any public law but on a private law provision (eg, governing the relationship between employer and employee)?*

9 A duty to take out liability insurance governing the relationship between employers and employees was contained in § 205d Labour Code No 65/1965 Coll (repealed by the Labour Code No 262/2006 Coll). The duty to take out liability insurance governing the relationship between employers and employees is currently stipulated in §§ 1 and 12 Decree of the Czech Ministry of Finance No 125/1993 Coll. Attorneys (§ 24a Act No 85/1996 Coll on the Legal Profession), notaries and court executors (distrainors acting under the authority of the state court)[6] are obliged to conclude liability insurance for damage caused by their employees in connection with the performance of their working duties.

d) *Duties to take out liability insurance that are not based on any public law but on a private law rule that is established by case law (and, eg, governs the relationship between employer and employee)?*

10 In the Czech Republic a duty to take out liability insurance that is based on a private law rule that is established by case law does not exist.

e) *Cases in which there is no duty to take out liability insurance but liability insurance cover is a prerequisite for the admissibility of carrying out a particular activity?*

11 Cases in which there is no duty to take out liability insurance but liability insurance cover is a prerequisite for the admissibility of carrying out a particular activity are rather exceptional. An example is the shipping of waste, which is subject to compulsory insurance only in the case of the cross border transport of waste (cf § 57 Act No 185/2001 Coll on Waste and amendments of certain other Acts and art 6 Regulation (EC) No 1013/2006 of the European Parliament and of the Council of 14 June 2006 on shipments of waste[7]).

6 § 11 Executory Order No 120/2001 Coll.
7 Official Journal (OJ) L 190, 12.7.2006, 1–98.

The duty to take out liability insurance is usually defined as a prerequisite for the admissibility of carrying out a particular (eg professional) activity (cf eg § 42 Act No 417/2004 Coll on Patent Attorneys and on a Modification of the Act on Measures for Protection of Industrial Property, §§ 6–8 Act No 159/1999 Coll on Certain Conditions for Undertakings in Travel Services). Another example is the insurance of operators of ships floating on inland waterways who must conclude liability insurance (§ 19 Act No 114/1995 Coll on Inland Navigation). However, small ships, which are not used for licensed passenger transport, are not subject to compulsory insurance (§ 8 Decree of Ministry of Transport on Operability of Ships on Inland Waterways No 223/1995 Coll). 12

According to § 24c para 1 Act No 85/1996 Coll on the Legal Profession, the 13 Czech Bar Association has to take out professional indemnity insurance against liability for damage for which the responsibility to the client exists under § 24 para 1 of the Act No 85/1996 Coll on the Legal Profession for attorneys practising as sole attorneys or as members of a Consortium; such insurance shall be insurance for the account of another according to the terms of the Act (No 37/2004 Coll) on Insurance Contracts (hereinafter referred to as 'common professional indemnity insurance of lawyers').[8] The Czech Bar Association has to publish the contract of common professional indemnity insurance of attorneys in the Official Journal of the Czech Bar Association. According to § 24c para 1 of the Act No 85/1996 Coll on the Legal Profession, an attorney shall be obliged to pay his common insurance premium to the Czech Bar Association by the end of the calendar year preceding the calendar year to be covered by the common professional indemnity insurance of attorneys. If an attorney refuses to be covered by the common professional indemnity insurance of lawyers, he shall, not later than in the mentioned time-limit (set in § 24c para 1 cited above), submit to the Czech Bar Association a counterpart, or verified copy, of his professional indemnity insurance contract or the document issued by the insurance company or other competent person proving that he is insured individually for the respective calendar year. According to the decision of the disciplinary senate of the Czech Bar Association No 8/99, it is a serious infringement of an attorney's duties if he does not fulfil his duty to be insured in the case of liability for damage caused by the legal service, because he did not pay the premium on time according to the common professional insurance contract, or individual insurance, on his own initiative. The conclusion of an insurance contract as the com-

8 Since 1.1.2014 this reference in § 24c Act on the Legal Profession is to be read as a reference to § 2767 Civil Code, because the First and Second Parts of Act No 37/2004 Coll on Insurance Contracts were repealed by the Civil Code.

pulsory prerequisite for the exercise of the profession of attorney is recognised by the Act on the Legal Profession and legal doctrine.[9]

14 Another example of the duty to take out liability insurance, where liability insurance cover is a prerequisite for the admissibility of carrying out a particular activity, is § 13 para 3 lit e Act No 18/1997 Coll on the Peaceful Use of Nuclear Energy and Ionising Radiation. A liability insurance policy in the case of nuclear damage or another proof of financial security has to be attached to the application to the State Office for Nuclear Safety for an official licence to be granted.

15 The final example is that of situations where an insurance holder has to prove to a public authority before commencing licensed trade (ie an activity requiring liability insurance) according to § 27 para 3 and § 50 Trades Licensing Act No 455/1991 Coll the conclusion of an insurance contract in the case of trade activities for which liability insurance is required according to Annex No 3 of the Trades Licensing Act No 455/1991 Coll (production and trading of heat energy – authority: State Energy Inspection) or specific law (eg travel agencies according to § 5 para 2 lit b Act No 159/1999 Coll on Certain Conditions for Undertakings in Travel Services – authority: Ministry of Regional Development).

16 In the Czech Republic there are three groups of bodies ensuring that insurance duties are fulfilled:

a) bodies of professional organisations (eg Czech Bar Association – Act on the Legal Profession; Chamber of Tax Advisers of the Czech Republic – Act on Tax Consulting and Chamber of Tax Advisers of the Czech Republic),
b) state bodies (eg Czech National Bank, Ministry of Finance, Ministry of Local Development and Police of the Czech Republic),
c) *sui generis* bodies (eg Czech Insurers Bureau).

17 The applicant must submit to the above-mentioned bodies/authorities the insurance agreement as an enclosure to the licence application. An exception is the insurance duty for operators of facilities for the production, manufacturing, storage, use or transport of dangerous substances, in which case there are specific time limits for the submission of the insurance agreement stipulated in § 12 Act No 59/2006 Coll on Control of Major Accidents.

9 Cf *L Lisse*, Několik poznámek k ust. § 3 zákona č. 85/1996 Sb., o advokacii, a k některým ustanovením souvisejícím, Bulletin advokacie 11–12/2006, 94.

f) *Cases of alternative financial security, in which the duty to provide for financial security may be fulfilled either by taking out liability insurance or other forms of financial security (eg, bank guarantees)?*

Indemnity insurance contracts and bank guarantees are used instead of financial securities in the framework of procedures for public awards:[10] The public authority can, according to § 67 para 1 Act No 137/2006 Coll on Public Awards (this Act will be repealed by the Act No 134/2016 Coll on Public Awards which contains similar regulation) in the framework of procedures for the award of public works contracts, public supply contracts and public service contracts,[11] demand security. The competitor shall provide security in the form of financial security, bank guarantee or insurance contract in order to secure the fulfillment of the competitors' obligations in the framework of the public award procedure. The public authority is, for example, the Czech Republic, organisations partially funded by the state or municipalities. The insurance guarantees are usually only granted to corporate clients of insurers as a supplement to property insurance. The insurance guarantee is a specific form of insurance which is based on the insurer assuming the risk if the policyholder is not able to fulfill his obligation towards the public authority. The insurance contract is, according to § 2868 para 2 Civil Code,[12] concluded for the purpose of fulfilling the guarantee obligation of the insured. The risk is, according to § 67 para 1 Act No 137/2006 Coll on Public Awards, defined as the failure of the insurance holder to perform obligations flowing from the provision of the supply contract or of the public awards procedure. 18

The financial guarantee may be provided instead of the conclusion of a liability insurance contract in the case of § 36 Act No 18/1997 Coll on the Peaceful Use of Nuclear Energy and Ionising Radiation by the holder of the authorisation, or in case of § 8b Act No 159/1999 Coll on Certain Conditions for Undertakings in Travel Services by the Travel Agency. 19

**10** A public award is defined as an award realised on the basis of a contract between the public authority and one or more suppliers. The subject matter of a public award is the supply of goods or services or public works for a payment (§ 7 para 1 Act No 137/2006 Coll).

**11** Cf Directives of the European Parliament and of the Council 2004/18/EC, 2005/75/EC, 2004/17/EC, 89/665/EEC, 92/13/EEC, 2007/66/EC, 2009/81/EC and Commission Directive 2005/51/EC.

**12** An unofficial translation of § 2868 para 2 Civil Code is as follows: 'The insurance guarantee is concluded in the case of the performance of a guarantee obligation of the insured, forfeiture of security or bail security, or performance/fulfillment of security or bail security or other similar reason.'

20 On the contrary the example of a cumulative duty to both conclude liability insurance and to ensure a bank guarantee is § 48a in connection with § 57 Act No 185/2001 on Waste. According to § 48a Act No 185/2001 on Waste, the operator of a waste dump has to take out liability insurance and simultaneously he must provide a bank guarantee against damage to the human environment in the first phase of operation of the waste dump.

*g) Cases in which the duty to have insurance has only been created by a contractual agreement between potential injuring party and victim?*

21 This case is not classified as an insurance contract in the Czech system of law.

## II. Aims

*5. What are the aims of the rules that impose an obligation to take out liability insurance:*

*a) the protection of the victim,*

22 The obligation to conclude a liability insurance contract is stipulated by law especially for activities which are connected with an increased danger of inflicting damage. The main goal is to compensate a victim's damage and therefore to protect the victim, especially if the insured person does not have sufficient financial resources.[13]

*b) the protection of the insurance holder,*

23 See above no 22.

*c) the protection of the victim and the insurance holder,*

24 See above no 22.

*d) other aims, eg internalising the costs in the interests of society?*

25 See above no 22.

---

13 Cf *Karfíková/Přikryl* (fn 4) 285.

6. *Do the rules that prescribe a form of alternative financial security (see above Question 4.f) pursue the same aims as those rules that exclusively set out a duty to have liability insurance (ie with no other alternative financial security options)?*

In accordance with § 57 Act No 185/2001 Coll on Waste and § 36 Act on the Peaceful Use of Nuclear Energy and Ionising Radiation, the financial guarantee pursues the same aims as those rules that set out a duty to have liability insurance. **26**

## III. Content of Insurance Cover

7. *Are the duties to take out liability insurance laid down by law only to cover extra-contractual compensation duties or also those arising out of contractual infringements?*

The rules on compulsory insurance in Czech law are designed to cover liability claims based on the statutory provisions granting protection of the insured regardless of the non-/contractual nature of the liability. According to § 2861 para 3 Civil Code, the liability insurance can only be concluded as indemnity insurance ('insurance against loss and damage'). **27**

8.a) *Are there duties to take out liability insurance aimed not only at the protection of absolutely protected rights (eg, property, bodily integrity) but additionally at compensating pure economic loss?*

According to Act No 168/1999 Coll on Liability Insurance for Damage Caused by the Operation of Vehicles and on Amendments to Some Related Acts (Motor Third-Party Liability Insurance Act), material and immaterial loss and lost profit shall be covered (cf § 2952 Civil Code and § 6 para 2 lit c Motor Third-Party Liability Insurance Act). Pure economic loss incurred by the injured party (victim) is also covered by the liability insurance according to § 6 paras 2 and 4 Motor Third-Party Liability Insurance Act. **28**

b) *Are there duties to take out liability insurance that are directed only or at least predominantly at the compensation of pure economic loss?*

The responsibility for pure economic loss is covered by the compulsory liability insurance for some professional activities (§ 22 Act No 93/2009 Coll on Auditors – auditors; § 24 para 1 Act No 85/1996 Coll on the Legal Profession – attor- **29** neys; § 10 lit a Act No 523/1992 Coll on Tax Consulting and Chamber of Tax Advisers of the Czech Republic – tax advisers; § 10 lit a Act No 358/1992 Coll on Notaries and their Work Activities – notaries, etc).

9. *Are there provisions that require the insurance of a third party's liability interest – for instance, that the employer must take out liability insurance for the benefit of an employee?*

30 Yes, in the Czech legal order there are provisions that require the insurance of a third party's liability interest. According to § 2779 para 2 Civil Code, if so stipulated by a special law, the insurer is obliged to conclude an insurance contract in such a way that the duty to provide the indemnity (insurance benefit) will arise in the case of the infliction of a loss by the wilful act of the insurance holder, insured or other person. Examples of liability insurance for wrongful acts of third parties can be found in § 24 para 1 Act No 85/1996 Coll on the Legal Profession. According to this provision, an attorney shall be responsible for damage caused to his client even if the damage was caused by a substitute attorney, employed attorney or an employee other than an employed attorney, in connection with the practice of the legal profession (a similar regulation exists in relation to notaries and their employees and notary clerks, which is contained in § 28 para 1 Act No 358/1992 Coll on Notaries and their Work Activities). Nevertheless, the attorney is, according to § 24a Act No 85/1996 Coll on the Legal Profession, obliged to take out liability insurance to cover his employees'/substitutes' liability interest. Court executors (§ 11 Act No 120/2001 Coll on Court Executors and Executive Activities) and insolvency administrators (§ 23 Act No 182/2006 Coll on Insolvency and Methods of its Settling) are also obliged to take out liability insurance to cover their employees' liability interest. According to the above-mentioned provisions, notaries and court executors have a duty to maintain a professional liability insurance policy to cover the risks of liability for damage to persons which was caused by activities of those for whom they are responsible (eg notarial clerks, notarial candidates and executory clerks).

10. *To what extent do the rules requiring the compulsory conclusion of a liability insurance policy also specify the specific contents of the insurance coverage:*

a) *Is there always a (sufficiently well-defined) specification of the risk to be insured?*

31 The specification of the risk to be insured is seldom well-defined. The majority of laws only stipulate the compulsory conclusion of an insurance liability con-

tract. In most laws the insured risk is defined very generally; for example, according to § 6 para 2 Act No 26/2000 Coll on Public Auctions, an auctioneer has to conclude a liability insurance contract in relation to damage which could be caused by the activities of auctioneers within 30 days of the granting of the concession. The insured risk is also defined in a similar manner in other laws regulating activities of the liberal professions (eg authorised inspector – § 146 para 2 Act No 183/2006 Coll on Town and Country Planning and Building Code, Building Act, or § 6 para 10 lit a Act No 523/1992 Coll on Tax Consulting and Chamber of Tax Advisers of Czech Republic). In § 9 para 2 lit e Act No 220/1991 Coll on Czech Medical Chamber, Czech Dental Chamber and Czech Chamber of Pharmacists there is no definition of the insured risk because the member of the Chamber has a duty to take out insurance in the cases stipulated by the Chamber.

*b) Are there provisions that require unlimited coverage?*

Provisions of Czech law do not require unlimited coverage. 32

*c) If unlimited coverage is not required (see above Question b), is a minimum or maximum insurance sum always specified?*

The minimum insurance sum is usually specified. For example, according to § 6 33
para 3 lit b Act on Public Auction, the amount of the policy must be at least CZK 35,000,000 (€ 1,275,743; a maximum insurance sum is never specified).[14] An exception from this rule is contained in § 24a Act on the Legal Profession (the Bar shall prescribe the minimum limit for the claim reimbursement from professional indemnity insurance for Consortium), § 22 Act No 93/2009 Coll on Auditors, § 10 para 6 lit f Act No 406/2000 Coll on Energy Management and § 45 para 2 lit n Act No 372/2011 Coll on Medical and Hospital Services and Conditions of its Provision (provider shall conclude insurance contract to the reasonable extent corresponding to liability which could be expected). In Act No 360/1992 Coll on the Professional Practice of Certified Architects and on the Professional Practice of Certified Engineers and Technicians Active in Construction and in the Act No 93/2009 Coll on Auditors there is no specified minimum insurance sum (Chamber of Auditors of the Czech Republic concluded group insurance with ČSOB *Pojišťovna, as, Kooperativa pojišťovna as* and *Česká pojišťovna as*; Czech Chamber of Architects concluded group insurance with ČSOB *Pojišťovna, as*). According to the § 22 Act on Auditors, the insured sum must be

14 Exchange rate of 14.2.2014: € 1 = CZK 27.435.

adequate in relation to the possible damage which can be predicted to a reasonable extent. In the Act on the Professional Practice of Certified Architects and on the Professional Practice of Certified Engineers and Technicians Active in Construction the insurance sum is not specified at all. The minimum insurance sum is in some cases not specified directly in the law, but by ministerial decree (eg § 8 Decree of the Ministry of Transport on the Operability of Ships on Inland Waterways No 223/1995 Coll in relation to § 19, § 30 para 2 Act No 114/1995 Coll on Inland Navigation). The liability is limited in exceptional cases (in § 35 Act No 18/1997 Coll on the Peaceful Use of Nuclear Energy and Ionising Radiation, the liability of the holder of the authorisation is limited for every nuclear incident up to CZK 8,000,000,000 (approx € 291,598,320) in the case of nuclear power plants, storages and repositories and for other nuclear sites and tranport up to CZK 2,000,000,000 (approx € 72,899,581)).

We can summarise the provisions of Czech law on limitations of insurance sum relating to compulsory liability insurance into three groups:

- laws prescribing a minimum insurance sum;
- laws that do not prescribe a minimum insurance sum but allow it to be prescribed by another legal act;
- laws that give no information at all or at least insufficient information about the minimum insurance sum: such as 'reasonable coverage', etc.

34 In the minority of laws there is no minimum sum stated and furthermore a complete lack of specification as regards the insurance sum (cf § 23 Act No 182/2006 Coll on Insolvency and § 146 para 2 Act No 183/2006 Coll on Town and Country Planning and Building Code).

*d) Are there general statutory rules to be applicable if the respective law that requires compulsory insurance only makes incomplete stipulations regarding the content of the insurance coverage? An example of this would be § 114 para 1 of the German Insurance Contract Act (Versicherungsvertragsgesetz, VVG) 2008.*

35 According to § 2779 para 1 Civil Code, the general statutory rules contained in Part IV Chapter 2 Section 15 Subsection 2 (Insurance) (= §§ 2758–2872) Civil Code shall be applied if the respective law that requires compulsory insurance only makes incomplete stipulations regarding the content of the insurance contract. A deviation from Part IV Chapter 2 Section 15 Subsection 2 in the case of compulsory insurance could be allowed only by law (§ 2779 para 1 Civil Code). None of the above-mentioned provisions (§§ 2758–2872 Civil Code) contain stipulations regarding the extent of the minimum insurance coverage in the case of incomplete stipulations in a specific law.

*11. Is it admissible to restrict the insurance cover by agreeing:*[15]

*a) risk exclusion clauses,*

Risk exclusion clauses are, in accordance with § 2779 para 1 Civil Code, admissible if they do not restrict the insurance cover stipulated in special laws. Usually only the exclusions stipulated by special law (eg § 7 Motor Third-Party Liability Insurance Act) are contained in the general terms of the insurance contract. The insurer shall not pay compensation for, for example, damage inflicted in the course of manipulation of the cargo of standing vehicles (§ 7 para 1 lit e Motor Third-Party Liability Insurance Act), damage caused to a vehicle by its use during a terror attack or act of war (§ 7 para 1 lit h Motor Third-Party Liability Insurance Act), etc. **36**

*b) deductibles,*

According to § 2779 para 1 Civil Code, it is not admissible to restrict the insurance cover stipulated in special laws. Thus, generally, deductibles are not allowed in compulsory liability insurance if they are not otherwise stipulated in a specific law. The deductibles are typically used in the case of motor third-party liability insurance, because they are allowed in accordance with § 3 para 1 Motor Third-Party Liability Insurance Act ('The parties may derogate in their insurance contract from the provision of this law if it will not lead to the reduction of the victim's claims ...'). **37**

*c) aggregate limits,*

According to § 2779 para 1 Civil Code, it is not admissible to restrict the scope of insurance cover stipulated in a special law. Aggregate limits are not allowed. **38**

---

**15** To answer Question 11, it is crucial to describe briefly the content of §§ 2777–2781 Civil Code. § 2777 Civil Code specifies the essentials of the insurance contract and policy. § 2778 Civil Code contains a list of provisions which cannot be derogated by the agreement of the parties. §§ 2779–2781 include provisions dedicated exclusively to compulsory insurance (cf above fn 1).

*d) claims series clauses,*

39 According to § 2779 para 1 Civil Code, it is not admissible to restrict the insurance cover stipulated in special laws. Claims series clauses are allowed (eg § 3a para 2 Motor Third-Party Liability Insurance Act and § 24 para 2 Act No 61/2000 Coll on Maritime Shipping).

*e) other clauses?*

40 According to § 2779 para 1 Civil Code, it is not admissible to restrict the insurance cover stipulated in special laws. In special laws it is also stressed that the extent of insurance cover stipulated by law must not be reduced in the general terms of an insurance contract (eg § 48 para 1 Act No 449/2001 Coll on Hunting – 'careless conduct of the insured' hunter must not be excluded by general conditions of the insurance contract).[16]

*12. What are the consequences if the liability insurance contract concluded in order to fulfil the insurance obligation contravenes what the law stipulates as to contents (see above Questions 10 and 11)?*

41 § 2778 Civil Code stipulates that, in the case of a deviation from § 2777[17] (essential terms of the contract), the divergent provisions of the contract shall be ignored.[18]

---

**16** The regulation in § 48 para 1 Act on Hunting is illusory because the main objective of the liability insurance is compensation in the case of damage caused by the negligent behaviour of the hunter. Thus the hunter must be insured for the case of his careless conduct. The purpose of this provision (§ 48 para 1 Act on Hunting) is insurance for the damage inflicted in the course of hunting especially in the case of bodily harm or the killing of another person (minimum insured sum CZK 20,000,000, approx € 728,996) or damage to goods (minimum insured sum CZK 500,000, approx € 18,225).

**17** An unofficial translation of § 2777 Civil Code is as follows:

§ 2777

(1) If the contract was not concluded in written form, the insurer shall specify in the policy at least:
   - a) number of the contract,
   - b) identification of the insurer and policyholder,
   - c) identification of the beneficiary or the method of his identification,
   - d) insured event and insured risk,
   - e) the amount of the premium, its maturity and information as to whether it is a regular premium or a lump-sum premium,
   - f) period of insurance,

*13.a) Are statutory stipulations as to the contents of the policy (eg, regarding the amount of the insurance sum, the ban on certain risk exclusion clauses, on deductibles, etc, see above Questions 10 and 11) also binding in favour of the insurance holder? Or is it nonetheless possible for the liability insurer and the insurance holder acting within their internal relationship to agree risk exclusion clauses, deductibles, aggregate limits, and claims series clauses, etc (see above Questions 10 and 11), releasing the insurer from its liability to pay?*

According to § 2779 Civil Code, statutory stipulations as to the contents of a policy are also binding in favour of the insurance holder.[19] According to this provision, derogations as to the scope of the insurance cover in favour of the insurance holder *are thus allowed.* Derogations to the detriment of the victim in relation to the scope of the insurance cover and extent of the deductibles are not allowed in relation to the victims, because this would go against basic principles of liability insurance (protection of the victim) and mandatory rules stipulating the minimum amount of the insurance sum. **42**

---

g) possible deviations from the general insurance conditions and
h) if by the insurance of persons it was agreed that the beneficiary will participate in the profit of the insurer, also the method to calculate the amount of his share.

(2) If the contract was concluded in written form, it shall contain the information listed in para 1 and the insurer shall specify in the policy at least
a) number of contract,
b) identification of the insurer and policyholder,
c) identification of the beneficiary or method of its identification,
d) insured event and insured risk,
e) period of insurance.

(3) For the identification of the persons according to para 1 or 2, their name or names, address of residence or seat and identification information shall be specified. It shall be applied also in case of the identification of the insured.

**18** § 2779 Civil Code is related exclusively to the regulation of compulsory insurance (for its content see fn 1). § 2778 Civil Code contains a list of provisions which cannot be derogated by the agreement of the parties even if the insurance is not compulsory (number of the contract, determination of the insurer and policy holder, determination of the beneficiary, insured event, insured risk, premium and its maturity, insurance period, deviations from insurance general terms and conditions and insurance trust revenue). No regard is taken in the case of deviation from these provisions. This rule applies also in the case of an insurance holder's waiver for the issuance of the policy.

**19** Cf *Bohman/Wawerková* (fn 5) 47.

*b) If it is possible for liability insurer and insurance holder acting within their internal relationship to agree a release from the obligation to pay (see above Question a): What consequences does this entail? Must the insurer first pay out to the victim and can then have recourse to the insurance holder? Or is another construction provided for the relationship between insurer, insurance holder and victim?*

43 See above answer to Question 13.a.

*14.a) Does your general (voluntary) liability insurance law include a statutory risk exclusion in respect of intentional damage by the insurance holder or the insured person?*

44 According to § 2779 para 2 Civil Code, if compulsory insurance cover is stipulated by a special (other) law, the insurer is obliged to conclude the insurance contract in such a way that the duty to provide the indemnity (insurance benefit) will also arise in the case of a loss by the wilful act of the insurance holder, insured or other person. § 2779 para 2 is applicable only in relation to compulsory insurance.

*b) If the general liability insurance law contains a statutory risk exclusion in respect of intentional damage inflicted by the insurance holder (see above Question a): Does this also apply in cases of compulsory liability insurance?*

45 See above answer to Question 14.a.

# IV. Protection Mechanisms

*15. Are insurers obliged to contract when they offer liability insurance policies covering a risk for which the insurance holder is obliged to obtain cover?*

46 Insurers are generally *not obliged to contract* when they offer liability insurance policies covering a risk for which the insurance holder is obliged to obtain cover.[20]

---

20 Formerly, the last provision on *statutory* compulsory liability insurance was contained in § 205d Labour Code No 65/1965 Coll (repealed by the new Labour Code No 262/2006 Coll). § 205d Labour Code stipulated the duty to take out liability insurance governing the relationship between employer and employee. Employers had to conclude insurance with Česká po-

One exception is § 3 para 1 the Motor Third-Party Liability Insurance Act. The insurer is always obliged to conclude the insurance contract, the content of which must not be contrary to the Motor Third-Party Liability Insurance Act, the law regulating insurance contracts (Civil Code) or general conditions of the insurer. 47

16. *If there is no obligation to contract: Are there comparable mechanisms provided to ensure that an insurance agreement is concluded?*

There are no comparable mechanisms in the Czech legal system. 48

17. *Is the insurance holder prohibited from disposing over his cover entitlement to the disadvantage of the victim (eg, by surrendering his entitlement)?*

According to § 2779 para 1 Civil Code, by way of contractual deviation from the provisions §§ 2758–2872[21] (Part IV Chapter 2 Section 15 Subsection 2 – Insurance) of the Civil Code, it is not allowed to reduce the extent of the insurance cover stipulated by special laws. In § 3 para 1 Motor Third-Party Liability Insurance Act it is explicitly stipulated that the contracting parties cannot reduce or limit the coverage to the disadvantage of the victim (after an accident which has to be covered by the insurer has occurred). 49

18. *Does the victim enjoy special protection against insolvency on the part of the insurance holder with regard to the sum payable by the liability insurer?*

The victim does not enjoy special protection against insolvency on the part of the insurance holder with regard to the sum payable by the liability insurer. The only provision contained in a specific law is the victim's direct action according to § 9 para 1 Motor Third-Party Liability Insurance Act. Thus also in the case of insolvency proceedings, the victim has a direct right of action. 50

jišťovna akciová společnost (contracts concluded until 31.12.1992), or Česká Kooperativa, družstevní pojišťovna (contracts concluded since 1.1.1993). Both insurance companies were obliged to conclude insurance contracts in the above-mentioned cases. The Czech Republic had the obligation to cover financial loss of the above-mentioned insurance companies from the state budget while the surplus was income of the state budget.

**21** The provisions of §§ 2758–2872 regulate insurance matters in the Civil Code.

*19.a) In what manner can the victim obtain the insurance payment?*

51 Under damage liability insurance the insured shall be entitled to the payment on his behalf by the insurer to the injured party, within the scope and in the amount set out by law or contract, upon the occurrence of an insured event, of damage or other loss for which the insured is liable under the law up to the limit of insurance benefits agreed in the insurance contract (§ 2861 para 1 Civil Code). The injured party shall be entitled to the payment of insurance benefits directly from the insurer only if it was provided by a special law (eg § 9 Motor Third-Party Liability Insurance Act) or the insurance contract. If the insured paid compensation for damage or other loss for which he is liable directly to the injured party, the insured shall be entitled to the reimbursement of the sum paid by the insurer up to the amount which the insurer would otherwise be obliged to pay to the injured party (§ 2865 para 1 Civil Code).

*b) Does the victim have a direct right of action against the liability insurer (action directe) in the case of voluntary or compulsory liability insurance?*

52 According to § 2861 para 1 Civil Code, the injured party shall be entitled to the payment of insurance benefits by ways of a direct action against the insurer only if this is provided by a special law (§ 9 Motor Third-Party Liability Insurance Act) or the insurance contract. In accordance with the relevant case law of the Supreme Court (File No 25 Cdo 1094/98, 7 June 2000), the injured party generally has no right of direct action against the insurer.

*20. When settling the claim, is the liability insurer obliged to observe a certain procedure in the interests of the victim? For instance, must it pay the victim an advance within a certain period?*

53 The insurer shall be obliged, following the notification of an event associated with a claim for insurance benefits, to commence, without unnecessary delay, the investigation needed for determining the existence and scope of his obligation to provide insurance benefits (§ 2797 para 1 Civil Code).

54 Unless provided (agreed) otherwise in the insurance contract, the insurance benefits shall be payable within 15 days after the termination of the above-mentioned investigation. According to § 2865 para 1, the insurer is only entitled to pay the indemnity to the injured party or the insured person who had already paid the indemnity to the injured person. It is irrelevant whether it is a case of compulsory liability insurance or voluntary insurance (§ 2861f Civil Code). The insurer shall be obliged to finalise the investigation within three months after

having been notified of the insured event according to § 2798 Civil Code. If the insurer is unable to finalise the investigation within this time period, he shall be obliged to notify the notifier (the insured or other person/s who have an interest in the indemnity) in writing of the reasons why the investigation cannot be finalised. The insurer provides the person who submits a claim for an insurance benefit (ie injured person), on her request, with an adequate advance payment after the above-mentioned three-month period. The insurer has to pay the advance payment if it is clear that the insurance claim is justified.[22] This does not apply if there is a valid reason to refuse the payment (§ 2798 paras 2, 3 Civil Code).

*21.a) In the context of its relationship with the victim, can the liability insurer rely on the fact that vis-à-vis the insurance holder (= damaging party) it is freed from the obligation to pay, eg, due to the insurance holder breaching an obligation of conduct/warranty (Obliegenheitsverletzung) or due to him defaulting on premiums?*

The insurer can (specifically), in the case of compulsory insurance, refuse to pay 55
the insurance benefit only if false information, incomplete answers to the insurer's written questions or deliberately untrue or severely distorted facts were provided by the victim or another person with the victim's knowledge (§ 2780 Civil Code). Otherwise the insurer must pay the victim despite being released from its obligation to pay vis-à-vis the insurance holder according to § 2781 Civil Code regardless of the insurance holder's breach of the compulsory liability insurance contract.

A special case is the default of the premium payment. Insurance shall be 56
suspended if the premium was not paid. The suspension period begins after expiry of a two-month period from the maturity of the premium and continues until the payment. In the case of delayed payment of the premium, there is no right to insurance benefits as a result of any events occurring during the suspension of insurance that would otherwise have been insured events. However, during the existence of the statutory grounds for duration of the compulsory insurance, the compulsory insurance must not be suspended (§ 2801 para 3 Civil Code).[23]

The insurer cannot, for example, according to § 7 para 3 Act No 159/1999 57
Coll on Certain Conditions for Undertakings in Travel Services, refuse or reduce

22 *Bohman/Wawerková* (fn 5) 112.

23 According to § 2861 para 2 Civil Code, in the case of liability insurance, the victim enjoys the right to perform from the insurer only if it was concluded in the insurance contract, or if it was stipulated by a specific law.

payment of the insurance benefit if the travel agency provided false information or incomplete answers to the insurer. This is so even when the insurer becomes aware that the travel agency wilfully provided incorrect information which was fundamental for the conclusion of the contract. The insurer can in this case bring a suit for damages against the insured travel agency.

*b) Does the law distinguish on the basis of the ground for the release from the obligation to pay so that in some cases the insurer may not invoke its release from such obligation vis-à-vis the victim?*

58 The law does not distinguish on the basis of the ground for the release from the obligation to pay in the above-mentioned situations.

*c) If the insurer must still pay the victim despite being released from its obligation to pay vis-à-vis the insurance holder (see above Question b), may it take recourse against the latter?*

59 Yes, the insurer may take recourse against the insurance holder if the insurer must still pay the victim despite being released from its obligation to pay vis-à-vis the insurance holder according to § 2781 Civil Code. The payment is based on § 2801 Civil Code.

*22.a) Within its relationship to the victim, can the liability insurer invoke the fact that the insurance agreement had already ended by the time relevant in respect of the duty to provide cover?*

60 The liability insurer can invoke the fact that the insurance agreement had already ended by the relevant time in respect of the duty to provide cover (cf, for example, §§ 12, 13 Motor Third-Party Liability Insurance Act).

*b) If the insurer must pay the victim despite the termination of the insurance agreement by the time relevant for the duty to provide cover (see above Question a), can it take recourse against the insurance holder?*

61 See above answer to Question 22.a.

*23.a) Are there cases in which a damaging party does not effectively conclude the required liability insurance and the victim injured by him nonetheless receives compensation for his loss from a liability insurer or another compensation scheme (eg, a guarantee fund)?*

The general rule is that there are no cases in which a damaging party does not effectively conclude the required liability insurance and the victim injured by him nonetheless receives compensation for his loss from a liability insurer or another compensation scheme (eg a guarantee fund). The exemption to this rule is motor liability insurance. For vehicles operated by persons who are exempt from motor liability insurance (eg joint rescue services according to § 5 para 1 lit b Motor Third-Party Liability Insurance Act), the Ministry of Finance shall provide compensation. In the case of damage caused by the operation of a motor vehicle, the victim can make a claim to the Czech Insurers Bureau, which shall provide compensation from a guarantee fund (§ 24 para 2 lit b Motor Third-Party Liability Insurance Act) if the damage was caused by a person without compulsory liability insurance for the damage caused by the operation of the motor vehicle. 62

*b) In the event that the policy taken out was not in fact effectively concluded, is it necessary to distinguish on the basis of the ground for this ineffectiveness, eg, whether the reason for the contract not coming into effect was:*

*i) a lack of legal capacity on the part of the insurance holder,*

See below no 65. 63

*ii) lack of consent,*

See below no 65. 64

*iii) falsa procuratio (unauthorised agency)?*

The above-mentioned circumstances are generally relevant for the validity of any contract and not only for the obligations arising from an insurance contract. 65

*c) Can the liability insurer (or the alternative compensation scheme) that must provide cover even though the insurance policy was not effectively concluded (see above Questions a and b) have recourse against the damaging party?*

**66** According to § 24 Motor Third-Party Liability Insurance Act, the alternative compensation scheme must provide cover despite the total absence of any insurance agreement and has recourse against the damaging party (eg Czech Insurers Bureau according to § 24 para 9 Motor Third-Party Liability Insurance Act).

*24.a) Are there cases in which a damaging party does not take out any liability insurance, ie not even an ineffective insurance policy (see above Question 23), and the victim whom he injured is still compensated for his damage by a liability insurer or another compensation scheme (guarantee fund, etc)?*

**67** As for the relation to the injured person, Czech law does not distinguish between a contract that is concluded but invalid and the case where no insurance contract was concluded. In the case of damage caused by the operation of a motor vehicle, the victim can file a claim with the Czech Insurers Bureau, which shall provide compensation from a guarantee fund.

*b) Can the liability insurer (or the alternative compensation scheme) that must provide cover despite the total absence of any insurance agreement (see above Question a) have recourse against the damaging party?*

**68** The alternative compensation scheme that must provide cover despite the total absence of any insurance agreement has recourse against the damaging party (eg Czech Insurers Bureau according to § 24 para 9 Motor Third-Party Liability Insurance Act).

*25. Is the victim protected against the insolvency of the liability insurer?*

**69** The Czech law on insolvency does not contain specific provisions on the protection of victims against the insolvency of the liability insurer. According to § 386 Act No 182/2006 Coll on Insolvency, indemnity claims against the insurer (insurance benefit) have priority over all other claims with the exception of claims brought by a liquidator.

*26. Are there rules that serve in particular the protection of the victim when the liability insurance was only concluded voluntarily – ie without it being compulsory?*

As a rule that in particular serves the protection of the victim when the liability insurance is concluded only on a voluntary basis, § 2865 para 1 Civil Code is relevant: If there was no limit to the insurance benefits payable by the insurer mentioned in the insurance contract, the insurer is obliged to provide payment to compensate the entire damage or other loss for which the insured is liable. 70

# V. Supervision and Sanctions

*27.a) In which cases must the insurance holder prove to an authority before commencing an activity requiring insurance that he has taken out the respective prescribed liability insurance cover (see above Question 4.e)?*

According to § 27 paras 3 and 50 Trades Licensing Act No 455/1991 Coll, the insurance holder shall prove to a public authority before commencing licensed trade (ie an activity requiring liability insurance) the conclusion of an insurance contract in the case of trading activities for which liability insurance according to the Annex No 3 of the Trades Licensing Act (production and trading of heat energy – authority: State Energy Inspection) or specific law (eg travel agencies according to § 5 Act on Certain Conditions for Undertakings in Travel Services – authority: Ministry of Regional Development) is required. The applicant for the licence must enclose to the application the insurance contract. The granting of the licence by the public authority is conditional upon the conclusion of this insurance contract. Another example of the duty to take out liability insurance, where liability insurance cover is a prerequisite for the admissibility of carrying out a particular activity, is § 13 para 3 lit e Act No 18/1997 Coll on the Peaceful Use of Nuclear Energy and Ionising Radiation. A liability insurance policy in the case of nuclear damage or other proof of financial security must be submitted with the application for the official licence granted by the State Office for Nuclear Safety. 71

The regulation whereby the liability insurance must be proven prior to the commencing of the professional activity is contained in specific laws on liberal professions. The required insurance must be submitted with the request for registration by the relevant professional chamber (lawyers – § 5, § 24a Act No 85/1996 Coll on the Legal Profession, notaries – § 9 para 1 lit d Act No 358/1992 Coll on Notaries and their Work Activities, architects – § 16 Act No 360/1992 Coll on 72 the Professional Practice of Certified Architects and on the Professional Practice of Certified Engineers and Technicians Active in Construction, doctors – § 9 para 2 lit e Act No 220/1991 Coll on the Czech Medical Chamber, the Czech Dental Chamber and the Czech Chamber of Pharmacists).

b) *Must the insurer inform an authority when liability insurance taken out to meet an insurance obligation ends?*

73 There is no general rule, but this obligation could be contained in specific laws. An instructive example is motor third-party liability insurance. The insurer shall inform the Czech Insurers Bureau according to § 15 para 1 Motor Third-Party Liability Insurance Act about the termination of the liability insurance contract. The Czech Insurers Bureau keeps information in a specific register (Information Centre – § 15a Motor Third-Party Liability Insurance Act: The Czech Insurers Bureau operates the Register for Liability Insurance and Information Centre, which sends and receives information [inter alia about suspension of the insurance contract] to/from the Central Register of Vehicles operated by the Ministry of Transport). As another example: the insurer shall inform the Ministry of Regional Development according to § 8 para 6 Act on Certain Conditions for Undertakings in Travel Services about the termination of the liability insurance contract for a travel agency.

c) *Is the insurer also under a duty to inform when a liability insurance agreement is in existence but it has no duty to provide cover – eg, due to defaults on premium payments?*

74 Yes, the insurer is also under a duty to inform when a liability insurance agreement is in existence but it has no duty to provide cover due to defaults on premium payments. The insurer shall inform the Czech Insurers Bureau (cf above no 73) according to § 15 para 1 Motor Third-Party Liability Insurance Act about the suspension (eg due to defaults on premium payments) of the liability insurance contract.[24] As another example: The insurer shall inform the Ministry of Regional Development according to § 8 para 6 Act on Certain Conditions for Undertakings in Travel Services about the suspension (or threatening termination) of the liability insurance contract.

---

**24** Cf also *L Jandová/P Vojtek*, Zákon o pojištění odpovědnosti z provozu vozidla – Komentář (2012) 278 ff.

d) *What are the consequences when the duties to inform of the end of contract or the release from payment obligations (see above Questions b and c) are violated?*

If, during supervisory activities of the domestic insurance undertaking (insurer) the Czech National Bank discovers an infringement of the obligations stipulated by Act No 277/2009 Coll on Insurance or specific laws (eg if an insurer fails to inform the Czech Insurers Bureau contrary to § 15 para 1 Motor Third-Party Liability Insurance Act), it shall order the removal of proven irregularities within a stipulated time limit (§ 95 para 1). Within the stipulated time limit as part of this measure, unless otherwise stipulated by the Act on Insurance, the Czech National Bank, based on the type of the irregularities, is authorised to request replacements of: 75

a) the person participating in the management,
b) the person in the capacity of proxy holder,
c) any member of the board of directors, supervisory board or control board,
d) the head of the organisational unit of an insurance undertaking in a foreign country,
e) responsible actuary, or
f) claims representative appointed to liquidate losses in motor third-party liability insurance,

if the proven irregularities in activities of the insurance company are connected with the activities of the persons listed above (§ 95 para 2 Act on Insurance). The imposition of the above-mentioned sanctions can hardly be expected to be executed in practice.

The insurance undertaking commits a tort if it does not adopt a measure 76 to remove irregularities according to § 95 Act on Insurance within the stipulated time limit. For this tort the Czech National Bank imposes a fine of up to CZK 50,000,000 (approx € 1,822,490; § 120 para 5 Act on Insurance). The Czech Insurers Bureau (cf above no 73) informs the Czech National Bank of all infringements of the duties according to § 18 para 8 Motor Third-Party Liability Insurance Act.

28. *Is there some official body (authority, professional chamber) where an injured party can find out whether and where the injuring party who inflicted damage upon him in the course of an activity requiring insurance has liability insurance?*

Not as a general rule. But, according to § 18a Motor Third-Party Liability Insur- 77 ance Act, the Czech Insurers Bureau has an information duty in relation to the injured party based on her request if this party is resident in the Czech Republic, in a Member State of the European Union or in any other state within the European Economic Area.

78 In this context, it can be mentioned that the Ministry of Local Development has a duty to publish a list of insured travel agencies on its websites (§ 5 para 5 lit d Act No 159/1999 Coll on Certain Conditions for Undertakings in Travel Services). Additionally the insured is obliged to prove to its clients the fulfilment of the obligation to conclude a compulsory liability insurance contract (eg § 9 para 2 Act No 159/1999 Coll on Certain Conditions for Undertakings in Travel Services). Another example is Act No 61/2000 Coll on Maritime Shipping. According to § 7 para 1, the marine register is publicly available. In the register, information on marine vessels is recorded in accordance with § 8 Act on Maritime Shipping. The documentation related to the ship has to be included in the collection of documents which is required for every registered ship. The operator of the ship is obliged to conclude a liability insurance contract and to pay premiums for the entire time that the ship is in operation (§ 24 para 1 lit l Act No 61/2000 Coll on Maritime Shipping), to make the documentation in relation to the conclusion of the liability insurance (§ 25 para 1 lit s Act No 61/2000 Coll on Maritime Shipping) available on the vessel. The original liability insurance policy must be available onboard the vessel with translated versions in English, French or Spanish (§ 27 para 2 Act on Maritime Shipping).

*29. Are there (public law) sanctions against the party who was required to take out insurance if such does not take out the compulsory liability insurance? Examples of this would be a ban on carrying out the activity that requires the insurance or the imposition of an administrative or judicial penalty.*

79 Yes, there are (public law) sanctions against a party who fails to take out the required compulsory liability insurance. In the case of an infringement of the obligation to conclude and to maintain liability insurance (on the part of the insurance holder), the public authorities have the power to suspend or cancel (withdraw) their permission (eg licence).

80 Examples of this are a ban on carrying out the activity that requires the insurance or the imposition of an administrative penalty; for example, the Trade Licensing Office may cancel a trade certificate (licence) on the motion of the Ministry of Local Development in the case of a serious infringement of the conditions specified in the decision on granting the licence (§ 58 para 2 Trade Licensing Act). Such an infringement of the conditions specified in the decision on granting the licence is, for example, considered serious according to § 11 Act No 159/1999 Coll on Certain Conditions for Undertakings in Travel Services, if

the Travel Agency has not concluded the required compulsory insurance for its business activities. Another example can be found in the Motor Third-Party Liability Insurance Act: a vehicle user commits a tort if he operates a vehicle without valid motor third-party liability insurance. If a tort is committed, the public authority can impose a fine up to CZK 40,000 (approx € 1,458; § 16 Motor Third-Party Liability Insurance Act).

## VI. Statutory Provisions required by the Constitution or the European Convention on Human Rights (ECHR)

*30. What has been said regarding the compatibility of the duties to take out liability insurance with your country's constitution and the ECHR? Please take into account case law and academic literature.*

In relation to the compatibility of the duty to take out liability insurance with **81** the Constitution of the Czech Republic No 1/1993 Coll, in a specific case (File No Pl 4/95, 7 June 1995) the Constitutional Court decided that the imposition of an obligation to conclude liability insurance for chartered engineers does not constitute a breach of art 1 (principle of equality) Charter of the Basic Rights and Freedoms (No 2/1993 Coll). In another case (File No I. ÚS 603/05, 19 April 2006) the information duty of the user of a motor vehicle in relation to the transfer of the ownership of a motor vehicle was found in accordance with basic rights and freedoms. The complainant (first defendant in proceedings before the Court of First Instance in Teplice and the Appellate Court in Ústí nad Labem) argued that his constitutional right to a fair trial (art 90 Constitution of the Czech Republic and art 36 Charter of Basic Rights and Freedoms) was violated because he was sued in court proceedings after an accident which was caused by a car which he had previously sold to another person (second defendant). The first defendant breached his duty to apply for the registration of the transfer of ownership of the vehicle in the Central Register of Vehicles. The second defendant did not conclude any compulsory liability insurance before the car accident. The constitutional complaint of the first defendant was not successful.

The Czech academic literature and case law are silent in regard to the com- **82** patibility of the duties to take out liability insurance with the ECHR.

*31. Does the constitution or the ECHR make any stipulations regarding the contents of such duties to take out liability insurance? Please take into account case law and academic literature.*

83 The Czech Constitution does not make any explicit stipulations regarding the contents of duties to take out liability insurance.

84 The Constitutional Court, in case File No II. ÚS 2221/07 of 19 March 2008 (the Constitutional Court argued and ruled recently identically in case File No I. ÚS 1902/13), ruled on the amount of the insurance benefit that should be paid as compensation to the victim of a car accident: The victim has a right to compensation covering the full price of new spare parts that had to be used by the motor vehicle repair service after an accident in order to restore a car to its original condition after an accident. The Constitutional Court declared a contravening decision of the Regional court in Ostrava void, because the Constitutional Court found a breach of the right to a fair trial (art 36 Constitution) and property right (art 11 Charter of the Basic Rights and Freedoms) due to a misinterpretation of the Civil Code and the Act on Motor Third-Party Liability Insurance in relation to the amount of the compensation for damage. In case File No III. ÚS 3162/12 of 24 January 2013, the Constitutional Court ruled that the insured was obliged to inform the claimant (insurer) without undue delay in writing that the insured event occurred specifying the facts related to this event, including the identity of the person who was driving the car at the time of the accident. If the insured did not fulfil this obligation and as a consequence prevented the insurers from properly investigating the incident according to § 9 para 3 Motor Third-Party Liability Insurance Act, the insurer is entitled to compensation of his performance by means of a recourse action against the insured. If the insured refused to provide the insurer with the requested information on matters of fact, it is correct with reference to art 37 (right to refuse testimony) of the Constitution, that he will bear the consequences arising from the breach of this legal obligation and he will have to reimburse to the insurer the insurance benefit paid to the injured. The principle *nemo tenetur* shall not apply in this civil law relationship.

## VII. Reform Efforts

*32. Are there efforts towards reforming the law regarding compulsory liability insurance?*

85 The general provisions in the Civil Code regulating liability insurance in general (§§ 2861–2867) and compulsory insurance (§§ 2779–2781) have been in force

since 1 January 2014. These provisions reformed (modernised and amended) the regulation formerly contained in § 5, §§ 43–46 Act No 37/2004 Coll on Insurance Contracts (which was repealed by the Civil Code on 1 January 2014).

# VIII. Compulsory Liability Insurance and Liability Law

*33. Is, at the legislative level, any connection discernible between the nature of liability (in particular in the case of strict liability) and the imposition of compulsory liability insurance?*

Compulsory liability insurance and liability law are to be found in the same Part of the Civil Code (Part IV – Relative property rights [ie Law of Obligations]). The regulation of liability law (§§ 2894–2990 Civil Code) includes definitions which are used in liability insurance law (eg § 2900: prevention, § 2906: exigency, § 2915: damage caused by several persons, § 2910: breach of the law, § 2913: breach of contractual obligation, § 2905: self-defence, § 2904: accidents). However, as regards strict liability, the regulation of non-contractual obligations (specific provisions: §§ 2920–2950) in the Civil Code (eg damage caused by a person who is not able to evaluate the consequences of his/her conduct, damage caused by a person with dangerous attributes, damage arising from operating activities, damage caused by extra-hazardous activities, damage to real property, damage caused by animals, damage caused by defective things, damage to discarded items) is not connected with compulsory liability insurance. Therefore most cases of strict liability are not linked to compulsory liability insurance. Nevertheless in many specific laws strict liability is covered by compulsory liability insurance, cf the Annex: Rules on Compulsory Liability Insurance in the Czech Republic. 86

Jaana Norio-Timonen

# Compulsory Liability Insurance in Finland

## I. The Term Compulsory Liability Insurance

1. *Indicate the rules within your legal system that set out a duty to take out liability insurance. In this context, also take into account the implementation of international treaties (eg, the International Convention on Civil Liability for Bunker Oil Pollution Damage, 2001).*

In Finland there are two types of legal rules that set out a duty to take out liability insurance. Firstly, there are rules which set out the duty without regulating in detail the contents of the insurance. Secondly, there are rules which also regulate the contents of the insurance (employment accidents insurance, motor liability insurance, nuclear liability insurance, patient injuries insurance). The latter type of insurance is called not only 'compulsory' but also 'statutory';[1] also cf below no 28. With some exceptions it is not subject to the general Insurance Contract Act (*vakuutussopimuslaki*, 28.6.1994/543, ICA), cf below no 25. 1

An overview of the following rules on compulsory liability insurance is provided in the Annex: Rules on Compulsory Liability Insurance in Finland (at the end of this book). 2

According to § 4 Patient Injuries Act (*potilasvahinkolaki*, 25.7.1986/585), all health care providers shall have patient insurance that provides compensation for injuries covered by this Act. The Act is mainly based on strict liability. This insurance is not only compulsory but also statutory. According to § 5 Act on Service Voucher for Social and Health Services (*laki sosiaali- ja terveydenhuollon palvelusetelistä*, 24.7.2009/569), a service provider, in order to be accepted to the service voucher system, must have either insurance according to the Patient Injuries Act or other liability insurance against personal injuries. 3

According to § 2 Environmental Damage Insurance Act (*laki ympäristövahinkovakuutuksesta*, 30.1.1998/81), any private corporation whose operations involve a material risk of environmental damage or whose operations cause harm to the environment in general shall be covered by insurance against loss com- 4

1 See eg Hallituksen esitys Eduskunnalle laeiksi vakuutussopimuslain ja eräiden siihen liittyvien lakien muuttamisesta 63/2009 (government proposal for amendments to the Insurance Contract Act, HE 63/2009) 15; *E Hoppu/M Hemmo*, Vakuutusoikeus (2006) 19 ff; *E af Hällström/H Ijäs/J Laasonen*, Vastuuvakuutus (3rd rev edn 2014) 168.

pensable under this Act.[2] This insurance is secondary in the sense that an environmental damage insurance policy issued by an insurer covers loss in cases where compensation cannot be recovered from the liable party or where the loss is not compensable under the liable party's liability insurance, if any (§ 5). This insurance is statutory.

5 According to § 23 Nuclear Liability Act (*ydinvastuulaki*, 8.6.1972/484), the operator of a nuclear installation must have liability insurance accepted by the Financial Supervisory Authority (*finanssivalvonta*).[3]

6 According to § 15 Motor Liability Insurance Act (*liikennevakuutuslaki*, 26.6.1959/279), the owner or permanent holder of a motor vehicle must have a valid statutory motor liability insurance policy. This obligation does not, however, apply to vehicles owned by the Finnish government, but the State Treasury processes the settlement and compensation of losses caused by them in compliance with the Act. Motor liability insurance is only partially liability insurance by nature: According to § 8, if in a traffic accident caused by one motor vehicle, another motor vehicle (or persons or property inside it) is damaged, the damage is not primarily compensated for by the first-mentioned vehicle's motor insurance policy unless the damage has been caused by negligence by its owner, holder, driver or passenger; by operating the vehicle in violation of traffic rules or the vehicle's location in violation of traffic rules, or by the vehicle's defective condition. However, personal injury is fully compensated even if it would not be compensated on a liability basis. This insurance is statutory.[4]

7 According to § 144 Aviation Act (*ilmailulaki*, 22.12.2009/1194), provisions on insurance for damage caused in aviation are laid down in Regulation (EC) No 785/2004 of the European Parliament and of the Council on insurance requirements for air carriers and aircraft operators (*Aviation Insurance Regulation*). Where the regulation is not applicable or certain issues related to insurance are not covered by it, § 145 containing national insurance requirements, shall apply.

8 According to § 3 Railway Act (*rautatielaki*, 8.4.2011/304), all railway undertakings must have liability insurance referred to in § 90 of the Act or other corresponding arrangement.

---

**2** See also Environmental Damage Insurance Decree (asetus ympäristövahinkovakuutuksesta, 2.10.1998/717).

**3** For more information see eg *Hoppu/Hemmo* (fn 1) 19 f; *Hällström/Ijäs/Laasonen* (fn 1) 172; *P Ståhlberg*, Ydinvastuusta – Vahingonkorvausoikeudellinen tutkimus erityisesti ydinvoimalaonnettomuudesta aiheutuvien vahinkojen kannalta (1993).

**4** For more information see eg *S Eskuri/J Jumppanen/A Nio/K Vihermaa*, Liikennevakuutus (2012).

The Maritime Act (*merilaki*, 15.7.1994/674) includes several requirements for insurance or security (Part 7 § 2: shipowners' liability; Part 10 §§ 10–11: oil tankers; Part 10a §§ 6–7: shipowners' liability for pollution by fuel).[5] 9

According to § 16 Assembly Act (*kokoontumislaki*, 22.4.1999/530), if the arrangement of the event may cause damage to persons or property, the police may order it to be a prerequisite of the arrangement of the event that the arranger has adequate liability insurance cover for possible damages.[6] 10

According to § 10b Medical Research Act (*laki lääketieteellisestä tutkimuksesta*, 9.4.1999/488), the party commissioning a clinical trial on medicinal products must ensure that there is an insurance policy or other appropriate guarantee to cover the liability of the party and the researcher. 11

According to § 1 Lawyers Act (*laki asianajajista*, 12.12.1958/496), lawyers must belong to the Finnish Bar Association, which is a public corporation. The obligation to take out liability insurance is based on § 11.7 Code of Conduct for Lawyers adopted by the Finnish Bar Association (*Hyvää asianajajatapaa koskevat ohjeet*, 15.1.2009, as amended 8.6.2012) and Guidelines on the Liability Insurance of a Lawyer (*Asianajajan vastuuvakuutusta koskevat ohjeet*, 11.6.1982, as amended 23.5.1997, 11.1.2001, 15.1.2009). See also Question 4.b (below no 30). 12

According to § 8 Act on Licensed Counsels (*laki luvan saaneista oikeudenkäyntiavustajista*, 17.6.2011/715), a professionally acting licensed counsel must have sufficient liability insurance cover for financial loss.[7] 13

According to § 28 Insurance Intermediation Act (*laki vakuutusedustuksesta*, 15.7.2005/570), an insurance broker must have liability insurance which fulfils the requirements listed in this paragraph.[8] 14

According to § 8 Act on Real Estate Agencies and Housing Rental Agencies (*laki kiinteistön ja vuokrahuoneiston välitysliikkeistä*, 15.12.2000/1075), a real estate agency and housing rental agency must have liability insurance.[9] According to § 15 Act on Building Projects in the Form of Joint Building Ventures (*ryhmärakennuttamislaki*, 6.3.2015/190), a joint building consultant must have liability insurance to cover the damage it is responsible for based on this law. 15

5 See eg *af Hällström/Ijäs/Laasonen* (fn 1) 172. See also Oil Damage Liability Decree (öljyvahinkovastuuasetus, 15.11.1996/852).

6 See eg *af Hällström/Ijäs/Laasonen* (fn 1) 170 f.

7 See the government proposal: Hallituksen esitys Eduskunnalle laiksi luvan saaneista oikeudenkäyntiavustajista ja eräiksi siihen liittyviksi laeiksi 318/2010, 32, *af Hällström/Ijäs/Laasonen* (fn 1) 169.

8 For more information see eg *af Hällström/Ijäs/Laasonen* (fn 1) 171; *M Määttä/R Forsman*, Vakuutusedustus – Asiamiesten ja vakuutusmeklarien toiminta (2005) 51, 55 f.

9 See eg *af Hällström/Ijäs/Laasonen* (fn 1) 170.

16 According to § 24a Electrical Safety Act (*sähköturvallisuuslaki*, 14.6.1996/410), an assessment body, authorised body or inspection body must have sufficient liability insurance cover with regard to the type and scope of its activity. According to § 24b, an authorised inspector must have sufficient liability insurance cover with regard to the type and scope of its activity.

17 According to § 60a Nuclear Energy Act (*ydinenergialaki*, 11.12.1987/990), an inspection body, a testing body and a qualification body must have liability insurance. An insurance requirement formulated in such a general manner in the law applies also to an inspection body for pressure equipment according to § 5 Pressure Equipment Act (*painelaitelaki*, 27.8.1999/869) as well as to an assay office for articles of precious metals (§ 6 Act on Articles of Precious Metals, *laki jalometallituotteista*, 1.12.2000/1029) and a conformity assessment body for toys (§ 48 Act on Safety of Toys, *laki lelujen turvallisuudesta*, 18.11.2011/1154).

18 According to § 12 Rescue Equipment Act (*laki pelastustoimen laitteista*, 12.1.2007/10), an assessment body or inspection body, in order to be approved, must have sufficient liability insurance cover or other arrangement deemed sufficient with regard to the type and scope of its activity. The same applies to an inspection body according to § 22 Act on Requirements for Ecodesign and Energy Labelling, or 'Ecodesign Act' (*laki tuotteiden ekologiselle suunnittelulle ja energiamerkinnälle asetettavista vaatimuksista*, 19.12.2008/1005). According to § 33 Act on the Type Approval of Certain Construction Products (*laki eräiden rakennustuotteiden tuotehyväksynnästä*, 21.12.2012/954) a type approval body, a body authorised to issue verification certificates as well as a certifying body for quality control, must have liability insurance for potential damages, or an equivalent arrangement. According to § 255 Information Society Code (*tietoyhteiskuntakaari*, 7.11.2014/917), a notified body for radio equipment and telecommunications terminal equipment must have liability insurance or some other corresponding arrangement that is adequate in view of the extent of its activities.

19 According to § 8 Act on Units of Measurement and the System of Measurement Standards (*laki mittayksiköistä ja mittanormaalijärjestelmästä*, 10.12.1993/1156), a national standards laboratory must have liability insurance unless the state is responsible for the damage. The same applies to a notified inspection body, according to § 12 Decree on Appliances Burning Gaseous Fuels (*kaasulaiteasetus*, 22.12.1993/1434).

20 According to § 30 Measuring Instruments Act (*mittauslaitelaki*, 17.6.2011/707), a notified body and an inspection body must have sufficient liability insurance cover or other arrangement deemed sufficient with regard to the type and scope of its activity. The same applies to an inspection body according to § 101 Act on the Safe Handling and Storage of Dangerous Chemicals and Explosives (*laki vaarallisten kemikaalien ja räjähteiden käsittelyn turvallisuudesta*,

3.6.2005/390), whereas only insurance is acceptable for manufacturers and importers of fireworks according to § 93 of the Act.

According to § 47a Vehicles Act (*ajoneuvolaki*, 11.12.2002/1090), a designated technical service shall have liability insurance which, in line with the scope of its activity, is to cover its liability against the manufacturer or third parties for any loss other than indirect loss. 21

According to § 38 Animal Welfare Act (*eläinsuojelulaki*, 4.4.1996/247), an animal protection supervisor is liable for any damage caused in an inspection as set down in the Tort Liability Act (*vahingonkorvauslaki*, 31.5.1974/412) and he/she must have insurance against the liability for any damage caused in an inspection. 22

According to § 3 Act on Employment Accidents and Occupational Diseases, (*työtapaturma- ja ammattitautilaki*, 24.4.2015/459), an employer must take out an insurance policy to cover the liability for compensation based on this Act. The cover includes both employment accidents and occupational diseases. This insurance is statutory. This insurance forms part of the social security system and usually attention is paid to the cover it provides, not to the form in which it does so. However, systematically this insurance can be characterised as liability insurance, the idea being that the employer is liable towards its employees for employment accidents and occupational diseases. 23

According to § 1 Act on the Accident and Pension Insurance Cover for an Athlete (*laki urheilijan tapaturma- ja eläketurvasta*, 24.4.2009/276), there is compulsory accident insurance until the age of 65 for those who derive their main income from sports if their annual income exceeds a certain amount. The sports association or organisation with which the athlete has an agreement has to take out the insurance. This insurance is statutory and forms part of the social security system. As for the character of this insurance see no 23 above. 24

## 2. *Is there a coherent 'law of compulsory liability insurance' in your legal system?*

There is no 'law of compulsory liability insurance'. However, the general Insurance Contract Act is, according to its § 1, applied to any insurance other than statutory insurance (as for the concept of statutory insurance, see no 1 above). Thus, each line of statutory insurance can be regulated exhaustively by special regulation.[10] There are, however, three exceptions to this rule: even insurance policies written under the Motor Liability Insurance Act (*liikennevakuutuslaki*, 25

---

**10** See also government proposal: Hallituksen esitys Eduskunnalle vakuutussopimuslaiksi ja laeiksi eräiden siihen liittyvien lakien muuttamisesta 114/1993, 21.

26.6.1959/279) (see no 6 above), the Patient Injuries Act (*potilasvahinkolaki*, 25.7.1986/585) (see no 3 above) and the Environmental Damage Liability Insurance Act (*laki ympäristövahinkovakuutuksesta*, 30.1.1998/81) (see no 4 above) are governed by this Act, unless otherwise provided in these three Acts. The Insurance Contract Act does not contain a special section on liability insurance. However, some special rules on liability insurance can also be found in this Act (see §§ 30, 31, 32, 67, 68, 73, 75).

3. *Is there a specific term for compulsory liability insurance in your legal system? How is it defined?*

26 There is no legal or official definition of compulsory insurance or compulsory liability insurance. However, what is usually meant by compulsory insurance is insurance which has to be taken out pursuant to laws or regulations issued by the authorities.[11]

27 A somewhat unclear issue is whether liability insurance should be considered compulsory only when it is the sole form of fulfilling the requirement based on laws or regulations issued by the authorities. This is the understanding of the Federation of Finnish Financial Services (*Finanssialan Keskusliitto*).[12] The very limited literature dealing with different forms of compulsory insurance seems to support a somewhat different view, namely that the decisive factor would be that the requirement is 'insurance or other arrangement' and not a more general 'financial guarantee'.[13] This paper is based on the latter opinion.

4. *In which of the following cases does compulsory liability insurance apply according to prevailing opinion?*

28 The question whether or not certain liability insurance is compulsory is discussed only very rarely. It seems that in Finland this question has neither been found theoretically interesting nor practically important or unclear. Therefore it is difficult to draw a precise borderline between compulsory and non-compulsory liability insurance. In addition, the wording of the government proposal

---

**11** See eg HE 114/1993 (fn 10) 66 and § 67 Insurance Contract Act, *Hoppu/Hemmo* (fn 1) 7; *J Häyhä* Sopimus, laki ja vakuutustoiminta (1996) 354. Cf HE 114/1993, 21.

**12** This is based on discussions with the personnel of the Federation. The Federation of Finnish Financial Services (FFI) is a trade body which represents financial companies, for more information see <http://www.finanssiala.fi/>.

**13** See *Hoppu/Hemmo* (fn 1) 19 f; *af Hällström/Ijäs/Laasonen* (fn 1) 169 ff; *K Lehtipuro/I Luukkonen/L Mäntyniemi/V Raulos/P Santavirta*, Vakuutuslainsäädäntö (4th rev edn 2010) 131 f.

for the current Insurance Contract Act has given rise to a certain lack of clarity as regards the meaning of and difference between 'compulsory' and 'statutory' insurance and therefore also of the concept of compulsory insurance.[14]

a) *Duties to take out liability insurance which are not directly based on the law but on an order or decision issued by administrative authorities?*

Yes, if the order or decision is based on a legal provision.[15] **29**

b) *Duties to take out liability insurance that are not based directly on the law but on the statutes of a professional or other self-governing body?*

Not exactly according to the definition, but often the liability insurance of law- **30**
yers is in any case considered to be compulsory insurance.[16] According to § 1 Lawyers Act, lawyers must be members of the Finnish Bar Association. The by-laws of the Bar Association have to be ratified by a decision of the Ministry of Justice (§ 2). The obligation to take out liability insurance is not based on the Lawyers Act or the ratified by-laws but on the Code of Conduct for Lawyers and Guidelines on the Liability Insurance of a Lawyer adopted by the Finnish Bar Association (see no 12 above). However, because of the position of the Bar Association as a public corporation, the liability insurance is usually considered compulsory.

c) *Duties to take out liability insurance that are not based on any public law but on a private law provision (eg, governing the relationship between employer and employee)?*

Yes. According to the definition (see no 26 above), it is irrelevant whether the **31**
legal provision is by nature public or private law.

**14** See HE 114/1993 (fn 10) 21 and 66; *P Karhu*, The injured party's right of direct action under the Finnish insurance contracts act, With particular reference to transport liability insurance, in: Scandinavian Institute of Maritime Law Yearbook SIMPLY (2005) 199, 212 ff; *J Könkkölä*, Vastuuvakuutus vahingonkorvausriidassa (2009) 12 f.

**15** *Af Hällström/Ijäs/Laasonen* (fn 1) 170; *Lehtipuro/Luukkonen/Mäntyniemi/Raulos/Santavirta* (fn 13) 131.

**16** See eg *Hoppu/Hemmo* (fn 1) 6 f, 315; *af Hällström/Ijäs/Laasonen* (fn 1) 168 f. For the opposite opinion see *Karhu* (fn 14) 199, 215.

d) *Duties to take out liability insurance that are not based on any public law but on a private law rule that is established by case law (and, eg, governs the relationship between employer and employee)?*

32 No. As mentioned above (see no 26), the duty to take out liability insurance must be based on laws or regulations issued by the authorities, not on case law.

e) *Cases in which there is no duty to take out liability insurance but liability insurance cover is a prerequisite for the admissibility of carrying out a particular activity?*

33 Yes, if the prerequisite is based on laws or regulations issued by the authorities.[17] In several cases the obligation is based on EU legislation.

f) *Cases of alternative financial security, in which the duty to provide for financial security may be fulfilled either by taking out liability insurance or other forms of financial security (eg, bank guarantees)?*

34 Based on the definition of statutory insurance, this kind of liability insurance could perhaps be considered compulsory. However, the understanding of the Federation of Finnish Financial Services is that liability insurance in these cases is not compulsory. Also the very limited literature on this issue seems to support this view.[18] See also the answer to Question 3 above.

g) *Cases in which the duty to have insurance has only been created by a contractual agreement between potential injuring party and victim?*

35 No. As mentioned above (see no 26) the duty to take out liability insurance must be based on laws or regulations issued by the authorities.

---

**17** See eg *Hoppu/Hemmo* (fn 1) 323.
**18** See *Hoppu/Hemmo* (fn 1) 19 f; *af Hällström/Ijäs/Laasonen* (fn 1) 169 ff; *Lehtipuro/Luukkonen/Mäntyniemi/Raulos/Santavirta* (fn 13) 131 f.

## II. Aims

5. *What are the aims of the rules that impose an obligation to take out liability insurance:*

a) *the protection of the victim,*

Compulsory liability insurance is often required in activities in which personal injuries are common (traffic, patient injuries), catastrophic loss is possible (nuclear plants) or risks are high (environmental damage). Also in the provision of consultation services considerable damage is possible. With the aim of protecting the victim in mind, liability insurance is often required as a prerequisite for certain lines of business;[19] also cf above no 33 (answer to Question 4.e). 36

b) *the protection of the insurance holder,*

Liability insurance can be seen as a means of protecting the insurance holder/ tortfeasor especially in cases where the risks are so high that the activity would not be possible without insurance cover, eg in nuclear liability.[20] 37

c) *the protection of the victim and the insurance holder,*

One could claim that all types of compulsory liability insurance also protect the insurance holder in the sense that they oblige potential tortfeasors in advance to take appropriate measures in the case that claims for damages are brought against them. 38

d) *other aims, eg internalising the costs in the interests of society?*

In this context patient insurance can be mentioned. As it is irrelevant whether or not the staff member of a health care provider has acted negligently, it is not 39

**19** See eg *af Hällström/Ijäs/Laasonen* (fn 1) 168; *J Könkkölä*, Vahingonkärsijän ja vakuutuksenantajan välisestä oikeussuhteesta vastuuvakuutuksessa (2005) Defensor Legis 454, 454 f; *H Strömberg*, Vastuuvakuutusten perusteella maksetut korvaukset, in: I Aalto-Setälä et al (eds), Yrityksen ja yhteisön vastuuriskit – Oikeudellisen riskienhallinnan perusteet (2nd rev edn 2004) 417, 419 f.

**20** See eg *Ståhlberg* (fn 3) 171.

necessary to deal with the question of negligence as a prerequisite for compensation.[21]

6. *Do the rules that prescribe a form of alternative financial security (see above Question 4.f) pursue the same aims as those rules that exclusively set out a duty to have liability insurance (ie with no other alternative financial security options)?*

40 The primary aim of the former rules is usually to protect the victim against the insolvency of the insurance holder and not against damage caused by the insurance holder in its activities as is the case with the latter rules.

## III. Content of Insurance Cover

7. *Are the duties to take out liability insurance laid down by law only to cover extra-contractual compensation duties or also those arising out of contractual infringements?*

41 Some of the duties are laid down to cover compensation duties arising out of contractual infringements, eg liability insurance for lawyers or insurance brokers.

8.a) *Are there duties to take out liability insurance aimed not only at the protection of absolutely protected rights (eg, property, bodily integrity) but additionally at compensating pure economic loss?*

42 Yes. For example, insurance cover of environmental damage includes both absolutely protected rights and pure economic loss.

b) *Are there duties to take out liability insurance that are directed only or at least predominantly at the compensation of pure economic loss?*

43 Yes, eg liability insurance for lawyers and insurance brokers.

21 See *J Mikkola/ M Mikkonen/I Suhonen/P Kallio*, Potilasvahinko – Lain sisältö ja soveltamiskäytäntö (2004) 9.

*9. Are there provisions that require the insurance of a third party's liability interest – for instance, that the employer must take out liability insurance for the benefit of an employee?*

Yes. According to § 4 Patient Injuries Act, patient injuries insurance is taken out by a health care provider. From a tort law point of view, the tortfeasor could be not only the health care provider itself but also its employee. **44**

*10. To what extent do the rules requiring the compulsory conclusion of a liability insurance policy also specify the specific contents of the insurance coverage:*

As mentioned above (no 1) 'statutory insurance' is a form of insurance the contents of which are regulated by law and not left to the contracting parties to be agreed on (eg motor liability insurance, patient insurance). However, the mere fact that some requirements are set for a certain line of compulsory liability insurance does not make it statutory. This is important to note as statutory forms of insurance are basically excluded from the scope of the Insurance Contract Act (§ 1), see above nos 25 and 28. **45**

*a) Is there always a (sufficiently well-defined) specification of the risk to be insured?*

The risk is often defined by just referring to the liability of the tortfeasor based on the relevant legislation. **46**

*b) Are there provisions that require unlimited coverage?*

Yes. According to § 18 Nuclear Liability Act, operators of nuclear power plants situated in Finland have unrestricted liability for nuclear damage occurring in Finland. **47**

*c) If unlimited coverage is not required (see above Question b), is a minimum or maximum insurance sum always specified?*

Sometimes but not always. For example, according to § 28 Insurance Intermediation Act, a minimum insurance sum for one damage event is € 1,250,600 and for all damage € 1,876,000 per year. According to § 18 Nuclear Liability Act, a plant operator's maximum liability for damage occurring elsewhere than in Finland amounts to 600 million Special Drawing Rights (for daily exchange **48** rates: http://www.imf.org/external/np/fin/data/rms_five.aspx). But there are no legal provisions stipulating maximum insurance sums.

*d) Are there general statutory rules to be applicable if the respective law that requires compulsory insurance only makes incomplete stipulations regarding the content of the insurance coverage? An example of this would be § 114 para 1 of the German Insurance Contract Act (Versicherungsvertragsgesetz, VVG) 2008.*

49 No.

*11. Is it admissible to restrict the insurance cover by agreeing:*

*a) risk exclusion clauses,*

50 The general Insurance Contract Act does not restrict this. However, as far as statutory liability insurance is concerned, the requirements of the respective legislation must be met. Even if the insurance is not statutory, restrictions based on special regulations or requirements by the authorities are possible. For example, according to § 2 Guidelines on the Liability Insurance of a Lawyer, the compulsory liability insurance must cover the whole spectrum of activities undertaken by a lawyer, but risk exclusions, mentioned in § 2, are possible (eg acting as a member of the board of directors of a company, acting as a trustee in bankruptcy in certain cases).

*b) deductibles,*

51 The general Insurance Contract Act does not restrict this. However, as far as statutory liability insurance is concerned, the requirements of the respective legislation must be met. Even if the insurance is not statutory, restrictions based on special regulations or requirements by the authorities are possible. For example, according to § 3 Guidelines on the Liability Insurance of a Lawyer, the maximum deductible amount is 2% of the sum insured. According to § 28 Insurance Intermediation Act, deductibles are allowed but the insurer must pay the insurance money to the victim without subtracting the amount of the deductible.

*c) aggregate limits,*

52 The general Insurance Contract Act does not restrict this. However, as far as statutory liability insurance is concerned, the requirements of the respective

legislation must be met. Even if the insurance is not statutory, restrictions based on special regulations or requirements by the authorities are possible. For example, according to § 28 Insurance Intermediation Act, the amount of the liability insurance must be at least € 1,250,600 applying to each claim and in aggregate € 1,876,000 per year for all claims.

*d) claims series clauses,*

The general Insurance Contract Act does not restrict this. However, as far as statutory liability insurance is concerned, the requirements of the respective legislation must be met. Even if the insurance is not statutory, restrictions based on special regulations or requirements by the authorities are possible. 53

*e) other clauses?*

The general Insurance Contract Act does not restrict this. However, as far as statutory liability insurance is concerned, the requirements of the respective legislation must be met. Even if the insurance is not statutory, restrictions based on special regulations or requirements by the authorities are possible. For example, according to § 28 Insurance Intermediation Act, the insurance of an insurance broker may not terminate within two months from the moment the insurer informed the Financial Supervisory Authority of the termination. 54

12. *What are the consequences if the liability insurance contract concluded in order to fulfil the insurance obligation contravenes what the law stipulates as to contents (see above Questions 10 and 11)?*

The contract would be binding and, in the case of insured events, insurance compensation would be paid according to the contract as concluded. In the case of statutory insurance, however, if according to the insurer the insurance contract concluded conformed with the requirements of the respective legislation, the insurer would probably be held liable according to these requirements, that is, terms and conditions contravening the law would be considered null and void. 55

In cases where the Insurance Contract Act is applicable (see no 25 above) also §§ 5 and 9 on an insurer's information duty prior to conclusion of a contract would apply. According to § 5, the insurer has to, before an insurance contract is concluded, provide the applicant with any information that the applicant may need to assess his insurance requirements and to select the appropriate form of insurance, such as details on the insurer's insurance products, insurance pre- 56 miums and insurance terms and conditions. When giving such information, the insurer shall point out all major exclusions in the cover provided. According to § 9, if the insurer or its representative has failed to provide the necessary information or has given incorrect or misleading information to the policyholder when marketing the insurance, the insurance contract is considered to be in force to the effect understood by the policyholder on the basis of the information received.

*13.a) Are statutory stipulations as to the contents of the policy (eg, regarding the amount of the insurance sum, the ban on certain risk exclusion clauses, on deductibles, etc, see above Questions 10 and 11) also binding in favour of the insurance holder? Or is it nonetheless possible for the liability insurer and the insurance holder acting within their internal relationship to agree risk exclusion clauses, deductibles, aggregate limits, and claims series clauses, etc (see above Questions 10 and 11), releasing the insurer from its liability to pay?*

**57** If there are statutory requirements, they are binding for both the insurer and the insurance holder.

*b) If it is possible for liability insurer and insurance holder acting within their internal relationship to agree a release from the obligation to pay (see above Question a): What consequences does this entail? Must the insurer first pay out to the victim and can then have recourse to the insurance holder? Or is another construction provided for the relationship between insurer, insurance holder and victim?*

**58** Not relevant, see Question a.

*14.a) Does your general (voluntary) liability insurance law include a statutory risk exclusion in respect of intentional damage by the insurance holder or the insured person?*

**59** According to § 30 para 1 Insurance Contract Act, the insurer is discharged from liability towards an insured that has willfully caused the occurrence of an insured event. However, the contracting parties are allowed to deviate from this provision in favour of the insurance holder and insured person. In practice the insurer might in some cases consider paying the insurance money despite this provision and a corresponding term and condition of the insurance contract.

b) *If the general liability insurance law contains a statutory risk exclusion in respect of intentional damage inflicted by the insurance holder (see above Question a): Does this also apply in cases of compulsory liability insurance?*

In cases where the Insurance Contract Act is applicable to compulsory liability insurance, § 30 para 1 is also applicable. 60

# IV. Protection Mechanisms

15. *Are insurers obliged to contract when they offer liability insurance policies covering a risk for which the insurance holder is obliged to obtain cover?*

Insurers are obliged to contract only when the liability insurance is not only compulsory but also statutory (see eg § 3 Motor Liability Insurance Decree [17.7.1959/324], § 4 Environmental Damage Insurance Act [30.1.1998/81]).[22] According to § 7 Patient Injuries Act (25.7.1986/585), the Finnish Patient Insurance Centre (*Potilasvakuutuskeskus*)[23] has to grant the patient insurance in cases where an insurance company has declined to do so. 61

16. *If there is no obligation to contract: Are there comparable mechanisms provided to ensure that an insurance agreement is concluded?*

According to Chapter 25 § 1 Insurance Companies Act (*vakuutusyhtiölaki*, 18.7.2008/521), an insurance company must always act in accordance with good insurance practice. This means that an insurer must always have an acceptable reason for not contracting. Even § 6 Constitution of Finland (*Suomen perustuslaki*, 11.6.1999/731) on equality requires that no one shall, without an acceptable reason, be treated differently from other persons on the grounds of sex, age, origin, language, religion, conviction, opinion, health, disability or other reason that concerns his or her person.[24] 62

22 See eg *Hoppu/Hemmo* (fn 1) 102; *af Hällström/Ijäs/Laasonen* (fn 1) 168.

23 Insurance companies in Finland providing patient insurance must be members of the Finnish Patient Insurance Centre. The Centre handles the compensation procedures for patient injuries which occur in Finland. It is a legal person directly founded by law. For more information see <http://www.pvk.fi/>.

24 See eg HE 63/2009 (fn 1) 10, 17 f; *Lehtipuro/Luukkonen/Mäntyniemi/Raulos/Santavirta* (fn 13) 124 ff; *J Norio-Timonen*, Vakuutussopimuslain pääkohdat (2010) 22 ff.

63 Even though it could be argued that an obligation to contract with some exceptions would in practice lead to the same result as the requirement to act in accordance with good insurance practice, the legislator decided to stick to the latter model. As far as consumer insurance is concerned, this issue was discussed when the Insurance Contract Act was amended in 2010 (see no 64 below) but it turned out to be impossible to create an exhaustive list of acceptable reasons not to contract.[25]

64 In addition, according to § 6a Insurance Contract Act, if no insurance is granted to a consumer or another person comparable to a consumer (see § 3 para 2)[26], the applicant has to be informed of the reason for the rejection of the application, unless the rejection was based on § 26 Act on Detecting and Preventing Money Laundering and Terrorist Financing (*laki rahanpesun ja terrorismin rahoittamisen estämisestä ja selvittämisestä*, 18.7.2008/503). The reason has to be given in writing. The reason for rejection shall be in compliance with law and good insurance practice.[27]

*17. Is the insurance holder prohibited from disposing over his cover entitlement to the disadvantage of the victim (eg, by surrendering his entitlement)?*

65 Not relevant as the victim has, according to § 67 Insurance Contract Act, a direct right of action against the insurer as far as compulsory liability insurance is concerned.

*18. Does the victim enjoy special protection against insolvency on the part of the insurance holder with regard to the sum payable by the liability insurer?*

66 As the victim has a direct right of action against the liability insurer (§ 67 Insurance Contract Act) the problem does not arise.

*19.a) In what manner can the victim obtain the insurance payment?*

67 In the case of compulsory liability insurance, the victim has a direct right of action against the liability insurer (§ 67 Insurance Contract Act/regulation on statutory insurance).

---

**25** See HE 63/2009 (fn 1) 10.

**26** According to this paragraph, this means another natural person or legal person that in terms of the nature and scope of its business or other activities or other circumstances can be compared to a consumer as a party to the contract signed with the insurer.

**27** See HE 63/2009 (fn 1) 17 f; *Lehtipuro/Luukkonen/Mäntyniemi/Raulos/Santavirta* (fn 13) 126; *Norio-Timonen* (fn 24) 21 ff.

*b) Does the victim have a direct right of action against the liability insurer (action directe) in the case of voluntary or compulsory liability insurance?*

The basic rule according to the Insurance Contract Act is that the victim does not have a direct right of action but it is the insurance holder who has a right to the insurance money. However, according to § 67 Insurance Contract Act, three exceptions exist: 1) the insurance policy was taken out pursuant to laws or regulations issued by the authorities; 2) the insured has been declared bankrupt or is otherwise insolvent; or 3) the general liability insurance has been mentioned in marketing efforts launched to promote the insured's business. Thus, in the case of compulsory insurance, a direct right of action does exist. 68

*20. When settling the claim, is the liability insurer obliged to observe a certain procedure in the interests of the victim? For instance, must it pay the victim an advance within a certain period?*

In the case of compulsory liability insurance, the victim has a direct right of action against the insurer. 69

In the case of voluntary liability insurance, it is legally the tortfeasor who is entitled to the insurance money. However, in practice the interests of the victim are taken into account so that the insurer usually pays the insurance money directly to the victim if he has not yet been compensated by the tortfeasor.[28] 70

*21.a) In the context of its relationship with the victim, can the liability insurer rely on the fact that vis-à-vis the insurance holder (= damaging party) it is freed from the obligation to pay, eg, due to the insurance holder breaching an obligation of conduct/warranty (Obliegenheitsverletzung) or due to him defaulting on premiums?*

Not necessarily. According to §§ 30–32 Insurance Contract Act, the insurer is still liable to pay damages to the injured party – which in this context refers to any natural person entitled to compensation in respect of any loss or injury covered by the insurance – to cover the portion that the injured party has not been able to claim from the insured because of its insolvency. This applies irrespective of whether the compensation has been refused or reduced. 71

Prerequisite for this is that the insurance holder has caused the insurance event through gross negligence, not complied with the precautionary guidelines 72

**28** *Af Hällström/Ijäs/Laasonen* (fn 1) 112 f.

or neglected his duty of salvage. The same applies if the terms and conditions of the policy include a provision to the effect that any compensation due to the insured may be reduced or refused, if use of alcohol or narcotics by the insured has affected the occurrence of an insured event, non-compliance with the precautionary guidelines or negligence of the duty of salvage. These rules do not, however, apply if the insurance holder has acted willfully whereas if the insurance holder has acted only with ordinary or slight negligence, the insurer is not allowed to reduce or refuse the insurance money, so in those cases the question addressed is not relevant. The rules apply also to voluntary liability insurance.

*b) Does the law distinguish on the basis of the ground for the release from the obligation to pay so that in some cases the insurer may not invoke its release from such obligation vis-à-vis the victim?*

73 See Question a above.

*c) If the insurer must still pay the victim despite being released from its obligation to pay vis-à-vis the insurance holder (see above Question b), may it take recourse against the latter?*

74 Neither the general provision on recourse rights in the Insurance Contract Act (§ 75) nor the government proposal for the Act[29] deal with this question. Therefore, in cases where the Insurance Contract Act is mandatory in favour of the insurance holder, a recourse right does not seem to exist. However, in cases where the insurance holder is not protected by the semi-mandatory character of the Insurance Contract Act, it is possible to agree on the recourse right.[30]

*22.a) Within its relationship to the victim, can the liability insurer invoke the fact that the insurance agreement had already ended by the time relevant in respect of the duty to provide cover?*

75 Yes, on the basis of the Insurance Contract Act, as it is the insurance holder and not the victim who is the insured. However, there are cases where the ter-

---

**29** HE 114/1993 (fn 10).

**30** According to § 3 Insurance Contract Act, any terms or conditions of an insurance contract that deviate from the provisions of this Act to the detriment of the policyholder shall be null and void if the policyholder is a consumer or another natural person or legal person that in terms of the nature and scope of its business or other activities or other circumstances can be compared to a consumer as a party to the contract signed with the insurer.

mination of the contract shall be postponed by law, cf above no 54 (Question 11.e).

In the case of statutory liability insurance, the victim is entitled to compen- 76
sation even if there is (for one reason or another) no valid insurance contract with an insurer, see Question 23.a.

*b) If the insurer must pay the victim despite the termination of the insurance agreement by the time relevant for the duty to provide cover (see above Question a), can it take recourse against the insurance holder?*

It is possible that a right of recourse exists. Penalty premiums can be seen as a 77
substitute for rights of recourse.

For example, according to § 16 Motor Liability Insurance Act, the insurance 78
holder must pay a penalty premium which can be at maximum tenfold. The penalty premium is calculated according to the instructions of the Financial Supervisory Authority. Also, according to § 4 Patient Injuries Act, the insurance holder must pay a penalty premium which can be at maximum tenfold.

*23.a) Are there cases in which a damaging party does not effectively conclude the required liability insurance and the victim injured by him nonetheless receives compensation for his loss from a liability insurer or another compensation scheme (eg, a guarantee fund)?*

No general guarantee fund or other compensation scheme exists. 79

However, in the case of statutory insurance, the victim is entitled to com- 80
pensation. For example, according to § 6 Act on Employment Accidents and Occupational Diseases, the Finnish Workers' Compensation Center (*Tapaturmavakuutuskeskus*)[31] is to pay accident compensation in cases where the employer did not have a valid insurance policy for the work provided. In the case of patient injury, the Finnish Patient Insurance Centre (*Potilasvakuutuskeskus*)[32] provides insurance cover when insurance has not been taken out (§ 5 Patient Insurance Act). According to § 10 Motor Liability Insurance Act, the Finnish Motor

---

**31** The Finnish Workers' Compensation Center coordinates the practical application of statutory accident insurance. It is a legal person directly founded by law. Pursuant to law, every insurance institution underwriting statutory accident insurance in Finland has to be a member of the Center. For more information see <http://www.tvk.fi/>.

**32** See no 61 above.

Insurers' Centre (*Liikennevakuutuskeskus*)[33] pays the compensation in the case of uninsured vehicles.

*b) In the event that the policy taken out was not in fact effectively concluded, is it necessary to distinguish on the basis of the ground for this ineffectiveness, eg, whether the reason for the contract not coming into effect was:*

*i) a lack of legal capacity on the part of the insurance holder,*

81 No. The above (Question a) mentioned compensation schemes apply.

*ii) lack of consent,*

82 No. The above (Question a) mentioned compensation schemes apply.

*iii) falsa procuratio (unauthorised agency)?*

83 No. The above (Question a) mentioned compensation schemes apply.

*c) Can the liability insurer (or the alternative compensation scheme) that must provide cover even though the insurance policy was not effectively concluded (see above Questions a and b) have recourse against the damaging party?*

84 Yes, see Question 22.b above.

*24.a) Are there cases in which a damaging party does not take out any liability insurance, ie not even an ineffective insurance policy (see above Question 23), and the victim whom he injured is still compensated for his damage by a liability insurer or another compensation scheme (guarantee fund, etc)?*

85 Yes, see Question 23.a above.

33 The Finnish Motor Insurers' Centre is a cooperation body of Finnish motor insurers. It also operates as the national Green Card Bureau and Guarantee Fund. It is a legal person directly founded by law. For more information see <http://www.lvk.fi/>.

b) *Can the liability insurer (or the alternative compensation scheme) that must provide cover despite the total absence of any insurance agreement (see above Question a) have recourse against the damaging party?*

Yes. 86

25. *Is the victim protected against the insolvency of the liability insurer?*

Not by any rules specific for liability insurance, but there is special regulation 87
concerning statutory lines of liability insurance. For example, according to § 5b–c Patient Insurance Act, if an insurance company's liquidation or bankruptcy results in a situation where an injured party does not receive all or any of the compensation due under this Act, the policyholder may be required to pay an additional premium. If this is not enough, the shortfall has to be paid jointly by all insurance companies involved in the patient insurance business.

26. *Are there rules that serve in particular the protection of the victim when the liability insurance was only concluded voluntarily – ie without it being compulsory?*

The rules of the general Insurance Contract Act are applicable to voluntary as 88
well as compulsory liability insurance. It is, however, worth noting that, in the case of voluntary liability insurance, the victim has a direct right of action against the insurer only if the insured has been declared bankrupt or is otherwise insolvent or if the general liability insurance has been mentioned in marketing efforts launched to promote the insured's business (§ 67 Insurance Contract Act).

According to § 68 Insurance Contract Act, in cases where the direct right of 89
action against the insurer does not exist, the insurer shall, however, dispatch a notice of its decision on a claim for compensation made under general liability insurance to the injured party. The injured party is then, in addition to the insured, entitled to take legal action against the insurer on account of the decision or refer the case to the Consumer Disputes Board or another similar body if the case otherwise falls under the responsibilities of such other body. Therefore, it remains for the insured to decide whether he wants to use his liability insurance or not. Only if he does so will the insurer make its decision on the claim and the victim has a right to take legal action against the insurer based on the decision. If the tortfeasor does not want to use his insurance, there is nothing the victim can do against the insurer.

## V. Supervision and Sanctions

*27.a) In which cases must the insurance holder prove to an authority before commencing an activity requiring insurance that he has taken out the respective prescribed liability insurance cover (see above Question 4.e)?*

90 In all cases mentioned in Question 4.e.

*b) Must the insurer inform an authority when liability insurance taken out to meet an insurance obligation ends?*

91 In general no, but there are cases in which this is required. For example, § 28 Insurance Intermediation Act includes such a requirement as well as § 5 Guidelines on the Liability Insurance of a Lawyer.

*c) Is the insurer also under a duty to inform when a liability insurance agreement is in existence but it has no duty to provide cover – eg, due to defaults on premium payments?*

92 Not according to the rules mentioned in Question b above.

*d) What are the consequences when the duties to inform of the end of contract or the release from payment obligations (see above Questions b and c) are violated?*

93 There are no sanctions.

*28. Is there some official body (authority, professional chamber) where an injured party can find out whether and where the injuring party who inflicted damage upon him in the course of an activity requiring insurance has liability insurance?*

94 A general body does not exist, but, for example, according to § 14f Motor Liability Insurance Act, the Finnish Motor Insurers' Centre acts as the Finnish Information Centre in motor vehicle liability insurance in accordance with the 4th Motor Insurance Directive (2000/26/EC).

*29. Are there (public law) sanctions against the party who was required to take out insurance if such does not take out the compulsory liability insurance? Examples of this would be a ban on carrying out the activity that requires the insurance or the imposition of an administrative or judicial penalty.*

There are no actual penalties. **95**

It is possible that a multiple insurance premium must be paid. For example, in accordance with § 16 Motor Liability Insurance Act, the Finnish Motor Insurers' Centre will collect a penalty premium from the owner or keeper of a vehicle for the entire time period when the vehicle was uninsured. **96**

In cases where liability insurance is one of the requirements for a certain activity, the question arises as to the general consequences according to the respective legislation of not fulfilling the requirements for an activity (for example, according to § 38 Insurance Intermediation Act: prohibition to carry out the activity or even withdrawal of the registration). However, one could assume that usually the party would have a possibility to immediately take out adequate insurance cover and only if this is not done does the question of sanctions and prohibition have to be dealt with. **97**

# VI. Statutory Provisions required by the Constitution or the European Convention on Human Rights (ECHR)

*30. What has been said regarding the compatibility of the duties to take out liability insurance with your country's constitution and the ECHR? Please take into account case law and academic literature.*

According to § 80 Constitution of Finland (*Suomen perustuslaki*, 11.6.1999/731), the principles governing the rights and obligations of private individuals shall be governed by laws enacted by Parliament. Thus, this requirement is stricter than what is required by the ECHR. Therefore there does not seem to have been any problems concerning acts, including a duty to take out liability insurance, either in Finland or against Finland. **98**

*31. Does the constitution or the ECHR make any stipulations regarding the contents of such duties to take out liability insurance? Please take into account case law and academic literature.*

99 The Constitution does not contain detailed stipulations such as those mentioned.

## VII. Reform Efforts

*32. Are there efforts towards reforming the law regarding compulsory liability insurance?*

100 As mentioned before there is no general legislation on compulsory liability insurance despite the few articles of the general Insurance Contract Law. There are no efforts towards reforming those rules.

101 A government proposal (*Hallituksen esitys eduskunnalle liikennevakuutuslaiksi ja eräiksi siihen liittyviksi laeiksi 123/2015*) for a major reform of the legislation on the insurance system in the case of traffic accidents has been approved by the Parliament (see no 6 above). The new Motor Liability Insurance Act (17.6.2016/460) comes into effect on 1 January 2017.

102 A committee has been nominated to make a proposal to reform the Patient Injuries Act (see no 3 above).

## VIII. Compulsory Liability Insurance and Liability Law

*33. Is, at the legislative level, any connection discernible between the nature of liability (in particular in the case of strict liability) and the imposition of compulsory liability insurance?*

103 In several cases the liability is strict when compulsory liability insurance is required, but in other cases there is strict liability without any liability insurance requirement, eg in product liability. It is also worth mentioning that there are also cases in which the liability is strict without any legislation, eg blasting.

Robert Koch*

# Compulsory Liability Insurance in Germany

## I. The Term Compulsory Liability Insurance

1. *Indicate the rules within your legal system that set out a duty to take out liability insurance. In this context, also take into account the implementation of international treaties (eg, the International Convention on Civil Liability for Bunker Oil Pollution Damage, 2001).*

In Germany, both at federal and state (*Länder*) level, there is quite a significant 1
number of rules stipulating a duty to take out liability insurance. For a (non-exhaustive) list of federal and state level rules setting out a duty to take out liability insurance, see Annex: Rules on Compulsory Liability Insurance in Germany (at the end of this book).

2. *Is there a coherent 'law of compulsory liability insurance' in your legal system?*

There are provisions on compulsory liability insurance in the German Insurance 2
Contract Act (*Versicherungsvertragsgesetz*, VVG). These provisions (§§ 113–124 VVG), however, do not establish the obligation to take out insurance but only provide a framework and determine inter alia the minimum content of cover whenever such obligation is imposed by a legal provision. Apart from this, there is no coherent regulatory regime of compulsory liability insurance, either at federal or state law level in terms of the reasons why they were established or with regard to different standards of liability or different types of damages. Compulsory liability insurance is foreseen for claims arising out of or relating to keeping vehicles (eg cars), animals (eg dogs) or weapons, the operation of (potentially) hazardous activities (eg the operation of air carriers, aircraft suppliers and other airplane owner's, railway companies and railway network operators, hunting) or a specific professional practice (eg lawyers, notaries). The aim of such insurance is to protect third parties against damages resulting from injury to life and limb, property, and/or against damages for pure economic loss. There is no general rule that, in cases where there is strict liability, compulsory liability insurance has been introduced (see no 83 below).

* The author wishes to thank Matthias von Kossak for his research assistance.

3. *Is there a specific term for compulsory liability insurance in your legal system? How is it defined?*

3 The term compulsory liability insurance can literally be translated with *Pflichthaftpflichtversicherung*. The provisions on compulsory liability insurance (§§ 113–124 VVG), however, only use the term *Pflichtversicherung*, which literally translated into English means 'compulsory insurance'. The use of the abbreviated expression in the VVG is somewhat misleading since there are other types of compulsory insurance in Germany such as private health insurance. The German Insurance Supervisory Act (*Versicherungsaufsichtsgesetz*, VAG) also uses the term *Pflichtversicherung* in a broader sense. For the avoidance of doubt, courts[1] and scholars[2] therefore generally use the German term *Pflichthaftpflichtversicherung* when referring to compulsory liability insurance.

4 § 113 para 1 VVG defines compulsory liability insurance as 'liability insurance which a policyholder is obligated by legal provision to take out'.

4. *In which of the following cases does compulsory liability insurance apply according to prevailing opinion?*

a) *Duties to take out liability insurance which are not directly based on the law but on an order or decision issued by administrative authorities?*

5 There is no case law on this question. According to prevailing opinion, where the duty to take out liability insurance follows from an order or a decision issued by administrative authorities, the application of the provisions on compulsory liability insurance depends on whether the order or decision is at the discretion of the authorities or not. In the first case, the provisions do not apply. By contrast, where the authorities are bound by a legal provision to issue an order or a decision to take out liability insurance, the provisions on compulsory liability insurance apply (see eg § 42 para 2 no 9 Air Traffic Licensing Regulations, *Luftverkehrs-Zulassungs-Ordnung*, LuftVZO) according to which the permission

1 See eg Federal Court of Justice (Bundesgerichtshof, BGH) 22.10.2003, Versicherungsrecht (VersR) 2003, 1565; BGH 17.9.2003, VersR 2003, 1389; BGH 19.3.2003, VersR 2003, 635.

2 See eg *O Brand* in: T Langheid/M Wandt (eds), Münchener Kommentar zum VVG (1st edn 2010) Vor §§ 113–124 VVG no 1; *RM Beckmann* in: H Baumann/RM Beckmann/K Johannsen/R Koch (eds), Bruck/Möller, Großkommentar zum Versicherungsvertragsrecht (9th edn 2013) Vor §§ 113–124 VVG no 7; *C Huber* in: HP Schwintowski/C Brömmelmeyer (eds), Praxiskommentar zum Versicherungsvertragsrecht (2nd edn 2010) Vor §§ 113–124 VVG no 1.

to operate an airport can only be granted by the competent authority contingent on the taking out of liability insurance).[3]

*b) Duties to take out liability insurance that are not based directly on the law but on the statutes of a professional or other self-governing body?*

There are again no cases on this question. There is, however, general consensus among scholars that, if statutes of self-governing bodies (such as regional or local authorities) impose a duty to take out liability insurance, such insurance is to be qualified as compulsory liability insurance.[4] Where the duty to take out liability insurance follows from a statute of a professional body (such as medical council), it is the prevailing opinion that the provisions on compulsory liability insurance only apply if the body is authorised by a legal provision to introduce such duty.[5] 6

*c) Duties to take out liability insurance that are not based on any public law but on a private law provision (eg, governing the relationship between employer and employee)?*

The definition of compulsory liability insurance in § 113 para 1 VVG does not require that the duty to take out liability insurance is based on public law but on a legal provision regardless of whether the provision can be classified as public or private law. In other words, for the definition of compulsory liability insurance, the distinction between 'public' and 'private' law is irrelevant. 7

---

3 Bruck/Möller/*Beckmann* (fn 2) § 113 VVG no 12; *P Schimikowski* in: W Rüffer/D Halbach/HP Schimikowski (eds), Versicherungsvertragsgesetz: Handkommentar (2nd edn 2011) § 113 VVG no 2; *U Knappmann* in: J Prölss/A Martin, Versicherungsvertragsgesetz (28th edn 2010) § 113 VVG no 2; for a different view see Langheid/Wandt/*Brand* (fn 2) § 113 VVG no 7; *B Späte*, Haftpflichtversicherung: AHB (1992) Vorbem no 107.

4 Prölss/Martin/*Knappmann* (fn 3) § 113 VVG no 1; *F Schwartze* in: D Looschelders/P Pohlmann, VVG-Kommentar (2nd edn 2011) § 113 VVG no 5; Langheid/Wandt/*Brand* (fn 2) § 113 VVG no 6; Drucksachen des Deutschen Bundestages (BT-Drucks) 16/3945, 87.

5 Bruck/Möller/*Beckmann* (fn 2) § 1h13 VVG no 13; Langheid/Wandt/*Brand* (fn 2) § 113 VVG no 10; Looschelders/Pohlmann/*Schwartze* (fn 4) § 113 VVG no 7; Rüffer/Halbach/*Schimikowski* (fn 3) § 113 VVG no 5; for a different view see: Prölss/Martin/*Knappmann* (fn 3) § 113 VVG no 2; *Späte* (fn 3) Vorbem no 107.

d) *Duties to take out liability insurance that are not based on any public law but on a private law rule that is established by case law (and, eg, governs the relationship between employer and employee)?*

8 There are a few cases where the courts found for a fiduciary duty to conclude liability insurance. For example, the German Supreme Court (*Bundesgerichtshof*, BGH) held that an employer owes a duty to his employee to close a gap in the motor vehicle insurance cover by concluding liability insurance.[6] In another case, the BGH held that the chairman of a horse riding club is obliged to insure the association in its capacity as the keeper of the horses against the risk of becoming liable for damage caused by horses.[7] It needs to be emphasised that the liability insurance contracts concluded for this purpose cannot be regarded as compulsory liability insurance in terms of § 113 para 1 VVG.

9 German courts do apply the provisions on compulsory Third-Party Liability Insurance for Keepers of Motor Vehicles (*Pflichtversicherungsgesetz*, PflVG) by means of analogy when a public legal entity (such as the Federal Republic of Germany, the German states, or municipalities) which is exempted from the compulsory insurance of vehicles (§ 2 para 1 PflVG) but has nonetheless taken out liability insurance.[8]

e) *Cases in which there is no duty to take out liability insurance but liability insurance cover is a prerequisite for the admissibility of carrying out a particular activity?*

10 Whenever the prerequisite is based on a legal provision and the decision about the admission to carry out a particular activity is not discretionary, the framework provisions (§§ 113–124 VVG) on compulsory liability insurance apply (see no 5 above).

f) *Cases of alternative financial security, in which the duty to provide for financial security may be fulfilled either by taking out liability insurance or other forms of financial security (eg, bank guarantees)?*

11 There is no case law on this question. According to prevailing opinion among scholars, the provisions on compulsory liability insurance do not apply to cases

---

6 See BGH 11.11.1969, VersR 1970, 63.

7 See BGH 26.11.1985, Neue Juristische Wochenschrift – Rechtsprechungs-Report: Zivilrecht (NJW-RR) 1986, 572.

8 BGH 17.2.1987, VersR 1987, 1034; Higher Regional Court (Oberlandesgericht, OLG) Düsseldorf 3.12.1992, VersR 1993, 1417.

where there is a duty to provide coverage either by taking out liability insurance or other forms of financial security and the right of option is exercised by taking out insurance.[9] This viewpoint seems to be endorsed by the fact that express reference to the provisions on compulsory liability insurance is made where the law allows a choice between the two options – see eg § 94 para 2 of the German Medicines Act (*Arzneimittelgesetz*, AMG), § 12 Digital Signature Act (*Signaturgesetz*, SigG) in conjunction with § 9 para 2 Digital Signature Ordinance (*Signaturverordnung*, SigV), § 2 para 1 Oil Pollution Damage Act (*Ölschadengesetz*, ÖlSG), art 7 International Convention on Civil Liability for Bunker Oil Pollution Damage, 2001 (*Internationales Übereinkommen von 2001 über die zivilrechtliche Haftung für Bunkerölverschmutzungsschäden*). The reference would be superfluous if the liability insurance were to be classified as compulsory liability insurance in terms of § 113 para 1 VVG. The same is true with regard to the Environmental Liability Act (*Umwelthaftungsgesetz*, UmweltHG) where express reference to § 117 para 2 VVG is made in § 20 para 1 no 5 UmweltHG, and the Atomic Energy Act (*Atomgesetz*, AtG) where express reference to § 117 and §§ 119 to 122 VVG is made in § 14 para 1 AtG.

*g) Cases in which the duty to have insurance has only been created by a contractual agreement between potential injuring party and victim?*

There is a general consensus that liability insurance taken out on the basis of a contractual agreement between the potential injuring party and the victim (eg a supplier and manufacturer agree that the former provide product liability coverage) cannot be regarded as compulsory liability insurance in terms of § 113 para 1 VVG.[10] 12

9 Langheid/Wandt/*Brand* (fn 2) § 113 VVG no 9; Looschelders/Pohlmann/*Schwartze* (fn 4) § 113 VVG no 5; Rüffer/Halbach/*Schimikowski* (fn 3) § 113 VVG no 3; *M Hübsch* in: Berliner Kommentar zum Versicherungsvertragsgesetz (1999) § 158b VVG no 2; Schwintowski/Brömmelmeyer/*Huber* (fn 2) § 113 VVG no 5; for a different view Bruck/Möller/*Beckmann* (fn 2) § 113 VVG no 15; *D Rubin* in: C Brömmelmeyer/H Heiss/U Meyer/D Rückle/HP Schwintowski/A Wallrabenstein (eds), Allgemeines Gleichbehandlungsgesetz – Private Krankenversicherung und Gesundheitsreform – Schwachstellen der VVG-Reform (2009) 285, 290 ff.

10 Prölss/Martin/*Knappmann* (fn 3) § 113 VVG no 2; Looschelders/Pohlmann/*Schwartze* (fn 4) § 113 VVG no 6; *T Langheid* in: W Römer/T Langheid, Versicherungsvertragsgesetz (3rd edn 2012) § 113 para 8; Langheid/Wandt/*Brand* (fn 2) § 113 VVG no 7 ff; Looschelders/Pohlmann/*Schwartze* (fn 4) § 113 VVG no 6; *Späte* (fn 3) Vorbem no 107.

## II. Aims

5. *What are the aims of the rules that impose an obligation to take out liability insurance: a) the protection of the victim, b) the protection of the insurance holder, c) the protection of the victim and the insurance holder, d) other aims, eg internalising the costs in the interests of society?*

13 Compulsory liability insurance, like any voluntary liability insurance, provides protection to the insurance holder against potential legal liability to third persons arising out of his acts, errors or omissions. It also provides protection to the victim because it constitutes a guarantee for the fulfilment of the latter's claim for compensation against the insurance holder for bodily injury, property damage or financial loss. Where compulsory liability insurance extends the coverage to the liability of third parties (eg motor vehicle insurance), it also serves their protection. In contrast to voluntary liability insurance, defences brought by the insurer based on the insured's non-compliance with policy terms or statutory duties have been eliminated in compulsory liability insurance (see eg § 117 para 1 VVG). Where the insurer would have been entitled to deny or limit coverage had there been no compulsory insurance, the insurance holder is liable vis-à-vis the insurer for the compensation paid out by the insurer to the victim (see eg § 116 para 1 VVG). Therefore, it can be reasonably concluded that the objective of compulsory liability insurance is primarily the protection of the victim.

14 With regard to bodily injury, compulsory liability insurance, like any voluntary liability insurance, helps the state social insurance system, which ultimately would have to shoulder the costs of, for example, victims' medical treatment.[11] Moreover, there will be no (cash) outflow of capital for the compensation of damage that may put the existence of enterprises at risk and lead to redundancies, which in turn puts a strain on the state social insurance system.[12]

6. *Do the rules that prescribe a form of alternative financial security (see above Question 4.f) pursue the same aims as those rules that exclusively set out a duty to have liability insurance (ie with no other alternative financial security options)?*

15 The question is, in principle, to be answered in the affirmative. Alternative financial security, such as bank guarantees, however, de facto does not provide

11 *R Koch* in: E Bruck/H Möller, Großkommentar zum Versicherungsvertragsrecht (9th edn 2013) Vor §§ 100–112 VVG no 38.

12 Bruck/Möller/*R Koch* (fn 11) Vor §§ 100–112 VVG no 38.

the same protection to the party who is obliged to take out liability insurance or a bank guarantee as liability insurance since the latter requires the insurer not only to indemnify the insured from existing liability but also to hold the insured harmless where his liability is only asserted by a third party.

# III. Content of Insurance Cover

7. *Are the duties to take out liability insurance laid down by law only to cover extra-contractual compensation duties or also those arising out of contractual infringements?*

The rules that impose an obligation to take out liability insurance are not related to extra-contractual or contractual liability. These rules generally require taking out insurance against liability claims on the grounds of statutory liability regardless of whether the liability is of an extra-/contractual nature. 16

8.a) *Are there duties to take out liability insurance aimed not only at the protection of absolutely protected rights (eg, property, bodily integrity) but additionally at compensating pure economic loss?*

There are only few provisions aimed at the protection of absolutely protected rights as well as the compensation of pure economic loss. For example, § 1 PflVG requires the keeper of a vehicle to take out compulsory insurance coverage not only for personal injury and damage to property but also pure economic loss. § 6 para 2 sent 1 Development Aid Workers Act (*Entwicklungshelfergesetz*, EhfG) also imposes on development services (*Träger des Entwicklungsdienstes*) the obligation to conclude insurance for the benefit of development aid workers against the liability for personal injury, damage to property and pure economic loss. § 34a para 2 no 3 c Industry Code (*Gewerbeordnung*, GewO) and § 26 para 1 no 8 General Railway Act (*Allgemeines Eisenbahngesetz*, AEG) empower the government to establish such duty for railway operators and security services by means of a regulation. The government, however, decided to obligate the railway operator only to take out insurance for personal injury and damage to property (see § 1 Ordinance concerning the Liability of Railways, *Verordnung über die Haftpflichtversicherung der Eisenbahnen*, EBHaftPflV). 17

*b) Are there duties to take out liability insurance that are directed only or at least predominantly at the compensation of pure economic loss?*

18 The duties for legal advisors (lawyers, notaries), tax advisors, and auditors to take out professional liability insurance are directed only at the compensation of pure economic loss. See eg § 51 Federal Lawyers' Act (*Bundesrechtsanwaltsordnung*, BRAO), § 67 Law on Tax Advisers (*Steuerberatungsgesetz*, StBerG), § 25 StBerG in conjunction with § 2 Ordinance on the Implementation of Provisions with regard to Wage Tax Societies (*Verordnung zur Durchführung der Vorschriften über Lohnsteuerhilfsvereine*, DVLStHV), § 54 Law regulating the Profession of Auditors (*Wirtschaftsprüferordnung*, WPO), § 19a para 1 sent 1 Federal Public Notaries Ordinance (*Bundesnotarordnung*, BNotO).

*9. Are there provisions that require the insurance of a third party's liability interest – for instance, that the employer must take out liability insurance for the benefit of an employee?*

19 There are provisions such as § 1 PflVG which require the keeper of a car to take out compulsory insurance coverage not only for himself but also for the owner and any driver of the car. § 6 para 1 EhfG imposes on development services the obligation to conclude liability insurance not only for the benefit of development aid workers but also for the benefit of their dependent spouses and children. Moreover, § 1908f German Civil Code (*Bürgerliches Gesetzbuch*, BGB) requires from social associations (*Betreuungsverein*) which have the task of finding and training voluntary citizens willing to become *Betreuer* (guardian of a disabled person) to insure its employees for any damage that they may cause to others in the course of their activity. Similar provisions exist for fairground workers (§ 55f GewO in conjunction with § 1 Ordinance on the Liability of Fairground Workers, *Schaustellerhaftpflichtverordnung*, SchauHV). According to § 19a para 1 sent 1 BNotO, notaries have a duty to maintain a professional liability insurance policy to cover the risks of liability for material damages arising out of the activity of persons for whom they are responsible (eg officially appointed representatives, notary clerks).

*10. To what extent do the rules requiring the compulsory conclusion of a liability insurance policy also specify the specific contents of the insurance coverage:*

*a) Is there always a (sufficiently well-defined) specification of the risk to be insured?*

In general, the provisions requiring the conclusion of a liability insurance policy specifically state that the insurance must cover risks of liability for damage arising out of or relating to the insured's (professional) activity (see eg § 51 BRAO, § 67 StBerG, § 54 WPO, § 19a para 1 sent 1 BNotO, § 1PflVG). In very few cases the types of damages that must be covered are not specified (eg § 1908f BGB, § 67 StBerG). **20**

*b) Are there provisions that require unlimited coverage?*

There are no rules that expressly require unlimited coverage. Where the rules on compulsory insurance necessitate 'adequate insurance' (see no 20 above), according to legal writers, the insurance holder is not obliged to take out insurance above the limits set forth in § 114 para 1 VVG (see no 22 below).[13] **21**

*c) If unlimited coverage is not required (see above Question b), is a minimum or maximum insurance sum always specified?*

The rules requiring the conclusion of a liability insurance policy often specify the minimum insurance sum but in no event the maximum one. For example, according to the annex to § 4 para 2 PflVG, compulsory motor vehicle insurance requires as a minimum coverage of € 7.5 million for personal injury, € 1.12 million for damage to property and € 50,000 for pure economic loss. § 19a para 2 sent 1 BNotO requires € 500,000, § 12 SigG in conjunction with § 9 no 2 SigV € 2.5 million and § 7a Road Haulage Act (*Güterkraftverkehrsgesetz*, GüKG) € 600,000 per claim as the minimum sum insured. § 102 LuftVZO does not stipulate a minimum insured sum. It rather states that the minimum insured sum is determined by the limits of liability prescribed in § 37 para 1 Air Traffic Act (*Luftverkehrsgesetz*, LuftVG). Where there is no specification of the minimum sum (eg § 3 para 2 no 4 Brandenburg Architects Act, *Brandenburgisches Architektengesetz*, or § 6 para 1 EhfG: 'adequate liability insurance'), this sum is **22**

**13** Bruck/Möller/*Beckmann* (fn 2) § 114 VVG no 9; Langheid/Wandt/*Brand* (fn 2) § 114 VVG no 9; Schwintowski/Brömmelmeyer/*Huber* (fn 2) § 114 VVG no 2.

determined by § 114 para 1 VVG according to which the minimum sum insured shall be € 250,000 per claim.

*d) Are there general statutory rules to be applicable if the respective law that requires compulsory insurance only makes incomplete stipulations regarding the content of the insurance coverage? An example of this would be § 114 para 1 of the German Insurance Contract Act (Versicherungsvertragsgesetz, VVG) 2008.*

23 Yes (see nos 2 and 21 above).

*11. Is it admissible to restrict the insurance cover by agreeing:*

24 According to § 114 para 2 sent 1 VVG, the contract of insurance may specify the content and scope of the compulsory insurance in more detail insofar as this does not endanger the fulfilment of the respective objective of the compulsory insurance (alt 1) and unless explicitly otherwise provided by legal provision (alt 2). In the absence of a legal provision, the test for all restrictions on coverage therefore will be whether the restrictions limit the rights of the victim and/or the (co-)insured to such an extent that the attainment of the purpose of the compulsory insurance is jeopardised. If the fulfilment is at risk, the clause is void. It is important to note that restrictions of the insurance cover are generally, that is, irrespective of the class of insurance or whether the risk insured is a large risk in terms of § 210 para 2 VVG, subject to the law on standard term clauses according to which surprising and ambiguous terms do not form part of the contract (§ 305c para 1 BGB), and terms unreasonably disadvantageous to the other party are void (§ 307 BGB).[14]

*a) risk exclusion clauses*

25 According to § 103 VVG, which is applicable to both voluntary liability and compulsory liability insurance, there is no coverage to the extent the insurance holder has intentionally and unlawfully caused the loss suffered by the victim.

26 The rules requiring the conclusion of a liability insurance policy for keepers of motor vehicles, lawyers, tax consultants, accountants and notaries contain a list of possible exclusion clauses. For example, according to § 4 para 2 PflVG in conjunction with § 4 Statutory Order on Compulsory Motor Vehicle Insurance

14 Langheid/Wandt/*Brand* (fn 2) § 114 VVG no 20.

(*Kfz-Pflichtversicherungsverordnung*, KfzPflVV), the motor vehicle insurer is allowed to exclude liability claims for

- damage to property or on account of pure economic loss of the policyholder, keeper or owner of the car against co-insured (§ 4 no 1 KfzPflVV),
- damage to or destruction of or loss of the insured car except for the damage to an inoperable car during towing (§ 4 no 2 KfzPflVV),
- damage to or destruction of or loss of items carried in the car except for such items normally used by passengers or intended for satisfying personal needs (§ 4 no 3 KfzPflVV),
- damage that occurs during the participation in car races or during test-drives for car races (§ 4 no 4 KfzPflVV),
- damage resulting from the failure to meet delivery deadlines (§ 4 no 5 KfzPflVV),
- damage due to nuclear energy (§ 4 no 6 KfzPflVV).

§ 51 para 3 BRAO and § 19a para 2 BNotO allow the insurer to exclude from 27
coverage claims for compensation of damage

- resulting from a deliberate breach of duty,
- arising out of or in connection with advice on or dealing with the law of, and out of activities at courts in countries outside Europe,
- as a result of fraud or of embezzlement by personnel, relatives or partners.

The express exclusions in the aforementioned acts indicate the reasons 28
why a restriction of coverage by means of exclusion is allowed when the rules requiring the compulsory conclusion of liability insurance are silent on this question.[15]

## *b) deductibles*

Pursuant to § 114 para 2 sent 2 VVG, deductibles on the part of the policyholder 29
cannot be invoked against the victim. As a consequence, clauses stipulating deductibles are permissible, albeit restricted to the internal relationship between insurer and policyholder (see no 30 below). § 114 para 2 sent 2 VVG further states that deductibles cannot be asserted against a co-insured person. For example, the employer/keeper of a car cannot demand from his employee reimbursement of the deductible in the case of an accident caused by the latter since, as a driver, he has co-insured status (§ 4 para 2 PflVG in conjunction with § 2 para 2 KfzPflVV).[16]

---

**15** Langheid/Wandt/*Brandt* (fn 2) § 114 VVG no 15.

**16** See Decisions of the Federal Labour Court (Entscheidungen des Bundesarbeitsgerichts, BAG) 31.12.2012, Neue Zeitschrift für Arbeits- und Sozialrecht (NZA) 2013, 622.

30 Although provisions on deductibles are permitted as between the insurer and the insurance holder, such clauses must conform to the requirements set forth in § 114 para 2 sent 1 VVG. Pursuant to § 114 para 2 sent 1 alt 2 VVG, they must comply with the rules requiring the conclusion of liability insurance. For example, according to § 19a para 4 BNotO, an agreement of a deductible up to 1% of the minimum sum insured, ie € 5,000 per claim is permissible. § 51 para 5 BRAO, § 5 para 1 Legal Services Act (*Rechtsdienstleistungsgesetz*, RDG) in conjunction with § 5 para 5 no 5 Legal Services Ordinance (*Rechtsdienstleistungsverordnung*, RDV) as well as § 45 para 2 Patent Attorney Code (*Patentanwaltsordnung*, PatAnwO), also allow a deductible up to 1% of the minimum sum insured.

31 In the absence of a legal provision specifying the maximum deductible, the parties, within the limits of § 114 para 2 sent 1 alt 1 VVG (see no 24 above), are free to agree on a deductible. Its amount, however, must not jeopardise the purpose of the compulsory insurance.[17] The threshold, however, is difficult to determine, and there is no case law on this point. It has been suggested by legal writers that deductibles up to € 5,000 are valid where the insurance holder is an individual.[18] In light of the provisions specifying the maximum deductible it seems more reasonable to allow deductibles up to 1% of the minimum sum insured unless rules requiring the compulsory conclusion of a liability insurance expressly prohibit agreements on deductibles (see eg § 6 para 2 sent 2 EhfG).

#### c) *aggregate limits*

32 Unless otherwise specified in the rules requiring the conclusion of a liability insurance, § 114 para 1 VVG provides that the minimum sum insured shall be € 1 million for all claims per insurance year. For example, according to § 7a GüKG, the minimum sum insured shall be € 1.2 million for all claims per insurance year.

#### d) *claims series clauses*

33 Like any other restrictions of coverage, claims series clauses must comply with the rules requiring the conclusion of liability insurance (see no 24 above). § 51 para 2 BRAO, § 19 para 3 sent 4 BNotO, § 45 para 2 PatAnwO and § 5 para 2 RDV, for example, permit clauses according to which two or more claims arising from or relating to one and the same mandate are considered a single claim. § 53

17 BT-Drucks 16/3945, 88; *WT Schneider* in: RM Beckmann/A Matusche-Beckmann, Versicherungsrechts-Handbuch (2nd edn 2009) § 24 no 167.

18 Bruck/Möller/*Beckmann* (fn 2) § 114 VVG no 44; Prölss/Martin/*Knappmann* (fn 3) § 114 no 3.

para 3 Regulation Implementing the Tax Consultants' Act (*Verordnung zur Durchführung der Vorschriften über Steuerberater, Steuerbevollmächtigte und Steuerberatungsgesellschaften*, DVStB) defines in more detail the permissible content of series clauses. According to this provision, the insurer is entitled to limit his liability to the sum insured for a single claim where the victim has a claim against more than one insured person (lit a), or where the same damage results from multiple breaches (lit b), or with regard to the consequences arising out of acts or omissions based on the same or a similar error if the matters concerned are legally or commercially related (lit c).

Series clauses modelled after § 53 para 3 DVStB should be permissible 34 where the rules requiring the conclusion of liability insurance keep silent on this issue. With regard to § 53 para 3 lit c) DVStB, it is to be noted that the German Supreme Court held that there is no legal or commercial connection where the insurance holder continued to make the same mistakes in different matters for one and the same client (eg annual tax declaration).[19]

According to legal writers, the objective of liability insurance would be en- 35 dangered if the same mistake vis-à-vis different clients were defined as a single claim by means of a claims series clause.[20] Some authors are critical of serial clauses under an events based policy. They hold the view that the insurer is sufficiently protected by his right to terminate the contract after the occurrence of an insured event as stipulated in § 111 para 1 VVG.[21]

### e) other clauses?

In order to eliminate long-tail claims, which only become apparent after many 36 years and possibly after the expiration of the policy, liability insurers generally introduce clauses according to which there is no coverage for wrongful acts, errors or omissions that occurred during the period of insurance but for which a claim was not made and/or reported within a certain period of time (eg three or five years) after the expiration of the policy. Such run-off coverage clauses can be found not only in voluntary insurance policies (eg product liability insurance, environmental liability insurance)[22] but also in professional compulsory

---

**19** BGH 15.5.1991, VersR 1991, 873, 875.

**20** Bruck/Möller/*Beckmann* (fn 2) § 114 VVG no 39; Langheid/Wandt/*Brandt* (fn 2) § 114 VVG no 15.

**21** Langheid/Wandt/*Brandt* (fn 2) § 114 VVG no 15; *F Dallwig*, Deckungsbegrenzungen in der Pflichtversicherung (2011) § 3 A III 2.

**22** For further details see Bruck/Möller/*R Koch* (fn 11) Produkthaftpflicht-Modell ch 7 no 1 ff, Umwelthaftpflicht-Modell ch 8 no 1 f.

insurance contracts such as architects' liability insurance. They may endanger the purpose (not only) of the compulsory insurance contract if first, in reality, there is a considerable time lag between the date on which a professional's act, error or omission took place and the date of its discovery and, second, the run-off period is shorter than the prescription period for a claim.[23] In any event, the clause is void when coupled with a provision that the insurance cover for the entire run-off period is limited to the available cover of the last year of the insurance period since the rules on compulsory liability insurance require a minimum coverage for each breach that occurred during the insurance period, or on an aggregate basis (see nos 22 and 32 above).

12. *What are the consequences if the liability insurance contract concluded in order to fulfil the insurance obligation contravenes what the law stipulates as to contents (see above Questions 10 and 11)?*

37 The rules requiring the compulsory conclusion of liability insurance as well as the framework rules in §§ 114–124 VVG are mandatory. Clauses which deviate from these rules to the detriment of the insurance holder or the (possible) victim are void.[24] Such clauses will be replaced by the applicable mandatory statutory provision while the remainder of the contract remains in force. If there is no statutory provision applicable and the continuance of the contract without a new clause would represent undue hardship for either party, it has been suggested by legal writers that the gap may be filled by means of supplementary interpretation (*ergänzende Vertragsauslegung*) with a clause the parties would have agreed on had they had known of the invalidity.[25] In light of the purpose of compulsory liability insurance, however, not only the intention of the insurer and insurance holder but also of the victim is relevant. It is therefore very debatable whether filling a gap by means of supplementary interpretation based

---

**23** Bruck/Möller/*Beckmann* (fn 2) § 114 VVG no 40; *C von Rintelen* in: RM Beckmann/A Matusche-Beckmann, Versicherungsrechts-Handbuch (2nd edn 2009) § 26 no 215; for a somewhat different, very debatable view see OLG Stuttgart 27.11.2008, VersR 2009, 669, 671: run-off clause shorter than the prescription is valid since the clause must be so construed that the insurer cannot invoke the limitation where the insurance holder acted without fault.
**24** Langheid/Wandt/*Brand* (fn 2) § 114 VVG no 13; *RM Beckmann* in: RM Beckmann/A Matusche-Beckmann, Versicherungsrechts-Handbuch (2nd edn 2009) § 113 no 41.
**25** Langheid/Wandt/*Brand* (fn 2) § 114 VVG no 22; *C Armbrüster/F Dallwig*, Die Rechtsfolgen übermäßiger Deckungsbegrenzungen in der Pflichtversicherung, VersR 2009, 150, 151 f; *H Feyock* in: H Feyock/P Jacobsen/DU Lemor, Kraftfahrtversicherung: KfzVers (3rd edn 2009) § 114 no 2.

on the intentions of the parties to the compulsory insurance contract is permissible.[26]

*13.a) Are statutory stipulations as to the contents of the policy (eg, regarding the amount of the insurance sum, the ban on certain risk exclusion clauses, on deductibles, etc, see above Questions 10 and 11) also binding in favour of the insurance holder? Or is it nonetheless possible for the liability insurer and the insurance holder acting within their internal relationship to agree risk exclusion clauses, deductibles, aggregate limits, and claims series clauses, etc (see above Questions 10 and 11), releasing the insurer from its liability to pay?*

Pursuant to § 113 para 3 VVG, the framework provisions on compulsory liability insurance (§§ 114–124 VVG) shall also apply insofar as the contract of insurance grants cover in excess of the minimum requirements set forth in these rules. It follows from that provision *a contrario* that derogations as to the contents of the contract in favour of the insurance holder are generally permitted. Even if there were no legal provision to that effect, such deviations, in light of the objectives of compulsory liability insurance, would be valid since they would not be detrimental to or, with regard to lower or higher deductibles, would be without effect for the victims. Within the limits set forth in § 114 para 2 sent 1 VVG (see no 24 ff above) the insurer and the insurance holder are free to agree on clauses which exempt the insurer from coverage vis-à-vis the insurance holder (in whole or in part). **38**

*b) If it is possible for liability insurer and insurance holder acting within their internal relationship to agree a release from the obligation to pay (see above Question a): What consequences does this entail? Must the insurer first pay out to the victim and can then have recourse to the insurance holder? Or is another construction provided for the relationship between insurer, insurance holder and victim?*

Whenever the insurer is exempted from coverage vis-à-vis the insurance holder, **39**
his liability to the victim, pursuant to § 117 para 1 VVG, nevertheless remains unaffected. The insurer must first compensate the victim and has the right to recourse against the insurance holder. This right arises in cases where the victim has a direct claim against the insurer in accordance with § 115 para 1 VVG, first,

---

**26** For a similar view see Bruck/Möller/*Beckmann* (fn 2) § 114 VVG no 3; Prölss/Martin/*Knappmann* (fn 3) § 114 VVG no 2; Looschelders/Pohlmann/*Schwartze* (fn 4) § 114 VVG no 8.

from § 115 para 1 sent 4 VVG according to which the insurer and the insurance holder are liable towards the victim as joint and several debtors, and, second, as regards the relationship between them, from § 116 para 1 sent 2 VVG according to which the insurance holder is solely liable. According to § 116 para 1 sent 3 VVG, the insurer is moreover entitled to claim for reimbursement of the expenses incurred (eg defence costs).

40 Where the victim has no direct claim against the insurer, there is no joint and several liability of the insurer and the insurance holder. It follows from § 117 para 5 VVG, according to which the victim's claim against the insurance holder shall be assigned to the insurer insofar as he satisfies the victim, that the insurer nonetheless must first compensate the victim and then may take recourse against the insured. Should the insurer (erroneously) compensate the victim because he was exempted from coverage vis-à-vis the insurance holder, he is entitled to claim repayment from the insurance holder on the grounds of unjust enrichment (§ 812 para 1 sent 1 alt 1 BGB).[27]

*14.a) Does your general (voluntary) liability insurance law include a statutory risk exclusion in respect of intentional damage by the insurance holder or the insured person?*

41 There is such exclusion in § 103 VVG (see no 25 above), which, pursuant to § 47 para 1 VVG, applies to all insured persons who have intentionally and unlawfully caused the loss suffered by the victim.

*b) If the general liability insurance law contains a statutory risk exclusion in respect of intentional damage inflicted by the insurance holder (see above Question a): Does this also apply in cases of compulsory liability insurance?*

42 Yes. The insurer is only liable within the risk assumed by him and it follows from § 103 VVG that compulsory liability insurance does not cover losses intentionally and unlawfully caused by the insurance holder or insured persons.

27 BGH 24.3.1976, VersR 1976, 480 f; Looschelders/Pohlmann/*Schwarze* (fn 4) § 117 VVG no 28; Langheid/Wandt/*Schneider* (fn 2) § 117 VVG no 53; Bruck/Möller/*Beckmann* (fn 2) § 117 VVG no 100.

# IV. Protection Mechanisms

15. *Are insurers obliged to contract when they offer liability insurance policies covering a risk for which the insurance holder is obliged to obtain cover?*

Except for motor vehicle insurance (§ 5 para 2 PflVG) there is no obligation of the insurer to accept an application for compulsory liability insurance (*Kontrahierungszwang*). According to § 5 para 3 PflVG, the application for motor vehicle insurance is deemed to have been accepted in accordance with the principles governing the insurer's business and the insurer's general business tariff provided that the insurer has not rejected the application within two weeks or the insurer has asked for a higher insurance premium due to a verifiable aggravation of risk (counter-offer). § 5 para 4 PflVG states that the insurer is only entitled to reject the application if there are territorial or material restrictions in the principles governing his business, or the applicant was already insured by him and the insurer 43

- has contested the insurance contract because of threat or fraudulent misrepresentation by the applicant (no 1), or
- has rescinded the contract because of an intentional breach of the obligation to provide information prior to conclusion of the contract or because of non-payment of the first insurance premium (no 2), or
- has terminated the contract due to delayed payment of (subsequent) premiums or because of the occurrence of an insured event (no 3).

16. *If there is no obligation to contract: Are there comparable mechanisms provided to ensure that an insurance agreement is concluded?*

No, not by operation of law. 44

17. *Is the insurance holder prohibited from disposing over his cover entitlement to the disadvantage of the victim (eg, by surrendering his entitlement)?*

Yes. According to § 108 para 1 VVG, the insurance holder may not dispose over his claim against the insurer to be released from liability towards the victim. Any disposition such as the alteration, transfer, encumbrance or forfeiture of the claim is ineffective vis-à-vis the victim (except for the assignment of the claim against the insurer to the victim; in that case the claim of the insurance holder against the insurer to be released from liability will be converted into a claim for compensation of the victim against the insurer by operation of law).[28] 45

---

**28** Bruck/Möller/*R Koch* (fn 11) § 100 VVG no 111 f and § 108 VVG no 11 ff.

*18. Does the victim enjoy special protection against insolvency on the part of the insurance holder with regard to the sum payable by the liability insurer?*

46 There is no need for special protection against insolvency on the part of the insurance holder where the victim has a direct right of action against the insurer (see no 49 below), who is liable as a joint and several debtor together with the insurance holder (see no 39 above).

47 Where the victim has no direct right of action against the insurer, in the event of insolvency proceedings being opened in respect of the assets of the insurance holder, the victim may request from the insurer separate satisfaction from the insurance holder's right against the insurer to be released from liability (§ 110 VVG).[29] Where the claim, prior to the opening of the insolvency proceedings, has been established with binding effect for the insurer by final judgment, acknowledgement or settlement (§ 106 sent 1 VVG), the victim is entitled to claim payment from the insurer (according to an analogous application of § 1282 BGB, ie no order of attachment and transfer of the insurance holder's claim against the insurer is necessary).[30] Where the claim has not been established prior to the opening of the insolvency proceedings and the insolvency administrator denies the liability of the insurance holder, the victim has two options to obtain the insurance payment.[31] Like any other creditor, he can bring an action for the determination of the liability claim against the insolvency administrator – § 179 Insolvency Act (*Insolvenzordnung*, InsO) – and, if he is successful, demand payment from the insurer. Alternatively, based on his right to separate satisfaction in accordance with § 110 VVG, he can bring an action for payment against the insolvency administrator, and demand payment from the insurer if he wins.[32] In both cases, no order of attachment and transfer of the insurance holder's right against the insurer to be released is necessary.

*19.a) In what manner can the victim obtain the insurance payment?*

48 Where the conditions for a direct right of action set forth in § 115 para 1 VVG (see no 49 below) are not met, the victim only has a derived right of action where

- the insurance holder has assigned his right against the insurer to be released from liability to the victim (see no 45 above),

---

**29** Ibid, § 110 VVG no 8.
**30** Ibid, § 110 VVG no 14.
**31** Ibid, § 110 VVG no 16.
**32** Ibid, § 110 VVG no 17.

- the victim has obtained an order of attachment and transfer of the insurance holder's right,[33] or
- the insurance holder is insolvent (see nos 46, 47 above).[34]

*b) Does the victim have a direct right of action against the liability insurer (action directe) in the case of voluntary or compulsory liability insurance?*

The victim has a direct right of action against the insurer only in the case of compulsory liability insurance. Pursuant to § 115 para 1 VVG this right, however, is limited to **49**

- motor vehicle liability insurance cases (no 1), or
- where insolvency proceedings have been instituted against the insurance holder's assets, where the request for such proceedings has been rejected due to lack of assets, where a temporary insolvency administrator has been appointed (no 2), or
- where the insurance holder's domicile is unknown (no 3).

In all other cases of voluntary or compulsory liability insurance the victim has only a derived right of action (see no 48 above).

*20. When settling the claim, is the liability insurer obliged to observe a certain procedure in the interests of the victim? For instance, must it pay the victim an advance within a certain period?*

Except for motor vehicle liability insurance, there are no statutory provisions **50** specifically establishing standards with regard to the settlement of liability claims. § 3a para 1 PflVG, in accordance with art 22 of the Directive 2009/103/EC[35], requires the motor vehicle insurer or its claims representative to make, without undue delay and in all cases within three months of the date when the victim presented his claim for compensation, a reasoned offer of compensation in cases where liability is not contested and the damages have been quantified. Where liability is denied or has not been clearly determined or the damages have not been fully quantified, the insurer has to provide a reasoned reply to the points made in the claim. If the insurer fails to make an offer within three

---

**33** Ibid, § 100 VVG no 109.

**34** Ibid, § 100 VVG no 112.

**35** Directive 2009/103/EC of the European Parliament and of the Council of 16 September 2009 relating to insurance against civil liability in respect of the use of motor vehicles, and the enforcement of the obligation to insure against such liability, Official Journal (OJ) L 263, 7.10.2009, 11–31.

months, pursuant to § 3a para 2 PflVG, default interest in the amount of five percentage points above the basic rate of interest per annum become due. The assertion of further damage is not excluded.

51 Where the claims for compensation to be paid on the basis of the same occurrence of loss are in excess of the sum insured, § 118 para 1 VVG establishes a ranking system on how claims are to be settled in the following order: first, claims arising from personal injury; second, claims arising from other injuries to natural or legal persons; third, claims arising from personal injury or other injuries assigned to insurers or other third parties; fourth, claims assigned to social insurance agencies and fifth, all other claims. In the event of equal-ranking claims, they will be settled in proportion to their amount.

*21.a) In the context of its relationship with the victim, can the liability insurer rely on the fact that vis-à-vis the insurance holder (= damaging party) it is freed from the obligation to pay, eg, due to the insurance holder breaching an obligation of conduct/warranty (Obliegenheitsverletzung) or due to him defaulting on premiums?*

52 According to § 117 para 1 and para 3 sent 1 VVG, the insurer remains liable to the third party within the framework of the prescribed minimum sum insured and the risk assumed by it, even if it is wholly or partially released from liability vis-à-vis the insurance holder due to a breach of an obligation (eg default in payment of the premium) and/or a duty (*Obliegenheitsverletzung*; eg duty of disclosure of risks prior to the conclusion of the contract, duty not to aggravate the risk insured, etc). It needs to be emphasised that the insurer is wholly or partially exempted from liability vis-à-vis both the insurance holder and the victim to the extent the amount insured exceeds the minimum sum as described in § 114 para 1 VVG. Moreover, according to § 117 para 3 sent 2 VVG, the insurer is not obligated to effect payment insofar as the victim may receive compensation for his loss from another indemnity insurer or from a social insurance agency.

*b) Does the law distinguish on the basis of the ground for the release from the obligation to pay so that in some cases the insurer may not invoke its release from such obligation vis-à-vis the victim?*

53 The law does not distinguish on the basis of the ground for the release from the obligation to pay. Therefore, the insurer can never invoke its release from such obligation vis-à-vis the victim.

c) *If the insurer must still pay the victim despite being released from its obligation to pay vis-à-vis the insurance holder (see above Question b), may it take recourse against the latter?*

Yes, the insurer may take recourse against the insurance holder if he satisfies the victim (see nos 39 and 40 above). 54

22.a) *Within its relationship to the victim, can the liability insurer invoke the fact that the insurance agreement had already ended by the time relevant in respect of the duty to provide cover?*

According to § 117 para 2 sent 1 VVG, circumstances which result in the non- 55
existence (eg due to lack of the insurance holder's legal capacity,[36] [hidden] lack of consent), or the cessation of the insurance contract (eg due to a revocation of or termination of or withdrawal from the insurance contract[37]) are only effective vis-à-vis the victim one month after the insurer has notified the competent agency of this circumstance (so-called *Nachhaftung*). The competent agency will be generally identified by the rules requiring the conclusion of liability insurance (eg vehicle registration authorities for motor vehicle liability insurance, § 7 PflVG in conjunction with § 25 para 1 Vehicle Admission Ordinance, *Fahrzeug-Zulassungsverordnung*, FZV, or the bar association for liability insurance taken out by lawyers, § 51 para 7 BRAO). The *Nachhaftung* shall also apply if the insurance contract has expired (§ 117 para 2 sent 2 VVG). The *Nachhaftung* by no means commences before the insurance contract has ended (for one of the afore-mentioned reasons) (§ 117 para 2 sent 3 VVG). The liability insurer, however, can invoke that the insurance agreement had already ended by the time relevant in respect of the obligation to provide cover if, at that point in time, the competent agency has received confirmation that a new contract has been concluded (§ 117 para 2 sent 4 VVG). It is to be noted that there will be no *Nachhaftung* where no competent agency has been appointed to receive the notification (§ 117 para 2 sent 5 VVG), as is the case, for example, with development aid workers' liability insurance (see § 6 EhfG).

**36** BGH 2.10.2002, VersR 2002, 1501.
**37** Prölss/Martin/*Knappmann* (fn 3) § 117 VVG no 9.

*b) If the insurer must pay the victim despite the termination of the insurance agreement by the time relevant for the duty to provide cover (see above Question a), can it take recourse against the insurance holder?*

56 Yes (see no 40 above).

*23.a) Are there cases in which a damaging party does not effectively conclude the required liability insurance and the victim injured by him nonetheless receives compensation for his loss from a liability insurer or another compensation scheme (eg, a guarantee fund)?*

57 There is general consensus among scholars that, whenever a contract of compulsory insurance, from the viewpoint of the competent agency, appears to be validly concluded, the victim receives compensation for his loss from the liability insurer.[38] In this respect, it is to be noted again that, where no competent agency has been appointed to receive the notification, the victim will not receive any compensation.

*b) In the event that the policy taken out was not in fact effectively concluded, is it necessary to distinguish on the basis of the ground for this ineffectiveness, eg, whether the reason for the contract not coming into effect was: i) a lack of legal capacity on the part of the insurance holder, ii) lack of consent, iii) falsa procuratio (unauthorised agency)?*

58 As stated before (no 57 above), the relevant criterion is not the ground for the ineffectiveness of the contract but whether the ineffectiveness was obvious for the agency. Therefore, the victim may receive compensation for his loss from a liability insurer even in the case of lack of legal capacity on the part of the insurance holder, or lack of consent, or unauthorised agency.[39]

*c) Can the liability insurer (or the alternative compensation scheme) that must provide cover even though the insurance policy was not effectively concluded (see above Questions a and b) have recourse against the damaging party?*

59 Yes (see no 40 above).

**38** Bruck/Möller/*Beckmann* (fn 2) § 117 VVG no 21; Langheid/Wandt/*Schneider* (fn 2) § 117 VVG no 13; Prölss/Martin/*Knappmann* (fn 3) § 117 VVG no 10.
**39** Bruck/Möller/*Beckmann* (fn 2) § 117 VVG no 21; Langheid/Wandt/*Schneider* (fn 2) § 117 VVG no 13; Prölss/Martin/*Knappmann* (fn 3) § 117 VVG no 10.

*24.a) Are there cases in which a damaging party does not take out any liability insurance, ie not even an ineffective insurance policy (see above Question 23), and the victim whom he injured is still compensated for his damage by a liability insurer or another compensation scheme (guarantee fund, etc)?*

Except for victims of car accidents, who will be compensated for the damage suffered by a guarantee fund (§ 12 para 1 no 2 PflVG), there is no compensation for damage. **60**

*b) Can the liability insurer (or the alternative compensation scheme) that must provide cover despite the total absence of any insurance agreement (see above Question a) have recourse against the damaging party?*

Yes, according to § 12 para 6 PflVG, the guarantee fund may take recourse against the holder, owner and/or driver of the car. Moreover, the guarantee fund may claim reimbursement of its expenses in accordance with § 12 para 5 PflVG.[40] **61**

*25. Is the victim protected against the insolvency of the liability insurer?*

Victims of car accidents again enjoy special protection. They will be compensated for their damage by the guarantee fund when the supervision authority has filed a petition for the institution of insolvency proceedings against the assets of the motor vehicle insurer (§ 12 para 1 no 4 PflVG). **62**

In all other cases of compulsory liability insurance, § 117 para 6 VVG provides that, where insolvency proceedings are opened against the assets of the insurer, the insurance contract does not end until one month after the insolvency administrator has notified the competent agency of this circumstance. Up until such time, it remains effective against the insolvency estate. This means that any claim arising out of an insured event which occurred during this period is considered to be a debt incumbent on the assets of the insurer in terms of § 55 para 1 no 2 InsO. Claims arising out of an insured event which occurred prior to the opening of insolvency proceedings, on the other hand, are to be filed with the insolvency administrator and entered in the insolvency register. If no competent agency has been appointed to take receipt of the notification, the insurance agreement ends one month after the insurance holder has been notified of the opening of insolvency proceedings. **63**

**40** Cf BT-Drucks IV/2252, 26.

*26. Are there rules that serve in particular the protection of the victim when the liability insurance was only concluded voluntarily – ie without it being compulsory?*

64 There are a couple of provisions applicable to both voluntary and compulsory liability insurance serving in particular the protection of the victim. First and foremost, there is § 108 para 1 VVG, according to which, any disposition of the insurance holder over his claim against the insurer to be released from liability is ineffective vis-à-vis the victim (see no 45 above). Moreover, § 109 VVG ensures that, where the claims for compensation to be paid on the basis of the same occurrence of loss are in excess of the sum insured, the claims will be settled in proportion to their amount. § 107 para 1 VVG ensures that the victim receives a partial payment whenever the insurance holder is obligated to pay the victim a pension and the sum insured is not equal to the capital value of the pension. Finally, § 110 VVG ensures that the victim may request separate satisfaction from the insurance holder's claim against the insurer to be released from liability in the event of insolvency proceedings being opened in respect of the assets of the insurance holder.

65 § 105 VVG and § 108 para 2 VVG also serve the protection of the victim to a certain extent because they invalidate clauses in the insurance contract according to which first, the insurer must not effect payment if the insurance holder satisfies the victim or acknowledges his entitlement without the insurer's consent, and second, the assignment of the insurance holder's claim against the insurer to be released from liability is excluded.

## V. Supervision and Sanctions

*27.a) In which cases must the insurance holder prove to an authority before commencing an activity requiring insurance that he has taken out the respective prescribed liability insurance cover (see above Question 4.e)?*

66 Whether or not there is a duty of the insurance holder to prove to the competent authority (see no 55 above) prior to the commencement of his activities that he has taken out the prescribed liability insurance depends on the respective law that requires insurance. In the area of liability insurance for professionals, for example, according to § 6a BNotO, without proof of the conclusion of a liability insurance contract in accordance with § 19a BNotO, an appointment as a notary is not possible. Similar rules can be found for lawyers (§ 12 para 2 sent 2 BRAO), tax consultants (§ 14 para 2 StBerG), auditors (§ 16 para 1 no 3 WPO), and patent

attorneys (§ 18 para 2 PatAnwO). Concerning the use of cars, the law requires that, prior to the registration of the car, the keeper must prove the conclusion of a motor vehicle insurance contract (§ 7 no 4 PflVG in conjunction with § 3 FZV). A similar rule exists for the keeper of an aircraft (§ 8 para 2 no 3 LuftVZO). Air carriers will be granted a licence to operate only on production of proof that the required liability insurance has been concluded (§ 20 para 1 LuftVG in conjunction with § 62 para 1 no 8 LuftVZO).

It is important to note that § 113 para 2 VVG obliges the insurer to provide 67 the insurance holder with a confirmation that there is a contract of liability insurance which corresponds to the rules requiring the conclusion of the insurance and indicates the sum insured (see also § 106 para 1 LuftVZO).

*b) Must the insurer inform an authority when liability insurance taken out to meet an insurance obligation ends?*

Whenever the insurance holder must prove to the competent authority prior to 68 the commencement of his activities that he has taken out the prescribed liability insurance, there is, in general, a corresponding duty of the insurer to inform the competent authority when the liability insurance contract ends (eg § 19a para 3 sent 3 BNotO, § 51 para 6 sent 1 BRAO, § 54 para 2 WPO, § 67 para 4 StBerG, § 102a LuftVZO). Motor vehicle insurers are, however, not obliged to notify the competent agency of the end of the insurance contract. § 25 FZV only states that the insurer may inform the vehicle registration authority.

*c) Is the insurer also under a duty to inform when a liability insurance agreement is in existence but it has no duty to provide cover – eg, due to defaults on premium payments?*

According to § 102a LuftVZO, both the insurer and the insurance holder must 69 notify the competent authority without delay of any suspension of insurance cover, the end of the insurance contract and the consumption of the sum insured if it concerns the operation of an airplane. There is no such express obligation in other cases where the insurer has to inform the competent agency of the end of the insurance. The rules for compulsory professional liability insurance, for example, only require the inclusion of a clause by which the insurer must inform the competent agency, without delay, of the inception of cover and the expiration or termination of the insurance contract as well as of any amendment which affects the minimum coverage requirements (see § 19a para 3 sent 3 BNotO, § 51 para 6 sent 1 BRAO, § 54 para 2 WPO, § 67 para 4 StBerG, § 45 para 6 PatAnwO). It is debatable whether default on premium payments exempting the insurer from liability in the case of an insured event falls within the scope of the afore-mentioned provisions.

*d) What are the consequences when the duties to inform of the end of contract or the release from payment obligations (see above Questions b and c) are violated?*

70 According to § 117 para 2 VVG, the insurer remains liable if he does not notify the competent authority. Where no competent authority has been appointed, the victim remains unprotected (see no 55 above). Motor vehicle insurers, which are not obliged to inform the vehicle registration authorities (see no 68 above), are not liable (in tort) towards the victim for non-notification.[41]

*28. Is there some official body (authority, professional chamber) where an injured party can find out whether and where the injuring party who inflicted damage upon him in the course of an activity requiring insurance has liability insurance?*

71 In line with art 23 no 3 Directive 2009/103/EC[42], there is an information centre (*Auskunftsstelle*) from which the injured party is entitled to obtain information regarding the name and address of the insurer and the keeper of the damaging automobile as well as the policy number and the validity of the insurance cover (§ 8a PflVG). Outside the area of motor vehicle insurance there are similar rules in the case of lawyers' and notaries' liability only. For example, according to § 19a para 6 BNotO, the regional administration of justice and the chamber of notaries, of which the notary committing malpractice is a member, provide victims with information about the name and address of his insurer as well as the number of the insurance policy insofar as the notary's interest not to provide this information does not prevail over the interest of the injured party. There are identical rules for (patent) lawyers (§ 51 para 6 sent 2 BRAO, § 45 para 6 sent 2 PatAnwO).

72 It is to be noted that, where no right to information about the insurance cover against an official body is granted by the rules that impose an obligation to take out liability insurance, the victim may have a claim to be informed about

41 *R Beckmann* in: Berliner Kommentar (fn 9) § 158c VVG no 24; Schwintowski/Brömmelmeyer/*Huber* (fn 2) § 117 VVG no 70; OLG Frankfurt/Main 18.5.1954, NJW 1955, 109.
42 See fn 35 above.

the damaging party in accordance with general rules of civil law (eg § 242 BGB).[43]

29. *Are there (public law) sanctions against the party who was required to take out insurance if such does not take out the compulsory liability insurance? Examples of this would be a ban on carrying out the activity that requires the insurance or the imposition of an administrative or judicial penalty.*

A person or company that fails to comply with its obligation to take out liability 73
insurance may be subject to a variety of sanctions. Such sanctions are often stipulated in the provisions governing the respective duty to take out liability insurance.[44] In most cases, the non-observance of an obligation to insure entails some sort of administrative penalty. For example, where the person or company needs an authorisation to carry out a particular activity and the admission is contingent on the taking out of the prescribed liability insurance, the competent authority (administrative authority, professional chamber) will revoke the authorisation (see § 14 para 2 no 9 BRAO, § 46 para 2 no 3 StBerG, § 20 para 2 no 4 WPO, § 21 para 2 no 10 PatAnwO, § 9 para 2 LuftVZO, § 20 para 3 LuftVG). Notaries will be removed from office (§ 50 para 1 no 10 BNotO).

Only in exceptional cases are criminal penalties imposed. For example, ac- 74
cording to § 6 para 1 PflVG, any person who fails to take out motor vehicle insurance in accordance with § 1 PflVG shall be guilty of an offence and shall be liable, on conviction, to a fine or to imprisonment for a term not exceeding one year (if the person acts negligently, the penalty is, pursuant to § 6 para 2 PflVG, reduced to a fine or imprisonment for a term not exceeding six months). In case of a deliberate failure, the car can be confiscated (§ 6 para 3 PflVG). A failure to take out liability insurance for participants in clinical studies conducted on humans and using pharmaceuticals or medical products is subject to a fine or to imprisonment for a term not exceeding one year (see §§ 96 no 10, 40 para 1 no 8, para 3 German Medicines Act, AMG, and §§ 41 no 4, 20 para 1 no 9, para 3 Medical Devices Act, *Medizinproduktegesetz*, MPG). In other cases the non-compliance is only regarded as a regulatory offence (*Ordnungswidrigkeit*) with a fine (eg § 3 SchauHV in conjunction with § 145 para 4 GewO: fine of up to € 5,000; § 16 para 1 no 1 Ordinance on Guard Services, *Verordnung über das Bewachungs-*

43 *J Keppel*, Die Pflichthaftpflichtversicherung nach der VVG-Reform (2010) 109; Rüffer/Halbach/*Schimikowski* (fn 3) § 115 VVG no 6.

44 Eg § 21 I no 3 Federal Pollution Control Act (Bundes-Immissionsschutzgesetz, BImSchG); § 17 para 4 Atomic Energy Act (Atomgesetz, AtG).

*gewerbe*, BewachV) in conjunction with § 144 para 2 no 1b GewO: fine of up to € 3,000).

75 Non-compliance with the duty to take out insurance may also lead to civil liability of the person or company where the compulsory liability insurance extends the coverage to third parties. German courts have held in several cases that the keeper of a car who has not concluded a motor vehicle insurance contract is liable (in tort, § 823 para 2 BGB in conjunction with §§ 1, 6 PflVG) towards the driver of the car in the case of an accident caused by the latter.[45] Where the rules do not expressly require taking out insurance for the benefit of third parties, the failure to conclude an insurance contract may lead to liability provided it follows from the *travaux préparatoires* that the rules are intended to protect a third party.[46]

## VI. Statutory Provisions required by the Constitution or the European Convention on Human Rights (ECHR)

30. *What has been said regarding the compatibility of the duties to take out liability insurance with your country's constitution and the ECHR? Please take into account case law and academic literature.*

76 The compatibility of the duty to take out liability insurance has been discussed with regard to the Constitution (*Grundgesetz*, GG) only. It has been argued that the rules requiring conclusion limit the freedom to conclude and to agree on the content of a contract that is protected by art 2 para 1 GG.[47] Where insurance is a precondition for providing services, to run a business or to operate eg power plants, the freedom to pursue an occupation (art 12 para 1 GG) as well as property rights (art 14 para 1 GG) of the persons concerned might be affected.[48] It has also been discussed whether the principle of equal treatment (art 3 para 1 GG) is concerned. This principle requires that the legislator as well as official bodies treat comparable situations in the same way and different situations in a differ-

---

**45** OLG Koblenz 28.1.2003, Beck'sche Rechtssammlung (BeckRS) 2003, 30303611; OLG Nürnberg 5.11.1992, Neue Zeitschrift für Verkehrsrecht (NZV) 1993, 273.

**46** See BGH 9.11.2004, NJW-RR 2005, 680 (denied with regard to § 7a GüKG).

**47** Bruck/Möller/*Beckmann* (fn 2) Vor §§ 113–124 VVG no 25; *F Hufen*, Staatsrecht II Grundrechte (3rd edn 2011) § 6 no 45 f.

**48** *KS Hedderich*, Pflichtversicherung (2011) 147.

ent way unless there is an objective reason not to do so (prohibition of arbitrary action, *Willkürverbot*).[49]

With regard to the limitation of the freedom to contract, to pursue an occupation and/or of ownership, the duty to take out liability insurance must be based on the enactment of a parliamentary statute (*Gesetzesvorbehalt*).[50] For that formal reason, professional and self-governing bodies do not have the competence to stipulate compulsory liability insurance.[51] Such bodies, however, may be authorised by a parliamentary statute to introduce compulsory liability insurance. 77

The so-called principle of materiality (*Wesentlichkeitsgrundsatz*), moreover, requires that the statute must not only designate the competent authority but also specify on which grounds the authority may introduce compulsory insurance as well as the risks to be insured.[52] In this regard it is interesting to note that the Hessian Higher Administrative Court (*Verwaltungsgerichtshof Kassel*) annulled a provision of the Hessian dogs' ordinance (*Hundeverordnung*) which imposed on keepers of dangerous breeds of dogs the obligation to conclude dog liability insurance. The court held that the Hessian Law for Safety and Public Order (*Hessisches Gesetz über die Sicherheit und Ordnung*, HessSOG) did not authorise the Hessian government to adopt a dogs' ordinance that requires keepers of such dogs to conclude dog liability insurance.[53] In the court's view, the provisions of an ordinance based on the HessSOG must be aimed at the protection of human life and health through prevention. Insurance, however, would not aim to prevent but to compensate for the damage suffered by the victim. From this the court concluded that there was no legislative basis for an ordinance's provision on dogs' liability insurance. In another case dealing with compulsory liability insurance for dangerous breeds of dogs, the Higher Administrative Court of Mecklenburg-Western Pomerania (*Oberverwaltungsgericht Greifswald*), before the entry into force of § 114 para 1 VVG (no 22 above), annulled the obligation to take out insurance in the dogs' ordinance of Mecklen- 78

**49** Ibid, 144 ff.

**50** Bruck/Möller/*Beckmann* (fn 2) Vor §§ 113–124 VVG no 26; see eg Higher Administrative Court (Verwaltungsgerichtshof, VGH) Kassel 29.8.2011, Neue Zeitschrift für Verwaltungsrecht, Rechtsprechungs-Report (NVwZ-RR) 2002, 650 (concerning the obligation of keepers of dogs to conclude insurance against dog liability).

**51** Federal Constitutional Court (Bundesverfassungsgericht, BVerfG) 9.5.1972, Decisions of the Federal Constitutional Court (Entscheidungen des BVerG, BVerfGE) 33, 125; Bruck/Möller/*Beckmann* (fn 2) Vor §§ 113–124 VVG no 26; *Hedderich* (fn 48) 244.

**52** Bruck/Möller/*Beckmann* (fn 2) Vor §§ 113–124 VVG no 26; *Hedderich* (fn 48) 238.

**53** VGH Kassel 29.8.2001, NVwZ-RR 2002, 650.

burg-Western Pomerania on the ground that, due to the non-specification of the minimum sum insured, it did not comply with the principle of legal certainty.[54]

*31. Does the constitution or the ECHR make any stipulations regarding the contents of such duties to take out liability insurance? Please take into account case law and academic literature.*

79 Like any other legal provision that affects fundamental rights (*Grundrechte*), the introduction of compulsory liability insurance must comply with the constitutional law requirements of proportionality, legal certainty and equal treatment. This means that compulsory insurance must serve a legitimate purpose, and it must be appropriate, necessary and proportionate to the specific and legitimate purposes pursued. Except for the afore-mentioned rulings, there have been no cases dealing with the constitutional compliance of compulsory liability insurance. Presumably for this reason, there is very little literature on the issue.[55] In light of the aims of the rules that impose an obligation to take out liability insurance (no 13 ff above), there can be no doubt that they serve public interest objectives, ie first and foremost victim protection, and second the internalisation of the costs resulting from damage in the interests of society (state social insurance system).

80 Taking into account also the jurisprudence of the Constitutional Court (*Bundesverfassungsgericht*, BVerfG), it is not surprising that the introduction of compulsory insurance has never been successfully challenged before the courts on the grounds of disproportionality or unequal treatment. The BVerfG has consistently held that the legislator has wide discretion when legislating, first, in setting the legitimate objectives and, second, with regard to the requirements of suitability, necessity, and proportionality.[56] Concerning the introduction of compulsory liability insurance, the legislator's discretion includes the determination of the areas where risks are particularly serious.

81 The legislator would exceed the limits of its discretion if it made the authorisation to carry out a particular activity or profession contingent on the taking out of the prescribed liability insurance, where coverage is not available on

---

**54** Higher Administrative Court (Oberverwaltungsgericht, OVG) Greifswald 6.4.2001, NVwZ-RR 2001, 752.

**55** Only *Hedderich* (fn 48) 144–246 has dealt with the question as to whether the Constitution limits the introduction of compulsory insurance including compulsory liability insurance in greater detail; see also Bruck/Möller/*Beckmann* (fn 2) Vor §§ 113–124 VVG no 25 ff.

**56** See eg BVerfG 16.5.2013, NJW 2013, 2674, 2681; BVerfG 27.2.2008, NJW 2008, 1293; BVerfG 12.12.2006, NJW 2007, 979; BVerfG 16.3.2004, NVwZ 2004, 597.

the market because the (re-)insurer considers the risks to be insured as uninsurable (eg catastrophic risks, gene technology risks, nanotechnology risks) or where coverage is not affordable.

# VII. Reform Efforts

*32. Are there efforts towards reforming the law regarding compulsory liability insurance?*

No. The framework rules on compulsory liability insurance have just been revised by the Insurance Code Act 2008. It is to be expected, however, that the number of compulsory liability insurance policies, both at state and federal law level, will continue to grow, particularly for professional indemnity[57], environmental risks, cyber risks, and damage to property resulting from natural catastrophes. Some scholars have proposed introducing an obligation for parents to take out liability insurance for their minor children over seven against everyday risks.[58] The legislator, however, did not take up this proposal. The position taken by the European Insurance and Reinsurance Federation (CEA) against the inclusion of a requirement for compulsory insurance into the environmental liability directive and into the directive on the geological storage of carbon dioxide, however, makes clear that the insurance sector has strong reservations against the introduction of compulsory liability insurance. In this regard, it again needs to be emphasised that no compulsory liability insurance (even if coupled with an insurer's obligation to contract) can be introduced where coverage is not available on the market or not affordable. 82

**57** See *J Müller*, Brauchen wir eine Pflichtversicherung für Insolvenzverwalter? Anwaltsblatt 2008, 536 (dealing with the question as to whether there is a need to introduce compulsory liability insurance for insolvency administrators).

**58** *D Looschelders*, Verfassungsrechtliche Grenzen der deliktischen Haftung, VersR 1999, 141, 151; *E Lorenz*, Zur haftungs- und versicherungsrechtlichen Problematik des § 828 Abs 2 BGB, VersR 1989, 711, 713.

# VIII. Compulsory Liability Insurance and Liability Law

*33. Is, at the legislative level, any connection discernible between the nature of liability (in particular in the case of strict liability) and the imposition of compulsory liability insurance?*

**83** As pointed out above (no 2 above), there is no coherent regulatory regime of compulsory liability insurance in terms of the reasons why they were established or with regard to different standards of liability or different types of damage. There is in particular no general rule that, in cases where there is strict liability, compulsory liability insurance has been introduced. For example, even though professional liability always requires fault, there is a duty to take out liability insurance. On the other hand, there is no duty to take out insurance for product liability and the liability of animal keepers where no fault is required (see § 1 para 1 Product Liability Act – *Produkthaftungsgesetz*, ProdHaftG, § 833 BGB).[59] Even if there is no direct connection between strict liability and the imposition of compulsory liability insurance, it appears, however, that outside of the area of fault-based professional liability, recently introduced obligations to take out liability insurance primarily relate to strict liability risks arising out of, for example, keeping dangerous breeds of dogs or the operation of (potentially) hazardous activities.

---

**59** Langheid/Wandt/*Brand* (fn 2) Vorbem zu §§ 113–124 VVG no 4.

Péter Takáts

# Compulsory Liability Insurance in Hungary

## I. The Term Compulsory Liability Insurance

1. *Indicate the rules within your legal system that set out a duty to take out liability insurance. In this context, also take into account the implementation of international treaties (eg, the International Convention on Civil Liability for Bunker Oil Pollution Damage, 2001).*

As a general rule, according to sec 129 para (1) of Law No LXXXVIII of 2014 on insurance business (hereinafter referred to as Bit[1]), compulsory insurance (ie an obligation to buy insurance) may be prescribed by an act of law (hereinafter referred to as 'Law'), passed by parliament only. Such obligation is further restricted to non-life insurance contracts. According to sec 129 para (2) Bit, an act of law may authorise the government to regulate the conditions of contracts of compulsory insurance in a decree.[2] Section 567 para (3) of the former Civil Code (Law No IV of 1959), which just recently ceased to be valid, further explicitly allowed compulsory insurance to be regulated differently than as set out by the Civil Code only by acts of statutory law.[3] A similar rule is now missing in the new Civil Code which entered into force on 15 March 2014 (Law No V of 2013). However, this would lead to no change in the merits as laws passed by parliament may have different contents from the Civil Code, and such a conflict can be resolved by the *lex specialis derogat legi generali* principle. In fact, the only comprehensive regulation on compulsory insurance, Law No LXII of 2009 on compulsory third-party motor liability insurance, provides for several rules differing from their counterparts in both the former and current Civil Code. 1

The list of compulsory insurance cover is highlighted in the Annex: Rules on Compulsory Liability Insurance in Hungary (at the end of this book). 2

---

1 'Bit', a term generally used in practice, stands for *biztosítási törvény* (insurance law). This law, that entered into force on 1 January 2016, replaced Law No LX of 2003 on the same subject.

2 It is noteworthy that Bit does not contain the list of cases of compulsory insurance any more, provided earlier in Appendix 7 of Law No LX of 2003.

3 Sec 129 para (1) Bit determines the form (rank) of the legislation, the Civil Code deals with its contents. Sec 129 Bit also contains further rules of an administrative nature on contracts of compulsory insurance to be discussed in other parts of this report.

*2. Is there a coherent 'law of compulsory liability insurance' in your legal system?*

3 There is no coherent 'law of compulsory liability insurance' in Hungary. Most of the legal acts referred to in the Annex contain rules of merely a procedural nature, specifying that a copy of liability insurance cover shall be attached to applications for certain licences.[4] Regarding the contents of this duty, the rules show great diversity. Whereas compulsory third-party motor liability insurance is regulated in detail[5] and there are also some cases where legal acts have been passed to determine the minimum content of, for example, aviation liability insurance[6] or the professional indemnity insurance of independent insurance intermediaries and insurance consultants,[7] most of the respective legal acts declare only that liability insurance has 'to be possessed'[8] or 'to be demonstrated'[9] or 'to be provided'[10] (cf also below no 18) in some cases, also as an alternative to other types of financial securities, as set out below in no 11.

4 Eg sec 2 para (3) item a) of Law No XXXII of 1995 on patent agents highlights, as one of the preconditions of becoming a member of the Chamber of Patent Agents, that the applicant 'has liability insurance for patent agency'.

5 Cf Law No LXII of 2009 on compulsory liability insurance for motor vehicles.

6 Cf Government Decree No 39/2001.(III.5.)Korm (Kormány) on compulsory liability insurance in air traffic. This rule of law defines the minimum limits of liability insurance relating to third-party and first-party loss in air traffic, also in the case of airport operators and air traffic controls. The decree maximises the acceptable amount of deductibles to 5% of the respective sums insured and renders the scope of cover to include war risks (risks of violence) as well.

7 Cf Government Decree No 44/2015.(III.12.)Korm on the minimum requirements of the contents of professional indemnity insurance of multi-agents and insurance brokers, replacing the Government Decree No 319/2004.(XII.1.)Korm on the same subject. This rule of law defines the scope of the cover and the minimum liability limits, the required territorial scope of the insurance, as well as the maximum amount of the deductible that is acceptable.

8 Cf sec 108 para (2) of Law No CLIV of 1997 on health care: 'The condition of a licence for pursuing the activity is that liability insurance to cover damages in the course of providing health care services is taken out'.

9 Cf sec 3 para (1) item h) of Government Decree No 188/1999.(XII.16.)Korm on the licensing of social institutions providing personal care ('in the case that the institution is not operated by the state, a copy of the liability insurance to cover damage caused in the course of providing professional services shall be demonstrated') and sec 4 para (6) item a) of Government Decree No 259/2002.(XII.18.)Korm on the licensing of children's welfare and children's care service providers ('a copy of the liability insurance to cover damage caused in the course of providing services shall be demonstrated').

10 Eg sec 5 para (1) item b) of Law No CXXXIII of 2005 requires 'liability insurance for the service to be provided', as a condition of a licence for private security services or private detectives. Obviously, the correct term would be 'professional indemnity insurance', as in the practice of insurers, 'service liability' refers to a product attached to general third-party liability insurance.

3. *Is there a specific term for compulsory liability insurance in your legal system? How is it defined?*

As sec 129 para (1) Bit explicitly rules that an obligation to buy insurance may be prescribed by an act of law only, the term 'compulsory insurance' (including compulsory liability insurance) only relates to cases where the source of the respective duty is an act of statutory law. Nevertheless, Hungarian law does not use a specific term describing compulsory liability insurance. Indeed, the terminology of the legal rules may be considered rather vague, because in some cases the nature of the insurance cover – eg that it is professional indemnity insurance – might only be determined by interpretation, as the legal act relates to 'liability insurance' only, cf above no 3. 4

4. *In which of the following cases does compulsory liability insurance apply according to prevailing opinion?*

a) *Duties to take out liability insurance which are not directly based on the law but on an order or decision issued by administrative authorities?*

Administrative authorities have not issued decisions to date instructing any party to take out liability insurance. This might also be explained by the abundance of legal acts to declare such duties, as listed in the Annex to this report. Authorities are rather restricted as to their supervision of whether a duty to take out and maintain liability insurance has been met. 5

b) *Duties to take out liability insurance that are not based directly on the law but on the statutes of a professional or other self-governing body?*

Professional bodies – eg the Hungarian Bar or the Hungarian Auditors' Chamber – are entitled by law to determine the details of the duty to take out liability insurance imposed on their members by the same law.[11] In such case, the deci- 6

11 Cf Guideline No 1/2000.(V.22.) of the Hungarian Bar on the liability insurance acceptable by the chambers of lawyers, further Regulation No 7/2011.(X.24.)MÜK of the Hungarian Bar specifying minimum limits of such liability insurance cover – based on sec 13 para (3) of Law No XI of 1998 on lawyers. There is a similar regulation in force in respect to auditors, established by sec 11 para (1) of Law No LXXV of 2007 on the Hungarian Chamber of Auditors and Auditing Business, referring the determination of the contents of compulsory professional indemnity insurance to the statutes of the chamber.

sion of the professional body becomes 'law', first, because it is derived from the legal act, second, because membership in these professional bodies is mandatory and the duty is thus enforced by the respective body itself.

7 If a professional association, not representing the profession as a whole, decides to take out professional indemnity insurance as a group insurance scheme on behalf of its members, without a duty prescribed by law, this insurance is considered voluntary. Most probably, however, if a professional body with a mandatory membership introduced such a scheme, this would, in my opinion,[12] be classified compulsory insurance by analogy.

c) *Duties to take out liability insurance that are not based on any public law but on a private law provision (eg, governing the relationship between employer and employee)?*

8 An act of private law is also an 'act of law' as, according to sec 129 para (1) Bit, such duty, if prescribed, would be considered compulsory insurance.

d) *Duties to take out liability insurance that are not based on any public law but on a private law rule that is established by case law (and, eg, governs the relationship between employer and employee)?*

9 Case law – a fact of sociology but officially not admitted in Hungary – would, in my opinion,[13] not lead to compulsory insurance, due to the wording of sec 129 para (1) Bit.

e) *Cases in which there is no duty to take out liability insurance but liability insurance cover is a prerequisite for the admissibility of carrying out a particular activity?*

10 In my opinion[14] such a case would clearly qualify as compulsory liability insurance, as it is an indirect method of imposing an obligation to take out insurance.

12 There are no debates or statements on the subject.
13 There are no debates or statements on the subject.
14 There are no debates or statements on the subject.

*f) Cases of alternative financial security, in which the duty to provide for financial security may be fulfilled either by taking out liability insurance or other forms of financial security (eg, bank guarantees)?*

In cases where liability insurance, as set out in a legal act, is optional to other forms of financial security and there is an obligation to demonstrate this, the respective liability insurance is considered to be compulsory. This is the case, for example, with multi-agents and insurance brokers as per sec 391 para (6) and sec 403 para (1) Bit.[15] 11

*g) Cases in which the duty to have insurance has only been created by a contractual agreement between potential injuring party and victim?*

Before the passing of Law No LX of 2003, sec 105 para (1) of which first regulated the level of statutory legislation to prescribe compulsory insurance, a rule repeated by sec 129 para (1) Bit, there was a general opinion that a duty to take out insurance might be derived from either an act of law or an agreement made between the parties.[16] Now, with the restrictive interpretation of the statutory rules referred to, in my opinion[17] it might not be considered as 'compulsory liability insurance' and obviously there would be no public law sanctions available should the obliged party not comply with this duty. In the latter case, the beneficiary could only sue the obliged party for breach of contract before a court of law. 12

## II. Aims

*5. What are the aims of the rules that impose an obligation to take out liability insurance:*

*a) the protection of the victim,*

In the socialist era (ie before 1990), the prevailing view in both theory and practice was that the primary aim of liability insurance cover was the protection of 13

15 In practice, there has not been any independent insurance intermediary yet to opt for a financial security instead of professional indemnity insurance. Cf also *J Zavodnyik*, A biztosítási szerződési jog alapjai [Fundaments of insurance contract law] (1999) 30. A different view is taken in the literature by *Z Kovács*, Biztosítási közjog [Public insurance law] (2006) 263.

16 Cf *Z Novotni*, A biztosítási szerződések joga [The law of insurance contracts] (1987) 137.

17 There are no debates or statements on the subject.

the potential victim, the protection of the insured being rather a 'side effect'.[18] The introduction of the market economy, however, seems to have brought about a shift in public opinion towards the acceptance of the protection of the insured, as an – at least, equal – aim.[19] However, the preamble of the Law No LXII of 2009 on compulsory third-party motor liability insurance defines the protection of the victim as the primary aim of the law. Other acts of law do not relate to the aim of this duty.

*b) the protection of the insurance holder,*

14 See above in no 13.

*c) the protection of the victim and the insurance holder,*

15 See above in no 13.

*d) other aims, eg internalising the costs in the interests of society?*

16 See above in no 13.

*6. Do the rules that prescribe a form of alternative financial security (see above Question 4.f) pursue the same aims as those rules that exclusively set out a duty to have liability insurance (ie with no other alternative financial security options)?*

17 Yes. It has also to be noted that the alternative financial security to liability insurance is usually a cash deposit, to provide for liquidity.[20]

---

**18** Cf *L Sólyom*, A polgári jogi felelősség hanyatlása [The decline of civil law liability] (1977) 36f. However, it was also maintained that 'liability insurance protects the victim of the accident at least to the same extent as it protects the tortfeasor' – *G Eörsi*, Összehasonlító polgári jog [Comparative civil law] (1975) 323.

**19** Cf *Zavodnyik* (fn 15) 31 and *P Takáts*, A biztosítás [Insurance], in: F Petrik (ed), Polgári jog – Kommentár a gyakorlat számára [Civil law – A commentary for the practice] (2008) 861.

**20** The cash deposit is proposed as an alternative to professional indemnity insurance in the case of multi-agents and insurance brokers (sec 391 para (6) and sec 403 para (1) Bit) and for traders of natural gas (sec 28 para (3) of Law No XL of 2008). In the case of company liquidators (receivers), a third option would be a bank guarantee (sec 2 para (3) item g) of Government Decree No 114/2006.(V.12.)Korm).

# III. Content of Insurance Cover

*7. Are the duties to take out liability insurance laid down by law only to cover extra-contractual compensation duties or also those arising out of contractual infringements?*

As already mentioned earlier, the wording of the vast majority of legal rules which render liability insurance mandatory are rather vague (see above no 3). Hence, in order to comply with these rules, a general liability insurance policy to cover third-party loss only would suffice, although the actual risk would necessitate covering contractual liability. This is the case when the respective legal rule relates to the duty to take out 'liability insurance' only, without further specification.[21] Should the legal rule in question, however, prescribe 'professional indemnity insurance', the insurance would cover the breach of contract (at least, certain types thereof), in which case, extra-contractual liability is either excluded completely or only restrictively covered. **18**

*8.a) Are there duties to take out liability insurance aimed not only at the protection of absolutely protected rights (eg, property, bodily integrity) but additionally at compensating pure economic loss?*

In the case of a duty to take out professional indemnity insurance, the policy covers pure economic loss, due to the nature of the risk. The wording of such policies usually exclude physical loss. **19**

*b) Are there duties to take out liability insurance that are directed only or at least predominantly at the compensation of pure economic loss?*

See above in no 19. **20**

*9. Are there provisions that require the insurance of a third party's liability interest – for instance, that the employer must take out liability insurance for the benefit of an employee?*

There are no such provisions in force in Hungary, not even for the holder of a vehicle in favour of its driver.[22] **21**

---

**21** Cf fn 10.

**22** The holder of the vehicle does not have to take out insurance protection for the driver since there is no duty in sec 4 para (1) of Law No LXII of 2009 that defines the obligation of the holder

*10. To what extent do the rules requiring the compulsory conclusion of a liability insurance policy also specify the specific contents of the insurance coverage:*

*a) Is there always a (sufficiently well-defined) specification of the risk to be insured?*

22 No. As mentioned earlier (no 3), it is rather an exception that a legal rule provides a description of the risk to be insured.[23] In the majority of cases, the legislator found it sufficient to refer to 'the liability in connection with' the named activity only. By way of exception, the legal rule setting out the duty to take out liability insurance may also contain some details of the cover in the form of laying down minimum standards.[24]

*b) Are there provisions that require unlimited coverage?*

23 No.

*c) If unlimited coverage is not required (see above Question b), is a minimum or maximum insurance sum always specified?*

24 No. The minimum sum insured is specified – either directly by the respective legal rule, or indirectly, via the professional body empowered – only in approx 50% of cases. Moreover these minimum sums are, as specified by statutory law, rather diverse and far from being adequate to the risk created by the profession or the activity in question. To demonstrate this, whereas the minimum sum insured is HUF 1 million (approx € 3,330) for an enforcer of judicial decisions (bailiff) for each loss, it is HUF 5 million (approx € 16,670) for auditors, and HUF 10 million (approx € 33,340) for each loss and HUF 100 million (approx € 333,400) in the annual aggregate of credit brokers, HUF 50 million (approx € 166,700) for public notaries and company liquidators (receivers). Apart from

---

of the vehicle to purchase liability insurance. This is because the holder's strict liability overrules the driver's fault – according to sec 6:535 para (1) of the Civil Code, the subject of the liability for loss caused by hazardous activities is the 'operator' (ie the holder of the vehicle). The fault of the driver could become relevant only if there is a subrogation claim by the insurer against the driver (drunk driving, etc). However, the driver does not have to be insured under the holder's policy.

**23** Cf fns 6, 7 and 9.

**24** Eg sec 391 para (8) and sec 403 para (3) Bit authorise the Government to pass a decree on the minimum requirements of the professional indemnity insurance of multi-agents and insurance brokers, respectively (cf Government Decree No 44/2015.(III.12.)Korm).

the liability insurance for aircraft and airport operators,[25] it may seem that the most dangerous profession is that of an insurance broker or multi-agent: the latter are obliged to maintain professional indemnity cover of € 1,251,000 for each and every loss and € 1,876,000 in the annual aggregate.

*d) Are there general statutory rules to be applicable if the respective law that requires compulsory insurance only makes incomplete stipulations regarding the content of the insurance coverage? An example of this would be § 114 para 1 of the German Insurance Contract Act (Versicherungsvertragsgesetz, VVG) 2008.*

No. **25**

*11. Is it admissible to restrict the insurance cover by agreeing:*

*a) risk exclusion clauses,*

Generally, yes. Legal rules only exceptionally define which risk exclusion **26** clauses are permitted.[26] The general practice of allowing exclusion clauses cannot be criticised as the legislator has seldom sufficient knowledge of insurance markets, hence ruling out standard exclusion clauses could make compliance at least difficult if not impossible. In Hungarian law, insurers are free to define the scope of the risk undertaken, a right limited only by the general principles of civil law. However, to define a risk in such a narrow way that would remove the essence of the institution would be null and void because this would be a breach of the prohibition of the abuse of law.[27]

---

**25** The minimum liability limits required by aircraft operators vary between HUF 50 million (approx € 166,700) and HUF 5 billion (approx € 16,670,000) for each loss, subject to the maximum take-off weight of the aircraft (cf sec 2 para (1) of Government Decree No 39/2001.(III.5.)Korm). Airport operators are obliged to maintain twice the amount of liability limit relating to the largest aircraft which uses the airport (cf sec 3 of the same Government Decree).

**26** Eg Government Decree No 44/2015.(III.12.)Korm on the minimum requirements of the contents of professional indemnity insurance of multi-agents and insurance brokers states an obligation to also cover the liability of employees and subcontractors and, additionally, does not allow the exclusion of lost profits; cf sec 2 para (2) and sec 7.

**27** This principle is regulated in art 1:5 of the new Hungarian Civil Code (Law No V of 2013) which entered into force on 15 March 2014.

*b) deductibles,*

27 Generally, yes. It is only with the professional indemnity insurance of multi-agents and insurance brokers that the respective legal rule provides for the maximum amount of the deductible permitted.[28] Also, in the case of third-party motor liability insurance, there is an interpretation given by the Financial Supervisory Authority (FSA – now a part of the Hungarian National Bank) that deductibles are not permitted.[29]

*c) aggregate limits,*

28 Generally, yes. Rules to define the minimum sum insured, if any, usually relate to the amount to be awarded for each loss (cf above Question 10.c, no 24). Only with the professional indemnity insurance of multi-agents and insurance brokers, further that of credit brokers is a minimum annual aggregate limit also defined.[30]

*d) claims series clauses,*

29 In my opinion,[31] yes.

*e) other clauses?*

30 In my opinion,[32] yes.

*12. What are the consequences if the liability insurance contract concluded in order to fulfil the insurance obligation contravenes what the law stipulates as to contents (see above Questions 10 and 11)?*

31 The consequence of non-compliance of the liability insurance contract with the respective legal rules is, in my opinion[33] the same as if no liability insurance had been concluded: A licence will not be granted or will be withdrawn should the

---

**28** The maximum amount of the deductible may not be higher than HUF 2 million (approx € 6,670) (sec 5 para (2) of Government Decree No 44/2015.(III.12.)Korm).

**29** Cf the decision of the FSA marked JE-II/IB 311/2009 (<www.felugyelet.mnb.hu/hatarozatok>).

**30** Cf above no 24 and fn 15.

**31** There are no debates or statements on the subject.

**32** There are no debates or statements on the subject.

**33** There are no debates or statements on the subject.

licensee fail to show the renewed policy or the certificate of the insurer that the premium has been paid (cf below no 57).

13.a) *Are statutory stipulations as to the contents of the policy (eg, regarding the amount of the insurance sum, the ban on certain risk exclusion clauses, on deductibles, etc, see above Questions 10 and 11) also binding in favour of the insurance holder? Or is it nonetheless possible for the liability insurer and the insurance holder acting within their internal relationship to agree risk exclusion clauses, deductibles, aggregate limits, and claims series clauses, etc (see above Questions 10 and 11), releasing the insurer from its liability to pay?*

Unless the rule of law to render liability insurance compulsory defines the contents of the cover required or some of its aspects,[34] there is nothing in the law to prohibit the parties from negotiating, for example, exorbitant deductibles or exclusion clauses to reduce insurers' liability and thus reduce the premium. However, neither literature nor judicial practice contains references to the existence of such practice. 32

b) *If it is possible for liability insurer and insurance holder acting within their internal relationship to agree a release from the obligation to pay (see above Question a): What consequences does this entail? Must the insurer first pay out to the victim and can then have recourse to the insurance holder? Or is another construction provided for the relationship between insurer, insurance holder and victim?*

According to sec 559 para (2) of the former Hungarian Civil Code (Law No IV of 1959) – a rule also upheld by sec 6:472 para (1) of the new Civil Code (Law No V of 2013) that entered into force on 15 March 2014 – the liability insurer may pay the insurance sum to the victim only. The insured may require payment from the insurer only upon demonstrating that he has already paid the victim himself. A recourse claim by the insurer would only be possible after the payment of the insurer. 33

34 Cf fns 6, 7 and 28.

*14.a) Does your general (voluntary) liability insurance law include a statutory risk exclusion in respect of intentional damage by the insurance holder or the insured person?*

34 Section 559 para (3) of the former Hungarian Civil Code (a semi-mandatory rule) explicitly rendered damage caused intentionally to be covered by the liability insurance, however, with an optional recourse against the insured. The new Civil Code does not repeat this rule. Actually, on the contrary, the rules in the new Civil Code relating to liability insurance allow parties to find an agreement otherwise as regulated by law; hence the insurer could exclude losses which were caused intentionally from the cover. This would, in my opinion,[35] also apply to compulsory liability insurance.[36] Anyhow, if there is no contractual exclusion clause, intentionally caused damage is still covered both in compulsory and non-compulsory liability insurance.

*b) If the general liability insurance law contains a statutory risk exclusion in respect of intentional damage inflicted by the insurance holder (see above Question a): Does this also apply in cases of compulsory liability insurance?*

35 In cases of compulsory liability insurance, the general rules prevail. Third-party motor liability is, however, an exception. Sections 12, 13 and 15 of the respective Law No LXII of 2009 define the scope of the mandatory cover[37] which clearly includes intentionally caused losses.

# IV. Protection Mechanisms

*15. Are insurers obliged to contract when they offer liability insurance policies covering a risk for which the insurance holder is obliged to obtain cover?*

36 Only in the case of third-party motor liability insurance.[38]

---

**35** There are no debates or statements on the subject.

**36** The exception being third-party motor liability insurance, where the rules of Law No LXII of 2009 apply as lex specialis (cf above no 35).

**37** Sec 12 sets out that the insurance covers costs to establish liability as well as justified claims in connection with the operation of the motor vehicle. The limit of the liability of the insurer is HUF 500 million (approx € 1,670,000) for each and every material loss and HUF 1,600 million (approx € 5,340,000) for each and every personal injury (sec 13). Sec 15 lists the risks excluded.

**38** Cf sec 5 para (1) of Law No LXII of 2009.

*16. If there is no obligation to contract: Are there comparable mechanisms provided to ensure that an insurance agreement is concluded?*

No. 37

*17. Is the insurance holder prohibited from disposing over his cover entitlement to the disadvantage of the victim (eg, by surrendering his entitlement)?*

In my opinion, no, as there is no prohibition rule and there has been no discus- 38
sion or statements on the subject matter.

*18. Does the victim enjoy special protection against insolvency on the part of the insurance holder with regard to the sum payable by the liability insurer?*

No. However, according to sec 6:472 para (1) of the Civil Code (Law No V of 39
2013), as a main rule, the insurer may pay out to the victim only (cf above no 33); the insolvency of the insured would not have an effect on the payment of the claim if the insolvency is declared after the claim was filed.

*19.a) In what manner can the victim obtain the insurance payment?*

See above in nos 33 and 39. 40

*b) Does the victim have a direct right of action against the liability insurer (action directe) in the case of voluntary or compulsory liability insurance?*

Only in the case of the third-party motor liability insurance.[39] 41

*20. When settling the claim, is the liability insurer obliged to observe a certain procedure in the interests of the victim? For instance, must it pay the victim an advance within a certain period?*

There is no standard procedure in force to observe, however, depending on the 42
facts, an advance payment is not infrequent. Interestingly, there used to be a general rule in earlier supervisory law that restricted the amount of advance payments to 60% of the calculated net loss in the case of third-party motor liability insurance claims.[40]

---

**39** Cf sec 28 para (1) of Law No LXII of 2009.

**40** Cf sec 96 para (9) of Law No XL of 2003. There is no regulation on the subject now in Bit.

*21.a) In the context of its relationship with the victim, can the liability insurer rely on the fact that vis-à-vis the insurance holder (= damaging party) it is freed from the obligation to pay, eg, due to the insurance holder breaching an obligation of conduct/warranty (Obliegenheitsverletzung) or due to him defaulting on premiums?*

43 Yes.[41] Please note that in the case of third-party motor liability insurance, there is a central compensation fund, created in accordance with European rules (the Fourth Motor Insurance Directive 2000/26/EC as amended by the Directive 2005/14/EC), which will deal with uninsured claims (see secs 35 and 36 of Law No LXII of 2009).

*b) Does the law distinguish on the basis of the ground for the release from the obligation to pay so that in some cases the insurer may not invoke its release from such obligation vis-à-vis the victim?*

44 No.

*c) If the insurer must still pay the victim despite being released from its obligation to pay vis-à-vis the insurance holder (see above Question b), may it take recourse against the latter?*

45 In third-party motor liability insurance, the central compensation fund can take full recourse against the uninsured tortfeasor.[42]

*22.a) Within its relationship to the victim, can the liability insurer invoke the fact that the insurance agreement had already ended by the time relevant in respect of the duty to provide cover?*

46 Yes, with the exception of third-party motor liability insurance (cf above no 43).

*b) If the insurer must pay the victim despite the termination of the insurance agreement by the time relevant for the duty to provide cover (see above Question a), can it take recourse against the insurance holder?*

47 This is only the case in motor liability insurance, cf no 45.

---

41 Cf *Zavodnyik* (fn 15) 184 and *Takáts* (fn 19) 845 and 861.
42 Cf sec 36 para (8) of Law No LXII of 2009.

*23.a) Are there cases in which a damaging party does not effectively conclude the required liability insurance and the victim injured by him nonetheless receives compensation for his loss from a liability insurer or another compensation scheme (eg, a guarantee fund)?*

This is only the case in third-party motor liability insurance, cf no 43. 48

*b) In the event that the policy taken out was not in fact effectively concluded, is it necessary to distinguish on the basis of the ground for this ineffectiveness, eg, whether the reason for the contract not coming into effect was:*

*i) a lack of legal capacity on the part of the insurance holder,*

No. 49

*ii) lack of consent,*

No. 50

*iii) falsa procuratio (unauthorised agency)?*

No. 51

*c) Can the liability insurer (or the alternative compensation scheme) that must provide cover even though the insurance policy was not effectively concluded (see above Questions a and b) have recourse against the damaging party?*

See above no 45. 52

*24.a) Are there cases in which a damaging party does not take out any liability insurance, ie not even an ineffective insurance policy (see above Question 23), and the victim whom he injured is still compensated for his damage by a liability insurer or another compensation scheme (guarantee fund, etc)?*

See above no 43. 53

*b) Can the liability insurer (or the alternative compensation scheme) that must provide cover despite the total absence of any insurance agreement (see above Question a) have recourse against the damaging party?*

See above no 45. 54

*25. Is the victim protected against the insolvency of the liability insurer?*

55 Only in the case of third-party motor insurance liability. Following the bankruptcy of the MAV ABE mutual insurance association, a law retroactively obliged MABISZ (the Hungarian Association of Insurers, handler of the central fund to respond to uninsured claims) to establish funds from which justified claims could be satisfied.[43] This fund is also the source of compensation in eventual future bankruptcies of motor insurers.[44]

*26. Are there rules that serve in particular the protection of the victim when the liability insurance was only concluded voluntarily – ie without it being compulsory?*

56 The same rules apply to both voluntary and compulsory liability insurance, cf above no 33.

# V. Supervision and Sanctions

*27.a) In which cases must the insurance holder prove to an authority before commencing an activity requiring insurance that he has taken out the respective prescribed liability insurance cover (see above Question 4.e)?*

57 Demonstration of, at least, the availability of insurance cover to the respective authority is a prerequisite of commencing activities requiring liability insurance. This follows from the wording of the respective legal acts rendering liability insurance mandatory in the case of certain professions (cf above no 3). In practice, although not foreseen by any legal provision, the minimum requirement is a letter of intent from an insurer stating that liability insurance cover will be provided immediately from the date the licence is issued.

*b) Must the insurer inform an authority when liability insurance taken out to meet an insurance obligation ends?*

58 It is a general rule, introduced by sec 129 para (3) Bit, that insurers shall inform the supervisory authorities in charge of the insured about the termination of

---

43 Cf sec 1 para (1) of Law No CLXII of 2012.

44 Cf sec 29 para (3) of Law No LII of 2009, as amended by sec 169 para (5) item i) of Law No CCLII of 2013.

their compulsory liability insurance. In the case of third-party motor liability insurance, there is a central register of insurance policies. Insurers are obliged to inform this register about the termination of the insurance contract.[45] In addition, this register has to be compared with the official register of motor vehicles on a quarterly basis and information about any uninsured vehicle has to be forwarded by the Ministry of the Interior, keeper of the register of motor vehicles, to the municipality according to the place of residence of the operator of the vehicle.[46]

c) *Is the insurer also under a duty to inform when a liability insurance agreement is in existence but it has no duty to provide cover – eg, due to defaults on premium payments?*

Generally, not. However, in compulsory third-party motor liability insurance, **59**
non-payment of premiums leads to the automatic termination of the contract after 60 days from the due date – hence the situation is similar to cancellation or non-renewal.[47] This leads to the insurer's duty to inform the register (above no 58).

d) *What are the consequences when the duties to inform of the end of contract or the release from payment obligations (see above Questions b and c) are violated?*

There are, however, no specific sanctions foreseen either in Law No LXII of 2009 **60**
on MTPL, or elsewhere against the insurer for a failure to inform the authorities. However, the Hungarian National Bank, in its capacity as the supervisory authority of insurers, may impose fines if serial failures of such kind have occurred and this information will be disclosed in the course of a regular supervisory review.

28. *Is there some official body (authority, professional chamber) where an injured party can find out whether and where the injuring party who inflicted damage upon him in the course of an activity requiring insurance has liability insurance?*

Such a possibility exists in the case of third-party motor liability insurance only. **61**
At the request of the victim, the Information Centre to be organised by motor in-

**45** Cf sec 49 of Law No LXII of 2009.
**46** Cf secs 45 para (2) and 48 of Law No LXII of 2009.
**47** Cf sec 21 para (4) of Law No LXII of 2009.

surers will provide the name and the contact data of the liability insurer of the tortfeasor, the policy number, the name and the contact data of the claims management agent of the liability insurer as well as the name and the address of the operator of the vehicle (in this respect only if the victim has a just interest in obtaining this information).[48]

*29. Are there (public law) sanctions against the party who was required to take out insurance if such does not take out the compulsory liability insurance? Examples of this would be a ban on carrying out the activity that requires the insurance or the imposition of an administrative or judicial penalty.*

62 As mentioned earlier (cf above no 57), there is a ban on carrying out the respective activity if compulsory liability insurance is not taken out. However, there would be no administrative or judicial penalty charged. In the case of third-party motor liability insurance, the municipality shall call upon the operator without delay to demonstrate the existence of liability insurance cover. Should the operator fail to do so, the licence of the car shall be withdrawn within eight days of the notice.[49] Moreover, the uninsured operator – in addition to its duty to make recourse payments to the central compensation fund (cf above no 45) – shall retroactively pay the premiums to the central fund via the liability insurer for the uninsured period in accordance with the official uniform tariff, which is significantly higher than insurers' individual tariffs.[50]

# VI. Statutory Provisions required by the Constitution or the European Convention on Human Rights (ECHR)

*30. What has been said regarding the compatibility of the duties to take out liability insurance with your country's constitution and the ECHR? Please take into account case law and academic literature.*

63 Neither case law nor academic literature exists on this question.

---

**48** Cf sec 54 para (2) of Law No LXII of 2009.
**49** Sec 45 para (3) of Law No LXII of 2009.
**50** Cf sec 22 of Law No LXII of 2009.

*31. Does the constitution or the ECHR make any stipulations regarding the contents of such duties to take out liability insurance? Please take into account case law and academic literature.*

Neither case law nor academic literature exists on this question. 64

# VII. Reform Efforts

*32. Are there efforts towards reforming the law regarding compulsory liability insurance?*

No such efforts are in place. 65

# VIII. Compulsory Liability Insurance and Liability Law

*33. Is, at the legislative level, any connection discernible between the nature of liability (in particular in the case of strict liability) and the imposition of compulsory liability insurance?*

No, since there are many cases of strict liability established by judicial practice 66
which are not linked to compulsory liability insurance. In general, these are either cases where machines, explosives, etc are involved or where an activity might become dangerous because of a lack of technology (eg digging tracks, wells).[51] Moreover, as a matter of interest, Hungarian civil law does not foresee liability of minors depending on the existence of liability insurance cover.

**51** To elaborate this topic in more detail would go beyond the scope of this study. For the most recent review of the judicial practice cf *P Havasi*, Felelősség szerződésen kívül okozott kárért [Tort liability], in: F Petrik/G Wellmann (eds), Az új Ptk. magyarázata [A commentary to the new Civil Code], vol VI (2013) 462ff.

Diana Cerini

# Compulsory Liability Insurance in Italy

## I. The Term Compulsory Liability Insurance

1. *Indicate the rules within your legal system that set out a duty to take out liability insurance. In this context, also take into account the implementation of international treaties (eg, the International Convention on Civil Liability for Bunker Oil Pollution Damage, 2001).*

1 Notwithstanding the relatively limited economic importance of the sector in term of aggregate premiums collected and intermediated, if compared to other branches of insurance (especially the life insurance sector), there is no doubt that liability insurance has an extremely relevant impact on the insured parties, such as enterprises, professionals as well as consumers who require a liability insurance contract. In fact, when liability insurance coverage exists, the insured can better plan their future economic duties and, consequently, they can realise a better management of the risk.

2 Equally, the existence of the insurance coverage is essential in the light of the protection of victims in order to ensure recovery in the case of insolvency or inability of the liable party to pay (see on this point no 33 below under Question 5). In fact, the scope and importance of liability insurance are clearly evident also in respect to third parties: liability insurance gives victims some comfort where the policy is triggered, as a corollary to its other function, ie to protect the insured policyholder. This is reversed when we talk about mandatory liability insurance, where the main function of insurance is to protect the victim.[1]

3 In addition to economic considerations, one also has to focus on the social impact of liability insurance spread all over the EU and the national market.

4 It is, in fact, common perception that the existence of liability insurance coverage plays an essential role in order to facilitate exchanges between the economic players of the EU.

5 For these reasons, in Italy the number of types of compulsory liability insurance is constantly growing. Even if there is not a 'law of liability insurance' (see no 10 below under Question 2), many rules establish the duty to require liability insurance for individuals and legal entities.[2]

---

1 See *AD Candian*, Responsabilità civile e assicurazione (1995) esp ch 1, passim.

2 See *D Cerini/A Memola*, Annex: Rules on Compulsory Liability Insurance in Italy (at the end of this book).

6 Some of these rules are to be found in the Code of Private Insurance (*Codice delle Assicurazione Private*, CAP – Legislative Decree no 209 of 2006). This text actually reunites the majority of the legal rules concerning insurance in Italy.

7 Nevertheless, the CAP does not include all the rules on mandatory liability insurance. In fact, in the majority of cases, rules establishing the duty to be insured against liability risks are to be found in numerous other special laws (please consider that in the Italian legal system, the term 'special law' refers to any law other than the Civil Code – herein also referred to as 'CC').

8 The list of the existing compulsory liability insurance is long, even if not as extensive as in other legal systems. A comprehensive list is provided in the Annex: Rules on Compulsory Liability Insurance in Italy (at the end of this book), as it is privately collected by the Italian Association of Insurance Companies (*Associazione Nazionale fra le Imprese Assicuratrici*, ANIA).[3] However, even the said list, nevertheless, does not include other forms of compulsory insurance that can be required at a regional level as a database or unique source does not exist.

9 In order to better understand the types of situations in which compulsory insurance is required, one can say that the duty to be insured may arise in the case of the exercise of specific activities as natural persons, as well as activities as legal entities (companies, associations, foundations, non-profit organisations). The involved businesses are quite varied. They may in fact include the exercise of many professional activities (insurance intermediaries and other operators of financial services), as well as the exercise of some dangerous activities, even those carried out by consumers (eg operating a motor vehicle, sport hunting, etc[4]).

*2. Is there a coherent 'law of compulsory liability insurance' in your legal system?*

10 In Italy, the idea of a '*law of compulsory liability insurance*', intended as a set of coherent or systematic rules in this area, does not exist.[5] In fact, not only does a law of compulsory liability insurance not exist, it is even impossible to talk about 'a *law of liability insurance*' in general (both compulsory and non-compulsory).

---

3 The list in the Annex is prepared according to the private collection of laws complied by ANIA. A public exhaustive list of compulsory insurance is not available. See <www.ania.it>.

4 For a complete list, see *Cerini/Memola*, Annex: Italy (fn 2).

5 *G Volpe Putzolu*, Le assicurazioni. Produzione e distribuzione (1995).

Actually, there is only one rule that expressly refers to liability insurance in general, and this rule is included in the Civil Code, in art 1917 CC (see following remarks). A number of specific rules exist with reference to some types of compulsory insurance and they are included either in the Code of Private Insurance or in special laws.[6] 11

The contract of liability insurance is consequently subject to all laws concerning the insurance contract in general (art 1882ff CC) plus the special rule of art 1917 CC specifically dedicated to liability insurance. This last rule can, nevertheless, be derogated by specific rules on certain types of compulsory liability insurance. 12

As said, the general rule dedicated to liability insurance is art 1917 of the Civil Code. The first paragraph of art 1917 CC defines the liability insurance contract as follows: '*In liability insurance the insurer is obliged to indemnify the insured for damages which he is obliged to pay because of events which occurred during the insured period and resulting in the liability covered by the insurance contract. Damages deriving from fraudulent acts are excluded*' (art 1917 para 1 CC). From a contractual point of view, liability insurance is a typical (or nominated) contract within the perimeter of the 'insurance contract', as such subject to the general rules contained in art 1882ff CC concerning insurance; the definition of insurance provided by art 1882 CC is as follows: '*A contract whereby one party, the insurer, on the payment of premium, binds himself to compensate the insured, within the limit agreed upon, for damages caused to the insured by an accident, or to pay a principal sum or annuity upon the occurrence of an event concerning human life*'. As is clear from the quotation, art 1882 CC distinguishes between life insurance and insurance against damages (in EU legislation, the term 'non-life insurance' is preferred to 'damages insurance', even if in practice they cover the same contracts): liability insurance is to be considered part of insurance against damages.[7] This clarification is not merely theoretical as it indicates that the rules provided by the Civil Code for non-life contracts are applicable to liability insurance, in addition to the special provision set by art 1917 CC. 13

Whenever compulsory insurance exists, the risk covered by each single contract is connected with the legal bases of the liability in question. In fact, policies offered and sold on the Italian market generally provide that the insured is covered in respect of sums he/she is legally liable to pay according to the law. There is no general limitation to a source of liability: in fact, the liability can be 14

---

6 See *Cerini/Memola*, Annex: Italy (fn 2).

7 See again *Candian* (fn 1) 87ff; *M Rossetti*, Commento Art 1932 c.c., in: Le assicurazioni. L'assicurazione nei codici. Le assicurazioni obbligatorie (2007) 389.

assessed according to *tort law* as well as *contractual liability*;[8] also cf the answer to Question 7.

15 A liability insurance contract does not cover risks that the insured has voluntarily assumed towards third parties or in the case of fault or fraud (*dolus directus* or *eventualis*). In addition, the limits of the covered risk relate to the insured person(s) as identified in the contract and to the kind of activities performed by the insured.

16 Further limits are set in the policies with reference to the types of damage recoverable. The coverage in general is limited to physical damage or damage to property, with exclusions for pure economic losses or damage for interruption of activity.

3. *Is there a specific term for compulsory liability insurance in your legal system? How is it defined?*

17 No, there is no definition or specific term for compulsory liability insurance. The relevant translation is *assicurazione obbligatoria.*

4. *In which of the following cases does compulsory liability insurance apply according to prevailing opinion?*

a) *Duties to take out liability insurance which are not directly based on the law but on an order or decision issued by administrative authorities?*

18 In the absence of a law provision, there is a common perception that an authority cannot impose a duty to take out liability insurance. In other words, a provision by law is necessary, while the 'sub-legal' source (ie a regulation by any administrative authority or other public entity) may only introduce specific requirements of the insurance coverage.[9] For example, Law 247/2012 has introduced mandatory insurance for all professional activities, including those of lawyers (see below no 23). The Code or Regulation to be introduced by the Bar Association will add specific requirements to the said insurance, as will also be the case for other involved professions according to their professional bodies.

19 When making reference to the 'law', both national laws and regional laws are included.

---

**8** See *D Cerini*, L'assicurazione della responsabilità civile da prodotti, in: D Cerini/V Gorla, Il danno da prodotto. Regole, responsabilità, assicurazione (2011) 231 ff.

**9** See *F de Strobel*/*V Ogliari*, L'assicurazione di responsabilità civile e il nuovo codice delle assicurazioni private (6th edn 2008) ch 1.

Where multiple solutions are provided (ie insurance and other financial guarantees), an administrative authority may in addition decide which form is the preferred one, but even in this case we can say that the law remains the main reference. 20

*b) Duties to take out liability insurance that are not based directly on the law but on the statutes of a professional or other self-governing body?*

The requirement of liability insurance coverage may be necessary for those registered or governed by a professional self-governing body. 21

The body may require liability insurance as an element for participation in the body. Nevertheless, in the absence of a provision by law, the non-performance cannot result in the impossibility to exercise a profession, which is a constitutionally granted right protected under art 41 of the Italian Constitution. 22

An interesting example on the said matter is the case of professional liability insurance for lawyers. In fact, until 2012, the professional liability insurance for lawyers had been completely voluntary even if mentioned by the Code of Conduct (see below no 25). In 2012, Law 247/2012, concerning many aspects of the regulation of the legal profession, was approved;[10] it entered into force on 2 February 2013. Article 12 of the Law 247/2012 provides for mandatory insurance for professional liability and for accidents[11] (the same duty was introduced by the same Law for other professions, for example: engineers, architects, medical professionals, and so on). The duty to take out insurance for lawyers 23

---

**10** See Official Journal (OJ) 18.1.2012.

**11** Here is the full text in Italian: Law 247/2012, Art 12: '1. L'avvocato, l'associazione o la società fra professionisti devono stipulare, autonomamente o anche per il tramite di convenzioni sottoscritte dal CNF, da ordini territoriali, associazioni ed enti previdenziali forensi, polizza assicurativa a copertura della responsabilità civile derivante dall'esercizio della professione, compresa quella per la custodia di documenti, somme di denaro, titoli e valori ricevuti in deposito dai clienti. L'avvocato rende noti al cliente gli estremi della propria polizza assicurativa.
2. All'avvocato, all'associazione o alla società tra professionisti è fatto obbligo di stipulare, anche per il tramite delle associazioni e degli enti previdenziali forensi, apposita polizza a copertura degli infortuni derivanti a sé e ai propri collaboratori, dipendenti e praticanti in conseguenza dell'attività svolta nell'esercizio della professione anche fuori dei locali dello studio legale, anche in qualità di sostituto o di collaboratore esterno occasionale.
3. Degli estremi delle polizze assicurative e di ogni loro successiva variazione è data comunicazione al consiglio dell'ordine.
4. La mancata osservanza delle disposizioni previste nel presente articolo costituisce illecito disciplinare.
5. Le condizioni essenziali e i massimali minimi delle polizze sono stabiliti e aggiornati ogni cinque anni dal Ministro della giustizia, sentito il CNF.'

was then postponed until August 2013; even now, in order to be effective, the duty to be insured requires a delegated regulation by the Italian Government, which is in fact still missing. Many lawyers still do not have an insurance contract, and the Bar does not sanction this, not even with disciplinary sanctions.[12]

24 Apart from this duty set by the Law in 2012, we might recall that references to insurance for professional liability are found in the Ethical Code of Conduct for lawyers, as approved by the *Consiglio Nazionale Forense* (ie the National Legal Council)[13] and these have been in force for years. In particular, art 17-bis referring to the information to be given to the client, mentions the duty to inform about the existence of professional liability insurance, here implicitly recognising the (ethical) duty to have such insurance. This was not required, nevertheless, as an element for the registration to the Bar in the absence of a provision by law. The said provision set by art 17-bis of the Code of Conduct was inspired by the Code of Conduct for European Lawyers, as adopted by the Council of Bars and Law Societies of Europe (CCBE) in Brussels in November 1985 and then amended, on the need for all lawyers in the Community to be insured against the risks arising from professional negligence claims against them.[14]

---

**12** The power of the Bar to sanction associates is provided by Law 247/2012 at arts 50–63.

**13** Codice deontologico forense (Code of conduct for lawyers) art 17-bis – Modalità dell'informazione: 'L'avvocato che intende dare informazione sulla propria attività professionale deve indicare: ... gli estremi della polizza assicurativa per la responsabilità professionale; ....' The National Legal Council is an independent body that regulates the legal profession.

**14** It is also important to consider art 2.4 (Respect for the Rules of Other Bars and Law Societies): 'When practising cross-border, a lawyer from another Member State may be bound to comply with the professional rules of the host Member State. Lawyers have a duty to inform themselves as to the rules that will affect them in the performance of any particular activity. Member organisations of the CCBE are obliged to deposit their codes of conduct at the Secretariat of the CCBE so that any lawyer can get hold of the copy of the current code from the Secretariat.'

Article 6.3 of the Lawyers Services Directive 98/5/EC of 16 February 1998 (OJ L 77, 14.3.1998, 36–43) contains the provisions with regard to the rules to be observed by a lawyer from one Member State providing services on an occasional or temporary basis in another Member State by virtue of art 49 of the consolidated EC treaty, as follows: 'The host Member State may require a lawyer practising under his home-country professional title either to take out professional indemnity insurance or to become a member of a professional guarantee fund in accordance with the rules which that State lays down for professional activities pursued in its territory. Nevertheless, a lawyer practising under his home-country professional title shall be exempted from that requirement if he can prove that he is covered by insurance taken out or a guarantee provided in accordance with the rules of his home Member State, insofar as such insurance or guarantee is equivalent in terms of the conditions and extent of cover. Where the equivalence is only partial, the competent authority in the host Member State may require that additional insurance or an additional guarantee be contracted to cover the elements which are not already

Notwithstanding the aforementioned rules, the lack of a duty by law to be insured (as Law 247/2012 is still not enforceable) could not result, until 2012–2013, in the impossibility to exercise the legal profession, but it could only result in a disciplinary sanction (even that, never applied). 25

*c) Duties to take out liability insurance that are not based on any public law but on a private law provision (eg, governing the relationship between employer and employee)?*

The mentioned situation may only be relevant as concerns the relation between the parties of a contract and the eventual non-compliance, according to the general rule of art 1372 CC, which provides that the contract is the law of the parties. 26

This is sometimes the case for land lease contracts, where the contract may provide for the duty of the tenant to take out insurance for all risks connected to the property, including liability coverage of the lessee for damage to the property. 27

The consequence of the violation of such duty to be insured has to be evaluated on the ground of contractual liability. 28

*d) Duties to take out liability insurance that are not based on any public law but on a private law rule that is established by case law (and, eg, governs the relationship between employer and employee)?*

No. We do not have examples of case law introducing a duty to be insured; if ever such a solution were to be adopted, the legitimacy of such a judge-made duty would be quite doubtful as the source of the duty to be insured can only be the law of the contract (which is the 'private law' between the parties, as set by art 1372 CC). 29

*e) Cases in which there is no duty to take out liability insurance but liability insurance cover is a prerequisite for the admissibility of carrying out a particular activity?*

The situation where, in order to exercise an activity, you have to be insured, is quite common. Nevertheless, as anticipated above in no 18, the duty to be in- 30

---

covered by the insurance or guarantee contracted in accordance with the rules of the home Member State.'

sured must be provided by law, or by the relevant professional body but only where the law allows it or delegates the professional body to regulate that duty.

f) *Cases of alternative financial security, in which the duty to provide for financial security may be fulfilled either by taking out liability insurance or other forms of financial security (eg, bank guarantees)?*

31 This is the case for the exercise of some specific activities, in particular in the transport sector. In other cases, the duty to be insured remains valid even if the existence of financial security is provided (see, for example, duties for insurance intermediaries, in particular agents and brokers registered under letter a) and b) of the Register of Insurance Intermediaries, as required by art 109ff of CAP).

g) *Cases in which the duty to have insurance has only been created by a contractual agreement between potential injuring party and victim?*

32 This may be the case in land lease contracts as well as in construction contracts. In these cases, the contractor might be required to have specific coverage, including liability insurance. Once again, even if such a duty exists, we do not refer to it as a 'compulsory liability regime'.

## II. Aims

5. *What are the aims of the rules that impose an obligation to take out liability insurance:*

a) *the protection of the victim,*

33 The protection of the victim is generally the main aim of compulsory liability insurance.[15]

b) *the protection of the insurance holder,*

34 The protection of the insurance holder, and of his/her assets in particular, is mainly a contractual matter, not essentially the primary goal of the law. In fact, this is proven by the fact that in many cases insurance is assumed on a volun-

15 See *M Rossetti*, Il diritto delle assicurazioni. Vol III. Le assicurazioni di responsabilità civile (2011) 6ff.

tary basis; on the contrary, when insurance is compulsory, the goal is essentially to protect the victim, especially with reference to possible victims of activities in 'sensitive' fields, such as the medical profession, motor accidents, etc. Nevertheless, the fact that the perspective of the insurance holder is also considered as relevant by the legislators and policymakers is, in our view, proven by the fact that mandatory rules are provided in order to protect the potential liable party in his/her role of insurance holder. In this sense, the idea that the insurance holder may be a 'weak party' is applied not only to consumers (for them, specific rules of the Code of Consumers are provided, even if not specifically for insurance) but to all insured parties, even if they have the legal status of legal persons or professionals.

*c) the protection of the victim and the insurance holder,*

As anticipated above in nos 33–34, all forms of compulsory insurance have a double-faced scope. 35

From one side, they protect the insured against costs for liability that can threaten his/her assets. 36

On the other side, they protect the victim of the insured event against the risk of the insolvency of the liable party. The existence of compulsory liability insurance also reduces (or should reduce) conflicts in order to provide more 'automatic recovery' for the victim. 37

Public policy therefore requires that, in certain situations, individuals should provide insurance so that, if they cause loss or damage to another, the injured will be compensated. 38

*d) other aims, eg internalising the costs in the interests of society?*

In addition, for society as a whole, compulsory insurance can protect the state against the duty to compensate those who suffer severe damage and who would otherwise need public care by the health system, as well as by public insurers. The risk is, in part, transferred to private insurers. 39

6. *Do the rules that prescribe a form of alternative financial security (see above Question 4.f) pursue the same aims as those rules that exclusively set out a duty to have liability insurance (ie with no other alternative financial security options)?*

Not completely. In fact, the existence of a financial security may improve the legal action and consequent recovery against the liable party. The existence of li- 40 ability insurance adds the existence of another professional subject who can be involved in the recovery.

## III. Content of Insurance Cover

*7. Are the duties to take out liability insurance laid down by law only to cover extra-contractual compensation duties or also those arising out of contractual infringements?*

41 In Italy, compulsory liability insurance does not make a distinction according to the source of the liability. The risk covered by each single contract is strictly connected with the legal bases of the liability in question, whether liability in torts or contractual liability. This is the case for all types of insurance (for a list, see the Annex at the end of this book). In fact, policies available on the Italian market generally provide that the insured is covered in respect of sums he/she is legally liable to pay, without mention of the source of that liability (which could be qualified as liability in tort as well as contractual liability).

42 Further, the liability insurance contract does not cover risks that the insured has voluntarily assumed towards third parties.

43 In addition, the limits of the covered risk relate to the insured person(s) as identified in the contract and to the kind of activities performed by the insured.

44 Further limits are set in the policies with reference to the types of recoverable damage. The coverage is often limited to physical damage or damage to property, with exclusions for pure economic losses or damage due to interruptions of activity. These types of damage can be the object of additional coverage (see below Questions 8.a and 8.b).

*8.a) Are there duties to take out liability insurance aimed not only at the protection of absolutely protected rights (eg, property, bodily integrity) but additionally at compensating pure economic loss?*

45 First of all, one should clarify the meaning of pure economic loss.

46 In the majority of cases the law does not limit the types of recoverable damage. In practical terms, pure economic loss is often excluded by a contract covering damage to persons or material things. Besides, it is true that many insurance contracts cover pure economic loss (see below under Question 8.b).

*b) Are there duties to take out liability insurance that are directed only or at least predominantly at the compensation of pure economic loss?*

Yes, there are examples of such liability insurance contracts. One important example is the coverage for insurance intermediaries as set by arts 110 para 3 and 112 para 3 CAP. 47

*9. Are there provisions that require the insurance of a third party's liability interest – for instance, that the employer must take out liability insurance for the benefit of an employee?*

Yes, this is in fact the case for many employment contracts, where the duty to stipulate a duty to take out insurance for the benefit of employees may be set by syndicate agreements or other contractual agreements. In more specific cases, the law requires that the contract of insurance makes a specific reference to the insured subjects other than the policyholder. This is, for example, the case for insurance intermediaries where the compulsory insurance must cover the liability directly assumed by the insured intermediary and the liability of the subsidiaries of the insurance intermediaries, as provided by arts 110 para 3 and 112 para 3 of the Code of Private Insurance. 48

*10. To what extent do the rules requiring the compulsory conclusion of a liability insurance policy also specify the specific contents of the insurance coverage:*

*a) Is there always a (sufficiently well-defined) specification of the risk to be insured?*

In many cases the duty to have insurance is also accompanied by a duty to include specific content in the coverage. 49

For example, in the case of motor liability insurance, governed by the CAP, the covered risk, as well as the possible exclusions of the coverage, are identified in detail by the law itself and the parties have limited power to modify these pre-identified elements:[16] For example, they can increase the maximum insured sum or add specific additional coverage whereas the CAP identifies the (minimum) recoverable damage (art 122), the persons who have to be insured, the territorial extension of the coverage, etc. 50

**16** See Code of Private Insurance, Titolo X, arts 122–143, esp arts 122, 128, 129.

51 In other cases, the law only imposes the duty to be insured upon the possible liable party and it identifies the minimum level of protection to be granted. This is, for example, the case of insurance for hunting accidents as provided by Law 11 February 1992 no 157.[17]

52 In some other cases, the provisions of law are even more superficial as they only provide for the duty to be insured, but the characteristics of the risk to be covered or the content and the perimeter of the coverage are not well defined.

*b) Are there provisions that require unlimited coverage?*

53 No, in general the duty to have liability insurance provides for a minimum coverage in absolute value or, possibly, the law sets the parameters in order to set the minimum coverage (cf below no 54). In Italy there are no duties to have unlimited coverage (not even for liability insurance).

*c) If unlimited coverage is not required (see above Question b), is a minimum or maximum insurance sum always specified?*

54 Not always. In fact, this is the case for motor liability insurance, where the CAP as well as some regulation specify the minimum limit of the coverage.[18] In other cases, the law only provides for the duty to be insured without indicating the

---

**17** Law 11 February 1992 no 157, OJ 25 February 1992, no 46; see also *Cerini/Memola*, Annex: Italy (fn 2).

**18** See art 128 CAP (Minimum amounts of cover): '1. The obligation to take out insurance against civil liability in respect of the use of motor vehicles and boats shall be regarded as fulfilled when the contract is taken out for amounts not lower than the following:
a) in the case of personal injury, a minimum amount of cover equal to 5,000,000 euros per claim, regardless of the number of victims;
b) in case of material damage, a minimum amount of cover equal to 1,000,000 euros per claim, regardless of the number of victims.
2. Compulsory insurance contracts against civil liability in respect of the use of motor vehicles and boats must be made compliant with the compulsory minimum amounts of cover for personal injury or material damage referred to in paragraph 1 before 11 June 2012.
3. Every five years from the date of 11 June 2012 referred to in paragraph 2, the amounts referred to in paragraph 1 shall be automatically indexed to the percentage shown by the European index of consumer prices (EICP) envisaged by Council Regulation (EC) N. 2494/95 of 23 October 1995 concerning harmonized indices of consumer prices. The increase shall be rounded up to a multiple of 10,000 euros.
4. The adjustment referred to in paragraph 3 shall be established by a measure taken by the Ministry of Economic Development to be published in the Italian Official Journal.
5. As at 11 December 2009 the minimum amounts must be equal to at least half of the amounts of cover referred to in paragraph 1.'

minimum insurance sum. This fact is quite peculiar, as the effectiveness of the coverage, in the interest of the damaged party, cannot be assured.

*d) Are there general statutory rules to be applicable if the respective law that requires compulsory insurance only makes incomplete stipulations regarding the content of the insurance coverage? An example of this would be § 114 para 1 of the German Insurance Contract Act (Versicherungsvertragsgesetz, VVG) 2008.*

No. One has to make reference to specific rules or regulations setting the duties 55
in order to be duly informed; if not, the parties are free to decide on the details of the contract.

*11. Is it admissible to restrict the insurance cover by agreeing:*

*a) risk exclusion clauses,*

In general, it is possible to have restrictions to the compulsory coverage, if not 56
prohibited by the law. This is always possible in voluntary liability coverage, as well as in many forms of compulsory insurance where there is not a complete and detailed description of the duty to be insured. For all the previous cases, one should, nevertheless, consider that, where exclusions or limitations of coverage are set, they can be opposed by the victim only if the general requirement of the insurance is respected. In other words, the said exclusions or limits to the coverage are valid only if they do not frustrate the duty to be insured and, respectively, the existence of comprehensive coverage. The evaluation of such principles is not always easy to assess.

*b) deductibles*

Yes, in the light of what has been said above no 56. For example, it would be 57
possible in the case of motor liability insurance (art 128 CAP)[19] to conclude a liability insurance contract with a deductible of € 10,000.

*c) aggregate limits*

Yes, in the light of what has been said above no 56. It should be clarified that 58
the contractual limits cannot be opposed to the victim in motor liability insur-

**19** See the previous fn.

ance as provided by art 144 para 2 CAP (see above no 50), but they represent a valid cause for recourse after payment towards the insured.

### d) *claims series clauses*

59 Yes, in the light of what has been said above no 56.

### e) *other clauses?*

60 Yes, in the light of what has been said above no 56.

61 The different 'triggers' for the liability insurance are of significance, ie whether the trigger for the coverage is on a *claims made clause* or an *occurrence based clause*, with all the consequences referring to the choice of one or the other model. Other triggers may also be considered including: causation, acts committed and manifestation, although these may be interpreted differently by the local courts. There can also be large variations in the wording of 'claims made' where some will be very restrictive, which can explain why claims made policies have attracted criticism from some courts.[20] This is especially true in contracts concluded between professionals and businessmen (so-called B2B contracts); the connection and interferences between the content of the coverage, especially with reference to minimum amount, and the substantial risk; the expertise and relation with liability regimes to be understood and known by the insurers.

62 'Triggers' are both an aspect of the insurance contract law solution and practice in local markets which can reflect historical developments in that market. With reference to Italy, one might say that the claims made clause is valid, but its validity is subject to the respect of the rules on unfair contract terms as provided by art 1341 CC.[21]

63 In some cases, compulsory liability insurance also requires a claims made clause by law, plus additional coverage for the period after the expiry of the insurance contract.

---

**20** See eg Court of Cassation, no 562/05, where the Court ruled that '*a claims made clause is valid but it requires a specific and written approval from the policyholder*'; in other cases courts, even after this decision in 2005, have ruled that the clause is void (see eg some local courts decisions, as Tribunale [Trib] Rome, no 17197/07); more recently, the majority of courts seem to consider the claims made clause as valid, but following the Court of Cassation rule they require a specific approval; in addition, it has been ruled that the application of the claims made clause has to be extended in time unless until the right of the victim is not barred by a prescription limit (see Trib Milan no 3527/10).

**21** See *D Cerini*, Italy, in: HA Cousy (ed), International Encyclopedia of Laws: Insurance Law (2014) §§ 331–333.

12. *What are the consequences if the liability insurance contract concluded in order to fulfil the insurance obligation contravenes what the law stipulates as to contents (see above Questions 10 and 11)?*

In some cases, clauses that contravene what the law stipulates are void, in other cases they are substituted by law provisions. There are also cases in which the stipulation of an insurance coverage not compliant with the legal requirements can be sanctioned. 64

13.a) *Are statutory stipulations as to the contents of the policy (eg, regarding the amount of the insurance sum, the ban on certain risk exclusion clauses, on deductibles, etc, see above Questions 10 and 11) also binding in favour of the insurance holder? Or is it nonetheless possible for the liability insurer and the insurance holder acting within their internal relationship to agree risk exclusion clauses, deductibles, aggregate limits, and claims series clauses, etc (see above Questions 10 and 11), releasing the insurer from its liability to pay?*

The law reference is to the insurance coverage, so the parties are bound to the provisions even in their internal relationship. 65

When dealing with compulsory liability insurance, the parties cannot agree on a complete release of the insurer, otherwise it would frustrate the duty to be insured. For this reason, the law in many cases provides for specific characteristics of the coverage. When such a description is not given, the contract cannot frustrate the aim of the policy and of the duty to be insured (see above no 63). A univocal answer is impossible as one has to refer to the different types of insurance involved. 66

b) *If it is possible for liability insurer and insurance holder acting within their internal relationship to agree a release from the obligation to pay (see above Question a): What consequences does this entail? Must the insurer first pay out to the victim and can then have recourse to the insurance holder? Or is another construction provided for the relationship between insurer, insurance holder and victim?*

Cf above the answer to Question 13.a, no 65f. 67

*14.a) Does your general (voluntary) liability insurance law include a statutory risk exclusion in respect of intentional damage by the insurance holder or the insured person?*

68 According to art 1900 CC, all types of non-life insurance contracts do not cover risk in the case of intentional damage provoked by the insured, as well as in the case of gross negligence of the insured. According to the same provision, while the exclusion of gross negligence can be derogated by the parties, this is impossible for intentional or fraudulent accidents.

69 In the field of liability insurance, the impossibility to cover intentional damage is confirmed by art 1917 para 1 CC, which expressly provides that intentional damage is not covered [by the liability insurance contract].

The exclusion of coverage in the case of *dolus* of the insured, which is confirmed for mandatory insurance in compliance with art 1917 CC, does not always mean that the insurer is not required to pay the victim in the first instance, as he/she may be required to do so by law, with the possibility to file a recourse claim against the liable party. This situation arises in motor liability insurance, where the *dolus* of the insured exception cannot be opposed to the victim, as can be assumed by art 144 para 2 CAP according to which: '*In relation to the insured amounts, the insurance undertaking shall neither raise any objections deriving from the contract nor envisage any clauses providing for the policyholder's contribution to damage. Nonetheless the insurance undertaking shall have a right of recourse against the policyholder to the extent to which it would have been entitled, by contract, to refuse or reduce its insurance benefit.*' According to the legal doctrine as well as the case law, the rule stated in art 144 para 2 also applies in the case of intentional damage.[22]

*b) If the general liability insurance law contains a statutory risk exclusion in respect of intentional damage inflicted by the insurance holder (see above Question a): Does this also apply in cases of compulsory liability insurance?*

70 As anticipated (see no 68 above the answer to Question 14.a), the exclusion of coverage in the case of intentional damage inflicted by the insurance holder generally applies to all liability insurance, whether voluntary or mandatory.

71 In limited situations, even if the coverage of intentional or fraudulent activities is not covered, there might be cases in which the insurer has to pay in favour of the victim, with a possibility to file a recourse claim against the liable

22 See *M Franzoni*, Il terzo danneggiato nell'assicurazione obbligatoria della responsabilità civile (1987) 18 ff.

party including the insured. In other words, the *dolus* exception cannot be opposed to the victim. It is said that the duty towards the damaged party derives from the law, not from the insurance contract. One relevant case where the exclusion of coverage for intentional damage cannot be opposed to the victim is that of motor liability insurance, as already described above.

# IV. Protection Mechanisms

*15. Are insurers obliged to contract when they offer liability insurance policies covering a risk for which the insurance holder is obliged to obtain cover?*

Only for motor liability insurance. The duty is stated in art 132 CAP (and was already provided by Law 990/1969, now included in the Code). 72

The text of art 132 CAP is as follows: 'Insurance undertakings shall be required, on the basis of the contract terms and insurance rates they must establish in advance for any risk in respect of the use of motor vehicles and boats, to accept the proposals regarding compulsory insurance which are submitted to them, without prejudice to the necessary assessment of correctness of the data shown in the certificate of claims experience, and the identification of the policyholder and the vehicle's owner, if other than the policyholder ...'. In fact, in practical terms, insurers are never able to refuse the coverage or the stipulation of the contract; whereas if they discover that data provided by the insured prior to the application have been manipulated, insurers will have a right to demand additional premiums but will not be able to declare the contract null and void. 73

Therefore, as far as motor liability insurance is concerned, the Italian legal system establishes this bilateral duty of insurance: while art 122 CAP affirms the duty to be insured on whoever drives a motor vehicle, the subsequent art 132 CAP provides that insurance companies operating in Italy are obliged to accept all motor liability insurance proposals that they receive from potential insured persons. 74

The consequence of a failure of an insurer to comply with the obligation to insure (that is to say, to accept the proposal for a motor liability insurance policy) represents a breach of statutory provisions and attracts heavy pecuniary sanctions: IVASS, the Supervisory Authority for insurance companies, has the power to supervise insurers in respect of the duty to insure and can impose sanctions on insurance companies for non-compliance with this duty. The sanctions are applicable both to Italian companies and to companies operating under the freedom to provide services. 75

76 In addition to the duty to accept insurance proposals coming from prospective insured, insurance companies operating in Italy are obliged to establish in advance all premiums applicable to motor insurance and to make them public at each point of sale and even via the Internet.

*16. If there is no obligation to contract: Are there comparable mechanisms provided to ensure that an insurance agreement is concluded?*

77 No, except for the eventual control of associations/professional bodies, where they may impose disciplinary sanctions.

*17. Is the insurance holder prohibited from disposing over his cover entitlement to the disadvantage of the victim (eg, by surrendering his entitlement)?*

78 Not by specific law. Nevertheless, the law provides for a privilege on the insured sum in favour of the victim (see below under no 79).

*18. Does the victim enjoy special protection against insolvency on the part of the insurance holder with regard to the sum payable by the liability insurer?*

79 The victim of damage is partially protected against the insolvency of the insurance holder. In fact, art 2767 Civil Code provides for a priority of the victim as a creditor for the sums due by the insurer to the insurance holder (see the text of art 2767 CC: '*Nel caso di assicurazione della responsabilità civile, il credito del danneggiato per il risarcimento ha privilegio, sull'indennità dovuta dall'assicuratore.*' – '*In the case of liability insurance, the sum due by the insurance company for the indemnity has to be paid in the first place to the victim and secondly to other creditors.*').

80 One should also remember that art 2778 CC provides a list of preferred creditors vis-à-vis the insolvent party. The victims as creditors for sums due by the liability insurer are ranked number 11 on the preferred creditors' list, before many others (employees, state as tax creditor, etc). The problem is, nevertheless, less relevant than it might appear in general terms; in fact, the rule set by art 2767 CC is only intended to operate when the insured sum is paid to the insured and there is a merger between that sum and the assets of the insured. In practical terms, the insurer always pays the victim directly, so that the insurance holder does not even get into possession of the insured sum.

81 In any case, some authors consider that art 2767 CC establishes a direct action of the victim against the insurers, even if the existence of a direct action is not a general solution in Italian law (see no 85 below under Question 19.b).

*19.a) In what manner can the victim obtain the insurance payment?*

The victim can sue the liable party. In general terms, the victim does not have a right to bring a direct action against the insurer. **82**

Nevertheless, one should mention once again the rule set by art 1917 CC (see above no 13), according to which the insurer, even if not obliged by law and in the absence of a direct action right from the victim, always has the choice to pay the insured sum directly to the victim; in addition, he/she is obliged to do so if the insured asks for this. This rule, as set in art 1917 of the Civil Code as well, applies to all types of liability insurance, whether voluntary or compulsory. **83**

Practice shows that the insurer normally pays the sum to the damaged party if he/she is aware of the insurance contract. **84**

*b) Does the victim have a direct right of action against the liability insurer (action directe) in the case of voluntary or compulsory liability insurance?*

In Italy the right to direct action of the victim towards the insurer of the liable party is not a general rule. Consequently, there is no general right afforded to a third party affected by a liable party to pursue any remedy or claim towards the insurer of the said party. **85**

The right to exercise a direct action must be specifically provided by law. This happens in some regulated types of insurance, which are of course compulsory, but not for all compulsory insurance. In fact, the existence of a direct action of the victim is provided, for example, for motor liability insurance, but the same direct action is not granted to victims of hunting activities, for which compulsory insurance exists but for which the law does not provide the express direct action. **86**

Where a direct action is provided by statutory law establishing the duty to be insured, the insurer is generally prevented from raising any objections or exceptions to payment based on the insurance contract if they do not refer to the existence of the insurance or the payment of the premium. The third party remains entitled to recover from the insured the amounts not paid under the policy. **87**

In light of the discriminating situation that may result for the victim of the different liability regimes, many scholars have tried to argue for the creation of a general direct action based on the rule of art 1917 CC (which allows the insurer to pay the victim directly and which obliges the insurer to do so where the insured demands it).[23] However, case law has refused such an interpretation, and **88**

**23** See eg *Candian* (fn 1) 219 ff; *de Strobel/Ogliari* (fn 9) 157; *Cerini* (fn 8) 242.

it is consequently impossible to talk about the existence of a direct action even in case law.[24]

89 When the rules on insurance were transposed into the Code of Private Insurances in 2005, the proposal of introducing a direct action by law was once again rejected.

*20. When settling the claim, is the liability insurer obliged to observe a certain procedure in the interests of the victim? For instance, must it pay the victim an advance within a certain period?*

90 Specific duties are stated only with reference to motor liability insurance by art 140 ff CAP.

91 With reference to motor liability insurance, both law and the applying regulations approved by the supervisory authority are very strict; numerous sanctions are provided for companies which do not respect the prescribed timetable and duties towards a victim of a motor accident.

*21.a) In the context of its relationship with the victim, can the liability insurer rely on the fact that vis-à-vis the insurance holder (= damaging party) it is freed from the obligation to pay, eg, due to the insurance holder breaching an obligation of conduct/warranty (Obliegenheitsverletzung) or due to him defaulting on premiums?*

*b) Does the law distinguish on the basis of the ground for the release from the obligation to pay so that in some cases the insurer may not invoke its release from such obligation vis-à-vis the victim?*

92 In general, the liability insurer is free to oppose all exceptions to the insured or third parties.

93 In some limited cases, the protection of the victim is extended to the impossibility for the insurer to oppose contractual exceptions, the most relevant case being that of motor liability insurance. In fact, the situation is not the rule and it is provided, with different perimeters, where the victim is granted a direct right of action against the insurer (see no 85 above under Question 19.b). In fact, if there are contractual exceptions that allow the insurer not to fulfil his obligations, in general the insurer can oppose to the beneficiaries the exceptions that may be opposed to the insured or policyholder.

---

24 See among many other Corte di Cassazione Civile (Cass Civ) 18 July 2002, no 10418, published in Foro Italiano, Repertorio 2002, 98.

*c) If the insurer must still pay the victim despite being released from its obligation to pay vis-à-vis the insurance holder (see above Question b), may it take recourse against the latter?*

Yes. This happens in general where the law provides the duty to pay regardless of the existence of contractual exceptions. If the choice to pay is voluntary, in principle the rules on unjust enrichment can be applied: also in this case, one should evaluate under which terms the insured had the duty to pay or not, and the insurer will have recourse against him under the same terms. 94

*22.a) Within its relationship to the victim, can the liability insurer invoke the fact that the insurance agreement had already ended by the time relevant in respect of the duty to provide cover?*

In general, yes. Even in motor liability insurance, this is in practice the only applicable exception from the insurer's duty to pay the victim that can be invoked referring to the contract of insurance. 95

*b) If the insurer must pay the victim despite the termination of the insurance agreement by the time relevant for the duty to provide cover (see above Question a), can it take recourse against the insurance holder?*

Yes. 96

*23.a) Are there cases in which a damaging party does not effectively conclude the required liability insurance and the victim injured by him nonetheless receives compensation for his loss from a liability insurer or another compensation scheme (eg, a guarantee fund)?*

Only where the law specifically provides for this solution, as is the case in motor liability insurance, in some forms of insurance for construction contracts, as well as for insurance intermediaries (see eg art 115 CAP, which establishes the Guarantee Fund for the activity of insurance intermediaries[25]). In these and a number of other limited cases, the victim can seek recovery not directly from the insurers, but from other entities, in particular the funds created by law and managed by CONSAP (Concessionaire for Public Insurance Services Ltd). 97

**25** The Fund pays the victim in the case of non-existence of the insurance policy or where the existing policy does not provide for the relevant coverage, for example, in the case of fraudulent acts of the insurance intermediaries.

CONSAP operates under the supervision of the Ministry of Productive Activities.

98 The *Fondo di garanzia per le vittime della strada*, set up within CONSAP, pays compensation for damage caused by motor vehicles and boats for which insurance is compulsory, in many cases where insurance is not effective, for example, when the accident was caused by an unidentified vehicle or boat; the vehicle or craft is not insured; the vehicle or craft is insured with an undertaking pursuing business in the territory of the Italian Republic by way of establishment or of free provision of services, which has been placed under compulsory winding up at the time of the accident or afterwards; the vehicle has been used against the will of the owner, usufructuary, buyer under reservation of title or lessee of an operating or financial leasing;the vehicle is involved in an accident while uninsured; the accident was caused by a foreign vehicle bearing a registration plate which does not correspond or no longer corresponds to the vehicle.[26]

99 CONSAP also pays victims in the case of other compulsory insurance, such as in the case where the relevant policy is ineffective or cannot operate for any other reason with reference to liability insurance for insurance intermediaries (art 115 CAP), insurance for hunting activities (art 302 CAP)[27], and others.

100 In the majority of cases, the fund within CONSAP pays compensation partially limited with respect to the limits of the minimum insurance sum set for the compulsory insurance law or by the specific contract of insurance. For example, it may only pay compensation for personal injury resulting in death or permanent disability. With reference to other specific cases, CONSAP pays material damages only within specific limits, even lower than those possibly provided for the compulsory insurance in question.

---

**26** See art 301 ff CAP.

**27** The Fondo di garanzia per le vittime della caccia (National guarantee fund for hunting victims), set up within CONSAP, pays compensation for damage caused by the practice of hunting for which insurance is compulsory, when:
a) the hunter is unidentified; b) the hunter liable for damage is not covered by compulsory insurance against civil liability; c) the hunter is insured with an undertaking pursuing business in the territory of the Italian Republic by way of establishment or of free provision of services, which has been placed under compulsory liquidation at the time of the accident or afterwards.

b) *In the event that the policy taken out was not in fact effectively concluded, is it necessary to distinguish on the basis of the ground for this ineffectiveness, eg, whether the reason for the contract not coming into effect was: i) a lack of legal capacity on the part of the insurance holder, ii) lack of consent, iii) falsa procuratio (unauthorised agency)?*

The law does not distinguish between different causes for ineffectiveness. **101**

c) *Can the liability insurer (or the alternative compensation scheme) that must provide cover even though the insurance policy was not effectively concluded (see above Questions a and b) have recourse against the damaging party?*

Yes, if the damaging party is known. **102**

24.a) *Are there cases in which a damaging party does not take out any liability insurance, ie not even an ineffective insurance policy (see above Question 23), and the victim whom he injured is still compensated for his damage by a liability insurer or another compensation scheme (guarantee fund, etc)?*

Once again, it is possible for some forms of liability insurance, such as motor li- **103**
ability insurance and some construction insurance (see above no 97).

b) *Can the liability insurer (or the alternative compensation scheme) that must provide cover despite the total absence of any insurance agreement (see above Question a) have recourse against the damaging party?*

In principle yes, even if considering the causes for the intervention of the fund, **104**
it is quite difficult to get effective recourse.

25. *Is the victim protected against the insolvency of the liability insurer?*

The victim is partially protected. In fact, provided that insurance companies are **105**
subjected to special procedures in the case of insolvency (ie administrative compulsory winding up, liquidation, etc, as per arts 245ff CAP), the same Code of Private Insurance provides for a priority of the insurer's assets – in addition to specific assets reserved for the insurance claims – in favour of insured parties, beneficiaries (in the case of life insurance contracts) as well as victims, such as in the case of liability insurance. The terms of such priority are, nevertheless, equivalent for all forms of liability insurance.

*26. Are there rules that serve in particular the protection of the victim when the liability insurance was only concluded voluntarily – ie without it being compulsory?*

106 No.

## V. Supervision and Sanctions

*27.a) In which cases must the insurance holder prove to an authority before commencing an activity requiring insurance that he has taken out the respective prescribed liability insurance cover (see above Question 4.e)?*

*b) Must the insurer inform an authority when liability insurance taken out to meet an insurance obligation ends?*

107 See no 18 above under Question 4.

108 Where the duty is provided, the duty to inform is a burden placed on the insured party, not on the insurer.

*c) Is the insurer also under a duty to inform when a liability insurance agreement is in existence but it has no duty to provide cover – eg, due to defaults on premium payments?*

109 No.

*d) What are the consequences when the duties to inform of the end of contract or the release from payment obligations (see above Questions b and c) are violated?*

110 See above under Question 27.c.

*28. Is there some official body (authority, professional chamber) where an injured party can find out whether and where the injuring party who inflicted damage upon him in the course of an activity requiring insurance has liability insurance?*

111 This is the case for insurance intermediaries, the website of the control authority giving evidence of existing insurance coverage. In some cases, it may also be the case for lawyers.

*29. Are there (public law) sanctions against the party who was required to take out insurance if such does not take out the compulsory liability insurance? Examples of this would be a ban on carrying out the activity that requires the insurance or the imposition of an administrative or judicial penalty.*

Yes, specific sanctions are provided. This may also be the case for transport operators. 112

# VI. Statutory Provisions required by the Constitution or the European Convention on Human Rights (ECHR)

*30. What has been said regarding the compatibility of the duties to take out liability insurance with your country's constitution and the ECHR? Please take into account case law and academic literature.*

There is no comprehensive literature on the matter, and no coherent or detailed case law exists. In many cases, the problem of the compatibility of the duties to take out liability insurance with constitutional principles or the protection and respect of rights as set by the ECHR was not raised before the constitutional court but it emerged incidentally with reference to other proceedings, for example, proceedings before a supervisory authority. This resulted only rarely in decisions by courts (national or supranational). 113

With reference to international courts, even if not specifically the European Court of Human Rights, there are some decisions from the European Court of Justice (ECJ) that have had an impact on liability insurance and in particular on motor liability insurance. 114

In the past, the ECJ had considered Italian Legislative Decree no 70/2000 (converted into Law 229/2000), that imposed upon insurance companies the so-called *blocco delle tariffe*, that is to say the impossibility to increase insurance premiums (see ECJ C-59/01) not to be compliant with EC law.[28] In this case, the principle of freedom to set contractual terms, including the premiums, is protected by the provisions under arts 6, 29, 39 of the Directive 92/49/EEC. 115

Another important decision is the case ECJ C-371/12 *Petillo and Petillo v Unipol Assicurazioni spa*: the case arose because Italian legislation (once again the 116

**28** [2003] European Court Reports (ECR) I-1759; for a comment see Assicurazioni 2003, II, 2–3.

Code of Private Insurance) fixes the maximum extent of the victim's right to compensation payable by the insurer for minor personal injuries (so-called micro-invalidity, that is to say from 1% to 9% of invalidity) deriving from motor accidents; the law does not limit the right towards the liable party, even if the two situations tend to coincide in practice. Nevertheless, the European Court of Justice ruled that a limitation to the compensation payable for non-material damage resulting from minor physical injuries caused by road traffic accidents is in accordance with EU law. On the same matter, a decision from the Italian Constitutional Court is actually pending.

117 The academic literature has also raised the problem. In addition, the focus on human rights, as well as the compatibility with fundamental rights as set by the Italian Constitution, has recently been directed towards insurance in general so that liability insurance is also more and more concerned.

118 On occasion, specific points have been addressed both in the political debate and in discussions and proceedings. It is impossible to give a comprehensive explanation here and report on the topics in question. One can, however, for example, mention:

- Problems of compatibility between the (Constitution as well as ECHR-based) principles of equality and non-discrimination and the peculiar situation in some areas of Italy, in particular in the south of the country, with reference to very high costs of insurance premiums for motor liability insurance.
- The *Test-Achats* decision has raised a limited debate with reference to costs of insurance and differences for men and women.

*31. Does the constitution or the ECHR make any stipulations regarding the contents of such duties to take out liability insurance? Please take into account case law and academic literature.*

119 Not directly with reference to the content of the duty to be insured.

120 Nevertheless, one can argue with reference to limits set for damages to be recoverable for personal injuries, as they have been recently introduced for motor liability insurance.

121 A great debate is currently ongoing.

## VII. Reform Efforts

*32. Are there efforts towards reforming the law regarding compulsory liability insurance?*

Insurance law as a whole was greatly modified at the time of the adoption of the Code of Private Insurance. This reform did not concern the rules set in the Civil Code – including art 1917 – but it touched other relevant contractual rules (eg the rules on the information to be given by insurers and by intermediaries). No other relevant and comprehensive reform of insurance law has been approved since 2005 or is currently the subject of debate. As a consequence, the law of liability insurance – in the sense clarified at the beginning of this paper – is not the subject of a reform or a project of law in order to introduce rules common to all forms of liability insurance. 122

Nevertheless, specific areas of liability insurance have been subject to important revisions over the last few years. They mainly refer to motor liability insurance, on the one hand, and professional liability insurance, on the other. 123

A number of provisions are constantly approved with reference to motor liability insurance. They concern the limits of the coverage, as well as the limits to indemnities to be paid to victims in the case of personal damage. 124

In addition, a number of types of compulsory liability insurance were introduced in 2012 (as explained with reference to professional liability insurance for lawyers). Some of them still need to be put into force as regulations have to be approved. 125

In addition, the medical liability insurance sector is still to be fully regulated and it is quite a topic of discussion. 126

## VIII. Compulsory Liability Insurance and Liability Law

*33. Is, at the legislative level, any connection discernible between the nature of liability (in particular in the case of strict liability) and the imposition of compulsory liability insurance?*

At a legislative level, there is no evident connection between the existence of a strict liability regime and the introduction of compulsory insurance for the subsequent risk. The main relevance of the regulations is, instead, focused on the degree of the risk that the specific activity introduces in society, on the one 127 hand, and the need for victims' protection, on the other. This said, one can discover that in practical terms, duties to be insured are often connected to the existence of a strict liability rule set by law: for example, this is the case for nuclear activities, hunting, (most cases of) liability of insurance intermediaries, liability of internet providers. Nevertheless, this is not an essential element for the introduction of a compulsory liability system. The counterproof is given by the fact that there are cases of strict or aggravated liability not accompanied by a duty to be insured: one of the most interesting cases in this perspective is the product liability regime, which is governed without a doubt (and for the majority of cases of liability provided by the law) by a strict liability rule but where no duty to be insured has been imposed (not even for specific kind of products, ie medicines). In fact, even if the basic idea for the introduction of a compulsory liability insurance is the need to assure a special protection of the victim on the one hand, and the need to increase the level of trust in a particular profession or activity on the other, there are other political or cultural elements that can influence the introduction of a compulsory insurance system. It is also important to clarify that the law establishing a duty to be insured generally does not qualify the nature of the liability in question: as a consequence, it is often up to the legal doctrine to try to qualify this liability and the case law can in its turn give different interpretations. One might also recall the fact that the same activity can give rise to strict or fault liability as is evident in the case of medical malpractice.

Andrea Stäubli*

# Compulsory Liability Insurance in Switzerland

## I. The Term Compulsory Liability Insurance

1. *Indicate the rules within your legal system that set out a duty to take out liability insurance. In this context, also take into account the implementation of international treaties (eg, the International Convention on Civil Liability for Bunker Oil Pollution Damage, 2001).*

At present the Swiss legal system contains an enormous amount of rules that set out a duty to take out liability insurance. Depending on the subject matter, the competence to legislate lies either with the federal state or the member states. Therefore, such rules may be found in federal law as well as in the law of the 26 states (*Kantone*). According to Beck, there are approximately 40 such rules to be found in federal law and an innumerable amount in states' law.[1] 1

There is no comprehensive act on compulsory insurance (see below no 5). Moreover, the Insurance Contract Act 1908 (*Versicherungsvertragsgesetz*, VVG) and the Code of Obligations 1911 (*Obligationenrecht*, OR) do not contain rules on compulsory liability insurance in general. Hence, duties to take out insurance as well as details of the cover required by law are found in various different laws.[2] A (non-exhaustive) overview is provided in the Annex: Rules on Compulsory Liability Insurance in Switzerland (at the end of this book). 2

However, there are two provisions in the Insurance Contract Act (arts 59 and 60) regulating liability insurance in general. Hence, these provisions apply to compulsory liability insurance as well. They are, however, not specific to 3

* This text is based on the statutory provisions prevailing in June 2014. However, the amendment to art 65 para 3 Road Traffic Act (Strassenverkehrsgesetz, SVG), entering into force on 1 January 2015, has been taken into account (see below nos 51, 52 and 70).

1 *R Beck*, Das patchworkartige System der Haftpflicht-Versicherungsobligatorien, in: S Fuhrer/C Chappuis (eds), Liber amicorum Roland Brehm (2012) 2.

2 *R Beck/S Furrer/H Heiss/S Läubli Ziegler/V Pribnow/A Scheurer/S Weber*, Pflichtversicherung – Entwurf einer gesetzlichen Regelung (2012) 124 ff.

compulsory insurance.[3] More detailed to art 59, see below no 38 and to art 60, see below nos 57 f and 61 f.

4 It is beyond the purpose of this paper to give an overview of duties to take out insurance for all 26 states, as this cannot be done within a reasonable period of time.[4] Hence, relevant state law will not be discussed.[5] Equally, international uniform law containing provisions on compulsory insurance will not be discussed in the following even if such law is in force in Switzerland.

### 2. *Is there a coherent 'law of compulsory liability insurance' in your legal system?*

5 As mentioned above, there is no comprehensive act on compulsory liability insurance at present and there are no specific legal rules on compulsory liability insurance in general (see above no 2). Instead, there are a large number of specific rules both on the federal and state level (see above no 1). The relevant provisions only apply to the subject matter of the specific act or regulation. However, there are private (academic) efforts towards reforming the law regarding compulsory liability insurance (see below no 100).

### 3. *Is there a specific term for compulsory liability insurance in your legal system? How is it defined?*

6 The term translates to *obligatorische Haftpflichtversicherung* or *Haftpflicht-Versicherungsobligatorium*, but no legal definition of these terms exists.

---

**3** These provisions read:
'Art. 59
Hat sich der Versicherungsnehmer gegen die Folgen der mit einem gewerblichen Betriebe verbundenen gesetzlichen Haftpflicht versichert, so erstreckt sich die Versicherung auch auf die Haftpflicht der Vertreter des Versicherungsnehmers sowie auf die Haftpflicht der mit der Leitung oder Beaufsichtigung des Betriebes betrauten Personen.
Art. 60
[1]An dem Ersatzanspruche, der dem Versicherungsnehmer aus der Versicherung gegen die Folgen gesetzlicher Haftpflicht zusteht, besitzt der geschädigte Dritte im Umfange seiner Schadenersatzforderung Pfandrecht. Der Versicherer ist berechtigt, die Ersatzleistung direkt an den geschädigten Dritten auszurichten.
[2]Der Versicherer ist für jede Handlung, durch die er den Dritten in seinem Rechte verkürzt, verantwortlich.'

**4** *Beck et al* (fn 2) 136.

**5** For an exemplary overview see: *Beck et al* (fn 2) 136 ff.

*4. In which of the following cases does compulsory liability insurance apply according to prevailing opinion?*

*a) Duties to take out liability insurance which are not directly based on the law but on an order or decision issued by administrative authorities?*

No such orders or decisions were found. However, in several federal acts and regulations, the legislator grants the Swiss federal council (*Bundesrat*) the competence to demand a financial security for certain risks. 7

For instance, the Swiss federal council (*Bundesrat*) may establish (by legislating in the form of a regulation) a duty to provide a financial security for a plant or a facility which poses a special risk for the environment according to art 59b lit a Environment Protection Act (*Umweltschutzgesetz*, USG).[6] In my opinion such duties should be considered to be compulsory liability insurance, as the competence to stipulate such a duty is established by a federal act even if the duty itself is based on a regulation by the federal council (*Bundesrat*), i.e. not by the parliament as the legislator. 8

*b) Duties to take out liability insurance that are not based directly on the law but on the statutes of a professional or other self-governing body?*

No such statutes were found. 9

*c) Duties to take out liability insurance that are not based on any public law but on a private law provision (eg, governing the relationship between employer and employee)?*

No. 10

*d) Duties to take out liability insurance that are not based on any public law but on a private law rule that is established by case law (and, eg, governs the relationship between employer and employee)?*

No such private law rule was found. 11

6 Full text in German: 'Zum Schutz der Geschädigten kann der Bundesrat: lit a: den Inhabern bestimmter Betriebe oder Anlagen sowie den bewilligungs- oder meldepflichtigen Personen, die mit pathogenen Organismen umgehen, vorschreiben, dass sie ihre Haftpflicht durch Versicherung oder in anderer Form sicherstellen.'

*e) Cases in which there is no duty to take out liability insurance but liability insurance cover is a prerequisite for the admissibility of carrying out a particular activity?*

12 It is quite common that liability insurance cover is a prerequisite for the admissibility of carrying out a particular activity. This does not apply, however, to professional activities. For these activities the liability insurance cover is in most cases not a prerequisite for the admissibility of carrying out the activity. Instead the professionals are required to take out insurance in order to comply with their professional duties (see the examples given in no 14).

13 An example in which there is no duty to take out liability insurance but liability insurance cover is a prerequisite for the admissibility of carrying out a particular activity is art 63 para 1 SVG (Road Traffic Act). According to this article, a motor vehicle may not be used on public roads before a liability insurance cover meeting the statutory standard has been provided.[7] Such a duty is considered to be compulsory liability insurance. Similar provisions exist, for example, for the liability insurance of the keeper of an aircraft[8], the liability insurance of the operator of railways[9] and the liability insurance of the keeper of a ship[10]. Furthermore, see below no 34 (carrying out certain activities involving radiation).

*f) Cases of alternative financial security, in which the duty to provide for financial security may be fulfilled either by taking out liability insurance or other forms of financial security (eg, bank guarantees)?*

14 Such provisions are also quite common and insurance taken out in compliance with such rules are likewise considered to be compulsory liability insurance. For instance, according to art 40 lit h Medical Professions Act (*Medizinalberufegesetz*, MedBG), a self-employed member of a medical profession which requires a university degree has the duty to either take out insurance with the cover depending on the nature and amounts of the risks associated with his practice or to provide an equivalent form of financial security.[11] Another example is art 27 lit f Psychology Professions Act (*Psychologieberufegesetz*, PsyG), according to

7 Full text in German: 'Kein Motorfahrzeug darf in den öffentlichen Verkehr gebracht werden, bevor eine Haftpflichtversicherung nach den folgenden Bestimmungen abgeschlossen ist.'
8 Art 18 para 1 lit c Aviation Regulation (Luftfahrtverordnung, LFV).
9 Art 8d para 1 lit b Railway Act (Eisenbahngesetz, EBG).
10 Art 153 para 1 Inland Shipping Regulation (Binnenschifffahrtsverordnung, BSV).
11 Full text in German: 'Sie haben eine Berufshaftpflichtversicherung nach Massgabe der Art und des Umfanges der Risiken, die mit ihrer Tätigkeit verbunden sind, abzuschliessen oder andere, gleichwertige Sicherheiten zu erbringen.'

which persons who practise psychology on a self-employed basis must either take out insurance with the cover depending on the nature and amount of the risks or must provide an equivalent form of financial security.[12] A further example is art 12 lit f Attorney Act (*Anwaltsgesetz*, BGFA; cf below no 24).

*g) Cases in which the duty to have insurance has only been created by a contractual agreement between potential injuring party and victim?*

Such a duty cannot be considered to be compulsory liability insurance *stricto sensu*, as the compulsion is not based on a provision of a law, but on a clause of a contract, which is only binding upon the parties involved. 15

For instance, it is quite common that lease contracts stipulate that the tenant has to take out liability insurance to cover the landlord's liability interest and such clauses are considered valid.[13] 16

# II. Aims

*5. What are the aims of the rules that impose an obligation to take out liability insurance:*

As the rules stem from numerous sources within federal law and their specific contents may vary, the following questions cannot be answered for all such rules in general. The answers hereafter apply to the majority of the rules. 17

*a) the protection of the victim,*

The primary purpose of the introduction of compulsory liability insurance is the protection of the victim, specifically the protection against the injuring party's insolvency.[14] 18

12 Full text in German: 'Sie haben eine Berufshaftpflichtversicherung nach Massgabe der Art und des Umfangs der Risiken abzuschliessen oder eine vergleichbare finanzielle Sicherheit zu erbringen.'

13 *P Heinrich* in: M Amstutz/P Breitschmid/A Furrer/D Girsberger/C Huguenin/M Müller-Chen/V Roberto/A Rumo-Jungo/A K Schnyder/H R Trüeb (eds), Handkommentar zum Schweizer Privatrecht, Vertragsverhältnisse Teil 1: Innominatkontrakte, Kauf, Tausch, Schenkung, Miete, Leihe (Art. 184–318 OR) (2nd edn 2012) art 257e no 1.

14 *Beck et al* (fn 2) 123; *K Oftinger/EW Stark*, Schweizerisches Haftpflichtrecht, Zweiter Band: Besonderer Teil, Zweiter Teilband (1989) 31f; *H Rey*, Ausservertragliches Haftpflichtrecht (2008) no 1335.

*b) the protection of the insurance holder,*

19 The original aim of (voluntary) liability insurance was mainly the protection of the insurance holder from the financial burden of having to pay damages to the injured party.[15] This aim is one of the purposes of compulsory liability insurance as well, but mostly as a secondary aim next to the primary aim, which is the protection of the victim.[16]

*c) the protection of the victim and the insurance holder,*

20 See, in particular concerning the relationship of these two aims, above no 18f.

*d) other aims, eg internalising the costs in the interests of society?*

21 None found.

*6. Do the rules that prescribe a form of alternative financial security (see above Question 4.f) pursue the same aims as those rules that exclusively set out a duty to have liability insurance (ie with no other alternative financial security options)?*

22 As the rules stem from numerous sources within federal law and their specific contents may vary, this question cannot be answered for all such rules in general.

23 However, one of the reasons to implement an option to choose between taking out liability insurance and other forms of financial security can be that it might be difficult to obtain cover in the insurance market.[17]

24 One example for a rule that prescribes a form of alternative financial security would be the duty of an attorney to take out liability insurance for his law practice. According to art 12 lit f BGFA (Attorney Act), an attorney must either take out insurance with the cover depending on the nature and amount of the risks associated with his practice or must provide another, equivalent form of financial security.[18] The aim of this provision is mainly the protection of poten-

15 *Rey* (fn 14) no 1335; *R Beck*, Haftpflicht II: Haftpflichtversicherung (2nd edn 2012) 45.
16 *Oftinger/Stark* (fn 14) 31f; *Beck* (fn 15) 45.
17 *Beck* (fn 1) 4; *Beck* (fn 15) 67 and 69.
18 Full text in German: 'Sie haben eine Berufshaftpflichtversicherung nach Massgabe der Art und des Umfangs der Risiken, die mit ihrer Tätigkeit verbunden sind, abzuschliessen; die Ver-

tial victims of malpractice, as it ensures that every attorney is able to pay damages in case of a lawsuit.[19] However, it furthermore serves to protect the assets of the attorney in question.[20]

# III. Content of Insurance Cover

7. *Are the duties to take out liability insurance laid down by law only to cover extra-contractual compensation duties or also those arising out of contractual infringements?*

This again depends on the specific type of duty, as they may have different aims 25
(see above Question 5) and their wordings often differ as well.

For instance, according to art 58 SVG (Road Traffic Act), the keeper of a mo- 26
tor vehicle is only liable if a person is killed or hurt or property is damaged. Article 63 para 2 SVG states that the compulsory liability insurance has to cover, amongst others, the liability of the keeper of the motor vehicle. Thus, the duty to insure under art 63 para 2 SVG is imposed with a view to a liability in tort. For examples of duties to take out liability insurance directed only or at least predominantly at the compensation of damage arising out of contractual infringements, see below no 29.

8.a) *Are there duties to take out liability insurance aimed not only at the protection of absolutely protected rights (eg, property, bodily integrity) but additionally at compensating pure economic loss?*

One of the general principles in Swiss extra-contractual liability law states that 27
only a person who unlawfully (*widerrechtlich*) causes a loss or damage is obliged to provide compensation (art 41 para 1 OR[21]). While any loss or damage to an absolutely protected right (*absolutes Recht*) is considered unlawful *per se*, a pure economic loss is only unlawful where the act causing the damage violates a so-called *Schutznorm*, which roughly translates to a norm with a protec-

sicherungssumme muss mindestens eine Million Franken pro Jahr betragen; anstelle der Haftpflichtversicherung können andere, gleichwertige Sicherheiten erbracht werden.'

**19** *W Fellmann* in: W Fellmann/GG Zindel (eds), Kommentar zum Anwaltsgesetz (2011) art 12 no 129c.

**20** Fellmann/Zindel/*Fellmann* (fn 19) art 12 no 130.

**21** Full text: Any person who unlawfully causes loss or damage to another, whether wilfully or negligently, is obliged to provide compensation.

tive purpose, aiming to avoid such damage. This principle also applies in the area of liability insurance. Consequently extra-contractual liability only covers damages caused by the violation of absolutely protected rights if no norm with a protective purpose was violated. Therefore, a duty to take out liability insurance for any form of extra-contractual liability generally only aims at the protection of absolutely protected rights. However, economic loss is also covered if brought about by the violation of an absolutely protected right.

**28** On the other hand, under Swiss law, any breach of contract is considered to be unlawful (*widerrechtlich*) *per se*, thus making a breaching party liable for pure economic loss as well. Consequently, any duty to take out liability insurance for a form of contractual liability aims not only at the protection of absolutely protected rights (eg, property, bodily integrity), but additionally at compensating pure economic loss. Most cases of compulsory professional liability insurance (eg, for attorneys or insurance brokers) are even predominantly directed at the compensation of pure economic loss as there typically is only damage to the fortune of the client (see below no 29).

### b) *Are there duties to take out liability insurance that are directed only or at least predominantly at the compensation of pure economic loss?*

**29** Yes, as mentioned above, most cases of compulsory professional liability are predominantly directed at the compensation of pure economic loss. For example, according to art 12 lit f BGFA (Attorney Act), an attorney has the duty to take out liability insurance for its law practice with the coverage depending on the nature and amount of the risks associated with it.[22] Usually, failure to comply with professional duties on the part of the attorney will result in its clients suffering pure economic loss. Another example is the professional liability insurance of insurance brokers. As per art 44 para 1 lit b Insurance Supervision Act (*Versicherungsaufsichtsgesetz*, VAG), only brokers who have taken out insurance cover or who provide an equivalent financial security may be entered into the official register of insurance brokers by the supervisory authority.[23] Their professional misconduct usually generates pure economic loss as well, because poor advice on their part results in absent or insufficient insurance coverage of their clients.

**22** For full text in German see fn 18.
**23** Full text in German: 'Ins Register eingetragen wird nur, wer: lit b: eine Berufshaftpflichtversicherung abgeschlossen oder gleichwertige finanzielle Sicherheiten geleistet hat.'

*9. Are there provisions that require the insurance of a third party's liability interest – for instance, that the employer must take out liability insurance for the benefit of an employee?*

Yes, there are. For example the duty of a keeper of a motor vehicle to insure the liability of the vehicle driver as well as his own liability,[24] because, according to art 63 para 2 SVG (Road Traffic Act), the keeper of a motor vehicle has to insure the liability of persons for whom it can be held accountable according to the Road Traffic Act.[25] **30**

Another example would be the duty of foster parents to take out liability insurance for a foster child according to art 8 para 3 Foster Care Regulation (*Pflegekinderverordnung*, PAVO).[26] The article states that the foster child needs to be adequately insured against the consequences of (illness, accidents and) liability. In contrast, the Swiss Civil Code, which stipulates the rules concerning family law, does not establish such a duty for legal parents. However, most Swiss households have in fact a (voluntary) household contents and personal liability insurance, which usually also covers the personal liability of children living in said household. **31**

Furthermore, art 59 VVG (Insurance Contract Act) should be mentioned in this context as this provision states that, if an insurance holder has voluntarily taken out insurance coverage for the liability concerning his business operations, the insurance contract also has to cover the liability of representatives of the insurance holder and of any persons entrusted with the management of said business operations (for more details see below no 38).[27] **32**

---

**24** *H Giger* in: H Giger (ed), SVG Strassenverkehrsgesetz (7th edn 2008) art 63 no 2.

**25** Full text in German: 'Die Versicherung deckt die Haftpflicht des Halters und der Personen, für die er nach diesem Gesetz verantwortlich ist, zumindest in jenen Staaten, in denen das schweizerische Kontrollschild als Versicherungsnachweis gilt.'

**26** Full text in German: 'Das Kind muss gegen die Folgen von Krankheit, Unfall und Haftpflicht angemessen versichert werden.'

**27** For full text in German see above fn 3.

*10. To what extent do the rules requiring the compulsory conclusion of a liability insurance policy also specify the specific contents of the insurance coverage:*

*a) Is there always a (sufficiently well-defined) specification of the risk to be insured?*

33 This depends on the specific duty to be insured, as they have different wordings. Although it can be said that the definitions vary quite considerably and there certainly are provisions which lack a sufficiently well-defined specification of the risk to be insured.

34 An example for an insufficient specification of the risk to be insured would be art 31 lit d Radiation Protection Act (*Strahlenschutzgesetz*, StSG) which states that, in order to be given authorisation for carrying out certain activities involving radiation, 'sufficient' liability insurance has to be provided for 'these activities'.[28] Similarly, the already mentioned (above no 31) art 8 para 3 PAVO (Foster Care Regulation) states only that the foster child needs to be 'adequately' insured against the consequences of illness, accidents and (civil) liability,[29] without specifying the necessary contents of the insurance coverage.

*b) Are there provisions that require unlimited coverage?*

35 No such provisions exist in Swiss federal law.

*c) If unlimited coverage is not required (see above Question b), is a minimum or maximum insurance sum always specified?*

36 Swiss federal legislation tends to specify a minimum insurance sum to ensure an adequate protection of the victim, but a minimum insurance sum is not always specified (cf below no 37).[30] A maximum insurance sum, on the other hand, is never specified. Examples for a specified minimum insurance sum are the liability of hunters[31], the liability of the keeper of a motor vehicle[32] and the liability of the owner of pipelines[33]. Furthermore, when a minimum insurance

---

28 Full text in German: 'Die Bewilligung wird erteilt, wenn: lit d: für den Betrieb eine ausreichende Haftpflichtversicherung besteht.'
29 For full text in German see above fn 26.
30 *Beck* (fn 1) 6; *Beck* (fn 15) 68.
31 Art 14 Hunting Regulation (Jagdverordnung, JSV).
32 Arts 3, 12 Road Traffic Insurance Regulation (Verkehrsversicherungsverordnung, VVV).
33 Art 35 para 2 Pipelines Act (Rohrleitungsgesetz, RLG).

sum is stipulated, it is often not done directly by the federal legislator in the act which provides the duty to take out liability insurance. Instead the federal legislator tends to grant the Swiss federal council the competence to decree executory provisions (*Ausführungsbestimmungen*) in the form of a regulation for certain details of the federal act, one of these details often being the required insurance sum. Examples of this legislative method are art 14 JSV (Hunting Regulation), art 3 Nuclear Liability Regulation (*Kernenergiehaftpflichtverordnung*, KHV) and art 3 VVV (Road Traffic Insurance Regulation).

Nonetheless, as mentioned above, there are provisions which do not specify 37
a minimum or maximum insurance sum, such as art 40 lit h MedBG (Medical Professions Act)[34] or art 27 lit f PsyG (Psychology Professions Act)[35].

*d) Are there general statutory rules to be applicable if the respective law that requires compulsory insurance only makes incomplete stipulations regarding the content of the insurance coverage? An example of this would be § 114 para 1 of the German Insurance Contract Act (Versicherungsvertragsgesetz, VVG) 2008.*

There are currently no such general statutory rules with the exception of art 59 38
VVG (Insurance Contract Act), which only applies to liability insurance for business activities.[36] This provision states that if an insurance holder has taken out insurance coverage for the liabilities concerning his business operations, such an insurance contract also covers the liability of representatives of the insurance holder and of any persons entrusted with the management of said business operations. However, this provision does not establish a compulsory duty to take out such insurance. It only stipulates the minimum content of the coverage if such an insurance contract was concluded voluntarily. In that case, however, it is binding as it may not be altered to the disadvantage of the insurance holder or the beneficiary according to art 98 para 2 VVG (Insurance Contract Act).

*11. Is it admissible to restrict the insurance cover by agreeing:*

*a) risk exclusion clauses,*

Apart from a few exceptions, such as the liability of the keeper of a motor vehi- 39
cle or the liability for nuclear material or nuclear plants, the provisions do not

34 For full text in German see above fn 11.
35 For more details see above no 14. For full text in German see above fn 12.
36 For full text in German see above fn 3.

explicitly specify whether risk restrictions are admissible. Consequently, at present there is legal uncertainty as to whether restrictions of the insurance cover are in fact admissible and to which extent.[37] However, Beck argues that if the provisions do not explicitly specify whether risk restrictions are admissible, risk restrictions should be admissible under certain conditions, which ensure that the intended protection of the victims will not be undermined. First, the risk restrictions need to comply with standard market-practices and secondly, the restrictions must not jeopardise the aim of the specific duty to take out liability insurance. Adversely, if one were to interpret the lack of specification as to whether risk restrictions are admissible or not to mean that risk restrictions are in fact inadmissible, it then would be difficult to obtain cover for such risks in the insurance market.[38]

**40** As mentioned above, the provisions on the liability of the keeper of a motor vehicle explicitly specify whether risk exclusion clauses are admissible. Article 63 para 3 SVG (Road Traffic Act) lists the admissible risk exclusions.[39] The same applies to the provisions regarding liability for nuclear material and nuclear plants as art 4 KHV (Nuclear Liability Regulation) also contains a list of the admissible risk exclusions.[40]

---

**37** *Beck* (fn 1) 6; *Beck et al* (fn 2) 125 f; *Beck* (fn 15) 68.

**38** *Beck* (fn 1) 6 f; *Beck* (fn 15) 68 f.

**39** Full text in German: 'Von der Versicherung können ausgeschlossen werden:

a. Ansprüche des Halters aus Sachschäden, die Personen verursacht haben, für die er nach diesem Gesetz verantwortlich ist;

b. Ansprüche aus Sachschäden des Ehegatten, der eingetragenen Partnerin oder des eingetragenen Partners des Halters, seiner Verwandten in auf- und absteigender Linie sowie seiner mit ihm in gemeinsamem Haushalt lebenden Geschwister;

c. Ansprüche aus Sachschäden, für die der Halter nicht nach diesem Gesetz haftet;

d. Ansprüche aus Unfällen bei Rennen, für welche die nach Artikel 72 vorgeschriebene Versicherung besteht.'

**40** Full text in German: 'Der private Versicherer darf gegenüber dem Geschädigten von der Deckung ausschliessen:

a. Nuklearschäden, die durch ausserordentliche Naturvorgänge oder kriegerische Ereignisse verursacht werden;

a^bis Nuklearschäden zwischen 500 Millionen und 1 Milliarde Franken, die durch terroristische Gewaltakte verursacht werden, gegen die mit zumutbarem Aufwand ein Schutz nicht möglich ist;

b. Ansprüche, für welche die Klage nicht innert zehn Jahren nach dem schädigenden Ereignis oder nach dem Aufhören einer andauernden Einwirkung erhoben wird;

c. Ansprüche, für welche die Klage nicht innert 20 Jahren nach dem Verlust, Diebstahl, Überbordwerfen oder nach der Besitzaufgabe von Kernmaterialien erhoben wird.'

*b) deductibles,*

None of the provisions in federal law specify whether deductibles are admissible, not even the provisions on the liability of the keeper of a motor vehicle. For the liability of the keeper of a motor vehicle it can be said that deductibles, irrespective of their amount, are therefore admissible.[41] However, according to art 65 para 2 SVG (Road Traffic Act) and a few other provisions, the insurer cannot hold the fact that it is freed from the obligation to pay vis-à-vis the insurance holder against the victim because the release is based on the insurance contract (for more details see below no 66f). For the general admissibility of risk restrictions see above no 39. **41**

*c) aggregate limits,*

As mentioned before, the federal legislator has a tendency to specify a minimum insurance sum (see above no 36). It can be said that the existing provisions predominantly stipulate either a minimum insurance sum or a 'sufficient' coverage.[42] The provisions in federal law do not explicitly state whether aggregate limits are admissible. Consequently, it is unclear as to whether aggregate limits are in fact admissible and to which extent. **42**

*d) claims series clauses,*

See above no 39. **43**

*e) other clauses?*

See above no 39. **44**

12. *What are the consequences if the liability insurance contract concluded in order to fulfil the insurance obligation contravenes what the law stipulates as to contents (see above Questions 10 and 11)?*

As mentioned before, apart from a few exceptions, the provisions do not explicitly specify whether risk restrictions are admissible and to what extent. Quite a few of them, however, specify a minimum insurance sum. **45**

**41** Giger/*Giger* (fn 24) art 64 no 4.
**42** *Beck* (fn 1) 6.

46 The consequences of a violation of such stipulations vary, as there are no generally applicable rules in administrative or civil law on such consequences.

47 For instance, an attorney whose insurance cover does not fulfil the legal requirements violates the rules of professional conduct. According to art 17 para 1 BGFA (Attorney Act), the supervisory authority for attorneys may take disciplinary action against the attorney in question. Disciplinary measures in general include formal warnings, reprimands, fines up to CHF 20,000 and temporary or permanent disbarment (art 17 para 1 lit a–e BGFA).[43] Other provisions make the violation of such stipulations a criminal offence, for example art 31 Nuclear Liability Act (*Kernenergiehaftpflichtgesetz*, KHG). However, for provisions which stipulate that liability insurance cover is a prerequisite for the admissibility of carrying out a particular activity (as opposed to provisions which only stipulate that liability insurance cover is needed to comply with the rules of professional conduct such as art 12 lit f BGFA (Attorney Act), art 40 lit h MedBG (Medical Professions Act) or art 27 lit f PsyG (Psychology Professions Act)), a violation of these stipulations generally leads to the refusal of the necessary authorisation by the supervisory authority. An example can be found in art 106 para 1 Aviation Regulation (*Luftfahrtgesetz*, LFV), which states that an air transport enterprise will only be granted an operational permit if it proves that it has taken out insurance to cover its liability and the legal requirements as to minimum insurance sums are fulfilled.[44] For further examples see above no 13 and no 34.

---

**43** Full text in German: 'Bei Verletzung dieses Gesetzes kann die Aufsichtsbehörde folgende Disziplinarmassnahmen anordnen:

a. eine Verwarnung;
b. einen Verweis;
c. eine Busse bis zu 20.000 Franken;
d. ein befristetes Berufsausübungsverbot für längstens zwei Jahre;
e. ein dauerndes Berufsausübungsverbot.'

**44** Full text in German: 'Eine Betriebsbewilligung wird einem Gesuchsteller nur erteilt, wenn er: lit. b: nachweist, dass er gegen die Folgen seiner Haftpflicht bis zu den Beträgen nach Buchstabe a versichert ist.'

*13.a) Are statutory stipulations as to the contents of the policy (eg, regarding the amount of the insurance sum, the ban on certain risk exclusion clauses, on deductibles, etc, see above Questions 10 and 11) also binding in favour of the insurance holder? Or is it nonetheless possible for the liability insurer and the insurance holder acting within their internal relationship to agree risk exclusion clauses, deductibles, aggregate limits, and claims series clauses, etc (see above Questions 10 and 11), releasing the insurer from its liability to pay?*

This again depends on the specific provision. The legislator may pronounce such statutory stipulations binding in favour of the insurance holder. For instance, the statutory stipulations of art 59 VVG (Insurance Contract Act) concerning liability insurance for business activities may not be altered to the disadvantage of the insurance holder or the beneficiary according to art 98 para 2 VVG (see above nos 32 and 38). **48**

The keeper of a motor vehicle may, on the other hand, agree on risk exclusion clauses which are not included in the list of admissible clauses in art 63 para 3 SVG (Road Traffic Act), thus releasing the insurer from its liability to pay within their internal relationship. The insurer, however, may not contest the claim of a victim of the insurance holder on the ground of such a risk exclusion clause.[45] **49**

*b) If it is possible for liability insurer and insurance holder acting within their internal relationship to agree a release from the obligation to pay (see above Question a): What consequences does this entail? Must the insurer first pay out to the victim and can then have recourse to the insurance holder? Or is another construction provided for the relationship between insurer, insurance holder and victim?*

This cannot be answered in a generally applicable manner, as it again depends on the specific provisions. **50**

In the above mentioned case of the liability of the keeper of a motor vehicle art 65 SVG (Road Traffic Act) applies. According to art 65 para 1 SVG, the victim has a direct claim against the insurer (see below nos 60 and 63) and as per art 65 para 2 SVG the insurer cannot hold the fact that vis-à-vis the insurance holder it is freed from the obligation to pay against the victim if said release is based on the insurance contract or the Insurance Contract Act 1908 (see below no 68). However, according to art 65 para 3 SVG, the insurer may – in certain cases is **51**

**45** Giger/*Giger* (fn 24) art 63 no 6.

even obliged to – then take recourse against the insurance holder as it would have been released from its obligation to pay according to the insurance contract (see below no 52 and no 70).

*14.a) Does your general (voluntary) liability insurance law include a statutory risk exclusion in respect of intentional damage by the insurance holder or the insured person?*

52 The general insurance law does include such a statutory risk exclusion, which also applies to liability insurance. According to art 14 para 1 VVG (Insurance Contract Act), the insurer is not liable (meaning it does not have to pay) for intentional damage by the insurance holder or the insured person.[46] The article requires that the insurance holder or the insured person intentionally caused the occurrence of an insured event. The definition of 'intentionally' is somewhat controversially discussed in case law and academic literature. It is generally acknowledged that the definition includes intent (*Absicht*) as defined by the criminal law, according to which intent is given if the aim of the actions of a person was the occurrence of the damage.[47] On the other hand, it is also acknowledged by the Swiss Supreme Court (*Bundesgericht*) and most of the academic literature that *dolus eventualis* (*Eventualvorsatz*), where the acting person does not want damage to occur, but accepts the possibility that damage could occur because of his or her actions, is excluded by the definition. Finally, there is legal uncertainty at present as to whether *dolus directus* (*direkter Vorsatz*) is also included by the definition.[48] Furthermore, if the insurance holder or the beneficiary acted with gross negligence, the insurer is authorised to reduce the compensation in proportion to the degree of culpability (art 14 para 2 VVG).[49] This penalty may be tightened by contractual agreement as art 14 para 2 VVG is not binding in favour of the insurance holder. However, up until 1 January 2015 full coverage could be obtained on the insurance market for most cases of gross negligence by paying an additional premium. This practice was restricted by a legislative amendment to art 65 para 3 SVG (Road Traffic Act) as part of a legislative project called *Via sicura* which aims to improve safety in road traffic. Ac-

46 Full text in German: 'Der Versicherer haftet nicht, wenn der Versicherungsnehmer oder der Anspruchsberechtigte das befürchtete Ereignis absichtlich herbeigeführt hat.'
47 *A Hönger/M Süsskind* in: H Honsell/NP Vogt/AK Schnyder (eds), Basler Kommentar Versicherungsvertragsgesetz (hereinafter BSK VVG) (2001) art 14 no 16 f.
48 BSK VVG/*Hönger/Süsskind* (fn 47) art 14 no 17.
49 Full text in German: 'Hat der Versicherungsnehmer oder der Anspruchsberechtigte das Ereignis grobfahrlässig herbeigeführt, so ist der Versicherer berechtigt, seine Leistung in einem dem Grade des Verschuldens entsprechenden Verhältnisse zu kürzen.'

cording to the amended art 65 para 3 SVG, insurers are obligated to take recourse against the damaging party which acted with gross negligence, although only if the cause of the damage is either driving under the influence of alcohol or impaired or speeding as defined by art 90 para 4 SVG.[50] The extent of the recourse depends on the degree of culpability and the economic standing of the person the recourse is taken against (art 65 para 3 sent 3 SVG). The amended article entered into force on 1 January 2015.

*b) If the general liability insurance law contains a statutory risk exclusion in respect of intentional damage inflicted by the insurance holder (see above Question a): Does this also apply in cases of compulsory liability insurance?*

Article 14 VVG (Insurance Contract Act) also applies to compulsory liability insurance. There are, however, some exceptions where the exclusion is valid in relation to the insurance holder, but void in relation to the injured party, one example being the liability of the keeper of a motor vehicle. According to art 65 para 2 SVG (Road Traffic Act), the insurer cannot hold the fact that vis-à-vis the insurance holder it is freed from the obligation to pay against the victim if said release is based on the Insurance Contract Act (for more details and a list of such exceptions see below no 67 f). 53

# IV. Protection Mechanisms

*15. Are insurers obliged to contract when they offer liability insurance policies covering a risk for which the insurance holder is obliged to obtain cover?*

The Swiss legislator may stipulate such an obligation and has done so in a number of cases in Swiss law in general.[51] 54

**50** Full text in German of the revised art 65 para 3 SVG (sents 2 and 3 are new): 'Der Versicherer hat ein Rückgriffsrecht gegen den Versicherungsnehmer oder den Versicherten, soweit er nach dem Versicherungsvertrag oder dem Bundesgesetz vom 2. April 1908 über den Versicherungsvertrag zur Ablehnung oder Kürzung seiner Leistung befugt wäre. Wurde der Schaden in angetrunkenem oder fahrunfähigem Zustand oder durch ein Geschwindigkeitsdelikt im Sinne des Artikels 90 Absatz 4 verursacht, so muss der Versicherer Rückgriff nehmen. Der Umfang des Rückgriffs trägt dem Verschulden und der wirtschaftlichen Leistungsfähigkeit der Person Rechnung, auf die Rückgriff genommen wird.'

**51** *P Gauch/W Schluep/J Schmid* (eds), Schweizerisches Obligationenrecht Allgemeiner Teil, Band I (9th edn 2008) no 1101a ff; *C Huguenin*, Obligationenrecht Allgemeiner und Besonderer Teil (2012) no 159 ff.

55 As of today, there are no such obligations in Swiss private insurance law (as opposed to the social insurance law).[52] While other countries at least stipulate such an obligation for the liability of the keeper of a motor vehicle, Swiss law does not stipulate any such obligations to contract in the area of compulsory liability insurance.[53]

*16. If there is no obligation to contract: Are there comparable mechanisms provided to ensure that an insurance agreement is concluded?*

56 No such mechanisms have been established by the legislator.

*17. Is the insurance holder prohibited from disposing over his cover entitlement to the disadvantage of the victim (eg, by surrendering his entitlement)?*

57 Article 60 para 1 VVG (Insurance Contract Act) stipulates that the injured party has a right of lien (*Pfandrecht*) on the claim of the insurance holder against the insurer.[54] This provision applies to all liability insurance and consequently prohibits the insurance holder from disposing over his cover entitlement to the disadvantage of the victim.[55]

*18. Does the victim enjoy special protection against insolvency on the part of the insurance holder with regard to the sum payable by the liability insurer?*

58 In the case of an insolvency of the insurance holder, art 60 VVG (Insurance Contract Act) also prohibits the other creditors of the insurance holder from disposing over the sum payable by the liability insurer, because it grants to the injured party a right to separate satisfaction from this sum.[56]

*19.a) In what manner can the victim obtain the insurance payment?*

59 This depends on the specific type of duty as the provisions vary. However, in most cases the victim has to proceed against the injuring party, as the insurer is

---

**52** *S Fuhrer*, Schweizerisches Privatversicherungsrecht (2011) no 3.63.

**53** *Oftinger/Stark* (fn 14) 360 f; *A Maurer*, Schweizerisches Privatversicherungsrecht (1995) 152 f.

**54** For full text in German see fn 3.

**55** *C Frey/S Eggenschwiler Suppan* in: H Honsell/NP Vogt/AK Schnyder/P Grolimund (eds), Basler Kommentar Versicherungsvertragsgesetz Nachführungsband (hereinafter BSK VVG Nachf Bd) (2012) art 60 ad no 13; *Beck* (fn 15) 66.

**56** BSK VVG Nachf Bd/*Frey/Eggenschwiler Suppan* (fn 55) art 60 ad no 13; *Beck* (fn 15) 66.

only obliged to make payments to the insurance holder based on the insurance contract.[57]

In a few cases the legislator stipulates a direct claim of the victim against the insurer, this, however, being the exception to the rule. These cases are the liability of hunters[58], the liability of the keeper of a motor vehicle[59], the liability concerning nuclear material und nuclear plants[60], the liability of the owner of pipelines[61], the liability of conductors of research on humans[62] and the liability of the keeper of a ship[63]. **60**

However, irrespective of whether a direct claim has been established by the legislator or not, the victim always has a right of lien on the claim of the insurance holder against the liability insurer according to art 60 para 1 VVG (Insurance Contract Act; see above no 57). In practice, it is often not necessary to enforce said right, as the insurer always has the right to pay the compensation directly to the injured third party irrespective of a contravening request of the insurance holder (art 60 para 1 sent 2 VVG). Furthermore, the insurer can be held accountable for his actions which harm this right of the victim (art 60 para 2 VVG), therefore it is in its interest to pay the compensation directly to the victim. Should the insurer, for example, pay out the insurance sum to the insurance holder without the approval of the victim, it risks having to pay out the insurance sum twice.[64] **61**

If the insurer refuses to pay, the victim can either file a suit against the insurance holder or initiate debt collection proceedings according to the Federal Law on Debt Collection and Bankruptcy (*Bundesgesetz über Schuldbetreibung und Konkurs*, SchKG). However, the court judgment against the insurance holder has no legal effect vis-à-vis the insurer. Therefore further legal proceedings have to be initiated.[65] **62**

---

**57** *S Fuhrer*, Die Totalrevision des Haftpflicht- und des Versicherungsvertragsrechts als Chance für eine Vereinheitlichung und Modernisierung der Bestimmungen zum Schutz geschädigter Personen, in: T Sutter-Somm/F Hafner/G Schmid/K Seelmann (eds), Risiko und Recht, Festgabe zum Schweizerischen Juristentag (2004) 6 ff and 15.

**58** Art 16 para 2 JSG (Hunting Act).

**59** Art 65 para 1 SVG (Road Traffic Act).

**60** Art 19 para 1 KHG (Nuclear Liability Act).

**61** Art 37 para 1 RLG (Pipelines Act).

**62** Art 13 para 4 Research on Humans Regulation (Humanforschungsverordnung, HFV); art 14 para 2 sent 1 Clinical Trials on Humans Regulation (Verordnung über klinische Versuche, KlinV).

**63** Art 33 para 1 BSG (Inland Shipping Act).

**64** *B Carron* in: H Honsell/NP Vogt/AK Schnyder (eds), Basler Kommentar Versicherungsvertragsgesetz (2001) art 60 no 30 f; *Beck* (fn 15) 66 f.

**65** For further information see: BSK VVG/*Carron* (fn 64) art 60 no 22 ff.

*b) Does the victim have a direct right of action against the liability insurer (action directe) in the case of voluntary or compulsory liability insurance?*

63 As mentioned above, there are a few provisions which establish such a direct right of action in the case of compulsory liability insurance (see above no 60).

*20. When settling the claim, is the liability insurer obliged to observe a certain procedure in the interests of the victim? For instance, must it pay the victim an advance within a certain period?*

64 Most provisions do not stipulate such obligations, the exception being the provisions on the liability of the keeper of a motor vehicle:

65 If a victim raises a claim against a liability insurer, the insurer has the obligations listed hereafter according to art 79c SVG (Road Traffic Act). If the liability is uncontested and the extent of the damage has been quantified, the insurer must, within three months, make an offer, stating its reasons, to settle the claim. If the liability is contested or has not (yet) been clearly established or the extent of the damage has not been fully quantified, the liability insurer has to provide an answer, stating its reasons, within three months.

*21.a) In the context of its relationship with the victim, can the liability insurer rely on the fact that vis-à-vis the insurance holder (= damaging party) it is freed from the obligation to pay, eg, due to the insurance holder breaching an obligation of conduct/warranty (Obliegenheitsverletzung) or due to him defaulting on premiums?*

66 This again depends on the specific provision. However, in most cases the liability insurer can indeed rely on the fact that vis-à-vis the insurance holder it is freed from the obligation to pay, with the hereafter introduced legal concept of the *Einredenausschluss* being the exception to this rule:

67 In a few cases the legislator stipulates that the insurer cannot hold the fact that vis-à-vis the insurance holder it is freed from the obligation to pay against the victim. In other words it cannot use this defence against the victim. In German this concept is therefore called *Einredenausschluss*. Such rules are stipulated for the liability of huntsmen[66], the liability of the keeper of a motor vehicle[67], the liability concerning nuclear material and nuclear plants[68], the liability

---

**66** Art 16 para 3 JSG (Hunting Act).

**67** Art 65 para 2 SVG (Road Traffic Act).

**68** Art 19 para 2 KHG (Nuclear Liability Act).

of the owner of pipelines[69], the liability of conductors of research on humans[70] and the liability of the keeper of a ship[71].

b) *Does the law distinguish on the basis of the ground for the release from the obligation to pay so that in some cases the insurer may not invoke its release from such obligation vis-à-vis the victim?*

Yes, it does. Article 16 para 3 JSG (Hunting Act), art 65 para 2 SVG (Road Traffic Act), art 19 para 2 KHG (Nuclear Liability Act), art 37 para 2 Pipelines Act (*Rohrleitungsgesetz*, RLG), art 14 para 2 sent 2 KlinV (Clinical Trials on Humans Regulation) and art 33 para 2 Inland Shipping Act (*Binnenschifffahrtsgesetz*, BSG) all specify that the insurer cannot hold the fact that vis-à-vis the insurance holder it is freed from the obligation to pay against the victim if said release is based on either the insurance contract or the VVG (Insurance Contract Act). Defences which are based on the insurance contract are, for example: risk exclusion clauses, agreed deductibles or the agreement that the legal costs of a law suit will be deducted from the payable insurance sum.[72] Defences which are based on the Insurance Contract Act are, for example: breaches of duties of disclosure according to arts 4 ff, 38 and 39 VVG, substantial increase in risk according to art 28 ff VVG, suspension of the insurance contract due to premium default according to art 20 para 3 VVG, fraudulent insurance claims according to art 40 VVG or intentional damage or gross negligence according to art 14 VVG (for more details see above no 52).[73] 68

c) *If the insurer must still pay the victim despite being released from its obligation to pay vis-à-vis the insurance holder (see above Question b), may it take recourse against the latter?*

Yes, such provisions normally allow the insurer to take recourse against the insurance holder. 69

For instance, as per art 65 para 3 SVG (Road Traffic Act), the insurer *may* (as of 1 January 2015 *is even obligated to* in certain cases, see no 52) take recourse against the insurance holder or the insured person if, according to the insur- 70

**69** Art 37 para 2 RLG (Pipelines Act).
**70** Art 13 para 4 HFV (Research on Humans Regulation); art 14 para 2 sent 2 KlinV (Clinical Trials on Humans Regulation).
**71** Art 33 para 2 BSG (Inland Shipping Act).
**72** *Fuhrer* (fn 57) 7 fn 30.
**73** *Fuhrer* (fn 57) 7 fn 29.

ance contract or the Insurance Contract Act, it would have been released from its obligation to pay or would have been authorised to reduce the compensation.[74]

71 Similar provisions exist for the liability of hunters[75], the liability concerning nuclear material and nuclear plants[76], the liability of the owner of pipelines[77], the liability of conductors of research on humans[78] and the liability of the keeper of a ship[79].

*22.a) Within its relationship to the victim, can the liability insurer invoke the fact that the insurance agreement had already ended by the time relevant in respect of the duty to provide cover?*

72 This again depends on the specific type of duty, but often the provisions do not specifically regulate this matter.

73 One exception is the liability of the keeper of a motor vehicle. Article 68 para 2 SVG (Road Traffic Act) states that, first of all, the insurer has to notify the road traffic licensing department if an insurance policy is suspended or has, for whatever reason, ended. Secondly, the provision states that, in the insurer's relationship with the victim, the suspension or cancellation only takes effect when the licence plates and the vehicle licence have been handed in to the road traffic licensing department or, at the latest, 60 days after the notification of the insurer has reached the road traffic licensing department.[80]

74 Similar provisions exist for the liability of air transport enterprises[81], the liability of the keeper of an aircraft for damage to third parties on the ground[82],

74 Full text in German: 'Der Versicherer hat ein Rückgriffsrecht gegen den Versicherungsnehmer oder den Versicherten, soweit er nach dem Versicherungsvertrag oder dem Bundesgesetz vom 2. April 1908 über den Versicherungsvertrag zur Ablehnung oder Kürzung seiner Leistung befugt wäre.'

75 Art 16 para 4 JSG (Hunting Act).

76 Art 20 KHG (Nuclear Liability Act).

77 Art 37 para 3 RLG (Pipelines Act).

78 Art 13 para 4 HFV (Research on Humans Regulation); art 14 para 3 KlinV (Clinical Trials on Humans Regulation).

79 Art 34 BSG (Inland Shipping Act).

80 Full text in German: 'Aussetzen und Aufhören der Versicherung sind vom Versicherer der Behörde zu melden und werden, sofern die Versicherung nicht vorher durch eine andere ersetzt wurde, gegenüber Geschädigten erst wirksam, wenn der Fahrzeugausweis und die Kontrollschilder abgegeben sind, spätestens jedoch 60 Tage nach Eingang der Meldung des Versicherers. Die Behörde hat Fahrzeugausweis und Kontrollschilder einzuziehen, sobald die Meldung eintrifft.'

81 Art 106 para 2 LFV (Aviation Regulation).

82 Art 128 lit b LFV (Aviation Regulation).

the liability concerning genetically modified or pathogenic organisms[83], the liability concerning nuclear material and nuclear plants[84], the liability of the owner of pipelines[85] and the liability of the keeper of a ship[86].

b) *If the insurer must pay the victim despite the termination of the insurance agreement by the time relevant for the duty to provide cover (see above Question a), can it take recourse against the insurance holder?*

In the above mentioned example of the liability of the keeper of a motor vehicle, 75
the provisions do not explicitly state so, but the above mentioned art 65 para 3 SVG (Road Traffic Act) applies to this case as well (cf above no 70). However, the insurer loses its right to take recourse against the insurance holder if it fails to comply with the obligation to notify the road traffic licensing department.[87]

23.a) *Are there cases in which a damaging party does not effectively conclude the required liability insurance and the victim injured by him nonetheless receives compensation for his loss from a liability insurer or another compensation scheme (eg, a guarantee fund)?*

Yes, such provisions exist for the liability of the keeper of a motor vehicle (cf 76 76
SVG).

The Swiss National Guarantee Fund (NGF) covers the damage caused by 77
unidentified or uninsured motor vehicles and trailers if liability insurance is required according to the Road Traffic Act (art 76 para 2 lit a no 1 SVG). This is financed through a contribution due by the vehicle holders (cf art 76a SVG). According to art 76 para 4 SVG, the NGF is only obliged to pay damages in the amount that exceeds other existing damage insurance claims or social insurance claims of the victim.

In addition, art 77 para 1 SVG establishes a liability of the States in the event 78
that they violate their obligations regarding the issuance and seizure of licence plates and vehicle licences. In certain cases both art 76 SVG and art 77 SVG might apply, for example if an uninsured motor vehicle which was wrongly is-

**83** Art 11 para 7, art 14 para 7 Regulation on the handling of organisms in the environment (Freisetzungsverordnung, FrSV); art 14 para 2 Regulation on the handling of organisms in closed systems (Einschliessungsverordnung, ESV).
**84** Art 21 KHG (Nuclear Liability Act).
**85** Art 36 RLG (Pipelines Act).
**86** Art 36 para 2 BSG (Inland Shipping Act).
**87** Giger/*Giger* (fn 24) art 68 no 5; *Oftinger/Stark* (fn 14) 400 ff.

sued a licence plate causes an accident. The provisions do not explicitly state whether in such a case one of the provisions must be considered as a *lex specialis* vis-à-vis the other or whether they are both applicable. However, art 77 SVG has to be considered as a *lex specialis* vis-à-vis art 76 SVG as the state has violated its obligations and is therefore at fault. Oftinger/Stark also consider that art 77 SVG takes precedence.[88]

*b) In the event that the policy taken out was not in fact effectively concluded, is it necessary to distinguish on the basis of the ground for this ineffectiveness, eg, whether the reason for the contract not coming into effect was:*

**79** Neither art 76 SVG nor art 77 SVG distinguish on the basis of the ground for this ineffectiveness.

*i) a lack of legal capacity on the part of the insurance holder,*

**80** See above no 79.

*ii) lack of consent,*

**81** See above no 79.

*iii) falsa procuratio (unauthorised agency)?*

**82** See above no 79.

*c) Can the liability insurer (or the alternative compensation scheme) that must provide cover even though the insurance policy was not effectively concluded (see above Questions a and b) have recourse against the damaging party?*

**83** Article 76 para 6 SVG states that, when the national guarantee fund pays damages to the victim, there will be subrogation to the rights of the victim for the amount of the compensation paid.[89]

**84** According to art 77 para 2 SVG, the state or its insurer has the right to take recourse for payments made based on the liability according to art 77 para 1 SVG

**88** *Oftinger/Stark* (fn 14) nos 389 and 396.

**89** Full text in German: 'Mit der Zahlung der Ersatzleistung an den Geschädigten tritt der Nationale Garantiefonds für die von ihm gedeckten gleichartigen Schadensposten in die Rechte des Geschädigten ein.'

(see above no 78) against the keeper of the motor vehicle if said keeper was not in good faith concerning the fact that it did not have the required insurance coverage.[90]

*24.a) Are there cases in which a damaging party does not take out any liability insurance, ie not even an ineffective insurance policy (see above Question 23), and the victim whom he injured is still compensated for his damage by a liability insurer or another compensation scheme (guarantee fund, etc)?*

Yes, arts 76 and 77 SVG also apply in this case (cf above no 76ff). **85**

*b) Can the liability insurer (or the alternative compensation scheme) that must provide cover despite the total absence of any insurance agreement (see above Question a) have recourse against the damaging party?*

See above no 83f. **86**

*25. Is the victim protected against the insolvency of the liability insurer?*

According to art 54a VAG (Insurance Supervision Act), claims of insured per- **87**
sons enjoy certain privileges in the bankruptcy proceedings of an insurer. This applies even if the claim is brought by the victim by way of a direct claim or in execution of the right of lien (*Pfandrecht*) according to art 60 VVG (Insurance Contract Act; cf above no 57) because the term insured persons (*Versicherte*) as used by the legislator in the Insurance Supervision Act in the area of liability insurance also encompasses victims.[91]

Furthermore, art 76 para 2 lit b SVG states that the national guarantee fund **88**
compensates damage if it was caused by a motor vehicle which is licensed in Switzerland and bankruptcy proceedings were opened over the liability insurer of said vehicle.[92]

---

**90** Full text in German: 'Der Kanton oder sein Versicherer hat den Rückgriff gegen den Halter, der nicht im guten Glauben war, er sei durch die vorgeschriebene Versicherung gedeckt.'

**91** *M Mächler* in: PC Hsu/E Stupp (eds), Basler Kommentar Versicherungsaufsichtsgesetz (2013) art 1 no 47.

**92** Full text in German: 'Er deckt die Haftung für Schäden, die durch in der Schweiz zugelassene Motorfahrzeuge und Anhänger verursacht werden, wenn über den leistungspflichtigen Haftpflichtversicherer der Konkurs eröffnet worden ist.'

*26. Are there rules that serve in particular the protection of the victim when the liability insurance was only concluded voluntarily – ie without it being compulsory?*

89 Yes, art 60 VVG (cf above no 57). This provision applies to compulsory as well as voluntarily concluded liability insurance.

# V. Supervision and Sanctions

*27.a) In which cases must the insurance holder prove to an authority before commencing an activity requiring insurance that he has taken out the respective prescribed liability insurance cover (see above Question 4.e)?*

90 As mentioned before, such provisions are quite common (see above no 12).

*b) Must the insurer inform an authority when liability insurance taken out to meet an insurance obligation ends?*

91 This depends on the specific provision, but it can be said that such a duty is the exception to the rule. An example is art 68 para 2 SVG (Road Traffic Act), which establishes such an obligation (see above no 73f).

92 Similar provisions exist for the liability of operators of cableways[93], the liability concerning genetically modified or pathogenic organisms[94], the liability concerning nuclear material and nuclear plants[95], the liability of the owner of pipelines[96], the liability of the keeper of a ship[97], the liability of trolley-bus corporations[98] and the liability concerning xenotransplantation[99].

*c) Is the insurer also under a duty to inform when a liability insurance agreement is in existence but it has no duty to provide cover – eg, due to defaults on premium payments?*

93 This again depends on the specific provisions, but it can be said that such a duty is the exception to the rule. Article 68 para 2 SVG (Road Traffic Act) estab-

**93** Art 21 para 4 Cableway Act (Seilbahngesetz, SebG).

**94** Art 11 para 6, art 14 para 6 FrSV (Regulation on the handling of organisms in the environment); art 14 para 1 ESV (Regulation on the handling of organisms in closed systems).

**95** Art 21 KHG (Nuclear Liability Act).

**96** Art 36 RLG (Pipelines Act).

**97** Art 36 para 2 BSG (Inland Shipping Act).

**98** Art 16 para 3 Trolley-bus Act (Trolleybus-Gesetz, TrG).

**99** Art 26 para 4 Xenotransplantation Regulation (Xenotransplantationsverordnung).

lishes such an obligation (for more details see above no 73f). Similar provisions exist for the liability of operators of cableways, the liability concerning genetically modified or pathogenic organisms, the liability concerning nuclear material and nuclear plants, the liability of the owner of pipelines, the liability of the keeper of a ship, the liability of trolley-bus corporations and the liability concerning xenotransplantation (see above no 92).

d) *What are the consequences when the duties to inform of the end of contract or the release from payment obligations (see above Questions b and c) are violated?*

This again depends on the specific provision. For instance, the liability insurer **94** of a motor vehicle will have to pay the victim if it violates the duty to inform the road traffic licensing department, because art 68 para 2 SVG (Road Traffic Act) states that a suspension or cancellation of an insurance contract only takes effect when the licence plates and the vehicle licence have been handed in to the road traffic licensing department or, at the latest, 60 days after the notification has reached the road traffic licensing department (see above no 73).

28. *Is there some official body (authority, professional chamber) where an injured party can find out whether and where the injuring party who inflicted damage upon him in the course of an activity requiring insurance has liability insurance?*

Yes, such an official body exists, though only for the liability of the keeper of a **95** motor vehicle. The so-called Information Centre gives road traffic victims and social insurance bodies the information they need in order to be able to introduce a compensation claim (art 79a SVG).[100]

29. *Are there (public law) sanctions against the party who was required to take out insurance if such does not take out the compulsory liability insurance? Examples of this would be a ban on carrying out the activity that requires the insurance or the imposition of an administrative or judicial penalty.*

There is a wide spectrum of measures to ensure compliance with duties to take **96** out compulsory liability insurance.[101] Bearing in mind the many cases in which liability insurance cover is a prerequisite for the admission to an activity (cf

**100** For further information see: <http://www.nbi.ch/en/nvb/auskunftsstelle>.
**101** *Beck* (fn 1) 5; *Beck* (fn 15) 72.

above no 12f), the refusal of the necessary authorisation by the respective supervisory authority (cf above no 47) can be seen as the most common sanction to the omission of taking out a compulsory liability insurance contract.

97 Another example is the already mentioned disciplinary measures the supervisory authority on attorneys may take in the case of non-compliance as this constitutes a violation of a professional duty (see above no 47). As for an example for a criminal offence see likewise no 47.

# VI. Statutory Provisions required by the Constitution or the European Convention on Human Rights (ECHR)

*30. What has been said regarding the compatibility of the duties to take out liability insurance with your country's constitution and the ECHR? Please take into account case law and academic literature.*

98 At the moment there is little to none academic or political discourse on this topic. Naturally, duties to take out liability insurance are restrictions on fundamental rights guaranteed by the Federal Constitution of the Swiss Confederation (*Bundesverfassung der Schweizerischen Eidgenossenschaft*, BV), such as economic freedom (art 27 BV). But, according to art 36 BV, restrictions on fundamental rights, such as economic freedom, are feasible if they have a legal basis (significant restrictions must have their basis in a federal act), are justified in the public interest or for the protection of the fundamental rights of others and are proportionate.[102] Restrictions on fundamental rights by the stipulation of duties to take out liability insurance are generally based on a federal or state law, are in the public interest and are in my opinion proportionate, therefore such restrictions are feasible according to art 36 BV.

---

**102** Full text: 'Art. 36 Restrictions on fundamental rights
[1]Restrictions on fundamental rights must have a legal basis. Significant restrictions must have their basis in a federal act. The foregoing does not apply in cases of serious and immediate danger where no other course of action is possible.
[2]Restrictions on fundamental rights must be justified in the public interest or for the protection of the fundamental rights of others.
[3]Any restrictions on fundamental rights must be proportionate.
[4]The essence of fundamental rights is sacrosanct.'

*31. Does the constitution or the ECHR make any stipulations regarding the contents of such duties to take out liability insurance? Please take into account case law and academic literature.*

The Federal Constitution of the Swiss Confederation does not specifically make any stipulations regarding the contents of such duties to take out liability insurance. 99

## VII. Reform Efforts

*32. Are there efforts towards reforming the law regarding compulsory liability insurance?*

As mentioned at the beginning of this report, there are private (academic) efforts towards reforming the law regarding compulsory liability insurance. The Swiss Association for Tort and Insurance Law has set up a group of experts which has drawn up a draft for a Compulsory Liability Act.[103] One of the main goals of this project is the systematisation of the currently existing patchwork of provisions. For this purpose, certain principles of the liability insurance of the keeper of a motor vehicle have been generalised, such as the introduction of a general direct right of action against the insurer. Furthermore, a general duty to take out insurance has been introduced by the draft for bodily injury. 100

On 5 March 2014 Claude Janiak submitted a motion (*Motion*) to the Council of States (*Ständerat*) which was aimed at, among other things, commissioning the federal council (*Bundesrat*) with the drafting of uniform rules for compulsory liability insurance based on federal law[104].[105] The motion was passed by the Council of States (*Ständerat*) on 3 June 2014[106] but later rejected by the National Council (*Nationalrat*)[107] and has therefore failed. 101

**103** This draft, along with an explanatory report, was published in 2012 (cf fn 2).

**104** The text of the motion in German: 'Der Bundesrat wird beauftragt, für die nach Bundesrecht obligatorischen Haftpflichtversicherungen ein einheitliches, sich am Vorbild des Strassenverkehrsgesetzes orientierendes Schutzniveau für geschädigte Personen einzuführen, die gesetzliche Grundlage für die Regulierung von Massenkollisionen im Strassenverkehr zu schaffen und die Einführung einer auf die Haftung für Personenschäden begrenzten obligatorischen Privathaftpflichtversicherung zu prüfen.'

**105** More information can be found under the reference no 14.3043 in the *Curia Vista* database of the Swiss Parliament: <http://www.parlament.ch/d/suche/seiten/curia-vista.aspx>.

**106** AB 2014 S 420.

**107** AB 2014 N 2327.

102 There might, however, be a chance that this topic will be considered to some degree in the ongoing legislative procedure on the revision to the VVG (Insurance Contract Act).[108]

# VIII. Compulsory Liability Insurance and Liability Law

*33. Is, at the legislative level, any connection discernible between the nature of liability (in particular in the case of strict liability) and the imposition of compulsory liability insurance?*

103 In federal law the legislator has established duties to take out liability insurance for most cases of strict liability (*Gefährdungshaftung*). However, there are numerous cases of compulsory liability insurance where the liability is not strict in nature (fault liability).

**108** Information on the current status of this procedure can be found here: <https://www.sif.admin.ch/sif/de/home/dokumentation/finweb/regulierungsprojekte/total revision-versicherungsvertragsgesetz--vvg--.html>.

Özlem Gürses

# Compulsory Liability Insurance in the United Kingdom

## I. The Term Compulsory Liability Insurance

1. *Indicate the rules within your legal system that set out a duty to take out liability insurance. In this context, also take into account the implementation of international treaties (eg, the International Convention on Civil Liability for Bunker Oil Pollution Damage, 2001).*

There are a number of laws imposing a duty to take out compulsory liability insurance. For a non-exhaustive list, please see Annex: Rules on Compulsory Liability Insurance in the United Kingdom (at the end of this book). None of the statutes say anything about liability. They are all based on the assumption that liability exists.[1] 1

International Conventions regulating liability on several matters impose liability insurance. One example of this is sec 153(1) of the *Merchant Shipping Act 1995* (MSA 1995) which incorporates the *International Convention on Civil Liability for Oil Pollution Damage* 1992.[2] Similarly, The *International Convention on Civil Liability for Bunker Oil Pollution Damage 2001* as implemented in the MSA 1995 imposes liability for bunker pollution caused by ships.[3] After imposing li-

---

**1** Some of the international conventions especially related to shipping law may refer to strict liability followed by a duty to take out compulsory insurance to cover such liability. For references please see *Özlem Gürses*, Annex: Rules on Compulsory Liability Insurance in the United Kingdom (at the end of this book).

**2** The relevant section provides: 'Where, as a result of any occurrence, any oil is discharged or escapes from a ship to which this section applies, then (except as otherwise provided by this Chapter) the owner of the ship shall be liable –

(a) for any damage caused outside the ship in the territory of the United Kingdom by contamination resulting from the discharge or escape; and

(b) for the cost of any measures reasonably taken after the discharge or escape for the purpose of preventing or minimising any damage so caused in the territory of the United Kingdom by contamination resulting from the discharge or escape; and

(c) for any damage caused in the territory of the United Kingdom by any measures so taken.'

**3** The MSA 1995, sec 153A (1) provides: 'Subject to subsection (3), where, as a result of any occurrence, any bunker oil is discharged or escapes from a ship (except as otherwise provided by this Chapter) the owner of the ship shall be liable –

ability, the MSA 1995, secs 163 and 163A require compulsory insurance for liability for oil pollution and bunker pollution respectively. In the pollution context the following international conventions are also relevant: the *Merchant Shipping (Compulsory Insurance: Ships Receiving Trans-shipped Fish) Regulations 2012/2267*, which cover various liabilities, and the *Nairobi International Convention on the Removal of Wrecks 2007* as implemented by the *Merchant Shipping Act 1995* as amended. Further, it is anticipated that in the near future the *International Convention on Liability and Compensation for Damage in Connection with the Carriage of Hazardous and Noxious Substances by Sea 2010* will come into force as well as its corresponding implementation in the *Merchant Shipping Act 1995*. Insurance for passenger claims is also compulsory under the *Athens Convention 1974* as amended by the 2002 Protocol and implemented in the *Merchant Shipping Act 1995*. In a general context, the *Merchant Shipping (Compulsory Insurance of Shipowners for Maritime Claims) Regulations 2012/2267* implementing *Directive 2009/20/EC* on the insurance of shipowners for maritime claims prescribe compulsory insurance. Mention also should be made here of the *British Waterways Act 1995, sec 17(3)(b)* in relation to inland navigation and houseboats.

Although the UK is party to the *Montreal Convention for the Unification of Certain Rules for International Carriage by Air 1999*, it is not bound by its art 50 on compulsory insurance. Provisions to the same effect are applicable under two European Regulations (Council Reg (EEC) No 2407/92, art 7; Reg (EC) No 785/2004, art 4) and the related *Civil Aviation (Insurance) Regulations 2005/1089, reg 4*.

The UK is party to the *Paris Convention on Nuclear Third Party Liability 1960* and the *Brussels Supplementary Convention 1963* (both as amended by their protocols except the 2004 protocols). The relevant insurance provision can be found in the *Nuclear Installations Act 1965, sec 19*.

Similarly to other jurisdictions, employers must maintain insurance for the benefit of their employees under the *Employers' Liability (Compulsory Insurance) Act 1969*, and users of motor vehicles must hold an insurance policy under the *Road Traffic Act 1988, sec 143*.

Compulsory insurance is required from certain professionals: those providing childcare, dentists, estate agents, notaries, optometrists and opticians, os-

---

(a) for any damage caused outside the ship in the territory of the United Kingdom by contamination resulting from the discharge or escape; and

(b) for the cost of any measures reasonably taken after the discharge or escape for the purpose of preventing or minimising any damage so caused in the territory of the United Kingdom by contamination resulting from the discharge or escape; and

(c) for any damage caused in the territory of the United Kingdom by any measures so taken.'

teopaths, and solicitors (for the particular provisions see the Annex mentioned above).

Certain particular cases also require compulsory insurance: church property while in the redundancy waiting period, parsonage houses, common parts of a commonhold; package travel, package holidays and package tours; licensees of riding establishments, and licensees of wild animals (for the particular provisions see the Annex mentioned above).

## 2. *Is there a coherent 'law of compulsory liability insurance' in your legal system?*

There are no rules setting out a general duty to take out liability insurance. There 2
are, however, rules setting out a duty in specific areas of activity such as the obligation imposed by the *Employers' Liability (Compulsory Insurance) Act 1969* (the ELCIA 1969),[4] sec 1(1) which requires '... every employer carrying on any business in Great Britain shall insure, and maintain insurance, under one or more approved policies with an authorised insurer or insurers against liability for bodily injury or disease sustained by his employees, and arising out of and in the course of their employment in Great Britain in that business'. There are areas where the law imposes compulsory insurance while at the same time the relevant legislation imposes strict liability. An example for this is shipowners' liability for bunker pollution according to the International Convention on Civil Liability for Bunker Oil Pollution Damage 2001 as implemented in the Merchant Shipping Act 1995.[5]

## 3. *Is there a specific term for compulsory liability insurance in your legal system? How is it defined?*

The legislation which imposes a duty to take out liability insurance does not de- 3
fine liability insurance, however, it indicates clearly that insurance is a requirement the absence of which will be met with some sanctions. For instance

4 The ELCIA 1969 is supplemented by the Employers' Liability (Compulsory Insurance) Regulations 1998 (ELCIR 1998). The ELCIR 1998 is a statutory instrument which consolidates with amendments the Employers' Liability (Compulsory Insurance) General Regulations 1971 and subsequent amending regulations made under the Employers' Liability (Compulsory Insurance) Act 1969. The ELCIR 1998 will be referred to in the following paragraphs where necessary. Statutory instruments, also known as SIs, are a form of legislation which allows the provisions of an Act of Parliament to be subsequently brought into force or altered without Parliament having to pass a new Act. They are also referred to as secondary, delegated or subordinate legislation. See <http://www.parliament.uk/business/bills-and-legislation/secondary-legislation/statutory-instruments/>.

5 For the wording of MSA 1995, sec 153A see above fn 3.

the *Road Traffic Act 1988* (RTA 1988), sec 143(1)(a) is worded as follows: 'a person must not use a motor vehicle on a road [or other public place] unless there is in force in relation to the use of the vehicle by that person such a policy of insurance or such a security in respect of third party risks as complies with the requirements of this Part of this Act', and the RTA 1988, sec 143(2) provides: 'If a person acts in contravention of subsec (1) above he is guilty of an offence.' As stated above (no 1), sec 163A(2) of the MSA 1995 requires ships which arrive at or leave a port in the United Kingdom to be insured and to carry a certificate which is proof of insurance. Breach of this provision may result in 'conviction on indictment to a fine, or on summary conviction to a fine not exceeding the statutory maximum' of the master or registered owner (the MSA 1995, sec 163A(5)). Similar requirements regarding compulsory insurance are imposed against oil pollution caused by tankers carrying oil.[6] Thus it is derived from the remedy imposed for the breach of the obligation in question that in some cases the duty to take out liability insurance is compulsory.

4. *In which of the following cases does compulsory liability insurance apply according to prevailing opinion?*

a) *Duties to take out liability insurance which are not directly based on the law but on an order or decision issued by administrative authorities?*

4 In the UK the duties to take out liability insurance are imposed by legislation. There is no duty derived from an order or decision issued by administrative authorities. There is a duty imposed by a self-governing body which is explained in no 5 below.

b) *Duties to take out liability insurance that are not based directly on the law but on the statutes of a professional or other self-governing body?*

5 The Solicitors Regulation Authority (SRA),[7] which is a self-governing body set up by statute, makes rules requiring solicitors to obtain professional indemnity insurance (PII). The SRA's power to make such rules derives from the *Solicitors Act 1974* and the *Administration of Justice Act 1985* and the *Legal Services Act 2007*. *SRA Indemnity Insurance Rules 2013*[8] were made on 13 June 2013 by the

6 For similar provisions in relation to oil pollution caused by tankers carrying oil, see the MSA 1995, secs 153, 154, 157 and 168.

7 <www.sra.org.uk>.

8 <http://www.sra.org.uk/solicitors/handbook/indemnityins/content.page>.

Solicitors Regulation Authority Board under secs 31, 37, 79 and 80 of the Solicitors Act 1974, sec 9 of the Administration of Justice Act 1985, and para 19 of Schedule 11 to the Legal Services Act 2007, with the approval of the Legal Services Board[9] under para 19 of Schedule 4 to the Legal Services Act 2007 (rule 1.1 of the Legal Services Act). These Rules came into force on 1 October 2013 (rule 1.2) and they require solicitors, RELs,[10] RFLs,[11] recognised bodies and their managers and licensed bodies (in respect of their regulated activities) in private practice in England and Wales to take out and maintain professional indemnity insurance with participating insurers with effect from 1 October 2013 (rule 1.3). All notaries in practice as such within England and Wales are required to hold insurance against civil liability for professional negligence incurred by the notary in connection with his or her practice as a notary; and insurance against financial loss suffered by a third party in consequence of any dishonest or fraudulent act or any omission by the notary in connection with his or her practice as a notary (Notaries (Practising Certificates) Rules 2012, rules 4.2.3, 6).

c) *Duties to take out liability insurance that are not based on any public law but on a private law provision (eg, governing the relationship between employer and employee)?*

The Financial Conduct Authority (FCA) regulates the financial services industry 6
in the UK.[12] FCA's aim is to protect consumers, ensure the industry remains stable and promote healthy competition between financial services providers. The FCA has rule-making, investigative and enforcement powers that it uses to protect and regulate the financial services industry. FCA's powers and objectives are given by the *Financial Services and Markets Act 2000* (FSMA), sec 2.[13] The

9 The Legal Services Board is an independent body responsible for overseeing the regulation of lawyers in England and Wales. Its goal is to reform and modernise the legal services market by putting the interests of consumers at the heart of the system, reflecting the objectives of the statute that created it, the Legal Services Act 2007 (see <http://www.legalservicesboard.org.uk/>).

10 REL is a Registered European Lawyer, namely, an individual registered with the SRA under Regulation 17 of the European Communities (Lawyer's Practice) Regulations 2000 (SI 2000/1119).

11 RFL is a Registered Foreign Lawyer, namely, an individual registered with the SRA under sec 89 of the Courts and Legal Services Act 1990.

12 <www.fca.org.uk>.

13 Sec 2 mentions the Financial Services Authority which was replaced in April 2013 by two new regulatory bodies that will carry forward the philosophy of outcomes-based regulation,

FCA Handbook, Prudential Sourcebook for Mortgage and Home Finance Firms, and Insurance Intermediaries (MIPRU) requires insurance brokers to take out professional indemnity insurance. MIPRU 3.2.1 provides: 'A firm must take out and maintain professional indemnity insurance' (see below no 8).

*d) Duties to take out liability insurance that are not based on any public law but on a private law rule that is established by case law (and, eg, governs the relationship between employer and employee)?*

7 There is no case law which has imposed a duty to purchase compulsory liability insurance. As referred to above, except for international conventions,[14] the statutory regimes do not define liability but assume that liability exists under the common law and the insurance obligation may be imposed by statute. It has not been seen in case law that courts have imposed compulsory liability insurance in addition to the duty. The only sources to rely upon for liability insurance are Acts which may impose a duty regarding compulsory liability insurance (see Annex: Rules on Compulsory Liability Insurance in the United Kingdom, at the end of this book) or the Financial Conduct Authority Handbook or the rules of self-governing authorities such as SRA as referred to above (no 5).

*e) Cases in which there is no duty to take out liability insurance but liability insurance cover is a prerequisite for the admissibility of carrying out a particular activity?*

**8** This does not apply in the UK for the reason that some professions are required to take out liability insurance which is also a prerequisite for the admissibility of carrying out a particular activity in order to protect third party rights against the professionals in question. Therefore, when there is such a prerequisite, this is also a duty on the professional in question. For instance MIPRU 3.2.1 (cf above no 6) provides: 'A firm must take out and maintain professional indemnity insurance that is at least equal to the requirements of this section from:

(1) an *insurance undertaking* authorised to transact professional indemnity insurance in the *EEA*; or

---

intensive firm supervision and credible deterrence: The Prudential Regulation Authority (PRA) for regulation of all deposit-taking institutions, insurers and investment banks and The Financial Conduct Authority (FCA) which is responsible for the regulation of conduct in retail, as well as wholesale, financial markets and the infrastructure that supports these markets.

**14** See Question 1 (no 1) above.

(2) a *person* of equivalent status in: (i) a *Zone A country*; or (ii) the Channel Islands, Gibraltar, Bermuda or the Isle of Man.'

This is a threshold condition to be able to carry out activities as insurance brokers. An assured may suffer loss if his broker acts negligently and does not purchase the cover required by the assured and the assured is not able to claim under the insurance policy when the risk occurs. In case the broker does not have financial abilities to compensate the assured's loss, the FCA Handbook aims to ensure that the assured's loss will be compensated by the broker's insurer.

Similarly, SRA Authorisation Rules for Legal Services Bodies and Licens- 9
able Bodies 2011, Part 2 is titled 'Authorisation applications and decision period'. Under this heading rule 6.2 provides: 'The *SRA* may only grant an application for *authorisation* if the conditions in (a) to (d) below are met and '(d)' provides: 'the SRA is satisfied that upon authorisation, the body will be in compliance with the following rules: (i) SRA Indemnity Insurance Rules' (cf above no 5). Additionally, MIPRU reiterates threshold condition 4 (adequate resources). This threshold condition provides that a firm must have, on a continuing basis, resources that are, in the opinion of the appropriate regulator, adequate in relation to the regulated activities that the firm carries on. This threshold condition is one that has to be satisfied to obtain authorisation to carry on a regulated activity under FSMA 2000. Thus, a firm will not get approval to act as an insurance broker (a regulated activity) without professional indemnity cover.

### *f) Cases of alternative financial security, in which the duty to provide for financial security may be fulfilled either by taking out liability insurance or other forms of financial security (eg, bank guarantees)?*

Section 144 of the RTA 1988 (cf above no 3) provides 'Exceptions from require- 10
ment of third-party insurance or security.' Accordingly, a compulsory policy is not required where the vehicle is owned by a person who has deposited and keeps deposited with the Accountant General of the Supreme Court the sum of £ 500,000 at a time when the vehicle is being driven under the owner's control. The amount may be varied by a statutory instrument (sec 144(1A)-(1B) of the RTA 1988). The formalities relating to deposits are set out in the UK *Motor Vehicles (Third-Party Risks Deposits) Regulations 1992* (SI 1992/1284) which regulate the permitted securities which must be deposited, the manner in which interest on the sum deposited is to be allocated and the documentation necessary to accompany a deposit: a person making a deposit must do so by means of statutory certificate which is issued by the Accountant General of the Supreme Court and

fulfils all of the functions of the certificate of insurance which has to be issued with a compulsory policy.

Optometrists and opticians are required to have an 'indemnity arrangement' which may be a) a policy of insurance, b) an arrangement made for the purposes of indemnifying a person, or c) a combination of the two (*Opticians Act 1989, sec 10A(2)*).

11 A similar alternative security is provided under sec 163(2) of the MSA 1995 (see above nos 1–3 with regard to liability for oil pollution).

*g) Cases in which the duty to have insurance has only been created by a contractual agreement between potential injuring party and victim?*

12 A contract may impose a duty on the parties to purchase a liability insurance policy to cover injuries that may arise as a result of performing the contractual obligations. For instance, in construction contracts, a contractor may be asked to take out insurance covering contractual liability or liability in tort for defective design of the subject matter of the contract. However, this is not compulsory insurance in the sense of, for example, motor insurance or employers' liability insurance. A contractual provision will only have a contractual effect and enforcement between the parties to the contract and its breach will result in contractual remedies.

## II. Aims

*5. What are the aims of the rules that impose an obligation to take out liability insurance:*

*a) the protection of the victim,*

13 Where a person of limited financial resources becomes liable for a substantial amount of damages to a third party, that liability is likely to be satisfied only if that person carries liability insurance.[15] In order to protect the victim, the law imposes a requirement that liability insurance be carried in respect of particular perils.[16] For instance, the application and purpose of the indemnity insurance requirement for Insurance Intermediaries is explained under FCA Hand-

15 *R Merkin*, Colinvaux's Law of Insurance (hereinafter: Colinvaux) (11th edn 2016) para 20-01.
16 These perils are referred to throughout this report, eg road traffic liability, employers' liability to employees, brokers' liability to their clients.

book MIPRU 3.1.4 (cf above no 6). Any breach of the duties of a firm or of its agents under the regulatory system or civil law can give rise to claims being brought against the firm. Professional indemnity insurance has an important role to play in helping to finance such claims and thus in protecting the victim. In so doing, this chapter emphasises the threshold condition. This threshold condition provides that a firm must have, on a continuing basis, resources that are, in the opinion of the appropriate regulator, adequate in relation to the regulated activities that the firm carries on. Another example is the *Estate Agents Act 1979, sec 16(1)* which provides that an estate agent may not accept a client's money in the course of estate agency work unless there is an insurance arrangement in force in the event of his failing to account for such money to his client. Moreover, a person who would like to keep a dangerous animal shall keep a licence granted by the local authority. One of the conditions of the application for the licence is to hold insurance against liability for any damage which may be caused by the animal (*Dangerous Wild Animals Act 1976, sec 1(6)*).

In order to protect the victim, art 12(1) of the *Consolidated Motor Insurance* **14**
*Directive 2009*[17] provides that compulsory insurance 'shall cover liability for personal injury to all passengers, other than the driver, arising out of the use of the vehicle'. Moreover, any judgment obtained against the driver may be enforced against the insurer under sec 151f of the RTA 1988 (cf above no 3) insofar as the liability is one which was required to be covered by insurance. Moreover, the victim may, in accordance with the European Communities (Rights against Insurers) Regulations 2002 (SI 2002/3061), bring a direct action against insurers without first having to obtain a judgment against the user of the vehicle which can then be enforced against the user's insurers.

*b) the protection of the insurance holder,*

See below no 16. **15**

---

**17** A series of five EU Motor Insurance Directives was consolidated by European Parliament and Council Directive 2009/103/EC of 16 September 2009 relating to insurance against civil liability in respect of the use of motor vehicles, and the enforcement of the obligation to insure against such liability, Official Journal (OJ) L 263, 7.10.2009, 11–31. The Directives established a harmonised system of compulsory insurance throughout the European Union; the sole objective of the Directives is to ensure that, if there is liability under the relevant law, such liability is covered by insurance. A number of important extensions have been made to the Road Traffic Act 1988 to implement the Directives.

*c) the protection of the victim and the insurance holder,*

16 Section 145(3) of the RTA 1988 (cf above no 3) provides that the policy must insure: 'Such person, persons or classes of person as may be specified in the policy'. The insurer's liability is thus not just to indemnify the assured, but to indemnify any person who is stated by the policy to be covered by it.[18] The right of other users covered by a policy to sue under it where there is compulsory insurance is conferred by sec 148(7).[19] The provision operates to create a contract between the insurers and the authorised user.[20] Section 148(7) does not demand that motor policies contain named or authorised user extensions, but states merely that if such an extension is present, the insurer is liable to adhere to it with respect to the persons stated to be covered.[21]

17 Similar aims can be seen in the professional indemnity insurance that insurance brokers are required to take out (cf above no 8). MIPRU 3.1.3 (2) states that its purpose is to meet the statutory objectives of consumer protection as well as to protect and enhance the integrity of the UK financial system by ensuring that firms have adequate resources to protect themselves, and their customers, against losses arising from breaches of its duties under the regulatory system or civil law. Professional indemnity insurance has an important role to play in helping to finance such claims. Similarly notaries are required to purchase insurance cover for their civil liability for professional negligence and financial loss suffered by a third party in consequence of any dishonest or fraudulent act or any omission by the notary in connection with his or her practice as a notary.

*d) other aims, eg internalising the costs in the interests of society?*

18 Most aims have been explained above in nos 13–17. In the case of environmental remediation, obligatory insurance can be regarded as a tool to make sure that the polluter-pays principle prevails.

---

**18** Colinvaux (fn 15) para 22-027.

**19** Sec 148(7) provides: 'Notwithstanding anything in any enactment, a person issuing a policy or insurance under s.145 of this Act shall be liable to indemnify the persons or classes of persons specified in the policy in respect of any liability which the policy purports to cover in the case of those persons or classes of persons.'

**20** Colinvaux (fn 15) para 22-027.

**21** *Tattersall v Drysdale* [1935] 2 King's Bench (KB) 174; *Digby v General Accident Fire and Life Assurance Corp Ltd* [1943] Appeal Cases (AC) 121.

6. *Do the rules that prescribe a form of alternative financial security (see above Question 4.f) pursue the same aims as those rules that exclusively set out a duty to have liability insurance (ie with no other alternative financial security options)?*

As referred to above (cf above no 10), sec 144(1) of RTA 1988 provides an exception if £ 500,000 is deposited with the Accountant General of the Senior Courts. The Motor Vehicles (Third-Party Risks Deposits) Regulations 1992 SI 1992/1284 set out the rules regarding the procedure and governance of such deposit. This exception aims to protect the victim but does not have any broader effect than that. It should be noted that in practice this exception does not apply. **19**

With regard to compulsory insurance for oil pollution, the owner of a ship that carries more than 2,000 tons of oil in bulk as cargo may either take out insurance or other type of financial security, such as a bank guarantee or a certificate delivered by an international compensation fund, in an amount equal to the sums fixed by applying the limits of liability prescribed in the MSA 1995.[22] **20**

# III. Content of Insurance Cover

7. *Are the duties to take out liability insurance laid down by law only to cover extra-contractual compensation duties or also those arising out of contractual infringements?*

The insured liability is extra-contractual and based on claims in tort. Liability policies are commonly expressed in terms of covering 'liability at law'[23] which refers to negligence ie liability in tort.[24] If the source of liability is extra-contractual, arising from a contractual infringement, this would mean that the liability may be tortious and may be covered by the policy depending on its wording. **21**

8.a) *Are there duties to take out liability insurance aimed not only at the protection of absolutely protected rights (eg, property, bodily integrity) but additionally at compensating pure economic loss?*

Pure economic loss is generally excluded from compulsory insurance regimes. Duties to take out liability insurance clearly state for which types of risk the in- **22**

---

**22** The MSA 1995, sec 163(2).

**23** Colinvaux (fn 15) para 20-009.

**24** *West Wake Price & Co v Ching* [1956] 2 Lloyd's Law Reports (Lloyd's Rep) 618.

surance is required and coverage for pure economic loss is not included. By way of example, ELCIA 1969 (cf above no 2) require employers to insure against their liability for personal injury to their employees. Section 145(3)(a) of RTA 1988 (cf above no 3) provides 'insurance is required in respect of any liability which may be incurred by him or them in respect of the death of or bodily injury to any person or damage to property caused by, or arising out of, the use of the vehicle on a road [or other public place] in Great Britain ...'.

Notaries insurance must cover 'against financial loss suffered by a third party in consequence of any dishonest or fraudulent act or any omission by the notary in connection with his or her practice as a notary' (Notaries (Practising Certificates) Rules 2012, rule 6.1.2).

*b) Are there duties to take out liability insurance that are directed only or at least predominantly at the compensation of pure economic loss?*

23 Professional indemnity insurance (PII) is liability insurance that covers businesses in the event that a third party claims to have suffered a loss as a result of professional negligence. Insurance brokers[25] and solicitors[26] are under an obligation to take out a type of PII which primarily covers pure economic loss. Insurance brokers are under a duty to exercise reasonable skill and care in carrying out their clients' instructions. If a broker negligently takes out a policy which was not in accordance with the assured's instructions, the latter may not be able to claim under the policy when the risk materialises. In such a case the assured's loss is economic in nature and, since it was a result of the broker's negligence, the broker's professional indemnity insurance may cover the claim.

*9. Are there provisions that require the insurance of a third party's liability interest – for instance, that the employer must take out liability insurance for the benefit of an employee?*

24 The RTA 1988, sec 143 (cf above no 3) does not require that the person using a vehicle is the holder of a policy; it is permissible, and is indeed often the case, for the owner of a vehicle to take out a policy under which the insurance is valid if named persons or indeed any persons acting with the assured's permission operate the vehicle.

25 See above no 6.
26 See above no 5.

As for solicitors, *Appendix 1 SRA Minimum Terms and Conditions of Professional Indemnity Insurance* (the SRA Appendix 1) (cf above no 5) the insured must include: 'each service, administration, trustee or nominee company owned as at the date of occurrence of relevant circumstances by the insured firm and/or the principals of the insured firm' (rule 1.3.(b)) and 'each employee, each former employee and each person who becomes during the period of insurance an employee of the insured firm or a company referred to in Rule 1.3.(b)' (rule 1.3.(d)). 25

*10. To what extent do the rules requiring the compulsory conclusion of a liability insurance policy also specify the specific contents of the insurance coverage:*

*a) Is there always a (sufficiently well-defined) specification of the risk to be insured?*

It is not always the case but there are examples where the risks are specified. 26
Section 145 of the RTA 1988 (cf above no 3) and MIPRU 3.2.4 (cf above no 6) provide such information. The SRA Appendix 1 rule 1.1 (cf above no 25) contains a definition in general terms: 'The insurance must indemnify each insured against civil liability to the extent that it arises from private legal practice in connection with the insured firm's practice ...'. The *British Waterways Act 1995* requires a vessel owner and such persons as is or as are authorised by the owner to have control of the vessel to be insured in respect of any liability which may be incurred by the owner or any such other person resulting from the presence of the vessel on any inland waterway in respect of the death of or bodily injury to any person or any damage to property. The insurance provided under the Notaries (Practising Certificates) Rules 2012 requires cover against civil liability for professional negligence incurred by the notary in connection with his or her practice as a notary; and insurance against financial loss suffered by a third party in consequence of any dishonest or fraudulent act or any omission by the notary in connection with his or her practice as a notary.

*b) Are there provisions that require unlimited coverage?*

The SRA Appendix 1 rule 2.2 (cf above no 25) states: 'There must be no monetary 27
limit on the cover for defence costs.' However, rule 2.3 adds that: 'the insurance may provide that liability for defence costs in relation to a claim which exceeds the sum insured is limited to the proportion that the sum insured bears to the total amount paid or payable to dispose of the claim.' Article 9 of the Consolidated Motor Insurance Directive 2009 (cf above no 14) permits Member States to cap liability at € 1,000,000 per victim, or in the alternative at € 500,000 for all per-

sonal injury claims irrespective of the number of claims and victims. This derogation has not been taken up, and the amount of cover for personal injury has been unlimited since the origins of the legislation in 1930.

c) *If unlimited coverage is not required (see above Question b), is a minimum or maximum insurance sum always specified?*

**28** The coverage required under the RTA 1988 (cf above no 3) is not unlimited in respect of liability for damage to property caused by, or arising out of, any one accident involving a vehicle. For such claims, insurance for a sum greater than £ 1,000,000 is not required.[27] The Civil Aviation (Insurance) Regulations 2005/1089 (implementing Regulation (EC) No 785/2004 of the European Parliament and of the Council of 21 April 2004 on insurance requirements for air carriers and aircraft operators) require minimum insurance cover of 250,000 SDRs per passenger. For liability in respect of baggage, the minimum insurance cover must be 1,131 SDRs per passenger in commercial operations. For liability in respect of cargo, the minimum insurance cover must be 19 SDRs per kilogramme in commercial operations.

**29** The SRA Appendix 1 rule 2.1 (cf above no 25) provides: The sum insured for any one claim (excluding defence costs) must be, where the insured firm is a relevant recognised body or a relevant licensed body (in respect of its regulated activities), at least £ 3 million, and in all other cases, at least £ 2 million. Under MIPRU 3.2.7 (cf above no 6), the minimum limits of indemnity are: (1) for a single claim, € 1,120,200; and (2) in aggregate, € 1,680,300 (per year) or, if higher, 10% of annual income up to £ 30 million. The Notaries (Practising Certificate) Rules 2012 provide that the minimum and maximum limit of cover will be fixed from time to time by the authorities mentioned under the Rules. See rule 6.2.

**30** As stated above (no 2), the ELCIA 1969 requires every employer carrying on any business in Great Britain to insure against liability for bodily injury or disease sustained by its employees, and arising out of and in the course of their employment in Great Britain in that business. The Employers' Liability (Compulsory Insurance) Regulations 1998 (ELCIR 1998),[28] reg 3(1) provides that the amount for such insurance shall be, or shall in aggregate be not less than, £ 5 million in respect of

(a) a claim relating to any one or more of those employees arising out of any one occurrence; and
(b) any costs and expenses incurred in relation to any such claim.

---

**27** The RTA 1988, sec 145(4)(b).
**28** To the ELCIR see fn 4.

d) *Are there general statutory rules to be applicable if the respective law that requires compulsory insurance only makes incomplete stipulations regarding the content of the insurance coverage? An example of this would be § 114 para 1 of the German Insurance Contract Act (Versicherungsvertragsgesetz, VVG) 2008.*

No, there are no statutory rules to this effect. 31

11. *Is it admissible to restrict the insurance cover by agreeing:*

a) *risk exclusion clauses,*

The Unfair Contract Terms Act 1977 prohibits excluding liability for personal injury claims. However, the Act does not apply to insurance contracts (Schedule 1(1)(a)). For employers' liability insurance, the ELCIR 1998,[29] reg 2 states the conditions which are not permitted. These include any condition which provides (in whatever terms) that no liability (either generally or in respect of a particular claim) shall arise under the policy, or that any such liability so arising shall cease if – 32

(a) some specified thing is done or omitted to be done after the happening of the event giving rise to a claim under the policy;
(b) the policy holder does not take reasonable care to protect his employees against the risk of bodily injury or disease in the course of their employment;
(c) the policy holder fails to comply with the requirements of any enactment for the protection of employees against the risk of bodily injury or disease in the course of their employment; or
(d) the policy holder does not keep specified records or fails to provide the insurer with or make available to him information from such records.

Moreover, it is prohibited to include in an insurance policy any condition which requires the first amount of any claim or any aggregation of claims to be paid either by –

(a) a relevant employee; or
(b) an insured employer to the relevant employee.

29 To the ELCIR see fn 4.

33 Similarly, sec 148 of the RTA 1988 (cf above no 3) is entitled: 'Avoidance of certain exceptions to policies or securities.' Accordingly, policies that contain restrictions regarding the following will be of no effect:

(a) the age or physical or mental condition of persons driving the vehicle,
(b) the condition of the vehicle,
(c) the number of persons that the vehicle carries,
(d) the weight or physical characteristics of the goods that the vehicle carries,
(e) the time at which or the areas within which the vehicle is used,
(f) the horsepower or cylinder capacity or value of the vehicle,
(g) the carrying on the vehicle of any particular apparatus, or
(h) the carrying on the vehicle of any particular means of identification other than any means of identification required to be carried by or under [the Vehicle Excise and Registration Act 1994].

The following is not permitted in an insurance contract concluded under the Package Travel, Package Holidays and Package Tours Regulations 1992, reg 19. Any provision which provides 'no liability shall arise under the policy, or that any liability so arising shall cease: –

(i) in the event of some specified thing being done or omitted to be done after the happening of the event giving rise to a claim under the policy;
(ii) in the event of the policy holder not making payments under or in connection with other policies; or
(iii) unless the policy holder keeps specified records or provides the insurer with or makes available to him information therefrom.'

34 The relevant legislation may require 'adequate and appropriate coverage' (cf eg Dentists Act 1984, sec 26A[30]). This has been interpreted as intended '*for liabilities which may be incurred in carrying out work as a dentist*', that is to say liabilities which a dentist may incur as a result of providing dental treatment, rather than, for example, liabilities which a dentist may incur as a result of employing other people to provide dental treatment.[31] In *Whetstone (Trading As Whelby House Dental Practice) v Medical Protection Society Limited (Sued As Dental Protection Limited)*[32] HHJ Richard Seymour QC (sitting as a Judge of the High Court) said '... what, in my judgment, the Dentists Act 1984 s.26A(1) requires is that a dentist be covered by insurance, as defined, in respect of the li-

---

**30** Introduced into the Dentists Act 1984 by the Dentists Act 1984 (Amendment) Order 2005, SI 2005/2011.

**31** *Whetstone (Trading As Whelby House Dental Practice) v Medical Protection Society Limited (Sued As Dental Protection Limited)* [2014] England & Wales High Court (EWHC) 1024 (Queen's Bench, QB).

**32** [2014] EWHC 1024 (QB) para 63.

abilities which may be incurred in performing dental treatment, and does not extend to vicarious liability for others who do so.'

*b) deductibles,*

No deductibles are permitted under the ELCIA 1969 (ELCIR 1998,[33] reg 2(2), cf below no 57). 35

In the case of death or personal injury, the RTA 1988 (cf above no 3) does not provide for any minimum amount of compulsory insurance. Moreover, the insurer cannot rely upon any policy deductible.[34] 36

Professional indemnity insurance which may aim to cover pure economic loss may permit excesses. For instance, the SRA Appendix 1 rule 3 (cf above no 25) permits excesses. Rule 3.1 provides: 'The insurance may be subject to an excess of such monetary amount and on such terms as the insurer and the insured firm agree. Subject to Rule 3.4, the excess may be "self-insured" or partly or wholly insured without regard to these MTC.' However, rule 3.4 adds: 'The insurance must provide that, if an insured fails to pay to a claimant any amount which is within the excess within 30 days of it becoming due for payment, the claimant may give notice of the insured's default to the insurer, whereupon the insurer is liable to remedy the default on the insured's behalf. The insurance may provide that any amount paid by the insurer to remedy such a default erodes the sum insured.' In other words, if the insurer has to pay the excess because the assured has failed to do so, the policy may provide that the excess payment by the insurer erodes the limit of indemnity. Thus, if there are other claims against the assured, the total amount paid – including the excess – is deducted from the total sum insured so that only the lower amount remains. This does not erode the sum payable to the victim, unless the victim's claim is in excess of the aggregate limit of indemnity. 37

In the case of insurance written on an excess of loss basis, there shall be no excess except in relation to the primary layer (rule 3.6). The excess must not apply to defence costs (rule 3.3). Moreover, MIPRU 3.2.10/11/12 (cf above no 6) provides an excess. 38

33 On the ELCIR see above fn 4.

34 Consolidated Motor Insurance Directive 2009 art 17.

*c) aggregate limits,*

39 Rules regarding aggregate limits can be found in the ELCIR 1998,[35] reg 3[36] (not less than £ 5 million in aggregate) and in the SRA Appendix 1 rule 2.4 (cf above no 25) (the sum insured for any one claim – excluding defence costs – must be at least £ 3 million in respect of the insured's regulated activities, and at least £ 2 million in all other cases; the insurance must not limit liability to any monetary amount (whether by way of an aggregate limit or otherwise) except as contemplated above). Under the RTA 1988, sec 145(4)(b) (cf above no 3) a policy which provides cover for £ 1,000,000 meets the compulsory insurance requirement. The assured is not required to (but may if he wishes to) purchase a policy covering more than £ 1,000,000 as this amount is sufficient to meet the requirement under the RTA 1988 in respect of all such liabilities as may be incurred in respect of damage to property caused by, or arising out of, any one accident involving the vehicle. MIPRU 3.2.7 (cf above no 29) (the minimum limits of indemnity are: £ 1,120,200 for a single claim and £ 1,680,300 in aggregate, or 10% of annual income up to £ 30 million).

*d) claims series clauses,*

40 There are no provisions regarding claims series clauses.

*e) other clauses?*

41 Some other clauses regarding the rights and obligations of the parties can be found in the relevant rules. For instance, under the SRA Appendix 1 rule 4.1 (cf above no 25), the insurance must provide that the insurer is not entitled to avoid or repudiate the insurance on any grounds whatsoever including, without limi-

---

**35** On the ELCIR see above fn 4.

**36** Reg 3 provides: 'Limit of amount of compulsory insurance
3. – (1) Subject to paragraph (2) below, the amount for which an employer is required by the 1969 Act to insure and maintain insurance in respect of relevant employees under one or more policies of insurance shall be, or shall in aggregate be not less than £ 5 million in respect of –
(a) a claim relating to any one or more of those employees arising out of any one occurrence; and
(b) any costs and expenses incurred in relation to any such claim.
(2) Where an employer is a company with one or more subsidiaries, the requirements of paragraph (1) above shall be taken to apply to that company with any subsidiaries together, as if they were a single employer.'

tation, non-disclosure or misrepresentation, whether fraudulent or not.[37] Moreover, SRA has a long list of exclusions which are not covered by the policy required under Appendix 1. Some of the exclusions are: death or bodily injury, directors' or officers' liability, fraud or dishonesty, war and terrorism and asbestos.

In the context of employer's liability insurance, it was held in *T&N Ltd, Re*[38] 42
that there was nothing in the ELCIA 1969 Act[39] which, following the termination of the policy for a given policy year, prevented the assured and insurers from entering into a commutation agreement which puts a financial cap on the amount of all claims against the insurers in that year. It was submitted that the reasoning of the court is open to severe doubt to the extent that it undermines the efficacy of the ELCIA 1969 Act.[40] The reasoning of the court was based on interpreting the Act as requiring no more than that liability insurance has to be in place at any one time: once the policy has lapsed (and has been replaced) it can be commuted even though this may have the effect of reducing or extinguishing the sums available to compensate employees who may subsequently submit claims based on exposure or injury as the case may be. Section 3 of the Third Parties (Rights against Insurers) Act 1930 was interpreted as recognising such release in other cases such as in the context of professional indemnity insurance.[41]

12. *What are the consequences if the liability insurance contract concluded in order to fulfil the insurance obligation contravenes what the law stipulates as to contents (see above Questions 10 and 11)?*

The RTA 1988, sec 148(1) (cf above no 3) provides that such a policy will be of no 43
effect and it is a criminal offence to drive without adequate insurance under the RTA 1988. In relation to SRA (cf above no 5), in order to be licensed as a solicitor, the indemnity insurance should meet the requirements of the SRA Appendix 1 (cf above no 25), otherwise, the candidate cannot meet the qualification requirements. The ELCIR 1998, reg 2 (cf above no 32) uses the word 'prohibited' for the clauses in question. It does not clearly state the faith of the policy which contains the prohibited clauses. It is arguable that a breach of such a regulation would mean a failure to meet the requirements of the ELCIR 1998. The ELCIA

**37** See also rule 4.2 'No adjustment of denial', 4.3 'No cancellation'.
**38** [2006] Lloyd's Rep IR 817.
**39** On this Act see above no 2.
**40** Colinvaux (fn 15) para 20-069.
**41** *Normid v Ralphs* [1989] 1 Lloyd's Rep 265.

1969, sec 5(1) (cf above no 2) provides: 'An employer who on any day is not insured in accordance with this Act when required to be so shall be guilty of an offence and shall be liable on summary conviction to a fine ...'. Under the *British Waterways Act 1995* the absence of the required insurance may result in the refusal of the application for a licence to use the vessel on any inland waterways (this includes being used as a pleasure boat or house boat) (sec 17(3)). Similarly, under the Notaries (Practising Certificate) Rules 2012, if the insurance requirement is not satisfied, the practising certificate as a notary shall cease to have effect immediately (rule 8). The Estate Agents Act 1979 provides that if the necessary insurance arrangements are not in place, the agent shall be liable on conviction on indictment or on summary conviction to a fine (sec 16(6)). Under the Civil Aviation (Insurance) Regulations 2005/1089, reg 4 an air carrier or aircraft operator shall be guilty of an offence if he fails to comply with the insurance requirement. Moreover, where EU countries are not satisfied that the conditions of this regulation are met, they must prohibit an aircraft from taking off until the air carrier or aircraft operator concerned has produced evidence of adequate insurance cover.

*13.a) Are statutory stipulations as to the contents of the policy (eg, regarding the amount of the insurance sum, the ban on certain risk exclusion clauses, on deductibles, etc, see above Questions 10 and 11) also binding in favour of the insurance holder? Or is it nonetheless possible for the liability insurer and the insurance holder acting within their internal relationship to agree risk exclusion clauses, deductibles, aggregate limits, and claims series clauses, etc (see above Questions 10 and 11), releasing the insurer from its liability to pay?*

**44** In motor insurance, in the internal relationship between the assured and insurer, such an agreement may be enforceable but will have no effect to the third party victim.[42] The insurer in any case will have to indemnify the victim but can subsequently seek compensation from the assured. The same applies in the case of employers' liability insurance.[43] In the case of professional indemnity insurance, it may be possible that the parties may freely draft their contract. When this is generally permitted, the insurance rules set out minimum coverage that has to be met: eg the SRA Appendix 1 rule 4 (cf above no 25). As long as the policy meets the minimum requirements, it may permit the parties to draft the contract as they wish (rule 7.1). Within the internal relationships regarding the

**42** The RTA 1988, sec 148(1).
**43** The ELCIR 1998, reg 2(3).

minimum cover stated above, the same rule as in motor and employers' liability insurance applies.

Excursus: In the case of non-compulsory insurance, reference can be made to *Normid v Ralphs*.[44] In this case, the third party victim, clients of the assured architects, sought an injunction restraining the assured from reaching a settlement with the insurer with regard to claims made by the third party victims. An injunction was granted by the trial judge but this was reversed by the Court of Appeal, which emphasised that the assured was not obliged to insure his contractual liability against the clients. Further, taking out such insurance imposes no duty upon the assured to act or not to act in a particular way in his relationship with the insurer. The Court emphasised that the policy was the assured's own asset and the assured was as free to deal with their rights under the policy as with any other assets. Moreover, the Court pointed out that sec 3 of the Third Parties (Rights against Insurers) Act 1930 implicitly indicates that, under normal circumstances, a third party will not be able to complain of an agreement made between insurer and insured even after liability has been incurred to the third party, if the agreement had been made before the commencement of the bankruptcy. The Court defined this as an ordinary case and stated that, if there is a lacuna in the 1930 Act, it is for Parliament, not this Court, to fill it. 45

*b) If it is possible for liability insurer and insurance holder acting within their internal relationship to agree a release from the obligation to pay (see above Question a): What consequences does this entail? Must the insurer first pay out to the victim and can then have recourse to the insurance holder? Or is another construction provided for the relationship between insurer, insurance holder and victim?*

See above no 44. 46

*14.a) Does your general (voluntary) liability insurance law include a statutory risk exclusion in respect of intentional damage by the insurance holder or the insured person?*

There is no statutory exception but it is a well settled fundamental principle in insurance law that the aim of insurance is to protect against contingencies, and not certain events.[45] Thus, the assured will be denied recovery if the loss resulted from the deliberate destruction of the insured subject matter by the as- 47

44 [1989] 1 Lloyd's Rep 265.
45 *Prudential Insurance Co v Inland Revenue Commissioners* [1904] 2 KB 658.

sured.[46] For example, directors' and officers' liability insurance does not provide cover if a director's own deliberate or reckless conduct caused the loss.[47]

*b) If the general liability insurance law contains a statutory risk exclusion in respect of intentional damage inflicted by the insurance holder (see above Question a): Does this also apply in cases of compulsory liability insurance?*

48 Insurers can generally rely upon intentional damage exclusions, but not in employment cases (ELCIR 1998,[48] reg 2(1)). With regard to motor insurance, the position is uncertain[49] but in any case the Motor Insurers Bureau will provide compensation if the insurer is found not to be liable to do so.[50] With regard to MIB, see below no 62f.

## IV. Protection Mechanisms

*15. Are insurers obliged to contract when they offer liability insurance policies covering a risk for which the insurance holder is obliged to obtain cover?*

49 Such an obligation is not imposed upon insurers. Freedom of contract is a prevailing principle in English contract law and insurers are free to make their own assessments in terms of an offer made by an assured with respect to compulsory or non-compulsory insurance.

*16. If there is no obligation to contract: Are there comparable mechanisms provided to ensure that an insurance agreement is concluded?*

50 There are no comparable mechanisms as such. As referred to above, insurers are free to accept or reject an offer made by an assured. In English contract law, applicable to the formation of insurance contracts, silence does not mean acceptance.[51]

46 Colinvaux (fn 15) para 5-01.
47 Colinvaux (fn 15) para 20-086.
48 To the ELCIR see above fn 4.
49 See Colinvaux (fn 15) para 22-028.
50 <http://www.mib.org.uk>.
51 *Selectmove Ltd, Re* [1995] 1 Weekly Law Reports (WLR) 474.

*17. Is the insurance holder prohibited from disposing over his cover entitlement to the disadvantage of the victim (eg, by surrendering his entitlement)?*

Please see above answer to Question 13.b (no 46). 51

*18. Does the victim enjoy special protection against insolvency on the part of the insurance holder with regard to the sum payable by the liability insurer?*

In the case of insolvency of the assured, its rights against the insurer under the 52
contract in respect of liability are transferred to and vested in the third party to whom the liability was so incurred.[52] This is a general measure which applies to all forms of liability insurance.[53]

In the case of motor insurance policies, under sec 151f of the RTA 1988 (cf 53
above no 3) once judgment has been obtained, the victim may bring proceedings against the insurers for payment of the amount in the judgment insofar as the liability is one which should have been covered by insurance. In such an action insurers cannot rely upon breach of policy conditions by the assured. The victim may, in accordance with the European Communities (Rights against Insurers) Regulations 2002,[54] bring a direct action against (motor vehicle) insurers without first having to obtain a judgment against the user which can then be enforced against the user's insurers. The Package Travel, Package Holidays and Package Tours Regulations 1992, reg 19 requires that the person who organises/sells the packages to consumers purchase insurance to protect the money paid by consumers under the contract in case the organiser/seller becomes insolvent.

*19.a) In what manner can the victim obtain the insurance payment?*

In motor insurance a third party is entitled to sue the insurer (sec 151f RTA 1988 and 54
the (UK) European Communities (Rights against Insurers) Regulations 2002[55]). In all other cases, they obtain the payment by suing the assured and enforcing the judgment against the insurers.[56]

---

52 Third Parties (Rights against Insurers) Act 1930, sec 1(1). As of 1 August 2016, the 1930 Act will be replaced by the Third Parties (Rights against Insurers) Act 2010.

53 International conventions on shipping law may also provide possibilities for direct action against insurers even without insolvency of the assured. Eg see the MSA 1995 (cf above no 1), sec 165.

54 SI 2002/3061.

55 SI 2002/3061.

56 Third Parties (Rights against Insurers) Act 1930, sec 1(1) was replaced by the more extensive Third Parties (Rights against Insurers) Act 2010 from 1 August 2010. The third party may sue

*b) Does the victim have a direct right of action against the liability insurer (action directe) in the case of voluntary or compulsory liability insurance?*

55 A victim has such rights under the Third Parties (Rights against Insurers) Act 2010 and the RTA 1988. In the case of motor insurance, a victim has a right to sue insurers directly under sec 151 of the RTA 1988 and also under the European Communities (Rights against Insurers) Regulations 2002.[57] A victim has a right of direct action under the RTA 1988 irrespective of the assured becoming insolvent. However, under the 2010 Act, a third party has a right of direct action against the insurer in the case of the assured's insolvency/bankruptcy.

*20. When settling the claim, is the liability insurer obliged to observe a certain procedure in the interests of the victim? For instance, must it pay the victim an advance within a certain period?*

56 There is no obligation as such. In the absence of express wording to the contrary, the assured's right to indemnification under a liability policy will be regarded as arising once the assured's liability to the third party has been ascertained, ie established and quantified.[58] This can happen by a judgment, an arbitration award or if the assured settles the claim with the third party. At the stage where the liability has not been established and quantified, the insurer is under no obligation to pay in advance to the victim. An insurance policy can provide otherwise. When the Motor Insurers' Bureau (MIB, see below no 62 f) is involved in substantial cases, the claimant may wish to apply for an interim payment.[59] The MIB will consider such applications on a voluntary basis but otherwise the claimant has a right to apply to the court for an interim payment order which, if granted, will be met by the MIB.[60]

---

both the assured and the insurer in one action and claim for a declaration of the assured's liability against the third party and also the insurer's liability under the insurance contract.

**57** Rule 3.2.

**58** *West Wake Price & Co v Ching* [1956] 2 Lloyd's Rep 618; *Post Office v Norwich Union Fire Insurance Society Ltd* [1967] 1 Lloyd's Rep 216.

**59** Uninsured Drivers Agreement, Notes for the guidance of victims of road traffic accidents, rule 8 <http://www.mib.org.uk/NR/rdonlyres/6867D357-D222-45E3-88C5-DCD054A8B49D/0/Uninsured_Agreement_1999_with_Notes_2002_version.pdf>. For the nature of the agreement see below no 63.

**60** Ibid.

*21.a) In the context of its relationship with the victim, can the liability insurer rely on the fact that vis-à-vis the insurance holder (= damaging party) it is freed from the obligation to pay, eg, due to the insurance holder breaching an obligation of conduct/warranty (Obliegenheitsverletzung) or due to him defaulting on premiums?*

In the case of motor insurance, the insurer is precluded from bringing a defence as such under the RTA 1988, sec 151(5) (cf above no 3).[61] The RTA does not permit a condition providing (a) that no liability shall arise under the policy or security, or (b) that any liability so arising shall cease, in the event of some specified act being committed or an omission taking place after the occurrence of the event giving rise to a claim under the policy or security. Any condition as such shall be of no effect in connection with such liabilities as are required to be covered by a policy under the Act.[62] A similar prohibition is seen in the ELCIR 1998, reg 2(1).[63] For instance, a condition is prohibited if it provides that the insurer will not be liable if some specific thing is done or not done after the occurrence of the event which gave rise to liability. **57**

No other restrictions can be found in other regulations or acts but similar prohibitions are contained in international conventions (eg MSA 1995, sec 165(1), cf above no 1).

*b) Does the law distinguish on the basis of the ground for the release from the obligation to pay so that in some cases the insurer may not invoke its release from such obligation vis-à-vis the victim?*

See above no 32f where it was explained that there are prohibited terms which cannot be included in a motor vehicle or employers' liability insurance policy. An insurer can enforce an exclusion clause also in its relationship to the victim unless the exclusion falls within the prohibitions referred to above no 32f. **58**

---

**61** Sec 151(5) provides 'Notwithstanding that the insurer may be entitled to avoid or cancel, or may have avoided or cancelled, the policy or security, he must, subject to the provisions of this section, pay to the persons entitled to the benefit of the judgment –
(a) as regards liability in respect of death or bodily injury, any sum payable under the judgment in respect of the liability, together with any sum which, by virtue of any enactment relating to interest on judgments, is payable in respect of interest on that sum,
(b) as regards liability in respect of damage to property, any sum required to be paid under subsection (6) below, and
(c) any amount payable in respect of costs.

**62** RTA 1988, sec 148(5).

**63** For the wording of ELCIR 1998, reg 2(1) see above no 32.

*c) If the insurer must still pay the victim despite being released from its obligation to pay vis-à-vis the insurance holder (see above Question b), may it take recourse against the latter?*

59 RTA 1988, secs 148 and 151(7) (cf above no 3) both give the insurer a right of recourse. An insurer under ELCIA 1969 (cf above no 2) may also have such right if (a) the policy provides so; and (b) the insurer is unable to rely upon a policy term that would otherwise have been enforceable but for the Regulations under the 1969 Act. There is no reference under ELCIA 1969 or ELCIR 1998 to this effect, however, this is a general principle that, as long as the employee is indemnified under the policy, the insurer can have a right of recourse against the employer if the contract so provides.[64]

*22.a) Within its relationship to the victim, can the liability insurer invoke the fact that the insurance agreement had already ended by the time relevant in respect of the duty to provide cover?*

60 Yes, a policy provides coverage only during the currency of the policy and once it has ended it has ended for all the parties, including third parties, concerned. It is, however, worth noting that whether the third party claim is covered is a matter of the wording of the policy. A liability insurance policy may be worded on a claims made basis or losses occurring or event occurring basis. A claims made policy provides cover for claims made against the assured during the currency of the policy irrespective of the date of the injury. A loss occurring policy requires that the loss or injury occurred during the currency of the policy. If the policy is an event occurring policy, the event which caused the third party to suffer has to have happened during the currency of the policy but the injury may arise after the policy expires. Therefore, whether a third party victim has a right under the policy – after the policy expires – may depend on the nature of the claim and the wording of the policy.

*b) If the insurer must pay the victim despite the termination of the insurance agreement by the time relevant for the duty to provide cover (see above Question a), can it take recourse against the insurance holder?*

61 This is not applicable in English law as, once the policy ends, the insurer's liability ceases.

---

64 Colinvaux (fn 15) para 20–117.

*23.a) Are there cases in which a damaging party does not effectively conclude the required liability insurance and the victim injured by him nonetheless receives compensation for his loss from a liability insurer or another compensation scheme (eg, a guarantee fund)?*

All insurers authorised to carry on motor insurance in the United Kingdom, or who provide motor insurance by way of services from elsewhere in the EU, are required to be members of the Motor Insurers' Bureau (MIB)[65] under the agreements referred to under no 63 below. As a member they will contribute to the MIB levy and supply data to the Motor Insurance Database. The MIB was established in 1946 as a central fund to provide a means of compensating victims of road accidents by negligent uninsured and untraced drivers. A claim is to be made against the MIB only where there is no insurer who can be held responsible for the victim's loss. Where the identity of the defendant is known but the claimant is unable to contact him or where the identity is unknown, in other words all attempts to establish the whereabouts of the defendant fail, the processing service of the MIB may be called upon. There is no similar scheme for other types of compulsory insurance. **62**

The MIB's liability is on the basis of two agreements between the MIB[66] and the Secretary of State: 1) Uninsured Drivers' Agreement England, Scotland and Wales 1999, 2) Untraced Drivers' Agreement England, Scotland and Wales 2003. The Uninsured Drivers Agreement is concerned with cases in which the driver responsible for causing a motor vehicle accident is identified but is not insured against the risks for which insurance is required under RTA 1988. The Uninsured Drivers Agreement requires the MIB to meet unsatisfied civil court judgments against identified motorists who may not have been insured as required by the RTA 1988 (cf above no 3). The Untraced Drivers' Agreement requires the MIB to consider compensation claims from victims of 'hit and run' motorists. Under these two separate agreements the MIB functions between the Government and the motor insurance industry. The MIB's obligations are linked to the compulsory insurance requirements of the Road Traffic Act, so the protection provided is limited to where there is a legal requirement to insure. **63**

65 <www/mib.org.uk>.
66 As for the MIB see above no 62 f.

*b) In the event that the policy taken out was not in fact effectively concluded, is it necessary to distinguish on the basis of the ground for this ineffectiveness, eg, whether the reason for the contract not coming into effect was:*

*i) a lack of legal capacity on the part of the insurance holder,*

64 Cf above answer to Question 23.a (no 62f).

*ii) lack of consent,*

65 Cf above answer to Question 23.a (no 62f).

*iii) falsa procuratio (unauthorised agency)?*

66 Cf above answer to Question 23.a (no 62f).

*c) Can the liability insurer (or the alternative compensation scheme) that must provide cover even though the insurance policy was not effectively concluded (see above Questions a and b) have recourse against the damaging party?*

67 Where the insurer is required to make payment to a third party under a policy which was voidable or cancellable as against the assured (eg see above no 62f), the insurer is given a right of recourse against the assured to recover from it the amount of its payment to the third party.[67] Similarly, if the insurer becomes liable under the policy as a result of its statutory obligation to meet a judgment passed against a person who had driven the vehicle without an appropriate driving licence but who would otherwise have been covered by the assured's policy, the insurer has a right of recourse against that person and not against the assured.[68] If the assured has caused or permitted an uninsured person to drive the vehicle, insurers have a right of recourse against the assured who caused or permitted such uninsured use in respect of liability incurred by the driver for which insurers are liable.[69] When the MIB meets the victim's claim, under general principles of subrogation, the MIB will subrogate into the third party's rights against the damaging party. However, in practice, this will be difficult given that, if the driver was classified as 'untraced', it will be likely that he will not be found.

67 RTA 1988, sec 151(7)(b).
68 RTA 1988, sec 151(7)(a).
69 RTA 1988, sec 151(8).

*24.a) Are there cases in which a damaging party does not take out any liability insurance, ie not even an ineffective insurance policy (see above Question 23), and the victim whom he injured is still compensated for his damage by a liability insurer or another compensation scheme (guarantee fund, etc)?*

See above answer to Question 23.a (no 62f). 68

*b) Can the liability insurer (or the alternative compensation scheme) that must provide cover despite the total absence of any insurance agreement (see above Question a) have recourse against the damaging party?*

It is not the insurer but the MIB who provides compensation in the absence of liability insurance. The Uninsured Drivers Agreement Clause 15 requires the victim to assign his rights to the MIB upon payment from the damaging party. Similarly under the Untraced Drivers Agreement 2003 Clause 11(4)(d), the applicant is obliged to assign to the MIB any judgments obtained by him in respect of death, bodily injury or damage to property as well as his rights against insurers. 69

*25. Is the victim protected against the insolvency of the liability insurer?*

The victim may recover from the Financial Services Compensation Scheme (the FSCS).[70] The FSCS is the UK's statutory fund of last resort for customers of financial services firms. The FSCS is an independent body, set up under the Financial Services & Markets Act 2000 (FSMA).[71] 70

All insurers are in the FSCS. The FSCS protects only individual policy holders and not corporate policy holders. A victim of a policy holder recovers 90% of his damages against the policyholder from the FSCS but an employee protected by compulsory insurance recovers 100%. 71

Under motor vehicle insurance, a victim of a motor accident can recover 100% from the MIB (see above no 62f). 72

*26. Are there rules that serve in particular the protection of the victim when the liability insurance was only concluded voluntarily – ie without it being compulsory?*

As referred to above (no 55), the Third Parties (Rights against Insurers) Act 2010 provides such protection. 73

70 See The Financial Services and Markets Act 2000, Part XV.

71 <http://www.fscs.org.uk/>.

# V. Supervision and Sanctions

*27.a) In which cases must the insurance holder prove to an authority before commencing an activity requiring insurance that he has taken out the respective prescribed liability insurance cover (see above Question 4.e)?*

74 It is a criminal offence not having employers' liability insurance (the ELCIA 1969, sec 5.1).[72] Similarly, it is a criminal offence driving a vehicle without having a satisfactory insurance (the RTA 1988,[73] sec 143(2)). It is a precondition for insurance brokers and solicitors to purchase professional indemnity insurance before being professionally active (see above MIPRU and SRA).[74] Under the international conventions (please see Annex: Rules on Compulsory Liability Insurance in the United Kingdom, at the end of this book) the shipowner has to have a certificate proving insurance against oil pollution, bunker pollution.[75] The Opticians Act 1989, sec 10A provides that where a registered optometrist or registered dispensing optician is in breach of subsec (1) (insurance requirements) or fails to comply with rules under this section 'the registrar may remove that person's name from the appropriate register; or the breach or failure may be treated as misconduct for the purposes of section 13D(2)(a), and the registrar may refer the matter to the Investigation Committee under section 13D(5).'

*b) Must the insurer inform an authority when liability insurance taken out to meet an insurance obligation ends?*

75 There is no obligation as such. It is the assured's obligation in motor insurance to take out a policy while driving and if the assured does not renew the policy it is the assured's responsibility and assured's criminal offence (see above no 74). The same analysis applies to all other cases. The relevant legislation does not impose such an obligation on insurers.

---

**72** To the ELCIA 1969 see above no 2.
**73** To the RTA 1988 see above no 3.
**74** To the SRA and MIPRU see above no 5f.
**75** The MSA 1995, secs 163 and 163A, respectively (see above no 1).

*c) Is the insurer also under a duty to inform when a liability insurance agreement is in existence but it has no duty to provide cover – eg, due to defaults on premium payments?*

There is no duty as such. Again, this is a contractual issue between the parties. If the policy never attached because the premium was a condition to the attachment of the insurer's liability, that means that there was never a binding insurance contract and the assured would be in breach of his duty which will result in a criminal offence under the relevant legislation. If the attachment of the risk does not depend on the payment of the premium, the risk will attach and the insurer will be liable. As stated above (cf Question 21.a–c, nos 57–59) the ELCIA 1969 (cf above no 2) and the RTA 1988 (cf above no 3) prohibit conditions such as non-liability for non-payment of premiums. 76

*d) What are the consequences when the duties to inform of the end of contract or the release from payment obligations (see above Questions b and c) are violated?*

This is non-applicable as there is no such duty. As stated above (no 75), this will be the responsibility of the assured who will have committed a criminal offence. 77

*28. Is there some official body (authority, professional chamber) where an injured party can find out whether and where the injuring party who inflicted damage upon him in the course of an activity requiring insurance has liability insurance?*

The Motor Insurance Database (MID) was set up by the insurance industry to help combat the use of motor vehicles without insurance thus reducing the number of uninsured motorists on the road, as well as the costs to the industry of compensating victims of accidents involving uninsured motorists. In January 2003 the EU Fourth Motor Insurance Directive was implemented, laying down 'special provisions applicable to injured parties entitled to compensation in respect of any loss or injury resulting from accidents occurring in a Member State other than the Member State of residence of the injured party which are caused by the use of vehicles insured and normally based in a Member State.' 78

The Fourth Directive and other Motor Insurance Directives now form part of the Codified Directive 2009/103/EC. 79

80 The Fourth Directive[76] required the setting up of an Information Centre (in the UK this is the UK Information Centre at MIB) and a Compensation Body (also MIB).[77]

81 The Information Centre is responsible for keeping a register of motor vehicles normally based in the country. In the UK, the register used is the MID – allowing the Information Centre to quickly identify the insurer of a UK vehicle by its registration number.

82 The Information Centre is responsible for maintaining a list of all claims representatives in each EU country for each UK insurer. The Information Centre facilitates cross-border claims by taking enquiries from UK victims about EU vehicles, and enquiries from EU victims about UK vehicles, communicating with all the corresponding Information Centres in the EU/EEA.

83 All insurers who underwrite motor insurance for vehicles on UK roads are obliged to be members of the MIB and to submit the policy details of all vehicles to the MID. The process of transferring the information to the MID is managed by the MIB but the data is loaded directly by the insurers and their representatives. The information is made available by the MID for insurers, brokers, and commercial policy holders. All the information as to how to access MID can be accessed at http://www.mib.org.uk/managing-insurance-data/the-motor-insurance-database-mid/public-access/.

*29. Are there (public law) sanctions against the party who was required to take out insurance if such does not take out the compulsory liability insurance? Examples of this would be a ban on carrying out the activity that requires the insurance or the imposition of an administrative or judicial penalty.*

84 See above nos 5, 8 and 43. Moreover, under sec 143(2) it is a criminal offence to drive a vehicle without holding the insurance required under the RTA 1988.

---

**76** The Fourth Motor Insurance Directive, European Parliament and Council Directive 2000/26/EC, has been implemented in the UK by the European Communities (Rights against Insurers) Regulations 2002 (SI 2002/3061) and by the Motor Vehicles (Compulsory Insurance) (Information Centre and Compensation Body) Regulations 2003 (SI 2003/37).

**77** <http://www.mib.org.uk/Customer+Services/en/UK+Information+Centre/default.htm>.

# VI. Statutory Provisions required by the Constitution or the European Convention on Human Rights (ECHR)

30. *What has been said regarding the compatibility of the duties to take out liability insurance with your country's constitution and the ECHR? Please take into account case law and academic literature.*

It has not been possible to find any comments on this issue. There is no single 85
written constitution document for the UK. If there was an obligation to pay a large proportion of insurance funds to a particular cause, Article 1 of Protocol 1 to ECHR might be considered. However, there is no case law which discussed this matter in the UK. One case from the European Court of Human Rights (ECtHR) discussed a similar matter. In *Allianz – Slovenska Poistovna v Slovakia*[78] (2010) the respective domestic Act which set an obligation for insurance companies doing business in the field of compulsory contractual insurance of liability for damage caused by the operation of motor vehicles to pay, on a yearly basis, 8% of the premiums collected in the previous year to the Ministry of the Interior was disputed. The insurers argued that the Act violated their property rights and the non-discrimination principle guaranteed by the Constitution and the Convention. Declaring the application inadmissible, the Court took into account the fact that the duty to transfer 8% of the collected premiums is imposed not only on the applicant companies but on all providers of insurance for liability for damage caused by the operation of motor vehicles and only in respect of premiums collected for providing this specific type of insurance. The Court also observed that no specific facts or arguments had been submitted which would allow the Court to establish, by means of calculation or other verifiable assessment, that the scope of the duty under the Act is prohibitive, oppressive or otherwise disproportionate. Under sec 2.1 of the Human Rights Act 1998, domestic courts in the UK are under a duty to take into account relevant decisions of the European Court of Human Rights.

**78** ECtHR *Allianz – Slovenská poisťovňa, a.s., and Others v Slovakia*, 9.11.2010, no 19276/05.

31. *Does the constitution or the ECHR make any stipulations regarding the contents of such duties to take out liability insurance? Please take into account case law and academic literature.*

86 It has not been possible to find case law discussing this point. The aims of compulsory liability insurance have been explained above. Accordingly, such insurance aims to protect the victim, the insurance holder and aims to internalise costs in the interests of society (see nos 13–17). In order to achieve its aims, the relevant legislation imposes certain obligations on the parties to an insurance contract, such as prohibiting the inclusion of certain clauses in contracts (see no 32f) and contributing from the premium eg in motor insurance to the MIB (see no 62f). Such duties should not be disproportionate and oppressive. Such duties have not been challenged before the UK Supreme Court and the literature has not touched upon the issue with the exception of the European Court of Human Rights case referred to above. It would seem that a compulsory obligation may be compatible with human rights provided that the obligation does not fall foul of the principle of proportionality, or is otherwise be oppressive.

## VII. Reform Efforts

32. *Are there efforts towards reforming the law regarding compulsory liability insurance?*

87 There have been efforts to reform employers' liability (EL) insurance. Mesothelioma is a long tail disease, resulting from exposure to asbestos, with symptoms developing up to 30–40 years after exposure. Due to this time lag, many people with mesothelioma who were exposed to asbestos by their employer negligently or in breach of statutory duties are unable to trace a liable employer or EL insurer from whom to claim damages. It was considered that government intervention is required to compel all EL insurers active in the EL market to contribute to a levy to finance a payment scheme and also to improve tracing to reduce the pool of untraced cases and the time between diagnosis and receipt of scheme payment or civil damages. The costs of the payment scheme should be met by the EL sector rather than from the general taxpayer. The scheme's aim is to provide payments to people with mesothelioma who were exposed to asbestos negligently or in breach of statutory duties by relevant employers, who are unable to bring actions for civil damages and who are not eligible for compensation from other specified sources, or to eligible dependents of such people and to improve tracing of EL insurers to allow civil claims to be resolved more

quickly. The preferred option to establish such a scheme is for the Government to introduce legislation to compel currently active EL insurers to contribute to a levy and fund a payment scheme and deliver improved tracing.[79] The relevant legislation, however, has not yet been enacted.

## VIII. Compulsory Liability Insurance and Liability Law

*33. Is, at the legislative level, any connection discernible between the nature of liability (in particular in the case of strict liability) and the imposition of compulsory liability insurance?*

88 Strict liability is imposed only in shipping cases. The International Convention on Civil Liability for Oil Pollution Damage,[80] Bunker Pollution,[81] Convention of Hazardous and Noxious Substances,[82] impose strict liability and compulsory insurance (see above nos 1–3). In other cases, liability is presumed to exist: that is liability in tort, which is a negligence based liability.

---

**79** <https://www.gov.uk/government/uploads/system/uploads/attachment_data/file/286525/mesothelioma-payment-scheme-ia-mar-2014.pdf>.

**80** Strict liability according to the MSA 1995, sec 153.

**81** Strict liability according to the MSA 1995, sec 63.

**82** Strict liability according to the MSA 1995, Schedule 5A, art VII.

# Special Reports

Stefan Perner

# Compulsory Liability Insurance and European Union Law

## I. Introduction

'Compulsory Liability Insurance and European Union Law' is a broad topic. 1
Therefore, it should be specified right from the start: This report deals with obligations to take out (liability) insurance in the light of European Union law. To be more precise, we speak about the *duty to conclude an insurance contract with a private insurance company* (eg as a prerequisite for the undertaking of a certain business). The field of social security (where compulsory membership is common) remains untouched by this report.[1]

A duty to conclude an insurance contract can derive from *European Union* 2
*law* itself (ie EU directive or EU regulation). In these cases, European law has a *regulatory effect*. This analysis is restricted to an overview of the respective duties in secondary law (see no 6 ff). As to be shown, the number of such provisions in European law is relatively small[2] and the most prominent obligations can be found in EU directives (which have to be transposed by the Member States). Most of the duties to take out insurance derive from the autonomous *national laws* of the Member States. The influence of European law on such provisions is twofold:

First, existing secondary law contains conflict of laws provisions (ie the Rome I 3
Regulation) which determine the law applicable. European Union law, therefore, has a *coordinating effect* on the law of compulsory liability insurance (see no 10 ff).

Second, the effect of primary law on national provisions setting out a duty 4
to take out insurance has to be taken into account. This is because such rules could be seen as a restriction of the freedom to provide services and the freedom of establishment (see no 16 ff). Should a national duty to take out insurance be qualified as an infringement of EU primary law, it is inapplicable.[3] In these cases, European law has a *deregulatory effect* on national laws.[4]

---

1 Cf the similar approach by *W-H Roth*, Pflichtversicherung, in: Hamburger Gesellschaft zur Förderung des Versicherungswesens (ed), Pflichtversicherung – Segnung oder Sündenfall (2005) 141, 143.

2 *KS Hedderich*, Pflichtversicherung (2011) 83 ff; *Roth* (fn 1) 153 f.

3 Cf only *D Chalmers/G Davies/G Monti*, European Union Law (2nd edn 2010) 203 ff.

4 However, liberalisation by abolishing obstacles for the cross-border provision of services is not restricted to primary law. Instead, the *establishing of an internal market* has been the core aim of EU legislation since its foundation. Therefore, provisions of a deregulatory nature can be

5 In recent years, the European Union has developed from a purely economic community into a political union.[5] The peak of this development was the entry into force of the *Charter of Fundamental Rights of the European Union* with the Lisbon Treaty in 2009.[6] The duty to take out insurance interferes with some of the freedoms granted under the Charter (especially the freedom of economic activities, property rights, and equal treatment).[7] Private persons (eg an insurance company or a service provider) can rely on the Charter and Member States are bound by it when 'implementing' Union law (art 51 para 1 of the Charter). Therefore, the influence of fundamental rights in the field of compulsory insurance is a topic also affected by European Union law. However, all of the aforementioned basic rights are also enshrined in the European Convention on Human Rights and 'the meaning and scope of those rights shall be the same as those laid down by the said Convention' (art 52 para 3 of the Charter). Therefore, reference can be made to the separate special report on constitutional law which also deals with the influence of the ECHR.[8]

## II. Duties to Take Out Insurance in European Secondary Law

6 As mentioned above (no 1 ff), European secondary law establishes duties to take out insurance only in few cases.[9] One of the reasons for this restraint of the European legislator is the *limited law-making competence of the European Union* (cf art 5 para 2 TEU: principle of limited singular competence).[10] Secondary law has to be based on a specific competence in the Treaties. According to prevailing opinion, there is no such general legal basis in the field of insurance law.[11] However, where the functioning of the internal market is affected by different

---

found in EU directives. In the field of (compulsory) insurance, the Solvency II Directive 2009/138/EC and its predecessors have to be highlighted. For instance, European secondary law led to the abolition of monopolies, coordinated the rules on supervision (home country control) and prohibited the requirement of the ex ante-control of terms and conditions.

**5** See *S Perner*, Grundfreiheiten, Grundrechte-Charta und Privatrecht (2013) 13 ff.

**6** Cf art 6 para 1 of the Treaty on the European Union (TEU).

**7** *F Merli*, Compulsory Liability Insurance and Constitutional Law (in this book) nos 2, 5.

**8** See *Merli* (fn 7).

**9** For an overview of other provisions in European secondary law see *Hedderich* (fn 2) 83 ff.

**10** Cf also *Hedderich* (fn 2) 88.

**11** Cf only *W-H Roth*, Rechtsetzungskompetenzen für das Privatrecht in der Europäischen Union (2008) Europäisches Wirtschafts- und Steuerrecht (EWS) 401.

legal standards in the Member States, measures can be based on art 114 of the Treaty on the Functioning of the European Union (TFEU). Moreover, the European legislator may issue directives to facilitate the taking up and pursuing of activities by self-employed persons as well as the cross-border provision of services (arts 53, 62 TFEU). The European legislator has based duties to take out insurance on both provisions.

The probably most prominent example of a duty to take out insurance in European secondary law is enshrined in art 3 of the *Motor Insurance Directive.*[12] The provision, which is based on [the predecessor of] art 114 TFEU, states that each Member State shall 'take all appropriate measures to ensure that civil liability in respect of the use of vehicles normally based in its territory is covered by insurance'. As the Annexes to the country reports (at the end of this book) show, the respective Member States have in principle fulfilled their obligation to transpose the directive. 7

Another example of a duty to take out insurance deriving from secondary law is art 4 no 3 of the *Insurance Mediation Directive* (IMD).[13] The provision, which is based on [the predecessors of] arts 53 and 62 TFEU, states that intermediaries 'shall hold professional indemnity insurance' or 'some other comparable guarantee' against liability arising from professional negligence. A similar provision will be included in the revised *Insurance Distribution Directive* (IDD) which replaces the current IMD.[14] The duty set out in the aforementioned Directive shows that compulsory insurance is not the only means of protecting the victim against the insolvency of the injuring party ('comparable guarantee'). However, it lies within the margin of appreciation of the (European) legislator how to shape the level of protection.[15] 8

Secondary law on compulsory liability insurance can also be found in *EU regulations*. As regulations are binding and directly apply in all Member States (art 288 para 2 TFEU), no transformation by Member States is needed. Such duties exist in the case of the *shipment of certain waste* (duty of the person who in- 9

**12** Directive 2009/103/EC of 16 September 2009 relating to insurance against civil liability in respect of the use of motor vehicles, and the enforcement of the obligation to insure against such liability, Official Journal of the European Union (OJ) L 263, 7.10.2009, 11–31.

**13** Directive 2002/92/EC of 9 December 2002 on insurance mediation, OJ L 9, 15.1.2003, 3–10.

**14** The text has not yet been published in the Official Journal of the European Union.

**15** Cf only *Merli* (fn 7) no 5: As for comparative equality, constitutional courts do not ask for coherence of the entire legal system: They are unlikely to question an insurance duty just because there is no such duty in a situation of comparable or even greater risk in another field of law.

tends to carry out a shipment)[16] as well as for *air carriers and aircraft operators*[17]. The latter obligations are rather comprehensive[18] as they comprise a minimum insurance sum, enforcement measures and sanctions.

## III. Conflict of Laws

10 The previous remarks have shown that the level of harmonisation in the field of the law of compulsory insurance is rather low. However, the reports indicate that Member States establish numerous different duties in various areas of the law. There is no common core of European duties to take out insurance. A reference to the Annexes to the country reports may serve as evidence.

11 As national laws differ from another, the focus lies even more on the rules of *international private law*. In principle, the law applicable to insurance contracts which are concluded in order to fulfil the duty to take out insurance is determined by the ordinary rules for insurance contracts.[19]

12 However, the Rome I Regulation takes into account that, in cases of compulsory insurance, the national legislator often aims at an application of the duty to take out insurance regardless of the law applicable to the insurance contract. In other words, such duties established by national laws are *overriding mandatory provisions*.[20] Taking this into account, it does not come as a surprise that art 7 para 4 lit a Rome I states that 'the insurance contract shall not satisfy the obligation to take out insurance unless it complies with the specific provi-

---

**16** Art 4 no 5 and art 6 of the Regulation (EC) No 1013/2006 of 14 June 2006 on shipments of waste, OJ L 190, 12.7.2006, 1–98.

**17** Art 4 ff of the Regulation (EC) No 785/2004 of 21 April 2004 on insurance requirements for air carriers and aircraft operators, OJ L 138, 30.4.2004, 1–16.

**18** See *Hedderich* (fn 2) 86.

**19** In detail see *C Armbrüster* in: J von Staudinger, Kommentar zum Bürgerlichen Gesetzbuch (2011) Vorbemerkungen zu Art 7 Rom I-VO and Art 7 Rom I-VO; *M Fricke*, Das Internationale Privatrecht der Versicherungsverträge nach Inkrafttreten der Rom-I-Verordnung (2008) Versicherungsrecht (VersR) 443; *UP Gruber*, Insurance Contracts, in: F Ferrari/S Leible (eds), Rome I Regulation. The Law Applicable to Contractual Obligations in Europe (2009) 109; *C Heinze*, Insurance Contracts under the Rome I Regulation (2009) Nederlands Internationaal Privaatrecht (NIPR) 445; *H Heiss*, Insurance Contracts in Rome I: Another Recent Failure of the European Legislator (2008) Yearbook of Private International Law 261; *D Looschelders/K Smarowos*, Das Internationale Versicherungsvertragsrecht nach Inkrafttreten der Rom-I-Verordnung (2010) VersR 1; *D Martiny* in: Münchener Kommentar zum Bürgerlichen Gesetzbuch, Band 10 (5th edn 2010) Art 7 Rom I; *S Perner*, Das Internationale Versicherungsvertragsrecht nach Rom I (2009) Praxis des Internationalen Privat- und Verfahrensrechts (IPRax) 218.

**20** See *Perner* (2009) IPRax 218, 221; *Heinze* (2009) NIPR 445, 451.

sions relating to that insurance laid down by the Member State that imposes the obligation'. According to the cited provision, where 'the law of the Member State in which the risk is situated [read as: the law applicable to the insurance contract[21]] and the law of the Member State imposing the obligation to take out insurance contradict each other, the latter shall prevail'. This is, for example, relevant if the minimum insurance sums of the duties set out by the states differ.

Article 7 para 4 lit a Rome I does not lead to an overall application of the in- 13 surance law of the Member State imposing the duty to take out insurance. Only the mandatory provisions on compulsory insurance are applicable. Therefore, the situation created by the cited provision can lead to a *law mix* in a manner similar to art 6 para 2 Rome I (mandatory provisions in the field of consumer protection) and art 9 para 2 Rome I (overriding mandatory provisions).[22] Article 7 para 4 lit b allows Member States to avoid the *law mix*: '... a Member State may lay down that the insurance contract shall be governed by the law of the Member State that imposes the obligation to take out insurance.' If a Member State takes advantage of this option, the whole insurance contract is governed by the law of the Member State which imposes the obligation to take out insurance.

What if a *non-EU country* requires compulsory insurance? From the wording 14 of the provision, art 7 para 4 does not apply. However, the distinction between EU and non-EU compulsory insurance appears inadequate for a regulation which aims at universal application.[23] According to prevailing opinion, the loophole has to be overcome either by an analogous application of art 7 para 4 Rome I[24], by applying the escape clause (art 4 para 3 or art 7 para 2 third subparagraph Rome I) in favour of the law of the country establishing the duty to take out insurance[25] or by applying the third-state rules as overriding mandatory provisions (art 9 Rome I).[26] All these suggestions lead to an application of the third-state provisions establishing a duty to take out insurance.

The above outlined legal framework in international private law shows that 15 it is impossible for the insurer to shape one single policy which can be used in all Member States and it obliges the insured person to meet different standards in different Member States. This conclusion is of double importance: *De lege ferenda*, it underlines the need for a harmonisation or (even better) unification of the laws on compulsory insurance. *De lege lata*, it shows that different legal

**21** *Heiss* (2008) Yearbook of Private International Law 279 fn 74.
**22** *Heinze* (2009) NIPR 445, 451.
**23** Ibid.
**24** Staudinger/*Armbrüster* (fn 19) Art 7 Rom I no 22.
**25** See *Heinze* (2009) NIPR 445, 450 f.
**26** *Heiss* (2008) Yearbook of Private International Law 261, 281.

standards can impede the cross-border provision of services (for the insurer as well as for the insured person). This brings European primary law into focus.

# IV. Primary Law (Four Freedoms)

## 1. General remarks

16 As mentioned above, the national standards in the field of compulsory insurance differ from one Member State to another. At first sight, this observation raises no concerns in the light of European law. To the contrary, the Treaties accept *different legal standards* set by Member States (cf art 5 TEU). A closer look that takes the *free movement provisions* into account paints a different picture. As to be shown (nos 19 ff and 24 ff), duties to take out insurance could be seen as an infringement of the right to free movement granted by the Treaties.

17 As the Annexes to the country reports reveal, obligations to take out insurance can not only be found in situations linked to the exercise of an *economic or professional activity*. Such duties exist, for instance, for holders of dogs or dog owners[27], private persons using firearms against certain species of birds[28], hunters[29] or fishermen[30].[31] If no economic or professional activity is exercised, arts 49 and 56 TFEU are inapplicable. However, arts 18 TFEU (general principle of non-discrimination) and 21 TFEU (citizenship of the union) extend the scope of the free movement provisions to cross-border situations regardless of the exercise of an economic or professional activity. Therefore, the results which are found in this report are also relevant for such duties as the aforementioned.

18 On closer examination, *two case groups* have to be distinguished. First, it has to be analysed whether duties to take out insurance are an infringement of the right to free movement (establishment, service provision) of the *person who*

---

**27** *D Rubin*, Annex: Rules on Compulsory Liability Insurance in Austria (at the end of this book) II.2; *R Koch*, Annex: Rules on Compulsory Liability Insurance in Germany (at the end of this book) II.1; *D Cerini/A Memola*, Annex: Rules on Compulsory Liability Insurance in Italy (at the end of this book) I.1.

**28** *H Cousy/C Van Schoubroeck*, Annex: Rules on Compulsory Liability Insurance in Belgium (at the end of this book) II.2.

**29** *P Dobiáš*, Annex: Rules on Compulsory Liability Insurance in the Czech Republic (at the end of this book) I.2; *Koch*, Annex: Germany (fn 27) I.2; *P Takáts*, Annex: Rules on Compulsory Liability Insurance in Hungary (at the end of this book) I.1.

**30** *Koch*, Annex: Germany (fn 27) II.2.

**31** The duty to take out insurance of a motor vehicle owner (see no 7 above) who uses a car for private purposes also belongs to this group.

*has to take out insurance.* For instance: Does a national duty that obliges a lawyer to take out insurance if he or she represents clients in the respective Member State infringe primary law? Second, obligations to take out insurance could also be seen as a *restriction of the insurer's business* as such duties often set out mandatory contents for the insurance contracts and, therefore, limit the contractual freedom of the insurer.

## 2. Free movement of the insured person

Certain duties to take out insurance infringe the right to free movement of the person who has to take out insurance. This observation needs no further explanation insofar as *discriminatory rules* are concerned. For instance, an obligation to take out insurance only for foreign – not for domiciled – undertakings would be discriminatory and, therefore, incompatible with European primary law.[32] Certainly, such discriminatory provisions are rare. However, it is common knowledge that European primary law not only prohibits any discrimination but also 'restrictions' of free movement by Member States. Therefore, non-discriminatory duties will have to be reviewed in the light of the case law of the Court of Justice of the European Union (CJEU). 19

According to consistent case law of the CJEU, primary law requires the removal of all restrictions – even if non-discriminatory – which are likely to *prohibit, impede or render less attractive* the establishment or the provision of services in another Member State.[33] This formula sounds rather vague and scholars have pointed out that it therefore seems difficult to assess whether a national provision is a restriction in the sense of the four freedoms.[34] However, in the field of compulsory liability insurance, the Court's view is clear. In an Austrian case,[35] the CJEU held that a national duty requiring *patent lawyers* wishing to 20

**32** Cf also art 23 para 2 of the Directive 2006/123/EC of 12 December 2006 on services in the internal market, OJ L 376, 27.12.2006, 36–68: 'When a provider establishes himself in their territory, Member States may not require professional liability insurance or a guarantee from the provider where he is already covered by a guarantee which is equivalent ...'.

**33** Cf CJEU C-76/90, *Säger v Dennemeyer & Co Ltd* [1991] European Court Reports (ECR) I-4221, para 12; C-168/04, *Commission v Austria* [2006] ECR I-9041, para 36. For the free movement of goods see the leading cases 8/74, *Procureur du Roi v Benoît and Dassonville* [1974] ECR 837, para 5; 120/78, *Cassis de Dijon* [1979] ECR 649, para 8; joined cases C-267/91 and 268/91, *Criminal proceedings against Keck and Mithouard* [1993] ECR I-6097, para 11.

**34** Cf *G Bachmann*, Nationales Privatrecht im Spannungsfeld der Grundfreiheiten (2010) Archiv für die civilistische Praxis (AcP) 424, 428 ff.

**35** CJEU C-564/07, *Commission v Austria* [2009] ECR I-100.

provide services temporarily in Austria to take out professional liability insurance[36] constitutes a restriction in the sense of the four freedoms. In the view of the Court, this requirement establishes an additional financial burden for the service provider and is therefore likely to impede the temporary provision of services in Austria by a patent lawyer lawfully established in another Member State, or at least to render the provision of such services less attractive.[37]

21 However, the CJEU acknowledges that *restrictions can be justified* if they fulfil the following requirements: They must be applied in a non-discriminatory manner, they must be justified by imperative requirements in the general interest, they must be suitable for securing the attainment of the objective which they pursue, and they must not go beyond what is necessary in order to attain it.[38] In the case at hand, the CJEU[39] held that the aim of protecting customers (potential victims) was a justification in the sense of the cited case law.[40] The Commission had argued that, by imposing a duty to take out insurance, the national legislator went beyond what was necessary to achieve the (in principle) justified purpose. According to the Commission, an obligation to inform the customer about the existence of (voluntary) liability insurance would be more appropriate. The Court discarded this argument and held that the *duty to take out liability insurance does not infringe primary law.*

22 The case law of the CJEU therefore shows that *compulsory liability insurance in principle complies with European primary law.* The Court acknowledges that such provisions – if non-discriminatory – are justified if they aim at protecting the victim. This finding is of the utmost importance as all country reports show that in fact the main aim[41] – or at least a very important purpose[42] – of national

**36** Sec 2 para 1 lit g, sec 21a Austrian Patent Lawyers Act.

**37** CJEU C-564/07, *Commission v Austria* [2009] ECR I-100, paras 22 ff, 28 ff.

**38** CJEU C-55/94, *Gebhard v Consiglio degli Avocati di Milano* [1995] ECR I-4165, para 37; C-564/07, *Commission v Austria* [2009] ECR I-100, para 31.

**39** C-564/07, *Austria* [2009] ECR I-100, para 34 ff.

**40** Art 23 of the Directive 2006/123/EC on services in the internal market (OJ L 376, 27.12.2006, 36–68) also gives an example for a justification: 'Member States may ensure that providers whose services present a direct and particular risk to the health or safety of the recipient or a third person, or to the financial security of the recipient, subscribe to professional liability insurance appropriate to the nature and extent of the risk, or provide a guarantee or similar arrangement which is equivalent or essentially comparable as regards its purpose.'

**41** *D Rubin*, Compulsory Liability Insurance in Austria (in this book) no 18; *P Dobiáš*, Compulsory Liability Insurance in the Czech Republic (in this book) no 22; *R Koch*, Compulsory Liability Insurance in Germany (in this book) no 13; *D Cerini*, Compulsory Liability Insurance in Italy (in this book) no 33; *A Stäubli*, Compulsory Liability Insurance in Switzerland (in this book) no 18.

**42** *H Cousy/C Van Schoubroeck*, Compulsory Liability Insurance in Belgium (in this book) no 23; *J Norio-Timonen*, Compulsory Liability Insurance in Finland (in this book) no 36; *P Takáts*,

provisions establishing compulsory liability insurance is to ensure that *victims will be adequately compensated.* Moreover, such duties, in principle, also pass the proportionality test.

As a result, this is convincing. However, it seems questionable whether such (non-discriminatory) provisions even qualify as 'restrictions' which need to be justified. A parallel to the case law on the free movement of goods could be drawn: In its famous *Keck* judgment, the Court distinguished between 'product requirements' and 'selling arrangements'.[43] Whereas the first restricted the free movement of the trader, the latter did not qualify as a charge 'having equivalent effect' to 'quantitative restrictions on imports' (art 34 TFEU), meaning that a *justification was not even required.* In other words: Not every mandatory national rule restricts free movement. For instance, national provisions prohibiting the opening of a shop on Sunday do not restrict the free movement of the shop-owner, even if this would be permitted in his/her home country. The situation is similar in the case of a duty to take out insurance: The 'product' (eg legal advice by a patent lawyer) is not affected by the duty: the obligation only affects the 'selling arrangement' (manner of practice of the profession) and does not hinder the exercise of the profession. However, the CJEU has so far not clarified whether it is willing to transpose the distinction between product requirements and selling arrangements to the field of services.[44] 23

## 3. Free movement of the insurer

Above (no 19 ff), restrictions of the free movement of the person who has to take out insurance have been examined. What about the free movement of the insurer? At first sight and in most cases, compulsory liability insurance seems to *promote the business of the insurer rather than to restrict it.*[45] Naturally, the specific design of a national provision has to be analysed in detail in order to give a final statement. For instance, an obligation to take out insurance from an insurer established in the territory of the Member State imposing the duty would not be compatible with European primary law[46] as foreign insurance companies would be discriminated. However, the remarks above (no 19 ff) have shown that 24

Compulsory Liability Insurance in Hungary (in this book) no 13; *Ö Gürses*, Compulsory Liability Insurance in the United Kingdom (in this book) no 13.

**43** CJEU joined cases C-267/91 and 268/91, *Keck* [1993] ECR I-6097, para 14 ff.

**44** See *Perner* (fn 5) 58.

**45** Cf *W-H Roth* (fn 1) 164.

**46** *Merli* (fn 7) no 7.

non-discriminatory provisions on compulsory liability insurance have to be analysed in the light of European primary law as well.

25 CJEU case law[47] provides a good example for a possible restriction of free movement: Italian national law sets out a duty to contract not only for the insured person (motor vehicle insurance) but also for the insurer.[48] Insurance undertakings were required to accept the proposals regarding compulsory insurance which were submitted to them (on the basis of the contract terms and insurance rates which they had to establish in advance for any risk in respect of the use of motor vehicles).[49] Does such an *obligation to contract* for the insurer qualify as a restriction of the free movement of the insurer?

26 In its judgment, the CJEU held that such a duty *restricted the freedom of establishment and the freedom to provide services* enshrined in arts 49 and 56 TFEU. In the view of the Court, such measures obstruct 'access to the market, in particular where it subjects insurance undertakings not only to an obligation to cover any risks which are proposed to them, but also to requirements to moderate premium rates'.[50] The meaning of the notion of 'market access' has remained controversial among scholars so far.[51] However, the Court seems to find the crucial argument in the classification of the provisions as *indirectly discriminatory*: 'Inasmuch as it involves changes and costs for those undertakings, the obligation to contract renders access to the market of that Member State less attractive and, if they obtain access to that market, reduces the ability of the undertakings concerned to compete effectively, from the outset, against undertakings traditionally established there.'[52] In the case at hand, the fact that *mandatory requirements for the insurance contract* exist was without a doubt pivotal. In other words: Whether an obligation to contract exists or not is less important, the restriction derives from the fact that the insurer has to design the product (insurance) in a specific manner.

27 However, the Court stated that the national legislator intends to achieve a 'social protection objective, which amounts, essentially, to ensuring that such victims will be adequately compensated [and this] can be taken into account as an overriding imperative relating to the public interest.'[53] Moreover, the provisions in question are not only in principle *justified*; they also pass the *propor-*

47 CJEU C-518/06, *Commission v Italy* [2009] ECR I-3491.
48 Ibid, para 20 ff.
49 CJEU C-518/06, *Italy* [2009] ECR I-3491, para 20.
50 Ibid, para 67.
51 Cf *J Snell*, The Notion of Market Access: A Concept or a Slogan? (2010) Common Market Law Review (CML Rev) 437.
52 CJEU C-518/06, *Italy* [2009] ECR I-3491, para 70.
53 Ibid, para 1 (Summary of the Judgment).

*tionality* test. The Court acknowledged that the national law 'is suitable for securing the attainment of the objective which it pursues and does not go beyond what is necessary to attain it. ... On the other hand, it is not indispensable, with regard to the proportionality criterion, that the restrictive measure laid down by the authorities of a Member State should correspond to a view shared by all the Member States concerning the means of protecting the legitimate interest at issue. Therefore, the fact that some Member States have chosen to establish a different system to ensure that every vehicle owner is able to take out third-party liability motor insurance for a premium that is not excessive does not indicate that the obligation to contract goes beyond what is necessary to attain the objectives pursued. Lastly, with regard to the criterion of proportionality, the obligation to insure does not prevent insurance undertakings from calculating a higher premium for a policyholder domiciled in an area characterised by a significant number of accidents than for a policyholder domiciled in an area where the risk is not so high.'[54]

The judgment of the CJEU has to be put into perspective. The duty to take 28 out motor insurance derives from European secondary law (see no 6 ff above) and is, therefore, without a doubt in principle compatible with European law. From the outset there is only the question whether the specific design of the national provisions – establishing an obligation to contract and specifying the content of the contract – infringe primary law. From this perspective, it seems understandable that the Court assumes a rather positive stance. The findings of the CJEU are nonetheless also highly relevant for duties to take out insurance which do not derive from secondary law. This is true especially for the justification test: As mentioned above (no 19 ff), the country reports show that the main – or at least a very important – aim of national provisions establishing compulsory liability insurance is to ensure that *victims will be adequately compensated*. Therefore, even if provisions on compulsory liability insurance qualify as 'restrictions' of the free movement of the insurer, they can in principle be justified according to the case law of the CJEU.

## V. Summary

A duty to take out insurance can derive from *European Union law* itself (ie an EU 29 directive or EU regulation). In these cases, European law has a *regulatory effect*. European secondary law establishes such obligations only in few cases. The most prominent example can be found in the *Motor Insurance Directive*.

54 CJEU C-518/06, *Italy* [2009] ECR I-3491, para 1 (Summary of the Judgment).

30 Article 7 para 4 of the Rome I Regulation unifies the *international private law* of compulsory insurance (*coordinating effect* of European Union law). In principle, the European legislator acknowledges that such national rules are *overriding mandatory provisions*.

31 An analysis of the case law of the CJEU shows that national provisions establishing a duty to take out insurance qualify as a restriction of the freedom to provide services (art 56 TFEU) and the freedom of establishment (art 49 TFEU). The freedom of both the insurer and the person who has to take out insurance are affected (*deregulatory effect* of European Union law). However, the Court recognises that such duties aim at *protecting the victim*. Therefore, they are justified and in principle *do not interfere with European primary law*.

Franz Merli

# Compulsory Liability Insurance and Constitutional Law

All national reports show that compulsory liability insurance has not been a constitutional problem so far. There are just a few cases, mostly dealing with details, and academic literature is sparse. 1

The duty to take out insurance interferes with fundamental freedoms under national constitutions, the European Convention on Human Rights and, where imposed by or in implementation of EU law, under the EU Charter of Fundamental Rights. The duty limits the freedom to contract,[1] the freedom of economic activities (where the insurance is a requirement to do business),[2] and property rights (where the insurance is a condition for a certain use of property, where the freedom to contract is qualified as a property right or where all public law duties leading to obligations to pay money are held to affect the right to property),[3] and it may be a question of equal treatment.[4] 2

Although constitutions differ in many respects, there is a common general European standard for restrictions of fundamental rights. On this basis the duty to take out insurance must be provided for by law. Whereas the European Court of Human Rights (ECtHR) is satisfied in this respect with an accessible and clear legal basis including executive-made and case law,[5] some constitutions are 3

1 *R Koch*, Compulsory Liability Insurance in Germany (in this book) no 76: the freedom to conclude and to agree on the content of a contract that is protected by art 2 para 1 Basic Law.

2 Eg for Austria art 6 of The Law on the Fundamental Rights of the Citizens of 1867; *Koch*, Report: Germany (fn 1) no 76: the freedom to pursue an occupation (art 12 para 1 Basic Law), *A Stäubli*, Compulsory Liability Insurance in Switzerland (in this book) no 98: economic freedom (art 27 of the Federal Constitution); the freedom to conduct a business under art 16 of the EU Charter of Fundamental Rights.

3 Eg for Austria art 5 of The Law on the Fundamental Rights of Citizens of 1867; see *B Raschauer*, Die Pflichthaftpflichtversicherung aus verfassungsrechtlicher Sicht, Versicherungsrundschau (VR) 2005, 35, 37 f; *Koch*, Report: Germany (fn 1) no 76: art 14 para 1 Basic Law; art 1 of Protocol 1 to the European Convention on Human Rights (ECHR); cf *Ö Gürses*, Compulsory Liability Insurance in the United Kingdom (in this book) no 85; art 17 of the EU Charter of Fundamental Rights.

4 *P Dobiáš*, Compulsory Liability Insurance in the Czech Republic (in this book) no 81: art 1 (principle of equality) Charter of the Basic Rights and Freedoms; *Koch*, Report: Germany (fn 1) no 76: art 3 para 1 Basic Law.

5 Eg ECtHR *Şahin v Turkey* [GC], 10.11.2005, no 44774/98, § 88: '[T]he Court observes that it has always understood the term "law" in its "substantive" sense, not its "formal" one; it has included both "written law", encompassing enactments of lower ranking statutes (see *De Wilde*,

stricter and require a *parliamentary* statute.[6] The statute may entrust administrative authorities or professional bodies with the duty to impose an obligation to take out insurance, but it has to make clear the purpose of the delegation and must specify the essential conditions such as the risks to be insured.[7]

4 From a substantive perspective, a duty of insurance, like any limitation of a basic freedom, may be imposed only if it serves a legitimate purpose and is compatible with the principle of proportionality.[8] The legislation enjoys a wide margin of appreciation, though. There is no doubt that the standard reasons for compulsory liability insurance such as protection of victims and insurance holders or the internalisation of costs for society are legitimate purposes.[9] The proportionality of respective regulations has not been seriously questioned in court so far.[10] In academic writing, compulsory insurance is held disproportionate if coverage is not available on the market.[11]

5 Equality of treatment demands that there is an objective reason for imposing a duty to take out insurance, eg the seriousness and size of the risk and the inability of the liable entity to pay damages. In this respect equality, as a prohibition of arbitrary burdens, to some extent duplicates the protection afforded by

---

*Ooms and Versyp v. Belgium*, judgment of 18 June 1971, Series A no. 12, pp. 45–46, § 93) and regulatory measures taken by professional regulatory bodies under independent rule-making powers delegated to them by Parliament (see *Barthold v. Germany*, judgment of 25 March 1985, Series A no. 90, pp. 21–22, § 46), and unwritten law. "Law" must be understood to include both statutory law and judge-made "law" (see, among other authorities, *The Sunday Times v. the United Kingdom (no. 1)*, judgment of 26 April 1979, Series A no. 30, p. 30, § 47; *Kruslin*, cited above, pp. 21–22, § 29 *in fine*; and *Casado Coca v. Spain*, judgment of 24 February 1994, Series A no. 285-A, p. 18, § 43).'

**6** Eg *J Norio-Timonen*, Compulsory Liability Insurance in Finland (in this book) no 98.

**7** Eg *Koch*, Report: Germany (fn 1) no 77. The cases cited there are the only ones in which a duty of insurance has been voided. For dubious cases under Austrian law, see *Raschauer*, VR 2005, 35, 37.

**8** Eg *Koch*, Report: Germany (fn 1) no 79; *Stäubli*, Report: Switzerland (fn 2) no 98; *Gürses*, Report: United Kingdom (fn 3) no 86; *C Grabenwarter*, European Convention on Human Rights (2014) art 1 of Protocol 1 no 20 for the jurisprudence of the ECtHR; art 52 para 1 of the EU Charter of Fundamental Rights.

**9** *D Rubin*, Compulsory Liability Insurance in Austria (in this book) no 87; see also Collection of cases of the Austrian Constitutional Court (Verfassungssammlung, VfSlg) 13.327/1993 for the protection of investors in securities, VfSlg 16.202/2001 for the protection of air passengers, and VfSlg 19.588/2011 for ensuring the confidence in the profession of private attorneys; *Koch*, Report: Germany (fn 1) no 79; *Gürses*, Report: United Kingdom (fn 3) no 86.

**10** For an unsuccessful attempt in regard of the intensity of financial burden, see VfSlg 16.202/2001 (Austria).

**11** *Koch*, Report: Germany (fn 1) no 81; for examples, but also for a detailed analysis of proportionality under German law, see *K Hedderich*, Pflichtversicherung (2011) 184, 158 f.

the basic freedoms. As for comparative equality, constitutional courts do not ask for coherence of the entire legal system: They are unlikely to question an insurance duty just because there is no such duty in a situation of comparable or even greater risk in another field of law. They rather focus on the equality of treatment of the concerned persons and entities within a given system of insurance or in the same business. So, to give an example, the equal treatment in insurance law of dog owners (depending on the dangerousness of their dogs) is a constitutional question whereas the equal treatment of cars and sports utilities is not (irrespective of the relative dangerousness of their use).[12] As a result there is a wide margin of appreciation for the legislator.

Some of the reported cases concerned not the duty to take out insurance as 6
such but questions of its design. Courts held that special rules on the opposability of defences against the injured party in compulsory liability insurance did not violate the right to equal treatment,[13] that rules on the transfer of liability and insurance in connection with the sale of a car and duties of the insured car owner to inform the insurance company of an accident were compatible with the right to a fair trial and the *nemo tenetur* principle,[14] that compensation covering the full price of new spare parts is required after a car accident,[15] that higher insurance rates for taxis are justified[16] and that insurance rates may depend on the development of damages caused by the insured vehicle (bonus malus system) as long as the character of the insurance is maintained.[17]

Compulsory liability insurance also restricts the EU market freedoms of es- 7
tablishment and services under arts 49 and 56 Treaty on the Functioning of the European Union (TFEU) if it is liable to prohibit, impede or render less advantageous commercial activities in another Member State. Secondary law notwith-

**12** Cf *Dobiáš*, Report: Czech Republic (fn 4) no 81. For Austria, Constitutional Court (Verfassungsgerichtshof, VfGH) 11 June 2012, G 71/11 (compulsory liability insurance for dangerous dogs) and generally *Raschauer*, VR 2005, 35, 39 f. In its decision of 12 July 2007, case 100/2007, <http://www.const-court.be>, the Belgian Constitutional Court compared architects who had to take out insurance with other actors in the construction business who did not; the court found discrimination against architects, because as the only group under an obligation to take out insurance they would risk being held liable to a larger extent than other actors in situations of joint liability.

**13** *H Cousy/C Van Schoubroeck*, Compulsory Liability Insurance in Belgium (in this book) no 98.

**14** *Dobiáš*, Report: Czech Republic (fn 4) nos 81, 84.

**15** *Dobiáš*, Report: Czech Republic (fn 4) no 84.

**16** VfSlg 10.492/1998 (Austria).

**17** VfSlg 8212/1977 (Austria). For the compatibility with EU secondary law, European Court of Justice (ECJ) C-347/02, *Commission v France* [2004] European Court Reports (ECR) I-7557.

standing,[18] a justification is possible under similar conditions to restrictions of fundamental rights: Insurance duties must be applied in a non-discriminatory manner (so an obligation to take out insurance from a provider or body established in the territory of the regulation Member State would not be compatible with the TFEU); they must be justified by imperative requirements in the general interest; they must be suitable to secure the attainment of the objective which they pursue; and they must not go beyond what is necessary in order to attain it.[19] On this basis, the ECJ accepted the duty of patent attorneys to take out insurance before offering services in Austria[20] and, because of specific problems in Southern Italy to find an insurer, an Italian duty imposing an obligation to contract not only upon car owners but also upon insurance undertakings.[21]

8 Although conceivable under certain circumstances,[22] the reports do not mention a possible positive obligation of the legislator to introduce compulsory liability insurance as a means to protect fundamental rights of victims. In an Austrian case[23] the Constitutional Court saw compulsory liability insurance as an instrument which the legislator may be required to provide in order to guarantee equal access to certain professional activities such as the scrutiny of public offer prospectuses. Similarly, the ECJ considered compulsory liability insurance a less restrictive measure under the EU freedom of establishment than minimum share capital requirements for private security activities and private vehicle inspection bodies.[24]

---

**18** See eg Directive 2006/123/EC of the European Parliament and of the Council of 12 December 2006 on services in the internal market, Official Journal (OJ) L 376, 27.12.2006, art 14 para 7 (Member States may not introduce a duty to take out insurance from a provider or body established in their territory) and art 23 (specific conditions for professional liability insurance imposed by the legislation of the Member States within the field of application of the Directive).

**19** ECJ C-564/07, *Commission v Austria* [2009] ECR I-100, para 31; C-518/06, *Commission v Italy* [2009] ECR I-3491, para 72.

**20** ECJ C-564/07, *Commission v Austria* [2009] ECR I-100.

**21** ECJ C-518/06, *Commission v Italy* [2009] ECR I-3491.

**22** See for Germany *Hedderich* (fn 11) 166 f; for the ECHR see ECtHR *Kotov v Russia* [GC], 3.4.2012, no 54522/00, § 109 ff on positive obligations of the state to set up a minimum legislative framework including a proper forum allowing persons to assert their rights effectively and have them enforced in the case of a person who suffered considerable loss because the private liquidator of an insolvent bank unlawfully distributed its assets (but without reference to compulsory liability insurance of the liquidator which was introduced too late for the applicant).

**23** VfSlg 13.327/1993.

**24** ECJ C-171/02, *Commission v Portugal* [2004] ECR I-5645, and C-438/08, *Commission v Portugal* [2009] ECR I-10219. For a general comparison of various means to secure the solvency of the liable entity see *Hedderich* (fn 11) 192 f.

Helmut Heiss

# Compulsory Liability Insurance in the Principles of European Insurance Contract Law (PEICL)

## I. Compulsory Liability Insurance: A 'Social Dimension' of Private Insurance Law

Liability insurance is an instrument with which an insured person's assets are protected against the risk of liability vis-à-vis an injured party.[1] Over time it has gained an important social dimension in that it also protects victims.[2] A victim will, first of all, benefit *de facto* from the mere existence of a private liability insurance contract, on the basis of which there is certainty as to the enforceability of a claim for indemnity, because the damage by the tortfeasor is underwritten by a solvent and typically easily accessible liability insurer. A cursory glance at liability insurance law reveals that benefiting the injured party is not merely a coincidental third party effect of liability insurance, but is also increasingly being guaranteed legally. Legal provisions in liability insurance often privilege the injured party with regard to the insurance benefit. This is particularly apparent when the law grants the victim a direct claim against the insurer. The institution of a direct claim was 'invented' by the French *Cour de Cassation* in 1926[3] and has since been applied in many jurisdictions.[4] Even where a direct claim is not granted by law, victims are usually given priority over the insured party's other creditors in respect of the insurance claim.[5] It is also typical for the insured party to be prevented from dealing with the indemnity arising from the third 1

1 Similarly *J Basedow*, Comment 1 on Article 16:101 PEICL, in: J Basedow/J Birds/M Clarke/H Cousy/H Heiss/L Loacker (eds), Principles of European Insurance Contract Law (PEICL) (2nd edn 2016).

2 See *H Heiss*, Comment 1 on Article 15:101 PEICL, in: J Basedow et al (eds), Principles of European Insurance Contract Law (PEICL) (2nd edn 2016).

3 Cour de Cassation, Chambre civile (Cass civ) 14.6.1926, Dalloz périodique (DP) 1927.J.57; today the direct claim against the liability insurer is codified in art L 124-3 Code des assurances (C ass).

4 A report on European legal systems as well as Union law is presented by *M Micha*, Der Direktanspruch im europäischen Internationalen Privatrecht (2010) 13 ff.

5 See art 60 Swiss Insurance Contract Act/ICA (Versicherungsvertragsgesetz, VVG); § 157 Austrian Insurance Contract Act/ICA (Versicherungsvertragsgesetz, VersVG); art 3:287 Dutch Civil Code.

party liability insurance to the detriment of the victim.[6] Based on these observations alone, the purpose of private liability insurance should not be viewed as only protecting the insured's assets, but also protecting the injured party and, thus, bearing a social element.[7]

2 The social element of liability insurance shifts to the fore especially where the conclusion of private liability insurance is compulsory.[8] Such compulsory insurance became particularly common in the first half of the 20th century and has since gained a great degree of popularity. For example, the Final Report[9] of the Commission Expert Group on European Insurance Contract Law[10] states that there are approximately 400 different types of compulsory insurance in Spain.[11] The trend over the past hundred years or so appears to have been to increase the level of liability and, at the same time, impose compulsory insurance.[12] The protective purpose of liability insurance has not fundamentally changed: As before, liability insurance is used in its compulsory form to protect the assets of the insured party as well as to protect the victim. There has merely been a shift in the accentuation of both these protective goals. In respect of compulsory insurance, protection of the victim plays a much more prominent role.[13] This protective goal is likely to be an important reason as to why the concept of compulsory insurance has found such high resonance amongst legislatures. At the same time and unfortunately, the abundance and diversity of compulsory insurance, which can be found in the various jurisdictions,[14] not only underscores the importance and rich blessings of this instrument, but also the lack of clear legislative planning with which different types of compulsory insurance have been created. It has been stated in legal commentary that there are no fixed parameters with which to assess the legitimacy of the introduction of compulsory insurance. Rather, a multitude of reasons might lead a legislator to impose du-

---

**6** See eg § 108 VVG (German ICA); § 156 VersVG (Austrian ICA).

**7** See PEICL/*Heiss* (fn 2) Comment 1 on Art 15:101 PEICL.

**8** See PEICL/*Heiss* (fn 2) Comment 1 on Art 15:101 PEICL.

**9** See Final Report of the Commission Expert Group on European Insurance Contract Law (2014) <http://ec.europa.eu/justice/contract/files/expert_groups/insurance/final_report_en.pdf>.

**10** See European Commission, Commission Decision of 17 January 2013 on setting up the Expert Group on a European Insurance Contract Law, Official Journal (OJ) C 16, 19.1.2013, 6–8.

**11** Final Report (fn 9) 18 para 31.

**12** With regard to this development, see eg PEICL/*Basedow* (fn 1) Comments 1, 2 on Art 16:101 PEICL.

**13** Similarly, PEICL/*Basedow* (fn 1) Comment 2 on Art 16:101 PEICL.

**14** Similarly, PEICL/*Basedow* (fn 1) Comment 8 on Art 16:101 PEICL.

ties to take out liability insurance.[15] Occasionally, initiatives to systemise the body of compulsory insurance law can be observed.[16] However, so far no coherent system has been established in national or Union law.

# II. Compulsory Liability Insurance and the Internal Market

## 1. Compulsory liability insurance in secondary Union law

Looking at the phenomenon of compulsory third party liability insurance from 3
the perspective of the internal market, it is initially striking that even the European legislature appears unable to escape the allure of compulsory insurance. Within the scope of its competence to harmonise legislation, it has itself namely created several types of compulsory insurance. The most significant example is likely the compulsory insurance imposed under art 3 of Directive 2009/103/EC (Motor Vehicle Liability Insurance).[17] It not only imposes a duty to take out such insurance but at the same time harmonises compulsory motor vehicle liability insurance law throughout the Union. Moreover, art 4 of Directive 2009/20/EC (Maritime Insurance),[18] the Regulation (EC) No 785/2004 (Insurance Requirements for Air Carriers and Aircraft Operators) and arts 4(h), 11 of Regulation (EC) No 1008/2008 (Operation of Air Services)[19] as well as art 10(4) of Directive (EU) 2016/97 (Insurance Distribution)[20] also impose compulsory insurance. Other di-

---

**15** See eg for German law *RM Beckmann* in: E Bruck/H Möller, Versicherungsvertragsgesetz, vol 4 Haftpflichtversicherung (9th edn 2013) vor §§ 113–124 no 18 ff.

**16** See the attempt to draft a comprehensive Swiss Compulsory Liability Insurance Act: Schweizerische Gesellschaft für Haftpflicht und Versicherungsrecht (SGHVR), Pflichtversicherung – Entwurf einer gesetzlichen Regelung (2012).

**17** Directive 2009/103/EC of the European Parliament and of the Council of 16 September 2009 relating to insurance against civil liability in respect of the use of motor vehicles, and the enforcement of the obligation to insure against such liability [2009] OJ L 263, 7.10.2009, 11–31.

**18** Directive 2009/20/EC of the European Parliament and of the Council of 23 April 2009 on the insurance of shipowners for maritime claims [2009] OJ L 131, 28.5.2009, 128–131.

**19** Regulation (EC) No 785/2004 of the European Parliament and of the Council of 21 April 2004 on insurance requirements for air carriers and aircraft operators [2004] OJ L 138, 30.4.2004, 1–6; Regulation (EC) No 1008/2008 of the European Parliament and of the Council of 24 September 2008 on common rules for the operation of air services in the Community (Recast) [2008] OJ L 293, 31.10.2008, 3–20.

**20** Directive (EU) 2016/97 of the European Parliament and of the Council of 20 January 2016 on insurance distribution (recast) [2016] OJ L 26, 2.2.2016, 19–59.

rectives do not make the taking out of liability insurance compulsory, but permit Member States to create duties to insure. An example of such a provision is art 6(3) of Directive 98/5/EC (Lawyers' Establishment).[21] Where there are no such substantive provisions governing compulsory insurance, Union law nevertheless still governs conflict of laws issues. For instance, art 7(4)(a) of Regulation (EC) No 593/2008 (Rome I)[22] ensures that an insurance contract, irrespective of the governing law, can only satisfy a (national) duty to take out insurance if 'it complies with the specific provisions relating to that insurance laid down by the Member State that imposes the obligation. Where the law of the Member State in which the risk is situated and the law of the Member State imposing the obligation to take out insurance contradict each other, the latter shall prevail'. Paragraph (b) of the same provision grants the Member State the option of subjecting the compulsory insurance contract entirely to the law of the Member State imposing the duty. Thus, the enforcement of national compulsory insurance requirements is in particular guaranteed by means of European conflict of laws.

## 2. Compulsory insurance as an obstacle to the freedoms under the TFEU

4 Compulsory insurance can affect the freedoms under the Treaty on the Functioning of the European Union (TFEU). In spite of the harmonisation of laws that took place in motor vehicle liability insurance but also in other areas of compulsory insurance, national rules differ to a considerable extent in that respect. EU citizens who make use of the fundamental freedoms, such as by moving from one Member State into another or by any cross-border activity (establishment or provision of services abroad), must comply with the compulsory insurance regimes applicable in the relevant Member State. Since this involves considerable costs, duties to take out insurance can constitute a serious obstacle to the internal market. More so, when no insurance cover satisfying local compulsory insurance regimes is available. This can be seen for example, but by no means solely, in the construction industry where the compulsory insurance prescribed for construction companies in some jurisdictions, for example in French law, severely hamper or even prevent foreign constructors from carrying out activity

21 Directive 98/5/EC of the European Parliament and of the Council of 16 February 1998 to facilitate practice of the profession of lawyer on a permanent basis in a Member State other than that in which the qualification was obtained [1998] OJ L 77, 14.3.1998, 36–43.
22 Regulation (EC) No 593/2008 of the European Parliament and of the Council of 17 June 2008 on the law applicable to contractual obligations (Rome I) [2008] OJ L 177, 4.7.2008, 6–16.

in France.[23] This is true, albeit in a much milder form, even where compulsory insurance law has been harmonised by EU law. The single premium principle[24] laid down in Directive 2009/103/EC (Motor Liability Insurance), for example, enables the insured party to use his vehicle to travel all over Europe without concern. The Directive obliges national legislators to ensure that 'all compulsory motor insurance policies cover, on the basis of a single premium and during the whole term of the contract, the entire territory of the Community, including any period in which the vehicle remains in other Member States during the term of the contract. Moreover, according to that article, Member States must take the necessary steps to ensure that those policies guarantee, on the basis of that single premium, in each Member State, the cover required by its law or the cover required by the law of the Member State where the vehicle is normally based when that cover is higher.'[25] In this way, EU law guarantees 'unlimited' mobility within the internal market. However, the single premium principle does not guarantee that the policyholder may keep its motor vehicle policy when moving to another Member State and thereby changing the habitual location of the vehicle. In such cases, the owner of the car will be required to obtain a new licence for the car in the Member State he moves into and, for that purpose, will have to take out a new motor vehicle insurance policy with an insurer which is admitted there. In this way, national compulsory insurance law hampers mobility in Europe. These obstacles can hardly be removed by force of the basic freedoms under the TFEU. Regularly, the purpose of protecting victims will provide a proper justification (a 'general interest') for the infringement of the freedoms.

Compulsory insurance also restricts the freedom of insurance companies to 5
provide services. As long as national compulsory insurance laws continue to lay down special substantive requirements for the insurance product (eg minimum insurance cover amounts; mandatory provisions on the substantive scope of cover, etc), such requirements will cause insurance companies to abstain from providing cross-border services. When an insurer nevertheless enters a foreign market by adjusting its product to the local regimes of compulsory insurance, the extra costs involved are considerable. By this means, compulsory insurance

**23** In this regard, see the example in the Final Report (fn 9) 18 para 33.
**24** Art 14 of Directive 2009/103/EC of the European Parliament and of the Council of 16 September 2009 relating to insurance against civil liability in respect of the use of motor vehicles, and the enforcement of the obligation to insure against such liability [2009] OJ L 263, 7.10.2009, 11–31.
**25** See European Court of Justice (ECJ) C-556/13, *'Litaksa' UAB v 'BTA Insurance Company' SE* (ECLI:EU:C:2015:202) para 18.

can lead to protectionist effects in favour of the national insurance industry. With a view to legal requirements for doing business in the area of motor vehicle liability insurance in Italy, the ECJ has qualified a rule of law obliging the insurer to contract for motor vehicle liability insurance as an infringement of the freedom to provide services because it 'affects the relevant operators' access to the market, in particular where it subjects insurance undertakings not only to an obligation to cover any risks which are proposed to them, but also to requirements to moderate premium rates'[26]. Such infringement was, however, considered to be justified by a general interest.

# III. The Role of the Principles of European Insurance Contract Law (PEICL)

## 1. General remarks on the PEICL

6 The second edition of the Principles of European Insurance Contract Law (PEICL) was published in 2016.[27] As the product of an academic research project, the Principles are to be viewed as a Restatement.[28] The rules laid down in the PEICL attempt to reflect the current status in the development of insurance law.[29] In so doing, the PEICL also attempt to provide a model law for a European insurance contract law.[30] The Project Group believes that it would be beneficial to the internal market for the European legislature to create a uniform European insurance contract law by means of a European regulation.[31] This applies especially to certain branches of insurance including liability insurance which is specifically regulated in the 2nd edition of the PEICL.

---

**26** ECJ C-518/06, *Commission of the European Communities v Italian Republic* [2009] European Court Reports (ECR) I-3491, para 67.

**27** *J Basedow/J Birds/M Clarke/H Cousy/H Heiss/L Loacker* (eds), Principles of European Insurance Contract Law (PEICL) (2nd edn 2016).

**28** For more detailed information about the idea behind the research project, see *H Heiss*, Introduction to PEICL, in: J Basedow et al (eds), Principles of European Insurance Contract Law (PEICL) (2nd edn 2016).

**29** See PEICL/*Heiss* (fn 28) para I7.

**30** See PEICL/*Heiss* (fn 28) para I8.

**31** For details, see PEICL/*Heiss* (fn 28) para I31.

## 2. The need for a uniform Insurance Contract Act

The need for a uniform European insurance contract law arises from the realisation that the differences between national insurance contract laws, in particular their mandatory provisions, constitute a significant barrier to the internal market and, not least, to the pursuit of the freedom to provide services in the internal market.[32] This situation is caused not the least by the conflict of laws situation in the EU. In short, insurance litigation is as a rule conducted in the place of the policyholder's residence and not in the country where the insurer's head office is located.[33] Furthermore, cross-border insurance contracts, at least in the bulk business sector, are usually governed by the law of the Member State in which the policyholder resides habitually and not by the law of the Member State in which the insurer is seated or established, as the case may be.[34] When providing their services across borders, insurance companies are therefore forced to adapt their insurance contracts to the law of the respective country targeted for such service provision.[35] Such adaptations are a prerequisite to any market entry into a Member State. This increases the costs incurred by insurers for a planned market entry. It almost completely hinders any occasional cross-border sale, for example upon request by a prospective foreign customer. This makes it considerably more difficult for the insurer to carry out cross-border activities; at the same time, it makes it largely impossible for policyholders to enquire into cross-border insurance products. This is mainly due to the often mandatory character of the provisions contained in national insurance contract laws because parties cannot deviate from those provisions, at least not to the detriment of the policyholder. This restriction on the internal market applies especially in the area of compulsory insurance,[36] where the pertinent mandatory provisions are particularly numerous and rigid. 7

## 3. The case for an optional European insurance contract law

In order to eliminate this restriction on the internal market without, in the process, removing the mandatory protection provided to policyholders and third parties, such as victims, legal harmonisation based on a high standard of pro- 8

32 This issue is discussed in more detail by PEICL/*Heiss* (fn 28) para I2 ff.
33 See PEICL/*Heiss* (fn 28) para I2.
34 See PEICL/*Heiss* (fn 28) para I2.
35 Similarly, PEICL/*Heiss* (fn 28) para I4.
36 Final Report (fn 9) 19 para 35.

tection for policyholders is required. In principle, this can be achieved using two different approaches:[37] The first is the creation of a uniform insurance contract law which supersedes national law. The second is the creation of a uniform insurance contract law which does not supersede national law, but merely provides the contracting parties with the option of ousting the application of national insurance contract laws by choosing the European law ('optional instrument'). Of these two alternatives, the 'optional instrument' should be favoured because it is politically feasible and more efficient.[38] It has greater political feasibility, because national law will not be displaced. Thus, national legal cultures will remain completely intact. Furthermore, it is more efficient because only those companies and policyholders actually wishing to sell or buy cross-border products will have to bring their contracts into line with a new European insurance contract law. Other companies and their customers who only act nationally will not have to make any changes in line with European law and will, therefore, not incur the associated costs.

9 For these reasons, the PEICL have been drafted as an optional instrument. If the European legislature were to mould them into the form of a European regulation, they would – pursuant to art 1:102[39] – always and only apply when the parties agree to their application by means of a choice of law. The choice of the PEICL would be exempt from all restrictions under private international law:

> 'Article 1:102 Optional Application
> The PEICL shall apply when the parties, notwithstanding any limitations of choice of law rules under private international law, have agreed that their contract shall be governed by it. In that event, subject to Article 1:103, the parties shall apply the PEICL as a whole and shall not exclude the application of particular provisions.'

10 In the event of such a choice, contrary national law would generally be completely superseded pursuant to art 1:105 para 1 PEICL:

---

**37** For more details about the possible approaches available, see PEICL/*Heiss* (fn 28) para I34 ff.

**38** For detailed analysis of the advantages of an optional instrument, see PEICL/*Heiss* (fn 28) para I36.

**39** As to the choice provided under art 1:102 and its effects, see *J Basedow*, Comments 1 to 7 on Article 1:102 PEICL, in: J Basedow et al (eds), Principles of European Insurance Contract Law (PEICL) (2nd edn 2016).

'Article 1:105 National Law and General Principles
No recourse to national law, whether to restrict or to supplement the PEICL, shall be permitted. This does not apply to mandatory national laws specifically enacted for branches of insurance which are not covered by special rules contained in the PEICL.'

In branches regulated by the PEICL, that is liability[40] and life insurance[41] (including group insurance[42]), this would allow insurers to distribute an insurance product developed in the country of their head offices anywhere within the EU/EEA without requiring adaptations to the respective local law. 11

## 4. Compulsory liability insurance in the PEICL

The diversity and complexity of national provisions governing compulsory insurance mentioned above do not allow for comprehensive harmonisation of compulsory insurance law from the outset. Even in the narrow field of motor liability insurance, which has already been subjected to a significant amount of harmonisation by the directives adopted, it would be a very lengthy and painful way to produce legal unity. This is, of course, not to deny that a uniform motor liability insurance law would definitely be beneficial to the internal market. In this context, it should be noted that, as a result of the European Court of Justice's (ECJ) so-called *Odenbreit* case law[43], direct action by foreign injured parties is normally litigated at the domicile of the victim. Whenever the underlying tort was committed in another Member State, the direct claim will be subject to foreign tort and insurance law. This imposes a heavy burden on courts to apply rather complex foreign laws. This burden would also be eliminated if there were a uniform motor liability insurance law in the EU, which consequently would clearly also have to deal with the tortious claims arising out of road traffic accidents.[44] 12

In view of the foregoing, the intention underlying the PEICL is not to unify compulsory insurance law,[45] nor therefore is it purported that they establish new types of liability insurance. The purpose is rather to make available a uni- 13

40 Art 14:101 ff PEICL.
41 Art 17:101 ff PEICL.
42 Art 18:101 ff PEICL.
43 ECJ C-463/06, *FBTO Schadeverzekeringen NV v Jack Odenbreit* [2007] ECR I-11321.
44 As to the relationship between tort and insurance law under the Motor Vehicle Liability Insurance Directive, see *H Heiss/L Loacker*, Verkehrsopferschutz und Staatshaftung, Zeitschrift für Europäisches Privatrecht (ZEuP) 2011, 684 (688 ff).
45 See PEICL/*Basedow* (fn 1) Comment 3 on Art 16:101 PEICL.

form model law, including for insurance contracts which are concluded in accordance with a duty to take out insurance. To this end, art 16:101 PEICL determines that the parties may also choose to apply the PEICL in the field of compulsory insurance. This provision reads:

> 'Article 16:101 Scope of Application
> (1) The PEICL may be chosen by the parties to an insurance contract concluded in performance of an obligation to insure
> (a) prescribed by Community law,
> (b) prescribed in a Member State, or
> (c) prescribed in a Non-Member State to the extent allowed by the law of that State.'

14 It is irrelevant whether the duty to take out insurance is imposed by Union law, the law of a Member State or the law of a Non-Member State.[46] In the latter case, a choice in favour of the PEICL is, however, only possible to the extent that the respective third country permits such a choice.[47] However, art 16:101 PEICL does not apply where the duty to insure arises out of a contract or the articles of association of a legal entity under private law.[48] There is also no need for an application of the said provision: In such cases, there is no doubt as to the availability of the option of choosing in favour of applying the PEICL anyway.[49]

## 5. The reservation in favour of national law on compulsory liability insurance

15 Especially since, as stated, the PEICL do not contain independent provisions governing compulsory insurance law, a choice in favour of the PEICL cannot result in the displacement of relevant national rules. Accordingly, art 16:101 para 2 PEICL provides that an insurance contract only satisfies the duty to take out insurance if the contract complies with the specific provisions requiring compulsory insurance. The provision reads:

> 'Article 16:101 Scope of Application
> (...)
> (2) The insurance contract shall not satisfy the obligation to take out insurance unless it complies with the specific provisions imposing the obligation.'

46 Art 16:101 paras 1(a)–(c) PEICL.
47 Art 16:101 para 1(c) PEICL.
48 PEICL/*Basedow* (fn 1) Comment 6 on Art 16:101 PEICL.
49 PEICL/*Basedow* (fn 1) Comment 6 on Art 16:101 PEICL.

This second paragraph in art 16:101 clearly indicates that any potential conflict between the PEICL, as chosen by the parties, and the law of the Member State prescribing the duty to take out insurance will be determined in favour of the latter. The provision is modelled on art 7(4)(a) of Regulation (EC) 593/2008 (Rome I):[50] 16

> 'The following additional rules shall apply to insurance contracts covering risks for which a Member State imposes an obligation to take out insurance:
> (a) the insurance contract shall not satisfy the obligation to take out insurance unless it complies with the specific provisions relating to that insurance laid down by the Member State that imposes the obligation. Where the law of the Member State in which the risk is situated and the law of the Member State imposing the obligation to take out insurance contradict each other, the latter shall prevail;'

Article 7(4)(b) of Regulation (EC) 593/2008 is even broader and permits Member States to subject an insurance contract entirely to their laws where it is intended to satisfy a duty to take out insurance in this Member State: 17

> '(b) by way of derogation from paragraphs 2 and 3, a Member State may lay down that the insurance contract shall be governed by the law of the Member State that imposes the obligation to take out insurance.'

This option, which has been used by Germany,[51] for example, does not prevent a choice in favour of the PEICL.[52] If the PEICL were adopted in the form of a European regulation, they would constitute directly applicable law in every Member State (art 288(2) TFEU) and a choice in favour of their application would, therefore, satisfy the requirement in a Member State that compulsory insurance must be subjected to national law entirely.[53] Overall, therefore, the following applies: Under the model of the PEICL and in the event of agreement upon the application of the PEICL, a compulsory insurance contract would be subject to the provisions of the PEICL and additionally to the national provisions governing compulsory insurance. 18

**50** PEICL/*Basedow* (fn 1) Comment 4 on Art 16:101 PEICL.
**51** See art 46c para 2 Introductory Law to the German Civil Code (Einführungsgesetz zum Bürgerlichen Gesetzbuch, EGBGB).
**52** See PEICL/*Basedow* (fn 1) Comment 5 on Art 16:101 PEICL.
**53** See PEICL/*Basedow* (fn 1) Comment 5 on Art 16:101 PEICL.

## 6. The importance of the provisions governing general liability insurance

### a) Why rules on general liability insurance are of relevance also for compulsory insurance

19 Due to art 16:101 para 2 PEICL, the relevant (national) provisions governing compulsory insurance would apply to a particular contract if the PEICL do not comply with the requirements imposed. As long as the PEICL comply, there is no need for having recourse to national law. In view of the fact that the PEICL apply a high level of policyholder as well as victim protection even to general liability insurance, the pertinent rules[54] will probably often be compliant with national requirements for compulsory insurance. Thus, the rules on general liability insurance will also play an important role in the area of compulsory insurance.

### b) Direct claims

20 Among all of the relevant provisions, art 15:101 PEICL (Direct Claims) should in particular be highlighted:

> 'Article 15:101 Direct Claims and Defences
> (1) To the extent that the policyholder or the insured, as the case may be, is liable, the victim shall be entitled to a direct claim for compensation against the insurer under the insurance contract provided that
> (a) the insurance is compulsory, or
> (b) the policyholder or insured is insolvent, or
> (c) the policyholder or insured has been liquidated or wound up, or
> (d) the victim has suffered personal injury, or
> (e) the law governing the liability provides for a direct claim.
> (2) As against the victim, the insurer may raise defences available under the insurance contract unless prohibited by specific provisions making the insurance compulsory. However, the insurer is not entitled to raise any defence based upon the conduct of the policyholder and/or the insured after the loss.'

21 Although this scheme should be regarded as a European compromise, and therefore does not have the same reach as, for example, French law, which generally confers a direct right on the injured party in respect of liability insur-

54 Chapter Fourteen: General Liability Insurance (arts 14:101–14:108) and Chapter Fifteen: Direct Claims and Direct Actions (arts 15:101–15:104).

ance[55], this provision is likely to extend the protection of victims across Europe.[56] Under art 15:101 para 1(a), such a direct right of action is namely available in all cases involving compulsory insurance. Thus, the provision already extends beyond the level of protection provided by the law in some Member States. Article 15:101 paras 1(b) to (e) extend the scope of direct claims further to other cases. The rule confers a direct right of action where the policyholder or the insured person is insolvent (b), the policyholder or the insured has been liquidated (c), the victim has suffered personal injury (d) or the law governing the liability claim provides for a direct claim (e). The necessity of subsection (e) is dictated by art 18 of Regulation (EC) 864/2007 (Rome II).[57]

According to art 15:101 para 2 PEICL, the direct claim will provide the victim with what the insured is entitled to under the insurance cover but no more. Any defence which the insurer has against the insured under the insurance contract may also be raised against the victim. Article 15:101 para 2 PEICL only applies one exception in order to avoid moral hazard on the side of the insured: The insured cannot create defences after the loss for which he is liable has occurred. Of course, specific provisions on compulsory insurance such as, for instance, art 13 of the Motor Vehicle Liability Insurance Directive (2009/103/EC) deeming certain exclusion clauses to be void in respect of claims brought by victims, will apply due to art 16:101 para 2 PEICL. 22

Article 15:102 PEICL[58] attempts to increase the effectiveness of direct claims by imposing a duty on the policyholder and the insured person to provide any information required for making a direct claim upon request by the victim. 23

---

**55** See art L 124-3 Cass.

**56** For comparisons to the legal situation in the Member States, see PEICL/*Heiss* (fn 2), Comment 1 on Art 15:101 PEICL.

**57** PEICL/*Heiss* (fn 2) Comment 7 on Art 15:101 PEICL.

**58** Article 15:102 Information Duties

(1) Upon request by the victim, the policyholder and the insured shall provide the information needed for making a direct claim.

(2) The insurer shall notify the policyholder in writing of any direct claim made against it without undue delay and, at the latest within two weeks following receipt of the claim. If the insurer breaches this obligation, a payment to or acknowledgement of debt towards the victim shall not affect the rights of the policyholder.

(3) If the policyholder fails to provide the insurer with information about the insured event within one month of receiving notice in accordance with para 2, the policyholder is deemed to agree to a direct settlement of the claim by the insurer. This rule also applies to insureds who have actually received such notice in time.

24 Under art 15:103 PEICL,[59] a payment by the insurer to the policyholder or insured person would only relieve the insurer vis-à-vis the victim where the latter has either waived his right of action or, upon request by the insurer, has not informed the insurer of his intention to bring a direct claim within four weeks of such request.

25 Victims are also treated favourably in issues concerning prescription. Under art 15:104 para 1 PEICL,[60] the prescription period for direct claims against insurers is brought into line with the prescription period for claims for indemnity against insured persons. Furthermore, the prescription period of claims for indemnity against an insured person is suspended once the insured person becomes aware that a direct claim against the insurer has been made.[61] The period of prescription will remain suspended until a final determination has been reached in respect of the direct claim made against the insurer.[62]

### c) Assignment of claim

26 In the instances where the PEICL do not provide a direct right of action, it is within the power of the insured person to enable a direct claim to be made by assigning the insurance claim to the victim.[63] Such assignment of the claim for indemnity is possible[64] and cannot be excluded pursuant to art 14:105

---

**59** Article 15:103 Discharge
The payment of insurance money to the policyholder or insured, as the case may be, will only discharge the insurer from its obligation towards the victim if the victim
(a) has waived his direct claim or
(b) has not notified the insurer about his intention to make a direct claim within four weeks of receiving the insurer's request in writing.

**60** Article 15:104 Prescription
(1) Action against the insurer, whether brought by the insured or by the victim, shall be prescribed when the victim's action against the insured is prescribed.
(2) The period of prescription for a claim made by the victim against the insured is suspended from the time, if any, that the insured becomes aware that a direct claim against the insurer has been made until the time that the direct claim is settled or unequivocally rejected by the insurer.

**61** Art 15:104 para 2 PEICL.

**62** Art 15:104 para 2 PEICL.

**63** With regard to the interests of the parties involved, see *M Clarke*, Comments 1 and 2 on Article 14:105 PEICL, in: J Basedow et al (eds), Principles of European Insurance Contract Law (PEICL) (2nd edn 2016).

**64** See PEICL/*Clarke* (fn 63) Comment 3 on Art 14:105 PEICL.

PEICL.[65] However, since art 15:101 para 1 lit a PEICL provides for a direct claim in all cases of compulsory insurance, art 14:105 PEICL will play no role in this sector.

## d) Settlements to the detriment of the victim (art 14:102 PEICL)

A major rule of protection for victims is provided in art 14:102 PEICL: 27

> 'Article 14:102 Protection of the Victim
> Unless the victim gives consent in writing, his position shall not be affected by any settlement of the insurance claim under the policy by the policyholder or the insured and the insurer, whether by agreement, waiver, payment or an equivalent act.'

While an agreement or act of the insurer and the policyholder will be of no 28 effect on a direct claim, it would affect the position of the victim where no such direct claim exists.[66] Thus, art 14:102 has its scope of application outside the scope of direct claims under art 15:101 PEICL. Thus, while this rule is of significant importance to general liability insurance, it will play no role for forms of compulsory insurance governed by the PEICL. This is due to the fact that, in the case of compulsory insurance governed by the PEICL, there will always be a direct claim of the victim.[67]

## e) Defence costs (art 14:101 PEICL)

Defence costs must be reimbursed by the insurer as costs for damage mitigation 29 even if the amount payable exceeds the sum insured (art 14:101 PEICL[68] together with art 9:102 PEICL[69]). This is also important for the victim, because it means that the sum insured available to him for liability cannot be reduced by defence costs.

---

**65** Article 14:105 Assignment
A clause in an insurance contract depriving the insured of his right to assign his claim under the policy shall be without effect.
**66** PEICL/*Heiss* (fn 2) Comment 3 on Art 14:102 PEICL.
**67** Art 15:101 para 1 lit a PEICL.
**68** Article 14:101 Defence Costs
The insurer shall reimburse defence costs incurred in accordance with Article 9:102.
**69** Article 9:102 The Costs of Mitigation
(1) The insurer shall reimburse the costs incurred or the amount of damage suffered by the policyholder or the insured in taking measures to mitigate insured loss, to the extent the

### f) Acknowledgement of liability (art 14:104 PEICL)

30 Article 14:104 PEICL,[70] in addition, precludes the inclusion of any clauses in insurance contracts prohibiting the acknowledgement of liability. Therefore, acknowledgment cannot lead to the insurer being released from or reducing its obligations.[71] Conversely, the insurer is, of course, not bound by such acknowledgment unless it gives its consent.[72]

### g) Liability exceeding insured sum

31 The PEICL also protect the victim in the event that the liability claims exceed the amount of the sum insured. In this case, the payments must be reduced proportionately (art 14:108 para 1 PEICL[73]). Thus, the PEICL aspire to protect a *par conditio* to all victims.

## IV. Summary

32 The PEICL are intended to provide insurers and their customers with a uniform legal framework for insurance contracts, especially when sold across borders. They regulate liability insurance specifically and allow for a choice of the PEICL as the law governing even liability insurance that is made compulsory. The PEICL provide a high level of victims' protection and, thus, will often prevail

policyholder or the insured was justified in regarding the measures as reasonable under the circumstances, even if they were unsuccessful in mitigating the loss.
(2) The insurer shall indemnify the policyholder or the insured, as the case may be, in respect of any measures taken in accordance with para. 1, even if together with the compensation for the loss insured the amount payable exceeds the sum insured.

70 Article 14:104 Acknowledgement of Liability
(1) A clause in the insurance contract releasing the insurer from its obligations in case the policyholder or insured, as the case may be, accepts or satisfies the victim's claim shall be without effect.
(2) Unless it consents, the insurer shall not be bound by an agreement between the victim and the policyholder or insured, as the case may be.

71 Art 14:104 para 1 PEICL.

72 Art 14:104 para 2 PEICL.

73 Article 14:108 Claims Exceeding the Sum Insured
(1) If the total payments due to several victims exceed the sum insured, the payments shall be reduced proportionately.

over national law as the better law for the victim. However, due to the multitude and variety of compulsory insurance forms in national laws, the PEICL cannot comprehensively regulate this subject but must refer to the specific provisions in each country.

Michael Faure*

# Compulsory Liability Insurance: Economic Perspectives

## I. Introduction

1 The question under which circumstances liability insurance should be made compulsory, what the particular advantage is, but equally potential dangers are, and how it should be structured are all issues that, at least to some extent, have been analysed in the law and economics literature. Compulsory liability insurance can in that respect be considered a relatively known topic in law and economics.[1] To some extent the Questionnaire that was drafted for the country reporters will be followed in the sense that some of the questions that are mentioned in the Questionnaire are equally relevant from a law and economics perspective.

2 Since there is already elaborate literature on compulsory liability insurance[2] also within the framework of earlier ECTIL projects,[3] this contribution will largely rely and expand upon those earlier studies. However, there have been some recent developments, also at the policy levels and in academic literature with which the previous studies will be updated.

3 As indicated, this special report on the law and economics aspects of compulsory liability insurance will not literally follow the Questionnaire, but try to analyse the relevant issues indicated in the Questionnaire. Hence after this introduction, the chapter will be structured as follows: first the aims of compulsory liability insurance from an economic perspective will be identified (II); next, the types and contents of the regulation of compulsory liability insurance

---

* I am grateful to W Liao (Maastricht University) for useful research assistance in the preparation of this chapter.

1 See in that respect inter alia *PJ Jost*, Limited liability and the requirement to purchase insurance (1999) 16 International Review of Law and Economics (IRLE) 259–276; *M Polborn*, Mandatory insurance and the judgment proof problem (1988) 18(2) IRLE 141–146 and *G Skogh*, Mandatory insurance: transaction costs analysis of insurance, in: B Bouckaert/G De Geest (eds), Encyclopedia of Law and Economics (2000) 521–537.

2 See inter alia *MG Faure*, Economic criteria for compulsory insurance (2006) 31 The Geneva Papers on Risk and Insurance 149–168 and *G Wagner*, Tort law and liability insurance, in: M Faure (ed), Tort Law and Economics (2009) 377–405.

3 See *M Faure*, The view from law and economics, in: G Wagner (ed), Tort Law and Liability Insurance (2005) 239–273.

will be addressed in further detail (III); the importance of controlling the moral hazard problem as a condition for an effective compulsory liability insurance will be stressed (IV) and the question will be asked at which level of governance compulsory liability insurance should be issued (V). It will equally be examined to what extent alternative mechanisms may support or replace compulsory liability insurance (VI) and a few limits of compulsory liability insurance will be discussed (VII). An effective compulsory liability insurance regime obviously requires detailed monitoring and enforcement (VIII). Recent literature will be discussed in IX and section X concludes.

## II. Aims of Compulsory Liability Insurance[4]

4 From an economic perspective, there are two criteria that could justify the introduction of compulsory liability insurance whereby the second is stronger than the first.

5 A first argument would be related to information problems and would then rather be an argument to protect the potential injurer, in other words the insurance holder, who would not be able to sufficiently judge the potential advantages of insurance.

6 Information problems might arise where the potential injurer cannot make an accurate assessment of the risk he is exposed to and the benefits of the purchase of insurance. An underestimation of the risk would in that case lead to the wrong decision of the injurer not to purchase liability insurance. The legislator could remedy this information problem by introducing a general duty to insure. This information problem is probably a valid argument to introduce a generalised duty to insure for motor vehicle owners. Maybe the average driver of a car underestimates the benefits of insurance. If there were no information problem and the legislator nevertheless introduced a duty to insure because this would be 'in the best interest' of the insured, this would of course be mere paternalism.

7 If empirical evidence existed that most injurers greatly underestimate the costs of damage related to specific risks they may cause, as well as the probability that they will be held liable for this damage, this would then lead injurers to reserve too few resources to cover their potential liability. If these conditions are met, and one can indeed assume that injurers underestimate the cost of accidents, this information deficiency may be considered an argument in favour of compulsory insurance.

4 This corresponds to some extent with some of the issues raised under Questions 1 to 6 of the Questionnaire.

This, however, may not be the strongest argument. If, after all, there were information problems on the side of potential injurers, the solution would rather be to provide them with adequate information (information remedies) rather than to force them to take out liability insurance cover. There may indeed be potential injurers who would not have a demand for liability insurance cover and for whom making this mandatory would thus not correspond with their preferences. The second reason, which is rather related to an internalisation of costs in the interest of society, is much stronger. 8

The argument goes that the magnitude of the harm will often exceed the individual wealth of an injurer, whereby a problem of undercompensation of victims will arise. Lawyers would, hence, push forward compulsory insurance as an argument to guarantee effective compensation to the victim. This – more distributional – argument obviously may play a role in the context of insurance of particular risks as well. Take the example of environmental pollution: if an injurer were to be found judgment proof and hence for example a polluted site would be 'orphaned', the costs would be borne by society. 9

It is, however, also possible to make an economic argument that insolvency will lead to underdeterrence problems which might be remedied through insurance. Indeed, this so-called 'judgment proof' problem has been extensively dealt with in the economic literature.[5] If the expected damage largely exceeds the injurer's assets, the injurer will only have incentives to purchase insurance up to the amount of his own assets. He is indeed only exposed to the risk of losing his own assets in a liability suit. The judgment proof problem may therefore lead to underinsurance and thus to underdeterrence. Jost has rightly pointed at the fact that, in these circumstances of insolvency, compulsory insurance might provide a better outcome.[6] By introducing a duty to purchase insurance coverage for the amount of the expected loss, better results will be obtained than with insolvency whereby the magnitude of the loss exceeds the injurer's assets.[7] In the latter case the injurer will indeed only consider the risk as one where he could at most lose his own assets and will set his standard of care accordingly. When the insurer is, under a duty to insure, exposed to full liability, he will have incentives to control the behaviour of the insured. Via the 10

5 More particularly by *S Shavell*, The judgment proof problem (1986) IRLE 43–58.

6 *Jost* (1999) 16 IRLE 259. A similar argument has been formulated by *Polborn* (1988) 18(2) IRLE 141ff and by *Skogh* (fn 1). Skogh has also pointed out that compulsory insurance may save on transaction costs.

7 See also *H Kunreuther/P Freeman*, Insurability, environmental risks and the law, in: A Heyes (ed), The Law and Economics of the Environment (2001) 316.

traditional instruments for the control of moral hazard,[8] the insurer can make sure that the injurer will take the necessary care to avoid an accident with the real magnitude of the loss. Thus Jost and Skogh argue that compulsory insurance can, provided that the moral hazard problem can be resolved adequately, provide better results than under the judgment proof problem. This is probably another explanation why, for instance for traffic liability, compulsory insurance was introduced. Uninsured and insolvent drivers who have little money at stake which they may lose compared to the possible magnitude of accidents they may cause may have little incentive to avoid an accident. Insurers might better be able to control this risk and could force the injurer to take care under the threat of shutting him out of the insurance.

11 From an economic perspective, it is hence neither the protection of the injurer, nor the protection of victims that would be the main argument in favour of making liability insurance compulsory. It is the risk of insolvency that would be created when the magnitude of the damage could largely outweigh the financial assets of the injurer. Without compulsory insurance the costs of accidents could be thrown on society and would hence be externalised instead of internalised. Internalisation of risks may hence be the most important argument in favour of making liability insurance compulsory.

## III. Types and Contents of the Duty

### 1. Form?

12 A first question that could arise is whether the problem created through a potential externalisation of accident costs should necessarily be resolved via the instrument of insurance. The problem to be resolved is the externalisation of accident costs resulting from the insolvency problem. That insolvency problem can obviously be solved through a variety of different forms of financial security other than insurance.[9]

13 From a policy perspective it would be indicated rather to refer to a duty to seek financial security instead of to impose compulsory liability insurance. Limiting the solution to the potential insolvency to insurance would have potential disadvantages. First, it would de facto make insurers the licensors of a particular activity. If no insurance cover were available, the activity could not take

8 These are discussed in no 25 below.

9 As is also recognised in the Questionnaire under Question 4.f, which equally refers to other forms of financial security.

place. From society's perspective it may not be desirable to put insurers in that powerful position. This relates to a second risk: if the financial security were limited to insurance, the policymaker would de facto become dependent upon the insurance market. If in that case the market refused to provide such cover, the regulatory duty to obtain compulsory liability insurance could de facto not be executed. This may be particularly problematic in cases where the insurance market is highly concentrated, but also where it is doubtful whether there is sufficient availability of insurance cover. Especially for particularly new risks it may be possible that insurance markets have not yet developed a sufficient number of new policies.

All these arguments underline the importance of formulating a regulatory 14
duty not as limited to liability insurance, but rather as a duty to seek financial security. This may have major advantages. First of all it may generate higher amounts, since in some cases cover on traditional insurance markets may only be available to a limited extent whereas cover via alternative techniques (more particularly self-insurance or cover via captives could be available to much higher amounts). Second, if a duty is imposed upon operators to seek financial security, leaving it basically free to them to offer a variety of instruments to guarantee their solvency, this will also provide incentives to the market to develop alternatives, such as for example pooling arrangements between operators. In this respect a wide variety of alternatives could be thought of that come to mind in addition to traditional liability insurance (and obviously re-insurance). Risk-sharing agreements between operators were already mentioned, as well as self-insurance by operators. But in addition other forms of financial security, like a guarantee by a parent company, or bank guarantees could be imagined as well. Moreover, in some cases the capital markets could be used to provide financial security, for example via a bond.

The crucial issue is that, especially when new risks are concerned, in some 15
cases the alternatives (like risk-sharing between operators or self-insurance) may for a variety of reasons be more attractive than liability insurance. It could for example be the case that insurers lack precise information on probabilities of the accident, given scientific uncertainty as a result of which they would not be able to set premiums. An advantage of risk-sharing is that this is possible even in the absence of precise information on probabilities.[10] Moreover, some

**10** The possibility to engage in risk-sharing without knowledge of probabilities was first stated by Göran Skogh. See *G Skogh*, Development risks, strict liability, and the insurability of industrial hazards (1998) 23 The Geneva Papers on Risk and Insurance. Issues and Practices 247–264; *G Skogh*, Risk-sharing institutions for unpredictable losses (1999) 155 Journal of Institutional and Theoretical Economics 505–515 and *G Skogh/H Wu*, The diversification theorem restated:

operators may have financial assets that are substantially larger than the assets of an insurance company. In this particular case forcing operators to take insurance coverage (via mandatory liability insurance) would not be effective since they could de facto generate higher amounts of cover via self-insurance.

16 Examples of such a flexible approach can also be found in practice, for example with respect to the cover for environmental risks. For example with respect to the risks created through so-called Carbon Capture and Storage (CCS), Directive 2009/31/EC on the geological storage of carbon dioxide[11] provides in art 7(10) that applications for storage permits must include proof that the financial security or other equivalent provision as required under art 19 of the Directive will be valid and effective before commencement of the injection.[12] A so-called Guidance Document 4, which provides further guidance concerning the implementation of the Directive, lists a large number of instruments that can be used to provide financial security for CCS-related risks such as funds, escrows, bank guarantees, bonds, deposits and letters of credit.[13] The Guidance Document explicitly refers to the many alternatives for insurance, being aware of the fact that insurance may only be available to a limited extent and amount and that other instruments may better deal with CCS-related risks than insurance.

17 Another example from the environmental area concerns the financial security for the risks created through offshore oil and gas activities. As in the case of CCS, a European Directive imposes a broad obligation upon Member States to require financial security from operators.[14] However, this is again not limited to

---

risk-pooling without assignment of probabilities (2005) 31(1) Journal of Risk and Uncertainty 35–51.

**11** Official Journal (OJ) L 140, 5.6.2009, 114–135.

**12** Article 19 of the Directive holds 'Member States shall ensure the proof that adequate provisions can be established, by way of financial security or any other equivalent, on the basis of arrangements to be decided by the Member States, is presented by the potential operator as part of the application for a storage permit'.

**13** Implementation of Directive 2009/31/EC on the geological storage of carbon dioxide, Guidance Document 4 4–6 and 26–28.

**14** According to art 7 of Directive 2013/30/EU of 12 June 2013 on safety of offshore oil and gas operations (OJ L 178, 28.6.2013, 66–106, referred to as the Offshore Safety Directive) Member States shall ensure that the licensee is financially liable for the prevention and the remediation of environmental damage caused by offshore oil and gas operations. Article 4(3) forces the Member States to ensure that the licensing authority will not grant a licence unless it is satisfied with evidence from the applicant that the applicant has made or will make adequate provision to cover liabilities potentially deriving from the applicant's offshore oil and gas operations.

insurance.[15] Interestingly, the way in which this financial cover is de facto provided in Europe, at least in the North Sea area, is through a voluntary agreement concluded between offshore operators, referred to as OPOL.[16] OPOL is an association of oil and gas producers that verifies whether, up to a limited amount, operators that are members of OPOL can provide financial security. This financial security can be provided via insurance, but again, also via other means such as a surety bond, a letter of guarantee from a parent company or a statement of self-insurance, to be verified by OPOL.[17] Although OPOL is a voluntary mechanism by oil and gas producers, it is taken seriously by the regulator as well. For example, in the UK, membership of OPOL has been made a condition to obtain a licence for offshore oil and gas drilling in the North Sea.[18]

These examples illustrate that regulators are also aware of the fact that **18**
mandatory financial security should not be limited to liability insurance, but that there are a wide variety of instruments available on the market that could be used by operators. Obviously the credibility of those instruments, ie that finances are also available to cover accident costs when it is needed, has to be verified by the authorities.

## 2. Amounts

As far as the amount to be required is concerned, from an economic perspective **19**
we can be brief: the amount should be sufficient to cover the magnitude of the potential damage in the case of an accident. Obviously it may be difficult to assess this *ex ante* and the type and magnitude of damage may also be strongly industry-related. Hence, this begs the question whether the amounts of financial security to be provided should be fixed *ex ante* by the legislator or whether they should rather be fixed by a licensing authority for every specific industry. Given the fact that licensing authorities may have better information on the nature of the potential risks posed by specific industries, there may be an argument in favour of having industry-specific limits concerning the duty to insure

**15** The Preamble (10) to the Directive just broadly states that 'Member States should verify that such entities have provided appropriate evidence that adequate provisions have been or are to be made to cover liabilities deriving from major accidents'.

**16** OPOL stands for the Offshore Pollution Liability Association Limited. Details of the scheme can be found on <http://www.opol.org.uk>.

**17** The maximum cover under OPOL is US$ 250 million.

**18** The UK Department of Energy and Climate Change (DECC) as the competent licensing authority requires all operators to have signed up to OPOL.

set in licences rather than providing this in statutes.[19] The disadvantage of a statutory limit on the duty to provide financial cover is that this amount may be too high (and thus too costly) for relatively small enterprises whereas it could be too low for the larger and riskier ones. Because of this, the legislator should rather provide a margin within which licensing authorities, taking into account the industry's specific information, can set specific amounts.

20 One point should be stressed as far as the amount of the financial security is concerned: the mere fact that either the legislator or a licensing authority would provide a limit on the amount to provide financial security does not imply that the liability of operators themselves should also be limited. That could create underdeterrence and other undesirable effects.[20] The better alternative is hence to leave liability unlimited but to limit the duty to provide financial cover to a specific amount of which a broader range is provided in the statute with a specific subsequent determination by regulatory authorities.

## 3. Duty to pay

21 A consequence of compulsory financial security is that the regulator also wants to ensure that accident costs can be covered by the financial security when the risk emerges.[21] As a consequence, all kinds of tools that insurers or other parties providing cover would normally be able to use to exclude particular risks from cover may no longer be available. Given the fact that the regulator will often ask for an unconditional guarantee that funds are available when the risk emerges, the right of insurers (or other providers of security) to invoke defences will often be limited.

22 Insurers (or other providers of financial security) may for example stipulate in the conditions for cover that cover will be excluded in the case of non-compliance of the operator with mandatory government regulations. As such this can be considered as an effective instrument to control moral hazard. The regulator will, however, often consider the third party victim a beneficiary of the financial cover and hence hold that defences (such as not following mandatory regulations) are not opposable to third parties. As a consequence, the insurer

**19** This would allow licensing authorities to base the amount on an objective assessment of the risk, taking into account technical criteria that relate a specific operation and operator to particular amounts of damage.

**20** See *Faure* (fn 3) 248–252.

**21** This is a problem in some cases of self-insurance. Since these are basically reserves set aside by an operator, there will be no guarantee that they cannot be seized by the trustee in bankruptcy and hence not available for the victims of an accident.

may have to compensate the victim and may then have a (contractual or statutory) right of recourse against the insured. That to some extent explains the reluctance of insurers towards mandatory liability insurance.[22]

Related to this is the fact that[23] victims often enjoy special protection against insolvency of the operator. One way of providing this protection is to grant the victim a direct right of action vis-à-vis the provider of the financial security, without the need to first call on the operator.[24] 23

## 4. Redress

The question equally arises whether the provider of financial security, after having fulfilled the obligation to provide compensation to the victim, can still have recourse against the operator. Recourse is in principle an important instrument, at least from an economic perspective, since it facilitates exposure of the operator to risk. Via recourse the costs that have been advanced by the provider of financial security will in principle be reallocated to the operator, thus providing him with incentives for prevention again. In this sense recourse can be considered as an important tool to control the moral hazard risk. However, the question to what extent recourse by insurers really serves social goals is heavily debated. Some argue that it only creates huge additional costs and in fact leads to few additional benefits as far as providing additional incentives for prevention is concerned.[25] Some therefore doubt the cost effectiveness of recourse actions.[26] 24

---

**22** See *Faure* (2006) 31 The Geneva Papers on Risk and Insurance 158 f.

**23** See also Question 18 of the Questionnaire.

**24** It is the 'action directe' to which Question 19.b of the Questionnaire refers.

**25** This is a point that was particularly powerfully made in the last century by the Dutch scholar Auke Bloembergen, who argued that redress would only lead to excessive costs, but would have no benefits whatsoever. See inter alia *AR Bloembergen*, Naar een nieuw verkeersongevallenrecht I (1973) Nederlands Juristenblad (NJB) 961–968; *AR Bloembergen*, Het rapport over het verkeersongevallenrecht (1978) NJB 693–705; *AR Bloembergen*, De invloed van verzekeringen (1980) NJB 182 and *AR Bloembergen*, Het SER-rapport over regresrechten: een fout verhaal (1994) NJB 118.

**26** What has happened in practice in order to reduce the costs of individual redress (eg in the Netherlands) is that redress has been 'collectivised'. That meant that for example social insurance carriers would no longer have individual redress against operators and their liability insurers, but that on a yearly basis an amount of money would be paid by the collectivity of liability insurers to the social insurance carriers, corresponding to the amount for which the insured of the liability insurers would be liable and obviously corresponding to the costs paid by social insurance carriers. For a discussion of this collectivisation of redress see *M Faure*, Regres in een rechtseconomisch perspectief, in: WH van Boom/T Hartlief/J Spier (eds), Regresrechten. Afschaffen, handhaven of uitbreiden? (1996) 45–71.

# IV. Control of Moral Hazard

## 1. *Ex ante* and *ex post* control

25 It should be remembered that insurance, but also other forms of financial security, always create a moral hazard problem. Moral hazard refers to the basic notion that, when an operator is no longer exposed to risk (because risk is shifted to the provider of the financial security), his incentives for prevention may be diluted.[27] If the moral hazard problem cannot be resolved, compulsory financial security would do more bad than good. In that case Shavell even goes as far as to state that if the moral hazard problem cannot be controlled, the only regulatory intervention should be a prohibition of liability insurance.[28]

26 The problem arises that, when the legislator introduces compulsory financial security, instruments should still be available to the security provider to differentiate risks in a sufficient manner in order to resolve the moral hazard problem. Shavell indicated in his seminal 1979 paper that the first best way of controlling moral hazard is via *ex ante* and *ex post* monitoring and an adaptation of the policy conditions to the risks posed by the insured.[29] Hence, also under a model of compulsory financial security, the security provider should still have the possibility to differentiate *ex ante* (by charging different prices for different types of risks) and *ex post* (for example by increasing prices (premiums) for financial cover after an accident) in order to make sure that the insured would behave as if no cover would be available.

27 In practice the regulator may in some cases find it more important to guarantee that financial cover is available than that moral hazard is also adequately insured. Some possibilities of risk differentiation may therefore be more limited under compulsory insurance. Some empirical research seems to indicate that compulsory insurance regulation in the US has led to serious moral hazard costs and thus to an increase in traffic fatalities in that country.[30]

---

**27** See *Wagner* (fn 2) 389–393.

**28** *Shavell* (1986) IRLE 43 ff.

**29** *S Shavell*, On moral hazard and insurance (1979) 93 Quarterly Journal of Economics 541–562.

**30** See *A Cohen/R Dehejia*, The effect of automobile insurance and accident liability laws on traffic fatalities (2004) 47(2) Journal of Law and Economics 357–393.

## 2. Duty to accept?

A question that is equally rightly asked in connection to compulsory financial security is whether a duty to have financial security also implies that insurers or other providers of financial security should accept the risk and would hence be obliged to offer cover since otherwise the activity could not be undertaken.[31] This point is obviously related to the issue that, under compulsory liability insurance, insurers would de facto become licensors of industry and would thus decide which activities to permit. If security providers would hence (all) exclude a particular operator from cover, this would mean that that activity could no longer be undertaken. 28

The answer to this particular problem is of course not to introduce an obligation to insurers or other security providers to accept particular risks. The answer is rather to guarantee, via competition policy, sufficient competition on insurance markets as a result of which a wide variety of differentiated policies will be available and, as indicated above, not to limit the duty to provide security to insurance. If a variety of other mechanisms can also be used by operators, there is less of a risk that the activity would not be undertaken anymore because no financial cover could be obtained. However, if on competitive markets all providers consider that the particular activity is too risky and if for that reason they collectively decide to refuse financial cover, this should provide a strong indication of the risky nature of the particular activity. The lack of available financial cover should then be a reason to reconsider whether that activity should be undertaken at all rather than obliging one provider to provide security cover. 29

Introducing a duty to accept certain operators as insured seems like an extremely dangerous exercise, given the importance of an effective control of moral hazard. One important instrument to control moral hazard is precisely to have the possibility to monitor the risk which a particular operator may pose. If that leads a provider of security to the decision that this particular operator poses too high risks, the security provider should have the right to freely decide who should and who should not be provided with security. A duty to accept certain risks would therefore collide with basic principles which have to be respected in order to guarantee an effective functioning of insurance markets.[32] 30

---

**31** See Question 15 of the Questionnaire.

**32** See *Faure* (2006) 31 The Geneva Papers on Risk and Insurance 157 f.

## 3. Deductibles

31 Although the first best technique to control the moral hazard risk is to expose the insured partially to risk and to adapt the premium conditions accordingly, a second tool, still exposing the insured partially to risk, is probably equally important. The latter can for example be done via the introduction of a deductible.[33] Again, since a deductible has to be considered as an instrument to control moral hazard, it remains important that deductibles can be charged to operators although this again will not limit the right of the victim to compensation. Eventually the consequence of a deductible would be that the victim is fully compensated by the security provider and that the security provider claims back the deductible from the operator. This is also current practice in many compulsory liability insurance regimes.

## 4. Competition policy and moral hazard

32 It is important to stress that the literature has indicated that the incentives of the insurance industry to adequately control moral hazard will to an important extent depend upon the competitiveness of the insurance market. If insurance markets are more concentrated, monopoly profits can be generated and the incentives to adequately control moral hazard are diluted.[34] From that perspective it is quite important to guarantee competition in insurance markets in order to provide adequate incentives to insurers to control moral hazard. Moreover, competition will equally lead to a more diversified portfolio and thus to a wider supply of cover.[35]

33 From a policy perspective it may be highly problematic to make liability insurance compulsory in a concentrated insurance market. That would on the one hand create moral hazard problems and would on the other hand reinforce the

---

**33** Hence the Questionnaire rightly asks to what extent deductibles can be reconciled with compulsory liability insurance in Question 11.b.

**34** For empirical evidence see inter alia *M Adams*, Ökonomische Analyse der Gefährdungs- und Verschuldenshaftung (1985) and *J Finsinger/E Hammond/J Tapp*, Insurance: competition or regulation? A comparative study of the insurance markets in the United Kingdom and the Federal Republic of Germany (1985).

**35** See on the importance of applying competition policy to the insurance industry *M Faure/R Van den Bergh*, Restrictions of competition on insurance markets and the applicability of EC antitrust law (1995) Kyklos 65–85. *MG Faure/R Van den Bergh*, Competition on the European Market for Liability Insurance and Efficient Accident Law (2002) 9(3) Maastricht Journal of European and Comparative Law 279–306.

feature that compulsory insurance de facto makes insurers become the licensors of industry.

This point underscores the importance of the application of competition policy to insurance markets generally, but also constitutes a warning that it may be dangerous to make liability insurance compulsory in highly concentrated insurance markets. Again, this once again underlines the point mentioned above that a duty to provide financial cover should surely not be limited to liability insurance but could constitute a much wider obligation to provide financial security through a variety of mechanisms, the adequacy of which of course has to be controlled by regulatory authorities. 34

## V. Level of Governance

The question of who should decide on financial security can be asked, ie it was already mentioned before that some authority should decide on an acceptable form of financial security[36] and on the appropriate amount.[37] This comes down to the question of whether the details of the specific design of the financial security should be laid down in legislation (via statutes) or in specific permit conditions, separately for each entity. The answer is probably that a flexible regime should be worked out making use on the one hand of a general legislative duty imposed by statutes but on the other hand of the superior informational advantage of regulatory authorities who may have better information on the types of risks posed by each specific operator and on the appropriateness of particular forms of financial security offered. From this discussion it follows that it may be important to fix the duty to provide financial security in legislation and to further provide guidance to administrative authorities on the types of security they can accept and on the relevant criteria to determine the appropriate amount. Such guidance could allow sufficient flexibility as far as the forms of financial security are concerned and again, they should not necessarily be limited to insurance. The guidance would assist local regulators to verify accurately whether the form and amount of financial security offered by operators would be adequate to cover the potential damage related to the specific activity. 35

This allows for a flexible system whereby licensing administrative authorities can judge in individual cases whether the obligation to provide financial security has been met. This allows the administrative authorities to decide the 36

36 See nos 12–18 above.
37 See no 19 f above.

specific form and amount of the financial obligation in a flexible way.[38] The authorities can then verify and monitor whether the type of financial assurance offered by the potentially responsible party will be adequate to meet his financial obligations. Under certain circumstances the duty to provide financial cover could even emerge from an obligation imposed by a self-governing body (such as a professional association regarding professional liability)[39] or the obligation to provide financial security could emerge from a contract.[40] In fact, many insurance policies which are purchased (although not necessarily liability insurance) are formally 'voluntary', but in fact imposed via contract. A well-known example is the situation where one takes a mortgage to secure a loan on a house. Usually the financial institution will at least require a fire or similar insurance on the house (in order to guarantee the property which serves as collateral to guarantee repayment of the loan) and in many cases a life insurance of the account holder will be required as well (to guarantee that the life insurance could cover the payments that would still be due in the case of the policy holder's death). Although not formally compulsory, many of these insurance policies are concluded on the basis of a contractual obligation. This will also often be the case under public procurement or other forms of contracting with the government whereby the government will oblige contractors to provide financial security to cover their obligations and responsibilities.

37 Many examples can be provided of such a flexible approach: for example, a Flemish Draft Decree, proposed by the Flemish Interuniversity Commission for the Reform of Environmental Law[41] provided the option for regulatory authorities to impose a duty on operators of a classified activity to provide a deposit in order to guarantee that specific obligations shall be complied with. The authority to fix the amount and to control the offer of financial assurance had to be the same as that which also granted the permit at the start of the operation of the activity.[42] As was mentioned earlier, the European Directives on Carbon Capture and Storage and on Offshore Safety also rely on such a flexible approach: a duty

**38** This was also advised with respect to damage related to offshore activities in *K De Smedt/M Faure/J Liu/N Philipsen/H Wang*, Civil Liability and Financial Security for Offshore Oil and Gas Activities, available at: <http://ec.europa.eu/dgs/energy/tenders/doc/2013/20131028_b3-978-1_final_report.pdf>, 306–312.

**39** As is rightly suggested in the Questionnaire under 4.b.

**40** See the Questionnaire under 4.e.

**41** See *H Bocken/D Ryckbost* (eds), Codification of Environmental Law. Draft Decree on Environmental Policy (1996).

**42** *H Bocken/D Ryckbost/S Deloddere*, Liability and financial guarantees, in: H Bocken/D Ryckbost (eds), Codification of Environmental Law. Draft Decree on Environmental Policy (1996) 214–223.

is imposed upon Member States to make sure that regulatory authorities will require financial security from operators before the start of the activity. However, the determination of the amount and form of the financial security is left to the individual Member State and ultimately to the regulatory authorities who may have better information. However, in order to provide these regulatory authorities with some guidance on the type of financial security that could be accepted and on the criteria to determine the potential magnitude of the damage, guidelines could be issued in order to facilitate the tasks of the regulatory authorities. This was also suggested in a recent study with respect to civil liability and compensation for the damage related to offshore installations.[43]

Obviously it should be stressed that the flexible mechanism proposed here as far as the determination of the amount and form of financial security is concerned mostly relates to industrial risks posed by hazardous installations. For more common risks such as, for example, motor vehicle liability, the administrative costs of such a detailed determination of the risk would obviously be too high. Moreover, in that case there are no regulatory authorities that could determine the amount and desirable form of financial security. A general rule, that is fixing the form and amount of financial security in a statute, may then be more effective, because it creates lower administrative costs. 38

## VI. Alternative Mechanisms

Since it was held above[44] that there should not be a duty on providers of financial security to accept risks (as that could have negative effects on the control of moral hazard), the question arises whether there are any alternative mechanisms that persons seeking financial security could then rely on.[45] As a starting point it should be repeated that the fact that particular dangerous activities (eg car drivers causing a great number of accidents) are excluded from that activity since they cannot meet the duty to provide financial security is as such a desirable consequence of the obligation to obtain financial security. Security providers screen the riskiness of the activity and when they hold that the activity is considered too dangerous to provide security, this could provide an important signal to the market. If, as a consequence, the activity cannot be performed, as a starting point one could even argue that security providers have then exercised 39

---

43 *De Smedt/Faure/Liu/Philipsen/Wang* (fn 38).

44 See nos 28–30 above.

45 An issue that is equally addressed in Question 16 of the Questionnaire.

a socially desirable function by screening out activities that are socially undesirable since they are considered too dangerous.

40 Nevertheless in many legal systems special regimes have been worked out, more particularly where the mandatory security only consists of liability insurance and where hence only insurers can provide the security, as in the case of motor vehicle insurance. The obligation to purchase liability insurance for example for motor vehicles raises questions concerning affordability and availability.[46] Many countries have installed special regimes to deal with these difficulties to insure risks. One reason to do so may be a distributional one: politicians may find it undesirable that, as a result of compulsory liability insurance (and an absence of a duty to accept), particular vulnerable groups in society would no longer have the possibility to exercise particular activities, for example driving a car. A second reason is that some risks are not necessarily bad risks, but are simply difficult to insure since their risk assessment may be relatively complicated and therefore costly.[47] Special insurance schemes have hence been created for those who find it difficult to obtain insurance on the voluntary insurance market; this is known as the residual or shared market.[48]

41 For these reasons special insurance arrangements have been created either voluntarily by the insurance industry (like in the Netherlands) or by statutes (like in Belgium).[49] From an economic perspective, the analysis of these special insurance regimes is rather straightforward: to the extent that they charge lower premiums to the insured than the actuarially fair ones, the schemes incite moral hazard and in fact lead to a negative redistribution whereby all car drivers (who contribute to the scheme) finance the risky drivers. In that sense the scheme would be highly problematic from a social welfare perspective since it allows dangerous drivers, not exposed to the full risk of their activity (by paying subsidised premiums), to stay on the road, thus decreasing traffic safety.[50] If, on the contrary the special scheme equally charges actuarially fair premiums, it leads

---

**46** See inter alia *L Regan/S Tennyson/M Weiss*, The relationship between auto-insurance rate regulation and insured low costs: an empirical analysis (2009) 27(1) Journal of Insurance Regulation 24.

**47** Take the example of ex-prisoners or Romas without a fixed residence, living in trailers. They should, as such, not necessarily be considered as uninsurable risks (causing more accidents than average), but risk assessment may require special attention and therefore be costly.

**48** *J De Mot/M Faure*, Special insurance systems for motor vehicle liability (2014) The Geneva Papers on Risk and Insurance 569–584.

**49** For a more detailed analysis of these special insurance schemes and for a comparative analysis of the regimes in Belgium and the Netherlands see *De Mot/Faure* (ibid).

**50** This is, as De Mot and Faure argue, the case in Belgium where contributions to the special scheme are subsidised and lower than average – *De Mot/Faure* (ibid).

neither to moral hazard nor to negative redistribution and should hence be considered largely unproblematic.[51]

## VII. Limits of Compulsory Liability Insurance

We have already mentioned repeatedly that although a duty to provide financial security can be considered as an important, adequate and even necessary instrument to prevent the externalisation of risks by operators[52] there are particular limits, more particularly to compulsory liability *insurance*. Those have to be taken into account since otherwise, as was equally argued, a duty to provide insurance cover for liability may on the whole do more bad than good. 42

A first limit concerns the fact that as every financial security implies a removal of risk from an operator, a moral hazard can be created. Hence a duty to provide financial cover should only be introduced when the moral hazard problem can be controlled and the duty to provide financial cover should be shaped in such a way that it does not limit the possibilities for the provider of financial security (like an insurer) to control moral hazard.[53] 43

Second, concentration in insurance markets may limit incentives to control moral hazard, but may equally limit the availability of a variety of insurance products. This obviously calls for an application of competition policy to insurance markets.[54] Moreover, when insurance markets are highly concentrated, one can question the desirability of the introduction of compulsory liability insurance. In the latter case it would more indicate formulating a duty to obtain financial security more broadly and not limiting this to liability insurance.[55] 44

This latter issue also relates to a third point, being that the regulator should avoid becoming dependent upon the insurance market. There are some more reasons to formulate such a cautious warning. One is that the legislator should be aware of the fact that as soon as it introduces compulsory insurance, it be- 45

---

**51** This was, so De Mot and Faure argued, the case with the scheme referred to as Rialto in the Netherlands – *De Mot/Faure* (ibid).

**52** See no 4 ff above.

**53** As was argued in nos 25–31 above.

**54** This warning is now taken seriously also by the European Commission. Whereas originally a regulation largely exempted the insurance industry from the application of competition policy (see more particularly Commission Regulation (EEC) No 3932/92 of 21 December 1992, OJ L 398, 31.12.1992, 7–14) more recent versions of the group exemption have already reduced its scope of application (see *M Faure/T Hartlief*, Insurance and Expanding Systemic Risks (2003) 87–88 and 222–225).

**55** This point was elaborated under nos 32–34 above.

comes dependent upon insurers to fulfil this duty to insure. The practical possibilities of an effective enforcement of a duty to insure will obviously to a large extent depend upon the willingness to insure in that particular market. It will ultimately be the insurance market who will decide whether they are willing to cover a certain risk. This may ultimately lead to the undesirable situation that the legislator would introduce a duty to take out compulsory insurance, but that the market would refuse to provide such coverage. Introducing a duty to insure leads to a high reliance of the policymaker upon the insurance market. This seems to have led to problems with the German Environmental Liability Act of 1990 (*Umwelthaftungsgesetz*) which requires the owner of an installation that can cause significant damage to take out liability insurance or to have sufficient financial guarantees.[56]

**46** There seems to be a trade off in that respect: introducing a duty to insure without any co-operation with the insurance world (which may have been the case in Germany) may lead to the catastrophic result that the government forces industry to take out a certain insurance coverage, where the market would not be willing to respond with the provision of such a coverage. However, a close co-operation between the insurers (usually represented via one insurance association) and the government only increases the risk of high concentration in insurance markets.

**47** These dangers of a dependence of the regulator upon the insurance market once more underscores the importance of not formulating a duty to obtain financial security as mandatory liability insurance, but rather as a more general duty to obtain financial security, which can include, but should not be limited to, liability insurance.[57]

**48** There is another remarkable fact with respect to mandatory financial security, which is the fact that first of all great differences remain between Member States as far as the activities for which mandatory financial security exists.[58] But in general it is striking that in some, even industrialised countries like the Netherlands, mandatory financial security is in fact only used to a relatively limited extent. For example in the Netherlands the literature has criticised the fact that no compulsory financial security exists for operators exercising hazardous activities. The consequences were shown when two major disasters occurred at

**56** See *G Wagner*, Umwelthaftung und Versicherung (1991) Versicherungsrecht (VR) 249–260 and *idem*, Die Zukunft der Umwelthaftpflichtversicherung (1992) VR 261–272.

**57** This point was stressed under no 12 ff above.

**58** A striking example concerns a comparison between Belgium and the Netherlands: in Belgium the number of activities subject to mandatory liability insurance is high, whereas in the Netherlands it is relatively low.

the turn of the century: an explosion in a fireworks factory in Enschede on 13 May 2000 and a fire in the De Hemel bar on 31 December 2000 in Volendam.[59] In both cases it appeared that the liable operator only had (voluntary!) liability insurance for relatively low amounts, which were largely insufficient to compensate the damage. As a consequence it was the Government who largely compensated most of the damage.[60]

One can wonder why such a duty to obtain financial security is not im- 49
posed upon operators on a larger scale. When inefficiencies are discovered in regulation, public choice theory holds that it is often special interest groups that would benefit. In that respect the lack of mandatory liability cover, for example in the Netherlands, at first blush poses somewhat of a puzzle. One would indeed assume that insurers as an interest group would want to lobby in favour of compulsory liability insurance. It seems like an ideal situation that the entire market would be forced via legislation to buy particular products or services, thus guaranteeing a steady demand. Given, moreover, high concentration in some insurance markets, profits on the supply side could be guaranteed as well. However, in practice one can notice that insurers are in fact not enthusiastic at all concerning the introduction of compulsory liability insurance. Cousy claims that it is related to the fact that, as a matter of law, under compulsory insurance the insurer can often not invoke defences against the third party beneficiary of insurance.[61] This has as a disadvantage for insurers that many of the normal tools controlling moral hazard may not be available. Moreover, many of the individuals who do not voluntarily purchase liability insurance may be a relatively difficult segment of the market (vulnerable and less financially viable groups) which could lead to problems related to the implementation and actual carrying out of the obligation to insure.[62] In that sense insurers often consider compulsory liability insurance more as a problem than as a benefit.

In addition, lobbying will obviously not only be undertaken by the insurers, 50
but by yet another powerful interest group as well, being the operators who

**59** See *M Faure/T Hartlief*, The Netherlands, in: M Faure/T Hartlief (eds), Financial Compensation for Victims of Catastrophes (2006) 218–221.

**60** See for a recent criticism also *T Hartlief*, Privaatrecht in nood, over de beperkte betekenis van het privaatrecht bij rampen en crisis en een rechtsgebied onder toenemende druk van het publiekrecht, NJV Preadvies (Report for the Dutch Lawyers Association) (2014).

**61** A point discussed under no 21 ff above.

**62** *H Cousy*, Recent developments in environmental insurance, in: F Abraham/K Deketelaere/J Stuyck (eds), Recent economic and legal developments in European environmental policy (1995) 241 and *J Rogge*, Les assurances en matière d'environnement (1997) 39.

would be exposed to the duty to provide financial security. A duty to purchase financial security may (depending on how it is formulated[63]) lead to additional costs for industry. From that perspective one may understand why industry would strongly oppose the imposition of a duty to provide financial security. In the absence of such a duty, they could continue (as the cases of Volendam and Enschede in the Netherlands show) to externalise risks to society and de facto let the general taxpayers pick up the bill for the risks they create. Hence one can understand that insurers and operators may join forces and jointly form an effective and strong lobby against the imposition of a duty to provide financial security, or at least compulsory liability insurance. Lobbying by industry and insurers may hence to a large extent explain why duties to provide financial security are not yet introduced (at least in some countries) to the extent that would be desirable from society's perspective, thus allowing industry to externalise the risks it creates.

## VIII. Enforcement

51 An important issue is obviously that it does not suffice to impose a duty to obtain financial cover; the fulfilment of that obligation should equally be monitored and enforced.[64] The ideal picture should be that dissuasive sanctions should prevent a duty holder from undertaking an activity without financial security. Moreover, in addition to sanctions, an *ex ante* control may be more effective. This would simply imply that a particular activity (such as running a waste incineration plant) may not be undertaken if the operator cannot show prior to the start of the activity that financial security is available. In order to guarantee that the security remains valid during the entire operation of the activity, a duty could be imposed upon the security provider to inform regulatory authorities of a suspension of the security, which would automatically lead to a suspension of the licensed activity as well.

52 As far as appropriate sanctions are concerned, the traditional economic model of crime and law enforcement indicates that appropriate sanctions should be introduced taking into account the probability of detection and the potential solvency of the wrongdoer. If compulsory insurance is introduced *inter alia* because insolvency is feared, then monetary sanctions may be inadequate.

63 If for example self-insurance by operators also is allowed, the costs for industry of a duty to obtain financial security could be relatively limited.
64 This aspect is rightly stressed in Question 27 of the Questionnaire as well.

However, since non-monetary sanctions may be costly to impose, economists would suggest increasing the probability of detection.

Indeed, if inadequate monitoring would still result in many potential injurers exposing others to risks without fulfilling the insurance obligation, the underdeterrence would still follow or they would still be able to externalise their costs upon others. In this respect still many differences seem to exist between even neighbouring European countries. For instance, as far as motor vehicle insurance in Belgium is concerned, no driver can obtain a licence plate for his car unless he shows that adequate insurance coverage is available. Moreover, at the occasion of a yearly technical control, the availability of sufficient coverage has to be shown again. In the Netherlands, on the other hand, the licence plate belongs to the car and drivers should take out insurance coverage, but monitoring is weak. One therefore has the impression that in the Netherlands the problem of uninsured driving is far more serious than in Belgium. This example shows that compulsory insurance needs to be accompanied by an *ex ante* monitoring system that guarantees as far as possible that no one can undertake the risky activity without the availability of insurance. 53

## IX. Reforms/Recent Literature

This chapter provided the basic economic perspectives with respect to compulsory liability insurance. Many of the basic arguments in favour of mandatory insurance, including the judgment proof problem, were in fact already stressed in publications by Shavell and Skogh in the 1980s. Obviously since then much more recent literature has emerged refining the starting points from earlier literature. In a recent literature overview, Wagner for example points at the fact that mandatory insurance is only a solution to the extent that the insurer is indeed adequately able to control moral hazard since otherwise the risk would simply have shifted onto the insurer, thus removing incentives from the tortfeasor.[65] Interestingly some literature has pointed at the fact that there are obviously remedies for the insolvency problem other than mandatory insurance. Dari-Mattiacci and Parisi have for example shown that to some extent vicarious liability or other techniques to shift liability from insolvent actors to solvent gatekeepers may constitute an alternative to mandatory insurance. The crucial trade-off, so they show, is between the different monitoring abilities of either insurers or other guarantors who function as gatekeepers. To the extent that those 54

65 See *Wagner* (fn 2) 397 f.

guarantors would be better able to control the behaviour of the liable tortfeasor, vicarious liability could be preferable to mandatory insurance, more particularly when (for a variety of reasons) insurers would have difficulties controlling the moral hazard risk.[66] A similar point has also been made by Shavell who compares minimum assets requirements and compulsory insurance as different tools to remedy potential insolvency problems.[67]

55 Many papers have, moreover, pointed at possible applications of mandatory insurance in specific areas. An often studied one, already mentioned above in the context of CCS and offshore related risks, is environmental liability. Wagner shows that, especially in the area of environmental liability insurance, insurers moved to detailed *ex ante* screening, especially in order to deal with so-called long-tail liabilities.[68] Others have equally examined the potential benefits of compulsory insurance, especially in a context where insurers would engage in active control of moral hazards, thus imposing additional conditions upon potential polluters and actively reducing environmental risks. One study sees a potential contribution of insurers in the reduction of greenhouse gas emissions.[69] Others have pointed at the potentially beneficial effects of compulsory pollution liability insurance in China.[70] One remarkable publication that merits mentioning is a study by Wray examining to what extent mandatory insurance would violate the free exercise of religion in the US.[71]

---

**66** See *G Dari-Mattiacci/F Parisi*, The cost of delegated control: vicarious liability, secondary liability and mandatory insurance (2003) 23(4) International Review of Law and Economics 453–475.

**67** See *S Shavell*, Minimum asset requirements and compulsory liability insurance as solutions to the judgment proof problem (2005) 36(1) Rand Journal of Economics 63–77.

**68** See *G Wagner*, (Un)insurability and the choice between market insurance and public compensation systems, in: WH van Boom/M Faure (eds), Shifts in Compensation between Private and Public Systems (2007) 87–112.

**69** See *A Telesetsky*, Insurance as a litigation mechanism: managing international greenhouse gases through nation-wide mandatory climate change, catastrophe insurance (2010) 27(3) Pace Environmental Law Review (Pace Envtl L Rev) 691.

**70** See *Y Feng et al*, Environmental pollution liability insurance in China: compulsory or voluntary? (2014) 70 Journal of Cleaner Production 211–219. See more generally on environmental insurance in China *MG Faure/J Liu*, Compensation for environmental damage in China: theory and practice (2014) 31(1) Pace Envtl L Rev 226–309.

**71** See *MP Wray*, Free exercise and compulsory insurance: the future of mandatory financial responsibility and religious observance (2010) 12 Lloyola Journal of Public International Law 239.

# X. Concluding Remarks

Compulsory liability insurance has received much attention in the law and economics literature. The foundation for a duty to seek financial security is relatively simple: if liable injurers were insolvent, they would be able to externalise risk upon society. However, as more recent literature indicates, there are means other than compulsory financial security which could equally remedy the insolvency risk, like vicarious liability. 56

Moreover, the literature equally indicates that there may be different forms in which a duty to seek financial security is shaped. In some cases (as with motor vehicle insurance), the duty can be of a relatively general nature, whereas in other cases it can be more detailed and tailored to the specific situation of an operator (eg in the case of environmental liability). 57

Compulsory liability insurance is increasingly becoming subject to debate, especially after significant (technological) disasters where operators appear insolvent (as in the case in the Netherlands). This leads to justified calls from society to impose duties on operators to provide financial guarantees. However, effective lobbying by operators (and insurers) means that those duties are less often imposed than would be indicated. 58

Practice, however, shows that it is equally important to remain flexible as far as the imposition of the duty to seek financial coverage is concerned. This should not be limited to liability insurance, but should be more widely formulated as a duty to seek financial security, which can equally provide incentives to operators to develop alternative forms (for example, risk pooling between operators). 59

There is, as was indicated, from an economic perspective, ample reason to largely consider the use of compulsory financial security. The mere fact that it is not imposed as often as would be desired from an economic perspective is often the result of effective lobbying by industry which means that industrial operators can continue exposing society to hazardous activities and at the same time also throw the costs of these activities (through their insolvency) largely on society. This implicit subsidy will continue to cause underdeterrence and undercompensation and is therefore from a societal perspective undesirable. 60

Bernard Tettamanti, Hubert Bär and Jean-Claude Werz

# Compulsory Liability Insurance in a Changing Legal Environment – An Insurance and Reinsurance Perspective

## I. Executive Summary

Many new liability regimes are starting to emerge both in the European Union and in individual European countries, and most of them are linked to a provision on financial security requirements. In discussions with both national and EU lawmakers, insurers and insurer associations often experience that, in the view of many lawmakers, financial security is equal to insurance.[1] 1

Insurance aims to transfer risks of financial losses as a result of unpredictable events from an individual or entity to an insurer in return for a premium. The belief that everything is insurable is a myth.[2] This article evaluates the possible liability insurance solutions available in Europe with a primary focus on the following lines of business: 2

- general third party liability,
- motor liability,
- professional indemnity.

From an economic and legal point of view, not all risks can be transferred from their source onto insurers or other third parties. This is particularly true for individual risks with a high moral hazard. 3

Moreover, any insurance contract has terms and conditions; it also contains exclusions and in most cases a maximum sum insured. An insurance contract is a bilateral agreement between an insurer and an insured. The insurer commits itself to pay out possible claims in line with the agreed insurance contract, and 4

1 The following example demonstrates the change of mind of the Swiss Parliament <https://www.admin.ch/opc/de/federal-gazette/2009/6013.pdf>: '... An Stelle einer ausreichenden Haftpflichtversicherung kann auch der Nachweis über eine gleichwertige finanzielle Sicherheit erbracht werden. Da kein Kontrahierungszwang auf Seite der Versicherungen besteht, erlaubt diese Möglichkeit auch dann die entsprechenden Aktivitäten anzubieten, wenn sich kein Sachversicherer bereit erklären sollte, eine Haftpflichtversicherung abzuschliessen. Die Gleichwertigkeit der finanziellen Sicherheit wird sich an der vom Bundesrat festzulegenden Mindesthöhe der Haftpflichtsumme orientieren. Der Bundesrat wird auch hier die Einzelheiten in der Verordnung regeln ...' (6039 f). The Swiss Parliament here also acknowledges that financial security may not always be available on the insurance market.

2 Cf fn 1 above.

the insured is committed to pay the corresponding premium. As a rule, the overall liability of the insured/tortfeasor extends beyond the liability covered by the insurance contract.

5 Most insurance solutions offered in the market have been developed on a voluntary basis in line with market demands, exposures of potential insureds and the risk capacity of the insurance industry. Compulsory insurance schemes cannot be created without taking technical constraints and market factors into account. Although compulsory insurance has a long-standing tradition in certain lines of business and is an important contributor to overall insurance premium income, it is not feasible for all types of insurance products.

6 The aim of this article is to outline how insurance works and to provide insights into the creation of voluntary and compulsory insurance markets.

7 The article closes with an outlook on trends towards new liability regimes and the related expectations of lawmakers towards the insurance industry. For this purpose, an evaluation grid for compulsory insurance has been included at the end of the article with the aim of stimulating discussion on when compulsory insurance can be meaningful.

## II. General Insurance Principles

8 Insurance aims to transfer risks of financial losses as a result of unpredictable events from an individual or entity to an insurer in return for a fee or premium. The insurer and the insured negotiate not only the terms and conditions, but also the limit the insurer will cover in the event of a loss. Negotiations involve finding a balanced relationship between risk and premium. The process of assessing the risk is referred to as underwriting. Generally: the higher the risk, the higher the premium. Risk assessment is an economic act and directly reflects the cost of providing insurance coverage.

9 In order to avoid smaller and more frequent insurance claims and to lower both premium and administrative costs, the contract parties often agree that the insured will bear smaller losses up to a specific amount as a so-called deductible. The agreed insurance amount then only covers losses that exceed this amount up to the agreed maximum insurance policy limit. How do such insured sums work? The mechanisms of agreed insurance limits can vary from country to country and between lines of business. Whereas in motor liability limits for 'each and every loss' is the standard, most general liability insurance policies not only have a limit for the individual loss, but also stipulate an overall aggregate limit for all losses in a single insurance year (respectively the insurance period), or at least stipulate it for product liability.

# III. Concept of Liability Insurance

## 1. Reasons to insure liability

All parties, whether legal entities or private persons, can be held liable for their 10
acts or omissions. In particular if they render a service to third parties or manufacture goods or products for consumers, they are exposed to being held liable for third party liability if this results in damage or injury. Such legal liability may be based on a contractual relationship, negligence or objective liability for hazardous activities. The potentially liable party needs to assess these challenges, which can constitute a financial exposure ranging from 'negligible' to 'significant' up to 'existentially threatening'. In a first step, the potentially liable party will (and must) seek to reduce the exposure by way of appropriate safety measures.

Depending on the result of its assessment of the remaining degree of finan- 11
cial risk, the party may decide to either bear these risks itself (ie without any insurance) by building up its own funds as necessary, or to transfer some of these risks to an insurance carrier. Insurance is thus at the end and not at the beginning of the evaluation process.

All insurance cover is financially capped with a maximum sum insured per 12
loss and/or in the aggregate over the insured period. It also needs to be affordable for the insured. 'Affordable' means that the necessary premium to cover losses in the long term must be in a reasonable relationship to the price of the insured activity or product. While in theory insurance costs can be passed on to the insured's customers, in practice this may not be the case (eg because they can no longer compete with product imports subject to lower insurance costs from outside the EU or because customers abandon the product or service as they consider it to be too expensive).[3] On the other hand, continuing the activity without insurance protection is often not a feasible alternative for a responsible small or medium enterprise.

---

3 For more details see the brochure of *Insurance Europe* (IE), How insurance works (<http://www.insuranceeurope.eu/sites/default/files/attachments/How%20insurance%20works.pdf>).

## 2. Purpose and content of liability insurance

### a) Purpose

13 Generally, the scope of a liability insurance contract covers the risks arising from exposure related to premises (eg the consequences of an accident in a factory) and to products (eg consequences of an unsafe or hazardous product injuring consumers) or risks relating to activities provided by a business or an individual (eg wrongful or inadequate advice to client). Its primary purpose is to protect the insured's assets against losses resulting from claims by injured third parties. Whereas in first party insurance (eg accident or fire insurance) the injured party is directly insured for the loss, in liability insurance the injured party is not insured, but indirectly protected by an assurance that the tortfeasor is able to indemnify the injured party. This fundamental difference between liability and compensation as well as first and third party insurance is material, but in the experience of the insurance industry is sometimes overlooked by politicians and/or lawmakers in discussions surrounding compulsory insurance.[4]

14 In liability insurance contracts, the sum of the liabilities assumed by the insurer is not identical to the insured's legal liabilities.

### b) Content

15 First of all it must be noted that legal liability is generally unlimited. Liability policies, however, contain limits of indemnity that – although adapted to the insured exposure – may in exceptional cases be insufficient to cover catastrophic losses (eg environmental or other catastrophes, mass bodily injury claims). Unlimited coverage is often neither feasible nor available, not only because it

4 For instance, Claude Janiak filed a motion in the Swiss Council of States on 5.3.2014 for the adoption of mandory construction defects liability insurance stating: 'Der Bundesrat wird beauftragt, für die nach Bundesrecht obligatorischen Haftpflichtversicherungen ein einheitliches, sich am Vorbild des Strassenverkehrsgesetzes orientierendes Schutzniveau für geschädigte Personen einzuführen ...'. The main arguments are: '... Obligatorische Haftpflichtversicherungen sind seit Jahrzehnten ein vom Gesetzgeber namentlich bei der Regulierung neuer technischer Entwicklungen bevorzugt eingesetztes Instrument zum Schutz geschädigter Personen ...'. The distinction between respective functions of *third party* liability insurance and *first party* insurance (such as surety, property) is ignored here (contrary to the French 'RC Décennale' the motion also did not foresee pre-financing by property insurance; cf fn 11 below). See <http://www.parlament.ch/d/suche/Seiten/geschaefte.aspx?gesch_id=20143043>.

would be unaffordable, but also because it could entail a real risk of insurer bankruptcy or even market failure.

An insurance contract, moreover, usually excludes all liability risks that are pure entrepreneurial risk. Entrepreneurial risk is an entrepreneur's business risk, that is the risk that his activities are not successful in an economic sense. In particular, this encompasses the insured's ability to fulfil its obligations and its liability for non-performance of contractual promises. Insofar as such risks are insurable, they fall into the domain of surety guaranties (see no 97 ff below). This includes a party's financial ability to perform, ie the risk of bankruptcy. 16

Entrepreneurial risks are generally not insurable, as this would lead to a distortion of competition: sound competition ensures that good firms thrive, while poor market performers fail. However, if an entrepreneur providing inferior quality were able to transfer his business risk to a liability insurer, this would put him at an unfair competitive advantage over competitors who provide a better but more expensive service. 17

### c) Actio directa

As in all contracts, it appears self-evident that legal rights and duties arising from such a contractual insurance relationship are limited to the two involved contract partners (ie the insurer and the insured) and that other third parties (ie the injured third parties/victims) have no right to seek compensation directly from the insurer. 18

This is correct as long as insurance law does not grant the victim a direct right of action (a so-called *actio directa*) giving a claimant the opportunity to seek compensation directly from the liable party's insurer. Such an *actio directa* does exist in motor liability on a broader European level and in some countries for other liability claims (eg France), or for some specific professional indemnity insurance schemes (eg Poland). 19

While the *actio directa* goes towards a full protection of the victim, it can also be seen as an intrusion into the bilateral contractual relationship between the insurer and the insured, and hence conflicts with the basic principle that liability insurance should primarily protect the insured. Compulsory liability insurance remains liability insurance; namely protects the insured's liability, ie the insured's assets. If the overwhelming purpose of compulsory insurance were to protect the victim, first party insurance should be mandated (eg accident insurance, workers' compensation or clinical trials insurance). When the stipulation of a direct action to claim is at issue, a distinction should be made between contractual and extra-contractual relationships between the claimant and the 20 original liable party. In a contractual relationship, there is a smaller need to protect the victim than in an extra-contractual relationship.[5] The contract partner (victim) is free to choose a counterparty and takes the corresponding risk of loss. In a contractual relationship, the potential victim can also discuss potential risks and claims with the partner and how to handle them. Moreover, a party can require potential risks to be covered by an insurance contract.

21 The situation is different in purely extra-contractual contexts, where the counterparty/claimant does not have any influence on the person of the liable party.

22 The insurer should not become the alter ego of the insured with the stipulation of a direct right of action. The insurance contract fulfils its purpose by ensuring that the insured's (ie the tortfeasor's) assets are sufficient to indemnify the victim. The *actio directa* is not necessary to protect the insured's interests. On the other hand, it leads to conflicts of interests between insurer and insured. Thus it may be in the insurer's economic interest to settle a claim quickly, admitting the insured's fault, rather than to defend an unfounded or exaggerated claim brought against the insured. This undermines the insurer's duty to defend. The insured also has a conflict of interest, in that it should assist the insurer in defending unfounded claims while it should support the injured party in coverage issues.[6]

23 In a compulsory insurance scheme, any applicable direct right of action against the insurer should not be coupled to a 'broadening' of the scope of an insurance policy to the extent where the insurer is no longer in a position to reject coverage due to stipulated coverage restrictions, such as a criminal offence or a wilful or intentional act committed by the insured. The insurer and the insured agree on specific terms and conditions, and this scope of cover forms the basis for the insurer to accept the risk and to calculate a commensurate premium. As the material foundations of the contract (declarations of insured, conditions of and restrictions on coverage, etc) determine whether an insurer accepts a given risk, the insurer should be in a position to apply the same defences as against the insured.

24 Again, once the terms of an insurance contract are agreed between the involved parties, this scope of the contract should form the basis for the agreed insurance period for any claim, irrespective of the existence of any direct right of action by the victim. If lawmakers interfere too much with the principle of freedom of contract and fail to respect the terms and conditions set out in an in-

---

5 *KS Hedderich*, Pflichtversicherung (2011) 250.

6 See *J-C Werz*, Versicherungspflicht und Pflichtversicherungsgesetz, Haftung und Versicherung (HAVE) 1/2013, 58 ff.

surance contract, insurers would potentially no longer be able to continue to cover their insureds.

A rare and well-founded exception to the above can be found in motor liability acts where, in connection with the direct right of action against the liability insurer (the *actio directa*), the injured claimant can seek compensation directly from the liable driver's/operator's insurer. Motor liability schemes are designed so as to place the risk of loss practically without exception upon the operator. The operator has few if any defences against the claimant. This is justified because, in a modern society, one cannot evade the unavoidable risks caused by the existence of motor traffic. Such exceptions are justified where universal, unavoidable, well-known, predictable and socially accepted operational hazards exist. As such, it can best be described as a socially accepted risk. Moreover, in cases of *actio directa* the insurer often cannot reject coverage vis-à-vis the injured party due to negligent or intentional acts of the operator.[7] Insurers can accept such risks – within certain limits (eg capacities) – only if they are calculable. Such situations do not exist for many other risks subject to compulsory insurance (eg medical malpractice, medical devices). 25

## 3. Types of liability insurance

There are many different types of policies available in liability insurance, depending on the insured's activities and perceived risks for transfer. This report focuses on the following main classes of insurance. Particularly, in general third party/product liability insurance and in professional indemnity insurance, there is an emerging trend towards compulsory insurance: 26

- *General third party/Product liability insurance (GTPL).* This combined insurance policy covers the damages a policyholder is obliged to pay due to bodily injury or property damage caused to another person or entity based on negligence, strict liability or contractual liability. This may arise from a range of activities and include general premises-related risks, as well as the product liability exposure for the manufacturer or supplier of goods for injury or damage caused by their products.
- *Professional indemnity insurance.* This type of liability insurance protects professional specialists such as architects, engineers, lawyers, accountants and others against third party claims arising from their professional activities. Contrary to GTPL insurance, the main exposures in most types of pro-

7 See art 65 para 2 Swiss Road Traffic Act (Strassenverkehrsgesetz, SVG).

fessional liability insurance are pure financial losses, for example in insurance policies covering the activities of lawyers or accountants.

- *Motor liability insurance*. This line of insurance offers coverage for bodily injury and property damage caused to third parties through the operation of motor vehicles.

# IV. Key Issues of Insurability

27 Insurers are often incorrectly perceived by the public and lawmakers as having identical and all-encompassing risk appetites, and as keen to underwrite every line of business and any risk. In fact, most insurers do not write all lines of liability (or other) insurance business. Certain risks even require specialised insurers, who may be few and far between. Even in 'bread and butter' motor insurance, individual insurers may decide not to write certain risks. Insurers must remain free to decide which risks they are willing and able to underwrite and which to reject. This very much depends on the nature of a given business item and on experience, expertise or available data and the insurer's financial strength.

28 The most fundamental underwriting consideration is the insurability of a loss. It is vital that insurers are in a position to assess with a reasonable degree of accuracy the claims amount to be paid out over a defined and realistically long period of time. The insured risk should also be random and independent.[8] It is not possible to insure against an event that definitively will occur since this involves no uncertainty. The occurrence of an insured event should be unpredictable and needs to be beyond the control of the beneficiary of insurance. For this reason, events that are caused voluntarily or intentionally by the insured cannot be covered.

29 Quite often it is not entirely clear which risks are insurable and to what extent. While one insurer may consider a risk to be uninsurable, another might be willing to underwrite the same risk, as it claims to understand the risk better, and may also have a larger risk appetite and the financial capacity to have such a risk in its book of business. By the same token, a risk may be insurable in one country but not in another due to different risk landscapes, which depend on criteria such as the scope of the national legal system (in particular regulation, liability law, procedural law, solvency requirements), the political environment and the welfare system.

8 See *Insurance Europe* (IE) (fn 3).

What criteria need to be met to fulfil the parameters of insurability? To assess a risk properly, the following key issues of insurability need to be fulfilled. They are issues which take their rationale from either objective or subjective criteria. 30

## 1. Objective criteria of insurability

### a) Legal clarity and certainty

As a general principle, legal clarity and certainty means that the law must be clear and precise. The law's consequences must be foreseeable, especially with respect to financial obligations. 31

The adoption of laws with effect in the European Union must have a proper legal basis, and they must be predictable. Legislation in Member States, implementing European Union law, must be worded in such a way that it is clearly understandable by those who are subject to the law. This requires that sufficient information must be available to enable subject parties to understand and comply with the legal requirements. 32

This principle is also of the utmost importance for insurers, as the insurance contract covers the legal liability of the insured. Legal certainty is an essential requirement to assess the potential exposure covered and to calculate a premium that is commensurate to the risk. 33

Motor third party liability insurance provides an excellent example for the need for legal clarity and certainty. Here, liability insurance is dependent upon the required expertise and authorisation to drive cars on public roads. This – together with the availability of accident statistics – enables insurers to differentiate risks and calculate risk-adequate premiums. 34

### b) Realistic objectives on insurability

Legal provisions which aim to introduce compulsory liability insurance for manufacturers (eg European Parliament text on medical devices and in-vitro diagnostic devices) often include subjective language such as 'appropriate liability insurance' and 'level of coverage proportionate to the potential risk'. While such language may be seen as vague and subject to varying interpretation, it does allow reasonable solutions to be reached in the context of the freedom of contract. However, lawmakers need to pursue realistic objectives on insurability, ideally with the involvement of the insurance industry. In particular, they must be aware that in determining what is 'appropriate' insurance, the realities 35 of the insurance market must also be taken into account. 'Appropriate' insurance does not mean that all losses – regardless of their cause or the total amount – can be indemnified.[9]

## 2. Subjective criteria of insurability

### a) Risk management

36 Understanding a risk and the corresponding risk management processes of the insureds – whether formalised or not – are key issues for insurance. After all, insurance cannot be a substitute for proper risk management which requires adherence to best risk management standards in any given class of business.

37 A proper risk management approach ideally consists of the following steps: risk identification, risk analysis, risk avoidance, risk control (which primarily involves loss prevention and loss reduction) and, as necessary, at least a partial risk transfer to an insurer. As risk management is not a standardised process, continuous training of staff and monitoring of work planning is essential. Finally, proper risk management must also include emergency and crisis reaction plans.

38 This allows an insurer to set an appropriate scope of insurance conditions in the insurance contract. Insurance does not serve as a substitute for loss prevention measures, nor does it replace the introduction of safety standards. But a risk with excellent risk management processes in place can be expected to reduce both the possible damage and costs. The quality of risk management may even determine whether a dangerous activity or installation is insurable or not.

### b) Underwriting and pricing

39 The underwriting process benefits the policyholder. The more information insurers have on a given risk, the better they can tailor the scope of the insurance contract and the premium to that risk. Insurers must be able to assess a risk properly, and to do so they must have access to statistics on the claims history. Detailed claims data covering a period of at least five years should be available in order to allow the premium to be calculated properly based on experience. This allows insurers to calculate the probability of the corresponding risk/

9 See also the PIP issue, no 71 ff below, and the Directive 2011/61/EU on Alternative Investment Fund Managers, no 104 below as illustrations of this issue.

claims (experience rating). In addition, costing must also include a fair calculation of the claims frequency and the severity of the risk exposure (exposure rating). This is particularly true for large, aggravated or non-standard risks.

If an insurer considers the financial impact of a loss to be too great, it can revert to other risk spreading instruments, such as sharing the risks with one or more direct insurers (known as co-insurance) or relying on reinsurance support (ie an insurer for insurers). **40**

However, the necessary basis for risk assessment and pricing is often lacking for future and unknown risks. Compulsory insurance thus often is not a feasible option for dealing with new or emerging risks or with novel liability laws. **41**

### c) Scope of cover

The policy wording determines the scope of cover the insurer grants the insured in the event of a loss occurring out of its business activities. By nature, coverage cannot be unlimited. The wording includes such important features as: **42**

- a detailed description of covered insured activity,
- a list of insured persons or entities,
- the geographical scope of the insurance contract, eg worldwide or limited to a specific geographical territory only,
- a definition of indemnification of third parties for bodily injury or property damage arising out of insured activities,
- a limit of the insurance contract per loss and as a maximum limit per year,
- the validity of indemnity over time (for details, see no 49 ff below) depending of the kind of activities of the insured,
- handling of a serial loss, ie when a large number of injured persons are affected by a single loss occurrence,
- exclusions: in liability insurance policies, a distinction can be made between absolute and relative exclusions in the 'exclusions' section. Absolute exclusions (eg fulfilment of the contract or the entrepreneurial risk of going bankrupt) are generally not negotiable as liability insurers do not cover such risks because they consider them to be uninsurable (see also no 16 above). Conversely, relative exclusions (such as pure financial loss or products' recall) can be 'bought back' by an insured if the insured's subjective risk justifies a corresponding coverage extension. The latter greatly depends on the detailed knowledge of the risk insured and the agreement of an additional premium charge.

#### d) Moral hazard

43 Moral hazard is traditionally defined as the hazard arising from the character and/or behaviour of the insured. It can generate extra layers of uncertainty in liability insurance which contribute significantly to the difficulties insurers experience with liability exposures. In addition to the traditional and most widely known form of hazard – the policyholder hazard – three other forms, ie the claimant hazard, the jurisprudential hazard and the underwriting hazard, also need to be considered[10] for a full evaluation of the moral hazard exposure from all angles:

- *Policyholder hazard.* The policyholder's hazard includes the risk that an insured may change his behaviour once an insurance contract is in force. This may lead to undesirable outcomes and can be driven by the fact that an insured might be less inclined to avoid damage from occurring as the costs are passed on to an insurer. A driver might drive more recklessly with a rented car than with his own car due to the renter's full physical damage insurance. This risk is even more inherent in compulsory insurance than in a voluntary market, as the law shifts the financial responsibility from the insured to the insurer at a relatively small economic charge.[11] Such moral risks can lead to unpredictable insurance losses. Having too many risks exposed to aggravated moral hazard in its book of business would also create severe losses for an insurer. Insurers therefore face the challenging task of having to avoid systematic adverse risk selection.
- *Claimant hazard.* The claimant's moral hazard concerns the effect that the existence of a liability insurance policy might have on actual or potential claimants. Claimants may be encouraged to target those who are insured as 'deep pockets' rather than those who are not and/or collude with policyholders to tap into insurance funds, or to launch unmeritorious suits in the hope that insurers will pay rather than risk incurring heavy defence costs.
- *Jurisprudential hazard.* The jurisprudential hazard concerns the extent to which judges (as well as legislative assemblies) might be influenced in the

---

**10** *C Parsons*, The Geneva Papers on Risk and Insurance, vol 28 no 3 (July 2003) 448–471.

**11** This may also be illustrated by the example of the 'RC Décennale' system in France. Under this compulsory insurance scheme, the building contractor has to buy compulsory liability insurance covering his contractual obligation to undertake work free from defects. Moreover, the insured's claims for improper performance of building work are pre-financed by a second compulsory (property) insurance to be taken out by the owner ('Dommages Ouvrage'). This scheme effectively transfers the contractor's business risk (providing work free from defects) to the insurer. As a result, French contractors are in practice far less likely to remedy defects than their counterparts in countries without such a system, such as Switzerland or Germany.

application, modification or expansion of liability rules by the existence of liability insurance either in a particular case or by the general availability of such insurance.

- *Underwriting hazard.* The underwriting hazard concerns the risk that underwriters may be encouraged to lower their normal underwriting standards for certain long-tail risks. A long time-span over which many liability claims develop means that an imprudent underwriter may not be faced immediately with the full consequences of his actions. An underwriter who writes long-tail business (eg pharmaceutical risks or employers' liability in the UK) for the first time may be tempted to underprice the risk. For an insurance company, such an underwriting hazard can also be viewed as an operational risk. The worst-case scenario is a financial meltdown situation leading to insurer failure and financial losses for society at large.

### e) Deductible/Self-insured retention (SIR)[12]

The moral hazard can be reduced by setting a deductible or self-insured retention limit. A deductible is the monetary amount deducted from the insurance limit which the insured agrees to bear prior to transferring the remaining amount of a loss to the insurer. A self-insured retention is a substantial amount which the insured bears prior to the insurance limit coming into force. Deductibles and self-insured retentions are both means to align the interests of the insured and the insurer and reduce the risk that an insured might be inclined to change his risk behaviour after having concluded an insurance contract. The size of the deductible should be determined jointly by the insured and the insurer on the basis of the financial strength and the risks of the insured. On the other hand, high deductibles may also make economic sense for large financially sound insureds who are able to carry a substantial part of the risk. 44

### f) Sum insured

Most insurance policies have a predefined maximum amount to cap the liability of the insurer. This enables the insurer to better calculate the risk and to cap its exposure in the event of a large individual loss, such as an accident or a large product liability claim with a large number of potential claimants. In principle, the insurance limit also applies to compulsory insurance schemes which should 45

12 A difference between a deductible and an SIR is that the SIR does not reduce available policy limits, whereas a deductible may reduce policy limits.

have an adequate minimum sum insured per claim linked to a maximum amount per year. Only few exceptions exist, for example in motor liability, which has an 'each and every event' limit per claim without an overall annual aggregate limit.

46 Insurers should be free to decide which sum insured they want to offer. Even in compulsory insurance schemes, where a minimum insurance limit is stipulated by law, it is of paramount importance that the limit is contractually stipulated in such a way that both serial losses (multiple losses resulting from the same cause or event) and a maximum insurance limit are fixed.

47 The stipulation of an annual aggregate limit in an insurance contract is the most common form for capping the amount of liability. Most insurance companies are joint stock companies and hence are able to offer only a limited amount of capacity. Moreover, insurers are bound by solvency requirements. An unlimited amount of capacity would therefore be an unreasonable – if not impossible – demand on the insurance market, and it would not correspond to the fact that only limited financial capacities are available.

48 The maximum available limits per event and in the aggregate in a given market also depend on the number of insurers and reinsurers willing to support a given risk.

### g) Trigger

49 The cause and/or the occurrence of any bodily injury, property damage or financial loss, as well as the resulting claim for indemnification often do not occur simultaneously. They may lie far apart in time (eg asbestosis). It is very common in liability insurance for claims to be initiated a substantial time after a loss is caused or occurs.

50 One of the core coverage elements in an insurance contract is the definition of the scope of indemnity along this timeline (trigger). When an event occurs that results in a later loss and/or claim, it is important to be clear as to which policy year it attaches to, ie which policy year is triggered. If the insurer or policy wording has been changed, the trigger will also determine the insurer and/or applicable policy terms.

51 Triggers are specific moments in time which determine the allocation of a loss to a specific policy period or policy. In the event of a loss, the policy terms need to be clear in terms of which policy period the loss will be allocated to.

52 Claims that are reported and settled within a relatively short period of time (eg 1–5 years) are referred to as short-tail business in the insurance industry. The opposite is long-tail business, and it is characterised by claims that take a

long time before they are caused/occur or are made/settled. This often happens in complex product liability losses, such as pharmaceutical losses or in medical malpractice. Long-tail risks can be problematical for insurers, as the probability and severity of the corresponding losses are often difficult to estimate.

The insurance industry operates with the following four different triggering events: 53

- *Damage is caused, ie causation or action committed principle.* According to this principle, cover is provided under the policy in effect upon causation of the event which ultimately results in the injury or damage, or when the action which initiated the loss was committed (eg exposure to a dangerous substance).
- *Loss occurs, ie occurrence principle.* On the losses occurring basis, the policy covers all losses occurring during the insurance period irrespective of when the original cause which led to the loss happened. This scope of indemnity in time is a valuable one if the occurrence can be allocated to a specific point in time (eg building collapse as a result of faulty planning).
- *Loss is discovered, ie manifestation principle.* The manifestation trigger constitutes the attempt to overcome the difficulties attached to causation/ action committed and occurrence triggers. The policy is triggered according to its manifestation at the point in time when the injury or damage is discovered or recorded (eg when symptoms of a victim's health impairment lead to a medical visit, when environmental damage resulting from a prior spill of pollutants is discovered).
- *Claim made against the insured or insurer, ie claims made principle.* The claims made principle (CM) focuses on the demand for indemnification: the triggering event is the notification of loss or the filing of a formal claim. This principle thus brings the insured event into a more present insurance period or triggers a later policy. Under some wording, the policy may already be triggered if the insured becomes aware of or notifies concrete circumstances that will probably lead to a claim.

  In principle, the causation or occurrence of the insured loss may lie before the inception of the CM policy. However, the policy may stipulate a retroactive date before which the insured occurrence – for which the claim is made during the policy period – must not have happened. On the other hand, the policy may contain an extended reporting period after the policy's termination (eg upon cessation of the insured's activities), allowing claims based on events occurring during the policy period to be nonetheless subsequently reported.
- *Determination of the triggering event.* It is not possible to say which trigger is generally more advantageous for the insurer, insured or victim. For in-

stance, while a loss causation policy has the advantage of providing insurance coverage into the far future, such coverage may prove insufficient – or even be exhausted by prior claims – eg in 10 years' time; for instance as a result of stricter liability or higher levels of indemnity awards by courts. Each trigger has its own inherent advantages and disadvantages which may well also depend upon the concrete circumstances of the loss.

The determination of the risk-adequate trigger also bears an influence on the pricing of a risk and on the risk appetite of insurers. Many insurers prefer to have primarily short-tail business in their portfolio rather than highly volatile long-tail exposures, such as pharmaceutical risks in product liability insurance. With regard to the availability of insurance, the choice of trigger may play an essential role. For short-tail business, occurrence is the most common trigger, whereas for long-tail business the most common triggers are either manifestation or claims made. Occurrence is the self-evident trigger where causation, injury and claim lie close together in time. On the other hand, the claims made principle allows insurers to provide coverage adapted to current liability standards and to rate long-term risks with late claims. Moreover, it is more practicable to determine the date of claim than the date of occurrence or causation (and to thus determine the applicable policy or wording) in such situations.

It is thus of paramount importance that legislators should not rule on which trigger insurers should base their product offerings. If they do, they could negatively influence product offerings and run the risk that no insurance market or only a limited market would emerge.

# V. Compulsory Insurance Schemes in Europe

## 1. Introduction

54 In the recent past, and in light of efforts currently being undertaken to broaden the protection of the injured party (ie the victim), many compulsory insurance schemes have been introduced and many more are under discussion on the national and European levels.[13] However, in essence there is no coherent regime of

13 See above, fn 4 and <https://www.news.admin.ch/message/?lang=de&msg-id=12966> '... Der Bundesrat hat die Botschaft zur Totalrevision des Kernenergiehaftpflichtgesetzes (KHG) zuhanden des Parlaments verabschiedet. Hauptpfeiler der Revision sind die Verbesserung des Opferschutzes durch die Erhöhung der Deckungssumme von bisher 1 Milliarde auf 1.8 Milliar-

compulsory liability insurance, neither on a national state level[14] nor on a broader European Union level, neither with respect to the reasons why such compulsory regimes were established nor with regard to different standards of liability or different types of damages. Compulsory insurance scheme requirements are set up in a rather unsystematic way, and the creation of compulsory insurance is often based on the occurrence of emotional events (eg a fatal dog bite attack on a child or severe environmental damage in the open sea).

The following four sectors are most suited for compulsory insurance 55
schemes with a particular focus on better protection of potential victims:[15]

- transportation such as motor vehicles, aircraft, boats, cable cars, railroads;
- potentially dangerous industrial plants, such as nuclear power plants, facilities with a high potential for bodily injury and environmental damage;
- hazardous activities or products, such as gene technology;[16]
- professional sectors such as physicians, lawyers and accountants.

In Switzerland for example, there are more than 40 compulsory insurance 56
schemes on a federal level and many more at a constituent state (cantonal) level, primarily in the above-mentioned sectors. On a constituent state level, it is difficult to understand why specific circumstances should necessitate a duty to insure in one canton but not in another.[17] Such compulsory constituent state insurance schemes are difficult to justify as the risk and liability for a specific activity within a given national state territory is uniform.

## 2. Motivation to regulate

The following four factors can serve as a possible motivation for regulators to in- 57
troduce such instruments:

– *Uninsured consumer claims.* The unavailability of insurance solutions, coverage gaps or an insurance market that is too small to grant cover

den Franken sowie die Anpassung des KHG an die internationalen Übereinkommen von Paris und Brüssel im Bereich der Kernenergiehaftung ...'.

**14** See eg *A Stäubli*, Compulsory Liability Insurance in Switzerland (in this book) nos 2 and 5, but in respect of private (academic) efforts towards reforming the law regarding compulsory liability insurance see also no 100. For an example of a systematic solution over a risk exposure approach see no 116 below.

**15** Swiss Re, Sigma 3/2011, 7 f <http://media.swissre.com/documents/sigma3_2011_en.pdf>.

**16** Swiss Federal Act on Non-Human Gene Technology, Art 34 (GTA) <https://www.admin.ch/opc/en/classified-compilation/19996136/index.html>.

**17** *R Beck*, Das patchworkartige System der Haftpflicht-Versicherungsobligatorien, Das Durlemann Dilemma – Liber Amicorum Roland Brehm (2012) 1–20.

for consumer claims could trigger the demand for better consumer protection.

- *Political or consumer pressure.* As a consequence of large loss scenarios, political and consumer pressure has increased with the aim to better protect victims. Recent examples are the Deepwater Horizon oil spill in the Gulf of Mexico in April 2010 and the French Poly Implant Prothèse (PIP) products liability scandal in France. The manufacturer of PIP deliberately used industry silicone that was not approved for breast/human body implants. Both events triggered demands to introduce adequate compulsory financial security. However, an EU-wide compulsory insurance system will not prevent fraudulent cases such as the PIP case.[18]
- *Re-assessment of existing non-mandatory insurance solutions.* A series of fatal attacks by dangerous dogs on small children occurred in Switzerland, resulting in compulsory insurance on a constituent state (cantonal) level[19] although this was already covered in the voluntary homeowners' policies taken out by over 90% of Swiss households.[20]
- *Self-regulation of professional associations (eg chambers, bar associations).* In some European countries (eg the Netherlands[21]), professional associations such as bar associations require their members take out insurance. The role of influential professional associations may lead to the de facto imposition of compulsory insurance.

## 3. Important elements

58 The following section highlights the most important elements to be taken into account in defining the extent of compulsory insurance.

---

**18** As an example, see the statement of Insurance Europe concerning Poly Implant Prothèse (PIP) case and resulting consequences: <http://www.insuranceeurope.eu/sites/default/files/attachments/Key%20messages%20on%20compulsory%20liability%20insurance%20for%20manufacturers%20of%20medical%20devices%20and%20in-vitro%20diagnostic%20devices.pdf>.

**19** <http://www.tierimrecht.org/de/tierschutzrecht/schweiz/hunde-recht/index.php>.

**20** <https://www.admin.ch/opc/de/federal-gazette/2010/4149.pdf>, 4152. Whereas Germany: <http://www.gdv.de/2014/11/15-prozent-aller-haushalte-verzichten-auf-die-privathaftpflicht versicherung/>.

**21** The basis for this is the 'Regulations concerning financial records and financial integrity' issued by the Dutch Bar Association. The minimum sum insured is € 500,000 per event with an aggregate limit of at least € 1 million per year.

### a) Limits

In principle, an adequate minimum sum insured may be stipulated in laws or legal ordinances. As outlined in no 45 ff above, the stipulation of unlimited sums insured is technically not possible in insurance. It should be left to the insurance industry and their insureds to decide what they consider to be a risk-adequate sum insured, taking into account the market conditions and its legal and societal environment. However, there are practical difficulties in legally stipulating minimum sums, resulting from the fact that insureds are of varying financial strength. Low minimum sums do not make sense for financially strong insureds (eg large corporations generating billions in revenues/profits such as multi-national pharmaceutical manufacturers or oil drilling companies), who can bear large losses themselves. On the other hand, high minimum sums may not make sense for small insureds (eg small and medium-sized enterprises), who generally have less exposure/revenues since they cannot afford it financially. 59

### b) Freedom to contract

It is important for contractual freedom to be secured. Lawmakers should not link compulsory insurance schemes with a legal duty of insurers to insure certain risks. Furthermore, the fundamental criteria for insurability need to be assured. If the insurance industry considers a given risk to be uninsurable, lawmakers should consider options other than insurance, such as prohibiting the pursuit of a given activity or granting permits subject to extensive conditions only. If insurance is not feasible, other financial security instruments[22] may be an option. 60

### c) Degree of contractual freedom

Insurers must be free to set adequate terms and conditions even for compulsory insurance schemes. They have the necessary expertise and skills to institute appropriate insurance schemes. This lies outside of the tasks and competence of lawmakers. Lawmakers should avoid mandating coverage elements that are not readily available on the commercial market. Moreover, they should generally avoid legislating coverage in detail. Overregulation can lead to a lack of insurers 61

22 See no 97 ff below.

willing to write the risk. On the other hand, flexibility in the mandated cover serves to secure competition within the insurance market, while boosting innovation, which is also in the interest of consumers. In this context, it must also be noted that both the insured and the injured party are 'consumers' of the insurance industry. Consumer protection thus also entails considering the interests of small and medium enterprises in their relationship with insurers.

62 If lawmakers rule on the scope of an insurance scheme or even propose specific terms in an insurance contract, this could lead to a situation in which individual insurers would withdraw from the market or stop writing a specific insurance segment, if the resulting uncertainty does not correspond to their risk appetite and/or their financial strength. Such situations could lead to a reduced capacity offering and have a negative impact on market competition.[23] This is not in anyone's interest.

#### d) Premium

63 One of the core competencies of an insurer is to determine the scope of the insurance contract, including the sum insured, and to calculate the respective risk-adequate premium. How is the premium calculated? If there is sufficient experience or knowledge of past events, insurers can use the resulting statistics to make sophisticated calculations. This process involves calculating the probability and severity of potential losses.

64 In the recent past, a trend has been observed among regulators to attempt to either come up with proposals for calculating premiums or at least to convey their expectations that the premium needs to be 'reasonable' or 'adequate' without defining what these terms should mean.[24] Premiums must be technically correct in order to ensure insurability in the long term. Lawmakers are well advised to leave the calculation of premiums to the insurance sector, which has far more experience in this respect than lawmakers and is the party assuming the risk.

65 If the market cannot offer reasonable or adequate premiums, the risk is obviously uninsurable and the activity must either be prohibited by the lawmaker

**23** Cf the difficulty for German midwives to obtain professional liability insurance: <http://www.gdv.de/2014/02/warum-bezahlbarer-versicherungsschutz-fuer-hebammen-immer-schwieriger-wird/>.

**24** Article 14.2 Directive 2004/35/EC on Environmental Liability: The EC Report to include 'availability at reasonable costs and conditions of insurance products' or art 9 Ciff 7 Directive 2011/61/EU Alternative Investment Funds Managers 'Insurance and funds appropriate to the risks'.

or the parties involved must bear the financial risks themselves. Primarily losses must be prevented and not insured (eg dangerous dogs must be controlled: insurance is not a substitute for control; see nos 36–38 above).

### e) Direct right of action

A direct right of action is considered to be an extended protection of the victim, improving the rights of the claimant by enabling him to seek compensation directly from the liability insurer. 66

Some compulsory liability insurance schemes (eg motor liability insurance in Switzerland, art 65 para 2 Swiss Road Traffic Act, SVG) stipulate a direct action to claim against the insurer. But this *actio directa* should not be combined with limiting the insurer's right to invoke coverage restrictions out of the insurance contract (as agreed with the insured) even when a direct claim is filed by a claimant. Not every compulsory insurance scheme needs to stipulate a direct right of action, and if it does so, it must not necessarily link this right to an exclusion of the insurer's coverage restrictions. 67

To illustrate: in Germany, there is a compulsory insurance requirement for members of selected professional associations, such as lawyers[25] or accountants.[26] However, this compulsory insurance requirement is not coupled with a direct action to claim, and the liability in the insurance contract is also limited, as the law excludes intentional acts among other items. 68

### f) Protection of the insured vs 'full' protection of the victim

The political discussion has put the main focus on protection of the victim.[27] This leads to very high expectations towards compulsory insurance which may exceed the contractual possibilities of an insurer. The existence of an insurance contract does not always lead to the compensation of victims. The sum of an insured's liabilities and the scope of an insurance contract are not always congruent, even with compulsory insurance. Moreover, it must be borne in mind that the primary purpose of liability insurance is to enable the insured to bear the consequences of its liability and not to unequivocally protect victims for any and every loss. 69

---

25 § 51 Federal Lawyers' Act (Bundesrechtsanwaltsordnung, BRAO).

26 § 54 Law regulating the Profession of Auditors (Wirtschaftsprüferordnung, WiPrO).

27 See for example *Werz*, HAVE 1/2013, 54 f.

70 In the example from Germany mentioned above, the compulsory insurance requirement for the said professions is linked to a provision of a minimum sum insured, eg € 500,000 or € 1 million. If a loss exceeds the agreed minimum sum insured, an insured needs to bear the additional loss amount if it did not buy higher insurance limits.

71 An example of ill-advised compulsory insurance is the recently adopted legislative resolution on medical devices and in-vitro diagnostic medical devices which the European Parliament adopted on 2 April 2014, introducing an obligation for manufacturers to acquire appropriate liability insurance, including coverage for the risk of insolvency driven by the PIP[28] loss in France. Even if they were made compulsory, product liability policies would not cover losses in which the manufacturer acted fraudulently or recklessly, thereby consciously accepting the occurrence of injuries. And the insolvency risk is considered an entrepreneurial risk which is not insurable as it does not meet the criteria of insurability (see above nos 17 and 42).

### g) Control mechanisms

72 The insurance policyholder needs to prove to the competent authority prior to commencement of his activities that he has taken out the prescribed liability insurance in line with the respective law that requires insurance. This may be linked with a corresponding duty of the insurer to inform the competent authority when the liability insurance contract ends.

73 The respective laws stipulate sanctions in the case of non-compliance with the professional obligation to have insurance. But in our view the lack of proof of compulsory insurance should not be linked to non-fulfilment of a licence requirement. This would have drastic consequences for the insurers, as they – as a practical matter – would be forced into the unwanted role of excluding professionals from the practice of their professions if they consider the moral hazard to be too high from an insurance perspective (not from a regulatory one!) and refuse or cancel cover. This cannot be the role of the insurance industry but should instead be the task of the competent authority. A link between compulsory insurance and a licence could lead to a factual obligation on insurers to cover the insured's professional services, as the insurer would have to assume

28 Poly Implant Prothèse (PIP), a French company, was specialised in manufacturing silicone breast implants. PIP deliberately used industry silicone not approved for use in breast implants/the human body.

that a cancellation of the insurance contract or a change of underwriting policy could lead to a prohibition of practice or even to an office closure.[29]

## VI. Compulsory Insurance in Economic Terms

On a European level, compulsory insurance has been successfully implemented for motor third party liability, railway liability, and aviation liability.[30] Many countries also have national and/or regional insurance requirements for individual activities (eg Switzerland, Spain) in the areas of general third party liability insurance including professional indemnity insurance. 74

The figures below illustrate that compulsory insurance is of considerable economic importance to the insurance industry, as it covers a broad range of activities. Within this sector, motor third party liability is by far the largest line, representing an average of 24% of total non-life premiums in the countries shown. Figure 1 also indicates that the share of motor liability in non-life premiums in the listed countries varies considerably. 75

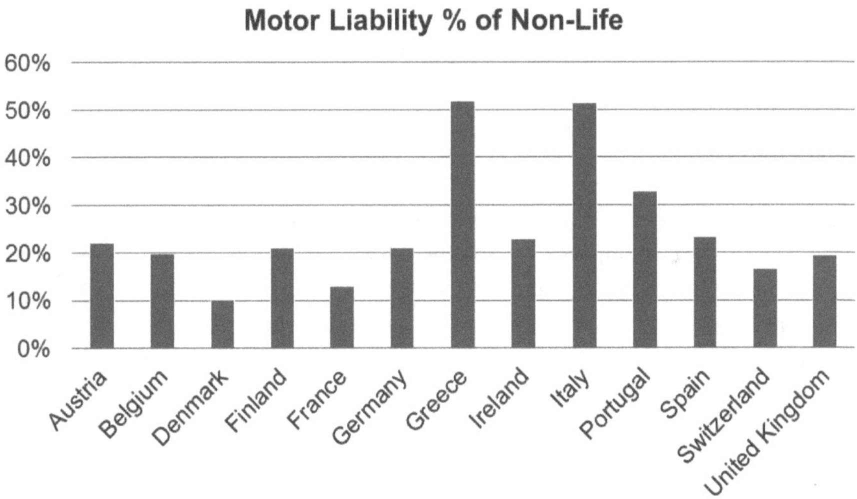


**Figure 1:** Share of motor third party liability (figures 2013) in % of non-life premiums in Europe[31]

29 *R Beck* in: Liber amicorum Roland Brehm (2012) 8: 'Die Pflichtversicherungen für die verschiedenen Berufsgattungen sollten als Berufspflicht und nicht als Bewilligungsvoraussetzung zur Berufsausübung festgelegt werden'.

30 *Swiss Re*, State involvement in insurance markets, Sigma No 3/2011, Table 3 p 8 <http://media.swissre.com/documents/sigma3_2011_en.pdf>.

31 Swiss Re Economic & Research Consulting (2013 Figures).

76 No precise figures are available for other compulsory insurance lines. However, Figure 2 below shows the proportion of premium income generated by general liability insurance in the form of professional indemnity and other third party liability as well as employers' liability insurance (eg UK). This should give some indication of its overall significance.

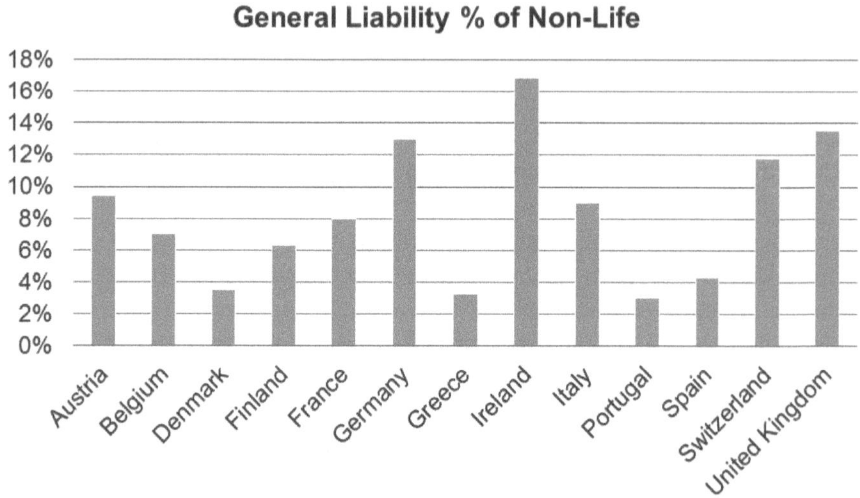


**Figure 2:** Share of general liability insurance in % of non-life premiums in Europe (encompassing professional indemnity, other third party liability as well as employers' liability, excluding marine and aviation liability)

77 There is even a trend, on a European Union level as well as on a national level,[32] to expand the number of activities that are subject to compulsory insurance – a trend that is likely to continue in the near future.[33] On the EU level, many of the recently proposed liability regimes have been linked to a provision on mandatory financial security. Here is a selection for illustration purposes:

- the EC public consultation on nuclear liability,
- the EC Directive on offshore oil in which the European Commission considers a form of mandatory financial security,
- the proposed new EC Regulation on medical devices.[34]

---

**32** Switzerland: 14.3043 – Motion Obligatorische Haftpflicht. Einheitliche Regelung und Anpassungen (<http://www.parlament.ch/d/suche/seiten/geschaefte.aspx?gesch_id=20143043>).
**33** <http://www.gdv.de/2009/12/wirtschaftspolitische-grenzen-von-haftungsausweitungen-und-pflichtversicherungen-fuer-unternehmen/>.
**34** See <http://www.en.gdv.de/wp-content/uploads/2015/05/GDV-Comments-MD-and-IVD_State-of-Play_042014.pdf> Section 'General concerns on compulsory insurance for manufacturers of medical devices'.

# VII. Prerequisites of Compulsory Insurance

## 1. Introduction

For the successful implementation of compulsory insurance schemes, some market preconditions are necessary. Compulsory insurance is often proposed when an existing liability regime is amended or a new liability regime is introduced (eg extension of the Environmental Liability Directive – ELD – to energy offshore;[35] EC proposed Regulation on medical devices[36] with respective comments from insurance associations). 78

However, compulsory insurance need not be primarily guided by the goal to better protect the victim. The primary purpose even of mandatory liability insurance contracts should be to protect the assets of the insured in the event of a loss, coupled with the positive secondary effect of protecting the victim by ensuring the existence of sufficient means to provide legally owed compensation. As outlined in section II, the scope of an insurance contract is based on the freedom of contract between the two parties involved, ie between the insurer and the insured. The insured liability risks are in line with the (financial) needs and the risk assessment of the insured party. This risk is determined by its potential exposure towards injured parties. The insured is best suited to assess the risks linked to its exposed activities and to evaluate its financial strengths and requirements. Conversely, the insurer also needs to make sure that its own interests (eg risk appetite, financial capacity, etc) and its assessment of the risk are clearly reflected in the scope of an insurance contract. 79

## 2. Established insurance market

An insurance market is considered to be established when insurers can adequately assess and meet the demand for insurance solutions. This requires the availability of sufficient and reliable data/information to predict the costs and frequency of claims. 80

Historical loss and exposure data is an essential factor for assessing and predicting the expected frequency and severity of claims. The absence of historical data makes this task more challenging as insurers then have to resort to making more assumptions, for example on the impact of technological, legal, 81

35 <http://www.insuranceeurope.eu/sites/default/files/attachments/Key%20messages%20on%20offshore%20oil%20liabilities.pdf>.

36 See fn 34 above.

political and societal changes, rather than to relying on firm information. If more than one such factor is subject to substantial change, a reasonable assessment may not be possible.

## 3. Sufficient supply of capacity

82 A sufficient supply of capacity with adequate limits means that sufficient capital is available to fund conceivable injuries or damage and/or severe loss scenarios. Moreover, insurers must also maintain sufficient capital for other business obligations, such as compliance with financial regulatory requirements (eg solvency laws). In evaluating compulsory insurance proposals, the insurance industry must first establish whether:

- it has sufficient capacity to satisfy an expected sudden increase in demand for cover, and
- if it can sustain this capacity in the long term.

## 4. Uniform risk characteristics

83 Standardised exposures, risks and protection needs are a prerequisite to adequately define the scope, sums, terms and costs of compulsory insurance (eg motor insurance).

84 Where claims are uniform or common and repetitive, it is easier for insurers to rely on standardised methods of cover. In liability cases where the risks are highly diverse, underwriting flexibility is essential to give insurers the freedom to contract policies with customers that are suitable for their regions or circumstances.

## 5. Competition in the market

85 The existence of a variety of insurers facilitates access to greater and more diverse insurance options and serves to foster competition. In such an environment, market diversity will be much more likely to remain effective when it comes to compulsory insurance proposals. Conversely, a small and highly specialised market limits the available insurance options to a small group of insurers with very special expertise. A variety of insurers fosters competition by encouraging cover offers based on the insurers' differing abilities to provide the statutory covers. Competition exists when insurers compete on price and on the ability to offer different products.

## 6. Alignment among stakeholders

Any stipulation on financial security solutions requires thorough discussions 86
and an agreement among all parties involved on possible solutions for the stakeholders concerned. Lawmakers in particular need to understand that financial security is not equal to an insurance solution. All other forms of financial security (see no 97 ff below) mechanisms also need to be evaluated in this process.

Again, it is the state which has to ensure the mitigation of hazards as a 87
whole with diverse solutions (including safety requirements). Insurance can well be part of a solution, but the extent needs to be negotiated with the insurance industry. For non-uninsurable risks or losses, other solutions need to be evaluated.

## 7. Reinsurance support

Similar to co-insurance, reinsurance enables insurers to reduce and spread their 88
own risk of loss by allowing them to share the loss with the reinsurer(s). As reinsurers provide insurance support in addition to that directly provided by the primary insurance market, the same considerations apply to the reinsurance market.

## 8. Affordability

Compulsory insurance is feasible only when insurers are able to provide prod- 89
ucts which meet the customers' needs at a premium which is affordable for the insureds.

## 9. Fall-back solution

Where an open market cannot provide the necessary cover, fall-back solutions 90
may offer relief. For instance:

- Assigning professional indemnity risks that have failed to secure professional indemnity insurance coverage in the open market can be placed in an assigned risk pool which ensures that they can remain in business; an option used in the UK for lawyers until the end of September 2013.[37]

---

**37** Solicitors in the UK usually have that cover arranged by the law firm they work for. The following is a statement from the PII Buyer's Guide 2014 published by the SRA (there is also a guide for the insurers – <http://www.lawsociety.org.uk/support-services/risk-compliance/pii/

- A fall-back solution (guarantee funds) also exists in motor liability insurance in the event that a loss involves an uninsured car.[38]

## 10. Non-fulfilment of prerequisites

91 If the conditions listed in nos 78–90 above are not met, the insurance market will not be able to respond to any sudden increase in demand for insurance, and undesired effects are likely to occur, such as premiums which do not accurately reflect risks, shortages of insurance capacity and a lack of insurers and products to adequately address consumer needs. In extreme cases, the compulsory insurance scheme may be doomed to failure.

# VIII. Advantages and Disadvantages of Compulsory Insurance

92 There are no black-and-white considerations when it comes to the evaluation of compulsory insurance.

93 This section is based on the considerations outlined in the Swiss Re publication 'Insights':[39] The statements made in this publication are still valid today.

## 1. Advantages of compulsory insurance

94 Advantages of compulsory insurance can include the following four consequences:

- *Rapid insurance penetration.* The high number of insureds involved in compulsory insurance facilitates technical calculations, as the market matures

guides/>): 'The 2012–13 indemnity period was the last time that firms unable to obtain open market insurance will be able to enter the assigned risks pool (APR). From 1 October 2013, if you are unable to obtain insurance on the open market, your previous insurer will have to provide you with a 30-day Extended Indemnity Period (EIP), a 60-day Cessation Period and then six years of run-off cover'.

**38** The Swiss National Guarantee Fund (NGF) covers losses caused in Switzerland and Liechtenstein by unidentified or uninsured motor vehicles, trailers or bicycles. The NGF also intervenes in the case of bankruptcy of the competent Swiss or Liechtenstein MTPL insurer and fulfils the tasks of the compensation body according to art 79d f of the Swiss Road Traffic Act (SVG).

**39** Swiss Re 'Insights' Compulsory non-life insurance in Europe, July 2003.

instantly and the law of large numbers applies from the outset. In a voluntary market situation, it would normally take years for the number of insureds to stabilise, allowing insurers to determine whether premium rates genuinely reflect their risk exposure accurately.

- *New outlets.* Introducing compulsory insurance may either create an entirely new market or significantly increase the size of an existing one.
- *'Full' protection of the victim and of the environment against any insolvency of the tortfeasor.* Third party liability insurance not only protects the assets of the policyholder as the liable party but also guarantees that the necessary funds to compensate the victims are available. The demand for compulsory insurance is at least in part being fuelled by governments' and society's increased desire to protect consumers or other potential victims.
- *Cross-subsidisation and redistribution of income in the absence of price differentiation.* As all are obliged to participate if insurance is compulsory, premiums tend to be lower as there is no selection bias. Good risks should allow lower premiums to be set, from which bad risks draw a benefit, while the burden is placed on the good ones. Making coverage compulsory can therefore be seen as an additional channel of income redistribution.

## 2. Disadvantages of compulsory insurance

Despite the advantages mentioned above, compulsory insurance is also associ- 95
ated with some less desirable consequences, some of which may be difficult to overcome.

The most important disadvantages are: 96

- *Over- or under-insurance.* The setting of a prescribed minimum insurance limit may be designed to reflect the need of large insureds, which would potentially be too high for many smaller insureds with limited or virtually no risk exposure. On the other hand, low limits may not be adequate for large insureds, or irrelevant for financially strong insureds.
- *Insurance cover can be tailored to the protection needs of the insured only to a limited extent.* In a voluntary free market, insurers can tailor the insurance cover to the needs and the exposure of the insured. In consequence, due to the lack of contractual freedom, in particular if the legislator seeks to impose terms of insurance, compulsory insurance can have a stifling effect on innovation (see also no 78 f above).
- *Aggravation of moral hazard.* Compulsory insurance aggravates the so-called moral hazard as outlined in no 43 above.

Having complied with the legal obligation to insure, the insured may feel that it has sufficiently complied with the law. The insured may be tempted to no longer weigh up the costs and benefits of insurance, and could refrain from adopting loss prevention measures if they involve further additional costs. Thus there is a danger that the insured might see the savings from neglecting prevention as a way of recovering some of the premium costs imposed by law.

- *Limited contractual flexibility*. Due to the mandatory nature of compulsory insurance, both the insurer and the insured are constrained when it comes to contractual flexibility. If compulsory acceptance and/or detailed terms are imposed, insurers are unable to turn down unfavourable risks and/or add appropriate provisions or exclusions. They will either write the class of business or not. In the latter case, a reduction of insurance availability for good risks will result. The same applies if pricing is mandated.
- *Hampering insurance innovation.* Contractual freedom gives insurers room to incorporate new developments or experience into innovative insurance solutions. Compulsory schemes may hinder or even prevent them from doing so.
- *Additional supervisory costs.* Authorities should take into account additional supervision costs when considering the introduction of compulsory cover. The costs and benefits should be weighed up against those of alternative solutions, such as surety or bank guarantees.
- *Delegation of supervisory obligations to insurers.* The criteria for granting a licence vary fundamentally from those which insurers apply in underwriting a risk; a fact which is often overlooked in practice. Public authorities are namely responsible for licensing and supervising activities that pose a hazard for consumers. Compulsory insurance tends to indirectly delegate such tasks to the insurance industry. This is the case where licensing authorities rely primarily on the existence of a compulsory insurance policy to approve a licence application. Moreover, supervisory authorities often seek to impose information or notification requirements on insurers, for which they are not responsible and may be ill-equipped to deal with (eg requirements that insurers inform authorities of contract modifications, non-payment of premiums etc).

# IX. Other Financial Security Instruments

## 1. Introduction

Financial security provisions are contained in various EU legislation such as the Environmental Liability Directive 2004/35/CE of 21 April 2004 (ELD Directive) which, for example, stipulates in art 14, sec 1 on financial security: 97

> 'Member States shall take measures to encourage the development of financial security instruments and markets by the appropriate economic and financial operators, including financial mechanisms in case of insolvency, with the aim of enabling operators to use financial guarantees to cover their responsibilities under this Directive.'

What is meant by the term 'financial security'? Generally, the most suitable financial coverage available is liability insurance, but in some Member States (eg Slovakia), the law also considers a bank guarantee as providing sufficient financial coverage. However, the general practice of banks to issue such bank guarantees for only a limited period of time may contradict the requirement to provide financial coverage for the entire time of operation, which can last up to several decades. 98

The following section briefly lists the most commonly known financial security instruments other than liability insurance. For this purpose, a distinction can be made between external and internal solutions. Under external solutions we understand insurance cover in the form of financial or surety guarantees typically issued by specialised insurance companies or products issued by banks (eg letters of credit or bank guarantees). Internal solutions are under the full control of the insured and independent of the solutions provided by external financial security providers. 99

The term 'financial guarantee', as mentioned in the EC ELD Directive, lacks clarity. In the practice of insurers, this term usually stands for guarantees issued by specialised insurance companies to cover pure financial obligations when granting loans or issuing securities. 100

## 2. External solutions

### a) Letters of credit or bank guarantees

A letter of credit is a document issued by a financial institution or a similar party assuring payment to a seller of goods and/or services, provided that certain 101 documents have been presented to the bank. These are documents that prove that the seller has performed the duties under an underlying contract (eg sale of goods contract) and the goods (or services) have been supplied as agreed. In return for these documents, the beneficiary receives payment from the financial institution that issued the letter of credit. The letter of credit serves as a guarantee to the seller that it will be paid regardless of whether the buyer ultimately fails to pay. In this way, the risk that the buyer will fail to pay is transferred from the seller to the issuer of the letter of credit. The letter of credit can also be used to ensure that all the standards and quality of goods agreed upon are met by the supplier, provided that these requirements are reflected in the documents described in the letter of credit. A letter of credit is not dependent on the risk evaluation but more on the obligor's financial strength.

#### b) Trade credit insurance and surety bonds

102 Credit insurance products cover losses from receivables and contractual obligations. Trade credit insurance products provide cover to the sellers of goods or services in the event that buyers fail to fulfil their payment obligations.

103 A surety bond is an insurance contract in which the insurer provides a guarantee to a beneficiary that a third party – the principal – will meet its contractual, legal or regulatory obligations. Such surety bonds mainly cover obligations from corporates and very rarely (financial) obligations/risks of individuals (eg consumer credits).

### 3. Internal solutions[40]

#### a) Dedicated funding or reserves

104 Dedicated funds are another option for financial security. Such an example can be found in the Directive 2011/61/EU on Alternative Investment Fund Managers (AIFM) art 9 cypher 7 lit (a):

> '... to cover potential professional liability risks resulting from the activities AIFMs may carry pursuant to this Directive shall either hold a professional indemnity insurance against liability arising from professional negligence which is appropriate to the risks

---

40 Internal solutions are under the full control of the insured and independent of solutions provided by external financial security providers ie insurance and/or banks.

covered or have additional own funds which are appropriate to cover potential liability risks arising from professional negligence.'

Given the choice, it is not likely that many fund managers would want to tie up capital in this way when insurance is viewed as an alternative. Moreover, difficulties may arise with determining cover that is 'appropriate to the risk covered', particularly bearing in mind that the size of such an alternative investment fund can easily reach a volume of hundreds of millions of euros. The Directive does not make any statement in this respect. **105**

### b) Pledge of assets

Assets are used as collateral for contractual obligations, typically a loan. A pledged asset[41] is transferred to the lender from the borrower to secure the debt. Ownership of the asset remains with the borrower during the loan period. When the debt has been repaid, the pledged asset is transferred back to the borrower. The lender assumes ownership of the loan if the borrower defaults on the loan. **106**

### c) Parental guarantee

A parent company guarantee is a declaration issued by a parent company in regard to one or more of its subsidiaries. Often, the guarantee is aimed at providing assurance to a potential client or partner of the subsidiary that the business is capable of honouring all obligations that are connected with the proposed business relationship. Unlike some other types of assurance, this guarantee commits the parent to stepping in and honouring the terms of the contract or settling liability obligations if the subsidiary should fail to do so for any reason. **107**

## 4. Additional protection by financial security instruments

Some of the external and internal financial instruments described above do not directly address the liability of exposed parties and compensation of their potential victims, as they focus primarily on the insolvency risk of the potentially liable party. Nonetheless, they serve to maintain or increase the potential tortfeasor's financial strength, and thus indirectly its capacity to settle possible claims. **108**

41 Read more: <http://www.businessdictionary.com/definition/pledged-asset.html#ixzz2rrXAXikz>.

109 Such financial security products, that offer protection beyond liability exposures, may serve as complementary protection – or even as an alternative – to pure liability cover.

# X. Buyer's Perspective on Compulsory Insurance

110 Insurance buyers and risk managers agree that compulsory insurance is in contradiction to any risk management philosophy, as it removes the incentives to prevent damage. Therefore, buyers should be free to decide which risks they want to transfer to insurers and which ones to keep.[42]

111 The Federation of European Risk Management Associations in Brussels (FERMA) argues that voluntary financial security must remain the rule and that the European Commission is not taking account of what market capacity is already available. If a given insurance market is working well, there is no specific reason to move to a mandatory financial security scheme. A free insurance market is better able to respond to the needs of insurance buyers at a fair price, and there is established law on many of the coverage issues that could arise.

112 Not only insurance buyers but also consumers may face disadvantages as compulsory insurance can distort competition if one state requires compulsory insurance for a specific product whereas another state does not. Such a product will be more expensive in the state requiring insurance, without improving quality.

# XI. Changing Legal Environment – Outlook

## 1. Increasingly consumer-friendly laws

113 The present developments on a national level and on the European Commission level for the EU Member States indicate that the trend to further strengthen consumer protection will increase and is most likely to lead to more consumer-friendly liability regimes. For illustration purposes, this can be seen in attempts

42 <http://www.ferma.eu/blog/2013/07/ferma-discourages-eu-from-compulsory-schemes-for-catastrophe-insurance/>.

of the European Commission to harmonise the liability regimes in the following sectors:

- nuclear liability,[43]
- energy offshore,[44]
- exploration and production of hydraulic fracturing.[45]

As in the recent past, most of these regimes will most likely be linked to a provision on financial security, and in the view of many lawmakers financial security is equal to insurance. 114

## 2. Expectations towards insurers will increase

As a result, the expectations towards insurers will increase, and the insurance industry is well advised to proactively get involved in the discussions on new liability regimes in order to bring in the realities and limits of insurance solutions. Although expectations towards insurers will increase, it must be stressed that insurance can only be part of the solution but not the sole solution for all consumer complaints or problems. The first aim of liability insurance continues to be the financial security of the insured. The request for an introduction of more compulsory insurance schemes will increase regardless of insurability. But not everything is insurable and compulsory insurance is not a viable requirement for all liability regimes. Whether a compulsory insurance scheme is justified often remains a matter of judgement. 115

## 3. Determining the need for and the content of compulsory insurance

To ensure that compulsory insurance is regulated in a consistent and objective manner, the Swiss Insurance Association (*Schweizerischer Versicherungsverband*, SVV) located in Zurich recommends in a strategy paper on compulsory insurance[46] systematically evaluating predefined criteria. For this purpose, the following evaluation grid has been developed to facilitate assessment. 116

43 <http://www.ensreg.eu/ensreg-conferences>.
44 <http://www.insuranceeurope.eu/key-messages-offshore-oil-liabilities>.
45 <http://eur-lex.europa.eu/legal-content/EN/TXT/?uri=CELEX:32014H0070>.
46 SVV Pflichtversicherungsgesetz: Strategie SVV Zurich, December 2013.

| | Evaluation grid for compulsory insurance | | | | | |
|---|---|---|---|---|---|---|
| | **Points** | **0** | **5** | **10** | **20** | |
| **Weighting factor** | **Criteria** | **Evaluation** | | | | **Score (weighted points)** |
| 2 | Avoidable exposure | Easily avoidable | Avoidable in certain conditions | Hardly avoidable | Unavoid-able | |
| 1.5 | Number of potential victims | Only one potential victim per event | Few poten-tial victims per event | Several potential victims per event | A large number of potential victims per event | |
| 1 | Loss po-tential – Bodily injury | Low to medium injury of the poten-tial victim | Medium injury of the poten-tial victim | Medium to severe in-jury of the potential victim | Severe in-jury of the potential victims | |
| 1 | – Property and/or pure fi-nancial losses | Low to medium impact for the poten-tial victim | Medium impact for the poten-tial victim | Medium to severe im-pact for the poten-tial victims | Severe impact for the poten-tial victim | |
| 1 | Know-ledge gap between tortfeasor and victim | No or neg-ligible knowledge gap be-tween tort-feasor and victim | Negligible to medium knowledge gap be-tween tort-feasor and victim | Significant knowledge gap be-tween tort-feasor and victim | Very large knowledge gap between tortfeasor and victim | |
| 1 | Risk evaluation skills of potential victims | Potential victim is fully able to assess potential risk | Potential victim can to a large extent as-sess po-tential risk | Potential victim cannot ade-quately assess the risk | Potential victim cannot assess the risk | |
| **Total score** | | | | | | |

**Figure 3:** Criteria for determining whether compulsory insurance is warranted (source SVV Zurich)

If a certain threshold is reached, the reviewed sector can be considered 'worthy of compulsory insurance': The SVV deems that compulsory insurance merits examination and may be appropriate if the above scoring grid for an evaluated sector/activity results in a total score of more than 75 points. This total score is the sum of the scores for each of the six criteria. The scores for the individual criteria are achieved by multiplying the points as per evaluation with the criteria's weighting factors. 117

The need for compulsory insurance is determined in the SVV model with the threshold of 75 points, but the affirmation of such a need must be distinguished from the content of such insurance. In particular, the affirmation of the need for compulsory insurance does not per se justify the statutory waiver of the insurer's defences against the victim's direct action. This requires a further aggregation of criteria scores above the threshold of 75 points (Figure 4 below). Apart from the criteria contained in the grid, further aggravation factors may also affect the aggregation level, for instance to what extent the applicable liability law allows any defences against the claim. 118

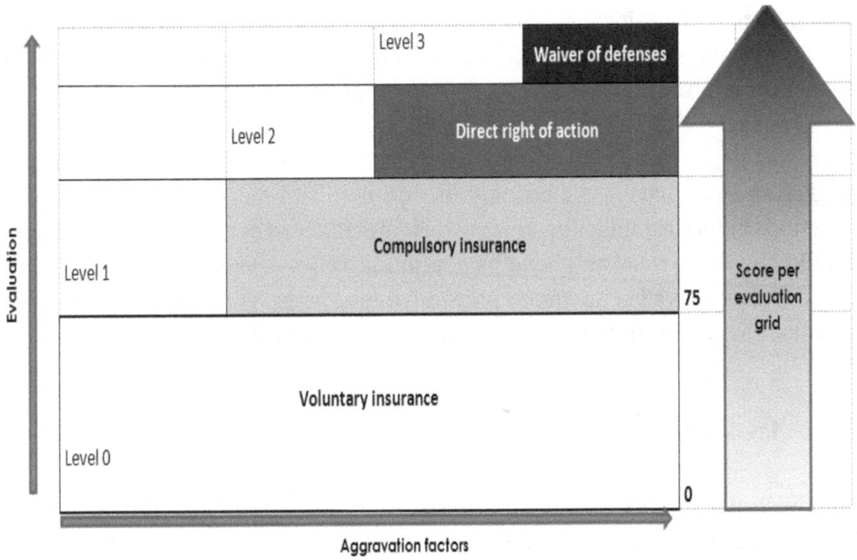


**Figure 4:** Evaluation of aggregation levels for compulsory insurance (source SVV Zurich)

To illustrate: The need for victim protection is much higher in road traffic events than it is, for example, for hunters or lawyers. Everybody is always and constantly exposed to perils related to road traffic accidents, as public roads 119 cannot be avoided. The situation is different with respect to hunting accidents, as such situations can be generally avoided and, in the case of a lawyer, one can even select the risk. As outlined above (see no 18 ff), in motor liability insurance the victim's direct right of action against the driver's liability insurer makes sense, as the insurer cannot even reject coverage for subjective risks linked to the insured (eg a criminal or intentional act). The other two examples demonstrate that the duty to have insurance is sufficient – if necessary with a minimum sum insured. The above escalation scheme of the SVV follows this approach. With respect to the underlying SVV evaluation grid, the criterion 'avoidable exposure' may be weighted with a maximum score of 40 points for motor liability, whereas hunters' and lawyers' liability will have far lower scores for this criterion. Thus the total score for motor liability will lie at a significantly higher aggregation level than for the other two examples which is an indication that intervention in the policy content is not justified for the latter two examples, in particular as motor accidents often also involve multiple victims, which is unusual in hunting accidents for example.

120 However, the criteria are not meant to be applicable at a regional level within a country, as local compulsory insurance schemes are undesirable. If an activity is dangerous in one province or constituent state, then surely it will be generally so in the country as a whole. An identified danger does not stop at internal borders. Compulsory insurance on a regional level within a country merely creates legal uncertainty. Such local rules threaten the existence of a single market and can have a distorting effect on competition in a national market. Here too, before establishing compulsory insurance schemes, local lawmakers should check the costs and benefits of alternative ways to ensure the protection of local consumers via adequate preventive measures, as in any event compulsory insurance cannot guarantee protection in all situations.

## XII. Conclusion

121 Compulsory insurance cannot be the primary measure to protect victims. Liability insurance essentially protects the liable party's (the insured's) assets, thereby ensuring that a set sum is available to satisfy its legal obligation to indemnify the victim. The primary emphasis must remain on loss prevention measures. If an activity is too dangerous to control, compulsory (liability) insurance is not a substitute for safety.

122 The introduction of compulsory liability insurance does not mean that all risks and losses can necessarily be covered. The insurance industry as a whole is constrained by technical considerations, capital requirements and capacities.

Moreover, each insurance company needs to evaluate which risks it considers to be insurable on what terms, based on its own risk assessment, risk appetite and portfolio mix. Insurers must be free to decide which risks and losses are insurable.

Insurance solutions must be provided in the context of freedom of contract 123
in order to enable insurers to offer products that are appropriate to individual risks. A free market is an indicator of the range and calculability of risk. Risks which are not insurable on a free market require detailed consideration of alternative solutions other than compulsory insurance. Measures to prevent or mitigate risks should precede the discussion of a potential transfer of risk costs to an insurer or other party.

Compulsory insurance must not lead to a rigid approach to the prescribed 124
scope of insurance, thus preventing insurance coverage that is commensurate to the risk.

Statutory standards interfere with the development of new insurance prod- 125
ucts. The limited flexibility of compulsory insurance schemes can interfere with insurance markets where underwriting considerations need to apply. Standardised compulsory insurance restricts the insurer's ability to negotiate terms of cover and leaves little room for competition other than on price differentiation.

Compulsory insurance may result in higher costs for customers if they must 126
buy insurance coverage at levels required by law whether they need it or not.

If compulsory insurance is to be meaningful, it must be adapted to the given 127
risk situation. There are risks where compulsory insurance may be an option, but not absolutely necessary. To ensure an objective approach to deciding whether insurance should be declared compulsory, consistent criteria should be systematically applied. The Swiss Insurance Association has developed assessment criteria for the evaluation of compulsory insurance (see no 116 above). Its basic principle is that compulsory insurance should be considered only if a specific exposure threshold is reached (see no 116 above, Figure 3, where a triggering score of 75 points is assumed). In specific cases where there is a particularly intense aggregation of exposure – and only then – material regulation of the contractual relationship between liability insurer and insured may be justified (see no 118 above, Figure 4).

Widespread compulsory liability insurance could even be contra-produc- 128
tive, leading to a lowered sense of responsibility if the erroneous impression is created that all losses can always be insured under all circumstances.

# Comparative Report and Conclusions

Daniel Rubin

# Comparative Report

## I. The Term Compulsory Liability Insurance

1. *Indicate the rules within your legal system that set out a duty to take out liability insurance.*

The number of rules that require a duty to take out liability insurance in the legal systems investigated does not by any means present a uniform picture: In *Germany*, *Switzerland* and *Italy*, especially in the laws of their federal states, there are – one is tempted to say – an almost uncountable number of (statutory) provisions stipulating compulsory liability insurance.[1] There are also copious numbers of regulations in *Belgium* with 150[2] and *Austria* with no less than 100[3] rules laying down a duty to take out liability insurance. In the middle of the field, approximately 40 examples for compulsory liability insurance are to be found in *Czech law*[4] and about 35 in *Finnish*[5] and in *Hungarian law*[6] respectively. 1

1 Regarding Germany cf *R Koch*, Compulsory Liability Insurance in Germany (in this book) no 1 ('quite a significant number of rules'); *R Koch*, Annex: Rules on Compulsory Liability Insurance in Germany (at the end of this book). Regarding Switzerland cf *A Stäubli*, Compulsory Liability Insurance in Switzerland (in this book) no 1 ('enormous amount of rules') and no 5; *A Stäubli*, Annex: Rules on Compulsory Liability Insurance in Switzerland (at the end of this book). Regarding Italy cf *D Cerini*, Compulsory Liability Insurance in Italy (in this book) nos 5–9; *D Cerini/A Memola*, Annex: Rules on Compulsory Liability Insurance in Italy (at the end of this book).

2 *H Cousy/C Van Schoubroeck*, Compulsory Liability Insurance in Belgium (in this book) no 1; *H Cousy/C Van Schoubroeck*, Annex: Rules on Compulsory Liability Insurance in Belgium (at the end of this book).

3 *D Rubin*, Compulsory Liability Insurance in Austria (in this book) no 1; *D Rubin*, Annex: Rules on Compulsory Liability Insurance in Austria (at the end of this book).

4 *P Dobiás*, Compulsory Liability Insurance in the Czech Republic (in this book) no 1 f; *P Dobiás*, Annex: Rules on Compulsory Liability Insurance in the Czech Republic (at the end of this book).

5 Cf *J Norio-Timonen*, Compulsory Liability Insurance in Finland (in this book) nos 2–24; *J Norio-Timonen*, Annex: Rules on Compulsory Liability Insurance in Finland (at the end of this book).

6 Cf *P Takáts*, Compulsory Liability Insurance in Hungary (in this book) no 1 f; *P Takáts*, Annex: Rules on Compulsory Liability Insurance in Hungary (at the end of this book).

On the other hand, we see merely approximately 20 examples of compulsory liability insurance in the *United Kingdom.*[7]

2. *Is there a coherent 'law of compulsory liability insurance' in your legal system?*

2 a) The question of whether there is a coherent system of rules on compulsory liability insurance arises, first of all, in connection with sectoral legislation, ie those provisions setting out duties to take out such insurance. Thus, there is a question of whether the *factual criteria triggering the duty are coherent*: It can very largely be said of all the legal systems investigated that there is virtually no *coherent regulatory system* as to *why* in certain cases compulsory liability insurance is *prescribed* and *why* in other cases it is *not.*[8] For instance, in some legal systems there is a tendency to link the implementation of strict liability with compulsory insurance[9] (cf below no 25) whereas in others[10] this is not the case. *Neither* do the legal systems *coordinate* the respective rules requiring compulsory liability insurance with each other as regards *content.*[11] This is true, for example, as regards the sums prescribed as minimum insurance amounts.[12] Nevertheless, it must be stressed that, in general, all this is not considered to be an infringement of the legislator's constitutional duty of equal treatment.[13]

3 b) Secondly, we face the question of whether legal systems provide for *coherent legal consequences* linked to the existence of duties to take out liability insurance (see above nos 1 and 2). In this context we can distinguish *two categories* among the *legal systems*:

4 The *first group* comprises those which, as well as having general rules for liability insurance, also contain a *separate law on compulsory liability insurance*, ie a framework of rules that uniformly attach specific legal consequences – mostly to protect the victim – to cases where there is compulsory liability insur-

7 Cf *Ö Gürses*, Compulsory Liability Insurance in the United Kingdom (in this book) nos 1–10; *Ö Gürses*, Annex: Rules on Compulsory Liability Insurance in the United Kingdom (at the end of this book).

8 Cf *Koch*, Report: Germany (fn 1) no 2; *Rubin*, Report: Austria (fn 3) no 2; also cf *Stäubli*, Report: Switzerland (fn 1) no 103.

9 Cf *Rubin*, Report: Austria (fn 3) no 3; *Cousy/Van Schoubroeck*, Report: Belgium (fn 2) no 27.

10 Cf eg *Takáts*, Report: Hungary (fn 6) no 66.

11 Cf *Dobiás*, Report: Czech Republic (fn 4) no 3; *Takáts*, Report: Hungary (fn 6) no 3; *Rubin*, Report: Austria (fn 3) no 2.

12 Cf *Takáts*, Report: Hungary (fn 6) no 24.

13 Cf *F Merli*, Compulsory Liability and Constitutional Law (in this book) no 5 and (to a certain extent) no 6.

ance. Such a system of rules can be found in particular in *German law* (§§ 113–124 VVG)[14] and in those legal systems that have *adopted* the German model, for instance *Austrian law* (§§ 158b–158i VersVG)[15] and, though not included in this study, *Turkish law*.

Within this first group there are also legal systems that do not provide a 5
comprehensive complex of rules but do at least have *scattered legal provisions* dealing with compulsory liability insurance. The *Czech Republic* is such an example, having some statutory provisions on compulsory liability insurance (see §§ 2779–2781 Civil Code).[16] *Belgian law*, on the other hand, basically provides no special rules for compulsory liability insurance[17] – with one important exception (art 151 Insurance Act [IA] 2014)[18] concerning the applicability of defences the insurer can raise against the injured party (on this exception, cf below no 84). One should not look at such legal systems with only scattered statutory provisions as a separate group, since they at least have *one rule* that *operates* with the *term compulsory liability insurance*. Therefore, it is also imperative in these legal systems that this term is defined for its meaning determines the scope of the relevant rules on compulsory liability insurance. Accordingly, the term needs to be applied in a uniform way.

Then there is a *second group of legal systems* which do *not distinguish* at the 6
statutory level between *voluntary* and *compulsory liability insurance*. These include *Switzerland* (art 59f Insurance Contract Act),[19] *Italy* (art 1917 Civil Code [CC])[20] and, as it seems, also *Hungary*.[21] In this group the legislature did not take the decision to link uniform legal consequences to statutory liability insurance duties. This means that *de lege lata* a separate law on compulsory liability insurance and therefore an autonomous definition of compulsory liability insurance is missing. This of course leaves unanswered essential questions[22] concerning the rules requiring compulsory liability insurance. It is rather surprising that Switzerland and Italy belong to this group given their dense regulation on compulsory liability insurance. Besides this, it is noticeable that the above cited le-

**14** Cf *Koch*, Report: Germany (fn 1) no 2.
**15** *Rubin*, Report: Austria (fn 3) nos 4–7.
**16** Cf *Dobiás*, Report: Czech Republic (fn 4) no 1 fn 1.
**17** Cf *Cousy/Van Schoubroeck*, Report: Belgium (fn 2) nos 5–7 (arts 150–152 Insurance Act 2014 [IA] for 'land insurance contracts').
**18** *Cousy/Van Schoubroeck*, Report: Belgium (fn 2) no 7f. See also no 9 regarding Compulsory Motor Liability Insurance.
**19** Cf *Stäubli*, Report: Switzerland (fn 1) nos 2 and 5.
**20** Cf *Cerini*, Report: Italy (fn 1) nos 11 and 13.
**21** Cf *Takáts*, Report: Hungary (fn 6) nos 1 and 3.
**22** As for these cf *D Rubin*, Introduction (in this book) no 4f.

gal systems also limit their rules on voluntary liability insurance to a few aspects.

7 Within the second group *Finland* occupies a somewhat special position: per se Finnish law does not have separate regulations on the legal consequences linked to compulsory liability insurance.[23] However, within the context of compulsory liability insurance, it does distinguish between ordinary 'compulsory liability insurance' and 'statutory liability insurance'.[24] The latter is different from the former in that the terms of mandatory cover are precisely laid out in special laws (on this see below no 31) and that the general Insurance Contract Act is basically not applicable to it.[25] Statutory liability insurance is to includes employment accidents insurance, motor liability insurance, nuclear liability insurance and patient injuries insurance.[26]

8 The law of the *United Kingdom* also falls into the *second category*. This legal system basically even has no *general rules* that link legal consequences to compulsory or indeed voluntary liability insurance[27] with the exception of the insurer's insolvency (on this see below no 66).

3. *Is there a specific term for compulsory liability insurance in your legal system? How is it defined?*

9 Those legal systems that have special rules on compulsory liability insurance – *Germany* and *Austria* (see above no 4) – also have a legal definition of the term. Both legal systems see compulsory liability insurance as a liability insurance which must by law be taken out.[28] *Hungarian law* has a very similar legal definition of compulsory insurance in general, as opposed to compulsory liability insurance specifically (§ 105 [1] Law on Insurers and Insurance Business [Bit]).[29]

10 In other countries – *Belgium*,[30] the *Czech Republic*,[31] *Finland*,[32] *Italy*[33] – there is no *statutory definition*. Nevertheless, legal doctrine and/or case law have

23 With its Insurance Contract Act containing only individual provisions (but no separate section as such) on liability insurance in general; cf *Norio-Timonen*, Report: Finland (fn 5) no 25.
24 *Norio-Timonen*, Report: Finland (fn 5) nos 1 and 25.
25 See in more detail *Norio-Timonen*, Report: Finland (fn 5) nos 1 and 25.
26 *Norio-Timonen*, Report: Finland (fn 5) no 1.
27 Cf *Gürses*, Report: United Kingdom (fn 7) nos 2 and 3.
28 Cf *Koch*, Report: Germany (fn 1) no 4; *Rubin*, Report: Austria (fn 3) no 4.
29 Cf *Takáts*, Report: Hungary (fn 6) no 1.
30 *Cousy/Van Schoubroeck*, Report: Belgium (fn 2) no 8.
31 *Dobiás*, Report: Czech Republic (fn 4) no 4.
32 *Norio-Timonen*, Report: Finland (fn 5) no 26.
33 *Cerini*, Report: Italy (fn 1) no 10.

found definitions *very similar* to the legal definitions in Germany and Austria (above no 9).[34]

In the *United Kingdom* legal *theory* has *not* developed any specific *definition* of compulsory liability insurance.[35] The same would seem on the face of it to be true of Italy.[36] 11

In general the above-described, *dissatisfactory situation* with regard to having a specific legal definition of the term can be *relativised* in that a separate legal term for compulsory liability insurance *only* fulfils a *function*, and thus makes sense, where specific legal consequences attach to this term. This is *not the case* in the majority of the legal systems discussed here, namely in all the states listed above in nos 6–8 (*Finland, Hungary, Italy, Switzerland, United Kingdom*). Logically, the question of whether liability insurance is to be qualified as compulsory accordingly plays no role in Finnish literature, for example, either.[37] 12

4. *In which of the following cases does compulsory liability insurance apply according to prevailing opinion?*

a) *Duties to take out liability insurance which are not directly based on the law but on an order or decision issued by administrative authorities?*

In the legal systems investigated, the question of whether liability insurance is compulsory depends on whether the decision or order prescribing the duty to have such insurance cover in its turn is based on a *general legal prescription.*[38] Parliamentary laws[39] or EU regulations[40] would certainly constitute such general 13

---

**34** Cf *Cousy/Van Schoubroeck*, Report: Belgium (fn 2) no 1 (adoption of the non-binding definition of the Belgian financial supervisory authority by legal doctrine); *Dobiás*, Report: Czech Republic (fn 4) no 4; *Norio-Timonen*, Report: Finland (fn 5) no 26.

**35** Cf *Gürses*, Report: United Kingdom (fn 7) no 3.

**36** Cf *Cerini*, Report: Italy (fn 1) no 17.

**37** Cf *Norio-Timonen*, Report: Finland (fn 5) no 28.

**38** Cf *Cousy/Van Schoubroeck*, Report: Belgium (fn 2) no 13; *Koch*, Report: Germany (fn 1) nos 5 and 77; *Rubin*, Report: Austria (fn 3) no 8 f. See further *Norio-Timonen*, Report: Finland (fn 5) no 29. Additionally, it is sometimes required that the law leaves the authority no leeway as to whether to prescribe liability insurance or not (cf *Koch*, Report: Germany [fn 1] no 5; *Rubin*, Report: Austria [fn 3] no 9).

**39** Cf *Stäubli*, Report: Switzerland (fn 1) no 7 f.

**40** Cf *Cousy/Van Schoubroeck*, Report: Belgium (fn 2) no 13; *Koch*, Report: Germany (fn 1) no 5; *Rubin*, Report: Austria (fn 3) no 8; *Cerini*, Report: Italy (fn 1) nos 18–20. Hungarian law, on the other hand, is more restrictive; cf *Takáts*, Report: Hungary (fn 6) no 5. The same applies for Czech law; cf *Dobiás*, Report: Czech Republic (fn 4) no 5 f (§ 2779 Civil Code: no 'duty to take out

legal prescriptions. However, royal decrees[41] and decrees of regional governments or communities[42] are also considered to fulfil this requirement. The decisive factor always seems to be whether the public law of the country concerned accords the respective body, that creates the legal rule on which the decision or order is based, independent competence to issue general rules.

14 However, one needs to bear in mind that here, as in all of the following subquestions under Question 4, it is important to refer to the relativisation made above in no 12.

b) *Duties to take out liability insurance that are not based directly on the law but on the statutes of a professional or other self-governing body?*

15 Some legal systems recognise this as compulsory liability insurance if the self-governing body has a statutory power in this respect.[43] For *Belgian law*, however, it is argued that even a statutory power would not be sufficient.[44] The same seems to be true in the *Czech Republic*.[45]

c) *Duties to take out liability insurance that are not based on any public law but on a private law provision (eg, governing the relationship between employer and employee)?*

16 This kind of duty to take out insurance is categorised as compulsory liability insurance in *Germany*,[46] *Finland*,[47] *Hungary*[48] and apparently also the *Czech*

---

liability insurance which is not directly based on the law but on an order or decision issued by administrative authorities').

41 Cf *Cousy*/*Van Schoubroeck*, Report: Belgium (fn 2) no 13.

42 Cf *Cousy*/*Van Schoubroeck*, Report: Belgium (fn 2) no 13.

43 Cf *Takáts*, Report: Hungary (fn 6) no 6 f; *Rubin*, Report: Austria (fn 3) no 10. Along the same lines *Norio-Timonen*, Report: Finland (fn 5) no 30 (only relevant for the Finnish Bar Association); *Gürses*, Report: United Kingdom (fn 7) no 5. Further-reaching for regional and local authorities *Koch*, Report: Germany (fn 1) no 6. The position of the Report: on Italian law seems to be unclear; cf *Cerini*, Report: Italy (fn 1) nos 21–25.

44 Cf *Cousy*/*Van Schoubroeck*, Report: Belgium (fn 2) no 14 f.

45 Cf *Dobiás*, Report: Czech Republic (fn 4) no 7 f.

46 *Koch*, Report: Germany (fn 1) no 7.

47 *Norio-Timonen*, Report: Finland (fn 5) no 31.

48 *Takâts*, Report: Hungary (fn 6) no 8.

*Republic,*[49] while the opposite is the case in *Belgium,*[50] *Austria*[51] and *Switzerland.*[52, 53]

d) *Duties to take out liability insurance that are not based on any public law but on a private law rule that is established by case law (and, eg, governs the relationship between employer and employee)?*

These types of duties, insofar as they even exist in the respective legal systems,[54] are consistently *not qualified* as compulsory liability insurance.[55] **17**

e) *Cases in which there is no duty to take out liability insurance but liability insurance cover is a prerequisite for the admissibility of carrying out a particular activity?*

This constellation is *regarded as compulsory* liability insurance in *Austria,*[56] *Finland,*[57] *Germany,*[58] *Hungary,*[59] and *Switzerland,*[60] while the same would seem to be true in the *Czech Republic*[61] and *Italy.*[62] In the *United Kingdom* this constellation is considered not to arise as, in those cases where liability insurance is a prerequisite for admission to some professions, it is always also linked to the legal duty to maintain liability insurance.[63] **18**

---

**49** *Dobiás*, Report: Czech Republic (fn 4) no 9.
**50** *Cousy/Van Schoubroeck*, Report: Belgium (fn 2) no 16.
**51** Critical on the prevailing rejection thereof in Austria *Rubin*, Report: Austria (fn 3) no 11.
**52** *Stäubli*, Report: Switzerland (fn 1) no 10.
**53** See further on the subject *Gürses*, Report: United Kingdom (fn 7) no 6; *Cerini*, Report: Italy (fn 1) nos 26–28.
**54** Thus for instance, rejecting this *Stäubli*, Report: Switzerland (fn 1) no 11; *Cerini*, Report: Italy (fn 1) no 29; *Gürses*, Report: United Kingdom (fn 7) no 7.
**55** Cf *Cousy/Van Schoubroeck*, Report: Belgium (fn 2) no 17; *Norio-Timonen*, Report: Finland (fn 5) no 32 (duty to take out liability insurance is not based on laws); *Takáts*, Report: Hungary (fn 6) no 9 (no act of law); *Koch*, Report: Germany (fn 1) no 8; *Rubin*, Report: Austria (fn 3) no 12.
**56** *Rubin*, Report: Austria (fn 3) no 13f.
**57** *Norio-Timonen*, Report: Finland (fn 5) no 33.
**58** *Koch*, Report: Germany (fn 1) no 10.
**59** *Takáts*, Report: Hungary (fn 6) no 10.
**60** Cf *Stäubli*, Report: Switzerland (fn 1) no 12.
**61** Cf *Dobiás*, Report: Czech Republic (fn 4) nos 11–17.
**62** Cf *Cerini*, Report: Italy (fn 1) no 30.
**63** Cf *Gürses*, Report: United Kingdom (fn 7) no 8.

*f) Cases of alternative financial security, in which the duty to provide for financial security may be fulfilled either by taking out liability insurance or other forms of financial security (eg, bank guarantees)?*

19 Prevailing opinion in *Germany*[64] and *Austria*[65] rejects the idea of compulsory insurance in such a case. However it is considered compulsory liability insurance in legal theory in *Belgium*,[66] *Hungary*,[67] *Switzerland*[68] and, it would appear, also in *Finland*.[69,70] The law of the *United Kingdom* also qualifies cases in which liability insurance is prescribed as an alternative as compulsory liability insurance.[71] No clear answer could be determined in respect of the *Czech Republic*.[72] As regards whether the categorisation as 'compulsory liability insurance' plays any legislative role in the various legal systems, see again above no 12.

*g) Cases in which the duty to have insurance has only been created by a contractual agreement between potential injuring party and victim?*

20 Here the categorisation as compulsory liability insurance is uniformly *rejected*.[73]

64 *Koch*, Report: Germany (fn 1) no 11.
65 Cf *Rubin*, Report: Austria (fn 3) no 15 f with criticism of the prevailing opinion.
66 *Cousy/Van Schoubroeck*, Report: Belgium (fn 2) nos 4 and 19 f.
67 *Takáts*, Report: Hungary (fn 6) no 11.
68 *Stäubli*, Report: Switzerland (fn 1) no 14.
69 Cf *Norio-Timonen*, Report: Finland (fn 5) nos 27 and 34.
70 The conclusion to be drawn from the submissions presented in the Italian report: is unclear; cf *Cerini*, Report: Italy (fn 1) no 31.
71 *Gürses*, Report: United Kingdom (fn 7) no 10 f.
72 Cf *Dobiás*, Report: Czech Republic (fn 4) nos 18–20 (no 18 seems to deal with only a contractual obligation; on this cf below no 20).
73 Cf *Cousy/Van Schoubroeck*, Report: Belgium (fn 2) no 21; *Dobiás*, Report: Czech Republic (fn 4) no 21; *Norio-Timonen*, Report: Finland (fn 5) nos 27 and 35; *Koch*, Report: Germany (fn 1) no 12; *Takáts*, Report: Hungary (fn 6) no 12; *Cerini*, Report: Italy (fn 1) no 32; *Stäubli*, Report: Switzerland (fn 1) no 15 f; *Gürses*, Report: United Kingdom (fn 7) no 12; *Rubin*, Report: Austria (fn 3) no 17.

# II. Aims

5. *What are the aims of the rules that impose an obligation to take out liability insurance:*

*a) the protection of the victim,*

Within all legal systems that are considered in this study one – if not the – *fundamental aim* of compulsory liability insurance is the protection of the injured party so as to ensure indemnification.[74] This is only very occasionally criticised.[75] 21

*b) the protection of the insurance holder,*

It is assumed that protection of the insurance holder is usually an *additional purpose* of compulsory liability insurance rules, alongside the protection of the victim.[76] The protection of the insurance holder is considered to be based on the fact of having a risk spread among the insured community by liability insurance and thus relieving the insurance holder of the burden of bearing damage.[77] In any case, it is at least convincingly pointed out that compulsory liability insurance also serves the protection of the insurance holder where the law not only imposes compulsory liability insurance but at the same time puts *a maximum limit on* the insurance holder's *liability* equal to the prescribed insurance sum.[78] 22

---

**74** *Cousy/Van Schoubroeck*, Report: Belgium (fn 2) nos 23 and 47; *Dobiás*, Report: Czech Republic (fn 4) no 22; *Norio-Timonen*, Report: Finland (fn 5) nos 36 and 40; *Koch*, Report: Germany (fn 1) no 13; *Stäubli*, Report: Switzerland (fn 1) no 18; *Rubin*, Report: Austria (fn 3) no 18; *Cerini*, Report: Italy (fn 1) no 33 (sometimes presenting contradictory submissions, however, in no 34); *Gürses*, Report: United Kingdom (fn 7) no 13 f.

**75** Relativising this *Takáts*, Report: Hungary (fn 6) no 13 (equal aim, if at all). Taking a totally opposing view *B Tettamanti/H Bär/J-C Werz*, Compulsory Liability Insurance in a Changing Legal Environment – An Insurance and Reinsurance Perspective (in this book) nos 13 and 20.

**76** *Cousy/Van Schoubroeck*, Report: Belgium (fn 2) no 24; *Koch*, Report: Germany (fn 1) no 13. See likewise *Norio-Timonen*, Report: Finland (fn 5) no 37 f; *Stäubli*, Report: Switzerland (fn 1) no 19; *Takáts*, Report: Hungary (fn 6) no 13 (at least equal aim); *Cerini*, Report: Italy (fn 1) nos 34–37. *Rubin*, Report: Austria (fn 3) no 21. Rejecting this, however, *Dobiás*, Report: Czech Republic (fn 4) no 22.

**77** *Cousy/Van Schoubroeck*, Report: Belgium (fn 2) no 25; *Rubin*, Report: Austria (fn 3) no 22.

**78** *Cousy/Van Schoubroeck*, Report: Belgium (fn 2) no 24.

*c) the protection of the victim and the insurance holder,*

23 It is uniformly assumed that rules on compulsory liability insurance normally protect the insurance holder *in addition to protecting the victim.*[79] It is the exception, on the other hand, that the insurance holder, ie the injuring party, alone should be protected.

*d) other aims, eg internalising the costs in the interests of society?*

24 Another additional goal may be that of *relieving the public burden*, in that the damage arising from a certain risk is allocated to the community of insurance holders (ie potential injuring parties).[80]

25 Ultimately the legislator may also seek to support the *enforceability of strict liability regimes based on dangerousness* by using compulsory liability insurance.[81]

*6. Do the rules that prescribe a form of alternative financial security (see above Question 4.f) pursue the same aims as those rules that exclusively set out a duty to have liability insurance (ie with no other alternative financial security options)?*

26 This is basically affirmed in respect of *Belgium*,[82] *Germany*,[83] *Hungary*,[84] *Austria*[85] and it would seem also *Switzerland*[86] and the *Czech Republic*[87] as well as the *United Kingdom*[88] and *Finland*,[89] but rejected for *Italy*.[90]

---

**79** Cf above the references in fn 76.
**80** Cf *Cousy/Van Schoubroeck*, Report: Belgium (fn 2) no 26; *Koch*, Report: Germany (fn 1) no 14; *Cerini*, Report: Italy (fn 1) no 39. This is considered to be the main aim of compulsory liability insurance from an economic analysis of law perspective; cf *M Faure*, Compulsory Liability Insurance: Economic Perspectives (in this book) no 11. On this see also *D Rubin*, Conclusions (in this book) no 1.
**81** Cf *Cousy/Van Schoubroeck*, Report: Belgium (fn 2) no 27.
**82** *Cousy/Van Schoubroeck*, Report: Belgium (fn 2) no 28.
**83** *Koch*, Report: Germany (fn 1) no 15.
**84** *Takáts*, Report: Hungary (fn 6) no 17.
**85** *Rubin*, Report: Austria (fn 3) no 23.
**86** *Stäubli*, Report: Switzerland (fn 1) nos 22–24.
**87** Cf *Dobiás*, Report: Czech Republic (fn 4) no 26.
**88** Cf *Gürses*, Report: United Kingdom (fn 7) no 19.
**89** *Norio-Timonen*, Report: Finland (fn 5) no 40.
**90** *Cerini*, Report: Italy (fn 1) no 40.

# III. Content of Insurance Cover

7. *Are the duties to take out liability insurance laid down by law only to cover extra-contractual compensation duties or also those arising out of contractual infringements?*

The answer is in the affirmative for *all legal systems* investigated.[91] It is sometimes emphasised that this follows from the fact that, according to the respective legal provisions, only the coverage of claims based on statutory liability is decisive regardless of its contractual or extra-contractual nature.[92] 27

8.a) *Are there duties to take out liability insurance aimed not only at the protection of absolutely protected rights (eg, property, bodily integrity) but additionally at compensating pure economic loss?*

This is affirmed for *Austria*,[93] *Belgium*,[94] the *Czech Republic*,[95] *Finland*,[96] *Germany*,[97] *Switzerland*[98] and it seems also *Italy*;[99] in the *United Kingdom*[100] and apparently in *Hungary*[101] there are no such duties. 28

---

**91** *Rubin*, Report: Austria (fn 3) no 24 f; *Cousy/Van Schoubroeck*, Report: Belgium (fn 2) nos 29 and 31; *Dobiás*, Report: Czech Republic (fn 4) no 27; *Norio-Timonen*, Report: Finland (fn 5) no 41; *Koch*, Report: Germany (fn 1) no 16; likewise *Takáts*, Report: Hungary (fn 6) no 18; *Cerini*, Report: Italy (fn 1) no 41; *Stäubli*, Report: Switzerland (fn 1) no 26; *Gürses*, Report: United Kingdom (fn 7) no 21 (with special terminology for claims/liability in tort).

**92** *Dobiás*, Report: Czech Republic (fn 4) no 27; *Koch*, Report: Germany (fn 1) no 16.

**93** *Rubin*, Report: Austria (fn 3) no 26 f.

**94** *Cousy/Van Schoubroeck*, Report: Belgium (fn 2) no 31 (no distinction in liability law between absolutely protected rights and [pure] economic loss).

**95** Cf *Dobiás*, Report: Czech Republic (fn 4) no 28.

**96** *Norio-Timonen*, Report: Finland (fn 5) no 42.

**97** *Koch*, Report: Germany (fn 1) no 17.

**98** Cf *Stäubli*, Report: Switzerland (fn 1) no 27 f (personal teleological deduction by the author).

**99** Cf *Cerini*, Report: Italy (fn 1) no 46 (not referring to statutory duties but to contractual habits).

**100** *Gürses*, Report: United Kingdom (fn 7) no 22.

**101** Cf *Takáts*, Report: Hungary (fn 6) no 19 (not referring to statutory duties but to contractual habits).

b) *Are there duties to take out liability insurance that are directed only or at least predominantly at the compensation of pure economic loss?*

29 This is affirmed for *all legal systems* in respect of professional indemnity insurance.[102]

9. *Are there provisions that require the insurance of a third party's liability interest – for instance, that the employer must take out liability insurance for the benefit of an employee?*

30 Examples of this type of rule can be found in *almost all legal systems* investigated,[103] in particular for the *liability interest of auxiliaries*, who are deployed by the person under the duty to take out insurance.[104] The situation is *different*, however, in *Hungary*, even in respect of third party liability insurance for motor vehicles.[105]

10. *To what extent do the rules requiring the compulsory conclusion of a liability insurance policy also specify the specific contents of the insurance coverage:*

a) *Is there always a (sufficiently well-defined) specification of the risk to be insured?*

31 There is widespread consensus that the legislator often makes even the requirements for *primary risk specifications* very *vague*.[106] For example, when it

---

**102** *Rubin*, Report: Austria (fn 3) no 28; going further *Cousy/Van Schoubroeck*, Report: Belgium (fn 2) no 31 (no distinction in liability law between consequential and pure economic loss); *Dobiás*, Report: Czech Republic (fn 4) no 29; *Norio-Timonen*, Report: Finland (fn 5) no 43; *Koch*, Report: Germany (fn 1) no 18; *Takáts*, Report: Hungary (fn 6) no 19; *Cerini*, Report: Italy (fn 1) no 47; *Stäubli*, Report: Switzerland (fn 1) no 28 f; *Gürses*, Report: United Kingdom (fn 7) no 23.

**103** *Rubin*, Report: Austria (fn 3) nos 19 f and 30 f; *Cousy/Van Schoubroeck*, Report: Belgium (fn 2) nos 32–38; *Dobiás*, Report: Czech Republic (fn 4) no 30; *Norio-Timonen*, Report: Finland (fn 5) no 44; *Koch*, Report: Germany (fn 1) nos 13 and 19; *Takáts*, Report: Hungary (fn 6) no 19; *Cerini*, Report: Italy (fn 1) no 48; *Stäubli*, Report: Switzerland (fn 1) nos 30–32; *Gürses*, Report: United Kingdom (fn 7) nos 16 f and 24 f.

**104** See on this *Rubin*, Report: Austria (fn 3) no 20; *Cousy/Van Schoubroeck*, Report: Belgium (fn 2) no 37; *Dobiás*, Report: Czech Republic (fn 4) no 30; *Norio-Timonen*, Report: Finland (fn 5) no 44; *Koch*, Report: Germany (fn 1) no 19; *Cerini*, Report: Italy (fn 1) no 48; *Gürses*, Report: United Kingdom (fn 7) nos 17 and 25.

**105** *Takáts*, Report: Hungary (fn 6) no 19.

**106** Cf *Rubin*, Report: Austria (fn 3) nos 33 f and 37; *Cousy/Van Schoubroeck*, Report: Belgium (fn 2) nos 39–41 (tendency for recent legal prescriptions to be more detailed and explicit); *Do-*

comes to professional indemnity insurance, lawmakers have a strong tendency to solely prescribe the duty to take out insurance to cover compensation claims arising out of the profession in question, without further clarification.[107] The case is *different* in *Finland* in respect of so-called 'statutory insurance'.[108]

### b) *Are there provisions that require unlimited coverage?*

Such very sweeping duties to insure are *not* found in the legal systems investigated.[109] *Exceptions* exist only in *Belgium* within the context of motor vehicle liability insurance for bodily injury,[110] and in *Finland* for the operators of nuclear power plants.[111] 32

### c) *If unlimited coverage is not required (see above Question b), is a minimum or maximum insurance sum always specified?*

*Minimum insurance* sums are a *widespread* tool used by the legislator whereas maximum insurance sums are not to be found.[112] Sometimes the laws on compulsory liability insurance do *not* specify *any limitations* of the insurance duty[113] or they only very *vaguely describe* the scope of the duty to insure. This is exemplified by formulations such as 'sufficient', 'adequate' or 'reasonable coverage' or 'coverage taking into account the risks of ...'.[114] In some legal systems the 33

*biás*, Report: Czech Republic (fn 4) no 31; *Norio-Timonen*, Report: Finland (fn 5) no 46; *Takáts*, Report: Hungary (fn 6) no 22; along these lines see also *Stäubli*, Report: Switzerland (fn 1) no 33f; likewise *Gürses*, Report: United Kingdom (fn 7) no 26; likewise *Cerini*, Report: Italy (fn 1) no 51f (however, taking the opposite view on the topic, but without references, in no 49).

**107** Cf *Rubin*, Report: Austria (fn 3) no 34; *Koch*, Report: Germany (fn 1) no 20.

**108** *Norio-Timonen*, Report: Finland (fn 5) nos 1 and 45.

**109** Cf *Rubin*, Report: Austria (fn 3) no 35; *Cousy/Van Schoubroeck*, Report: Belgium (fn 2) no 43; *Dobiás*, Report: Czech Republic (fn 4) no 32; *Koch*, Report: Germany (fn 1) no 21; *Takáts*, Report: Hungary (fn 6) no 23; *Cerini*, Report: Italy (fn 1) no 53; *Stäubli*, Report: Switzerland (fn 1) no 35; see also *Gürses*, Report: United Kingdom (fn 7) nos 28–30.

**110** *Cousy/Van Schoubroeck*, Report: Belgium (fn 2) no 43.

**111** *Norio-Timonen*, Report: Finland (fn 5) no 47.

**112** Cf *Rubin*, Report: Austria (fn 3) nos 36–38; *Dobiás*, Report: Czech Republic (fn 4) no 33; *Norio-Timonen*, Report: Finland (fn 5) no 48; *Koch*, Report: Germany (fn 1) no 22; *Takáts*, Report: Hungary (fn 6) no 24 (minimum insurance: approx 50% of cases); *Stäubli*, Report: Switzerland (fn 1) no 36; *Gürses*, Report: United Kingdom (fn 7) nos 28–30; leaving this open *Cerini*, Report: Italy (fn 1) no 54 ('not always').

**113** Cf *Dobiás*, Report: Czech Republic (fn 4) no 34; *Cerini*, Report: Italy (fn 1) no 54.

**114** For examples cf *Stäubli*, Report: Switzerland (fn 1) nos 14 (fn 11 f), 34, 36f, 42; *Rubin*, Report: Austria (fn 3) no 37f; *Koch*, Report: Germany (fn 1) no 22; *Gürses*, Report: United Kingdom (fn 7) no 34.

scope of the insurance duty is even predominantly limited in this latter fashion.[115]

d) *Are there general statutory rules to be applicable if the respective law that requires compulsory insurance only makes incomplete stipulations regarding the content of the insurance coverage? An example of this would be § 114 para 1 of the German Insurance Contract Act (Versicherungsvertragsgesetz, VVG) 2008.*

34 *No such rules* can be found within the legal orders that took part in this study, other than in *Germany.*[116]

11. *Is it admissible to restrict the insurance cover by agreeing:*

a) *risk exclusion clauses,*

35 Above all, in relation to *compulsory motor vehicle liability insurance*, there are rules that set out which risk exclusion clauses are admissible.[117] In *other cases of compulsory liability insurance*, however, the legislator only *seldom* explicitly addresses to what extent risk exclusion clauses are admissible.[118] Nevertheless, it is *predominantly assumed* – and in *Germany* even ruled by law (§ 114 para 2 sent 1 VVG 2008)[119] – that such clauses are allowed as long as they do *not undermine the scope of the respective duty* to take out liability insurance.[120] In general there is no *distinction* explicitly made by law between the insurer's internal

**115** Cf eg *Cousy/Van Schoubroeck*, Report: Belgium (fn 2) no 44.
**116** Cf *Rubin*, Report: Austria (fn 3) no 39; *Cousy/Van Schoubroeck*, Report: Belgium (fn 2) no 45; *Dobiás*, Report: Czech Republic (fn 4) no 35; *Takáts*, Report: Hungary (fn 6) no 25; *Cerini*, Report: Italy (fn 1) no 55; *Stäubli*, Report: Switzerland (fn 1) no 38; *Gürses*, Report: United Kingdom (fn 7) no 31.
**117** Cf *Rubin*, Report: Austria (fn 3) no 40; *Dobiás*, Report: Czech Republic (fn 4) no 36; *Koch*, Report: Germany (fn 1) no 26; *Stäubli*, Report: Switzerland (fn 1) no 40; *Gürses*, Report: United Kingdom (fn 7) no 33. No explicit statements on this for Belgium, Finland, Hungary, Italy.
**118** Cf *Rubin*, Report: Austria (fn 3) no 40; *Cousy/Van Schoubroeck*, Report: Belgium (fn 2) no 46; *Takáts*, Report: Hungary (fn 6) no 26; *Stäubli*, Report: Switzerland (fn 1) no 38. For examples of these provisions cf *Rubin*, Report: Austria (fn 3) no 40; *Dobiás*, Report: Czech Republic (fn 4) nos 36 and 40; *Norio-Timonen*, Report: Finland (fn 5) no 50; *Koch*, Report: Germany (fn 1) nos 26–28; *Stäubli*, Report: Switzerland (fn 1) no 39; *Gürses*, Report: United Kingdom (fn 7) nos 32–34 and 41.
**119** Cf *Koch*, Report: Germany (fn 1) no 24.
**120** Cf *Rubin*, Report: Austria (fn 3) no 41; *Takáts*, Report: Hungary (fn 6) no 26; *Cerini*, Report: Italy (fn 1) no 56; *Stäubli*, Report: Switzerland (fn 1) no 39.

relationship to the insured party and the external relationship of the insurer to the injured.[121] Notwithstanding this, it is certainly often the case that the *relationship to the injured party* is primarily considered when assessing whether a certain risk exclusion clause jeopardises the purpose of the compulsory liability insurance provision in question (on the purpose of compulsory liability insurance cf above no 21ff).[122] It is also *sometimes* argued that risk exclusion clauses, in order to be admissible, have to be allowed by *special legal provisions.*[123]

*b) deductibles,*

36 With the *exception of Switzerland,*[124] there are *sectoral laws* in the legal systems investigated that include rules on the amount and thus the admissibility of deductibles.[125] In *German law* there is even a *general rule* (§ 114 para 2 sent 2 VVG): The insurer *cannot* invoke deductibles *against the victim at all.* They are likewise prohibited in the relationship to a *co-insured* person if a duty to co-insure that person exists.[126]

37 If there is no statutory rule on deductibles, the admissibility of such will basically be examined on the basis of *the same principles* as *risk exclusion clauses* (see above no 35).[127] Above all in *Austria* this applies only in relation to the *insurance holder* as deductibles are not effective in relation to the *victim.*[128]

38 For an examination of deductibles as a means of *reducing moral hazard* within liability insurance contracts cf the special reports by Faure and Tettamanti/Bär/Werz.[129]

**121** Cf *Rubin*, Report: Austria (fn 3) no 41; *Koch*, Report: Germany (fn 1) nos 24 and 28.
**122** Cf *Koch*, Report: Germany (fn 1) no 24.
**123** Cf *Dobiás*, Report: Czech Republic (fn 4) no 36.
**124** *Stäubli*, Report: Switzerland (fn 1) no 41. Leaving this open *Cousy/Van Schoubroeck*, Report: Belgium (fn 2) no 46.
**125** Cf *Rubin*, Report: Austria (fn 3) no 42; *Dobiás*, Report: Czech Republic (fn 4) no 37; *Norio-Timonen*, Report: Finland (fn 5) no 51; *Koch*, Report: Germany (fn 1) no 30; *Takáts*, Report: Hungary (fn 6) no 27; *Cerini*, Report: Italy (fn 1) no 57; *Gürses*, Report: United Kingdom (fn 7) nos 35–38.
**126** Cf *Koch*, Report: Germany (fn 1) no 29.
**127** Cf *Cousy/Van Schoubroeck*, Report: Belgium (fn 2) no 46; *Dobiás*, Report: Czech Republic (fn 4) no 37; *Norio-Timonen*, Report: Finland (fn 5) no 51; *Koch*, Report: Germany (fn 1) no 31; *Takáts*, Report: Hungary (fn 6) no 27; *Cerini*, Report: Italy (fn 1) no 57; *Stäubli*, Report: Switzerland (fn 1) no 41. *Gürses*, Report: United Kingdom (fn 7) nos 32–34.
**128** Cf *Rubin*, Report: Austria (fn 3) no 42. The same is also assumed in respect of Switzerland in some selected cases; cf *Stäubli*, Report: Switzerland (fn 1) no 41.
**129** See *Faure* (fn 80) no 31; *Tettamanti/Bär/Werz* (fn 75) nos 9 and 44.

### c) *aggregate limits,*

39 In some of the jurisdictions investigated, there are also *sectoral laws*, which lay down that aggregate limits in the insurance contract must have a *certain minimum threshold*.[130] *German law* has a *general rule* that, unless otherwise specified by a provision requiring compulsory liability insurance, the minimum sum insured shall be € 1 million for all claims per insurance year (§ 114 para 1 VVG).[131] If there are no express statutory rules, aggregate limits are – as is the case for deductibles (see above no 37) – basically treated like risk exclusion clauses.[132] Regarding the United Kingdom, see also below no 42.

40 As for the technical function of aggregate limits cf the special report by Tettamanti/Bär/Werz.[133]

### d) *claims series clauses,*

41 The admissibility of such is only explicitly regulated in *Germany*[134] and the *Czech Republic*.[135] Otherwise, where *regulation is absent*, claim series clauses are also judged according to essentially the same criteria as risk exclusion clauses (above no 35),[136] insofar as they are dealt with at all.[137]

---

**130** Cf *Rubin*, Report: Austria (fn 3) no 43; *Norio-Timonen*, Report: Finland (fn 5) no 52; *Koch*, Report: Germany (fn 1) no 32; *Takáts*, Report: Hungary (fn 6) no 28; *Cerini*, Report: Italy (fn 1) no 58 (motor liability insurance: solely protection of the injured); *Gürses*, Report: United Kingdom (fn 7) no 39.

**131** Cf *Koch*, Report: Germany (fn 1) no 32.

**132** Cf *Rubin*, Report: Austria (fn 3) no 43; *Cousy/Van Schoubroeck*, Report: Belgium (fn 2) no 46; *Dobiás*, Report: Czech Republic (fn 4) no 38; *Norio-Timonen*, Report: Finland (fn 5) no 52; *Koch*, Report: Germany (fn 1) no 30; *Takáts*, Report: Hungary (fn 6) no 28. This would also appear to be the position of *Gürses*, Report: United Kingdom (fn 7) no 39. Leaving this open *Stäubli*, Report: Switzerland (fn 1) no 42.

**133** See *Tettamanti/Bär/Werz* (fn 75) nos 9, 12, 45, 47 f.

**134** *Koch*, Report: Germany (fn 1) nos 33–35.

**135** *Dobiás*, Report: Czech Republic (fn 4) no 39.

**136** Cf *Rubin*, Report: Austria (fn 3) no 44; *Cousy/Van Schoubroeck*, Report: Belgium (fn 2) no 46; *Norio-Timonen*, Report: Finland (fn 5) no 53; *Koch*, Report: Germany (fn 1) no 35; *Takáts*, Report: Hungary (fn 6) no 29; *Cerini*, Report: Italy (fn 1) no 59; *Stäubli*, Report: Switzerland (fn 1) no 42.

**137** This is not the case in the United Kingdom, cf *Gürses*, Report: United Kingdom (fn 7) no 40.

*e) other clauses?*

Under *Austrian law*[138] there are provisions stipulating compulsory liability insurance that deal with *subsequent coverage* of *long-tail claims*: These provisions prohibit contractual limitations of subsequent coverage or set out a minimum period for such.[139] *German* literature considers these clauses to a large extent to be void.[140] *Italian* literature also looks at this subject.[141] Case law in the *United Kingdom*, albeit criticised by academic literature, holds that, once the insurance contract has expired, *commutation agreements* on reduced aggregate limits during the period of subsequent coverage are valid.[142] **42**

The admissibility of clauses in insurance contracts that *limit* the insurance cover in *other manners* is also assessed basically according to the *same principles* as *risk exclusion clauses* (see above no 35).[143] **43**

12. *What are the consequences if the liability insurance contract concluded in order to fulfil the insurance obligation contravenes what the law stipulates as to contents (see above Questions 10 and 11)?*

In all legal systems investigated there are no *uniform legal consequences* explicitly prescribed by law which would apply every time when liability insurance is taken out. **44**

Nevertheless, the *rules* prescribing compulsory liability insurance are necessarily *mandatory*.[144] Therefore, contractual clauses deviating from these rules are *void*.[145] In the case of an inadmissible *restriction of the insurance cover* this means either that – for instance, according to *Austrian law* – the relevant contractual clause is void only to the extent of its deviation while the remainder of **45**

**138** *Rubin*, Report: Austria (fn 3) no 45.
**139** *Rubin*, Report: Austria (fn 3) no 45.
**140** *Koch*, Report: Germany (fn 1) no 36.
**141** Cf *Cerini*, Report: Italy (fn 1) no 62 f.
**142** Cf *Gürses*, Report: United Kingdom (fn 7) no 42.
**143** Cf *Cousy/Van Schoubroeck*, Report: Belgium (fn 2) no 46; *Dobiás*, Report: Czech Republic (fn 4) no 40; *Norio-Timonen*, Report: Finland (fn 5) no 54; *Takáts*, Report: Hungary (fn 6) no 30; *Stäubli*, Report: Switzerland (fn 1) no 44.
**144** *Cousy/Van Schoubroeck*, Report: Belgium (fn 2) no 47; *Koch*, Report: Germany (fn 1) no 37; also cf *Dobiás*, Report: Czech Republic (fn 4) nos 36–40.
**145** Cf *Rubin*, Report: Austria (fn 3) no 46; *Cousy/Van Schoubroeck*, Report: Belgium (fn 2) no 47; *Koch*, Report: Germany (fn 1) no 37; *Dobiás*, Report: Czech Republic (fn 4) no 41; *Norio-Timonen*, Report: Finland (fn 5) no 55; *Cerini*, Report: Italy (fn 1) no 64. As for motor vehicle liability insurance in the United Kingdom cf *Gürses*, Report: United Kingdom (fn 7) no 43.

the clause stays in force,[146] or – as according to *German law* – the deviating contractual clause is entirely void and must be replaced by applicable mandatory provisions.[147] This difference is in fact a mere question of dogmatic construction, the result being virtually the same in both cases. More difficult to solve is the question of how to deal with contractual clauses that, already on the level of *(primary) risk description*, provide for inadmissibly *short cover* (such as with an agreement on an insurance sum that is too low): in this case *Belgium law* also completes the contractual clause with the respective legal provision on compulsory liability insurance.[148] The same solution seems to be possible under *German law*[149] as well as under *Austrian law*. *Finnish law*, on the other hand, provides a similar solution already on the grounds of an *interpretation* of the insurance contract.[150]

46 As for the *consequences* within *public law* (such as administrative penalties; a ban on carrying out the respective activity), cf below no 119.

*13.a) Are statutory stipulations as to the contents of the policy (eg, regarding the amount of the insurance sum, the ban on certain risk exclusion clauses, on deductibles, etc, see above Questions 10 and 11) also binding in favour of the insurance holder? Or is it nonetheless possible for the liability insurer and the insurance holder acting within their internal relationship to agree risk exclusion clauses, deductibles, aggregate limits, and claims series clauses, etc (see above Questions 10 and 11), releasing the insurer from its liability to pay?*

47 For the *majority of legal orders* taking part in this study it is assumed that statutory stipulations prohibiting contractual clauses restricting the insurance are also *binding* in favour of the insurance holder. Therefore, these clauses are *also prohibited within the internal relationship* between the insurer and the insurance holder.[151] It ought to be stressed that the contrary is the case in *Ger-*

146 *Rubin*, Report: Austria (fn 3) no 46.

147 *Koch*, Report: Germany (fn 1) no 37. As for Italy, the question as to which of the two solutions would be adopted is left open; cf *Cerini*, Report: Italy (fn 1) no 64.

148 *Cousy/Van Schoubroeck*, Report: Belgium (fn 2) nos 48–50; but, on the other hand, also cf ibid no 64 ('The non-opposability however does not extend to defences that are based on ... the exceeding of the scope of the cover').

149 Cf *Koch*, Report: Germany (fn 1) no 37.

150 Cf *Norio-Timonen*, Report: Finland (fn 5) no 56.

151 *Cousy/Van Schoubroeck*, Report: Belgium (fn 2) no 50; *Dobiás*, Report: Czech Republic (fn 4) no 42 (with unclear argumentation); *Norio-Timonen*, Report: Finland (fn 5) no 57 (answer for statutory rules in the specific sense of ibid no 1); likewise as it seems *Takáts*, Report: Hungary (fn 6) no 32. Leaving this open *Cerini*, Report: Italy (fn 1) no 65 f.

*many*[152] and *Austria,*[153] as well as partly in *Belgium* (only as far as deductibles are concerned),[154] the *United Kingdom* (motor vehicle liability insurance and employers' liability insurance)[155] and *Switzerland* (motor vehicle liability insurance[156] and the respective liability insurances of keepers of nuclear plants or nuclear material, of pipeline owners, hunters, keepers of ships and of conductors of clinical research on humans[157]).

b) *If it is possible for liability insurer and insurance holder acting within their internal relationship to agree a release from the obligation to pay (see above Question a): What consequences does this entail? Must the insurer first pay out to the victim and can then have recourse to the insurance holder? Or is another construction provided for the relationship between insurer, insurance holder and victim?*

This question is *not relevant* for most of the legal orders subject to this study since they do not draw a distinction between the external and internal relationship (cf above no 47).[158] **48**

The situation is different for *Germany* and *Austria*: if the insurer was able to refuse its obligation to provide insurance cover within the internal relationship to the insurance holder but not in the external relationship to the third-party victim (cf above no 47), then it may have *recourse to the insurance holder* as soon as he has paid out the insurance sum to the third party.[159] This solution is also applied in the above-mentioned cases (see no 47) in *Belgium,*[160] in the *United Kingdom* (motor liability insurance, employers' liability insurance)[161] and *Switzerland* (motor liability insurance and the respective liability insurances of **49**

**152** *Koch*, Report: Germany (fn 1) no 38.
**153** *Rubin*, Report: Austria (fn 3) no 47.
**154** *Cousy/Van Schoubroeck*, Report: Belgium (fn 2) no 63f; whereas for the general rule see above fn 151.
**155** Cf *Gürses*, Report: United Kingdom (fn 7) no 44.
**156** *Stäubli*, Report: Switzerland (fn 1) no 48f.
**157** Cf *Stäubli*, Report: Switzerland (fn 1) no 68.
**158** *Cousy/Van Schoubroeck*, Report: Belgium (fn 2) no 51; *Dobiás*, Report: Czech Republic (fn 4) no 43; *Norio-Timonen*, Report: Finland (fn 5) no 58; not going into this *Takáts*, Report: Hungary (fn 6) no 33. On Italy see (leaving this open) *Cerini*, Report: Italy (fn 1) no 67.
**159** Cf *Koch*, Report: Germany (fn 1) no 39f; *Rubin*, Report: Austria (fn 3) no 48.
**160** *Cousy/Van Schoubroeck*, Report: Belgium (fn 2) no 64.
**161** Cf *Gürses*, Report: United Kingdom (fn 7) no 44.

keepers of nuclear plants or nuclear material, of pipeline owners, hunters, keepers of ships and of conductors of clinical research on humans[162]).

*14.a) Does the general (voluntary) liability insurance law include a statutory risk exclusion in respect of intentional damage by the insurance holder or the insured person?*

50 Most of the legal orders in the study prescribe by law a *subjective risk exclusion* in this case.[163] The rule is *ius cogens* in some legal orders,[164] in others not.[165] For this risk exclusion, even *dolus eventualis* is sufficient in some legal orders.[166]

51 If, for example, *only the (co-)insured* acted intentionally, but not the insurance holder, the risk exclusion would only apply to the (co-)insured (and vice versa if there was intention solely on the insurance holder's side).[167] This is relevant especially if the insurance holder is vicariously liable for the (co-)insured's acts.[168]

52 According to *Hungarian*[169] and *Czech law*,[170] on the other hand, there is no such *statutory* risk exclusion, so that it is up to the insurance companies to set up a corresponding exclusion clause by contract.

53 *Swiss law* even allows a proportional reduction of the insurance payment in the case of damage caused with *gross negligence*. This provision (art 14 para 2 VVG) may be varied by agreement between the parties and thus may theoretically be made more stringent at the expense of the insurance holder in insurance contracts.[171]

---

**162** See art 65 para 3 SVG (Road Traffic Act); cf *Stäubli*, Report: Switzerland (fn 1) no 50f; as for the other examples mentioned cf ibid no 67f.

**163** *Rubin*, Report: Austria (fn 3) no 49; *Cousy/Van Schoubroeck*, Report: Belgium (fn 2) no 52 (with the exception of minors below a certain age); *Norio-Timonen*, Report: Finland (fn 5) no 59; *Koch*, Report: Germany (fn 1) no 41; *Cerini*, Report: Italy (fn 1) no 68; *Stäubli*, Report: Switzerland (fn 1) no 52; *Gürses*, Report: United Kingdom (fn 7) no 47.

**164** Cf *Cousy/Van Schoubroeck*, Report: Belgium (fn 2) no 52.

**165** *Norio-Timonen*, Report: Finland (fn 5) no 59.

**166** *Rubin*, Report: Austria (fn 3) no 49. More strictly, on the other hand, *Cousy/Van Schoubroeck*, Report: Belgium (fn 2) no 52. This is not the case for Swiss law, cf *Stäubli*, Report: Switzerland (fn 1) no 52.

**167** *Rubin*, Report: Austria (fn 3) no 49; *Cousy/Van Schoubroeck*, Report: Belgium (fn 2) no 52.

**168** Cf *Cousy/Van Schoubroeck*, Report: Belgium (fn 2) no 53.

**169** *Takáts*, Report: Hungary (fn 6) no 34.

**170** Cf *Dobiás*, Report: Czech Republic (fn 4) no 44.

**171** *Stäubli*, Report: Switzerland (fn 1) no 52.

b) *If the general liability insurance law contains a statutory risk exclusion in respect of intentional damage inflicted by the insurance holder (see above Question a): Does this also apply in cases of compulsory liability insurance?*

It does in the majority of the legal orders so that it also *applies* in the insurer's relationship to the *victim*.[172] 54

Under *Belgian*[173] and *Czech law*[174] the insurer is *not allowed* to invoke against the *injured party* the defence that the damage was intentionally caused by the insurance holder. In such a case the insurer can initiate a *recourse* action against the latter.[175] 55

In *Switzerland* said rule on the *mandatory inclusion* of intentionally caused damage in relation to the victim applies in motor liability insurance[176] and in the liability insurance of keepers of nuclear plants or nuclear material, of pipeline owners, hunters, keepers of ships and of conductors of clinical research on humans.[177] The proportional reduction of cover in the case of gross negligence (see above no 53) is likewise prohibited in respect of such insurance.[178] In *Hungary* the rule on mandatory inclusion of intentionally caused damage in relation to the injured party only applies in *motor liability insurance*.[179] It would seem that the same applies for *Italy*.[180] In the *United Kingdom* there is mandatory inclusion of the risk of intentionally caused damage in respect of employers' liability.[181] 56

**172** *Rubin*, Report: Austria (fn 3) no 49; *Norio-Timonen*, Report: Finland (fn 5) no 60; *Koch*, Report: Germany (fn 1) no 42; *Cerini*, Report: Italy (fn 1) no 70; *Stäubli*, Report: Switzerland (fn 1) no 53; *Gürses*, Report: United Kingdom (fn 7) no 48.
**173** *Cousy/Van Schoubroeck*, Report: Belgium (fn 2) no 54.
**174** *Dobiás*, Report: Czech Republic (fn 4) no 44.
**175** *Cousy/Van Schoubroeck*, Report: Belgium (fn 2) no 54.
**176** *Stäubli*, Report: Switzerland (fn 1) no 53.
**177** *Stäubli*, Report: Switzerland (fn 1) nos 53 and 67 f.
**178** *Stäubli*, ibid.
**179** *Takáts*, Report: Hungary (fn 6) no 34 f.
**180** *Cerini*, Report: Italy (fn 1) nos 69 and 71.
**181** *Gürses*, Report: United Kingdom (fn 7) no 48.

# IV. Protection Mechanisms

*15. Are insurers obliged to contract when they offer liability insurance policies covering a risk for which the insurance holder is obliged to obtain cover?*

57 In all legal orders in this study, insurers offering compulsory liability insurance policies enjoy *freedom to contract* in principle,[182] with the *exception* being *motor liability insurance* in the *vast majority* of jurisdictions[183] *apart from Belgium* (see also below no 59),[184] *Switzerland*[185] and the *United Kingdom*.[186] These legal orders grant full freedom to underwrite even in the case of motor liability insurance.

58 Only *Finnish law* provides for exceptions from the freedom to contract not only for motor liability insurance but also for all other cases of so-called *statutory liability* insurance (above no 7).[187] Moreover, it is pointed out that, notwithstanding, in all cases of *compulsory insurance* (above no 7), the insurer must act in accordance with *good insurance practice*. The consequence of this is that the insurer has to have an acceptable reason for not contracting,[188] which, so it is emphasised by legal doctrine, can be argued to accomplish the same result as an obligation to contract with appropriate exceptions.[189]

*16. If there is no obligation to contract: Are there comparable mechanisms provided to ensure that an insurance agreement is concluded?*

59 There is a mechanism under *Belgian law* in respect of *motor vehicle liability insurance*, which certainly comes close to an obligation to contract.[190] In the other legal systems of the study, however, there are no comparable mechanisms.[191]

---

**182** *Rubin*, Report: Austria (fn 3) no 51 f; *Cousy/Van Schoubroeck*, Report: Belgium (fn 2) no 56; *Dobiás*, Report: Czech Republic (fn 4) no 46; *Norio-Timonen*, Report: Finland (fn 5) no 61; *Koch*, Report: Germany (fn 1) no 43; *Takáts*, Report: Hungary (fn 6) no 36; *Cerini*, Report: Italy (fn 1) no 72.

**183** *Rubin*, Report: Austria (fn 3) no 51; *Dobiás*, Report: Czech Republic (fn 4) no 47; *Koch*, Report: Germany (fn 1) no 43; *Takáts*, Report: Hungary (fn 6) no 36; *Cerini*, Report: Italy (fn 1) nos 72–76.

**184** Cf *Cousy/Van Schoubroeck*, Report: Belgium (fn 2) no 56.

**185** *Stäubli*, Report: Switzerland (fn 1) no 54.

**186** *Gürses*, Report: United Kingdom (fn 7) no 49.

**187** *Norio-Timonen*, Report: Finland (fn 5) no 61.

**188** *Norio-Timonen*, Report: Finland (fn 5) no 62.

**189** *Norio-Timonen*, Report: Finland (fn 5) no 63.

**190** *Cousy/Van Schoubroeck*, Report: Belgium (fn 2) no 57 f.

**191** *Dobiás*, Report: Czech Republic (fn 4) no 48; *Koch*, Report: Germany (fn 1) no 44; *Takáts*, Report: Hungary (fn 6) no 37; *Cerini*, Report: Italy (fn 1) no 77; *Stäubli*, Report: Switzerland

*17. Is the insurance holder prohibited from disposing over his cover entitlement to the disadvantage of the victim (eg, by surrendering his entitlement)?*

*German* and *Austrian law* each contain an (identical) regulation applicable both for voluntary and compulsory insurance *explicitly* ruling that dispositions by the insurance holder over his claim against the insurer are *ineffective* vis-à-vis the victim.[192] Such dispositions include, for example, the alteration, transfer, encumbrance or forfeiture of the claim.[193] From this rule, it thus follows that only paying the insurance sum to the victim can have the effect of discharging the insurer from its duty to perform.[194] *Swiss law* achieves the same effect (also for voluntary and compulsory insurance) by way of the victim's right of lien on the claim of the insurance holder against the insurer.[195] 60

*Belgian law* prohibits, according to legal doctrine, the insurance holder from disposing over his claim to the detriment of the victim – the reason being that the claim provides the victim with a separate right (*ius proprium*) and therefore a *direct action* against the insurer both for voluntary and compulsory insurance.[196] The same answer can, so it seems, be given for *Finnish law* as far as *compulsory liability insurance* is concerned.[197] The above opinion on *Belgium* is, in my view, supported by the fact that the Belgian Insurance Act, even as far as voluntary liability insurance is concerned, allows the insurer in its relationship to the victim only to rely upon defences having their cause in an *act occurring prior to the insured event.*[198] On this see below no 82. 61

Legal doctrine answers the question of whether the insurance holder is prohibited from disposing over his insurance claim under *Italian law* in the positive, too. This can be inferred from the fact that the insurer is obliged to pay the victim first (before all creditors).[199] As for the *United Kingdom*, legal doctrine in principle seems to answer this question in the positive as well, although not for all compulsory insurance but for motor vehicle, employers' liability and profes- 62

(fn 1) no 56; *Gürses*, Report: United Kingdom (fn 7) no 50. As for Finland see above no 58 (duty to comply with 'good insurance practice' [*Norio-Timonen*, Report: Finland (fn 5) nos 62–64]).

**192** *Koch*, Report: Germany (fn 1) no 45; *Rubin*, Report: Austria (fn 3) no 53.

**193** *Koch*, Report: Germany (fn 1) no 45.

**194** *Rubin*, Report: Austria (fn 3) no 53; *Koch*, Report: Germany (fn 1) no 45. Only if the insurance holder has already done so does the insurer have to pay the compensation to him; see below no 77.

**195** Cf *Stäubli*, Report: Switzerland (fn 1) no 57.

**196** *Cousy/Van Schoubroeck*, Report: Belgium (fn 2) nos 59 and 61f.

**197** *Norio-Timonen*, Report: Finland (fn 5) no 65.

**198** *Cousy/Van Schoubroeck*, Report: Belgium (fn 2) nos 8, 52, 65.

**199** *Cerini*, Report: Italy (fn 1) no 78.

sional indemnity insurance.[200] *Czech law* in turn explicitly forbids contractual dispositions over the claim by the parties to the insurance contract once the insured event has taken place.[201]

63 Legal doctrine answers the question in the negative for *Hungary*.[202]

*18. Does the victim enjoy special protection against insolvency on the part of the insurance holder with regard to the sum payable by the liability insurer?*

64 Legal doctrine states that there is no *need* for this kind of protection if the victim is invested with a *direct right of action* against the insurer.[203] That is especially true under *Belgian law* which has implemented the direct action in both voluntary and compulsory insurance.[204] It should be noted that one could also, by looking at cause and effect from the opposite side, understand the direct action as a possible tool that has, among others, been provided by the legislator to grant the victim protection from the insurance holder's insolvency. This view is adopted by the law of the *United Kingdom* where a right of direct action for the victim is foreseen in the case of the insurance holder's insolvency in all forms of liability insurance (see below no 74 in conjunction with no 66).[205] The same applies in *Germany*, albeit only for compulsory liability insurance (also below no 74). On the scope of the direct action (this still being rather the exception within the different legal orders of this study) in general see below no 71ff.

65 In some legal orders the victim is protected against the insolvency of the damaging party separately from a direct action against the insurer (on this see below no 69). Thus, under *Swiss law* (*right of lien*) as well as under *Austrian* and *German law*, the victim is granted a *right to separate satisfaction* out of the insurance holder's claim against the insurer to be released from liability towards the victim.[206]

66 Moreover, *German law* additionally *ex lege transfers* to *and vests* in the injured party the insolvent injuring party's entitlement to cover from the insurer

**200** *Gürses*, Report: United Kingdom (fn 7) no 51 referring to no 44.
**201** *Dobiás*, Report: Czech Republic (fn 4) no 49 (with a lack of clarity regarding all other liability insurances).
**202** *Takáts*, Report: Hungary (fn 6) no 38.
**203** *Cousy/Van Schoubroeck*, Report: Belgium (fn 2) no 61; *Dobiás*, Report: Czech Republic (fn 4) no 50; *Koch*, Report: Germany (fn 1) no 46; *Norio-Timonen*, Report: Finland (fn 5) no 66.
**204** Cf *Cousy/Van Schoubroeck*, Report: Belgium (fn 2) no 61.
**205** *Gürses*, Report: United Kingdom (fn 7) no 52.
**206** *Stäubli*, Report: Switzerland (fn 1) no 58; *Rubin*, Report: Austria (fn 3) no 54; *Koch*, Report: Germany (fn 1) no 47; on this see also *Rubin*, Conclusions (fn 80) no 25.

without order of attachment and transfer.[207] The same rule exists under *United Kingdom law* even for voluntary liability insurance.[208] *German literature* infers this legal consequence for all forms of liability insurance (by analogy to § 1282 BGB) from the victim's right to separate satisfaction against the insurer under the condition that, prior to the opening of the insolvency proceedings, the victim's claim against the insurance holder had been established with binding effect vis-à-vis the insurer.[209]

*Italian law* as well, as a rule, seems to protect the victim against the insolvency of the insurance holder both in respect of voluntary and compulsory insurance.[210] This also applies, within limits, to *Hungarian law* where the insolvency of the insured party would (only) be devoid of effect on the payment of the claim if the insolvency is declared after the claim was filed.[211] **67**

*19.a) In what manner can the victim obtain the insurance payment?*

As far as procedural economy is concerned, the most efficient way to give the victim access to the insurance payment is by means of a *direct action* against the insurer;[212] for the scope of this action see below no 71 ff. **68**

Where no direct action is provided, the victim's access to the injuring party's cover claim from the liability insurer is, as a rule, subject to the *general rules* of the law of obligations and of debt and enforcement law: The insurance holder might *assign* to the victim his claim against the insurer to be released from liability. Otherwise the victim has to obtain an *order of attachment and transfer* of the insurance holder's claim.[213] As for the *exception* to this rule under German and United Kingdom law in the case of the injuring party's *insolvency*, see above no 66. **69**

**207** *Koch*, Report: Germany (fn 1) no 47.
**208** *Gürses*, Report: United Kingdom (fn 7) no 52.
**209** *Koch*, Report: Germany (fn 1) no 47.
**210** Cf *Cerini*, Report: Italy (fn 1) no 79 f (though lacking clarity by indicating that the victim enjoys greater protection against the insolvency of the insurance holder if the insurance benefit has been paid to the insurance holder compared to the insurer holding it back for direct payment to the victim).
**211** Cf *Takáts*, Report: Hungary (fn 6) no 39.
**212** Recital 30 of the Directive on Motor Vehicle Liability Insurance (2009/103/EC) (on this Directive see below fn 227); also cf *Cousy/Van Schoubroeck*, Report: Belgium (fn 2) no 62; *Norio-Timonen*, Report: Finland (fn 5) nos 66 and 69; *Gürses*, Report: United Kingdom (fn 7) no 54.
**213** *Koch*, Report: Germany (fn 1) no 48 (also referring to an order of attachment and transfer with further examples); cf also *Rubin*, Report: Austria (fn 3) no 55; *Stäubli*, Report: Switzerland (fn 1) nos 59 and 62; *Gürses*, Report: United Kingdom (fn 7) no 54.

70 Finally, the *Swiss law's particularity* of the victim's *right of lien* on the insurance holder's claim against the insurer must be mentioned.[214]

### b) *Does the victim have a direct right of action against the liability insurer (action directe) in the case of voluntary or compulsory liability insurance?*

71 A direct action of the victim against the injuring party's liability insurer does not derive from the general civil law rules and therefore needs to be granted to the victim by special (insurance law) rules.[215] Such rules can be identified in each legal order, albeit to a very different extent. In any case, a direct action against the insurer is factually still rather the exception.[216] According to prevailing opinion, a direct action creates a *joint obligation* between injuring party and insurer.[217]

72 Hence, the victim is rarely vested with a direct action against the insurer as a general measure in both *voluntary* and *compulsory liability insurance*. Such a constellation is only to be found in *Belgian law* where the direct action is a procedural consequence of the victim's substantive individual right against the insurer.[218] As for the conditions for this action, see below no 82.

73 Apart from this, only *Finnish law* orders a direct action even for *voluntary* insurance – and even then only in two specific cases: One is when (general) liability insurance is mentioned in *marketing efforts* launched to promote the insurance holder's business.[219] The other example being the *insolvency* of the insurance holder (on this, see the following no 74).

74 On a rather general level, the victim can, under *Finnish law*, file a direct action in *all cases of compulsory* liability insurance.[220] Moreover, the victim has protection *in compulsory* as well *in voluntary* liability insurance against the *injuring party's insolvency* by way of a direct action against the liability insurer (once the insolvency proceedings over the injuring party's assets are opened).[221]

---

**214** Cf *Stäubli*, Report: Switzerland (fn 1) no 61 f.
**215** Cf eg *Cerini*, Report: Italy (fn 1) nos 85 f and 88 f.
**216** Cf eg *Koch*, Report: Germany (fn 1) no 49; *Dobiás*, Report: Czech Republic (fn 4) nos 50 and 52; *Cerini*, Report: Italy (fn 1) nos 85 and 88 f; *Stäubli*, Report: Switzerland (fn 1) no 59; *Rubin*, Report: Austria (fn 3) no 55 f.
**217** Cf *Rubin*, Report: Austria (fn 3) no 56; *Cousy/Van Schoubroeck*, Report: Belgium (fn 2) no 62.
**218** *Cousy/Van Schoubroeck*, Report: Belgium (fn 2) nos 6 and 59–66 (there especially nos 60 and 61).
**219** *Norio-Timonen*, Report: Finland (fn 5) no 68.
**220** *Norio-Timonen*, ibid.
**221** *Norio-Timonen*, ibid.

This is the case in *Germany* only in respect of *compulsory liability insurance.*[222] It appears to be doubtful that – apart from the transfer of rights already mentioned above in no 66 – *United Kingdom law* provides for a direct action in this case.[223]

Further, under *German law* the victim is granted a direct action if the compulsory insurance holder's *domicile* is *unknown.*[224] 75

The legal orders of this study vary in the number of *individual* compulsory liability insurance provisions granting a direct action for specific activities.[225] Nevertheless, *all legal orders* have in common that they provide a direct action for one specific case: *motor vehicle liability.*[226] They do so – except for Switzerland – by transposing art 18 of the (6th) Directive on Motor Vehicle Liability Insurance.[227] For some legal orders, this is the only example of a direct action.[228] 76

20. *When settling the claim, is the liability insurer obliged to observe a certain procedure in the interests of the victim? For instance, must it pay the victim an advance within a certain period?*

In all legal orders, albeit for different legal reasons, the insurer is obliged to pay compensation (ie the insurance sum) not to the insurance holder but *to the victim only* unless the latter was already paid by the insurance holder: see *Austrian* 77

**222** *Koch*, Report: Germany (fn 1) no 49.

**223** Cf contrary *Gürses*, Report: United Kingdom (fn 7) no 55 (in conjunction with no 52) apparently equating the transfer of the insurance holder's rights to the victim with a direct action of the victim.

**224** *Koch*, Report: Germany (fn 1) no 49.

**225** Cf, for example, the enumerations provided by *Rubin*, Report: Austria (fn 3) no 56 f; *Stäubli*, Report: Switzerland (fn 1) no 60.

**226** *Rubin*, Report: Austria (fn 3) no 56; *Cousy/Van Schoubroeck*, Report: Belgium (fn 2) no 60; *Dobiás*, Report: Czech Republic (fn 4) no 52; *Norio-Timonen*, Report: Finland (fn 5) no 67; *Koch*, Report: Germany (fn 1) no 49; *Takáts*, Report: Hungary (fn 6) nos 36 and 41; *Cerini*, Report: Italy (fn 1) no 86; *Stäubli*, Report: Switzerland (fn 1) no 60; *Gürses*, Report: United Kingdom (fn 7) nos 53 and 55.

**227** Directive 2009/103/EC of 16 September 2009 relating to insurance against civil liability in respect of the use of motor vehicles, and the enforcement of the obligation to insure against such liability, Official Journal (OJ) L 263, 7.10.2009, 11–31. On this directive also see *S Perner*, Compulsory Liability Insurance and European Union Law (in this book) nos 7 and 29; *Cousy/Van Schoubroeck*, Report: Belgium (fn 2) nos 32 and 78; *Koch*, Report: Germany (fn 1) no 50 fn 35.

**228** Cf *Dobiás*, Report: Czech Republic (fn 4) no 52; *Takáts*, Report: Hungary (fn 6) nos 36 and 41.

and *German law* (above no 60),[229] *Belgian law* (above no 61), *Czech law,*[230] *Hungarian law,*[231] *Swiss law* (above nos 60, 65, 70) and, seemingly within limits, *Italian law.*[232] Under *Finnish law*, there is no obligation but a common practice that the compensation is paid directly to the victim in voluntary lines of insurance (as for compulsory liability insurance, see above no 74).

**78** Under *Austrian* and *German law*, once the victim's claim against the insurance holder – especially by final judgment (on the liability action between them) – has been *established with binding effect on the insurer* too, the latter must pay compensation to the victim within two weeks.[233] A comparable rule is to be found in *United Kingdom* law.[234]

**79** It must be assumed that *all EU legal orders*, in line with art 22 of the Directive on *Motor Vehicle Liability Insurance,*[235] provide for an *advance payment* to the victim in motor vehicle liability insurance by means of a detailed procedure if the claim is undisputed and the insurer has not offered the compensation payment to the victim within three months upon notice of the damaging event.[236] The same advance payment system has also been established under *Swiss law.*[237] Interestingly, *Hungarian supervisory law* restricts the amount of advance payments to 60% of the calculated net loss (damage) in the case of third-party motor liability insurance claims.[238]

**80** In the event of a plurality of victims with a total amount of compensation exceeding the sum insured, *Belgian law* provides a rule for all liability insurance (proportional settlement).[239] In *German law* there is also a rule on *compulsory* liability insurance (in general) for this situation, firstly establishing a ranking on

---

**229** As for Austrian law cf also *Rubin*, Report: Austria (fn 3) no 58.
**230** Cf *Dobiás*, Report: Czech Republic (fn 4) nos 51 and 54.
**231** *Takáts*, Report: Hungary (fn 6) no 39 f.
**232** *Cerini*, Report: Italy (fn 1) nos 79 and 83 f.
**233** *Rubin*, Report: Austria (fn 3) no 59 (with further examples apart from the judgment in the liability action).
**234** *Gürses*, Report: United Kingdom (fn 7) no 56.
**235** On this Directive see above fn 227.
**236** *Rubin*, Report: Austria (fn 3) no 60; *Cousy/Van Schoubroeck*, Report: Belgium (fn 2) no 71; *Koch*, Report: Germany (fn 1) no 50; *Takáts*, Report: Hungary (fn 6) no 42. It must be assumed that this also applies to *Italian law*, cf, rather vague, *Cerini*, Report: Italy (fn 1) no 90 f. For somewhat divergent advance payment rules in the *United Kingdom* cf *Gürses*, Report: United Kingdom (fn 7) no 56.
**237** *Stäubli*, Report: Switzerland (fn 1) no 65.
**238** *Takáts*, Report: Hungary (fn 6) no 42.
**239** *Cousy/Van Schoubroeck*, Report: Belgium (fn 2) no 72.

how the compensation claims against the insurer have to be settled and, only secondly, in the case of equal-ranking claims, a proportional settlement.[240]

Under *Belgian law* the insurer has to follow the *general civil law rule* of contractual performance according to good faith. This also obliges him to indemnify the victim within reasonable time.[241] Moreover, *Belgian law* has implemented a special ad hoc (advance) compensation system in the case of technological disasters involving third party liability.[242] *Czech law* in turn has, for *all forms of liability insurance*, adopted the advance payment procedure, in the other jurisdictions usually only applicable in motor vehicle liability (see above no 79).[243] **81**

*21.a) In the context of its relationship with the victim, can the liability insurer rely on the fact that vis-à-vis the insurance holder (= damaging party) it is freed from the obligation to pay, eg, due to the insurance holder breaching an obligation of conduct/warranty (Obliegenheitsverletzung) or due to him defaulting on premiums?*

With the exception of *Hungarian law*,[244] the question is to be answered in the **82**
negative, though the extent to which the victim is protected varies greatly depending on the legal order concerned. In any case, in all EU legal orders, in accordance with art 3 of the Directive on *Motor Vehicle Liability Insurance*,[245] the insurer of such vehicle cannot, in its relation to the victim, rely on a release from its obligation to perform due to a *breach of policy conditions* by the insurance holder.[246] Apart from this, the following can be said in respect of each legal order respectively:

In *Swiss law*, in a manner comparable to *Hungarian law*, the insurer may as **83**
a general rule, likewise vis-à-vis the insurance holder and the victim, rely on the fact that it is freed from its obligation to pay compensation.[247] Additionally, however, *Swiss law* contains a number of exceptions to this rule. Examples are

**240** *Koch*, Report: Germany (fn 1) no 51.
**241** *Cousy/Van Schoubroeck*, Report: Belgium (fn 2) no 69.
**242** *Cousy/Van Schoubroeck*, Report: Belgium (fn 2) no 70.
**243** *Dobiás*, Report: Czech Republic (fn 4) no 54.
**244** *Takáts*, Report: Hungary (fn 6) no 43.
**245** On this Directive see above fn 227.
**246** *Cerini*, Report: Italy (fn 1) no 93; *Gürses*, Report: United Kingdom (fn 7) no 53. Cf also *Cousy/Van Schoubroeck*, Report: Belgium (fn 2) no 60; *Takáts*, Report: Hungary (fn 6) no 43. For non EU Swiss law see the following no 83.
**247** *Stäubli*, Report: Switzerland (fn 1) no 66.

the liability of the keeper of a motor vehicle or a ship and liability concerning nuclear material and nuclear plants.[248]

84 Under *Belgian law*, the victim is granted his own right (accompanied with a direct action) against the liability insurer (see above nos 61 and 72): As for *voluntary liability insurance*, the victim is invested with this right and action as long as a valid insurance contract exists at the time of the occurrence of the insured event.[249] This means that *defences* (such as nullities or forfeitures deriving from law or the insurance contract) may only be raised by the insurer against the injured party if they are caused by an *act prior to the insured event* (on this see above no 61).[250] Remarkably, therefore, the victim does not lose the right even in the case of nullity of the contract as long as the judge only decided upon the nullity after the insured event occurred.[251] *Belgian law* further *strengthens* the position of the victim in cases of *compulsory liability insurance*. Here, the insurer is *additionally* cut off from raising defences against the victim insofar as such are based on acts either prior or *subsequent to the insured event*.[252] Examples of such non-admissible defences are netting, forfeiture for intentional fault by the insurance holder (above no 55), and nullity of the contract because of intentional non-disclosure of the risk (unless the nullity was already judicially decided before the insured event).[253] Moreover, as far as the content of cover in compulsory liability insurance is concerned,[254] the insurer, in relation to the victim, is *prohibited from relying* on *deductibles*.[255] Nevertheless, he has, on the other hand, no *duty to compensate* if there was no *insurance contract* at the time of the *insured event* – be it for lack of contract at all or the expiry, cancellation or annulment of the contract.[256]

85 Under *German* and *Austrian law*, notwithstanding the fact that a direct action is not granted by any general rule (see above no 71), the legal position of the injured party in compulsory liability insurance is – with the exception of intentional fault (see above no 54 [Germany and Austria] and no 55 [Belgium]) – very similar to the position under *Belgian law*: in these legal orders too, the in-

248 The other cases being the liability of hunters, of pipeline owners and of conductors of research on humans; cf *Stäubli*, Report: Switzerland (fn 1) no 67.
249 *Cousy/Van Schoubroeck*, Report: Belgium (fn 2) nos 8, 61, 65.
250 *Cousy/Van Schoubroeck*, Report: Belgium (fn 2) nos 8 and 65.
251 *Cousy/Van Schoubroeck*, Report: Belgium (fn 2) no 61.
252 *Cousy/Van Schoubroeck*, Report: Belgium (fn 2) no 63f. For examples in detail see ibid no 64.
253 *Cousy/Van Schoubroeck*, Report: Belgium (fn 2) no 64.
254 As for the otherwise applicable general rule under Belgian law see above no 47.
255 *Cousy/Van Schoubroeck*, Report: Belgium (fn 2) nos 7 and 63f.
256 *Cousy/Van Schoubroeck*, Report: Belgium (fn 2) no 64.

surer *remains liable* to the victim within the framework of the legally prescribed minimum insurance sum and the risk to be covered according to the insurance contract, even if it is wholly or partially released from liability vis-à-vis the insurance holder. The release from liability may be founded on a breach of an *obligation* (eg default on payment of the premium) or a *duty of conduct* (*Obliegenheitsverletzung*) (eg the duty to inform the insurer of the occurrence of the insured event).[257] Thus, according to prevailing opinion, the legislator *simulates*, in the interest of the victim, the *obligation of the insurer to provide cover* that would otherwise not exist on the grounds of the insurance contract.[258] As already indicated, this fictional cover is only provided within the framework of the minimum sum insured: if it is exceeded by the actual amount insured, this has no effect on the fictional cover.[259]

Under *Czech law*, as far as compulsory liability insurance is concerned, the **86** insurer is prohibited from raising defences against the injured party which are based on a breach of duty of conduct by the insurance holder, unless the injured party participated in the insurance holder's breach.[260] A default on payment of the *premium* can be relied on neither vis-à-vis the injured party nor the insurance holder.[261]

*Finnish law*, through the inadmissibility of defences against the injured **87** party, in compulsory as well as in voluntary liability insurance, establishes the insurer's *subsidiary liability* to cover the portion that the injured party has not been able to claim from the insurance holder because of the *insolvency* of such.[262] The prerequisite for this is that the victim is a natural person and the insurance holder has either by virtue of gross negligence caused the insured event, not complied with the precautionary guidelines, or neglected his duty of salvage.[263] The same applies if the terms and conditions of the policy free the insurer partly or in total from its obligation to compensate due to the use of alcohol or narcotics by the insurance holder who acted with gross negligence.[264]

In the *United Kingdom*, the insurer is precluded from raising certain kinds of **88** defences under a *motor vehicle liability insurance* (above no 82) or *employers' liability insurance* policy: In these two cases *United Kingdom* law *prohibits* insurance clauses providing that the insurer will not be liable under the policy if

**257** *Koch*, Report: Germany (fn 1) no 52; *Rubin*, Report: Austria (fn 3) nos 61 and 63.
**258** *Rubin*, Report: Austria (fn 3) no 62.
**259** *Koch*, Report: Germany (fn 1) no 52.
**260** *Dobiás*, Report: Czech Republic (fn 4) no 55.
**261** *Dobiás*, Report: Czech Republic (fn 4) no 56.
**262** *Norio-Timonen*, Report: Finland (fn 5) no 71.
**263** Cf *Norio-Timonen*, Report: Finland (fn 5) no 72.
**264** *Norio-Timonen*, ibid.

some specified action is taken or omitted after the occurrence of the event insured or if the employer does not take reasonable care to protect his employees against bodily harm in the course of their employment.[265] At least the former such clause seems to refer to what is to be seen as an obligation of conduct (*Obliegenheit*) under *German* and *Austrian law*. No other similar prohibitions are seen under *United Kingdom law* but they are found in some international conventions.[266]

89 Where a direct action is provided for under *Italian law*[267] by statutory law establishing the duty to be insured, the insurer is generally *prevented* from raising any *objections or exceptions* to payment based on the contract of insurance, except those referring to the *existence of the insurance* or the *payment of the premium*.[268] Compared to other legal orders, the admissibility of a default on payment as a ground not to pay out vis-à-vis the victim seems to be rather exceptional.

*b) Does the law distinguish on the basis of the ground for the release from the obligation to pay so that in some cases the insurer may not invoke its release from such obligation vis-à-vis the victim?*

90 In general, no such distinction is made.[269] For *German* and *Austrian law* this is correct as far as the insurer's release from payment in the technical sense of the word is concerned.[270] Additionally, it is pointed out that the fictional cover to the benefit of the victim (see above no 85) only exists within the framework of the prescribed minimum sum insured and the risk contractually assumed by the insurer. Therefore (admissibly agreed) risk exclusion clauses also have effect vis-à-vis the victim.[271] Accordingly, the release from the obligation to pay due to breach of an *obligation of conduct* must be precisely distinguished from such freedom on the basis of the applicability of a *risk exclusion clause*.[272] The same is

**265** *Gürses*, Report: United Kingdom (fn 7) no 57.
**266** *Gürses*, Report: United Kingdom (fn 7) no 57 (second para).
**267** See above fn 215 f.
**268** *Cerini*, Report: Italy (fn 1) nos 87 and 93.
**269** *Dobiás*, Report: Czech Republic (fn 4) no 58; *Koch*, Report: Germany (fn 1) no 53; *Stäubli*, Report: Switzerland (fn 1) nos 53 and 68; *Gürses*, Report: United Kingdom (fn 7) no 58. This does not apply to *Hungary* (see above no 82). To a certain extent, *Finnish law* also draws a distinction; cf *Norio-Timonen*, Report: Finland (fn 5) no 72 f.
**270** Cf *Koch*, Report: Germany (fn 1) no 53.
**271** Cf *Koch*, Report: Germany (fn 1) no 52.
**272** *Rubin*, Report: Austria (fn 3) no 63.

true of *Belgian law*[273] whereas the contrary view is to be found in *Swiss law*[274] and, so it would seem, under *Italian law* (on the latter see above no 89). Moreover, *Italian law* draws a distinction between default on payment and other contractual breaches (see above no 89).

*c) If the insurer must still pay the victim despite being released from its obligation to pay vis-à-vis the insurance holder (see above Question b), may it take recourse against the latter?*

The insurer can take recourse against the insurance holder upon satisfaction of the victim.[275] In respect of *Finnish* and partly *United Kingdom law*, it is assumed that the right to recourse needs to be contractually stipulated,[276] while it remains ambiguous whether this is also the case for *Belgian law*.[277] 91

*22.a) Within its relationship to the victim, can the liability insurer invoke the fact that the insurance agreement had already ended by the time relevant in respect of the duty to provide cover?*

The legal orders of this study show an inhomogeneous picture: Some allow the insurer to raise this defence even for compulsory liability insurance (as is the case under *Czech*,[278] *Hungarian*,[279] *Italian*[280] and *United Kingdom law*[281]), whereas other legal orders preclude this (see below no 93 f). In any case, as far as a *motor vehicle liability insurer* is exempted from the duty to compensate, the special compensation scheme to protect victims of accidents involving uninsured cars 92

273 *Cousy/Van Schoubroeck*, Report: Belgium (fn 2) no 64 (at the end).
274 *Stäubli*, Report: Switzerland (fn 1) nos 53 and 68 (inadmissibility of risk exclusions as well). It is to be noted that *Swiss law* does not distinguish between the grounds of the release but between the statutory provisions stipulating compulsory liability insurance (cf *Stäubli*, ibid).
275 *Rubin*, Report: Austria (fn 3) no 64; *Dobiás*, Report: Czech Republic (fn 4) no 59; *Koch*, Report: Germany (fn 1) no 54; *Takáts*, Report: Hungary (fn 6) no 45; *Cerini*, Report: Italy (fn 1) no 94; *Stäubli*, Report: Switzerland (fn 1) nos 69–71.
276 *Norio-Timonen*, Report: Finland (fn 5) no 74; *Gürses*, Report: United Kingdom (fn 7) no 59 (only as far as employers' liability insurance is concerned, but not for motor vehicle insurance).
277 *Cousy/Van Schoubroeck*, Report: Belgium (fn 2) no 64.
278 *Dobiás*, Report: Czech Republic (fn 4) no 60.
279 *Takáts*, Report: Hungary (fn 6) no 46.
280 *Cerini*, Report: Italy (fn 1) no 95. On Italian law see also above no 89 of this text.
281 *Gürses*, Report: United Kingdom (fn 7) no 60.

must be borne in mind in respect of each legal order;[282] on this scheme see below no 97.

93 *Austrian* and *German law* statutorily *simulate* the *continued existence* of the insurance cover.[283] The insurer may, in short,[284] *only end* its further liability thus effected by *informing* the *supervisory authority* responsible for the insurance holder about the termination of the insurance contract. One month after this information is received by the authority, the fictional cover is extinguished. Comparable rules are to be found under *Swiss law* for *specific cases* (such as for keepers of motor vehicles, aircraft or ships, transport enterprises, keepers of nuclear plants or nuclear material, owners of pipelines).[285]

94 Interestingly, *Finnish law* contains a rule – albeit not applicable in general but relating for instance to insurance brokers – that is very similar to the described rule under *German*, *Austrian* and, partly, *Swiss law*: The liability insurance contract of an insurance broker may not terminate before two months from the moment the insurer has informed the Finnish Financial Supervisory Authority of the contract's termination.[286] However, the liability insurer can usually invoke the termination of the contract in other cases.[287] *Belgian law* likewise provides a rule reminiscent of the legal situation in *Germany* and *Austria*. This rule relates to the compulsory liability insurance for fire and explosions occurring in (certain) places accessible to the general public. Remarkably, the rule distinguishes according to how long after the insurer's notification the victim asserts his claim.[288] Further for *Belgium* see above no 84 (no insurer's duty to compensate).

*b) If the insurer must pay the victim despite the termination of the insurance agreement by the time relevant for the duty to provide cover (see above Question a), can it take recourse against the insurance holder?*

95 The insurer's recourse is provided for in this case by all legal orders stipulating the continued existence of the insurer's duty to compensate vis-à-vis the victim.[289]

---

**282** Cf eg *Takáts*, Report: Hungary (fn 6) nos 43 and 46.

**283** As for the simulation of cover vis-à-vis the victim when an insurance contract is effective but dysfunctional, see above no 85.

**284** Cf in more detail for Germany *Koch*, Report: Germany (fn 1) no 55.

**285** *Stäubli*, Report: Switzerland (fn 1) nos 72–74.

**286** *Norio-Timonen*, Report: Finland (fn 5) no 54.

**287** *Norio-Timonen*, Report: Finland (fn 5) no 75.

**288** Cf *Cousy/Van Schoubroeck*, Report: Belgium (fn 2) no 66.

**289** *Rubin*, Report: Austria (fn 3) no 66; *Koch*, Report: Germany (fn 1) no 56; *Stäubli*, Report: Switzerland (fn 1) no 75 (only relating to § 65 para 3 SVG [Road Traffic Act] but not to the similar

*23.a) Are there cases in which a damaging party does not effectively conclude the required liability insurance and the victim injured by him nonetheless receives compensation for his loss from a liability insurer or another compensation scheme (eg, a guarantee fund)?*

For all legal orders the same applies as has been said above under nos 92–94.[290] 96
This means for *Austrian* and *German law* (cf above no 93) that, as a rule, the compulsory liability insurer remains liable as long as there is the mere appearance (as seen from the viewpoint of the supervisory authority) of an insurance contract validly concluded.[291] On the other hand, under *Swiss law* in the situation of an ineffective contract, other than its ending as described above in no 93, no liability of an insurer seems to be prescribed. An exception to this rule can be found for motor liability insurance.[292] As for the liability of a guarantee fund, see the following no 97.

Further, it must be noted that, as a rule, no guarantee fund or other com- 97
pensation scheme is a legal tool generally provided for within the framework of compulsory liability insurance.[293] Nevertheless, each EU legal order has, in accordance with art 10 of the Directive on *Motor Vehicle Liability Insurance*,[294] established a compensation scheme in order to protect victims of car accidents, dealing with *uninsured claims* related to motor vehicle liability.[295] A guarantee fund solution is equally to be found under *Swiss law* for this case.[296]

Additionally, *Belgian law* has also established a compensation fund for 98
*medical accidents*, in particular in the case of the provider of care being liable for mistreatment without having taken out sufficient insurance.[297]

---

cases mentioned in no 74). This also seems to be the case for *Belgian law*, cf *Cousy/Van Schoubroeck*, Report: Belgium (fn 2) no 77 in conjunction with no 64. Some ambiguity remains for *Finnish law*, cf *Norio-Timonen*, Report: Finland (fn 5) no 77 f ('penalty premium').

**290** Cf *Dobiás*, Report: Czech Republic (fn 4) no 62; *Takáts*, Report: Hungary (fn 6) no 48.

**291** *Koch*, Report: Germany (fn 1) no 57; also cf *Rubin*, Report: Austria (fn 3) nos 67 and 69.

**292** Firstly, art 68 SVG (Road Traffic Act) (cf *Stäubli*, Report: Switzerland [fn 1] no 73) is also applied if the insurance contract is invalid under the condition that the insurer has confirmed to the supervisory authority the existence of the insurance contract. Secondly; cf below no 97 fn 296.

**293** Cf eg *Norio-Timonen*, Report: Finland (fn 5) no 79; *Cerini*, Report: Italy (fn 1) no 97.

**294** On this Directive see above fn 227.

**295** *Cousy/Van Schoubroeck*, Report: Belgium (fn 2) no 78; *Dobiás*, Report: Czech Republic (fn 4) no 62; *Norio-Timonen*, Report: Finland (fn 5) no 80; *Takáts*, Report: Hungary (fn 6) nos 43 and 48; *Cerini*, Report: Italy (fn 1) nos 97 f and 100; *Gürses*, Report: United Kingdom (fn 7) no 62 f.

**296** *Stäubli*, Report: Switzerland (fn 1) nos 76–78.

**297** *Cousy/Van Schoubroeck*, Report: Belgium (fn 2) no 79.

99 Moreover, *Finnish law* has established guarantee fund solutions for all *statutory liability insurance* (on these see above no 7) in the event of a lack of valid insurance policy, such as – apart from motor vehicle liability – for *employers' liability* and *medical injuries*.[298]

100 In order to protect the victim in the event of ineffective liability insurance, *Italy* too has established guarantee fund solutions not only for motor vehicle liability but also for a few other cases such as the liability of *insurance intermediaries* or *hunters*.[299]

*b) In the event that the policy taken out was not in fact effectively concluded, is it necessary to distinguish on the basis of the ground for this ineffectiveness, eg, whether the reason for the contract not coming into effect was:*

*i) a lack of legal capacity on the part of the insurance holder,*

101 In general, no distinction is made as far as the cause of ineffectiveness is concerned.[300] Therefore the answers given above under nos 92–94 and 96–100 are likewise relevant for Questions i–iii.

*ii) lack of consent,*

102 See the preceding no 101.[301]

*iii) falsa procuratio (unauthorised agency)?*

103 See above no 101.[302]

---

**298** *Norio-Timonen*, Report: Finland (fn 5) no 80.
**299** *Cerini*, Report: Italy (fn 1) no 99.
**300** Cf *Cousy/Van Schoubroeck*, Report: Belgium (fn 2) no 80; *Norio-Timonen*, Report: Finland (fn 5) no 81; *Koch*, Report: Germany (fn 1) no 58; *Takáts*, Report: Hungary (fn 6) no 49; *Cerini*, Report: Italy (fn 1) no 101; *Stäubli*, Report: Switzerland (fn 1) no 79 ff; *Gürses*, Report: United Kingdom (fn 7) no 64.
**301** Cf *Rubin*, Report: Austria (fn 3) no 69 (differentiating); *Cousy/Van Schoubroeck*, Report: Belgium (fn 2) no 81; *Norio-Timonen*, Report: Finland (fn 5) no 82; *Koch*, Report: Germany (fn 1) no 58; *Takáts*, Report: Hungary (fn 6) no 50; *Stäubli*, Report: Switzerland (fn 1) no 81; *Gürses*, Report: United Kingdom (fn 7) no 65.
**302** Cf *Rubin*, Report: Austria (fn 3) no 70 (differentiating); *Cousy/Van Schoubroeck*, Report: Belgium (fn 2) no 82; *Norio-Timonen*, Report: Finland (fn 5) no 83; *Koch*, Report: Germany (fn 1) no 58; *Takáts*, Report: Hungary (fn 6) no 51; *Stäubli*, Report: Switzerland (fn 1) no 82; *Gürses*, Report: United Kingdom (fn 7) no 66.

c) *Can the liability insurer (or the alternative compensation scheme) that must provide cover even though the insurance policy was not effectively concluded (see above Questions a and b) have recourse against the damaging party?*

This can be answered in the positive.[303] 104

24.a) *Are there cases in which a damaging party does not take out any liability insurance, ie not even an ineffective insurance policy (see above Question 23), and the victim whom he injured is still compensated for his damage by a liability insurer or another compensation scheme (guarantee fund, etc)?*

The answers given above under nos 92–94 and 96–100 predominantly also 105
apply to this question as they did above under no 101.[304] However, *German* and *Austrian law* present exceptions: Here, other than described above in no 96 for an invalidly concluded insurance contract, no *liability of the insurer* is possible.[305] In motor liability insurance a *guarantee fund* has to pay compensation.[306]

b) *Can the liability insurer (or the alternative compensation scheme) that must provide cover despite the total absence of any insurance agreement (see above Question a) have recourse against the damaging party?*

Likewise, this is to be answered in the affirmative.[307] 106

---

**303** *Rubin*, Report: Austria (fn 3) no 71; *Cousy/Van Schoubroeck*, Report: Belgium (fn 2) nos 83–85; *Dobiás*, Report: Czech Republic (fn 4) no 66; *Norio-Timonen*, Report: Finland (fn 5) no 84; *Koch*, Report: Germany (fn 1) no 59; *Takáts*, Report: Hungary (fn 6) no 52; *Cerini*, Report: Italy (fn 1) no 102; *Gürses*, Report: United Kingdom (fn 7) no 67.

**304** Cf *Cousy/Van Schoubroeck*, Report: Belgium (fn 2) no 86; *Dobiás*, Report: Czech Republic (fn 4) no 67; *Norio-Timonen*, Report: Finland (fn 5) no 85; *Takáts*, Report: Hungary (fn 6) no 53; *Cerini*, Report: Italy (fn 1) no 103; *Gürses*, Report: United Kingdom (fn 7) no 68.

**305** *Rubin*, Report: Austria (fn 3) no 72; *Koch*, Report: Germany (fn 1) no 60.

**306** *Rubin*, ibid; *Koch*, ibid.

**307** *Rubin*, Report: Austria (fn 3) no 73; *Dobiás*, Report: Czech Republic (fn 4) no 68; *Norio-Timonen*, Report: Finland (fn 5) no 86; *Koch*, Report: Germany (fn 1) no 61; *Takáts*, Report: Hungary (fn 6) no 54; *Cerini*, Report: Italy (fn 1) no 104; *Stäubli*, Report: Switzerland (fn 1) no 83f; *Gürses*, Report: United Kingdom (fn 7) no 69.

*25. Is the victim protected against the insolvency of the liability insurer?*

107 The victim is *specifically protected* against the insurer's insolvency solely as far as *motor vehicle liability* is involved.[308] Apart from this, the victim is protected in some legal orders insofar as claims to the insurance sum (on this see above nos 68–76) are privileged before any other insolvency claims.[309] More comprehensive protection of the victim is seen under *United Kingdom law*,[310] *German law* (albeit factually for a very limited number of cases)[311] and *Finnish law* (for so-called statutory liability insurance [on this see above no 7]).[312]

*26. Are there rules that serve in particular the protection of the victim when the liability insurance was only concluded voluntarily – ie without it being compulsory?*

108 *Dispositions* by the insurance holder over the compensation claim against the insurer are *ineffective* vis-à-vis the victim under *German* and *Austrian law* (see above no 60).[313] From this rule, it follows that *only paying out compensation to the victim* can have the effect of discharging the insurer's debt. It is thus ensured that the insurance holder's cover entitlement is reserved to satisfy the insurance holder's duty to compensate the victim (above no 60). For the very same reason, in the case of the insurance holder's insolvency, the victim is granted a *right to separate satisfaction* out of his claim against the liability insurer (see above no 65).[314] Further, there is a rule on *pro rata satisfaction* of claims of several victims arising from the same insured event if the *insurance sum is not sufficient* to cover their damage in full. This rule also serves the protection of the victim.[315] Moreover, clauses in policies that, for example, forbid the satisfaction of the victim or (for Austria: subject to certain requirements) the acknowledgement of the victim's entitlement[316] are *invalid.*

---

**308** *Rubin*, Report: Austria (fn 3) no 74; *Cousy/Van Schoubroeck*, Report: Belgium (fn 2) no 90; *Koch*, Report: Germany (fn 1) no 62; *Takáts*, Report: Hungary (fn 6) no 55; *Stäubli*, Report: Switzerland (fn 1) no 88; *Gürses*, Report: United Kingdom (fn 7) no 72.
**309** Cf *Rubin*, Report: Austria (fn 3) no 75; *Dobiás*, Report: Czech Republic (fn 4) no 69; *Cerini*, Report: Italy (fn 1) no 105; *Stäubli*, Report: Switzerland (fn 1) no 87.
**310** *Gürses*, Report: United Kingdom (fn 7) no 71.
**311** *Koch*, Report: Germany (fn 1) no 63.
**312** *Norio-Timonen*, Report: Finland (fn 5) no 87.
**313** Also cf *Koch*, Report: Germany (fn 1) no 64.
**314** *Koch*, ibid.
**315** Cf more in detail *Koch*, ibid; *Rubin*, Report: Austria (fn 3) no 76.
**316** Cf *Koch*, Report: Germany (fn 1) no 65.

To a large extent *Swiss law* achieves the same effects as said *German* and *Austrian law* by way of the victim's *right of lien* on the claim of the insurance holder against the insurer (see above nos 60 and 65).[317] The *Belgian system* of an *own right* including the victim's *direct action* as well as the *limited admissibility* of the insurer's *defences* in respect of the victim also brings about similar results (see above nos 61 and 64).[318] 109

Under *Finnish law*, in respect of voluntary insurance, the victim is given a *direct right of action* against the insurer in two specific cases. This is either if the insurance holder has been declared *insolvent* or if he mentioned the (general) liability insurance in *marketing efforts* launched to promote his business (see above nos 64 and 74).[319] Furthermore, *Finnish law* protects the victim in a very specific way: He may take (direct) legal action against the liability insurer once he has been notified by the latter of its decision on the insurance holder's claim of compensation.[320] 110

*Hungarian law* protects the victim insofar as the liability insurer may pay the insurance sum to him only (see above no 77).[321] This leads to limited protection of the victim in the case of the insurance holder's insolvency (see above no 67). 111

In the law of the *United Kingdom* the victim has a right of direct action against the liability insurer in the event of the insurance holder's insolvency (see above no 74).[322] 112

# V. Supervision and Sanctions

*27.a) In which cases must the insurance holder prove to an authority before commencing an activity requiring insurance that he has taken out the respective prescribed liability insurance cover (see above Question 4.e)?*

It may be noted for all legal orders in this study that, in many cases, compulsory liability insurance is imposed as a *condition* for obtaining *authorisation* to carry out the respective activity or profession (see also above no 18).[323] 113

---

**317** Also cf *Stäubli*, Report: Switzerland (fn 1) no 89.
**318** Cf also *Cousy/Van Schoubroeck*, Report: Belgium (fn 2) no 91.
**319** Further cf *Norio-Timonen*, Report: Finland (fn 5) no 88.
**320** *Norio-Timonen*, Report: Finland (fn 5) no 89.
**321** Also cf *Takáts*, Report: Hungary (fn 6) no 56.
**322** Cf also *Gürses*, Report: United Kingdom (fn 7) no 73.
**323** *Rubin*, Report: Austria (fn 3) no 77 f; *Cousy/Van Schoubroeck*, Report: Belgium (fn 2) no 92; *Dobiás*, Report: Czech Republic (fn 4) no 71 f; *Norio-Timonen*, Report: Finland (fn 5) no 90;

b) *Must the insurer inform an authority when liability insurance taken out to meet an insurance obligation ends?*

114 Under *German law*, whenever the insurance holder must prove to the competent authority prior to the commencement of his activities that he has taken out the prescribed liability insurance, there is, in general, a corresponding duty of the insurer to inform the authority when the liability insurance contract ends.[324] This can also be discerned, as a tendency, in *Austria* among more recently enacted provisions establishing compulsory liability insurance.[325] However, neither in Germany nor in Austria is there a general rule imposing this kind of information duty on compulsory liability insurers.[326] For example, under German law, unlike in Austria,[327] *motor vehicle insurers* are not obliged to notify the competent authority.[328] In any case, under German and Austrian law, this has no impact on the victim's position due to the *fictional cover* that applies if the insurer does not inform the supervisory authority of the insurance contract's termination (on this see above no 93).[329]

115 *Belgian law* rarely prescribes any duty on the part of compulsory liability insurers to give such information.[330] Some examples of this duty are to be found under *Czech,*[331] *Finnish*[332] and *Swiss law*[333] whereas no such obligation is foreseen under *United Kingdom*[334] or, as it seems, *Italian law.*[335] Under *Hungarian law* the duty appears to exist only for motor vehicle liability insurance, though it is common practice among *Hungarian* insurers to inform the supervisory authorities even without a firm rule of law.[336]

---

*Koch*, Report: Germany (fn 1) no 66; *Takáts*, Report: Hungary (fn 6) no 57; *Stäubli*, Report: Switzerland (fn 1) no 90; *Gürses*, Report: United Kingdom (fn 7) no 74; vaguely *Cerini*, Report: Italy (fn 1) no 107.

**324** *Koch*, Report: Germany (fn 1) no 68.

**325** Cf *Rubin*, Report: Austria (fn 3) no 80.

**326** Cf *Rubin*, Report: Austria (fn 3) no 79.

**327** Cf *Rubin*, Report: Austria (fn 3) no 80.

**328** *Koch*, Report: Germany (fn 1) no 68.

**329** *Rubin*, Report: Austria (fn 3) no 79.

**330** *Cousy/Van Schoubroeck*, Report: Belgium (fn 2) no 93 (especially relating to motor vehicle liability insurance).

**331** *Dobiás*, Report: Czech Republic (fn 4) no 73.

**332** *Norio-Timonen*, Report: Finland (fn 5) no 91.

**333** *Stäubli*, Report: Switzerland (fn 1) no 91 f (especially motor vehicle liability insurance).

**334** *Gürses*, Report: United Kingdom (fn 7) no 75.

**335** *Cerini*, Report: Italy (fn 1) no 108.

**336** *Takáts*, Report: Hungary (fn 6) no 58.

c) *Is the insurer also under a duty to inform when a liability insurance agreement is in existence but it has no duty to provide cover – eg, due to defaults on premium payments?*

Such obligation is *rather rare* to find: Under *Czech*[337] and *Austrian law*, it does exist in some cases, though for the latter to a lesser extent than the aforementioned duty to inform about the contract's termination.[338] *Belgian law* rarely prescribes this duty.[339] Under *German law*, only one example for the insurer's duty to inform about its release from providing cover is to be found.[340] The obligation does not exist under *Hungarian law*[341] or, as it seems, under *Finnish law*.[342] Under *Swiss law* in contrast, this duty has the same scope as that relating to the termination of the insurance contract (see the preceding no 115).[343] Again, no such duty exists under *Italian* or *United Kingdom law*.[344] 116

d) *What are the consequences when the duties to inform of the end of contract or the release from payment obligations (see above Questions b and c) are violated?*

Under *German* and *Austrian law*, the insurer remains liable due to its statutorily *simulated cover duty* (see above nos 93 and 114).[345] But if the legal rule establishing a specific compulsory liability insurance scheme has omitted to appoint an authority competent to receive the insurer's notification, no simulated cover duty is set forth under *German law*.[346] Moreover, the breach of the information duty may lead to administrative penalties under *Austrian law*[347] as is also the case for *Czech*[348] and *Hungarian law*.[349] Under *Belgian law*, in a manner comparable to the *German* and *Austrian* schemes, the insurer's omission to notify trig- 117

---

**337** *Dobiás*, Report: Czech Republic (fn 4) no 74.
**338** *Rubin*, Report: Austria (fn 3) no 81.
**339** *Cousy/Van Schoubroeck*, Report: Belgium (fn 2) no 94.
**340** *Koch*, Report: Germany (fn 1) no 69 (liability insurance for the operator of an aircraft).
**341** *Takáts*, Report: Hungary (fn 6) no 59 with more detailed information about motor vehicle liability insurance.
**342** *Norio-Timonen*, Report: Finland (fn 5) no 92.
**343** *Stäubli*, Report: Switzerland (fn 1) no 93.
**344** *Cerini*, Report: Italy (fn 1) no 109; *Gürses*, Report: United Kingdom (fn 7) no 76.
**345** Also cf *Koch*, Report: Germany (fn 1) no 70; *Rubin*, Report: Austria (fn 3) no 82.
**346** *Koch*, ibid.
**347** *Rubin*, Report: Austria (fn 3) no 82.
**348** *Dobiás*, Report: Czech Republic (fn 4) no 76.
**349** *Takáts*, Report: Hungary (fn 6) no 60.

gers the non-applicability of defences in the specific case of compulsory liability insurance for fire and explosions occurring in (certain) places accessible to the general public (as described above in no 94).[350] The same applies for *Swiss law* relating to motor vehicle liability insurance and, as it appears, the other Swiss cases of compulsory liability insurance mentioned above in no 93.[351] No sanctions are to be found under *Finnish law.*[352] As for the *United Kingdom*, the question does not arise as there is no duty to inform in the first place.[353]

*28. Is there some official body (authority, professional chamber) where an injured party can find out whether and where the injuring party who inflicted damage upon him in the course of an activity requiring insurance has liability insurance?*

118 This is generally answered in the *negative*. However, in line with art 23 of the Directive on *Motor Vehicle Liability Insurance*,[354] all EU Member States have set up such a body to enable the victims of car accidents to file their claims against the relevant insurer that is under an obligation to indemnify them.[355] Such a scheme also exists in *Switzerland.*[356] Additionally, under *Austrian law*, this is likewise established for the liability insurer of *insurance brokers*,[357] under *German law* for the liability insurers of *lawyers*, *patent lawyers* and *notaries*,[358] under *Czech law* for *travel agencies* and *operators* of *maritime ships.*[359] Further, such a duty appears to have been established for *insurance intermediaries* under *Italian law.*[360]

**350** *Cousy/Van Schoubroeck*, Report: Belgium (fn 2) no 95.
**351** Cf *Stäubli*, Report: Switzerland (fn 1) no 94 (though limiting this effect to motor vehicle liability insurance which might seem to be difficult to harmonize with the information given ibid no 73).
**352** *Norio-Timonen*, Report: Finland (fn 5) no 93.
**353** *Gürses*, Report: United Kingdom (fn 7) no 77.
**354** Cf *Koch*, Report: Germany (fn 1) no 71. On this Directive see also above fn 227.
**355** *Rubin*, Report: Austria (fn 3) no 83; *Cousy/Van Schoubroeck*, Report: Belgium (fn 2) no 96; *Dobiás*, Report: Czech Republic (fn 4) no 77; *Norio-Timonen*, Report: Finland (fn 5) no 94; *Koch*, Report: Germany (fn 1) no 71; *Takáts*, Report: Hungary (fn 6) no 61; *Gürses*, Report: United Kingdom (fn 7) nos 78–83. Contrary to *Cerini*, Report: Italy (fn 1) no 111, it is to be assumed that such scheme has also been established in Italy.
**356** *Stäubli*, Report: Switzerland (fn 1) no 95.
**357** *Rubin*, Report: Austria (fn 3) no 83.
**358** *Koch*, Report: Germany (fn 1) no 71.
**359** *Dobiás*, Report: Czech Republic (fn 4) no 78.
**360** Cf *Cerini*, Report: Italy (fn 1) no 111. Regarding motor vehicle liability insurance, see above fn 355.

*29. Are there (public law) sanctions against the party who was required to take out insurance if such does not take out the compulsory liability insurance? Examples of this would be a ban on carrying out the activity that requires the insurance or the imposition of an administrative or judicial penalty.*

In all the *legal orders* investigated there are professions or activities which legally *require* valid liability insurance cover. The non-fulfilment of this precondition often ultimately entails a *prohibition* on carrying out the respective profession/activity either by the refusal or revocation of the authorisation to engage in such.[361] This might be enforced by imposing *administrative penalties*[362] or, as is sometimes the case for motor vehicle liability insurance, a *penalty premium.*[363] In exceptional cases even *criminal penalties* are foreseen.[364] For example, in the *United Kingdom* it is a *criminal offence* to drive a motor vehicle or to employ people without having sufficient liability insurance covering the employer's liability for bodily injury or disease sustained by his employees.[365] The failure to *take out motor vehicle insurance* likewise constitutes a criminal offence under *German law.*[366] 119

As for *civil law sanctions*: Where legal rules require taking out insurance for the *benefit of third parties*, non-compliance with the duty to take out insurance leads to *civil liability* towards the third party for the pure economic loss which consists in the lack of liability insurance cover.[367] See also above nos 96–106. 120

**361** *Rubin*, Report: Austria (fn 3) no 85; *Cousy/Van Schoubroeck*, Report: Belgium (fn 2) no 97; *Dobiás*, Report: Czech Republic (fn 4) no 80; *Koch*, Report: Germany (fn 1) no 73; *Norio-Timonen*, Report: Finland (fn 5) no 97; *Takáts*, Report: Hungary (fn 6) no 62; *Stäubli*, Report: Switzerland (fn 1) nos 47 and 96; *Gürses*, Report: United Kingdom (fn 7) no 43.
**362** *Rubin*, Report: Austria (fn 3) no 86; *Dobiás*, Report: Czech Republic (fn 4) no 80; *Koch*, Report: Germany (fn 1) no 73; *Stäubli*, Report: Switzerland (fn 1) no 47.
**363** *Norio-Timonen*, Report: Finland (fn 5) no 96; *Takáts*, Report: Hungary (fn 6) no 62.
**364** Cf *Koch*, Report: Germany (fn 1) no 74; *Stäubli*, Report: Switzerland (fn 1) no 47.
**365** *Gürses*, Report: United Kingdom (fn 7) nos 43 and 74. As for the employer's duty to take out liability insurance, cf *Gürses*, ibid no 2.
**366** *Koch*, Report: Germany (fn 1) no 74.
**367** Cf *Koch*, Report: Germany (fn 1) no 75.

## VI. Statutory Provisions required by the Constitution or the European Convention on Human Rights (ECHR)

*30. What has been said regarding the compatibility of the duties to take out liability insurance with the investigated countries' constitutions and the ECHR?*

121 These topics are specifically dealt with in a report by Franz Merli on constitutional law in this book.[368] Duties to take out liability insurance *interfere* with *fundamental freedoms* provided for by national constitutions just as by the ECHR: Above all, property rights as well as the freedom to contract and to engage in economic activities are affected.[369] Merli shows that the problems related to compulsory liability insurance on a constitutional level can all be solved without great difficulty.[370]

*31. Do the constitutions or the ECHR make any stipulations regarding the contents of such duties to take out liability insurance?*

122 National constitutions and the ECHR make such stipulations but the legislator enjoys a *wide margin of discretion.*[371]

## VII. Reform Efforts

*32. Are there efforts towards reforming the law regarding compulsory liability insurance?*

123 Ongoing reform efforts on the level of framework provisions for compulsory liability insurance can be seen in *Switzerland,*[372] whereas such reforms have been recently implemented in the *Czech Republic*[373] and *Germany.*[374]

---

**368** *Merli* (fn 13) no 1 ff.
**369** *Merli* (fn 13) no 2.
**370** *Merli* (fn 13) no 3 ff; see also *Rubin*, Conclusions (fn 80) nos 2–4.
**371** *Merli*, ibid; *Rubin*, ibid.
**372** *Stäubli*, Report: Switzerland (fn 1) nos 100–102.
**373** *Dobiás*, Report: Czech Republic (fn 4) no 85.
**374** *Koch*, Report: Germany (fn 1) no 82.

# VIII. Compulsory Liability Insurance and Liability Law

*33. Is, at the legislative level, any connection discernible between the nature of liability (in particular in the case of strict liability) and the imposition of compulsory liability insurance?*

In the majority of jurisdictions there is no *legal rule* or *factual experience* to the effect that, in cases of strict liability, compulsory liability insurance must be introduced.[375] It appears, however, that some legal orders have (at least) in recent times shown a *tendency* not to introduce strict liability without a compulsory liability insurance scheme.[376] 124

**375** *Dobiás*, Report: Czech Republic (fn 4) no 86; *Norio-Timonen*, Report: Finland (fn 5) no 103; *Koch*, Report: Germany (fn 1) no 83; *Takáts*, Report: Hungary (fn 6) no 66; *Cerini*, Report: Italy (fn 1) no 127.

**376** *Rubin*, Report: Austria (fn 3) no 90; *Koch*, Report: Germany (fn 1) no 83; *Cerini*, Report: Italy (fn 1) no 127; *Stäubli*, Report: Switzerland (fn 1) no 103. Also cf *Gürses*, Report: United Kingdom (fn 7) no 88.

Daniel Rubin

# Conclusions

## I. The Purpose of Compulsory Liability Insurance

1 The *function* of compulsory liability insurance is to ensure that *indemnity claims can be met.*[1] However, legislators very seldom disclose which goal(s) they are pursuing when establishing a particular compulsory liability insurance provision.[2] Nevertheless, the country reports show that the *predominant aim* is to ensure that victims are sufficiently indemnified.[3] In other words: compulsory liability insurance basically aims at *protecting the victim* from the *insolvency* of the *injuring* (= the insured) party. The protection of the latter, on the other hand, is mostly seen merely as an additional purpose for the establishment of compulsory liability insurance regimes.[4] In contrast, it is widely concluded from an economic analysis of law point of view that compulsory liability insurance provisions aim less at the victim's or the injuring party's protection than at the internalisation of damage risks (within the funds of the injuring party) for the sake of relieving society of the burden of the costs caused by these risks.[5] The economic analysis of law's perspective that compulsory liability insurance is a means to relieve public funds from the negative effects caused by a tortfeasor's insolvency, seems persuasive. However, this does not necessarily conflict with the prevailing opinion within insurance law literature that compulsory liability insurance mainly serves to protect the victim. Therefore the arguments in the following are based on this view.

---

1 See *D Rubin*, Introduction (in this book) no 2 f; *H Heiss*, Compulsory Liability Insurance in the Principles of European Insurance Contract Law (PEICL) (in this book) no 1.

2 Cf *H Cousy/C Van Schoubroeck*, Compulsory Liability Insurance in Belgium (in this book) no 22; *P Takáts*, Compulsory Liability Insurance in Hungary (in this book) no 13. See also in depth *Heiss* (fn 1) no 2.

3 See *D Rubin*, Comparative Report (in this book) no 21.

4 See *Rubin*, Comparative Report (fn 3) no 22 f; *Heiss* (fn 1) no 2.

5 *M Faure*, Compulsory Liability Insurance: Economic Perspectives (in this book) no 11; *I Gilead*, Israel, in: BA Koch/H Koziol (eds), Unification of Tort Law: Strict Liability (2002) no 52; *BA Koch/H Koziol*, Comparative Conclusions, in: BA Koch/H Koziol (eds), Unification of Tort Law: Strict Liability (2002) no 19; cf also *R Koch*, Compulsory Liability Insurance in Germany (in this book) no 14.

# II. Establishment of Duties to Take out Liability Insurance

## 1. Framework supplied by constitutions and the European Convention on Human Rights

2 In respect of the establishment of compulsory liability insurance, it has to be borne in mind that – as the legal flip side of the coin – such a duty *interferes* with *fundamental freedoms* under national constitutions and the European Convention on Human Rights.[6] Therefore, any duty to take out liability insurance must be provided for by law[7] which is to be understood as a sufficiently clear legal basis.[8] Thus, a *general legal prescription* is required, such as laid down, to give the most notable examples, in the form of a *parliamentary statute* or an *EU regulation* though also, for example, a *royal decree* (this is the case in *Belgium*).[9] However, *administrative authorities* or *professional bodies* may also be *authorised* on such legal bases, especially by parliamentary statute, to impose compulsory liability insurance.[10]

3 Moreover, if lawmakers decide to introduce a duty to take out liability insurance, this not only needs to serve a *legitimate purpose* – which would mainly be the (potential) injured parties' protection[11] – but also has to be a *proportionate measure.*[12] Hence, an *objective reason* is necessary to justify the interference with fundamental rights caused by the creation of mandatory liability insurance.[13] Such a reason would mainly be seen in the seriousness and size of the *risk of damage* attributed to the relevant activity (operation or profession).[14] In any case, the requirement of proportionality can only set very broad boundaries since it is acknowledged that lawmakers do enjoy a *wide margin of discretion* when it comes to the establishment of new cases of compulsory liability insurance.[15]

6 *F Merli*, Compulsory Liability Insurance and Constitutional Law (in this book) no 2.
7 *Merli* (fn 6) no 3.
8 Cf *Merli* (fn 6) no 3.
9 See more in detail *Rubin*, Comparative Report (fn 3) no 13 and *Merli*, (fn 6) no 3.
10 On this again see *Rubin*, ibid and *Merli*, ibid.
11 See above no 1.
12 *Merli* (fn 6) no 4.
13 *Merli* (fn 6) no 5.
14 Cf *Merli* (fn 6) no 5.
15 *Merli* (fn 6) no 4. See also *Rubin*, Comparative Report (fn 3) no 2.

## 2. Framework supplied by EU primary law

*Similar questions* to those just described[16] are raised by *EU primary law*. According to the case law of the CJEU, national provisions imposing an additional financial burden on enterprises by establishing a duty to take out insurance restrict their freedom of establishment and to provide services.[17] However, these insurance duties normally have a non-discriminatory content, mostly aiming at the *protection of the victim* and pursue this goal in a proportionate manner so that the Court, as a rule, acknowledges them to be *justified* and therefore *in compliance* with European primary law.[18] The same applies for the insurer's freedom of establishment and services.[19] It must be noted that in the context at hand too – the EU right to freedom of movement – national legislators, in judging the proportionality of their measures, enjoy at least a certain degree of discretional freedom.[20] 4

## 3. Creating a consistent system

Even though above we saw it unquestioned on the level of constitutions,[21] virtually all legal orders in this study suffer from a *lack of a consistent system* for the introduction of compulsory liability.[22] This structural deficiency not only applies for the 'if' but also the 'how' – ie the mandatory content – of compulsory liability insurance regulations.[23] However, it goes without saying that there is a need for a consistent and therefore risk-adequate system of compulsory liability insurance rules (be it on national levels or be it on the level of EU law).[24] This entails *three aspects*: *First*, guidelines on the severity and quality of *risks* are nec- 5

**16** See above no 3.
**17** *S Perner*, Compulsory Liability Insurance and European Union Law (in this book) nos 20 and 23 (with, in my view, convincing criticism). See also *Heiss* (fn 1) no 4.
**18** *Perner* (fn 17) nos 21 f and 31. See also *Heiss* (fn 1) no 4.
**19** *Perner* (fn 17) no 24 ff. See also *Heiss* (fn 1) no 5.
**20** Cf *Perner* (fn 17) no 27.
**21** See above no 3.
**22** *Rubin*, Comparative Report (fn 3) no 2. See also *Heiss* (fn 1) nos 2 and 12; *B Tettamanti/H Bär/J-C Werz*, Compulsory Liability Insurance in a Changing Legal Environment – An Insurance and Reinsurance Perspective (in this book) no 54. As for lobbying as a possible explanation for this insufficiency, see *Faure* (fn 5) no 48 ff.
**23** See *Rubin*, Comparative Report (fn 3) no 2.
**24** Cf *Tettamanti/Bär/Werz* (fn 22) no 127. Different national standards for the duty to take out liability insurance do, as a rule, not come into conflict with EU law; see on this *Perner* (fn 17) no 16 ff.

essary. It must be acknowledged that these guidelines can only provide a fairly general framework in the shape of a flexible system[25] consisting of the relevant aspects for the assessment of which liability risks should be insured against and which not (on this see the following no 6f). *Second*, framework provisions on the mandatory *content of insurance cover* (for instance, definition of the insured event, minimum insurance sum, admissibility of defences in relation to the insurance holder/the injured party etc) are needed[26] (on this see below no 17ff). *Third*, the same applies to framework provisions on the *legal consequences* linked to any *duty to take out liability insurance*[27] and, likewise, to the existence of an *insurance contract concluded* in fulfilment of such duty[28] (on both see below no 20ff).

6 The above-described *systematic deficiencies* seem to originate from the frequently observed *lack of the lawmakers' knowledge* on how (compulsory) liability insurance markets work, especially risk assessment and – in close connection with this – premium calculations within these markets.[29] One way to solve the problem would be that lawmakers, before establishing duties to take out liability insurance, should consult experts from the insurance industry who would provide the necessary technical knowledge.[30] In so doing, lawmakers would be better able to create duties that correspond with the economic realities of insurance markets.[31] This could also reduce the risk of establishing insurance duties that are impossible to fulfil since no insurer would be available to cover the specific risk.[32] In assessing whether a particular risk is insurable, it needs to be taken into account that duties to insure can lead to the creation of new insurance markets that would otherwise economically not be feasible for insurers.[33]

7 Moreover, a helpful tool for the *systematic assessment* of whether the introduction of compulsory liability insurance is advisable can be found in the

---

**25** On the flexible system as a methodological approach, cf *H Koziol*, Basic Questions of Tort Law from a Germanic Perspective (2012) no 1/28 ff.

**26** As for the present status in the legal systems investigated, see *Rubin*, Comparative Report (fn 3) nos 27–56.

**27** As for the present status in the legal systems investigated, see *Rubin*, Comparative Report (fn 3) nos 57–59 and 113–120.

**28** As for the present status in the legal systems investigated, see *Rubin*, Comparative Report (fn 3) nos 60–107.

**29** Cf eg *Cousy/Van Schoubroeck*, Report: Belgium (fn 2) no 22.

**30** Cf *Tettamanti/Bär/Werz* (fn 22) no 87; *Faure* (fn 5) no 46.

**31** *Tettamanti/Bär/Werz* (fn 22) no 35.

**32** *Faure* (fn 5) no 45f; *Tettamanti/Bär/Werz* (fn 22) no 41; also cf ibid no 28 ff.

**33** Cf on this phenomenon *Cousy/Van Schoubroeck*, Report: Belgium (fn 2) no 25; *Tettamanti/Bär/Werz* (fn 22) no 94.

evaluation scheme with predefined criteria that was developed by the *Swiss Insurance Association* (*Schweizerischer Versicherungsverband*, SVV) in 2013:[34] This scheme might serve as a good basis for further discussion on how to create a consistent – ie risk-adapted – system of compulsory liability insurance statutes.

## 4. Controlling the problem of moral hazard

A structural problem inherent to any compulsory liability insurance is the fact 8
that its establishment creates *moral hazard*, meaning that the mere existence of liability insurance cover automatically increases the risk of liability due to its generally observed negative effect on the level of care exercised by the insured.[35] Lawmakers can best solve the problem of moral hazard by leaving sufficient contractual freedom to insurers so that they remain able to differentiate the subjective risk of the insured and to formulate the insurance contract accordingly.[36] In this respect, there are *two different ways* of controlling moral hazard through the design of the contractual content.

One possibility would be to expose the insurance holder to the liability 9
risk and thus *tighten the conditions for cover*, be it by means of *risk exclusion clauses* (especially for intentional damage by the insured[37] or the insured's non-compliance with mandatory government regulations),[38] or be it by setting a *deductible*.[39] Both kinds of cover limitations might have a *diluting* effect on the *protection* of the *victim*.[40] As for a solution to this problem, see below nos 18 and 20.

The second means of risk differentiation in order to control moral hazard is 10
an *ex post adaptation of the price* of the cover (through a bonus malus system).[41]

A *combination* of both possibilities seems to be the most effective tool to re- 11
duce moral hazard in compulsory liability insurance as far as possible. Moreover, legal doctrine points out that a *functioning competitive insurance market*

**34** Cf on this *Tettamanti/Bär/Werz* (fn 22) nos 116–119 and 127.
**35** See *Rubin*, Introduction (fn 1) nos 2–4.
**36** Cf *M Faure*, Economic Criteria for Compulsory Insurance, The Geneva Papers 2006, 149, 157; *Faure* (fn 5) nos 26 and 43.
**37** On this very special risk exclusion, see *Rubin*, Comparative Report (fn 3) nos 54–56.
**38** *Faure* (fn 5) no 22.
**39** As for deductibles as a means of reducing moral hazard, see *Faure* (fn 5) no 31; *Tettamanti/Bär/Werz* (fn 22) nos 9 and 44.
**40** Cf *Faure* (fn 5) no 27.
**41** Cf *Faure* (fn 5) no 26.

that forces insurers to keep their costs low is a rather strong incentive for them to invest in measures against moral hazard.[42]

12 From what has been said so far, the conclusion must be drawn that a *free insurance market* with each *insurer's right to refusal* appears to be essential for the control of the insurance holder's moral hazard. Therefore, the introduction of an insurer's *duty to contract* would be fairly *problematic*[43] and, indeed, the legal systems in our study do not in general impose such a duty on insurers when it comes to concluding compulsory liability insurance contracts.[44]

13 Additionally, it should be borne in mind that the prevention of moral hazard can be, and in fact is, effectuated not only by contractual tools agreed on between the parties of the insurance contract but *also by means* of *criminal* and *administrative law* (penalties).

## 5. Compulsory liability insurance as an optional tool (alternative liability insurance)

14 As far as the *type or form of mandatory financial securities* is concerned, the aim of protecting the injured party from the injuring party's insolvency[45] does not necessarily require the legislator to prescribe compulsory liability insurance as the exclusive legal tool to be used by operators of hazardous activities. Another solution worth considering for legislators is to stipulate a duty to provide for financial security that may be fulfilled either by taking out liability insurance or *other forms of financial security* (eg bank guarantees,[46] pooling arrangements[47] between operators or other tools to secure the position of the victim).[48]

15 The main advantage of this *flexible scheme* as compared to compulsory liability insurance without alternative is that optional instruments might *better fit* the *financial situation of the individual operator* and also be more suitable for *risks with no established liability insurance market.*[49] The greater flexibility of

---

**42** Cf *Faure* (fn 5) no 32 ff.

**43** *Faure* (fn 5) no 30. Cf also, albeit rather generally addressing insurers' freedom to contract, *Tettamanti/Bär/Werz* (fn 22) no 60.

**44** See *Rubin*, Comparative Report (fn 3) no 57 f.

**45** As for this goal, see above no 1.

**46** Cf *Tettamanti/Bär/Werz* (fn 22) nos 96 and 101.

**47** On these, see *Faure* (fn 5) no 14.

**48** Strongly in favour of this solution *Faure* (fn 5) no 12 ff. As for the various types of financial security appropriate as a possible alternative to compulsory liability insurance *stricto sensu*, see further *Tettamanti/Bär/Werz* (fn 22) no 97 ff.

**49** See *Faure* (fn 5) no 14 f.

such a scheme might, on the other hand, create *higher costs of supervision* if the supervisory authority is forced to assess and monitor non-standardised financial security tools.[50] This problem could be solved by the legislator stipulating a certain *pool of standardised financial securities* out of which the most appropriate tool can be chosen by each operator under a duty to provide for a financial security according to his individual financial situation.[51]

The above-described scheme of alternative financial security *already exists* in respect of various activities in most legal systems in this study.[52] While it is partly disputed whether liability insurance that is optional to other forms of financial security actually qualifies as compulsory liability insurance in a technical sense,[53] there seem to be no convincing reasons why it should not.[54] 16

## III. Content of the Insurance Cover

### 1. Mandatory content of cover and recourse against the insured

*Mandatory* minimum requirements for *the content of cover* are in any case *necessary* for the sake of achieving the main aim of compulsory liability insurance, the protection of the victim.[55] Accordingly, all legal systems stipulate such *mandatory content* for compulsory liability insurance contracts. They relate, for example, to a ban on risk exclusions[56], deductibles[57] or aggregate limits[58]. The degree to which such restrictions of cover have to be prohibited is a matter open for further discussion in detail. As for the present status of such provisions within the legal systems at issue in this study, see the Comparative Report (in this book) no 35ff. It must be noted that these statutory rules set *limits to the contractual freedom* not only of the injuring party obligated to buy insurance cover but also of the *insurer*.[59] Interestingly, such cover-related requirements are 17

50 Cf also *Tettamanti/Bär/Werz* (fn 22) no 96.
51 This solution was brought forward by H Koziol during the discussion on this paper.
52 See *Rubin*, Comparative Report (fn 3) no 19; *Faure* (fn 5) no 15 f.
53 See *Rubin*, ibid.
54 Cf also *Faure* (fn 5) no 14 ff.
55 Cf likewise *Faure* (fn 5) no 24 for the achievement of externalisation (see above no 1).
56 On these, see *Rubin*, Comparative Report (fn 3) no 35.
57 On these, see *Rubin*, Comparative Report (fn 3) no 36 ff; *Faure* (fn 5) no 31.
58 On these, see *Rubin*, Comparative Report (fn 3) no 39 f.
59 Cf also *Perner* (fn 17) no 18.

to be found as a *general statutory rule* only under *German law*.[60] This rule specifies the necessary content of compulsory liability insurance regarding the minimum sum[61] and deductibles[62]. In all other cases, such rules are instead scattered in individual provisions regulating particular cases of compulsory liability insurance.[63]

18 The aforesaid stands in *conflict* with another requirement regarding compulsory liability insurance: Limitations of cover are required to control the risk of *moral hazard*.[64] The need to reconcile the aims of protecting the injured party and control of moral hazard leads rather unavoidably to the consequence that restrictions of cover are necessary and therefore allowed in relation to the insured, but they are (at least to a certain extent[65]) *not valid in relation to the victim*.[66] Thus, the insurer has a contractual duty only to provide cover in relation to the victim, meaning he must first pay out to the victim. The insurer's payment triggers his (contractual or statutory) right of *recourse against the insurance holder*.[67] This model is known for specific aspects of cover under *German*, *Austrian*, *Belgian*, *Swiss* and *United Kingdom* law.[68]

## 2. Minimum insurance sum

19 As for the *quantitative degree of protection* – ie the *amount of cover* – the most comprehensive way to reach compulsory liability insurance's aim of protecting the victim would be insurance which exactly corresponds to the possible amount of liability. However, this would lead, as a rule, to unlimited cover which cannot be feasible from an insurer's point of view.[69] And, indeed, the legal systems in this study very rarely prescribe compulsory liability insurance without limits.[70] From the victim's point of view, the next best solution would be a duty to purchase insurance coverage for the *amount of the expected loss*. The

---

**60** See § 114 of the German Insurance Contract Act (*Versicherungsvertragsgesetz*, VVG). On this provision in detail *Koch*, Report: Germany (fn 5) nos 22 ff, 28 ff and 35 ff.
**61** § 114 para 1 VVG.
**62** § 114 para 2 VVG.
**63** See *Rubin*, Comparative Report (fn 3) no 35 ff; see also *Faure* (fn 5) no 22.
**64** See above no 8 ff.
**65** See above no 17.
**66** Cf *Faure* (fn 5) no 21.
**67** Cf *Faure* (fn 5) nos 22 and 31 (deductibles).
**68** See *Rubin*, Comparative Report (fn 3) no 48 f.
**69** *Tettamanti/Bär/Werz* (fn 22) nos 15, 42, 59.
**70** See *Rubin*, Comparative Report (fn 3) no 32.

legislator will in general, however, face great difficulty in assessing the minimum insurance sum that can be seen as risk-adequate ex ante; the reason being that the magnitude of the liability risk at stake strongly depends on the size and exact operations of the particular enterprise that is the object of a particular duty to take out liability insurance.[71] Therefore, it would appear wise for the legislator to stipulate only a *margin*, within which it is at the licensing (supervisory) authority's discretion to prescribe a specific minimum insurance sum for the individual operator of a hazardous activity.[72]

# IV. Protection Mechanisms

## 1. Non-applicability of releases from payment as regards the victim and recourse against the insured

As mentioned above,[73] it is the victim that is usually the beneficiary of compulsory liability insurance cover. This entails certain mechanisms to secure the victim's interest in being indemnified. One of these is that the victim's position needs to be *independent from the internal relationship* between the parties to the insurance contract, as far as this is justifiable taking also into account the legitimate interests of the insurer. The insurer should therefore, in its relationship to the victim, *not be entitled* to rely on the fact that, vis-à-vis the insurance holder, it is *released from the obligation to pay*, for example, due to the insurance holder breaching an obligation of conduct/warranty (*Obliegenheitsverletzung*) or due to him defaulting on premiums. This is widely acknowledged by the legal orders in this study[74] and leads to the same consequences as shown above for restrictions of cover (above no 18): The insurer has to compensate the victim and can then take *recourse* against the insurance holder.[75] 20

71 Cf *Faure* (fn 5) no 19.
72 See the proposal put forward by *Faure* (fn 5) no 19.
73 See above no 1.
74 See *Rubin*, Comparative Report (fn 3) no 82 ff.
75 Cf *Faure* (fn 5) nos 22 and 24.

## 2. The victim's exclusive claim over the cover entitlement

21 As mentioned above, compulsory liability insurance mainly aims at ensuring the indemnification of the victim.[76] Consequently, the *exclusivity of the victim's claim for cover* against the insurer is essential: It is necessary to ensure that the insurance holder's cover entitlement is *reserved to satisfy* the insurance holder's duty to compensate *the victim*. This entails the following consequences.

22 a) The insurer's *payments to the insurance holder* cannot relieve the insurer of his cover obligation in relation to the victim unless the payment is effected with the victim's consent or the insurance holder has already indemnified the latter.[77] The same rule is also foreseen by the *Principles of European Insurance Contract Law* (PEICL).[78]

23 b) Further, the insurance holder is *prohibited from disposing over this claim* – be it by settlement with the insurer or with third parties – to the detriment of the victim, for example by surrendering his entitlement or by assigning it to a third party.[79] This is likewise foreseen as a rule by the PEICL.[80]

24 c) The victim also needs to enjoy priority over any enforcement proceedings in favour of the insured's other creditors on the insured's claim of cover.[81]

25 To a large extent compulsory liability insurance serves the purpose of protecting the victim against the injuring party's insolvency.[82] It therefore goes without saying that this protection needs to expand into the cover entitlement against the insurer. One efficient way to achieve this goal is the establishment of the *victim's direct action* against the insurer,[83] as is also foreseen by the PEICL for all compulsory liability insurance.[84] The other possible way is to grant the

---

**76** Above no 1.

**77** On this, see *Rubin*, Comparative Report (fn 3) no 60 ff.

**78** *Heiss* (fn 1) no 24. The PEICL are to be seen as model for a European insurance contract law designed by European academics to serve as an optional instrument available to be chosen by the parties to an insurance contract; cf *Heiss* (fn 1) nos 6 and 8 ff.

**79** See *Rubin*, Comparative Report (fn 3) no 60 ff on the current situation in the legal systems of this study.

**80** *Heiss* (fn 1) no 27 f. However, this rule would play no role within the scope of the PEICL since they grant the victim a direct action which is not subject to the insurance holder's dispositions; cf *Heiss*, ibid no 28.

**81** See also *Heiss* (fn 1) no 1.

**82** See above no 1.

**83** See *Rubin*, Comparative Report (fn 3) no 64; *Faure* (fn 5) no 23; *Heiss* (fn 1) no 1. On the scope of this *action directe* in the legal systems in this study, see *Rubin*, Comparative Report (fn 3) no 71 ff.

**84** As to the PEICL see *Heiss* (fn 1) no 20 ff.

victim a *right to separate satisfaction* out of the insurance holder's claim against the insurer, as is the case, for example, in *Germany, Austria* and *Switzerland*.[85]

### 3. Necessity of the insurer's obligation to contract?

26 As already stated,[86] the *insurer's duty to contract* is not a necessary tool to protect the victim's interests and would even be counterproductive.

## V. Supervision

### 1. Compulsory liability insurance as authorisation requirement

27 Any lawmaker imposing compulsory liability insurance has to make sure that the liability to be insured against is covered, otherwise the establishment of mandatory insurance would be without effect.[87] The most effective tool – and thus not to be seen as a disproportional restriction of the insured's freedoms[88] – to achieve this aim is to impose liability insurance as a *condition to obtain authorisation* for the commencement of an activity or profession. And indeed, such requirements are widespread within the legal systems in our study: it is already rather often the case that the authorising body has to check *ex ante whether* the insurance has been taken out and whether the conditions are in accordance with the legal requirements.[89]

28 This may lead to the consequence that insurers de facto become licensors of industry,[90] which is considered by some as problematic.[91] However, another view seems more appropriate: If in a competitive insurance market (so that a market failure can be excluded as the reason for insurers' refusal to contract) no insurer is willing to underwrite the specific liability risk in question, this would

---

**85** See *Rubin*, Comparative Report (fn 3) no 65.
**86** See above no 12.
**87** Also cf *Faure* (fn 5) no 21.
**88** See above no 3 (constitutional law) and no 4 (EU primary law) as well as *Perner* (fn 17) no 20 f.
**89** See *Rubin*, Comparative Report (fn 3) no 113. As for the understanding of such requirement as compulsory liability insurance, see *Rubin*, ibid no 18.
**90** Cf *Faure* (fn 5) nos 33 and 45.
**91** *Tettamanti/Bär/Werz* (fn 22) no 73.

seem to indicate that the underlying activity might be *too hazardous* and should therefore not be undertaken.[92]

## 2. Monitoring of the maintenance of cover

29 Further, compliance with compulsory liability insurance regulations needs regular monitoring after the commencement of the activity or profession subject to the duty to obtain liability insurance.[93] Therefore, it would also seem to be essential for the protection of victims that *insurers inform the supervisory authority* when insurance *cover ends*.[94] However, such a duty is not yet widespread among the legal systems in this study.[95] In any case, according to the *German* model that was also adopted by *Austria*, insurance cover does not end in relation to the injured party until a certain time span has elapsed after the contract's termination has been notified to the supervisory authority.[96] This maintains the protection of the victim while the authority has time to force the operator of the hazardous activity to obtain new insurance cover or to cease the activity in question.

## 3. Official body for the victim's inquiries about compulsory liability insurance

30 The victim's difficulty in enforcing claims would be greatly reduced if an official body existed where a victim could find out whether and where the injuring party who inflicted damage upon him in the course of an activity requiring insurance has liability insurance cover. Generally, such information bodies are not foreseen by our legal systems.[97]

---

**92** Cf *Faure* (fn 5) no 29.
**93** Cf eg *Cousy/Van Schoubroeck*, Report: Belgium (fn 2) no 22.
**94** Cf also *Tettamanti/Bär/Werz* (fn 22) no 72.
**95** See *Rubin*, Comparative Report (fn 3) no 114 f.
**96** See *Rubin*, Comparative Report (fn 3) no 93 and, for further examples in other legal systems, ibid no 94.
**97** See *Rubin*, Comparative Report (fn 3) no 118.

# Annex: Rules on Compulsory Liability Insurance

Daniel Rubin

# Austria

## I. Federal Law

The following laws may be downloaded in the original German at http://www.ris.bka.gv.at/Bundesrecht/.

### 1. Strict liability

| | |
|---|---|
| Aircraft, aerial vehicles or aerial devices<br>keepers of ~ | §§ 164, 166 ff Aviation Act (*Luftfahrtgesetz*, LFG) |
| Cableway enterprises | §§ 29, 103 Cableway Act (*Seilbahngesetz*, SeilbG) 2003 |
| Genetically modified organisms<br>working with/release of ~ | § 79j Gene Technology Act (*Gentechnikgesetz*, GTG) |
| Land, water and air vehicles<br>keepers of ~ | Art 56 Vienna Convention on Diplomatic Relations |
| Military aircraft, motor vehicles, and water vehicles<br>keepers of ~ | § 4 no 13 Act on the Stationing of Troops (*Truppenaufenthaltsgesetz*, TrAufG) |
| Motor vehicles<br>keepers of ~ | § 36 lit d, § 59, § 62 Motor Vehicles Act (*Kraftfahrgesetz*, KFG) 1967 |
| Motor vehicles<br>owners and users of ~ | Art 7 no 5 and art 8 no 6 Protocol on the Privileges and Immunities of the International Seabed Authority<br>Art 5 (4), art 13 (5), art 14 (3) Agreement on the Privileges and Immunities of the International Tribunal for the Law of the Sea |
| Natural gas networks<br>operators of ~ | § 44 para 1 no 2, § 51, § 58 para 1 no 19, § 62 para 1 no 13 Natural Gas Act (*Gaswirtschaftsgesetz*, GWG) |
| Nuclear material<br>carriers of ~ | §§ 6, 7 Nuclear Liability Act (*Atomhaftungsgesetz*, AtomHG) (alternative liability insurance) |
| Nuclear plants located in Austria<br>operators of ~ | §§ 6, 8 Nuclear Liability Act (AtomHG) (alternative liability insurance) |

| | |
|---|---|
| Pipelines<br>operation of ~<br>or transportation of goods in ~ | §§ 13, 21, 33 Pipelines Act (*Rohrleitungsgesetz*)<br>§ 78 para 3 Trade Act (*Gewerbeordnung*, GewO) |
| Producers/importers | § 16 Product Liability Act (*Produkthaftungsgesetz*, PHG) |
| Radionuclides<br>holders of ~ | §§ 9, 10 Nuclear Liability Act (AtomHG) |
| Space activities<br>operators of ~ | § 4 Austrian Space Act (*Weltraumgesetz*) |
| Tow lift enterprises | § 6 no 6 Tow Lift Ordinance (*Schepplifteverordnung*, SchleppVO) 2004 |

## 2. Fault liability

| | |
|---|---|
| Accountants<br>self-employed ~ | § 7 para 1 no 4 and § 10 Accountancy Act (*Bilanzbuchhaltungsgesetz*, BiBuG) |
| Air carriers | Regulation (EC) No 785/2004 on insurance requirements for air carriers and aircraft operators<br>Art 7 Regulation (EEC) No 2407/92 licensing of air carriers |
| Air transport enterprises | § 106 para 1 lit c Aviation Act (LFG) |
| Airfields<br>operators of civil ~ | § 72 para 1 lit c Aviation Act (LFG) |
| Airports<br>ground services at ~ | § 7 para 2 no 4 Airport Ground Service Act (*Flughafen-Bodenabfertigungsgesetz*, FBG) |
| Attorneys-at-law | § 1 para 2 lit g, § 21a Attorney Code (*Rechtsanwaltsordnung*, RAO) and § 87c para 1 Notary Code (NO) (voluntary auction of real properties) |
| Austrian Aero Club | § 6 Austrian Aero Club Competence Ordinance (*ÖAeC-Zuständigkeitsverordnung*) |
| Builders | § 99 (7–10) Trade Act (GewO) |
| Dentists<br>self-employed ~ | § 26c Dentists Act (*Zahnärztegesetz*, ZÄG) |
| Development aid organisations | § 7 para 2 Development Aid Workers Act (*Entwicklungshelfergesetz*) |
| Doctors<br>self-employed ~ | § 52d Medical Doctors Act (*Ärztegesetz*, ÄrzteG) |

| | |
|---|---|
| Expert witnesses, interpreters | § 2 para 2 lit l, § 2a Expert Witnesses and Interpreters Act (*Sachverständigen- und Dolmetschergesetz*, SDG) |
| Financial advisors<br>commercial ~ | § 136a para 12 Trade Act (GewO) |
| Hospitals and outpatient clinics<br>operators of ~ | § 3 para 4 lit f, § 3b para 1 no 5, § 5c Hospitals and Health Resorts Act (*Krankenanstalten- und Kuranstaltengesetz*, KAKuG) |
| Insurance brokers | § 137c Trade Act (GewO) (alternative liability insurance) |
| Investment services providers | § 4 paras 2 and 3, § 9 para 2 Securities Supervision Act (*Wertpapieraufsichtsgesetz*, WAG) (alternative liability insurance) |
| Medicinal products<br>specified body for the development of ~ | § 37 para 8 Medical Devices Act (*Medizinproduktegesetz*, MPG) (alternative liability insurance) |
| Music therapists<br>self-employed ~ | § 34 Music Therapy Act (*Musiktherapiegesetz*) |
| Natural gas networks<br>responsible party of a balance group of the users of ~ | § 93 para 1 no 5 Natural Gas Act (GWG) (alternative liability insurance) |
| Notaries | § 14 para 1 no 3, § 30, § 109a para 6 Code on Notaries (*Notariatsordnung*, NO) |
| Patent attorneys | § 2 para 1 lit g, § 21a Patent Attorneys Act (*Patentanwaltsgesetz*) |
| Pharmaceutical products | § 32 para 1 nos 11 and 12 Pharmaceutical Products Act (*Arzneimittelgesetz*, AMG) |
| Pharmacists | § 4a Pharmacy Act (*Apothekengesetz*) |
| Postal services<br>providers of ~ | § 28 para 1 no 2 Postal Market Act (*Postmarktgesetz*) |
| Psychologists<br>self-employed ~ | § 39 Psychologists Act 2013 (*Psychologengesetz* 2013) |
| Psychotherapists<br>self-employed ~ | § 16b Psychotherapy Act (*Psychotherapiegesetz*) |
| Railway companies (insurance duty for the benefit of the head of operations and his/her deputy) | § 6 para 2, § 14 no 7 Railway Ordinance 2003 (*Eisenbahnverordnung*, EisbVO 2003) |

| | |
|---|---|
| Real estate trustees = real estate brokers, administrators and real estate developers | § 117 para 7 Trade Act (GewO) |
| Shipowners | § 18 Maritime Shipping Act (*Seeschifffahrtsgesetz*, SeeSchFG)<br>Art 7 International Convention on Civil Liability for Bunker Oil Pollution Damage 2001 |
| Ships<br>holders of ~ | Art 6 para 3 of the Agreement on Shipping on Lake Constance (*Übereinkommen über die Schifffahrt am Bodensee*) |
| Signature and certification services | § 7 para 1 no 6, § 25 no 2 Signature Act (*Signaturgesetz*, SigG)<br>§ 2, § 14 para 2 no 3 Signature Ordinance (*Signaturverordnung*, SigV) 2008 (alternative liability insurance) |
| Tax advisors and auditors | § 8 para 1 no 4, § 11, § 65 para 1 no 6, § 70 para 1 no 6, § 111 para 1 no 5, § 231 para 1 no 4 Certified Public Accountants and Tax Advisors Act (*Wirtschaftstreuhandberufsgesetz*, WTBG)<br>§ 9 para 2 lit a Takeover Act (*Übernahmegesetz*, ÜbG) (for auditors)<br>§§ 25, 25b, 25c Audit Quality Assurance Act (*Abschlussprüfungs-Qualitätssicherungsgesetz*, A-QSG) (for auditors from the EU, EEA and third countries) |
| Transportation of people with certain trailers<br>commercial ~ | § 156 Trade Act (GewO) |
| Transportation of waste across borders | § 68 para 1 nos 4 and 5, § 70 Waste Management Act (*Abfallwirtschaftsgesetz*, AWG) 2002 (partly alternative liability insurance) |

## 3. Insurance duties in respect of recourse duties vis-à-vis the state on the part of entrepreneurs entrusted with sovereign functions (fault liability)

| | |
|---|---|
| Accredited bodies evaluating conformity (in particular, testing laboratories, inspection bodies, calibration bodies and certification bodies) | § 12 para 7 Accreditation Act (*Akkreditierungsgesetz*, AkkG) 2012<br>Ordinance on Accreditation Insurance (*Akkreditierungsversicherungsverordnung*, AkkVV) |
| Air traffic control organisations | § 120b para 4 Aviation Act (LFG) |

| | |
|---|---|
| Aircraft, aerial vehicles or aerial devices<br>producers of ~ | § 140b para 5 no 3 Aviation Act (LFG) |
| Cableway parts<br>specific body to test EC conformity of ~ | § 72 para 2 no 6 Cableway Act (SeilbG) 2003 |
| Civil airfields<br>keepers of ~ | § 5 no 4 Aviation Security Act (*Luftfahrtsicherheitsgesetz*, LSG) 2011 |
| Pressure equipment approval and pressure equipment inspection bodies | § 28 Boiler Act (*Kesselgesetz*) |
| Security enterprises (security checks in courts) | § 10 no 7 Court Organisation Act (*Gerichtsorganisationsgesetz*, GOG) |

# II. Laws of the Provinces (State Laws)

The following laws may be downloaded in the original German at http://www.ris.bka.gv.at/Land/.

## 1. Strict liability

It appears that there are no cases of strict liability on the level of the laws of the provinces.

## 2. Fault liability

| | |
|---|---|
| Beekeepers | §§ 11, 12 Burgenland Act on Beekeeping (*Burgenländisches Bienenzuchtgesetz*)<br>§§ 9, 17 Carinthian Apiculture Act (*Kärntner Bienenwirtschaftsgesetz*)<br>§§ 6, 12 Lower Austrian Act on Beekeeping (*Niederösterreichisches Bienenzuchtgesetz*)<br>§§ 8, 11a Salzburg Apiculture Act (*Salzburger Bienenwirtschaftsgesetz*)<br>§§ 14, 15 Styrian Act on Beekeeping (*Steiermärkisches Bienenzuchtgesetz*) |

| | |
|---|---|
| | §§ 10, 17 Upper Austrian Act on Beekeeping (*Oberösterreichisches Bienenzuchtgesetz*)<br>§ 10 Vienna Act on the Keeping and Breeding of Bees (*Wiener Gesetz über die Haltung und Zucht von Bienen*) |
| Dog owners | § 4 Lower Austrian Dog Owners Act (*Niederösterreichisches Hundehaltegesetz*) 2002<br>§ 9 Upper Austrian Dog Owners Act (*Oberösterreichisches Hundehaltegesetz*) 2002<br>§ 5 Viennese Act on the Protection and Keeping of Animals (*Wiener Tierhaltegesetz*) |
| Event organisers | § 6 Burgenland Events Act (*Burgenländisches Veranstaltungsgesetz*)<br>§ 3 Carinthian Events Act (*Kärntner Veranstaltungsgesetz*) 2010<br>§ 5 Lower Austrian Events Act (*Niederösterreichisches Veranstaltungsgesetz*)<br>§ 7 Salzburg Events Act (*Salzburger Veranstaltungsgesetz*) 1997<br>§ 4 Styrian Events Act (*Steiermärkisches Veranstaltungsgesetz*) 2012<br>§ 6 Tyrolean Events Act (*Tiroler Veranstaltungsgesetz*) 2003<br>§ 5 Vorarlberg Events Act (*Vorarlberger Veranstaltungsgesetz*) |
| Fisheries | § 31 Lower Austrian Fisheries Act (*Niederösterreichisches Fischereigesetz*) 2002<br>§ 10 Vorarlberg Fisheries Ordinance (*Vorarlberger Fischereiverordnung*) |
| Hackney carriagemen ('Fiaker') | § 3 Salzburg Regulations for 'Fiakers' (*Salzburger Fiaker-Betriebsordnung*)<br>§§ 3, 14 Viennese 'Fiaker' and Horsedrawn Hackney Carriages Act (*Wiener Fiaker- und Pferdemietwagengesetz*) |
| Hunters | §§ 122, 123 Salzburg Hunting Act (*Salzburger Jagdgesetz*) 1993<br>§§ 27, 28 Tyrolean Hunting Act (*Tiroler Jagdgesetz*)<br>§§ 51, 58 Viennese Hunting Act (*Wiener Jagdgesetz*) |
| Mountain guides | §§ 4, 16, 21 Tyrolean Mountain Sport Guide Act (*Tiroler Bergsportführergesetz*)<br>§ 31 Tyrolean Mountain Sport Guide Ordinance (*Tiroler Bergsportführerverordnung*)<br>§ 12 Vorarlberg Mountain Guide Act (*Vorarlberger Bergführergesetz*) |

| | |
|---|---|
| Ski schools | §§ 4, 13 Carinthian Ski School Act (*Kärntner Schischulgesetz*, K-SschG)<br>§§ 15, 32 Lower Austrian Sports Act (*Niederösterreichisches Sportgesetz*)<br>§§ 3, 8 Salzburg Ski School and Snowboarding School Act (*Salzburger Schischul- und Snowboardschulgesetz*)<br>§§ 5, 29 Styrian Ski School Act (*Steiermärkisches Schischulgesetz*) 1997<br>§§ 4a, 4b, 5, 8 Tyrolean Ski School Act (*Tiroler Schischulgesetz*) 1995<br>§ 52 Tyrolean Ski Instructor Ordinance (*Tiroler Schilehrerverordnung*)<br>§§ 3e, 8, 16 Vorarlberg Ski School Act (*Vorarlberger Schischulgesetz*)<br>§ 1 Ordinance Issued by the Government of Vorarlberg regarding the Liability Insurance of Instructors at Ski Schools (*Verordnung der Vorarlberger Landesregierung über die Haftpflichtversicherung für Lehrkräfte an Schischulen*) |

## 3. Insurance duties in respect of recourse duties vis-à-vis the state on the part of entrepreneurs entrusted with sovereign functions (fault liability)

| | |
|---|---|
| Fire brigades | § 41a Carinthian Fire Brigade Act (*Kärntner Feuerwehrgesetz*, K-FWG)<br>§ 20 Upper Austrian Fire Brigade Act (*Oberösterreichisches Feuerwehrgesetz*) |

Herman Cousy and Caroline Van Schoubroeck

# Belgium

## I. Federal Law

The following laws may be downloaded in the original Dutch and French versions at http://www.ejustice.just.fgov.be/cgi_wet/wetgeving.pl (Dutch) or http://www.ejustice.just.fgov.be/loi/loi.htm (French).

The list of all compulsory insurance, organised according to the subject matter, including a reference to the origin of each act or regulation in 'Belgisch Staatsblad/Moniteur belge', may be downloaded from the Financial Services and Market Authority (FSMA) website at http://www.fsma.be/nl/Supervision/finbem/vohvo/Article/wetteksten/verp.aspx (Dutch) or http://www.fsma.be/fr/Supervision/finbem/vohvo/Article/wetteksten/verp.aspx (French).

Nearly all laws and regulations, hereafter listed, simply refer to the compulsory insurance of the 'civil liability' of the person in question, a term which refers to fault liability or strict liability and often to both.

Following the instructions of the editors of the Questionnaire, an effort is made to separate those types of compulsory insurance where the insured liability is exclusively or mainly 'strict' from the others. Nevertheless the reader must be warned that the following classification is neither accurate nor complete.

### 1. Strict liability

| **Buildings and locations open to the public** | |
|---|---|
| Buildings usually open to the public<br>holders of ~ | Art 7 Act (on prevention of fire and explosions in public buildings) 30 July 1979 (*prévention des incendies et explosions*)<br>Royal Decree (RD) 28 February 1991 (definition of 'building and location open to the public'), implementing art 7 of the Act (*prévention des incendies et explosions*)<br>RD 5 August 1991 (insured amounts), implementing art 7 of the Act (*prévention des incendies et explosions*) |
| Dwellings under construction<br>sellers or contractors of~<br>(guarantee of achievement of the building) | Art 12 Act 9 July 1971 (on dwellings under construction) (*vente d'habitation à construire*)<br>RD 21 September 2012 implementing art 12 of the Act (*vente d'habitation à construire*) |

| | |
|---|---|
| **Health care** | |
| Medical experiments on humans<br>liability of research instances for damage suffered by participants in direct or indirect connection with ~ | Art 5, 9° and art 29 Act (on medical experiments on humans) 7 May 2004 (*expérimentations sur la personne humaine*) |
| **Nuclear installations** | |
| Ionising radiation<br>institutions working with ~ | Arts 6, 7 and 8 RD (on the protection of the population and workers against ionising radiation) 20 July 2001 (*rayonnements ionisants*) |
| Nuclear installations<br>operators of ~ | Paris Convention (29 July 1960) on civil liability in the domain of nuclear energy, and complementary Convention of Brussels (31 January 1963), and Protocols (incl strict liability) (*énergie nucléaire*)<br>Act of 1 August 1966 ratifying the Paris Convention (arts 4 and 10 of the Convention) (*approbation d'actes internationaux*)<br>Art 8 Act (on civil liability in the domain of nuclear energy) 22 July 1985 (*domaine de l'énergie nucléaire*) |
| **Transport** | |
| Foreign aircraft<br>carriers/operators of ~ | Art 3 Act 14 July 1966 ratifying arts 1 and 15 Rome Convention (on damage caused by foreign aircraft to third parties on the surface) 7 October 1952 (*dommages causés au tiers à la surface par aéronefs étrangers*) |

## 2. Fault liability

| | |
|---|---|
| **Accountancy and tax professions** | |
| Accounting experts and tax advisors | Arts 33 and 50 Act (on accountancy and tax professions) 22 April 1999 (*professions comptables et fiscales*) |
| **Animals** | |
| Animal farms<br>operators of ~ | Art 5 Act (on animal welfare) 14 August 1986 (*protection et bien-être des animaux*) |
| Veterinarians | Art 4 Act (on the practice of veterinary medicine) 28 August 1991 (*médecine vétérinaire*) |
| Zoos (authorisation requirement)<br>operators of ~ | Art 2, § 2, 7° RD 10 August 1998 (*parcs zoologiques*) |

| | |
|---|---|
| **Architects and contractors** | |
| Architects | Art 9 Act (on the profession of architect) 20 February 1939 (*profession d'architecte*)<br>RD 25 April 2007 implementing art 9 of the Act (*profession d'architecte*) |
| **Civil security (*Sécurité civile*)** | |
| Financial requirements for special accounting officers (*comptable spécial*) | Art 77, § 2 Act 15 May 2007 concerning civil security (*sécurité civile*) |
| **Environment** | |
| Applicants for domain concessions for installations of hydro-electrical energy on the sea-floor | Art 2, 7° and art 15, 12° RD 8 May 2014 (*stockage d'énergie dans les espaces marins*) |
| Biological resources of the sea-floor<br>operators of ~ | Art 9, § 2 Act (on the exploitation of resources of the sea-floor) 17 August 2013 (*ressources des fonds marins*)<br>RD 4 October 2013 (*ressources des fonds marins*) |
| Plant protection and adjuvants<br>sustainable use of ~ | Annex 1, art 1, j RD 19 March 2013 (*produits phytopharmaceutiques et adjuvants*) |
| Shipment of waste | Art 6 Regulation (EC) No 1013/2006 (*transferts de déchets*) |
| **Health care** | |
| Banks for human body material for medical and scientific purposes<br>liability of operators of ~ towards donors | Art 17, § 4 Act (on human body material for medical and scientific purposes) 19 December 2008 (*matériel corporel humain*) |
| Blood banks<br>operators of ~ | Art 3, § 2, 6° RD 4 April 1996 (*sang et dérivés du sang*) |
| Medical control of occupational<br>disability<br>consulting physicians for the ~ | Art 16 RD no 35 20 July 1967 (*soins de santé*) |
| Non-conventional medicine<br>practitioners of ~ | Art 5 RD 26 March 2014 (*pratiques non-conventionelles*) |
| Psychologists | Art 27 RD 2 April 2014 (*psychologues*) |
| Supervisors of apprentice medical specialists | Art 38 Ministerial Decree 23 April 2014 (*médecins spécialistes*) |

| | |
|---|---|
| **Intermediation** | |
| Apprentice real estate agents<br>registration of ~ | Art 4, 6° RD 23 July 2013 (concerning the Professional Institute of Real Estate Agents) (*Institut professionnel des agents immobiliers*) |
| Debt collectors | Arts 4 and 19 Act (on the amicable recovery of debts and guarantees) 20 December 2002 (*médiation de dettes*)<br>Art 2, 3° RD 17 February 2005, implementing arts 4 and 19 of the Act (*recouvrement amiable de dettes*) |
| Independent financial planners[1] | Art 14 Act 25 April 2014 (*planificateurs financiers*)<br>Art 3, 4°, art 4, 6° and art 9 RD 8 July 2014, implementing the Act (*planificateurs financiers*) |
| Insurance and reinsurance intermediaries | Art 10 (1) Act (on insurance distribution) 27 March 1995 (*intermédiation en assurances*)<br>Art 18 RD 25 March 1996, implementing art 10 of the Act (*intermédiation en assurances*) |
| Intermediaries in banking and investment services and financial instruments | Art 8, 5° Act (on intermediation in banking and investment services) 22 March 2006 (*intermédiation en services bancaires et d'investissement*)<br>Arts 11 and 12 RD 1 July 2006, implementing the Act (*intermédiation en services bancaires et d'investissement*) |
| Mortgage credit intermediaries | Art VII, 180, § 1, 4° Code of Economic Law (2014) (*crédit hypothécaire*) |
| Real estate agents | Art 4 Act (on the profession of real estate agent) 11 February 2013 (*agents immobiliers*) |
| **Land surveyors** | |
| Land surveyors (access to the profession) | Art 1 RD 25 April 2007 (implementing RD of 15 December 2005) (*géomètre-expert*) |
| **Local public institutions** | |
| Electoral bureaus<br>members of ~ | Art 24, § 2 RD 21 March 2014 (*opérations en vue des élections simultanées*) |
| Emphyteutic lessee of a specific immovable property in the city of Nieuwpoort | Art 6 RD 18 July 2013 (*mise à disposition d'un bien immobilier*) |
| **Notaries** | |
| Notaries | Arts 34ter and 50, § 4 Act of 25 Ventôse Year XI, as modified by the Act of 25 April 2014 (*notaires*) |

1 Considered as intermediaries in the FSMA classification.

| | |
|---|---|
| **Payment services and institutions for collective investment** | |
| Cover of cash deposits with a payment institution | Art 78, § 1, c Act (on payment services) 21 December 2009 (as amended by the Act of 27 November 2012) (*établissements de paiement*) |
| Institutions for collective investment and their managers | Art 22, § 5, 2° Act (on alternative investment funds) 19 April 2014 (*organismes de placement collectif alternatifs*) |
| Payment institutions | Art 22, § 1, c Act (on payment services) 21 December 2009 (as amended by the Act of 27 November 2012) (*établissements de paiement*)<br>Art 15 RD 7 December 2010, implementing art 22, § 1, c of the Act (*sicafi*) |
| Real estate companies<br>subsidiaries of publicly registered ~ | Art 6, 7° Act (on registered real estate companies) 12 May 2014 (*sociétés immobilières réglementées*) |
| **Public procurement** | |
| Public works and supplies in the field of defence and security<br>providers of ~ | Act (on public procurement) 13 August 2011 (*marchés publics*)<br>Art 69 RD 23 January 2012, implementing the Act (*marchés publics*) |
| **Service providers** | |
| Electronic service providers<br>confidential advisors of ~ | Art 10 Act (on the legal framework for providers of confidential services) 15 May 2007 (*services de confiance*) |
| Providers whose services present a direct and particular risk to the health or safety of the recipient or a third person, or to the financial security of the recipient<br>(No double requirement of liability insurance and proof of existing insurance in other Member State) | Art 23 European Directive 2006/123/EC on services in the internal market (*services dans le marché intérieur*)<br>Arts 8 and 14, 7° Services Act 26 March 2010, implementing the Services Directive |
| **Sports** | |
| Organisers of cycling competitions | Art 14 RD 21 August 1967 (*courses cyclistes*) |
| **Surveillance and security firms and services** | |
| Maritime security companies | Art 6, 3° Act (on maritime piracy) 16 January 2013 (*piraterie maritime*)<br>Art 3, 3° RD 2 September 2013, implementing art 6, 3° of the Act (*entreprise de sécurité maritime*) |

| | |
|---|---|
| Surveillance firms and internal surveillance services | Art 3 Act (on private safety) 10 April 1990 (*sécurité privée*)<br>RD 27 June 1991, arts 2 and 7 (insurance certificate) implementing art 3 of the Act (*entreprise de gardiennage*) |
| **Syndicus** | |
| Syndicus (property manager of an apartment building) | Art 577–8, § 4, 10° Civil code (*Code civil*) |
| **Technical control organisms** | |
| Construction sites<br>safety coordinators of temporary or mobile ~ | Art 65sexies RD 25 January 2001 (*chantiers temporaires ou mobiles*) |
| Containers<br>control organisms of safety of ~ | Art 10 RD 4 June 1984 (*sécurité des conteneurs*) |
| Financial Services and Market Authority (FSMA)<br>compliance officers of ~ | Art 4 RD 12 March 2012 (*agrément des compliance officers*) |
| Inspection bodies | Art 1/3, 5° RD 18 January 1990 (*ouvrages en métaux précieux*) |
| Instances charged with safety assessment procedures for railways | Art 3 RD 8 December 2013 (*organismes de vérification de sécurité*) |
| Laboratories responsible for safety of the food chain<br>licensing of ~ | Art 5, 16° RD 3 August 2012 (*sécurité de la chaîne alimentaire*) |
| Licensed organisms<br>liability of directors of ~ | Art 829bis lit e General Regulation on employment protection 27 September 1947 (*protection du travail*)<br>Ministerial Decree 26 August 1971 (*protection du travail*) |
| Measuring instruments<br>controlling organisms for ~ | Art 12, 7° RD 13 June 2006 (*instruments de mesure*) |
| Motor vehicle inspection<br>organisms for ~ | Art 19 RD 23 December 1994 (*contrôle des véhicules en circulation*) |
| Pleasure boats<br>gas and sound emissions of ~ | Art N14 RD 23 February 2005 (*bateaux de plaisance*) |
| Safety of toys,<br>control organisms for ~ | Annex N3 RD 4 March 2002 (*sécurité des jouets*) |
| Security firms | Art 7, 7° RD 27 May 2014 (*sécurité privée et particulière*) |

| | |
|---|---|
| Workplace<br>external services for technical inspection of the ~ | Art 6, § 7 RD 29 April 1999 (*contrôles techniques sur le lieu de travail*) |
| **Tourism** | |
| Travel agencies and intermediaries | Art 37 Act (on travel organisations and intermediation) 16 February 1994 (*agences de voyage*)<br>RD 1 February 1995 (insurance conditions), implementing the Act (*agences de voyage*) |
| **Transport** | |
| Air carriers<br>licensing of ~ | Art 7 Regulation (EEC) No 2407/92 23 July 1992 (*transporteurs aériens*) |
| Airfields for paramotors<br>operators of ~ | Art 37, § 1, 2° and § 2, 2° RD 10 June 2014 (*circulation aérienne des paramoteurs*) |
| Carriers of passengers by sea | Art 4 RD 13 June 2012 (*responsabilité des transporteurs par mer en cas d'accident*) |
| Carriers of passengers by sea<br>evaluation organisms of ~ | Act 26 November 2012 ratifying the 2002 Protocol to the 1974 Athens Convention, art 4bis of the Convention (*transport par mer de passagers*) |
| Dangerous and harmful substances<br>transport by sea of ~ | HNS (Hazardous and Noxious Substances) Convention 1996 (liability for damage caused by transport by sea of dangerous and harmful substances) (*substances nocives et dangereuses*) |
| Driving schools<br>liability of learner drivers and passengers of ~ | Art 15 RD 20 September 2012 (*écoles de conduite des véhicules*) |
| International air carriers | Art 6 Regulation (EC) No 785/2004 (insurance requirements for air carriers and aircraft operators) (*transporteurs aériens et exploitants d'aéronefs*) |
| Maintenance of railway vehicles<br>operators of ~ | Art 4 RD 21 December 2010 (*maintenance des véhicules ferroviaires*) |
| Motor vehicles<br>holders of ~ | Act (on compulsory motor vehicle liability insurance) 21 November 1989 (*assurance obligatoire de responsabilité*)<br>RD 14 December 1992 (on model contract) (*assurance obligatoire de responsabilité*) |
| Museum railways<br>liability of operators of ~ | Art 21 Act (on the safety of museum railway lines) 26 March 2014 (*lignes ferroviaires musées*)<br>Art 5 RD 8 May 2014 (*lignes ferroviaires musées*) |

| | |
|---|---|
| Railway inspection bodies | Annex N21.6 Act 30 August 2013 (Rail Codex) (*Code ferroviaire*) |
| Railway undertakings | Art 14 Act (on the use of railway infrastructure) 4 December 2006 (*infrastructure ferroviaire*) |
| Railway undertakings<br>liability towards railway passengers of ~ | Art 12 EU Regulation (EC) No 1371/2007 23 October 2007 (*voyageurs par chemin de fer et par route*)<br>Art 9, 10° Act 15 May 2014, implementing the EU Regulation (*voyageurs ferroviaires*) |
| Safety verification<br>organisms charged with ~ | Annex 1, art 6 Act (on interoperability of EU railway system) 26 January 2010 (*interopérabilité du système ferroviaire*) |
| School transport<br>providers of ~ | Art 7, 12° RD 28 June 1962 (*transport commun des élèves*) |
| Ships under Belgian flag<br>owners of ~ | Art 5 Act (of insurance of shipowners against maritime claims) 30 January 2012 (*créances maritimes*) |
| Transport of gaseous and other products through pipelines | Art 2, § 1, 6° RD 14 May 2002 (*transport de produits gazeux*) |
| Transport of passengers by road | Art 35 RD 21 April 2007 (*transport de personnes par route*) |
| Transport of travellers by bus<br>providers of remunerated ~ | Decree-law 30 December 1946 (*transport de personnes par autobus*)<br>Art 6 Decree of the Regent 20 September 1947 (*transport de personnes par autobus*) |
| **Volunteers** | |
| Organisations working with volunteers | Art 5 Act 3 July 2005 (*droit des volontaires*) |

# II. Regional Legislation and Regulation (Laws of Local Entities in the Federal State: 'Regions' and 'Communities')[2]

The following laws may be downloaded in the original Dutch and French version at http://www.ejustice.just.fgov.be/cgi_wet/wetgeving.pl (Dutch) or http://www.ejustice.just.fgov.be/loi/loi.htm (French).

---

2 There are communities and regions in Belgium. In both there are bodies with legislative power and bodies with executive power.

The list of all compulsory insurance, organised according to the subject matter, including a reference to the origin of each act or regulation in 'Belgisch Staatsblad/Moniteur belge', may be downloaded from the FSMA website at http://www.fsma.be/nl/Supervision/finbem/vohvo/Article/wetteksten/verp.aspx (Dutch) or http://www.fsma.be/fr/Supervision/finbem/vohvo/Article/wetteksten/verp.aspx (French).

## 1. Strict liability

See the note here above (under the heading federal law) on the distinction between fault and strict liability.

| **Environment** | |
|---|---|
| Toxic waste<br>liability of licensed organisms for ~ | Art 6, 2° RD 9 February 1976 (repealed in the Brussels Region) (*déchets toxiques*) |

## 2. Fault liability

| **Control organisms** | |
|---|---|
| Energy performance of buildings<br>energy experts for ~ | Legislative Decree (Flemish community) 22 December 2006 (*performance énergétique des bâtiments*)<br>Annex 2, art 10 Ministerial Decree 13 June 2008 (*certificat de prestation énergétique*) |
| Energy performance of buildings<br>energy experts for ~ | Art 552 Legislative Decree (Wallonia) 19 April 2007 (*performance énergétique des bâtiments*)<br>Executive Decree (Ex D) (Wallonia) 17 April 2008 (*performance énergétique des bâtiments*) |
| Health requirements in sport activities<br>inspection services and laboratories for ~ | Legislative Decree (Flemish community) 13 July 2007 (*pratiques du sport et impératifs de santé*)<br>Ex D (Flemish government) 20 June 2008 (*pratiques du sport et impératifs de santé*)<br>Decision of the Secretary-General of the Flemish Authority of 29 August 2008 (*pratiques du sport et impératifs de santé*)<br>Decision of the Secretary-General of 17 December 2008 (applicability of approval requirements in the WADA [World Anti-Doping Agency] code) (*pratiques du sport et impératifs de santé*) |

| | |
|---|---|
| Home energy experts | Annex art 8 Ex D (Flemish government) 17 June 2005 (*agrément des experts énergétiques*) |
| **Education, formation and child care** | |
| Apprentices in employment services<br>liability of ~<br>(insurance to be taken out by the employer) | Art 7, 5° Ex D (Wallonia) 18 July 2013 (*stages de transition*) |
| Centres for childcare and family support<br>(liability of the centre and of its members) | Art 12 Ex D (Flemish government) 9 November 2012 (*subventionnement des centres d'aide aux enfants*) |
| Certain jobseekers (identified in art 4, § 1 of the decree of 20 February 2014)<br>liability of ~<br>(insurance to be taken out by the employer) | Legislative Decree on alternative training programmes for jobseekers (Wallonia) 20 February 2014, art 12, 7° (*insertion de demandeurs d'emploi*)<br>Annex 2 Ex D (Wallonia) 20 March 2014, implementing the Legislative Decree (*demandeurs d'emploi*) |
| Child and family support services | Legislative Decree (Flanders) 29 May 1984 and Legislative Decree (Flanders) 30 April 2004 (*organisme enfant et famille*)<br>Art 25 Ex D (Flemish government) 1 March 2002 (liability insurance of directors) (*bureaux de consultation pour le jeune enfant*)<br>Art 12 Ex D (Flemish government) 16 December 2011 (liability insurance of doctors) (*bureaux de consultation pour le jeune enfant*) |
| Educational personnel | Art 10 RD 27 October 1967 (*organisations de jeunesse*) |
| Foster care services, foster children and those who provide foster care<br>liability of ~<br>(insurance to be taken out by the foster care service) | Art 25 Ex D (Flemish government) 8 November 2013 (*placement familial*) |
| Graduate nurses in clinical training<br>(traineeship agreement must refer to liability insurance) | Art 4, § 1, e Ex D (French-speaking community) 2 September 1997 (*diplôme d'infirmièr(e) gradué(e)* (*enseignement de promotion sociale*)) |
| Home childminders (day care centres) | Art 63 Ex D (German-speaking community) 18 January 2007 (*accueil des enfants*) |

| | |
|---|---|
| Organisers of childcare facilities | Art 29 Ex D (Flemish government) 22 November 2013 (*accueil familial et de groupe*) |
| Public educational institutions<br>liability of ~ and of their personnel | Arts 12bis and 13 Legislative Decree (Flemish community) 27 March 1991 (*personnel de l'enseignement communautaire*) |
| Students in alternative forms of professional education<br>liability of ~ | Art 6, 10° Legislative Decree (Wallonia) 28 April 2014 ratifying the cooperation agreement of 24 October 2008 (*formation alternée*) |
| Teaching staff in vocational education | Art 21 of the regulation attached to Ex D (Flemish government) 6 July 2012 (*enseignement fondamental et secondaire ordinaire*) |
| **Environment** | |
| Centres for disassembly of used vehicles | Art 20, § 5 Ex D (Brussels-Capital Region) 15 April 2004 (*véhicules hors d'usage*) |
| Collection and transport of toxic waste<br>liability of brokers and traders for the ~ | Legislative Decree (Wallonia) 27 June 1996 (*Décret relatif aux déchets*) |
| Collectors and transporters of dangerous waste | Art 32 Ex D (Wallonia) 9 April 1992 (*déchets toxiques et dangereux*) |
| Demolition firms | Art 43 Ex D (Flemish government) 23 May 2014 (*la gestion durable de cycles de matériaux et de déchets*), amending Ex D (Flemish government) 17 February 2012 |
| Environmental health<br>– Environmental experts<br>– Environmental coordinators<br>– Waste processing facilities<br>– Waste disposal site<br>– Manufacturers of paints<br>– Coating firms<br>– Thermal treatment firms | Ex D (Flemish government) 1 June 1995 (VLAREM [*Vlaams Reglement betreffende de Milieuvergunningen*]) (*hygiène de l'environnement*) |
| Environmental protection organisations | Art 10, 6° Legislative Decree (Wallonia) 23 January 2014 (*reconnaissance et subventionnements des associations environnementales*) |

| | |
|---|---|
| Fluoridised refrigerating agents (licensed as specialised refrigeration firm) | Art 3, 6° Ex D (Wallonia) 12 July 2007 (*équipements frigorifiques*) |
| Installers of renewable energy installations | Art 5, 8° Ex D (Brussels-Capital Region) 24 April 2014 (*certifications des installateurs*) |
| Institution for the disposal of waste | Art 11, § 1, 1°, c Ex D Brussels-Capital Region 19 September 1991 (*élimination des déchets dangereux*) |
| Land management organisations and soil cleaning centres | Arts 202, 203 Ex D (Flemish government) 14 December 2007 (*assainissement et protection du sol*) |
| Organisms for taking back electronic equipment | Art 14, § 2, 7° Environmental Policy Agreement (Brussels-Capital Region) 6 February 2012 (*reprise de déchets d'equipements électriques*) |
| Personnel (experts, technicians, coordinators) in ecological matters | Art 34, § 3 Ex D (Flemish government) 19 November 2010, Flemish regulation concerning environmental licensing (VLAREL [*Vlaams Reglement inzake Erkenningen met betrekking tot het Leefmilieu*]) (*agréments relatifs à l'environnement*) |
| Producers<br>obligation of ~ to take back portable and industrial batteries | Art 14, § 6 Environmental Policy Agreement concerning the taking back of portable and industrial batteries (Wallonia) 5 December 2013 (*reprise de piles et accumulateurs portables et industriels*) |
| Producers and importers<br>obligation of ~ to take back waste oils | Art 11, § 3 Environmental Policy Agreement concerning the taking back of waste oils (Wallonia) 5 December 2013 (*reprises des huiles usagées*) |
| Soil remediation experts and organisations<br>licensing of ~ | Art 8, 2° and art 13 Ex D (Wallonia) 27 May 2009 (*gestion des sols*) |
| Storage of plant protection products for professional use | Art 19 Ex D (Wallonia) 13 June 2013 (*dépôt de produits phytopharmaceutiques*) |
| Waste<br>export, import and transit of ~ | Art 3, 1°, c RD 2 June 1987 (repealed in the Brussels-Capital Region) (*transit des déchets*)<br>Art 5, § 1 Ex D (Brussels-Capital Region) 7 July 1994 (*importation et exportation de déchets*) |
| Waste<br>prevention and handling (export) of ~ | Art 6.2.5 Ex D (Flemish government) 17 February 2012 (*règlement flamand sur la gestion durable de cycles de matériaux et de déchets*) |
| Waste<br>transfer of ~ | Art 6 Ex D (Wallonia) 19 July 2007 (*transferts de déchets*) |

| | |
|---|---|
| **Homes for the elderly** | |
| Accommodation and reception of elderly people | Legislative Decree (Brussels-Capital Region) 22 March 2007 (*hébergement et accueil des personnes âgées*) |
| liability of directors of ~ | Art 23 Ex D (commission communautaire française)[3] 2 April 2009 (*hébergement et accueil des personnes âgées*) |
| Homes for the elderly<br>liability of directors and personnel of ~ | Art 3, 7° Ex D (commission communautaire commune of the Brussels-Capital Region)[3] 7 October 1993 (*établissements hébergeant des personnes âgées*)<br>Art 13 Ex D (Collège réuni of the Brussels-Capital Region) 14 March 1996 (*établissements hébergeant des personnes âgées*) |
| **Hunting** | |
| Hunting licence<br>holder of ~ | Arts 18 and 19 Ex D (Flemish government) 25 April 2014 (*organisation de la chasse*) |
| Private persons using fire-arms against certain species of bird | Art N3 Annex 3, *in fine*. Ex D (Flemish government) 15 May 2009 (*protection des espèces*) |
| **Local public institutions** | |
| Decentralised institutions | Art L 1241–3 Code of local democracy (Wallonia) 22 April 2004 (*démocratie locale*) |
| Energetic performance advisor | Art 3, 9° Ex D 10 October 2013 (Brussels-Capital Region) (*agrément de conseillers PEB* [*Performance Energétique des Bâtiments*]) |
| General social assistance<br>centres for ~ | Art 3, § 1, 3° Ex D (Flemish government) 21 June 2013 (*aide sociale générale*) |
| Mayors and aldermen<br>personal liability of ~<br>(insurance to be taken out by the municipality) | Art 329bis Municipalities Act 24 June 1988 (Brussels-Capital Region) (*nouvelle loi communale*) |
| Mayors and aldermen and municipal councillors<br>personal liability of ~<br>(insurance to be taken out by the municipalities) | Art 74 Legislative Decree 15 July 2005 (Flemish Region), as modified by the Decree of 23 January 2009, art 13 (*Décret communal Flandres*) |

3 This is one of the bodies with regulatory power in the Brussels-Capital Region.

| | |
|---|---|
| Members and chairperson of the council of social welfare<br>personal liability of ~ (insurance to be taken out by the social welfare body) | Art 27, § 5 and art 73 Legislative Decree (Flemish government) 19 December 2008 (*centres publics d'aide sociale*) |
| Members of provincial councils<br>personal liability of ~ (insurance to be taken out by the province) | Art 127 Legislative Decree (Wallonia) 12 February 2004 (*provinces wallonnes*) |
| Provincial deputies<br>personal liability of ~ (insurance to be taken out by the province) | Art 72 Legislative Decree 9 December 2005 (Flemish government) (*Décret provincial Flandres*) |
| **Mediation** | |
| Debt mediation institutions | Art 3, 11° Ex D (Commission communautaire française) 11 June 1998 (*médiation de dettes*) |
| **Service providers** | |
| Service providers<br>(No double requirement of liability insurance in EU Member States) | Implementation of the European Services Directive 2006/123/EC by:<br>– Arts 8 and 14, 7° Legislative Decree (Walloon Region) 10 December 2009<br>– Arts 8 and 14 Legislative Decree (French-speaking community) 10 December 2009<br>– Legislative Decree (German-speaking community) 15 March 2010 |
| **Service stations** | |
| Operators of service stations | Art 73 Ex D (Brussels-Capital Region) 21 January 1999 (*exploitation des stations-service*) |
| **Slag heaps** | |
| Applicants for development of old slag heaps | Ministerial Decree (Wallonia) 22 October 1985 (*valorisation des terrils*) |
| **Social development** | |
| Foster care services | Legislative Decree (Flemish community) 29 June 2012 (*placement familial*) |
| Service of help with daily life activities<br>providers of ~ | Art 49 Ex D (Walloon government) 10 January 2008 (*aide aux activités de vie journalière*) |

| | |
|---|---|
| Services for handicapped people<br>liability of the personnel of ~ | Art 26 Ex D of the Joint Community Commission (Brussels-Capital Region) 25 October 2007 (*centres pour personnes handicapées*) |
| Social housing agencies | Annex art 8 Ex D (Brussels-Capital Region) 28 February 2008 (*agences immobilières sociales*) |
| Social rent<br>(liability of tenants) | Art 31 Ex D (Flemish government) 12 October 2007<br>(title VII of the Flemish Housing Code) (*location sociale*) |
| Social student housing<br>tenants of ~ | Annex 3, art 16 Ex D (Wallonia) 19 July 2012 (*logement de service public*) |
| **Sports** | |
| Doping<br>liability of organisers of sports events in the case of ~ | Art 24 Ordinance (Brussels-Capital Region) 21 June 2012 (*interdiction de dopage*) |
| Trainers and participants in cycling sport events<br>(insurance to be taken out by the trainer) | Ex D (German-speaking community) 7 July 2000 (*sport cycliste*) |
| **Tourism** | |
| Camping and caravanning grounds<br>operators of ~ | Art 9 Ex D (French community) 4 September 1991 (*camping-caravaning*) |
| Camping sites<br>operators of ~ | Art 15 Ex D (German-speaking community) 10 June 2004 (*permis de camping*) |
| Holiday centres<br>organisation of ~ | Art 7 Decree (French-speaking community) 17 May 1999 (*centres de vacances*) |
| Sites for outdoor recreational accommodation<br>operators of ~ | Art 5, 9° Ex D (Flemish government) 23 February 1995 (*exploitation de terrains pour résidences de loisirs*) |
| Tourist accommodation<br>operators of ~ | Art 5, 1°, c Ordinance (Brussels-Capital Region) 8 May 2014 (*hébergement touristique*) |
| Tourist accommodation<br>operators of ~ | Art 4 Decree (Flemish Region) 10 July 2008 (*hébergement touristique*) |
| Travel agencies | Art 6, § 2, 2° Ordinance (Brussels-Capital Region) 22 April 2010 (*statut des agences de voyage*)<br>Art 11, § 2, 6° Ex D (Brussels-Capital Region) 27 September 2012 (*statut des agences de voyage*) |

| | |
|---|---|
| Travel agencies | Art 5 Decree (Flemish Region) 2 March 2007 (*agences de voyage*)<br>Art 9 Ex D (Flemish government) 19 July 2007 (*agences de voyage*) |
| Travel agencies | Decree (Wallonia) 22 April 2010 (*agences de voyage*)<br>Art 6, § 2, 2°, a Ex D (Walloon government) 27 May 2010 (*agences de voyage*) |
| **Transport** | |
| Non-urgent transportation of patients | Art 3, § 3 Decree (German-speaking community) 4 June 2007 (*transport non urgent de patients*)<br>Art 2, § 1, 4° Ex D (German-speaking community) 7 May 2009 (*transport non urgent de patients*) |
| Taxis and lease of vehicles with drivers | Art 5, 3° Ex D (Brussels-Capital Region) 29 March 2007 (*location de voiture avec chauffeur*) |
| Taxis and lease of vehicles with drivers | Art 19, § 1 and art 31, § 1 Decree (Wallonia) 18 October 2007 (*taxis et voitures avec chauffeur*)<br>Art 4, § 1, 3° Ex D (Wallonia) 3 June 2009 as modified by Ex D 11 July 2013 |

Petr Dobiáš
# Czech Republic

## I. Federal Law

The following laws may be downloaded in the original Czech at www.portal.gov.cz/app/zakony/?path=/portal/obcan. Neither online nor print official translations are available in English yet.

### 1. Strict liability

| | |
|---|---|
| Aircraft<br>keepers of ~ | § 12 para 2 lit d, § 71 para 2 lit c, § 84c para 6 lit d, § 92 para 1 lit s and t, § 93 para 1 lit u and v, § 98 para 3 Act No 49/1997 Coll on Civil Aviation and on Amendment of Trade Licensing Act No 455/1991 Coll Subsequently Amended (*Zákon o civilním letectví a o změně a doplnění zákona č. 455/1991 Sb., o živnostenském podnikání [živnostenský zákon], ve znění pozdějších předpisů*)<br>§ 1a para 4 lit c, § 18 para 2 lit d, § 18a para 2 lit c, § 21 para 2 lit g, § 23 para 2 lit g, § 31 Decree of Ministry of Transport and Communications No 108/1997 Coll providing the Act on Civil Aviation No 49/1997 Coll and on Amendment of Trade Licensing Act No 455/1991 Coll Subsequently Amended (*Vyhláška Ministerstva dopravy a spojů, kterou se provádí zákon č. 49/1997 Sb., o civilním letectví a o změně a doplnění zákona č. 455/1991 Sb., o živnostenském podnikání [živnostenský zákon] ve znění pozdějších předpisů*) |
| Clinical evaluation<br>examiner and submitter of ~ | § 52 para 3 lit f Act No 378/2007 Coll on Pharmaceuticals and on Amendments of Certain Related Acts (Act on Pharmaceuticals) (*Zákon o léčivech a o změnách některých souvisejících zákonů [zákon o léčivech]*) |
| Clinical tests<br>provider of ~ | § 10 para 1 lit i, § 12 para 2 lit h, § 13 para 1 no 8 Act No 123/2000 Coll on Medical Instruments and on Amendments of Certain Related Acts (*Zákon o zdravotnických prostředcích a o změně některých souvisejících zákonů*) |
| Dangerous substances<br>operators of facilities for production, manufacturing, storage, use or transport of ~ | § 12 Act No 59/2006 Coll on Control of Major Accidents Caused by Selected Dangerous Chemical Substances or Chemical Preparations and on Amendment Act No 258/2000 Coll on Protection of Public Health and on Amendments of Certain Related Acts, as Amended, and Act No 320/2002 Coll, on Amendments |

| | |
|---|---|
| | and Repeal of Certain Acts in Connection with Terminating of Activities of District Authorities, as Amended (Act on Control of Major Accidents) (*Zákon o prevenci závažných havárií způsobených vybranými nebezpečnými chemickými látkami nebo chemickými přípravky a o změně zákona č. 258/2000 Sb., o ochraně veřejného zdraví a o změně některých souvisejících zákonů, ve znění pozdějších předpisů, a zákona č. 320/2002 Sb., o změně a zrušení některých zákonů v souvislosti s ukončením činnosti okresních úřadů, ve znění pozdějších předpisů [zákon o prevenci závažných havárií]*) |
| Heat energy (production and distribution)<br>operators of ~ | Enclosure No 3 to Act No 455/1991 Coll Trade Licensing Act (*Příloha č. 3 k živnostenskému zákonu*) |
| Motor vehicles<br>keepers of ~ | §§ 1–29 Act No 168/1999 Coll on Liability Insurance for Damage Caused by Operation of Vehicles and on Amendments to Some Related Acts (Motor Third-Party Liability Insurance Act (*Zákon o pojištění odpovědnosti za škodu způsobenou provozem vozidla a o změně některých souvisejících zákonů [zákon o pojištění odpovědnosti z provozu vozidla]*) |
| Motor vehicles<br>owners and users of ~ | Art 7 no 5 and art 8 no 6 Protocol on the Privileges and Immunities of the International Seabed Authority 1998 (*Protokol o výsadách a imunitách Mezinárodního úřadu pro mořské dno z roku 1998*) |
| Nuclear material<br>carriers of ~ | § 13 para 3 lit e, §§ 36–38 Act No 18/1997 Coll on the Peaceful Use of Nuclear Energy and Ionising Radiation (*Zákon o mírovém využívání jaderné energie a ionizujícího záření [atomový zákon ] a o změně a doplnění některých zákonů*)[1]<br>Art VII Vienna Convention on Civil Liability for Nuclear Damage 1963 (*Vídeňská úmluva o občanskoprávní odpovědnosti za jaderné škody z roku 1963*) |
| Nuclear plants<br>operators of ~ | § 13 para 3 lit e, §§ 36–38 Act No 18/1997 Coll on the Peaceful Use of Nuclear Energy and Ionising Radiation (*Zákon o mírovém využívání jaderné energie a ionizujícího záření / atomový zákon / a o změně a doplnění některých zákonů*)[1]<br>Art VII Vienna Convention on Civil Liability for Nuclear Damage 1963 (*Vídeňská úmluva o občanskoprávní odpovědnosti za jaderné škody z roku 1963*) |

**1** § 13 contains a list of compulsory enclosures/documents which must be enclosed with the application for the permit/licence to operate the nuclear plant. § 13 para 3 lit e transforms art VII para 1 (first sentence) and requires proof of the conclusion of an insurance liability contract for the official licence granted by the State Office for Nuclear Safety or other proof of financial security.

| | |
|---|---|
| Railways undertakings | § 27a para 4, § 35 para 2 lit d Act No 266/1994 Coll on Railways (*Zákon o drahách*) |
| Ships<br>operators of ~ | § 19, § 30 para 2 Act No 114/1995 Coll on Inland Navigation (*Zákon o vnitrozemské plavbě*)<br>§ 8 Decree No 223/1995 Coll of Ministry of Transport on Operability of Ships on Inland Waterways No 223/1995 Coll (*Vyhláška Ministerstva dopravy o způsobilosti plavidel k provozu na vnitrozemských vodních cestách*)<br>§ 24 para 1 lit l, § 24 paras 2 and 3, § 25 para 1 lit s, § 27 para 2, § 78 para 3 lit a Act No 61/2000 Coll on Maritime Shipping (*Zákon o námořní plavbě*)<br>§ 4 Decree of Ministry of Transport No 327/2011 Coll on Data Provided in Connection with Operating of Ship and Reports and Notifications of Maritime Accidents or Emergency Events, on Minimum Insurance Sum Concluded for Damages Arising from the Operating of Ships and on Amendment of the Decree of Ministry of Transport and Communications No 278/2000 Coll on Navy Register and Documentation of Maritime Vessels (*Vyhláška o údajích poskytovaných v souvislosti s provozem lodě a ve zprávách a oznámeních o námořní nehodě nebo mimořádné události, o minimální výši sjednaného pojištění za škody z provozu lodě a o změně vyhlášky Ministerstva dopravy a spojů č. 278/2000 Sb., o námořním rejstříku a dokladech námořních plavidel*)<br>§ 29a Decree of the Ministry of Transport, No 278/2000 Coll on Marine Register and Documentation of the Marine Vessels<br>Art 7 International Convention on Civil Liability for Bunker Oil Pollution Damage 2001 (*Mezinárodní úmluva o občanskoprávní odpovědnosti za škody způsobené znečištěním ropnými palivy z roku 2001*) |

## 2. Fault liability

| | |
|---|---|
| Attorneys-at-law | §§ 24a–24c Act No 85/1996 Coll on the Legal Profession (*Zákon o advokacii*) |
| Auctioneers | § 6 para 2 Act No 26/2000 Coll on Public Auctions (*Zákon o veřejných dražbách*) |
| Authorised inspectors | § 146 para 2 Act No 183/2006 Coll on Town and Country Planning and Building Code (Building Act) (*Zákon o územním plánování a stavebním řádu [stavební zákon]*) |

| | |
|---|---|
| Certified architects, certified engineers and technicians active in construction | § 16, § 23 para 6 lit t, § 30b para 3, § 30i para 2 lit c Act No 360/1992 Coll on the Professional Practice of Certified Architects and on the Professional Practice of Certified Engineers and Technicians Active in Construction (*Zákon České národní rady o výkonu povolání autorizovaných architektů a o výkonu povolání autorizovaných inženýrů a techniků činných ve výstavbě*) |
| Dentists, doctors and pharmacists<br>self-employed ~ | § 9 para 2 lit e Act No 220/1991 Coll of the Czech National Council on Czech Medical Chamber, Czech Dental Chamber and Czech Chamber of Pharmacists (*Zákon České národní rady o České lékařské komoře, České stomatologické komoře a České lékárnické komoře*) |
| Energy specialists | § 10 para 6 lit f Act No 406/2000 Coll on Energy Management (*Zákon o hospodaření energií*) |
| Exercise activities of children[2]<br>providers of ~ | § 122 para 4 Act No 435/2000 Coll on Employment (*Zákon o zaměstnanosti*) |
| Flying training<br>instructors for~ | § 22j para 2 lit e Act No 49/1997 on Civil Aviation and on Amendment of Trade Licensing Act No 455/1991 Coll Subsequently Amended (*Zákon o civilním letectví a o změně a doplnění zákona č. 455/1991 Sb., o živnostenském podnikání [živnostenský zákon], ve znění pozdějších předpisů*) |
| Hunters | § 47 para 3 lit e, § 48 Act No 449/2001 Coll on Hunting (*Zákon o myslivosti*) |
| Insolvency administrators | § 23 Act No 182/2006 Coll on Insolvency and Methods of its Settling (Insolvency Act) (*Zákon o úpadku a způsobech jeho řešení [insolvenční zákon]*) |
| Insurance brokers and loss adjusters | § 7 para 4, § 8 para 5, § 10 para 4 Act No 38/2004 Coll on Insurance Brokers and Independent Loss Adjusters and on Amendments to the Trade Act (Insurance Brokers and Loss Adjusters Act) (*Zákon o pojišťovacích zprostředkovatelích a samostatných likvidátorech pojistných událostí a o změně živnostenského zákona [zákon o pojišťovacích zprostředkovatelích a likvidátorech pojistných událostí]*) |
| Medical and hospital services<br>providers of ~ | § 24 para 2 lit b, § 45 para 2 lit n Act No 372/2011 Coll on Medical and Hospital Services and Conditions of its Provision (*Zákon o zdravotních službách a podmínkách jejich poskytování*) |

2 Artistic, sports or cultural activities which can be practised by children younger than 15 years of age under specific conditions listed in § 121 para 2 Act on Employment.

| | |
|---|---|
| Non-transferred housing units for which a bank loan was granted | § 12 Act No 311/2013 Coll on Transfer of Property in Relation to the Housing Units and Group Buildings of Certain Housing Co-operatives and Amendments of Certain Acts (*Zákon o převodu vlastnického práva k jednotkám a skupinovým rodinným domům některých bytových družstev a změně některých zákonů*) |
| Notaries | § 9 para 1 lit d, § 15 para 2, § 18 para 1 Act No 358/1992 Coll on Notaries and their Work Activities (*Zákon České národní rady o notářích a jejich činnosti [notářský řád]*) |
| Patent attorneys | § 42 Act No 417/2004 Coll on Patent Attorneys and on Modification of the Act on Measures for Protection of Industrial Property (*Zákon o patentových zástupcích a o změně zákona o opatřeních na ochranu průmyslového vlastnictví*) |
| Retraining schemes<br>providers of ~ | § 108 para 7 lit h Act No 435/2004 Coll on Employment (*Zákon o zaměstnanosti*) |
| Tax advisors and auditors | § 6 para 10 lit a, § 8 para 1 lit c Act No 523/1992 Coll on Tax Consulting and Chamber of Tax Advisers of the Czech Republic (*Zákon České národní rady o daňovém poradenství a Komoře daňových poradců České republiky*)<br>§ 22 Act No 93/2009 Coll on Auditors and Amendments of Certain Acts (*Zákon o auditorech a o změně některých zákonů*) |
| Travel Agencies<br>operators of ~ | §§ 6–10 Act No 159/1999 Coll on Certain Conditions for Undertakings in the Travel Services and on Amendments of Act No 40/1964 Coll Civil Code, and Act No 455/1991 Coll Trade Licensing Act as Amended (*Zákon o některých podmínkách podnikání v oblasti cestovního ruchu a o změně zákona č. 40/1964 Sb., občanský zákoník, ve znění pozdějších předpisů, a zákona č. 455/1991 Sb., o živnostenském podnikání [živnostenský zákon], ve znění pozdějších předpisů*) |
| Veterinarians | § 6 para 2 lit d Act No 381/1991 Coll on the Chamber of Veterinary Surgeons of the Czech Republic (*Zákon České národní rady o Komoře veterinárních lékařů České republiky*) |
| Volunteer services[3]<br>sending organisations of ~ | § 7 para 1 Act No 198/2002 Coll on Volunteer Service and on Amendments of Certain Acts (Act on Volunteer Service) (*Zákon o dobrovolnické službě a o změně některých zákonů [Zákon o dobrovolnické službě]*) |
| Waste<br>notifier providing cross border transport of ~ | § 48a, § 57 Act No 185/2001 Coll on Waste and Amendments of Certain Other Acts (*Zákon o odpadech a o změně některých dalších zákonů*) |

3 Volunteer Service (organisations) to help in the case of eg natural disasters.

## 3. Insurance duties in respect of recourse duties vis-à-vis the state on the part of entrepreneurs entrusted with sovereign functions (fault liability)

| | |
|---|---|
| Accredited persons evaluating conformity | § 11 para 3 Act No 22/1997 Sb on Technical Requirements on Products and on Amendments on Certain Acts (*Zákon o technických požadavcích na výrobky a o změně a doplnění některých zákonů*) |
| Agricultural public store<br>providers of ~ | § 15 para 2 lit k, § 23 Act No 307/2000 Coll on Agricultural Warehouse Warrant and Agricultural Public Storehouses and on Amendments on Certain Related Acts (*Zákon o zemědělských skladních listech a zemědělských veřejných skladech a o změně některých souvisejících zákonů*) |
| Airfields<br>air traffic services of ~<br>detection check in service for ~<br>ground handling facility service of ~<br>keepers of civil ~ | § 46, § 49c para 1 lit e, § 85d para 4 Act No 49/1997 Coll on Civil Aviation and on Amendment of Trade Licensing Act No 455/1991 Coll Subsequently Amended (*Zákon o civilním letectví a o změně a doplnění zákona č. 455/1991 Sb., o živnostenském podnikání [živnostenský zákon], ve znění pozdějších předpisů*) |
| Airfields<br>co-ordinators of ~ | § 32 para 4, § 93 para 1 lit m Act No 49/1997 Coll on Civil Aviation and on Amendment of Trade Licensing Act No 455/1991 Coll Subsequently Amended (*Zákon o civilním letectví a o změně a doplnění zákona č. 455/1991 Sb., o živnostenském podnikání [živnostenský zákon], ve znění pozdějších předpisů*) |
| Court executors | § 11, § 15 para 2 lit b, § 18 para 1 lit b Act No 120/2001 Coll on Court Executors and Executive Activities (Executory Order) (*Zákon o soudních exekutorech a exekuční činnosti [exekuční řád] a o změně dalších zákonů*) |
| Highways and roads<br>concessionary administrators of ~ | § 18e lit g Act No 13/1997 Coll on Motorways (*Zákon o pozemních komunikacích*) |
| Labour agencies[4] | § 58a Act No 435/2004 Coll on Employment (*Zákon o zaměstnanosti*) |

4 Labour agencies are, according to § 14 para 3 lit b, legal or physical persons who have a licence for concrete forms of procurement of employment.

| | |
|---|---|
| Labour Bureaus[5]<br>public service by the district office of the ~ | § 18a para 2 Act No 111/2006 Coll on Aid in Material Distress (*Zákon o pomoci v hmotné nouzi*) |
| Legal person providing help to the victims of criminal acts | § 41 para 2 lit e of Act No 45/2013 Coll on the Victims of Criminal Acts (*Zákon o obětech trestných činů*) |
| Social and legal protection of children<br>authorized persons[6] for ~ | § 49 para 9 Act No 359/1999 Coll on Social and Legal Protection of Children (*Zákon o sociálně-právní ochraně dětí*) |
| Social services<br>providers of ~ | § 80 Act No 108/2006 Coll on Social Services (*Zákon o sociálních službách*) |

# II. Laws of the Provinces (State Laws)

In the Czech Republic are no rules in the laws of provinces that set out a duty to take out liability insurance.

5 District Office of the Labour Bureau is the local branch of the Labour Bureau, which is a state body providing help for jobseekers (eg procurement of employment). The Labour Bureau has a nationwide sphere of authority and its seat is Prague. The powers of the District Office of the Labour Bureau are defined in § 8 Act No 435/2004 Coll.

6 Authorised persons are legal or physical persons, which are entrusted with the social and legal protection of children.

Jaana Norio-Timonen

# Finland

## I. National Law

The following laws may be downloaded in the original Finnish and Swedish versions at http://www.finlex.fi/. Official English translations do not exist, but a number of unofficial ones are available at http://www.finlex.fi/en/. It may also be possible to find some translations on the websites of Ministries, other authorities or other bodies.

### 1. Strict liability

| | |
|---|---|
| Air carriers and aircraft operators | § 144 Aviation Act (*ilmailulaki*, 22.12.2009/1194) |
| Employers | § 3 Act on Employment Accidents and Occupational Diseases (*työapaturma- ja ammattitautilaki*, 24.4.2015/459) |
| Environmental damage<br>private corporation whose operations involve a material risk of ~ or whose operations cause harm to the environment in general | § 2 Environmental Damage Insurance Act (*laki ympäristövahinkovakuutuksesta*, 30.1.1998/81) |
| Health care providers | § 4 Patient Injuries Act (*potilasvahinkolaki*, 25.7.1986/585) |
| Motor vehicles<br>owner or permanent holder of ~ | § 15 Motor Liability Insurance Act (*liikennevakuutuslaki*, 26.6.1959/279) |
| Nuclear installation<br>operator of ~ | § 23 Nuclear Liability Act (*ydinvastuulaki*, 8.6.1972/484) |
| Oil tanker owners | Part 10 §§ 10–11 Maritime Act (*merilaki*, 15.7.1994/674) |
| Pollution by fuel<br>shipowners against ~ | Part 10a §§ 6–7 Maritime Act (*merilaki*, 15.7.1994/674) |
| Railway undertakings | § 3 Railway Act (*rautatielaki*, 8.4.2011/304) |
| Sports associations or organisations with which the athlete has an agreement | § 1 Act on the Accident and Pension Insurance Cover for an Athlete (*laki urheilijan tapaturma- ja eläketurvasta*, 24.4.2009/276) |

## 2. Fault liability

| | |
|---|---|
| Animal protection supervisor<br>damage caused by an ~ in an inspection | § 38 Animal Welfare Act (*eläinsuojelulaki*, 4.4.1996/247) |
| Appliances burning gaseous fuels<br>notified inspection body for ~ | § 12 Decree on Appliances Burning Gaseous Fuels (*kaasulaiteasetus*, 22.12.1993/1434) |
| Articles of precious metals<br>assay office for ~ | § 6 Act on Articles of Precious Metals (*laki jalometallituotteista*, 1.12.2000/1029) |
| Construction products<br>approved body (body authorised to issue verification certificates) for ~<br>certifying body for quality control of ~<br>type approval body for ~ | § 33 Act on the Type Approval of Certain Construction Products (*laki eräiden rakennustuotteiden tuotehyväksynnästä*, 21.12.2012/954) |
| Counsels<br>licensed ~ | § 8 Act on Licensed Counsels (*laki luvan saaneista oikeudenkäyntiavustajista*, 17.6.2011/715) |
| Dangerous chemicals and explosives<br>inspection body for ~ | § 101 Act on the Safe Handling and Storage of Dangerous Chemicals and Explosives (*laki vaarallisten kemikaalien ja räjähteiden käsittelyn turvallisuudesta*, 3.6.2005/390) |
| Electrical safety<br>assessment body for ~<br>authorised inspection body for ~<br>authorised inspector (as a person) for ~<br>inspection body for ~ | § 24 a–b Electrical Safety Act (*sähköturvallisuuslaki*, 14.6.1996/410) |
| Energy labelling<br>inspection body for ~ | § 22 Act on Requirements for Ecodesign and Energy Labelling (*laki tuotteiden ekologiselle suunnittelulle ja energiamerkinnälle asetettavista vaatimuksista*, 19.12.2008/1005) |
| Event organisers | § 16 Assembly Act (*kokoontumislaki*, 22.4.1999/530) |
| Fireworks<br>producers and importers of ~ | § 93 Act on the Safe Handling and Storage of Dangerous Chemicals and Explosives (*laki vaarallisten kemikaalien ja räjähteiden käsittelyn turvallisuudesta*, 3.6.2005/390) |

| | |
|---|---|
| Insurance brokers | § 28 Insurance Intermediation Act (*laki vakuutusedustuksesta*, 15.7.2005/570) |
| Joint Building Consultants | § 15 Act on Building Projects in the Form of Joint Building Ventures (*ryhmärakennuttamislaki* 6.3.2015/190) |
| Lawyers | § 1 Lawyers Act (*laki asianajajista*, 12.12.1958/496), § 11.7 Code of Conduct for Lawyers adopted by the Finnish Bar Association (*Hyvää asianajajatapaa koskevat ohjeet*, 15.1.2009 as amended 8.6.2012) and Guidelines on the Liability Insurance of a Lawyer (*Asianajajan vastuuvakuutusta koskevat ohjeet*, 11.6.1982, as amended 23.5.1997, 11.1.2001, 15.1.2009) |
| Measurement units and system of measurement standards, National Standards Laboratories | § 8 Act on Units of Measurement and the System of Measurement Standards (*laki mittayksiköistä ja mittanormaalijärjestelmästä*, 10.12.1993/1156) |
| Measuring instruments<br>inspection bodies for ~<br>notified bodies for ~ | § 30 Measuring Instruments Act (*mittauslaitelaki*, 17.6.2011/707) |
| Medicinal products<br>party commissioning[1] clinical trial on ~ | § 10b Medical Research Act (*laki lääketieteellisestä tutkimuksesta*, 9.4.1999/488) |
| Motor vehicles<br>owner or permanent holder of ~ | § 15 Motor Liability Insurance Act (*liikennevakuutuslaki*, 26.6.1959/279)<br>– traffic accident caused by the motor vehicle concerns another motor vehicle |
| Nuclear plants<br>inspection body for ~<br>qualification body for ~<br>testing body for ~ | § 60 a Nuclear Energy Act (*ydinenergialaki*, 11.12.1987/990) |
| Pressure equipment<br>inspection body for ~ | § 5 Pressure Equipment Act (*painelaitelaki*, 27.8.1999/869) |
| Radio equipment and telecommunications terminal equipment<br>notified body for ~ | § 255 Information Society Code (*tietoyhteiskuntakaari*, 7.11.2014/917) |
| Real estate agencies, housing rental agencies | § 8 Act on Real Estate Agencies and Housing Rental Agencies (*laki kiinteistön ja vuokrahuoneiston välitysliikkeistä*, 15.12.2000/1075) |

1 This is the party who is responsible for the insurance; the insurance must also cover the liability of the researcher.

| | |
|---|---|
| Rescue equipment<br>assessment bodies for ~<br>inspection bodies for ~ | § 12 Rescue Equipment Act (*laki pelastustoimen laitteista*, 12.1.2007/10) |
| Shipowners | Part 7 § 2 Maritime Act (*merilaki*, 15.7.1994/674) |
| Social and health service providers | § 5 Act on Service Vouchers for Social and Health Services (*laki sosiaali- ja terveydenhuollon palvelusetelistä*, 24.7.2009/569) |
| Toys<br>conformity assessment bodies for ~ | § 48 Act on Safety of Toys (*laki lelujen turvallisuudesta*, 18.11.2011/1154) |
| Vehicles<br>designated technical services for ~ | § 47a Vehicles Act (*ajoneuvolaki*, 11.12.2002/1090) |

## II. Laws of the Provinces (State Laws)

Laws of the provinces (state laws) do not exist in Finland.

Robert Koch

# Germany

## I. Federal Law

The following laws may be downloaded in the original German at http://www.gesetze-im-internet.de/. The list follows the classification of risks according to classes of insurance set forth in Annex A of the Law on the Supervision of Insurance Undertakings (*Versicherungsaufsichtsgesetz*, VAG). An English translation of the VAG is available at http://www.iuscomp.org/gla/statutes/VAG.htm.

Please note that this list, which also includes cases where the duty to provide for financial security may be fulfilled either by taking out liability insurance or other forms of financial security, makes no claim to be exhaustive.

### 1. Strict liability

| | |
|---|---|
| Air traffic passengers | § 50 Air Traffic Act (*Luftverkehrsgesetz*, LuftVG)<br>§ 106 Air Traffic Licensing Regulations (*Luftverkehrs-Zulassungs-Ordnung*, LuftVZO) |
| Air transportation companies and other keepers of aircraft | §§ 2 (1) no 3, 37 (1), 43 (1) and 50 LuftVG in conjunction with §§ 102–104 LuftVZO |
| Airports<br>ground handling services at ~ | § 3 Ground Handling Ordinance (*Verordnung über Bodenabfertigungsdienste auf Flugplätzen*, BADV) in conjunction with Annex 3 no 2 B (6) |
| Clinical studies conducted on humans and using pharmaceuticals or medical products<br>participants in ~ | § 40 (1) no 8, (3) German Medicines Act (*Arzneimittelgesetz*, AMG) and<br>§ 20 (1) no 9, (3) Medical Devices Act (*Medizinproduktegesetz*, MPG) |
| Dangerous goods<br>transport of ~ | § 3 (1) fourth sentence Dangerous Goods Transportation Act (*Gefahrgutbeförderungsgesetz*, GGBefG) |
| Landfill sites | § 19 (2) Landfill Ordinance (*Deponieverordnung*, DepV) requires a 'deposit of security' made by the owner of the landfill, but not imperatively in the form of liability insurance |
| Motor vehicles<br>foreign ~ | § 1 Act on Third-Party Liability Insurance for Vehicles and Trailers Based Abroad (*Gesetz über die Haftpflichtversicherung für ausländische Kraftfahrzeuge und Kraftfahrzeuganhänger*, AuslPflVG) |

| | |
|---|---|
| Motor vehicles<br>third-party liability insurance for keepers of ~ | §§ 1, 4 Compulsory Insurance Act (*Pflichtversicherungsgesetz*, PflVG) |
| Nuclear plants and owners of nuclear fuels and other radioactive substances, as well as users of ionising radiation<br>operating liability for ~ | § 13 Atomic Energy Act (*Atomgesetz*, AtG) in conjunction with the Nuclear Financial Security Ordinance (*Atomrechtliche Deckungsvorsorgeverordnung*, AtDeckV) and § 24 (1) no 5 Radiation Protection Ordinance (*Strahlenschutzverordnung*, StrlSchV) and § 28b (1) no 5 X-Ray Ordinance (*Röntgenverordnung*, RöV) |
| Oil in sea transport<br>damage caused by ~ | § 2 Oil Pollution Damage Act (*Ölschadengesetz*, ÖlSG), see also Act on Liability and Compensation for Oil Pollution (*Ölhaftungsgesetz*) |
| Pharmaceutical manufacturers | §§ 88 (1), 94 AMG |
| Plants that may pose a hazard to the environment<br>operating liability for certain ~ | § 19 (1) and (2) no 1 Environmental Liability Act (*Umwelthaftungsgesetz*, UmweltHG) in conjunction with Annex 2 (the regulations on coverage provisions have not yet come into force as the relevant ordinance has still to be issued) |
| Road haulage<br>commercial ~ | § 7a (1) Road Haulage Act (*Güterkraftverkehrsgesetz*, GüKG) |
| Waste management companies<br>operating liability for specialised ~ | § 6 Ordinance on Specialised Waste Management Companies (*Entsorgungsfachbetriebeverordnung*, EfbV) requires proof of adequate insurance cover |
| Waste shipment | § 3 (1) Waste Shipment Act (*Abfallverbringungsgesetz*, AbfVerbrG) |
| Waste transport | § 7 (2) no 1e Ordinance on Transport Licences (*Beförderungserlaubnisverordnung*, BefErlV) concerning third-party liability insurance and specific environmental impairment liability insurance |

## 2. Fault liability

| | |
|---|---|
| Auditors and auditing companies | § 54 of the Law regulating the Profession of Auditors (*Wirtschaftsprüferordnung*, WPO) in conjunction with §§ 1 and 2 Ordinance on the Professional Liability of Auditors (*Wirtschaftsprüfer-Berufshaftpflichtversicherungsverordnung*, WPBHV) |

| | |
|---|---|
| *Betreuungsvereine* (social associations which have the task of finding and training volunteers willing to become 'Betreuer' [guardian of a disabled person]) | § 1908f Civil Code (*Bürgerliches Gesetzbuch*, BGB) |
| Brokers and building contractors | § 2 Broker and Building Contractor Ordinance (*Makler- und Bauträgerverordnung*, MaBV) |
| Control organisations | Annex VIII b no 2.6 Regulation on the Entry into Service of Motor Vehicles (*Straßenverkehrs-Zulassungs-Ordnung*, StVZO) |
| Development aid institutions for the benefit of development aid workers (combined with corresponding health insurance) | § 6 Development Aid Workers Act (*Entwicklungshelfergesetz*, EhfG) |
| Digital signatures<br>certification services for ~ | § 12 Digital Signature Ordinance (*Signaturgesetz*, SigG) in conjunction with § 9 Digital Signature Ordinance (*Signaturverordnung*, SigV) |
| Equipment and Product Safety<br>agencies and institutions for the control of installations and equipment within the meaning of § 2 no 17 of the ~ | § 13 (8) and § 37 (5) no 4 Equipment and Product Safety Act (*Gesetz über die Bereitstellung von Produkten auf dem Markt*, ProdSG) |
| Fairground workers | § 55 Industry Code (*Gewerbeordnung*, GewO) in conjunction with the Ordinance on the Liability of Fairground Workers (*Schaustellerhaftpflichtverordnung*, SchauHV) concerning conveyance of passengers: show driving with motor vehicles, Wall of Death motordromes, shooting galleries, circuses, performances with dangerous animals, horse-riding businesses |
| Firearms certificates, shooting permits | § 4 (1) no 5 Weapons Act (*Waffengesetz*, WaffG) |
| Guard services | § 34a (2) no 3c Industry Code (GewO) in conjunction with § 6 Ordinance on Guard Services (*Verordnung über das Bewachungsgewerbe*, BewachV) |
| Hunters | § 17 (1) no 4 Federal Hunting Act (*Bundesjagdgesetz*, BJagdG) |
| Industrial safety and health control agencies | § 21 (2) no 1 Ordinance on Industrial Safety and Health (*Betriebssicherheitsverordnung*, BetrSichV) |

| | |
|---|---|
| Inspection, control and certification agencies | § 7 (1) Ordinance on the Installation of Heating Boilers and Equipment in accordance with the Construction Products Act (*Verordnung über das Inverkehrbringen von Heizkesseln und Geräten nach dem Bauproduktegesetz*, BauPGHeizkesselV) |
| Inspection of gas systems and their installation by state-approved garages<br>liability concerning the ~ | Annex VIIa nos 2.8 and 2.9 StVZO |
| Lawyers | § 51 Federal Lawyers' Act (*Bundesrechtsanwaltsordnung*, BRAO) and § 7 of the Law regulating the Activity of European Lawyers in Germany (*Europäisches Rechtsanwaltsgesetz*, EuRAG) |
| Legal Services | § 5 (1) Legal Services Act (*Rechtsdienstleistungsgesetz*, RDG) in conjunction with § 5 (1) Legal Services Ordinance (*Rechtsdienstleistungsverordnung*, RDV) concerning the provision of out of court legal services |
| Motor vehicles<br>control organisations for ~ | Annex VIIIb no 2.6 StVZO |
| Notaries | §§ 19a, 67 (3) no 3 Federal Public Notaries Ordinance (*Bundesnotarordnung*, BNotO) |
| Patent attorneys | § 45 Patent Attorney Code (*Patentanwaltsordnung*, PatAnwO) |
| Publicly appointed and sworn experts | § 36 (3) no 3b GewO |
| Receivers<br>official ~ | § 1 (4) Official Receivers Ordinance (*Zwangsverwalterverordnung*, ZwVwV) |
| Shooting ranges<br>operating liability for ~ | § 27 (1) Weapons Act (WaffG) |
| Sport boats<br>liability for ~ | Annex 7 no 1 to § 9 (2) no 2 Ordinance on the Rental of Lake Sport Boats (*Binnenschiffahrts-Sportbootvermietungsverordnung*, BinSch-SportbootVermV) |
| Tax advisors, tax agents, tax consultancy services | § 67 Law on Tax Advisors (*Steuerberatungsgesetz*, StBerG) |
| Technical equipment and consumer products | § 37 (5) no 4 Equipment and Product Safety Act (ProdSG) |
| Test engineers (construction engineering) | § 15 (2) no 7 Regulation on Building Specifications, Engineering Inspections and Tests (*Anordnung über Bauvorlagen, bautechnische Prüfungen und Überwachung*, BauPÜAnO)<br>(Note: This ordinance is part of the laws of the former GDR still applicable in the states that joined the Federal Republic of |

| | |
|---|---|
| | Germany in accordance with art 3 no 32a of the Unification Treaty Act of 18.9.1990 (BGBl II 1239) and art 9 Unification Treaty of 31.8.1990 in conjunction with art 1 G of 23.9.1990 (BGBl II 885, 1239 effective as of 3.10.1990; cf also part II of this listing)) |
| Training courses<br>approval of ~ | § 33 First Ordinance on the Explosives Act (*Erste Verordnung zum Sprengstoffgesetz*, 1. SprengV) |
| Verification of weights and measures/inspection authorities | § 63 (2) Verification Ordinance (*Eichordnung*, EO) |

# II. Laws of the (Federal) States (*Bundesländer*)

The following laws may be downloaded in the original German at http://www.gesetze-im-internet.de/. There are no English translations available on the internet. Please note that this list makes no claim to be exhaustive.

## 1. Strict liability

| | |
|---|---|
| Dog owners | Berlin: Dog owners pursuant to § 1 (6) Act concerning Dog-Keeping and Dog-Walking in Berlin (*Gesetz über das Halten und Führen von Hunden in Berlin*, HundeHaltG Bln)<br>Brandenburg: Dog owners pursuant to § 17 (5) Act on Regulatory Authorities (*Ordnungsbehördengesetz*, OBG)<br>Bremen: Dog owners pursuant to § 1 (6) Bremen Act on the Keeping of Dogs (*Bremisches Gesetz über das Halten von Hunden*, BremHundeG)<br>Hamburg: Dog owners pursuant to § 2 (2) Hamburg Dangerous Dogs Ordinance (*Hundeverordnung*, HundeVO)<br>Hessen: Pursuant to § 71a (2) of the Hessian Law and Order Act (*Hessisches Gesetz über die Sicherheit und Ordnung*, HSOG), owners of dogs subject to permit under the Control of Dogs Ordinance (*Hundeverordnung*) must have liability insurance with a minimum limit of € 500,000.<br>Lower Saxony: Dog owners' liability pursuant to § 10 Lower Saxony Act on the Keeping of Dogs (*Niedersächsisches Gesetz über das Halten von Hunden*, NHundG)<br>North Rhine-Westphalia: Dog owners' liability pursuant to § 5 North Rhine-Westphalian Act on the Keeping of Dogs (*Landeshundegesetz NRW*, LHhundG NRW) |

| | |
|---|---|
| | Rhineland-Palatinate: Dog owners pursuant to § 4 (2) Rhineland-Palatinatian Act on the Keeping of Dogs (*Landeshundegesetz*, LHundG)<br>Saarland: Dog owners pursuant to § 2 (3) Ordinance on the Protection of the Public from Dangerous Dogs (*Polizeiverordnung über den Schutz der Bevölkerung vor gefährlichen Hunden*)<br>Saxony: Dog owners pursuant to § 5 Saxony Dangerous Dogs Act (*Sächsisches Gefahrhundegesetz*, SächsGefHG)<br>Schleswig Holstein: Dog owners' liability as per § 9 Dangerous Dogs Act Schleswig Holstein (*Gefahrhundegesetz*) |
| Mountain railways and cableways<br>operation of ~ | Lower Saxony: Cableways pursuant to § 19 Lower Saxony Act on Railways and Cableways (*Niedersächsisches Gesetz über Eisenbahnen und Seilbahnen*, NESG)<br>Thuringia: § 14 Thuringian Mountain Railways Act (*Thüringer Bergbahngesetz*, ThürBBahnG) |
| Railways, mountain railways and tow lifts<br>operation of private ~ | Baden-Württemberg: § 15 of the State Law on Railways in Baden-Württemberg (*Landeseisenbahngesetz*, LEisenbG)<br>Bavaria: Art 14 Act on the Legal Relations of Non-Federally Owned Railways and Cableways in Bavaria (*Bayerisches Eisenbahn- und Seilbahngesetz*, BayESG), the Ordinance on the Liability Insurance of Railways (*Verordnung über die Haftpflichtversicherung der Eisenbahn*, EBHaftPflV) adopted as per § 26 (1) no 8 General Railway Act (*Allgemeines Eisenbahngesetz*, AEG) applies *mutatis mutandis* to all non-federally owned railways. In accordance with art 1 (1) second sentence BayESG, this also applies to rack railways. Operators of cableways must have liability insurance as per art 31 (1) BayESG in conjunction with arts 5 (1) no 5 and 10 (1) no 4 Third Ordinance on the Implementation of the BayESG (*Seilbahnverordnung*, SeilvB)<br>Rhineland-Palatinate: § 33 of the State Law on Railways in Rhineland-Palatinate (*Landeseisenbahngesetz*, LEisenbG) in conjunction with the State Ordinance on Minimum Sums Insured under the LEisenbG (*Landesverordnung über die Mindestversicherungssummen*) |
| Waterway carriers<br>inland ~ | Bavaria: Art 72 (1) Bavarian Water Act (*Bayerisches Wassergesetz*, BayWG)<br>Thuringia: § 4 (1) no 8 Thuringian Regulations on Inland Waterway Vessels and Rafts (*Thüringer Verordnung zur Regelung der Schiff- und Floßfahrt*, ThürSchiffFloßVO) |

## 2. Fault liability

| | |
|---|---|
| Architects, town planners, engineers, issuers of structural certificates and engineering inspectors | Baden-Württemberg: § 8 (3) Act on Limited Liability Partnerships (*Partnerschaftsgesellschaftsgesetz*, PartGG) in conjunction with § 2a (3) Architects Act of Baden-Württemberg (*Architektengesetz*, ArchG BW): architectural firms<br>Berlin: Independent architects and town planners accredited in building and construction as defined in § 4 (5) no 5 of the Berlin Architects and Chamber of Construction Act (*Berliner Architekten- und Baukammergesetz*, ABKG); town planners, and architectural and town planning firms pursuant to § 7 (9) ABKG (with regard to incorporated companies) and § 7 (2) ABKG (with regard to professional partnerships as per § 8 (3) PartGG), both in conjunction with § 19 ABKG<br>Brandenburg: Independent architects pursuant to § 3 (2) no 4 Brandenburg Architects Act (*Brandenburgisches Architektengesetz*, BbgArchG); Architects pursuant to § 5 (2) no 4 BbgArchG, professional partnerships pursuant to § 8 (3) PartGG in conjunction with § 8 (3) and (4) BbgArchG, companies pursuant to § 9 (2) no 7 BbgArchG; § 24 (2) no 4 BbgIngKamG; § 8 (3) PartGG in conjunction with § 19 (3) and (4), and § 20 (3) Brandenburg Chamber of Engineers Act (*Brandenburgisches Ingenieurkammergesetz*, BbgIngKamG)<br>Bremen: Architects §§ 9 (6) and 25 (2) no 5 Bremen Engineers Act (*Bremer Ingenieursgesetz*, BremIngG), Town planners, and architectural and town planning firms pursuant to § 4 (1) no 4 Bremen Architects Act (*Bremer Architektengesetz*, BremArchG)<br>Hamburg: Members of the Hamburg Chamber of Architects § 19 (2) no 5 Hamburg Architects Act (*Hamburgisches Architektengesetz*, HmbArchG), town planners, and architectural and town planning firms pursuant to § 10 (3) and (12) HmbArchG<br>Hessen: Independent architects pursuant to § 4 (6) no 5 and § 17 (1) sent 2 no 8 Hessian Architects and Town Planners Act (*Hessisches Architekten- und Stadtplanergesetz*, HASG). Pursuant to § 6 (4) of the Hessian Chamber of Architects and Town Planners Act (*Hessisches Gesetz über die Architekten- und Stadtplanerkammer*), architectural and town planning firms must take out professional liability insurance (with a minimum sum insured of € 1 million for personal injury and € 500,000 for property damage and financial loss. § 17 (1) sent 2 no 8 of that Act requires natural persons to take out 'adequate' professional liability insurance without specifying a minimum sum insured. Pursuant to § 16 (2) no 5 of the Hessian Chamber of Engineers Act (*Hessisches Ingenieurkammergesetz*, IngKammG), engineers must show proof of having adequate professional liability |

| | |
|---|---|
| | insurance in order to be listed in the register of consulting engineers. The Chamber of Engineers may specify a minimum sum insured by issuing appropriate guidelines; Pursuant to § 18a (3), 18b (2) no 5 IngKammG, consulting engineers who work in a professional partnership must take out professional liability insurance. In accordance with § 19a (3) no 3 and (6) no 2, this obligation also applies to persons listed in the Chamber of Engineers' register of engineers qualified to set up building specifications. § 19b (5) no 5, (7) and (8) no 5 extends this obligation also to persons listed in the town planners' register, § 80 of the Hessian Building Regulations (*Hessische Bauordnung*, HBO) comprises the authorisation to issue ordinances concerning adequate and proper liability insurance. § 6 (3) Ordinance concerning Issuers of Structural Certifications (*Nachweisberechtigten-Verordnung*, NBVO) and § 7 (2) no 9 Hessian Ordinance on Structural Engineering Inspections (*Bautechnische Prüfungsverordnung*, BautechPrüfVO) make liability insurance obligatory for issuers of structural certificates and engineering inspectors. The same will apply in future to experts who will have to take out liability insurance under Regulations concerning experts still to be issued<br>Lower Saxony: Architects of residential buildings not requiring building consent pursuant to § 62 (4) Lower Saxony Building Code (*Niedersächsische Bauordnung*, NbauO); Issuers (architects and engineers) of safety certificates for residential buildings not requiring building consent, as well as town planners and architectural and town planning firms pursuant to § 62 (4) NbauO; Consulting engineers pursuant to § 29 (2) no 4 Lower Saxony Engineers Act (*Niedersächsisches Ingenieurgesetz*, NIngG); Companies within the meaning of § 4a (2) Lower Saxony Architects Act (*Niedersächsisches Architektengesetz*, NArchtG)<br>Mecklenburg-Western Pomerania: Independent architects pursuant to § 29 (1) no 3, § 30 Architects Act of Mecklenburg-Western Pomerania (*Architektengesetz des Landes Mecklenburg-Vorpommern*, ArchG M-V) of 12 March 1998, Legal and Regulatory Gazette (*Gesetz- und Verordnungsblatt*, GVBl M-V) pp 364, 549 as amended by § 2 of the Act of 27 June 2002, GVBl M-V p 510, 2003 p 107), companies pursuant to § 6 (5), and professional partnerships pursuant to § 13 (2) ArchG M-V; Persons in charge of technical surveillance pursuant to § 6 (13) third and fourth sentence Ordinance on the Organisation of Technical Surveillance (*Verordnung über die Organisation der technischen Überwachung*), GVBl M-V 1992, p 301<br>North Rhine-Westphalia: Architects who write building specifications within the meaning of § 70 (3) no 1 Building Regulations of North-Rhine-Westphalia (*Bauordnung NRW*, BauO NRW) in |

| | |
|---|---|
| | conjunction with § 19 Implementing Regulation of the Chamber of Construction Act of North-Rhine Westphalia (*Baukammergesetz*, BauKaG NRW); Members of the Chamber of Architects North-Rhine-Westphalia pursuant to § 22 (2) no 5 BauKaG NRW in conjunction with § 19 Implementing Regulation of the BauKaG NRW, town planners, and architectural and town planning firms pursuant to § 8 BauKG NRW and § 20 of the relevant Implementing Regulation |
| | Rhineland-Palatinate: Engineers working in a professional partnership pursuant to § 10 (2) IngKammG; To be listed in the register of consulting engineers as stipulated in § 1 (4) no 3 State Ordinance on the Register Maintained by the Chamber of Consulting Engineers of Rhineland-Palatinate (*Landesverordnung über die von der Kammer der Beratenden Ingenieure zu führenden Listen*), consulting engineers must show proof of adequate professional liability insurance |
| | Rhineland-Palatinate: § 2 (1) no 7 Architects Act of Rhineland-Palatinate (*Architektengesetz Rheinland Pfalz*, ArchitektenG R-Pf): members of the Chamber of Architects of Rhineland-Palatinate |
| | Saarland: § 86 (3) second sentence no 6 and (5) no 2 Building Regulations (*Landesbauordnung*, LBO) Saarland: architects; § 43 (1) no 5 Saarland Act on the Chamber of Architects and Engineers (*Saarländisches Architekten- und Ingenieurskammergesetz*, SAIG): architects and engineers; town planners, and architectural and town planning firms pursuant to §§ 7 (3) and 43 (1) no 5 SAIG; § 8 sent 3 no 2 in conjunction with § 7 (3) SAIG: companies not accredited in Germany |
| | Saxony: §§ 3 (2) no 2 and 9 (3) no 2 Saxony Architects Act (*Sächsisches Architektengesetz*, SächsArchG): architects and town planners; Inspection, control and certification agencies pursuant to §§ 88 (4) no 4 and 25 (1) LBO Saxony |
| | Saxony Anhalt: § 33 (2) no 4 Engineers Act of Saxony-Anhalt (IngenieurG LSA): engineers; § 16 (2) no 3 Architects Act of Saxony-Anhalt (ArchtG LSA): members of the Chamber of Architects, as well as architects not accredited in Germany; § 16 (3) in conjunction with § 16 (2) no 3 ArchtG-LSA: companies and companies not accredited in Germany |
| | Schleswig Holstein: §§ 71 (6), 91 (1) no 7 LBO Schleswig Holstein: architects; § 3 (1) no 10 Act on the Chamber of Architects and Engineers Schleswig Holstein (*Architekten- und Ingenieurkammergesetz Schleswig-Holstein*, ArchIngKG): architects and engineers; town planners, and architectural and town planning firms pursuant to § 10 (2) ArchIngKG |

| | |
|---|---|
| | Thuringia: Architects pursuant to § 29 (1) Thuringian Architects and Engineers Act (*Thüringer Architekten- und Ingenieurkammergesetz*, ThürAIKG), town planners, and architectural and town planning firms pursuant to § 10 in conjunction with § 29 (1) ThürAIKG |
| Conciliation agencies | Hessen: Pursuant to § 5 Act on the Establishment and Recognition of Conciliation Agencies (*Gesetz zur Errichtung and Anerkennung von Gütestellen*) by the Land administration of justice, conciliation agencies that are not funded by public corporations or institutions have to take out financial loss liability insurance with a minimum sum insured of € 250,000 per loss event |
| Experts | Baden-Württemberg: Experts within the meaning of § 22 (3) no 5 Ordinance on Installations Handling Substances Constituting a Hazard to Water (*Anlagenverordnung wassergefährdende Stoffe*, VAwS)<br>Bavaria: Experts within the meaning of § 19i (2) third sentence Water Resources Act (*Wasserhaushaltsgesetz*, WHG) in conjunction with the Ordinance concerning Private Experts in Water Management (*Verordnung über private Sachverständige in der Wasserwirtschaft*, VPSW); Experts in soil protection and contaminated soil pursuant to art 6 Bavarian Soil Protection Act (*Bayerisches Bodenschutzgesetz*, BayBodSchG) in conjunction with the Ordinance on Experts and Examination Centres for Soil Protection and Contaminated Sites (*Verordnung über Sachverständige und Untersuchungsstellen für den Bodenschutz und die Altlastenbehandlung*, VSU)<br>Berlin: Experts within the meaning of § 19i (2) third sentence WHG working in expert organisations for the inspection of oil tanks pursuant to the Ordinance governing the Handling of Water Polluting Substances and Specialised Facilities (*Verordnung über Anlagen zum Umgang mit wassergefährdenden Stoffen*, VAwS) and § 5 Ordinance on Discharge of Waste Water into Public Waste-Water-Treatment Installations (*Indirekteinleiterverordnung*, IndV)<br>Brandenburg: Experts in construction and evaluation pursuant to § 80 (3) no 7 Brandenburg Building Regulations (*Brandenburgische Bauordnung*, BbgBO) in conjunction with § 3 (6) of the Brandenburg Ordinance concerning Experts in Construction and Evaluation (*Brandenburgische Prüfverständigenverordnung*, BbgPrüfSV); Experts within the meaning of § 19i (2) third sentence WHG in conjunction with § 21 (3) no 5 VAwS<br>Hamburg: Asbestos experts pursuant to § 4 (1) no 4 Hamburg Ordinance on Asbestos Abatement Experts (*Asbest-Sachverständigenverordnung*, Asbest-SvVO) |

| | |
|---|---|
| | Hessen: Pursuant to § 15 Hessian Water Act (*Hessisches Wassergesetz*, HWG) the competent authority may require holders of a licence relating to water rights to take out liability insurance to the extent necessary to ensure that requirements, conditions or other obligations are fulfilled and financial risks arising in the course of accidents or business interruption are covered. In accordance with § 15 Ordinance on the Public Appointment of Experts on Agriculture and Forestry including Horticulture (*Verordnung über die öffentliche Bestellung von Sachverständigen auf dem Gebiet der Land- und Forstwirtschaft einschließlich des Gartenbaues*), experts are required to take out professional liability insurance to cover financial losses incurred in the course of their occupation; Publicly appointed and sworn experts in the field of engineering in accordance with § 14 (2) Experts Code of Practice (*Sachverständigenordnung*, SVO), pursuant to § 14 (7) second sentence IngKammG in conjunction with the Ordinance on the Appointment of Experts pursuant to the Chamber of Engineers Act (*Verordnung über die Bestellung von Sachverständigen nach dem Ingenieurkammergesetz*)<br>Lower Saxony: Experts as defined by § 19i (2) third sentence WHG in conjunction with § 16 (2) no 4 VAwS<br>Mecklenburg-Western Pomerania: Experts pursuant to § 116 Water Act of Mecklenburg-Western Pomerania (*Landeswassergesetz*, LWG)<br>North Rhine-Westphalia: Liability of particular state-approved experts in accordance with § 3 (2) North Rhine-Westphalian Regulation governing Experts (*Sachverständigenverordnung*, SvVO) in conjunction with § 20 Implementing Regulation of the BauKaG NRW; Experts within the meaning of § 19i (2) third sentence WHG in conjunction with § 11 no 5 VAwS<br>Rhineland-Palatinate: Experts in structural fire protection in accordance with §§ 3, 65 (4), 87 (5) no 6 LBauO in conjunction with § 2 (1) no 6 State Ordinance concerning Experts in Structural Fire Protection (*Landesverordnung über Sachverständige für baulichen Brandschutz*, BauBrSchSVVO); Experts in earthworks and foundations pursuant to § 2 (1) no 7 State Ordinance on Experts in Earthworks and Foundations (*Landesverordnung über Sachverständige für Erd- und Grundbau*, SEGBauVO); Organisations appointing experts in water contamination as per § 22 (3) no 5 State Ordinance on Installations and Certified Specialists Handling Substances Constituting a Hazard to Water (*Anlagenverordnung*, VAwS)<br>Saxony: Publicly appointed and sworn experts in agriculture, forestry, horticulture and viticulture pursuant to § 1 (3) no 4 and |

| | |
|---|---|
| | § 4 (6) of the Saxony Ordinance on the Public Appointment and Swearing-in of Experts in Agriculture, Forestry, Horticulture and Viticulture of 29 October 2001 (*Sächsische Landwirtschaftssachverständigenverordnung*, SächsLandwSachVO); Experts within the meaning of § 19i (2) third sentence WHG in conjunction with the Saxony Ordinance on Installations Handling Substances Constituting a Hazard to Water of 18 April 2000 (*Sächsische Anlagenverordnung*, SächsVAwS)<br>Schleswig Holstein: Organisations appointing experts in water contamination as per § 22 (3) no 5 State Ordinance on Installations and Certified Specialists Handling Substances Constituting a Hazard to Water (*Anlagenverordnung*, VAwS)<br>Thuringia: Experts pursuant to § 22 (3) no 6 Ordinance on Installations Handling Substances Constituting a Hazard to Water (*Thüringer Anlagenverordnung*, ThürVAwS); Testing experts in charge of the testing of technical systems and installations and experts in earthworks and foundations as per § 82 (2) in conjunction with § 5 (1) Ordinance on Inspection Engineers and Expert Inspectors (*Thüringer Verordnung über die Prüfingenieure und Prüfsachverständigen*, ThürPPVO) |
| Hunters, falconers, fishermen | Berlin: Hunting licence holders pursuant to § 20 State Hunting Act of Berlin (*Berliner Jagdgesetz*) in conjunction with § 17 Federal Hunting Act (*Bundesjagdgesetz*, BJagdG); Falconers' and hunters' liability in accordance with the Ordinance concerning Falconry and Hunting Exams (*Verordnung über die Jäger- und Falknerprüfung*)<br>Rhineland-Palatinate: Fishing liability pursuant to § 13 (2) no 3 State Ordinance concerning the Implementation of the Rhineland-Palatinatian Fishing Law (*Landesverordnung zur Durchführung des Rheinland-Pfälzischen Landesfischereigesetzes*, LFischG-DVO); Candidates taking courses for the hunting exam must maintain adequate liability and accident insurance pursuant to § 23 (3) State Ordinance concerning the Implementation of the Rhineland-Palatinatian Hunting Law (*Landesjagdverordnung*, LJVO)<br>Thuringia: Hunting liability pursuant to § 9 Thuringian Ordinance on Hunting (*Verordnung zur Ausführung des Thüringer Jagdgesetzes*, ThJGAVO); Fishing liability as per § 18 (2) item 3 of the Thuringian Fishing Regulations (*Thüringer Fischereiverordnung*, ThürFischVO) |
| Medical professions, midwives, obstetric nurses | Mecklenburg-Western Pomerania: Midwives and obstetric nurses pursuant to § 8 of the Code of Conduct for Midwives and Obstetric Nurses (*Berufsordnung für Hebammen und Entbindungspfleger*, HebBO) |

| | |
|---|---|
| | Rhineland-Palatinate: Independent midwives and obstetric nurses pursuant to § 7 (1) State Ordinance on Professional Duties and Activities of Midwives and Obstetric Nurses (*Landesverordnung über die Berufspflichten und die Berufsausübung der Hebammen und Entbindungshelfer*)<br>Saxony: Pursuant to § 9 (3) no 1 State Birth Aides Law (*Sächsisches Hebammengesetz*, SächsHebG), midwives must maintain adequate professional indemnity insurance<br>The Saxony Law on Medical Professions (*Sächsisches Heilberufekammergesetz*, SächsHKaG) and the code of conduct for members of healing professions provide that healing professionals must maintain adequate professional indemnity insurance as stipulated in:<br>– § 17 (1) no 9 SächsHKaG in conjunction with § 23 Code of Conduct of the Saxony Regional Dental Society;<br>– § 17 (1) no 9 SächsHKaG in conjunction with § 21 Code of Conduct of the Saxony Regional Medical Society;<br>– § 17 (1) no 9 SächsHKaG in conjunction with § 7 Code of Conduct of the Saxony Regional Pharmacists Society;<br>– § 17 (1) no 9 SächsHKaG in conjunction with § 19 Code of Conduct of the Saxony Regional Veterinary Society;<br>– § 16 (4) second sentence SächsHKaG (not yet entered into force): Adequate professional indemnity insurance will be required for all who perform operations as legal persons under private law;<br>– § 5a SächsHKaG: Liability insurance is required for the Saxony Regional Medical Society when acting as ethic commission |
| Pupils | Bavaria: School sponsors pursuant to art 89 (2) no 8 Bavarian Education and School Act (*Bayerisches Gesetz über das Erziehungs- und Unterrichtungswesen*, BayEUG): This provision permits schools to call for pupils' liability insurance for particular types of schools or school events that include increased liability risks. Provisions concerning pupils' liability were included in the following school regulations: School Regulations for Elementary Schools in Bavaria, § 72; Vocational School Regulations, § 72; Regulations for Vocational Schools for Home Economics, Nursing and Social Care, § 95; Regulations concerning Non-Medical Therapeutic Vocational Schools, § 65; Regulations for Vocational Schools for Medical/Pharmaceutical Technologists, § 75; Regulations concerning Vocational Schools for Medical Education and Nursing Care, § 66; Regulations for Vocational Schools for Elderly and Family Care, § 65; Technical College and Upper Vocational School Regulations, § 100; Regu- |

| | |
|---|---|
| | lations governing Schools for the Disabled, § 90; School Regulations for Elementary Schools providing Special Pedagogical Care, § 72 |
| Sports facilities | Berlin: Clubs and associations pursuant to §§ 7 and 8 of the framework agreement on the autonomous use of sports facilities based on the Regulations for the Use of Sports Facilities (*Sportanlagen-Nutzungsvorschriften*, SPAN) in conjunction with § 14 (2) Act on the Promotion of Sports (*Sportförderungsgesetz*, SportFG) |
| Voluntary helpers | Rhineland-Palatinate: Voluntary helpers pursuant to § 3 (1) no 3 State Ordinance on Recognition of Low Threshold Service Proposals as per § 45b SGB, Book XI (*Landesverordnung über die Anerkennung von niedrigschwelligen Betreuungsangeboten*) |
| Volunteer fire brigade members | Hessen: § 11 (5) Hessian Act on Fire Protection, General Aid and Disaster Prevention (*Hessisches Gesetz über den Brandschutz, die Allgemeine Hilfe und den Katastrophenschutz*, HBKG) |

# III. Codes of Conduct (based on the Law of the Federal States)

Please note that the following list makes no claim to completeness. There are no English translations available on the internet.

## 1. Strict liability

In the Codes of Conduct (based on the law of the Federal States) there are no examples concerning strict liability available.

## 2. Fault liability

| | |
|---|---|
| Architects, engineers, designers, landscape gardeners, and town planners | Baden-Württemberg: § 15 (2) no 7 and § 17 sent 2 Architects Act Baden-Württemberg (*Architektengesetz BW*, ArchG BW) in conjunction with para 1 (9) Code of Conduct for Architects and Engineers in Baden-Württemberg: Independent architects<br>Bavaria: Art 1 (6) sents 2 and 3 no 8 Bavarian Architects Act (*Bayerisches Architektengesetz*, BayArchG), art 24 (1) sent 2 no 3 and sent 3 Bavarian Chamber of Construction Act (*Bayerisches Baukammerngesetz*, BauKaG Bayern) in conjunction with item 9 |

| | |
|---|---|
| | Code of Conduct of the Bavarian Chamber of Architects: Independent architects and members of the Bavarian Chamber of Architects<br>Berlin: § 10 Code of Conduct of the Berlin Chamber of Construction: Members of the Berlin Chamber of Construction (engineers)<br>Bremen: § 13 (2) no 5 BremArchG in conjunction with § 8 Code of Conduct of the Bremen Chamber of Architects: Independent architects<br>Saxony: Manual on the awarding and execution of professional services of engineers and landscape architects in road and bridge construction (HVA F-StB): Engineers and landscape architects in road and bridge construction<br>Thuringia: § 29 (1) ThürAIKG in conjunction with the Code of Conduct of the Thuringian Chamber of Architects: Independent architects, interior designers, landscape gardeners and architects, as well as town planners; § 29 (1) ThürAIKG in conjunction with the relevant Code of Conduct: Consulting engineers and engineers writing building specifications |
| Psychotherapists, physicians, dentists, and veterinarians | Berlin: § 6 (8) Code of Conduct of the Berlin Chamber of Psychotherapists: Psychological psychotherapists, child and adolescent therapists; § 21 Code of Conduct of the Berlin Chamber of Physicians; § 1 (11) Code of Conduct of the Berlin Chamber of Dentists<br>Rhineland-Palatinate: Codes of Conduct of their respective chambers in Rhineland-Palatinate for physicians, dentists and veterinarians<br>Thuringia: § 23 no 16 Thuringian Healing Professions Act (*Thüringer Heilberufegesetz*, ThürHeilBG): Veterinarians must have adequate liability insurance |
| Publicly appointed surveyors | Berlin: § 17 (1) Code of Conduct for Publicly Appointed Surveyors<br>Brandenburg: § 9 (3) Code of Conduct for Publicly Appointed Surveyors in Brandenburg<br>Hessen: § 12 Code of Conduct for Publicly Appointed and Sworn Surveyors: publicly appointed and sworn surveyors<br>Rhineland-Palatinate: § 8 (4) Code of Conduct for Publicly Appointed Sworn Surveyors in conjunction with § 6 (2) of the pertinent implementing regulation |

Péter Takáts

# Hungary

## I. National Law

The following Laws may be downloaded in the original Hungarian at http://net.jogtar.hu/, quoting the numbers of the respective legislative acts. No English translations are available online and translations, if any, are not for public access.

### 1. Strict liability

| | |
|---|---|
| Airports and aircraft<br>operators of ~ | Sec 69 of Law No XCVII of 1995 on air traffic (*a légiközlekedésről*); for details, see also Government Decree No 39/2001.(III.5.)Korm on compulsory liability insurance in air traffic (*a légiközlekedési kötelező felelősségbiztosításról*) |
| Gas supply systems<br>operators of ~ | Sec 126 para (4) of Government Decree No 19/2009.(I.30.)Korm on the execution of Law No XL of 2008 on the supply of natural gas (*a földgázellátásról szóló 2008. évi XL. törvény rendelkezéseinek végrehajtásáról*) |
| Hazardous materials<br>users of ~ on protected areas of nature | Sec 73 paras (1) and (2) of Law No LIII of 1996 on the protection of nature (*a természet védelméről*) |
| Hunters | Sec 60 para (1) item c) and sec 62 para (1) item d) of Law No LV of 1996 on the protection of game, its development and hunting (*a vad védelméről, a vadgazdálkodásról valamint a vadászatról*) |
| Motor vehicles<br>operators of ~ | Sec 4 para (1) of Law No LXII of 2009 on compulsory third-party motor liability insurance (*a kötelező gépjármű-felelősségbiztosításról*) |
| Nuclear facilities<br>concessionaires of ~ | Sec 54 para (1) and sec 67 item g) of Law No CXVI of 1996 on nuclear energy (*az atomenergiáról*) |
| Shooting ranges<br>operators of ~ | Sec 1 para (4) of the Decree of the Minister of Interior No 49/2004.(VIII.31.)BM on shooting ranges, the storage of shooting weapons and ammunition, further theoretical and training requirements of possessing shooting weapons (*a lőterekről, a lőfegyverek, lőszerek hatósági tárolásáról, a fegyvertartáshoz szükséges elméleti és jártassági követelményekről*) |

## 2. Fault liability

| | |
|---|---|
| Auditors | Sec 11 para (1) item g) of Law No LXXV of 2007 on the Hungarian Chamber of Auditors, the activity of auditors and on the public supervision of the same (*a Magyar Könyvvizsgálói Kamaráról, a könyvvizsgálói tevékenységről, valamint a könyvvizsgálói közfelügyeletről*) |
| Bonded warehouses<br>operators of ~ | Sec 4 para (3) of Law No XLVIII of 1996 on bonded warehousing (*a közraktározásról*) |
| Enforcers of judicial decisions (bailiffs) | Sec 236 para (2) of Law No LIII of 1994 on the enforcement of judicial decisions (*a bírósági végrehajtásról*) |
| Health care services providers | Sec 108 para (2) of Law No CLIV of 1997 on health care (*az egészségügyről*) |
| Insurance intermediaries and multi-agents<br>independent ~ | Sec 391 para (6) item a) and sec 403 para (1) item a) of Law No LXXXVIII of 2014 on insurance business (*a biztosítási tevékenységről*) |
| Intermediaries of financial services and credit brokers<br>independent ~ | Sec 21 para (3) item b) and para (5) item b) of Law No CCXXXVII of 2013 on credit institutions and financial enterprises (*a hitelintézetekről és a pénzügyi vállalkozásokról*) |
| Lawyers | Sec 13 para (3) item f) of Law No XI of 1998 on lawyers (*az ügyvédekről*) |
| Lifts, elevators and conveyors<br>supervisors of ~ | Sec 6 para (5) of Government Decree No 113/1998.(VI.10.)Korm on the licensing of elevators and conveyors by building authorities, the operation and supervision of the same and on the supervisors of the same (*a felvonók és a mozgólépcsők építésügyi hatósági engedélyezéséről, üzemeltetéséről, ellenőrzéséről és az ellenőrökről*) |
| Liquidators (receivers) of businesses | Sec 2 para (3) item g) of Government Decree No 114/2006.(V.12.)Korm on the list of liquidators (*a felszámolók névjegyzékéről*) |
| Medical research on human subjects<br>providers of ~ | Sec 164 para (2) of Law No CLIV of 1997 on health care (*az egészségügyről*) |
| Non-governmental welfare institutions<br>operators of ~ | Sec 3 item h) of Government Decree No 188/1999.(XII.16.)Korm on the licensing of the operation of social institutions providing personal care and village caretakers, further the licensing of social enterprises (*a személyes gondoskodást nyújtó szociális intézmény és a falugondnoki szolgálat működésének engedélyezéséről, továbbá a szociális vállalkozás engedélyezéséről*) |

| | |
|---|---|
| Non-governmental welfare institutions for children<br>operators of ~ | Sec 4 para (6) item a) of Government Decree No 259/2002. (XII.18.)Korm on the licencing of service activities relating to the welfare and protection of children, further the children's welfare and protection entrepreneurs' licence (*a gyermekjóléti és gyermekvédelmi szolgáltató tevékenység engedélyezéséről, valamint a gyermekjóléti és gyermekvédelmi vállalkozói engedélyről*) |
| Notaries<br>public~ | Sec 10 para (2) of Law No XLI of 1991 on public notaries (*a közjegyzőkről*) |
| Patent agents | Sec 2 para (3) item a) of Law No XXXII of 1995 on patent agents (*a szabadalmi ügyvivőkről*) |
| Pharmaceuticals<br>manufacturers of ~ for human use | Sec 4 para (3) of Law No XCV of 2005 on medicines to be applied to humans and on the amendment of other laws to regulate the medicines market (*az emberi alkalmazásra kerülő gyógyszerekről és egyéb, a gyógyszerpiacot szabályozó törvények módosításáról*) |
| Pharmaceuticals<br>wholesale traders of ~ | Sec 5 para (1) item j) of Decree of the Minister for Health Care No 53/2004.(VI.2.)ESzCsM on the wholesale and parallel import activities relating to medicines (*a gyógyszerekkel folytatott nagykereskedelmi és párhuzamos import tevékenységről*) |
| Printers of promissory notes | Sec 3 para (1) item a) of Government Decree No 98/1995. (VIII.24.)Korm on the security rules of the production, handling and physical destruction of promissory notes (*az egyes értékpapírok előállításának, kezelésének és fizikai megsemmisítésének biztonsági szabályairól*) |
| Public procurement tenders for construction works<br>offerors on ~ | Sec 9 of Government Decree No 306/2011.(XII.23.)Korm on the detailed rules on the public procurement of construction works (*az építési beruházások közbeszerzésének részletes szabályairól*) |
| Roads<br>service providers on public ~ | Sec 5 para (8) item b) of Government Decree No 89/1988. (XII.20.)MT on services related to public roads and the operation of road vehicles (*a közúti közlekedési szolgáltatásokról és a közúti járművek üzemben tartásáról*) |
| Security services<br>providers of ~, bodyguards and private detectives | Sec 5 para (1) item b) of Law No CXXXIII of 2005 on the rules of the activities to safeguard persons and property, further those of private detectives (*a személy- és vagyonvédelmi, valamint a magánnyomozói tevékenység szabályairól*) |
| Sports events<br>organisers of ~ | Sec 70 para (5) of Law No I of 2004 on sports (*a sportról*), further sec 7 item a) of Government Decree No 54/2004.(III.31.)Korm on the safety of sports events (*a sportrendezvények biztonságáról*) |
| Technical products<br>examiners, supervisors and certifiers of ~ | Sec 5 para (1) item c) of Government Decree No 182/1997.(X.17.)Korm on the appointment of the organisations examining, supervising and certifying the suitability of technical products (*a műszaki termékek megfelelőségét vizsgáló,* |

| | |
|---|---|
| | *ellenőrző és tanúsító szervezetek kijelöléséről*), further Appendix 7 to Joint Decree No 3/2003.(I.25.)BM-GKM-KvVM on the detailed rules of the technical requirements, certification of suitability, further marketing and use of construction products (*az építési termékek műszaki követelményeinek, megfelelőség igazolásának, valamint forgalomba hozatalának és felhasználásának részletes szabályairól*) |
| Trainees of physical professions<br>organisers of practical courses for ~ | Sec 70 para (3) of Law No CLXXXVII of 2011 on the training of skilled workers (*a szakképzésről*) |
| Veterinarians | Sec 34 para (1) item c) of Law No CXXVII of 2012 on the Hungarian Chamber of veterinarians and the veterinary services' activities (*a Magyar Állatorvosi Kamaráról, valamint az állatorvosi szolgáltatói tevékenység végzéséről*) |

## II. Laws of the Provinces (State Laws)

Laws of the provinces (state laws) do not exist in Hungary.

Diana Cerini and Anna Teresa Memola

# Italy

a) The following list of laws* was compiled by collecting information from the website of the Italian Authority for Private Insurance – IVASS (at www.IVASS.it) and from the website of the National Association of Insurers – ANIA (www.ANIA.it); in addition, research of relevant areas of insurance law was referred to. Nevertheless, there is not an official list of compulsory insurance available and the reader may find some repetition.

b) The text of each mentioned law can be downloaded from www.gazzettaufficiale.it (the Official Journal of Law and Statutory Acts in Italy), or from www.camera.it (the Parliament web site).

c) No website with a comprehensive English translation of the listed laws is available, apart from the reference of Legislative Decree D.lgs.209/2005 also named Codice delle Assicurazioni Private, which can be downloaded from www.IVASS.it. Other laws might have been translated partially in private websites.

d) The laws and equivalent acts (delegated legislation, ministry and presidential decrees in application of laws) establishing liability insurance do not generally distinguish between the type of liability in question (fault, strict, absolute liability) or the source (tort, contract) of the liability. Consequently, the distinction is based on the interpretation of the relevant rule of law setting the liability.

## I. National Law

### 1. Strict liability

| | |
|---|---|
| Agricultural assistance centres<br>reform of ~ | Art 5 – Decree of the Ministry of Agriculture 27.3.2008 for the reform of agricultural assistance centres (*Decreto del Ministero delle politiche agricole alimentari e forestali 27 marzo 2008. Riforma dei centri autorizzati di assistenza agricola*) |

* Editors' note: Other than in the other Annexes, in this Annex legal provisions stipulating compulsory insurance both for strict and for fault liability are not only mentioned under the heading 'strict liability' but also under the heading 'fault liability'.

| | |
|---|---|
| Anti-crisis provisions<br>approval of ~ | Art 25 – Law Decree 1.7.2009, no 78 (converted in Law 3.8.2009, no 102) for the approval of anti-crises provisions (*Decreto convertito, con modificazioni, in legge 3 agosto 2009, n. 102 – provvedimenti anticrisi, nonché proroga di termini. Visto di conformità*) |
| Audit companies and requisites of head positions in financial companies | Art 4 – Decree of the Ministry of Economics and Finance 5.4.2012, no 66 for the organisation of audit companies and for the requisites of head positions in financial companies (*Decreto del Ministero dell'Economia e delle Finanze del 5 aprile 2012, n. 66 – Regolamento di disciplina dei requisiti patrimoniali e di indipendenza delle società di consulenza finanziaria, nonché dei requisiti di professionalità, onorabilità e indipendenza degli esponenti aziendali delle società di consulenza finanziaria*) |
| Cars and elevators | Art 11 para 2 and attachment XI – Legislative Decree 27.1.2010, no 17 in relation to cars and modifying the Directive concerning elevators (*Attuazione della direttiva 2006/42/CE, relativa alle macchine e che modifica la direttiva 95/16/CE relativa agli ascensori*) |
| Certification, inspection and testing of building products | Art 2 – Decree of the Ministry of Productive Activities 9.5.2003, no 156 for the release of the licence for certification, inspection and testing in the field of building products (*Criteri e modalità per il rilascio dell'abilitazione degli organismi di certificazione, ispezione e prova nel settore dei prodotti da costruzione, ai sensi dell'articolo 9, comma 2, del decreto del presidente della repubblica 21 aprile 1993, n. 246*) |
| Certification of laboratories | Art 2 para 4 letter c) – Ministerial Decree 25.2.2002, no 84 on the certification of laboratories (*Decreto del ministero delle comunicazioni 25 febbraio 2002, n. 84. Regolamento concernente la procedura di accreditamento dei laboratori di prova*) |
| Certified e-mail account service providers | Art 14 para 6 letter i) – Presidential Decree 11.2.2005, no 68 under art 27 of the Law 16.1.2003, no 3 for the certified e-mail account (*Decreto del Presidente della Repubblica 11 febbraio 2005, n. 68. Regolamento recante disposizioni per l'utilizzo della posta elettronica certificata, a norma dell'articolo 27 della legge 16 gennaio 2003, n. 3*) |
| Certified organisms not depending on the Ministry of Infrastructure and Transport authorised for the release of transport instruments for dangerous products | Decree of the Ministry of Infrastructure and Transport 2.4.2003, pursuant to Legislative Decree 2.2.2002, no 23 for certified and authorised organisms not depending on the Ministry of Infrastructure and Transport (*Decreto del Ministero delle Infrastrutture e dei Trasporti 2 aprile 2003. Procedure per la designazione degli organismi notificati e autorizzati non dipendenti dal ministero delle infrastrutture e dei trasporti ai sensi del decreto legislativo 2 febbraio 2002, n. 23*) |

| | |
|---|---|
| Clinical experimentation of medicines<br>protection of patients of ~ | Arts 1 and 3 – Decree of the Ministry of Labour, Health and Social Politics 14.7.2009 for the insurance coverage and protection of patients subject to clinical experimentation of medicines (*Requisiti minimi per le polizze assicurative a tutela dei soggetti partecipanti alle sperimentazioni cliniche dei medicinali*) |
| Commercialisation of explosive materials for civil use | Art 5 – Decree of the Ministry of the Interior 19.9.2002, no 272 pursuant to Legislative Decree 2.1.1997, no 7 for the harmonisation of the commercialisation of explosive materials for civil use (*Decreto del ministro dell'interno 19 settembre 2002, n. 272. Regolamento di esecuzione del decreto legislativo 2 gennaio 1997, n. 7, recante le norme di recepimento della direttiva 93/15/cee relativa all'armonizzazione delle disposizioni in materia di immissione sul mercato e controllo degli esplosivi per uso civile*) |
| Consumer credit contracts<br>donors of ~ | Art 6 para 1 letter b) – Legislative Decree 19.9.2012, no 169 modifying Legislative Decree 13.8.2010, no 141 on Consumer credit contracts (*Ulteriori modifiche ed integrazioni al decreto legislativo 13 agosto 2010, n. 141, recante attuazione della direttiva 2008/48/CE, relativa ai contratti di credito ai consumatori, nonché modifiche del titolo v del testo unico bancario in merito alla disciplina dei soggetti operanti nel settore finanziario, degli agenti in attività finanziaria e dei mediatori creditizi*) |
| Cooperative practicality of the European railway system | Arts 4 and 8 – Legislative Decree 8.10.2010, no 191 on the cooperative practicality of the European railway system (*Attuazione della direttiva 2008/57/CE e 2009/131/CE relativa all'interoperabilità del sistema ferroviario comunitario*) |
| Cross-border health care<br>rights of patients to ~ | Arts 4 and 7 – Directive 2011/24/EU of the European Parliament and of the Council of 9.3.2011 on the application of patients' rights in cross-border health care (*Direttiva UE del Parlamento europeo e del Consiglio del 9 marzo 2011, n. 24 concernente l'applicazione dei diritti dei pazienti relativi all'assistenza sanitaria transfrontaliera*) |
| Cycle races on roads<br>organisers of ~ | Art 8 – Provision of the Ministry of Infrastructure and Transport 27.11.2002 on cycle races on roads (*Provvedimento del Ministero delle Infrastrutture e dei Trasporti 27 novembre 2002 per le scorte tecniche alle competizioni ciclistiche su strada*) |
| Dentistry and partial denture<br>apprenticeship of ~ | Art 1 – Law 20.3.1984, no 47 (unique article) on the apprenticeship of dentistry and partial denture (*Tirocinio pratico di cui alla tabella XVIII-bis dell'ordinamento didattico universitario per gli studenti del corso di laurea in odontoiatria e protesi dentaria*) |
| Development of the country through a higher level of health | Art 3 – Law Decree 12.9.2012, no 158 converted in Law 8.11.2012, no 189 for the development of the country through a higher level of health (*disposizioni urgenti per promuovere lo sviluppo del paese mediante un più alto livello di tutela della salute – Decreto Sanità*) |

| | |
|---|---|
| Dogs<br>holders of ~ | Art 3 para 4 – Public injunction of the Ministry of Labour, Health and Social Policy 3.3.2009 concerning public safety in the case of aggressive dogs (*Ordinanza del Ministero del Lavoro, della Salute e delle Politiche Sociali 3 marzo 2009. Ordinanza contingibile ed urgente concernente la tutela dell'incolumità pubblica dall'aggressione dei cani*) |
| Electrical nuclear energy and storage of radioactive waste<br>providers of ~ | Art 17 – Legislative Decree 15.2.2010, no 31 on electrical nuclear energy and the storage of radioactive waste under art 25 of Law 23.7.2009, no 99 (*Decreto legislativo 15 febbraio 2010, n. 31. Disciplina [della localizzazione, della realizzazione e dell'esercizio nel territorio nazionale di impianti di produzione di energia elettrica nucleare, di impianti di fabbricazione del combustibile nucleare], dei sistemi di stoccaggio del combustibile irraggiato e dei rifiuti radioattivi, nonché benefici economici [e campagne informative al pubblico], a norma dell'articolo 25 della legge 23 luglio 2009, n. 99*) |
| Electromagnetic compatibility | Art 5 and attachment VI – Legislative Decree 6.11.2007, no 194 concerning electromagnetic compatibility (*Attuazione della direttiva 2004/108/CE concernente il ravvicinamento delle legislazioni degli Stati membri relative alla compatibilità elettromagnetica e che abroga la direttiva 89/336/CEE*) |
| Energy consumption<br>planning, installation, maintenance of buildings in order to control ~ | Attachment I para 7 – Decree of the President of the Republic 21.12.1999, no 551 modifying the Presidential Decree 26.8.1993, no 412 for planning, installation, maintenance of buildings in order to control energy consumption (*Decreto del Presidente della Repubblica 21 dicembre 1999, n. 5. Regolamento recante modifiche al decreto del Presidente della Repubblica 26 agosto 1993, n. 412, in materia di progettazione, installazione, esercizio e manutenzione degli impianti termici degli edifici, ai fini del contenimento dei consumi di energia*) |
| Energy deriving from liquefied natural gas<br>construction of sites for ~<br>distribution and selling of ~ | Art 16 – Legislative Decree 22.2.2006, no 128 for the construction of sites, distribution and selling of liquefied natural gas (*Riordino della disciplina relativa all'installazione e all'esercizio degli impianti di riempimento, travaso e deposito di gpl, nonché all'esercizio dell'attività di distribuzione e vendita di gpl in recipienti, a norma dell'articolo 1, comma 52, della legge 23 agosto 2004, n. 239*) |
| European rail passengers' rights | Art 12 – Regulation (EC) No 1371/2007 of the European Parliament and Council 23.10.2007, on rail passengers' rights and obligations (*Diritti e obblighi dei passeggeri nel trasporto ferroviario*) |
| Financial assistance<br>specialised centres and professionals for ~ | Art 22 – Ministerial Decree 31.5.1999, no 164 on financial assistance provided by specialised centres and professionals (*Regolamento recante norme per l'assistenza fiscale resa dai centri di* |

| | |
|---|---|
| | *assistenza fiscale per le imprese e per i dipendenti, dai sostituti d'imposta e dai professionisti ai sensi dell'art. 40 del decreto legislativo 9 luglio 1997, n. 241*) |
| Financial consultants | Art 6 – Ministerial Decree 24.12.2008, no 206 in relation to financial consultants' requirements (*Regolamento di disciplina dei requisiti di professionalità, onorabilità, indipendenza e patrimoniali per l'iscrizione all'albo delle persone fisiche consulenti finanziari*) |
| Fiscal measuring instruments | Fiscal provision in relation to fiscal measuring instruments (of 28.7.2003), modifying Ministerial Decree 23.3.1983 and pursuant to fiscal provision 4.3.2002, point 5.1 letters b) and c) in relation to fiscal measuring instruments (*Provvedimento dell'Agenzia delle Entrate 28 luglio 2003. Modifica del decreto ministeriale 23 marzo 1983 e successive integrazioni e modificazioni, concernente norme di attuazione delle disposizioni di cui alla legge 26 gennaio 1983, n. 18. Attuazione delle disposizioni contenute nelle lettere b) e c) del punto 5.1 del provvedimento 4 marzo 2002 dell'Agenzia delle Entrate*) |
| Free circulation of people and workers in the EU after the entrance of Bulgaria and Romania<br>professional qualifications for ~ | Art 17 para 7 – Legislative Decree 9.11.2007, no 206 for the identification of professional qualifications and free circulation of people in the EU after the entrance of Bulgaria and Romania (*Attuazione della direttiva 2005/36/CE relativa al riconoscimento delle qualifiche professionali, nonché della direttiva 2006/100/CE che adegua determinate direttive sulla libera circolazione delle persone a seguito dell'adesione di Bulgaria e Romania*) |
| Gas distributors via local pipelines<br>liability of ~ to final clients | Decision of the Authority for Gas and Electrical Energy 79/10 on final clients of gas distributed via local pipelines (*Delibera arg/gas 79/10 – disposizioni per l'estensione dell'assicurazione dei clienti finali civili del gas distribuito a mezzo di gasdotti locali e di reti di trasporto fino al 31 dicembre 2013*) |
| Health professionals (doctors, biologists, chemists, psychologists) for the assistance of navigational, maritime and civil aviation personnel | Art 15 – Decree of the Ministry of Health 3.10.2012, no 202 concerning the agreement between the Ministry of Health and health professionals (doctors, biologists, chemists, psychologists) for the assistance of navigational, maritime and civil aviation personnel (*Regolamento recante accordo collettivo nazionale per la disciplina dei rapporti tra il ministero della salute, i medici ambulatoriali, specialisti e generici e le altre professionalità sanitarie – biologi, chimici e psicologi – operanti negli ambulatori direttamente gestiti dal Ministero della Salute per l'assistenza sanitaria e medico-legale al personale navigante, marittimo e dell'aviazione civile*) |
| Housing complexes<br>administration of ~ | Art 9 – Law 11.12.2012, no 220 for the administration of housing complexes (*Modifiche alla disciplina del condominio negli edifici*) |

| | |
|---|---|
| Hunting and protection of warm-blooded animals | Art 12, para 8 – Law 11.2.1992, no 157 on the protection of omeotermic animals and hunting (*Norme per la protezione della fauna selvatica omeoterma e per il prelievo venatorio*) |
| In vitro diagnostic medical devices | Art 8 para 6 and attachment no 3 – Legislative Decree 8.9.2000, no 332 pursuant to EU Directive 98/79/EC on in vitro diagnostic medical devices (*Attuazione della Direttiva 98/79/CE relativa ai dispositivi medicodiagnostici in vitro*) |
| Inspection bodies of type 'a' | Art 3 letter g) – Directive of the Ministry of the Productive Activities 11.3.2002 on the identification of inspective bodies of type 'a' under arts 4, 6 and 7 of the Presidential Decree 22.10.2001, no 462 (*Direttiva del Ministero delle Attività Produttive 11 marzo 2002. Procedure per l'individuazione, ai sensi degli articoli 4, 6 e 7 del decreto del Presidente della Repubblica 22 ottobre 2001, n. 462, degli organismi di ispezione di tipo 'a'*) |
| Insurance intermediaries | Art 110 para 3 – Legislative Decree 7.9.2005, no 209 (Private Insurance Code) on professional insurance for insurance intermediaries (*Codice delle assicurazioni private – r.c. professionale per gli intermediari assicurativi*) |
| Internal auditors | Art 15 – Legislative Decree 27.1.2010, no 39 on the implementation of Directive 2006/43/EC on statutory audits of annual accounts and consolidated accounts (*Attuazione della Direttiva 2006/43/CE, relativa alle revisioni legali dei conti annuali e dei conti consolidati, che modifica le Direttive 78/660/CEE e 83/349/CEE, e che abroga la Direttiva 84/253/CEE*) |
| Labour contracts<br>training activities and orientation activities in ~ | Art 3 – Ministerial Decree 25.3.1998, no 142 on training activities and orientation activities in labour contracts (*Decreto ministeriale 25 marzo 1998, n. 142. Regolamento recante norme di attuazione dei princìpi e dei criteri di cui all'articolo 18 della l. 24 giugno 1997, n. 196, sui tirocini formativi e di orientamento*) |
| Legal professionals | Art 12 – Law 31.12.2012, no 247 for the organisation of the legal profession (*Nuova disciplina dell'ordinamento della professione forense*) |
| Liquefied natural gas<br>producers and suppliers of (eg ENI) ~ | Art 19 – Presidential Decree 9.11.1991, no 404, pursuant to Laws 8.7.1950 no 640 and 7.6.1990 no 145 on liquefied natural gas (*Decreto del Presidente della Repubblica 9 novembre 1991, n. 404. Regolamento di esecuzione delle leggi 8 luglio 1950 n. 640 e 7 giugno 1990 n. 145, sulla disciplina delle bombole per metano*) |
| Measuring instruments | Art 9 – Legislative Decree 2.2.2007, no 22 putting into effect EU Directive 2004/22/EC on measuring instruments (*Attuazione della Direttiva 2004/22/CE relativa agli strumenti di misura*) |

| | |
|---|---|
| Mediators | Art 3 para 5bis – Law 3.2.1989, no 39 modifying Law 21.3.1958, no 253 concerning the profession of mediators (*Modifiche ed integrazioni alla legge 21 marzo 1958, n. 253, concernente la disciplina della professione di mediatore*) |
| Mediators/arbitrators and their indemnities/subscription to conciliation boards | Art 4 para 2 letter b) and art 4 para 5 – Decree of the Ministry of Justice 18.10.2010, no 180 pursuant to art 16 of the Legislative Decree 4.3.2010, no 28 concerning mediators and their indemnities (*Regolamento recante la determinazione dei criteri e delle modalità di iscrizione e tenuta del registro degli organismi di mediazione e dell'elenco dei formatori per la mediazione nonché' l'approvazione delle indennità spettanti agli organismi, ai sensi dell'articolo 16 del decreto legislativo 4 marzo 2010, n. 28*)<br>Decree of the Ministry of Justice 23.7.2004, no 222 on subscription and registrar's office rules of the conciliation boards under art 38 of the Legislative Decree 17.1.2003, no 5 (*Decreto del ministero della giustizia 23 luglio 2004, n. 222. Regolamento recante la determinazione dei criteri e delle modalità di iscrizione nonché di tenuta del registro degli organismi di conciliazione di cui all'articolo 38 del decreto legislativo 17 gennaio 2003, n. 5*) |
| Medical devices and biocides | Art 2.2 – Legislative Decree 25.1.2010, no 37 regarding active medical devices and biocides (*Attuazione della direttiva 2007/47/CE che modifica le direttive 90/385/CEE per il ravvicinamento delle legislazioni degli Stati membri relative ai dispositivi medici impiantabili attivi, 93/42/CE concernente i dispositivi medici e 98/8/CE relativa all'immissione sul mercato dei biocidi*) |
| New hot-water heaters | Attachment V para 6 – Presidential Decree 15.11.1996, no 660 pursuant to EU Directive 92/42/EEC on efficiency requirements for new hot-water boilers fired with liquid or gaseous fuels (*Regolamento per l'attuazione della direttiva 92/42/CEE concernente i requisiti di rendimento delle nuove caldaie ad acqua calda, alimentate con combustibili liquidi o gassosi*) |
| Noise emission in the environment caused by equipment for use outdoors | Arts 3 and 9 – Legislative Decree 4.9.2002, no 262 pursuant to EU Directive 2000/14/EC on noise emission in the environment caused by equipment for use outdoors (*Decreto legislativo 4 settembre 2002, n. 262. Attuazione della direttiva 2000/14/CE concernente l'emissione acustica ambientale delle macchine ed attrezzature destinate a funzionare all'aperto*) |
| Non-automatic weighing instruments<br>organisms certifying the compliance of ~ | Art 9 and attachment V – Directive 2009/23/EC of the European Parliament and the European Council on non-automatic weighing instruments (*Direttiva 2009/23/CE del Parlamento Europeo e del Consiglio del 23 aprile 2009 relativa agli strumenti per pesare a funzionamento non automatico*) |
| Non-profit activities | Art 4 – Law 11.8.1991, no 266 on non-profit activities (*Legge-quadro sul volontariato*) |

| | |
|---|---|
| Non-registered professions | Art 7 letter e) – Law 14.1.2013, no 4 for the exercise of non-registered jobs (*Disposizioni in materia di professioni non organizzate*) |
| Notaries<br>civil liability of ~ | Art 2 – Legislative Decree 4.5.2006, no 182 on civil liability insurance in relation to notarial activity for the establishment of a guarantee fund (*Norme in materia di assicurazione per la responsabilità civile derivante dall'esercizio dell'attività notarile ed istituzione di un fondo di garanzia in attuazione dell'articolo 7, comma 1, della legge 28 novembre 2005, n. 246*) |
| Organ transplant from living donors | Art 12 para 3 – Decree of the Ministry of Health 16.4.2010, no 116 on organ transplant from living donors (*Regolamento per lo svolgimento delle attività di trapianto di organi da donatore vivente*) |
| Personal protective equipment | Attachment V para 6 – Legislative Decree 4.12.1992, no 475 pursuant to EU Directive 89/686/EEC on the approximation of the laws of the Member States relating to personal protective equipment (*Attuazione della Direttiva 89/686/CEE del Consiglio del 21 dicembre 1989, in materia di ravvicinamento delle legislazioni degli Stati Membri relative ai dispositivi di protezione individuale*) |
| Pressure vessels | Attachment III para 6 – Legislative Decree 27.9.1991, no 311 pursuant to EU Directives 87/404/EEC and 90/488/EEC under art 56 of the Law 29.12.1990, no 428 in relation to simple pressure vessels (*Decreto legislativo 27 settembre 1991, n. 311. Attuazione delle direttive n. 87/404/CEE e n. 90/488/CEE in materia di recipienti semplici a pressione, a norma dell'art. 56 della legge 29 dicembre 1990, n. 428*) |
| Protection disposals and systems to be used in explosive atmosphere | Art 3 – Ministerial Decree 12.3.1999 on the compliance of protection disposals and systems which are going to be used in explosive atmosphere (*Requisiti per l'autorizzazione degli organismi ad espletare le procedure per la valutazione di conformità di apparecchi e sistemi di protezione destinati ad essere utilizzati in atmosfera potenzialmente esplosiva*) |
| Public security companies and their employees | Attachment A art 6 – Decree of the Ministry of the Interior 1.12.2010, no 269 concerning the requisites for the organisation of public security companies and for the quality of institutes as well as for the professional requirements of the employed personnel (*Regolamento recante disciplina delle caratteristiche minime del progetto organizzativo e dei requisiti minimi di qualità degli istituti e dei servizi di cui agli articoli 256-bis e 257-bis del regolamento di esecuzione del testo unico delle leggi di pubblica sicurezza, nonché dei requisiti professionali e di capacità tecnica richiesti per la direzione dei medesimi istituti e per lo svolgimento di incarichi organizzativi nell'ambito degli stessi istituti*) |

| | |
|---|---|
| Pyrotechnical products<br>introduction on the market of ~ | Arts 6 and 11 – Law Decree 4.4.2010, no 58 for the introduction on the market of pyrotechnical products (*Attuazione della direttiva 2007/23/CE relativa all'immissione sul mercato di prodotti pirotecnici*) |
| Recreation units and their components<br>planning, building and selling of ~ | Art 5 – Decree of the Ministry of Productive Activities 30.4.2003, no 175 concerning the granting of a licence with regard to the activity of planning, building and selling of recreation units and their components (*Regolamento recante disposizioni per il rilascio dell'autorizzazione agli organismi di certificazione in materia di progettazione, di costruzione e immissione in commercio di unità da diporto e loro componenti*) |
| Registered professional activities | Art 5 – Presidential Decree 7.8.2012, no 137 on the organisation of registered professional activities (*Regolamento recante riforma degli ordinamenti professionali*) |
| Rescue teams<br>speleologic and mountain ~ | Art 2 – Law 21.3.2001, no 74 on improving activities of speleologic and mountain rescue teams (*Disposizioni per favorire l'attività svolta dal corpo nazionale soccorso alpino e speleologico*) |
| School<br>managing and organisation (limited to financial activities [not for other forms of liabilities]) ~ | Art 50 para 3 – Decree of the Ministry of Education 1.2.2001, no 44 on school managing and organisation limited to financial activities (*Decreto del Ministero della pubblica istruzione 1 febbraio 2001, n. 44. Regolamento concernente le 'istruzioni generali sulla gestione amministrativo-contabile delle istituzioni scolastiche'*) |
| Sport competitions | Art 124 – Legislative Decree 7.9.2005, no 209 (Private Insurance Code) on sport competitions (*Decreto legislativo 7 settembre 2005, n. 209. Codice delle assicurazioni private. Gare e competizioni sportive*) |
| Tourism activities' organisers and long term holiday contracts | Art 19 – Legislative Decree 23.5.2011, no 79 on tourism activities and on the implementation of long term holiday contracts (*Codice della normativa statale in tema di ordinamento e mercato del turismo, a norma dell'articolo 14 della legge 28 novembre 2005, n. 246, nonché attuazione della direttiva 2008/122/CE, relativa ai contratti di multiproprietà, contratti relativi ai prodotti per le vacanze di lungo termine, contratti di rivendita e di scambio*) |
| Toys<br>safety duties upon producers of ~ | Arts 3 and 8 – Legislative Decree 11.4.2011, no 54 on the safety of toys (*Attuazione della Direttiva 2009/48/CE sulla sicurezza dei giocattoli*) |
| Winter ski sports<br>organisers of the practice of ~ | Art 4 – Law 24.12.2003, no 363 on the practice of winter ski sports (*Legge 24 dicembre 2003, n. 363 norme in materia di sicurezza nella pratica degli sport invernali da discesa e da fondo*) |

## 2. Fault liability

| | |
|---|---|
| Active medical devices and biocides<br>producers of ~ | Art 2.2 – Legislative Decree 25.1.2010, no 37 regarding active medical devices and biocides (*Attuazione della direttiva 2007/47/CE che modifica le direttive 90/385/CEE per il ravvicinamento delle legislazioni degli Stati membri relative ai dispositivi medici impiantabili attivi, 93/42/CE concernente i dispositivi medici e 98/8/CE relativa all'immissione sul mercato dei biocidi*) |
| Anti-crises provisions<br>approval of ~ | Art 25 – Law Decree 1.7.2009, no 78 converted in Law 3.8.2009, no 102 for the approval of anti-crises provisions (*Decreto convertito, con modificazioni, in legge 3 agosto 2009, n. 102 – provvedimenti anticrisi, nonché proroga di termini. Visto di conformità*) |
| Audit companies and requisites of head positions in financial companies | Art 4 – Decree of the Ministry of Economics and Finance 5.4.2012, no 66 for the organisation of audit companies and for the requisites of head positions in financial companies (*Decreto del Ministero dell'Economia e delle Finanze del 5 aprile 2012, n. 66. Regolamento di disciplina dei requisiti patrimoniali e di indipendenza delle società di consulenza finanziaria, nonché dei requisiti di professionalità, onorabilità e indipendenza degli esponenti aziendali delle società di consulenza finanziaria*) |
| Cars and elevators | Art 11 para 2 and attachment XI – Legislative Decree 27.1.2010, no 17 in relation to cars and modifying the discipline concerning elevators (*Attuazione della direttiva 2006/42/CE, relativa alle macchine e che modifica la direttiva 95/16/CE relativa agli ascensori*) |
| Certification, inspection and testing of building products<br>licences for the ~ | Art 2 – Decree of the Ministry of Productive Activities 9.5.2003, no 156 for the granting of a licence for certification, inspection and testing in the field of building products (*Criteri e modalità per il rilascio dell'abilitazione degli organismi di certificazione, ispezione e prova nel settore dei prodotti da costruzione, ai sensi dell'articolo 9, comma 2, del decreto del presidente della repubblica 21 aprile 1993, n. 246*) |
| Certified and authorised organisms not dependent on the Ministry of Infrastructure and Transport authorised for the granting of transport instruments for dangerous products | Decree of the Ministry of Infrastructure and Transport 2.4.2003, pursuant to Legislative Decree 2.2.2002, no 23 for certified and authorised organisms not dependent on the Ministry of Infrastructure and Transport (*Decreto del Ministero delle Infrastrutture e dei Trasporti 2 aprile 2003. Procedure per la designazione degli organismi notificati e autorizzati non dipendenti dal ministero delle infrastrutture e dei trasporti ai sensi del decreto legislativo 2 febbraio 2002, n. 23*) |
| Certified e-mail accounts<br>providers of ~ | Art 14 para 6 letter i) – Presidential Decree 11.2.2005, no 68 under art 27 of the Law 16.1.2003, no 3 for certified e-mail accounts (*Decreto del Presidente della Repubblica 11 febbraio 2005, n. 68.* |

| | |
|---|---|
| | *Regolamento recante disposizioni per l'utilizzo della posta elettronica certificata, a norma dell'articolo 27 della legge 16 gennaio 2003, n. 3*) |
| Clinical tests of medicines<br>protection of patients subject to ~ | Arts 1 and 3 – Decree of the Ministry of Labour, Health and Social Politics, 14.7.2009 for the insurance coverage and protection of patients subject to clinical experiments of medicines (*Requisiti minimi per le polizze assicurative a tutela dei soggetti partecipanti alle sperimentazioni cliniche dei medicinali*) |
| Commercialisation of explosive materials for civil use<br>harmonisation of ~ | Art 5 – Decree of the Ministry of the Interior 19.9.2002, no 272 pursuant to Legislative Decree 2.1.1997, no 7 for the harmonisation of the commercialisation of explosive materials for civil use (*Decreto del ministro dell'interno 19 settembre 2002, n. 272. Regolamento di esecuzione del decreto legislativo 2 gennaio 1997, n. 7, recante le norme di recepimento della direttiva 93/15/CEE relativa all'armonizzazione delle disposizioni in materia di immissione sul mercato e controllo degli esplosivi per uso civile*) |
| Compliance of protection disposals and systems to be used in explosive atmosphere | Art 3 – Ministerial Decree 12.3.1999 on the compliance of protection disposals and systems to be used in explosive atmosphere (*Requisiti per l'autorizzazione degli organismi ad espletare le procedure per la valutazione di conformità di apparecchi e sistemi di protezione destinati ad essere utilizzati in atmosfera potenzialmente esplosiva*) |
| Consumer credit contracts<br>donors of ~ | Art 6 para 1 letter b) – Legislative Decree 19.9.2012, no 169 modifying Legislative Decree 13.8.2010, no 141 on consumer credit contract (*Ulteriori modifiche ed integrazioni al decreto legislativo 13 agosto 2010, n. 141, recante attuazione della direttiva 2008/48/CE, relativa ai contratti di credito ai consumatori, nonché modifiche del titolo v del testo unico bancario in merito alla disciplina dei soggetti operanti nel settore finanziario, degli agenti in attività finanziaria e dei mediatori creditizi*) |
| Cross-border health care<br>rights of patients to ~ | Arts 4 and 7 – Directive 2011/24/EU of the European Parliament and of the Council 9.3.2011, on the application of patients' rights in cross-border health care (*Direttiva UE del Parlamento europeo e del Consiglio del 9 marzo 2011, n. 24 concernente l'applicazione dei diritti dei pazienti relativi all'assistenza sanitaria transfrontaliera*) |
| Cycle races on roads<br>organisers of ~ | Art 8 – Provision of the Ministry of Infrastructures and Transports 27.11.2002 on cycle races on roads (*Provvedimento del Ministero delle Infrastrutture e dei Trasporti 27 novembre 2002 per le scorte tecniche alle competizioni ciclistiche su strada*) |
| Dentistry and partial denture<br>apprenticeship of ~ | Art 1 – Law 20.3.1984, no 47 (unique article) on the apprenticeship of dentistry and partial denture (*Tirocinio pratico di cui alla tabella XVIII-bis dell'ordinamento didattico universitario per gli studenti del corso di laurea in odontoiatria e protesi dentaria*) |

| | |
|---|---|
| Development of the country through a higher level of health | Art 3 – Law Decree 12.9.2012, no 158 converted in Law 8.11.2012, no 189 for the development of the country through a higher level of health (*Disposizioni urgenti per promuovere lo sviluppo del paese mediante un più alto livello di tutela della salute – Decreto Sanità*) |
| Dogs<br>holders of ~ | Art 3 para 4 – Public injunction of the Ministry of Labour, Health and Social Policy 3.3.2009 concerning public safety in the case of aggressive dogs (*Ordinanza del Ministero del Lavoro, della Salute e delle Politiche Sociali 3 marzo 2009. Ordinanza contingibile ed urgente concernente la tutela dell'incolumità pubblica dall'aggressione dei cani*) |
| Electromagnetic compatibility | Art 5 and attachment VI – Legislative Decree 6.11.2007, no 194 concerning electromagnetic compatibility (*Attuazione della direttiva 2004/108/CE concernente il riavvicinamento delle legislazioni degli Stati membri relative alla compatibilità elettromagnetica e che abroga la direttiva 89/336/CEE*) |
| European rail passengers' rights | Art 12 – Regulation (EC) No 1371/2007 of the European Parliament and of the Council 23.10.2007, no 1371 on rail passengers' rights and obligations (*Diritti e obblighi dei passeggeri nel trasporto ferroviario*) |
| Financial assistance<br>specialised centres and professionals for ~ | Art 22 – Ministerial Decree 31.5.1999, no 164 on financial assistance provided by specialised centres and professionals (*Regolamento recante norme per l'assistenza fiscale resa dai centri di assistenza fiscale per le imprese e per i dipendenti, dai sostituti d'imposta e dai professionisti ai sensi dell'art. 40 del decreto legislativo 9 luglio 1997, n. 241*) |
| Financial consultants | Art 6 – Ministerial Decree 24.12.2008, no 206 in relation to financial consultants' requirements (*Regolamento di disciplina dei requisiti di professionalità, onorabilità, indipendenza e patrimoniali per l'iscrizione all'albo delle persone fisiche consulenti finanziari*) |
| Free circulation of people and workers in the EU after the entrance of Bulgaria and Romania<br>professional qualifications for ~ | Art 17 para 7 – Legislative Decree 9.11.2007, no 206 for the identification of professional qualifications and free circulation of people in the EU after the entrance of Bulgaria and Romania (*Attuazione della direttiva 2005/36/CE relativa al riconoscimento delle qualifiche professionali, nonché della direttiva 2006/100/CE che adegua determinate direttive sulla libera circolazione delle persone a seguito dell'adesione di Bulgaria e Romania*) |
| Housing complexes<br>administration of ~ | Art 9 – Law 11.12.2012, no 220 for the administration of housing complexes (*Modifiche alla disciplina del condominio negli edifici*) |
| Hunting and protection of warm-blooded animals | Art 12 para 8 – Law 11.2.1992, no 157 on the protection of omeotermic animals and hunting (*Norme per la protezione della fauna selvatica omeoterma e per il prelievo venatorio*) |

| | |
|---|---|
| In vitro diagnostic medical devices | Art 8 para 6 and attachment no 3 – Legislative Decree 8.9.2000, no 332 pursuant to EU Directive 98/79/EC on in vitro diagnostic medical devices (*Attuazione della Direttiva 98/79/CE relativa ai dispositivi medicodiagnostici in vitro*) |
| Inspection bodies of type 'a' | Art 3 letter g) – Directive of the Ministry of the Productive Activities 11.3.2002 on the identification of inspection bodies of type 'a' under arts 4, 6 and 7 of the Presidential Decree 22.10.2001, no 462 (*Direttiva del Ministero delle Attività Produttive 11 marzo 2002. Procedure per l'individuazione, ai sensi degli articoli 4, 6 e 7 del decreto del Presidente della Repubblica 22 ottobre 2001, n. 462, degli organismi di ispezione di tipo 'a'*) |
| Insurance intermediaries | Art 110 para 3 – Legislative Decree 7.9.2005, no 209 (Private Insurance Code) on professional insurance for insurance intermediaries (*Codice delle assicurazioni private – r.c. professionale per gli intermediari assicurativi*) |
| Internal auditors | Art 15 – Legislative Decree 27.1.2010, no 39 on the implementation of Directive 2006/43/EC on statutory audits of annual accounts and consolidated accounts (*Attuazione della Direttiva 2006/43/CE, relativa alle revisioni legali dei conti annuali e dei conti consolidati, che modifica le Direttive 78/660/CEE e 83/349/CEE, e che abroga la Direttiva 84/253/CEE*) |
| Labour contracts<br>training activities and orientation activities in ~ | Art 3 – Ministerial Decree 25.3.1998, no 142 on training activities and orientation activities in labour contracts (*Decreto ministeriale 25 marzo 1998, n. 142. Regolamento recante norme di attuazione dei princìpi e dei criteri di cui all'articolo 18 della l. 24 giugno 1997, n. 196, sui tirocini formativi e di orientamento*) |
| Legal professionals | Art 12 – Law 31.12.2012, no 247 for the organisation of the legal profession (*Nuova disciplina dell'ordinamento della professione forense*) |
| Measuring instruments | Art 9 – Legislative Decree 2.2.2007, no 22 putting into effect EU Directive 2004/22/EC on measuring instruments (*Attuazione della Direttiva 2004/22/CE relativa agli strumenti di misura*) |
| Mediators | Art 3 para 5bis – Law 3.2.1989, no 39 modifying Law 21.3.1958, no 253 concerning the profession of mediators (*Modifiche ed integrazioni alla legge 21 marzo 1958, n. 253, concernente la disciplina della professione di mediatore*) |
| Mediators/arbitrators and their indemnities/subscription to conciliation boards | Art 4 para 2 letter b) and art 4 para 5 – Decree of the Ministry of Justice 18.10.2010, no 180 pursuant to art 16 of the Legislative Decree 4.3.2010, no 28 concerning mediators and their indemnities (*Regolamento recante la determinazione dei criteri e delle modalità di iscrizione e tenuta del registro degli organismi di mediazione e dell'elenco dei formatori per la mediazione nonché' l'approvazione delle indennità spettanti agli organismi, ai sensi dell'articolo 16 del decreto legislativo 4 marzo 2010, n. 28*) |

| | |
|---|---|
| | Decree of the Ministry of Justice 23.7.2004, no 222 on subscription and registrar's office rules of the conciliation boards under art 38 of Legislative Decree 17.1.2003, no 5 (*Decreto del ministero della giustizia 23 luglio 2004, n. 222. Regolamento recante la determinazione dei criteri e delle modalità di iscrizione nonché di tenuta del registro degli organismi di conciliazione di cui all'articolo 38 del decreto legislativo 17 gennaio 2003, n. 5*) |
| Noise emission in the environment caused by equipment for use outdoors<br>producers of ~ | Arts 3 and 9 – Legislative Decree 4.9.2002, no 262 pursuant to EU Directive 2000/14/EC on noise emission in the environment caused by equipment for use outdoors (*Decreto legislativo 4 settembre 2002, n. 262. Attuazione della direttiva 2000/14/CE concernente l'emissione acustica ambientale delle macchine ed attrezzature destinate a funzionare all'aperto*) |
| Non-automatic weighing instruments<br>producers of ~ | Art 9 and attachment V – Directive 2009/23/EC of the European Parliament and of the Council on non-automatic weighing instruments (*Direttiva 2009/23/CE del Parlamento Europeo e del Consiglio del 23 aprile 2009 relativa agli strumenti per pesare a funzionamento non automatico*) |
| Non-profit activities | Art 4 – Law 11.8.1991, no 266 on non-profit activities (*Legge-quadro sul volontariato*) |
| Non-registered professions<br>exercise of ~ | Art 7 letter e) – Law 14.1.2013, no 4 for the exercise of non-registered professions (*Disposizioni in materia di professioni non organizzate*) |
| Notaries<br>civil liability of ~ | Art 2 – Legislative Decree 4.5.2006, no 182 on civil liability insurance in relation to notarial activity for the establishment of a guarantee fund (*Norme in materia di assicurazione per la responsabilità civile derivante dall'esercizio dell'attività notarile ed istituzione di un fondo di garanzia in attuazione dell'articolo 7, comma 1, della legge 28 novembre 2005, n. 246*) |
| Organ transplants from living donors | Art 12 para 3 – Decree of the Ministry of Health 16.4.2010, no 116 on organ transplants from living donors (*Regolamento per lo svolgimento delle attività di trapianto di organi da donatore vivente*) |
| Personal protective equipment | Attachment V para 6 – Legislative Decree 4.12.1992, no 475 pursuant to EU Directive 89/686/EEC on the harmonisation of the legislation of the Member States relating to personal protective equipment (*Attuazione della Direttiva 89/686/CEE del Consiglio del 21 dicembre 1989, in materia di ravvicinamento delle legislazioni degli Stati Membri relative ai dispositivi di protezione individuale*) |
| Pressure vessels<br>producers of ~ | Attachment III para 6 – Legislative Decree 27.9.1991, no 311 pursuant to EU Directives 87/404/EEC and 90/488/EEC under art 56 of the Law 29.12.1990, no 428 in relation to simple pressure |

| | |
|---|---|
| | vessels (*Decreto legislativo 27 settembre 1991, n. 311. Attuazione delle direttive n. 87/404/cee e n. 90/488/cee in materia di recipienti semplici a pressione, a norma dell'art. 56 della legge 29 dicembre 1990, n. 428*) |
| Public security companies and their employees | Attachment A art 6 – Decree of the Ministry of the Interior 1.12.2010, no 269 concerning the requisites for the organisation of public security companies and for the quality of institutes as well as for the professional requirements of the employed personnel (*Regolamento recante disciplina delle caratteristiche minime del progetto organizzativo e dei requisiti minimi di qualità degli istituti e dei servizi di cui agli articoli 256-bis e 257-bis del regolamento di esecuzione del testo unico delle leggi di pubblica sicurezza, nonché dei requisiti professionali e di capacità tecnica richiesti per la direzione dei medesimi istituti e per lo svolgimento di incarichi organizzativi nell'ambito degli stessi istituti*) |
| Pyrotechnical products<br>introduction on the market of ~ | Arts 6 and 11 – Law Decree 4.4.2010, no 58 for the introduction on the market of pyrotechnical products (*Attuazione della direttiva 2007/23/CE relativa all'immissione sul mercato di prodotti pirotecnici*) |
| Recreation units and their components<br>planning, building and selling of ~ | Art 5 – Decree of the Ministry of Productive Activities 30.4.2003, no 175 concerning the granting of a licence with regard to the activity of planning, building and selling of recreation units and their components (*Regolamento recante disposizioni per il rilascio dell'autorizzazione agli organismi di certificazione in materia di progettazione, di costruzione e immissione in commercio di unità da diporto e loro componenti*) |
| Registered professional activities | Art 5 – Presidential Decree 7.8.2012, no 137 on the organisation of registered professional activities (*Regolamento recante riforma degli ordinamenti professionali*) |
| Rescue teams<br>speleologic and mountain ~ | Art 2 – Law 21.3.2001, no 74 on improving activities of speleologic and mountain rescue teams (*Disposizioni per favorire l'attività svolta dal corpo nazionale soccorso alpino e speleologico*) |
| School<br>managing and organisation (limited to financial activities [not for other forms of liabilities]) ~ | Art 50 para 3 – Decree of the Ministry of Education 1.2.2001, no 44 on school managing and organisation limited to financial activities (*Decreto del Ministero della pubblica istruzione 1 febbraio 2001, n. 44. Regolamento concernente le 'istruzioni generali sulla gestione amministrativo-contabile delle istituzioni scolastiche'*) |
| Sport competitions | Art 124 – Legislative Decree 7.9.2005, no 209 (Private Insurance Code) on sport competitions (*Decreto legislativo 7 settembre 2005, n. 209. Codice delle assicurazioni private. Gare e competizioni sportive*) |

| | |
|---|---|
| Tourism activities' organisers and long term holiday contracts | Art 19 – Legislative Decree 23.5.2011, no 79 on tourism activities and on the implementation of long term holiday contracts (*Codice della normativa statale in tema di ordinamento e mercato del turismo, a norma dell'articolo 14 della legge 28 novembre 2005, n. 246, nonché attuazione della direttiva 2008/122/CE, relativa ai contratti di multiproprietà, contratti relativi ai prodotti per le vacanze di lungo termine, contratti di rivendita e di scambio*) |
| Toys<br>safety duties upon producers ~ | Arts 3 and 8 – Legislative Decree 11.4.2011, no 54 on the safety of toys (*Attuazione della Direttiva 2009/48/CE sulla sicurezza dei giocattoli*) |
| Winter ski sports<br>practice of ~ | Art 4 – Law 24.12.2003, no 363 on the practice of winter ski sports (*Legge 24 dicembre 2003, n. 363 norme in materia di sicurezza nella pratica degli sport invernali da discesa e da fondo*) |

# II. Regional Laws

Regional laws can be found on the www.normativa.it website, where they are organised region by region.

There are many rules concerning public bodies' duty to insure, or subjects exercising specific activities, or hospitals and specific medical professions, or schools (therefore, it is impossible to reproduce a comprehensive list).

Note: all the provisions above, concerning compulsory insurance in the field of tourism and accommodation, have been adopted and implemented by the single Regions pursuant to the national Legislative Decree 23.5.2011, no 79 (*administration of the public real estate, accounting and tourism*). To this decree see above under I.1/2.

## 1. Strict liability

Example: tourism and accommodation

| | |
|---|---|
| Abruzzo | Art 12 modified by art 37.1 of the Regional Law 18.2.2010, no 5 – Regional Law 12.1.1998, no 1 on professions and vocations (*Nuova normativa sulla disciplina delle agenzie di viaggio e turismo e della professione di Direttore Tecnico*) |
| Basilicata | Art 13 – Regional Law 29.3.1999, no 8 on tourism and accommodation (*Organizzazione ed intermediazione di viaggi e soggiorni turistici*) |

| | |
|---|---|
| Calabria | Art 23 – Regional Law 5.4.2008, no 8 on tourism and accommodation (*Riordino dell'organizzazione turistica regionale*) |
| Campania | Art 9 – Regional Law 26.3.1993, no 13 on tourism and accommodation (*Disciplina dei complessi turistico-recettivi all'aria aperta*) |
| Emilia-Romagna | Art 33 – Regional Law 27.6.2014, no 7 on tourism and accommodation (*Modifiche alla legge regionale 31 marzo 2003, n. 7 – Disciplina delle attività di produzione, organizzazione e vendita viaggi, soggiorni e servizi turistici. Abrogazione della legge regionale 26 luglio 1977, n. 23 – Disciplina delle attività delle agenzie di viaggio e turismo*) |
| Friuli – Venezia Giulia | Art 2 – Regional Law 16.1.2002, no 2 on tourism and accommodation (*Disciplina organica del turismo*) |
| Lazio | Art 33 – Regional Law 6.8.2007, no 13 on tourism and accommodation modifying Regional Law 6.8.1999, no 14 (*Organizzazione del sistema turistico laziale*) |
| Liguria | Arts 7 and 17 – Regional Law 1.4.2014, no 7 on tourism and accommodation (*Organizzazione ed intermediazione di viaggi e soggiorni turistici*) |
| Lombardia | Arts 88 and 89 – Regional Law 16.7.2007, no 15 on tourism and accommodation (*Testo unico delle leggi regionali in materia di turismo*) |
| Marche | Art 67.3 – Regional Law 11.7.2006, no 9 on tourism and accommodation (*Testo unico delle norme regionali in materia di turismo*) |
| Molise | Art 26 – Regional Law 25.10.1996, no 32 on tourism and accommodation (*Disciplina dell'esercizio di attività professionali delle agenzie di viaggio e di turismo*) |
| Piemonte | Art 5-bis – Regional Law 30.12.2009, no 38 on tourism and accommodation (*Disposizioni di attuazione della direttiva 2006/123/CE del Parlamento europeo e del Consiglio relativa ai servizi del mercato interno*) |
| Puglia | Art 15 – Regional Law 15.11.2007, no 34 on tourism and accommodation (*Recupero di sottotetti, porticati e locali seminterrati*) |
| Sardegna | Art 11 – Regional Law 13.7.1988, no 13 on tourism and accommodation (*Disciplina in Sardegna delle agenzie di viaggio e di turismo*) |
| Sicilia | Art 6 – Regional Law 13.3.1982, no 14 on tourism and accommodation (*Disciplina dei complessi ricettivi all'aria aperta*) |
| Toscana | Art 16 – Regional Law 23.3.2000, no 42 on tourism and accommodation (*Testo unico delle leggi regionali in materia di turismo*) |
| Trentino Alto Adige | Art 8 – Regional Law 17.3.1988, no 9 on tourism and accommodation (*Disciplina delle agenzie di viaggio e di turismo*) |

| | |
|---|---|
| Umbria | Art 56 – Regional Law 12.7.2013, no 13 on tourism and accommodation (*Testo unico in materia di turismo*) |
| Valle d'Aosta | Art 5 – Regional Law 30.6.2010, no 19 on tourism and accommodation (*Disposizioni urgenti in materia di strutture, imprese e operatori turistici*) |
| Veneto | Arts 37 and 38 – Regional Law 14.6.2013, no 11 on tourism and accommodation (*Sviluppo e sostenibilità del turismo veneto*) |

## 2. Strict and fault liability

Example of skiing: mandatory insurance coverage of skiing schools as regards liability towards third parties

| | |
|---|---|
| Abruzzo | Art 18 – Regional Law 18.2.2010, no 5 on ski schools and teachers (*Ordinamento delle professioni*) |
| Basilicata | Regional Law 29.3.1993, no 16 on ski schools and teachers (*Disciplina della professione di maestro di sci e dell'esercizio delle scuole di sci in Basilicata*) |
| Campania | Art 13 – Regional Law 23.2.2012, no 4 on ski schools and teachers (*Ordinamento della professione di maestro di sci e delle scuole di sci*) |
| Friuli-Venezia Giulia | Arts 136 and 138 – Regional Law 16.1.2002, no 2 on tourism (*Disciplina organica del turismo*) |
| Lombardia | Art 14 – Regional Law 8.10.2002, no 26 on sports and sport professionals (*Norme per lo sviluppo dello sport e delle professioni sportive in Lombardia*) |
| Marche | Art 31 – Regional Law 23.1.1996, no 4 on tourism and related professionals (*Disciplina delle attività professionali nei settori del turismo e del tempo libero*) |
| Molise | Art 7 – Regional Law 8.1.1996, no 1 on ski schools and teachers (*Disciplina della professione di maestro di sci nella regione Molise*) |
| Piemonte | Art 14 – Regional Law 23.11.1992, no 50 on tourism and ski schools (*Accertamento dell'abilitazione alla professione di maestro di sci*) |
| Toscana | Art 156.1 letter d) – Regional Law 23.3.2000, no 42 on tourism (*Testo unico sul turismo*) |
| Trentino Alto Adige | Art 4 – Regional Law 8.3.1991, no 81 on ski schools and teachers (*Legge-quadro per la professione di maestro di sci e ulteriori disposizioni in materia di ordinamento della professione di guida alpina*) |

| | |
|---|---|
| Valle d'Aosta | Art 27 – Regional Law 31.12.1999, no 44 on ski schools and teachers (*Disciplina della professione di maestro di sci e delle scuole di sci in Valle d'Aosta*) |
| Veneto | Art 7 – Regional Law 3.1.2005, no 2 on ski schools and teachers (*Nuovo ordinamento della professione di maestro di sci*) |

Andrea Stäubli

# Switzerland

## I. Federal Law

The following laws may be downloaded in German, French or Italian at https://www.admin.ch/gov/de/start/bundesrecht/systematische-sammlung.html. Under the same link some laws can be found in English by selecting the English language option. However, as English is not an official language of the Swiss Confederation, translations are provided for information purposes only and have no legal force.

The *systematische Rechtssammlung* (in the following abbreviated as SR), which translates to systematic compilation of laws, contains every Swiss law which is currently in force. As every law is assigned a specific reference number (eg SR 748.0 for the Aviation Act), the following laws may be found by entering either their name abbreviation or reference number into the search engine.

### 1. Strict liability

| | |
|---|---|
| Air transport enterprises | Arts 27, 76a Aviation Act (*Luftfahrtgesetz*, LFG, SR 748.0)<br>Art 106 Aviation Regulation (*Luftfahrtverordnung*, LFV, SR 748.01) |
| Aircraft<br>keepers of ~ | Arts 70, 71, 74 Aviation Act (LFG, SR 748.0)<br>Arts 123, 125–129, 131 Aviation Regulation (LFV, SR 748.01) |
| Cableways<br>operators of ~ | Art 21 Cableway Act (*Seilbahngesetz*, SebG, SR 743.01) |
| Cycle and motor sport races<br>organisers of ~ | Art 72 Road Traffic Act (*Strassenverkehrsgesetz*, SVG, SR 741.01)<br>Art 30 Traffic Insurance Regulation (*Verkehrsversicherungs-verordnung*, VVV, SR 741.31) |
| Genetically modified or pathogenic organisms<br>working with ~<br>release of ~<br>first-time distribution of ~ | Art 34 Genetic Engineering Act (*Gentechnikgesetz*, GTG, SR 814.91)<br>Art 59b lit a Environmental Protection Act (*Umweltschutzgesetz*, USG, SR 814.01)<br>Art 13 Regulation on the handling of organisms in closed systems (*Einschliessungsverordnung*, ESV, SR 814.912)<br>Arts 11, 14 Regulation on the handling of organisms outside closed systems (*Freisetzungsverordnung*, FrSV, SR 814.911) |

| | |
|---|---|
| Hang gliders, pilotless aircraft and other aerial devices<br>keepers of ~ | Art 74 para 2 Aviation Act (LFG, SR 748.0)<br>Arts 123, 125–129, 131 Aviation Regulation (LFV, SR 748.01)<br>Arts 10, 11, 13, 14, 20 Regulation on special categories of aircraft (*Verordnung des UVEK über Luftfahrzeuge besonderer Kategorien*, VLK, SR 748.941) |
| Hunters | Art 16 Hunting Act (*Jagdgesetz*, JSG, SR 922.0)<br>Art 14 Hunting Regulation (*Jagdverordnung*, JSV, SR 922.01) |
| Motor vehicles<br>enterprises in the ~ industry (eg garages, repair enterprises) | Art 71 Road Traffic Act (SVG, SR 741.01)<br>Art 27 Traffic Insurance Regulation (VVV, SR 741.31) |
| Motor vehicles<br>keepers of ~ | Art 63 ff Road Traffic Act (SVG, SR 741.01)<br>Arts 3, 12 Traffic Insurance Regulation (VVV, SR 741.31) |
| Nuclear material<br>carriers of ~ | Arts 11–21 Nuclear Liability Act (*Kernenergiehaftpflichtgesetz*, KHG, SR 732.44)<br>Arts 3, 4 Nuclear Liability Regulation (*Kernenergiehaftpflichtverordnung*, KHV, SR 732.441) |
| Nuclear plants<br>possessor of ~<br>property owner of ~ | Arts 11–21 Nuclear Liability Act (KHG, SR 732.44)<br>Arts 3, 4 Nuclear Liability Regulation (KHV, SR 732.441) |
| Pipelines<br>owners of ~ | Arts 35–38, 41 Pipelines Act (*Rohrleitungsgesetz*, RLG, SR 746.1) |
| Railways<br>operators of ~ | Art 8d para 1 lit b Railway Act (*Eisenbahngesetz*, EBG, SR 742.101)<br>Art 5a Regulation on the access to the railway network (*Eisenbahn-Netzzugangsverordnung*, NZV, SR 742.122) |
| Research on humans<br>conductors of ~ | Art 20 Research on Humans Act (*Humanforschungsgesetz*, HFG, SR 810.30)<br>Art 13 Research on Humans Regulation (*Humanforschungsverordnung*, HFV, SR 810.301)<br>Arts 10, 12–14 Clinical Trials on Humans Regulation (*Verordnung über klinische Versuche*; KlinV, SR 810.305) |
| Shipping corporations<br>state-licensed ~ | Arts 31–37 Inland Shipping Act (*Bundesgesetz über die Binnenschifffahrt*, BSG, SR 747.201)<br>Arts 153, 155a Inland Shipping Regulation (*Binnenschifffahrtsverordnung*, BSV, SR 747.201.1) |
| Trolley-bus corporations | Art 16 Trolley-bus Act (*Trolleybus-Gesetz*, TrG, SR 744.21)<br>Art 3 Traffic Insurance Regulation (VVV, SR 741.31) |

## 2. Fault liability

| | |
|---|---|
| Aircraft<br>keepers of ~ (liability in respect of passengers) | Arts 106, 132a Aviation Regulation (LFV, SR 748.01) |
| Aircraft events<br>organisers of ~ | Arts 133, 134 Aviation Regulation (LFV, SR 748.01) |
| Attorneys-at-law | Art 12 lit f Attorney Act (*Anwaltsgesetz*, BGFA, SR 935.61) |
| Cable test centres<br>accredited ~ | Art 8 Cableway Regulation (*Seilbahnverordnung*, SebV, SR 743.011) |
| Calibration offices<br>operators of state-licensed ~ | Art 20 lit d Regulation on competence in metrology (*Verordnung über die Zuständigkeiten im Messwesen*, ZMessV, SR 941.206) |
| Certification bodies<br>accredited ~ | Annex 5 no 6 Accreditation Regulation (*Akkreditierungs- und Bezeichnungsverordnung*, AkkBV, SR 946.512) |
| Consumer credits<br>brokers of ~<br>lenders of ~ | Art 40 para 1 lit c Consumer Credit Act (*Bundesgesetz über den Konsumkredit*, KKG, SR 221.214.1)<br>Arts 7–7b Consumer Credit Regulation (*Verordnung zum Konsumkreditgesetz*, VKKG, SR 221.214.11) |
| Electronic signatures<br>accredited certification enterprises for ~ | Art 3 para 1 lit f Electronic Signature Act (*Bundesgesetz über die elektronische Signatur*, ZertES, SR 943.03)<br>Art 2 Electronic Signature Regulation (*Verordnung über die elektronische Signatur*, VZertES, SR 943.032) |
| Enforcement duties of the Swiss civilian service<br>executing third parties with ~ | Art 4 para 1 lit e Regulation on the transfer of enforcement duties of the civilian service to third parties (*Verordnung betreffend die Übertragung von Vollzugsaufgaben des Zivildienstes auf Dritte*, ZDUeV, SR 824.091) |
| Foster care facilities<br>operators of ~ | Art 15 para 1 lit f Foster Care Regulation (*Pflegekinderverordnung*, PAVO, SR 211.222.338) |
| Foster parents | Art 8 para 3 Foster Care Regulation (PAVO, SR 211.222.338) |
| High-risk activities including mountain guidance<br>operators of ~<br>organisers of ~ | Art 13 High-Risk Activities Act (*Bundesgesetz über das Bergführerwesen und Anbieten weiterer Risikoaktivitäten*, SR 935.91)<br>Arts 18, 20 High-Risk Activities Regulation (*Risikoaktivitätenverordnung*, SR 935.911) |
| Insurance brokers | Art 44 Insurance Supervision Act (*Versicherungsaufsichtsgesetz*, VAG, SR 961.01)<br>Art 186 Insurance Supervision Regulation (*Aufsichtsverordnung*, AVO, SR 961.011) |

| | |
|---|---|
| Medical professionals<br>self-employed ~ | Art 40 lit h Medical Professions Act (*Medizinalberufegesetz*, SR 811.11) |
| Military clubs as organisers of voluntary private (non-military) events | Art 14 Regulation on private activities in military clubs (*Verordnung über die ausserdienstliche Tätigkeit in den militärischen Gesellschaften und Dachverbänden*, VATV, SR 512.30)<br>Art 11 Regulation of the Department of Defence and Sports on private activities in military clubs (*Verordnung des VBS über die ausserdienstliche Tätigkeit in den militärischen Gesellschaften und Dachverbänden*, VATV- VBS, SR 512.301) |
| Military shipping material<br>use of ~ by nautical clubs | Art 22 para 3 Military Shipping Regulation (*Verordnung über die militärische Schifffahrt*, VMSch, SR 510.755) |
| Nautical events<br>organisers of ~ | Art 155 para 6 Inland Shipping Regulation (*Binnenschifffahrtsverordnung*, BSV, SR 747.201.1) |
| Psychotherapists<br>self-employed ~ | Art 27 lit f Psychology Professions Act (*Psychologieberufegesetz*, PsyG, SR 935.81) |
| Radiation Protection Act<br>activities in need of a permit according to the ~ | Art 31 lit d Radiation Protection Act (*Strahlenschutzgesetz*, StSG, SR 814.50) |
| Security enterprises assigned with protection duties by the federal state | Art 5 para 1 lit f Regulation on the assignment of private security enterprises (*Verordnung über den Einsatz privater Sicherheitsfirmen*, VES, SR 124) |
| Ships<br>keepers of ~ | Arts 31–37 Inland Shipping Act (*Bundesgesetz über die Binnenschifffahrt*, BSG, SR 747.201)<br>Arts 153, 155 Inland Shipping Regulation (BSV, SR 747.201.1) |
| Shooting clubs<br>officially recognized ~ | Art 19 para 2 lit f Non-Military Shooting Regulation (*Schiessverordnung*, SR 512.31) |
| Shooting events outside of officially recognized shooting clubs<br>organisers of ~ | Arts 4, 5 Regulation of the Department of Defence and Sports on non-military shooting (*Schiessverordnung des VBS*, SR 512.311) |
| Showmen and carnival owners | Art 5 para 1 lit a Travelling Trade Act (*Bundesgesetz über das Gewerbe der Reisenden*, SR 943.1)<br>Art 24, Annex 3 Travelling Trade Regulation (*Verordnung über das Gewerbe der Reisenden*, SR 943.11) |
| Xenotransplantation<br>performance of ~<br>transfer of organs for ~ | Art 46 Transplantation Act (*Transplantationsgesetz*, SR 810.21)<br>Art 26 Xenotransplantation Regulation (*Xenotransplantationsverordnung*, SR 810.213) |

| | |
|---|---|
| Yacht owners | Art 8 Regulation on Swiss yachts on sea (*Jachtenverordnung*, SR 747.321.7) |

## II. Laws of the Provinces (State Laws)

It is beyond the purpose of this paper to give an exhaustive overview on duties to take out insurance for all 26 cantons (*Kantone*), as it cannot be done within a reasonable period of time. Hence, only an exemplary overview of duties to take out insurance for notaries as well as dog keepers will be given.

As all 26 cantons have their own compilation of laws, a list of links for these compilations will be provided. In all cantons, laws are given a specific reference number (like at federal level) and may be found by entering either their name abbreviation or reference number into the respective search engine.

The following laws may be downloaded in the original German, French or Italian version from:

| | |
|---|---|
| Aargau/Argovia: | https://gesetzessammlungen.ag.ch/ |
| Appenzell Ausserrhoden: | http://www.bgs.ar.ch/ |
| Appenzell Innerrhoden: | http://www.ai.ch/de/politik/gesetzessammlung/ |
| Basel-City: | http://www.gesetzessammlung.bs.ch/ |
| Basel-Country: | http://bl.clex.ch/ |
| Berne: | https://www.belex.sites.be.ch/ |
| Fribourg: | http://bdlf.fr.ch/ |
| Geneva: | http://www.ge.ch/legislation/rsg/main.html |
| Glarus: | http://gesetze.gl.ch/ |
| Grisons/Graubünden: | http://www.gr-lex.gr.ch/?locale=de |
| Jura: | http://rsju.jura.ch/extranet/common/rsju/index.html |
| Lucerne: | http://srl.lu.ch/ |
| Neuchâtel: | http://rsn.ne.ch |
| Nidwalden: | http://www.navigator.ch/nw/lpext.dll?f=templates&fn=main-h.htm |
| Obwalden: | http://gdb.ow.ch/ |
| Schaffhausen: | http://rechtsbuch.sh.ch/index.php?id=89 |
| Schwyz: | http://www.sz.ch/xml_1/internet/de/application/d999/d29129/d24457/p24456.cfm |
| Solothurn: | http://bgs.so.ch/ |
| St. Gallen: | http://gesetzessammlung.sg.ch/ |
| Thurgau/Thurgovia: | http://www.rechtsbuch.tg.ch/ |

| | |
|---|---|
| Ticino: | http://www3.ti.ch/CAN/RLeggi/public/index.php/raccolta-leggi |
| Uri: | http://ur.lexspider.com |
| Valais: | https://www.vs.ch/de/web/accueil/legislation-cantonale |
| Vaud: | http://www.rsv.vd.ch/rsvsite/rsv_site/index.xsp |
| Zug: | http://bgs.zg.ch/ |
| Zurich: | http://www.zh.ch/internet/de/rechtliche_grundlagen/gesetze.html |

## 1. Example: Dog Keepers

The liability of animal keepers is regulated by federal law in Art 56 Code of Obligations 1911 (*Obligationenrecht*, OR). The question of its legal qualification as strict liability or fault liability is currently being somewhat controversially discussed in academic literature. According to the prevailing doctrine, this liability is strict, but some qualify it as fault liability with an opportunity for exculpation (*Verschuldenshaftung mit Exkulpationsmöglichkeit*).

However, the competence to legislate regarding the keeping of dogs lies with the cantons. Therefore, rules which stipulate compulsory liability insurance for the keepers of dogs can only be found in the laws of the 26 cantons or sometimes even exclusively on the municipal level (for example in the canton of Uri).

| | |
|---|---|
| Aargau/Argovia:<br>Dogs with an increased hazard potential (dangerous dog; depends on breed)<br>keepers of ~ | § 11 para 1 lit c Dog Act (*Hundegesetz*, HuG, 393.400)<br>§ 12 para 1 lit c Dog Regulation (*Hundeverordnung*, HuV, 393.411) |
| Appenzell Ausserrhoden: | At the moment, there is no duty to take out liability insurance.<br>However, the Dog Act is under revision at the moment, with the current draft as of May 2014 stipulating a duty to take out liability insurance for all dogs (not just dangerous ones). |
| Appenzell Innerrhoden:<br>Dogs<br>keepers of ~ | Art 17 para 2 Dog Act (*Hundegesetz*, HuG, 560.100) |

| | |
|---|---|
| Basel-City:<br>Dogs<br>keepers of ~ | § 2 para 4 Dog Act (*Hundegesetz*, 365.100)<br>§ 16 Dog Regulation (*Hundeverordnung*, 365.110) |
| Basel-Country:<br>Dogs<br>keepers of ~ | § 2 paras 4 and 5, § 3a para 1 lit d Dog Act (*Hundegesetz*, SGS 342 / GS 32.289) |
| Berne:<br>Dogs<br>keepers of ~ | Art 11 Dog Act (*Hundegesetz*, 916.31)<br>Art 29 Animal Welfare and Dog Regulation (*Verordnung über den Tierschutz und die Hunde*, THV, 916.812) |
| Fribourg:<br>Dogs<br>keepers of ~ | Arts 39–43 Dog Keeping Act (*Gesetz über die Hundehaltung*, HHG, 725.3)<br>Arts 50, 51 Dog Keeping Regulation (*Reglement über die Hundehaltung*, HHR, 725.31) |
| Geneva:<br>Dogs<br>keepers of ~ | Art 16 para 2, art 16 para 4 lit a Dog Act (*Loi sur les chiens*, LChiens, M 3 45)<br>Art 9 para 7 Dog Regulation (*Règlement d'application de la loi sur les chiens*, RChiens, M 3 45.01) |
| Glarus:<br>Dogs<br>keepers of ~ | Arts 29, 30 Animal Welfare and Epizootic Diseases Execution Act (*Kantonales Tierschutz- und Tierseuchengesetz*, EG zum TSchG und TSG, IV G/3/2)<br>Art 23 para 1 lit c Animal Welfare and Epizootic Diseases Regulation (*Verordnung zum kantonalen Tierschutz- und Tierseuchengesetz, Veterinärverordnung*, IX D/633/2) |
| Grisons/Graubünden: | There is no duty to take out liability insurance.<br>However, according to art 66 para 1 lit b Veterinary Act (*Veterinärgesetz*, VetG, 914.000), the keeper of a dog considered dangerous may be ordered to take out liability insurance. |
| Jura: | There is no duty to take out liability insurance. |
| Lucerne: | There is no duty to take out liability insurance.<br>However, according to § 7a para 2 lit d Dog Keeping Regulation (*Verordnung über das Halten von Hunden*, 849), the keeper of a dog considered dangerous may be ordered to take out liability insurance. |
| Neuchâtel: | There is no duty to take out liability insurance. |
| Nidwalden: | There is no duty to take out liability insurance. |
| Obwalden: | There is no duty to take out liability insurance. |
| Schaffhausen:<br>Dogs<br>keepers of ~ | Arts 7, 9 para 4 lit d Dog Keeping Act (*Gesetz über das Halten von Hunden*, 455.200) |

| | |
|---|---|
| Schwyz:<br>Dogs<br>keepers of ~ | § 1 para 3 Dog Keeping Act (*Gesetz über das Halten von Hunden*, 546.100) |
| Solothurn:<br>Dogs<br>keepers of ~ | § 7 para 2, § 10 Dog Keeping Act (*Gesetz über das Halten von Hunden*, 614.71) |
| St. Gallen: | There is no duty to take out liability insurance.<br>However, according to art 9 para 2 lit a Dog Act (*Hundegesetz*, HG, 456.1), the keeper of a dog who neglects his duties according to the Dog Act may be ordered to take out liability insurance. |
| Thurgau/Thurgovia:<br>Dogs<br>keepers of ~ | § 1a, § 3b para 1 no 7 Dog Keeping Act (*Gesetz über das Halten von Hunden*, 641.2)<br>§ 7c para 1 no 6 Dog Keeping Regulation (*Verordnung des Regierungsrates über das Halten von Hunden*, 641.21) |
| Ticino:<br>Dogs<br>keepers of ~ | Art 5 Dog Act (*Legge sui cani*, 8.3.1.2)<br>Art 6 Dog Regulation (*Regolamento sui cani*, 8.3.1.2.1) |
| Uri: | The canton of Uri did not legislate concerning the keeping of dogs. Rules may be found at the municipal level. |
| Valais:<br>Dogs<br>keepers of ~ | Art 10a para 4 Animal Welfare Execution Act (*Gesetz welches das eidgenössische Tierschutzgesetz vollzieht*, 455.1) |
| Vaud:<br>Dogs<br>keepers of ~ | Art 15 Dog Act (*Loi sur la police des chiens*, LPolC, 133.75)<br>Art 9 para 1 lit c Dog Regulation (*Règlement d'application de la loi du 31 octobre 2006 sur la police des chiens*, RLPolC, 133.75.1) |
| Zug: | At the moment, there is no duty to take out liability insurance, as there is no legislation on this topic.<br>However, new legislation is pending with the current draft of the executive council (*Regierungsrat*) stipulating a duty to take out liability insurance for all dogs (not just dangerous ones). |
| Zurich:<br>Dogs<br>keepers of ~ | § 3 para 2 lit e, § 6, § 30 para 2 lit d Dog Act (*Hundegesetz*, 554.5)<br>§ 23 para 1 lit h, § 25 para 1 lit e Dog Regulation (*Hundeverordnung*, 554.51) |

## 2. Example: Notaries

The competence to legislate in this area lies fully with the cantons. This has led to the establishment of different systems in the cantons.

A notary can be either a civil servant, a so-called *Amtsnotar*, which roughly translates to 'official notary', or a professional, a so-called *freiberuflicher Notar*, which roughly translates to 'professional notary'. The cantons know either only the *Amtsnotar* (so-called *Amtsnotariat*) or only the *freiberuflicher Notar* (so-called *freiberufliches Notariat*) or both (mixed system).

In the cantons where there are *Amtsnotare*, the state is generally liable for damage caused by them in their official capacity. Therefore, those cantons tend not to stipulate a duty to take out liability insurance for these *Amtsnotare* or 'official notaries'.

| | |
|---|---|
| Aargau/Argovia: | Professional notaries:<br>§ 6 para 2 lit i, § 12 Certification and Authentication Act (*Beurkundungs- und Beglaubigungsgesetz*, BeurG, 295.200)<br>§ 1 para 2 lit g, §§ 4–5, § 19 para 1 lit b Certification and Authentication Regulation (*Beurkundungs- und Beglaubigungsverordnung*, BeurV, 295.211) |
| Appenzell Ausserrhoden: | Mixed system:<br>Art 25 para 2 Certification Act (*Beurkundungsgesetz*, BeurkG, 211.2) |
| Appenzell Innerrhoden: | Mixed system:<br>There is no duty to take out liability insurance. |
| Basel-City: | Professional notaries:<br>§ 7 para 1 Notary Act (*Notariatsgesetz*, 292.100) |
| Basel-Country: | Professional notaries:<br>§ 3 para 1 lit l, § 56 para 1 lit e Notary Act (*Notariatsgesetz*, SGS 217 / GS 37.1057)<br>§ 1 para 2 lit g, § 4, § 6 para 2 lit f Notary Regulation (*Notariatsverordnung*, NotV, SGS 217.11 / GS 37.1088) |
| Berne: | Professional notaries:<br>Art 9 para 1 lit f, art 59 Notary Act (*Notariatsgesetz*, NG, 169.11)<br>Art 2 para 1 lit g, art 3 para 3 lit f, art 11, art 20 para 1 lit b Notary Regulation (*Notariatsverordnung*, NV, 169.112) |
| Fribourg: | Professional notaries:<br>Art 11 para 2 Notary Act (*Gesetz über das Notariat*, NG, 261.1) |

| | |
|---|---|
| Geneva: | Professional notaries:<br>Art 45 Notary Act (*Loi sur le notariat*, LNot, E 6 05)<br>Art 15 Notary Regulation (*Règlement d'exécution de la loi sur le notariat*, RNot, E 6 05.01) |
| Glarus: | Mixed system:<br>Art 32 para 1 Certification and Authentication Act (*Gesetz über Beurkundung und Beglaubigung*, Beurkundungsgesetz, III B/3/1) |
| Grisons/Graubünden: | Mixed system:<br>Art 43 para 3 Notary Act (*Notariatsgesetz*, 210.300)<br>Art 8 Notary Regulation (*Notariatsverordnung*, 210.350) |
| Jura: | Professional notaries:<br>Art 7 para 2 no 1 Notary Act (*Loi sur le notariat*, 189.11) |
| Lucerne: | Mixed system:<br>§ 7, § 55 para 3 Certification Act (*Beurkundungsgesetz*, BeurkG, 255)<br>§ 1 para 2 lit b, § 3 Certification Regulation (*Beurkundungsverordnung*, BeurkV, 256) |
| Neuchâtel: | Professional notaries:<br>Art 41 Notary Act (*Loi sur le notariat*, LN, 166.10)<br>Art 6 Notary Regulation (*Règlement d'exécution de la loi sur le notariat*, RELN, 166.101) |
| Nidwalden: | Mixed system:<br>§ 51 para 2, § 52 para 2 Certification Regulation (*Beurkundungsverordnung*, BeurkV, 268.11)<br>§ 17 Certification Rules (*Beurkundungsreglement*, BeurkR, 268.111) |
| Obwalden: | Mixed system:<br>Art 7 para 1 Certification Act (*Beurkundungsgesetz*, 210.3)<br>Art 6 Certification Regulation (*Beurkundungsverordnung*, 210.31) |
| Schaffhausen: | Official notaries:<br>There is no duty to take out liability insurance. |
| Schwyz: | Mixed system:<br>There is no duty to take out liability insurance. |
| Solothurn: | Mixed system:<br>§ 61 Notary Regulation (*Notariatsverordnung*, 129.11) |
| St. Gallen: | Mixed system:<br>Art 1 para 3 Attorney Act (*Anwaltsgesetz*, AnwG, 963.70) |

| | |
|---|---|
| Thurgau/Thurgovia: | Mixed system:<br>§ 18a Attorney Act (*Anwaltsgesetz*, AnwG, 176.1) |
| Ticino: | Professional notaries:<br>There is no duty to take out liability insurance. |
| Uri: | Professional notaries:<br>There is no duty to take out liability insurance. |
| Valais: | Professional notaries:<br>Art 17 lit f, art 19 Notary Act (*Notariatsgesetz*, 178.1)<br>Arts 26, 27 Notary Regulation (*Reglement betreffend das Notariatsgesetz*, 178.101) |
| Vaud: | Professional notaries:<br>Art 17 para 1 no 6, art 29 para 1 no 1, arts 109, 110 Notary Act (*Loi sur le notariat*, LNo, 178.11)<br>Art 16 para 1 no 2, arts 39–42 Notary Regulation (*Règlement d'application de la loi du 29 juin 2004 sur le notariat*, RLNo, 178.11.1) |
| Zug: | Mixed system:<br>There is no duty to take out liability insurance. |
| Zurich: | Official notaries:<br>There is no duty to take out liability insurance. |

Özlem Gürses

# United Kingdom

## I. United Kingdom Legislation

The following laws may be downloaded in the original English language at http://www.legislation.gov.uk/ukpga.

### 1. Strict liability

| | |
|---|---|
| Air carrier and aircraft operator insurance | Civil Aviation (Insurance) Regulations 2005/1089 |
| Bunker pollution (liability for registered shipowners) | The Merchant Shipping (Oil Pollution) (Bunkers Convention) Regulations 2006 (incorporating the International Convention on Civil Liability for Bunker Oil Pollution Damage 2001), sec 17 |
| Carriage of hazardous and noxious substances by ship | Not yet in force. Sec 16 Merchant Shipping and Maritime Security Act 1997 (implementing The International Convention on Liability and Compensation for Damage in Connection with the Carriage of Hazardous and Noxious Substances by Sea, 1996), sch 5A to the Merchant Shipping Act 1995 |
| Carriage of passengers by ship[1] | The Merchant Shipping (Carriage of Passengers by Sea) Statutory Instrument (SI)[2] 2012/3152, reg 5 (implementing the regime relating to liability and insurance for the carriage of passengers by sea as set out in the relevant provisions of the Athens Convention relating to the Carriage of Passengers and their Luggage by Sea, 1974, as amended by the Protocol of 2002 – 'the Athens Convention'), sch 6 to Merchant Shipping Act 1995 |
| Nuclear installations licensees of ~ | Nuclear Installations Act 1965, sec 19(1) where a nuclear site licence has been granted in respect of any site, the licensee shall make such provision (either by insurance or by some other means) as the Minister may with the consent of the Treasury approve for sufficient funds to be available at all times to ensure that any claims which have been or may be duly established against the licensee as licensee of that site by virtue of sec 7 of this Act or any relevant foreign law made for purposes corresponding to those of sec 10 of this Act (excluding, but without prejudice to, any claim in |

1 Fault is assumed unless the contrary is proved, art 3(3) of the Convention.
2 As for the meaning of statutory instruments, see *Ö Gürses*, Compulsory Liability Insurance in the United Kingdom (in this book) fn 4.

| | |
|---|---|
| | respect of interest or costs) are satisfied up to an aggregate amount of five million pounds in respect of each severally of the following periods, that is to say –<br>(a) the current cover period, if any;<br>(b) any cover period which ended less than ten years before the time in question;<br>(c) any earlier cover period in respect of which a claim remains to be disposed of, being a claim made –<br>(i) within the relevant period within the meaning of sec 16 of this Act; and<br>(ii) in the case of a claim such as is mentioned in sec 15(2) of this Act, also within the period of twenty years so mentioned;<br>and for the purposes of this section the cover period in respect of which any claim is to be treated as being made shall be that in which the beginning of the relevant period aforesaid fell |
| Oil pollution<br>liability for ~ | The Merchant Shipping Act 1995, secs 153–163 |
| Various shipping liabilities | Merchant Shipping (Compulsory Insurance: Ships Receiving Trans-shipped Fish) Regulations 1998/209, reg 4 |
| Wreck removal | Wreck Removal Convention Act 2011, sec 1(1) amending The Merchant Shipping Act 1995 by inserting sec 255J |

## 2. Fault liability

| | |
|---|---|
| Common parts of a commonhold | Commonhold and Leasehold Reform Act 2002, sec 26(b)<br>Commonhold Regulations 2004 (SI 2004/1829), sch 3 pt 4 para 4.4.1 |
| Dentists | Dentists Act 1984, sec 26A |
| Employers | Employers' Liability (Compulsory Insurance) Act 1969, sec 1. Insurance is required 'against liability for bodily injury or disease sustained by his employees, and arising out of and in the course of their employment in Great Britain in that business'<br>Offshore Installations and Pipeline Works (Management and Administration) Regulations 1995/738, reg 21 |
| Estate agents | Insurance cover for clients' money, Estate Agents' Act 1979, sec 16 |
| Inland navigation and houseboats | British Waterways Act 1995, sec 17(3)(b) |
| Maritime claims | Merchant Shipping (Compulsory Insurance of Shipowners for Maritime Claims) Regulations 2012/2267, reg 4 |

| | |
|---|---|
| Motor vehicles<br>users of ~ | Road Traffic Act 1988, sec 143 et al (criminal liability – no civil liability under the RTA 1988 other than for failing to insure)<br>Direct action of a victim against the insurers without first having to obtain a judgment against the user of a motor vehicle (European Communities (Rights against Insurers) Regulations 2002 (SI 2002/3061))<br>Formalities relating to deposits under sec 144 of the RTA 1988 (Motor Vehicles (Third-Party Risks Deposits) Regulations 1992 (SI 1992/1284)) |
| Notaries | Notaries (Practising Certificates) Rules 2012, rules 4.2.3, 6 |
| Optometrists and opticians | Opticians Act 1989, sec 10A |
| Osteopaths | Osteopaths Act 1993, sec 37 |
| Package travel, package holidays and package tours | Package Travel, Package Holidays and Package Tours Regulations 1992, reg 19 |
| Riding establishments<br>licensees of ~ | The Riding Establishments Act 1964, sec 1(4A)(d) the licence holder shall hold a current insurance policy which insures him against liability for any injury sustained by those who hire a horse from him for riding and those who use a horse in the course of receiving from him, in return for payment, instruction in riding and arising out of the hire or use of a horse as aforesaid and which also insures such persons in respect of any liability which may be incurred by them in respect of injury to any person caused by, or arising out of, the hire or use of a horse as aforesaid |
| Solicitors | Solicitors Act 1974, sec 37 |
| Wild animals | Dangerous Wild Animals Act 1976, sec 1(6)(a)(iv) |

## II. Devolved Legislation

The compulsory insurance legislation applies to the United Kingdom as a whole.

# List of Contributors and Editors

Hubert Bär
Swiss Insurance Association, Zurich, Switzerland

Diana Cerini
Università degli Studi di Milano Bicocca, Dipartimento di Giurisprudenza (School of Law), Italy

Herman Cousy
KU Leuven University, Belgium

Petr Dobiáš
Charles University, Prague, Czech Republic

Michael Faure
Maastricht University, METRO and Erasmus University Rotterdam, The Netherlands

Attila Fenyves (Editor)
Vienna and Graz University, Austria

Özlem Gürses
Southampton University, United Kingdom

Helmut Heiss
Zurich University, Switzerland

Christa Kissling (Editor)
Institute for European Tort Law, Austrian Academy of Sciences and University of Graz, Vienna, Austria

Robert Koch
Hamburg University, Germany

Anna Teresa Memola
Università degli Studi di Milano Bicocca, Dipartimento di Giurisprudenza (School of Law), Italy

Franz Merli
Vienna University, Austria

Jaana Norio-Timonen
Helsinki University, Finland

Stefan Perner (Editor)
Linz University, Austria

Daniel Rubin (Editor)
Vienna University, Austria

Andrea Stäubli
Zurich University, Switzerland

Péter Takáts
Eötvös Loránd University, Budapest, Hungary

Bernard Tettamanti
Swiss Re, Zurich, Switzerland

Caroline Van Schoubroeck
KU Leuven University, Belgium

Jean-Claude Werz
AXA-Winterthur, Winterthur, Switzerland

# Index

In this Index, the numbers refer to the marginal numbers (not to pages) and the letters refer to the reports: **A** stands for Austria, **B** for Belgium, **CC** for the Conclusions, **CH** for Switzerland, **CONST** for Constitutional Law, **CR** for the Comparative Report, **CZ** for the Czech Republic, **D** for Germany, **EP** for the Economic Perspectives, **EU** for the European Union, **FIN** for Finland, **H** for Hungary, **I** for Italy, **INTR** for the Introduction, **PEICL** for the Principles of European Insurance Contract Law, **REINS** for the Insurance and Reinsurance Perspective, and **UK** for the United Kingdom.

1 *In this index, 'contract' is used to describe the legal agreement in general, whereas 'insurance contract' is used when referring to a legal agreement concerning insurance only.*

2 *This notion might be used in different shades of meaning in the different reports.*

3 *References can also be found under the respective activity (eg 'hunting' or 'hydraulic fracturing').*

4 *In this index, 'insurance contract' is used when referring to a legal agreement concerning insurance only, whereas 'contract' is used to describe the legal agreement in general.*

5 *Depending on the context, 'insurance holder' and 'insured' can be used synonymously or not in the different reports.*

6 *Depending on the context, 'insurance holder' and 'insured' can be used synonymously or not in the different reports.*

7 *References can also be found under the respective profession or professional activity (eg 'dentist' or 'railway').*

8 *This notion might be used in different shades of meaning in the different reports.*

# Publications

## Principles of European Tort Law Series

**Volume 1:** *The Limits of Liability: Keeping the Floodgates Shut*
Edited by Jaap Spier
Kluwer Law International, The Hague. Hardcover
ISBN 90-411-0169-1. 1996, 162 pp

**Volume 2:** *The Limits of Expanding Liability. Eight Fundamental Cases in a Comparative Perspective*
Edited by Jaap Spier
Kluwer Law International, The Hague. Hardcover
ISBN 90-411-0581-6. 1998, 244 pp

**Volume 3:** *Unification of Tort Law: Wrongfulness*
Edited by Helmut Koziol
Kluwer Law International, The Hague. Hardcover
ISBN 90-411-1019-4. 1998, 144 pp

**Volume 4:** *Unification of Tort Law: Causation*
Edited by Jaap Spier
Kluwer Law International, The Hague. Hardcover
ISBN 90-411-1325-8. 2000, 161 pp

**Volume 5:** *Unification of Tort Law: Damages*
Edited by Ulrich Magnus
Kluwer Law International, The Hague. Hardcover
ISBN 90-411-1481-5. 2001, 225 pp

**Volume 6:** *Unification of Tort Law: Strict Liability*
Edited by Bernhard A Koch and Helmut Koziol
Kluwer Law International, The Hague. Hardcover
ISBN 90-411-1705-9. 2002, 444 pp

**Volume 7:** *Unification of Tort Law: Liability for Damage Caused by Others*
Edited by Jaap Spier
Kluwer Law International, The Hague. Hardcover
ISBN 90-411-2185-4. 2003, 335 pp

**Volume 8:** *Unification of Tort Law: Contributory Negligence*
Edited by Ulrich Magnus and Miquel Martín-Casals
Kluwer Law International, The Hague. Hardcover
ISBN 90-411-2220-6. 2004, 300 pp

**Volume 9:** *Unification of Tort Law: Multiple Tortfeasors*
Edited by WV Horton Rogers
Kluwer Law International, The Hague. Hardcover
ISBN 90-411-2319-9. 2004, 313 pp

**Volume 10:** *Unification of Tort Law: Fault*
Edited by Pierre Widmer
Kluwer Law International, The Hague. Hardcover
ISBN 90-411-2098-X. 2005, 393 pp

# Tort and Insurance Law Series

**Volume 1:** *Cases on Medical Malpractice in a Comparative Perspective*
Edited by Michael Faure and Helmut Koziol
Verlag Österreich, Vienna
Softcover. ISBN 978-3-7046-6056-5
2001, 331 pp

**Volume 2:** *Damages for Non-Pecuniary Loss in a Comparative Perspective*
Edited by WV Horton Rogers
Verlag Österreich, Vienna
Softcover. ISBN 978-3-7046-6057-2
2001, 318 pp

**Volume 3:** *The Impact of Social Security on Tort Law*
Edited by Ulrich Magnus
Verlag Österreich, Vienna
Softcover. ISBN 978-3-7046-6083-1
2003, 312 pp

**Volume 4:** *Compensation for Personal Injury in a Comparative Perspective*
Edited by Bernhard A Koch and Helmut Koziol
Verlag Österreich, Vienna
Softcover. ISBN 978-3-7046-6082-4
2003, 501 pp

**Volume 5:** *Deterrence, Insurability and Compensation in Environmental Liability. Future Developments in the European Union*
Edited by Michael Faure
Verlag Österreich, Vienna
Softcover. ISBN 978-3-7046-6891-2
2003, 405 pp

**Volume 6:** *Der Ersatz frustrierter Aufwendungen. Vermögens- und Nichtvermögensschaden im österreichischen und deutschen Recht*
by Thomas Schobel
Verlag Österreich, Vienna
Softcover. ISBN 978-3-7046-6093-0
2003, 342 pp

**Volume 7:** *Liability for and Insurability of Biomedical Research with Human Subjects in a Comparative Perspective*
Edited by Jos Dute, Michael G Faure and Helmut Koziol
Verlag Österreich, Vienna
Softcover. ISBN 978-3-7046-5812-8
2004, 445 pp

**Volume 8:** *No-Fault Compensation in the Health Care Sector*
Edited by Jos Dute, Michael G Faure and Helmut Koziol
Verlag Österreich, Vienna
Softcover. ISBN 978-3-7046-5821-0
2004, 492 pp

**Volume 9:** *Pure Economic Loss*
Edited by Willem H van Boom, Helmut Koziol and Christian A Witting
Verlag Österreich, Vienna
Softcover. ISBN 978-3-7046-5790-9
2004, 214 pp

**Volume 10:** *Liber Amicorum Pierre Widmer*
Edited by Helmut Koziol and Jaap Spier
Verlag Österreich, Vienna
Softcover. ISBN 978-3-7046-5792-3
2003, 376 pp

**Volume 11:** *Terrorism, Tort Law and Insurance. A Comparative Survey*
Edited by Bernhard A Koch
Verlag Österreich, Vienna
Softcover. ISBN 978-3-7046-5795-4
2004, 313 pp

**Volume 12:** *Abschlussprüfer. Haftung und Versicherung*
Edited by Helmut Koziol and Walter Doralt
Verlag Österreich, Vienna
Softcover. ISBN 978-3-7046-5822-7
2004, 180 pp

**Volume 13:** *Persönlichkeitsschutz gegenüber Massenmedien/The Protection of Personality Rights against Invasions by Mass Media*
Edited by Helmut Koziol and Alexander Warzilek
Verlag Österreich, Vienna
Softcover. ISBN 978-3-7046-5841-8
2005, 713 pp

**Volume 14:** *Financial Compensation for Victims of Catastrophes*
Edited by Michael Faure and Ton Hartlief
Verlag Österreich, Vienna
Softcover. ISBN 978-3-7046-5849-4
2006, 466 pp

**Volume 15:** *Entwurf eines neuen österreichischen Schadenersatzrechts*
Edited by Irmgard Griss, Georg Kathrein and Helmut Koziol
Verlag Österreich, Vienna
Softcover. ISBN 978-3-7046-5849-4
2006, 146 pp

**Volume 16:** *Tort Law and Liability Insurance*
Edited by Gerhard Wagner
Verlag Österreich, Vienna
Softcover. ISBN 978-3-7046-5850-0
2005, 361 pp

**Volume 17:** *Children in Tort Law. Part I: Children as Tortfeasors*
Edited by Miquel Martín-Casals
Verlag Österreich, Vienna
Softcover. ISBN 978-3-7046-5870-8
2006, 476 pp

**Volume 18:** *Children in Tort Law. Part II: Children as Victims*
Edited by Miquel Martín-Casals
Verlag Österreich, Vienna
Softcover. ISBN 978-3-7046-5869-2
2007, 320 pp

**Volume 19:** *Tort and Regulatory Law*
Edited by Willem H van Boom, Meinhard Lukas and Christa Kissling
Verlag Österreich, Vienna
Hardcover. ISBN 978-3-7046-5870-8
2007, 477 pp

**Volume 20:** *Shifts in Compensating Work-Related Injuries and Diseases*
Edited by Saskia Klosse and Ton Hartlief
Verlag Österreich, Vienna
Hardcover. ISBN 978-3-7046-5913-2
2007, 236 pp

**Volume 21:** *Shifts in Compensation for Environmental Damage*
Edited by Michael Faure and Albert Verheij
Verlag Österreich, Vienna
Hardcover. ISBN 978-3-7046-5911-8
2007, 338 pp

**Volume 22:** *Shifts in Compensation between Private and Public Systems*
Edited by Willem H van Boom and Michael Faure
Verlag Österreich, Vienna
Hardcover. ISBN 978-3-7046-5912-5
2007, 246 pp

**Volume 23:** *Tort Law of the European Community*
Edited by Helmut Koziol and Reiner Schulze
Verlag Österreich, Vienna
Hardcover. ISBN 978-3-7046-5935-4
2008, 693 pp

**Volume 24:** *Economic Loss Caused by Genetically Modified Organisms*
Edited by Bernhard A Koch
Verlag Österreich, Vienna
Hardcover. ISBN 978-3-7046-5937-8
2008, 747 pp

**Volume 25:** *Punitive Damages*
Edited by Helmut Koziol and Vanessa Wilcox
Verlag Österreich, Vienna
Hardcover. ISBN 978-3-7046-6117-3
2009, 322 pp

**Volume 26:** *Aggregation and Divisibility of Damage*
Edited by Ken Oliphant
Verlag Österreich, Vienna
Hardcover. ISBN 978-3-7046-6116-6
2009, 568 pp

**Volume 27:** *Damage Caused by Genetically Modified Organisms. Comparative Survey of Redress Options for Harm to Persons, Property or the Environment*
Edited by Bernhard A Koch
de Gruyter, Berlin/New York
Hardcover. ISBN 978-3-89949-811-0
eBook. ISBN 978-3-89949-812-7
2010, 954 pp

**Volume 28:** *Loss of Housekeeping Capacity*
Edited by Ernst Karner and Ken Oliphant
de Gruyter, Berlin/Boston
Hardcover. ISBN 978-3-89949-813-4
eBook. ISBN 978-3-89949-814-1
2012, 339 pp

**Volume 29:** *Medical Liability in Europe. A Comparison of Selected Jurisdictions*
Edited by Bernhard A Koch
de Gruyter, Berlin/Boston
Hardcover. ISBN 978-3-11-026010-6
eBook. ISBN 978-3-11-026016-8
2011, 701 pp

**Volume 30:** *Tort Law in the Jurisprudence of the European Court of Human Rights*
Edited by Attila Fenyves, Ernst Karner, Helmut Koziol and Elisabeth Steiner
de Gruyter, Berlin/Boston
Hardcover. ISBN 978-3-11-025966-7
eBook. ISBN 978-3-11-026000-7
2011, 906 pp

**Volume 31:** *Employers' Liability and Workers' Compensation*
Edited by Ken Oliphant and Gerhard Wagner
de Gruyter, Berlin/Boston
Hardcover. ISBN 978-3-11-026996-3
eBook. ISBN 978-3-11-027021-1
2012, 619 pp

**Volume 32:** *Medical Malpractice and Compensation in a Global Perspective*
Edited by Ken Oliphant and Richard W Wright
de Gruyter, Berlin/Boston
Hardcover. ISBN 978-3-11-026997-0
eBook. ISBN 978-3-11-027023-5
2013, 573 pp

**Volume 33:** *Proportional Liability: Analytical and Comparative Perspectives*
Edited by Israel Gilead, Michael D Green and Bernhard A Koch
de Gruyter, Berlin/Boston
Hardcover. ISBN 978-3-11-028253-5
eBook. ISBN 978-3-11-028258-0
2013, 376 pp

**Volume 34:** *Mass Torts in Europe: Cases and Reflections*
Edited by Willem H van Boom and Gerhard Wagner
de Gruyter, Berlin/Boston
Hardcover. ISBN 978-3-11-034945-0
eBook. ISBN 978-3-11-034946-7
2014, 311 pp

# European Tort Law Yearbook

*European Tort Law 2001*
Edited by Helmut Koziol and Barbara C Steininger
Verlag Österreich, Vienna
Softcover. ISBN 978-3-7046-6085-5
2002, 571 pp

*European Tort Law 2002*
Edited by Helmut Koziol and Barbara C Steininger
Verlag Österreich, Vienna
Softcover. ISBN 3-211-00486-6
2003, 596 pp

*European Tort Law 2003*
Edited by Helmut Koziol and Barbara C Steininger
Verlag Österreich, Vienna
Softcover. ISBN 978-3-7046-5825-8
2004, 493 pp

*European Tort Law 2004*
Edited by Helmut Koziol and Barbara C Steininger
Verlag Österreich, Vienna
Softcover. ISBN 978-3-7046-5847-0
2005, 674 pp

*European Tort Law 2005*
Edited by Helmut Koziol and Barbara C Steininger
Verlag Österreich, Vienna
Softcover. ISBN 978-3-7046-5871-5
2006, 711 pp

*European Tort Law 2006*
Edited by Helmut Koziol and Barbara C Steininger
Verlag Österreich, Vienna
Softcover. ISBN 978-3-7046-6162-3
2008, 576 pp

*European Tort Law 2007*
Edited by Helmut Koziol and Barbara C Steininger
Verlag Österreich, Vienna
Hardcover. ISBN 978-3-7046-6168-5
2008, 661 pp

*European Tort Law 2008*
Edited by Helmut Koziol and Barbara C Steininger
Verlag Österreich, Vienna
Hardcover. ISBN 978-3-7046-6120-3
2009, 708 pp

*European Tort Law 2009*
Edited by Helmut Koziol and Barbara C Steininger
de Gruyter, Berlin/New York
Hardcover. ISBN 978-3-11-024606-3
eBook. ISBN 978-3-11-024607-0
2010, 735 pp

*European Tort Law 2010*
Edited by Helmut Koziol and Barbara C Steininger
de Gruyter, Berlin/Boston
Hardcover. ISBN 978-3-11-023941-6
eBook. ISBN 978-3-11-023942-3
2011, 702 pp

*European Tort Law 2011*
Edited by Ken Oliphant and Barbara C Steininger
de Gruyter, Berlin/Boston
Hardcover. ISSN 2190-7773
eBook. ISSN 2190-7781
2012, 789 pp

*European Tort Law 2012*
Edited by Ken Oliphant and Barbara C Steininger
de Gruyter, Berlin/Boston
Hardcover. ISSN 2190-7773
eBook. ISSN 2190-7781
2013, 816 pp

*European Tort Law 2013*
Edited by Ernst Karner and Barbara C Steininger
de Gruyter, Berlin/Boston
Hardcover. ISSN 2190-7773
eBook. ISSN 2190-7781
2014, 824 pp

*European Tort Law 2014*
Edited by Ernst Karner and Barbara C Steininger
de Gruyter, Berlin/Boston
Hardcover. ISSN 2190-7773
eBook. ISSN 2190-7781
2015, 758 pp

*European Tort Law 2015*
Edited by Ernst Karner and Barbara C Steininger
de Gruyter, Berlin/Boston
Hardcover. ISSN 2190-7773
eBook. ISSN 2190-7781
forthcoming Oct 2016, approx 800 pp

# European Group on Tort Law

*Principles of European Tort Law. Text and Commentary*
Edited by the European Group on Tort Law
Verlag Österreich, Vienna
Softcover. ISBN 978-3-7046-5837-1
2005, 282 pp

*The Liability of Public Authorities in Comparative Perspective*
Edited by Ken Oliphant
Intersentia, Cambridge/Antwerp/Portland
Softcover. ISBN 978-178068-238-9
forthcoming 2016, approx 800 pp

# Digest of European Tort Law

**Volume 1:** *Essential Cases on Natural Causation*
Edited by Bénédict Winiger, Helmut Koziol, Bernhard A Koch and Reinhard Zimmermann
Verlag Österreich, Vienna
Hardcover. ISBN 978-3-7046-5885-2
2007, 632 pp

**Volume 2:** *Essential Cases on Damage*
Edited by Bénédict Winiger, Helmut Koziol, Bernhard A Koch and Reinhard Zimmermann
de Gruyter, Berlin/Boston
Hardcover. ISBN 978-3-11-024848-7
eBook. ISBN 978-3-11-024849-4
2011, 1175 pp

# Others

*European Tort Law. Basic Texts*
Edited by Ken Oliphant and Barbara C Steininger
Jan Sramek Verlag, Vienna
Softcover. ISBN 978-3-902638-50-2
2011, 330 pp

*Medienpolitik und Recht. Bd I Media Governance, Wahrhaftigkeitspflicht und sachgerechte Haftung*
Edited by Helmut Koziol, Josef Seethaler and Thomas Thiede
Jan Sramek Verlag, Vienna
Hardcover. ISBN 978-3-902638-36-6
2010, 214 pp

*Medienpolitik und Recht. Bd II Presserat, WikiLeaks und Redaktionsgeheimnis*
Edited by Helmut Koziol, Josef Seethaler and Thomas Thiede
Jan Sramek Verlag, Vienna
Hardcover. ISBN 978-3-902638-63-2
2013, 216 pp

*Grundfragen des Schadenersatzrechts*
by Helmut Koziol
Jan Sramek Verlag, Vienna
Hardcover. ISBN 978-3-902638-28-1
2010, 371 pp

*Basic Questions of Tort Law from a Germanic Perspective*
by Helmut Koziol
Jan Sramek Verlag, Vienna
Hardcover. ISBN 978-3-902638-85-4
2012, 380 pp

*Grundfragen des Schadenersatzrechts aus rechtsvergleichender Sicht*
Edited by Helmut Koziol
Jan Sramek Verlag, Vienna
Hardcover. ISBN 978-3-7097-0048-8
2014, 941 pp

*Basic Questions of Tort Law from a Comparative Perspective*
Edited by Helmut Koziol
Jan Sramek Verlag, Vienna
Hardcover. ISBN 978-3-7097-0040-2
2015, 867 pp

*Comparative Stimulations for Developing Tort Law*
Edited by Helmut Koziol
Jan Sramek Verlag, Vienna
Hardcover. ISBN 978-3-7097-0060-0
2015, 273 pp

*Essays in Honour of Jaap Spier*
Edited by Helmut Koziol and Ulrich Magnus
Jan Sramek Verlag, Vienna
Hardcover. ISBN 978-3-7097-0101-0
2016, 325 pp

*Österreichisches Haftpflichtrecht Band III*
by Helmut Koziol, Peter Apathy and Bernhard A Koch
Jan Sramek Verlag, Vienna
Hardcover. ISBN 978-3-7097-0022-8
2014, 596 pp

*Mangelfolgeschäden in Veräußerungsketten. Am Beispiel der Aus- und Einbaukosten*
by Ernst Karner and Helmut Koziol
Jan Sramek Verlag, Vienna
Softcover. ISBN 978-3-902638-84-7
2012, 96 pp

*Zur Anwendbarkeit des UN-Kaufrechts bei Werk- und Dienstleistungen. Am Beispiel der Maschinen- und Industrieanlagenlieferungsverträge*
by Helmut Koziol and Ernst Karner
Jan Sramek Verlag, Vienna
Softcover. ISBN 978-3-7097-0052-5
2015, 91 pp

*Obsoleszenzen im österreichischen Recht. Geltendes Recht, Schutzlücken und Reformbedarf*
by Helmut Koziol
Jan Sramek Verlag, Vienna
Softcover. ISBN 978-3-7097-0108-9
2016, 152 pp

# Journal of European Tort Law

The Journal of European Tort Law (JETL) is published three times a year. The General Editor is Professor Ken Oliphant, University of Bristol.

Further information, including subscription details and instructions for authors, is available on the JETL website <http://www.degruyter.com/view/j/jetl>.

Queries may be addressed to <information@jetl.eu>. Articles, comments and reviews should be submitted for consideration to <submissions@jetl.eu>. The Journal applies a policy of double blind peer review.

# Eurotort

EUROTORT is the first comprehensive database of European cases on tort law. Access to the database is free (subject to prior registration) at <www.eurotort.org>.

# European Tort Law Blog

A new feature recently added to the ECTIL/ETL homepages is the European tort law blog (<www.europeantortlaw.net>). This highlights important legislative changes and case law developments in the European tort law field, as well as forthcoming events, new publications, useful web links and other items of topical interest. Suggestions of items for posting are always welcome.

FSC
www.fsc.org
MIX
Papier | Fördert
gute Waldnutzung
FSC® C083411

Kolibri 360 GmbH
Ferdinand-Jühlke-Straße 7
99095 Erfurt, Deutschland
produktsicherheit@kolibri360.de